European Integration, 1950–2003

Integration is the most significant European historical development of the past fifty years, eclipsing in importance even the collapse of the USSR. Yet, until now, no satisfactory explanation is to be found in any single book as to why integration is significant, how it originated, how it has changed Europe, and where it is headed. John Gillingham corrects the inadequacies of the existing literature by cutting through the genuine confusion that surrounds the activities of the European Union and by looking at his subject from a truly historical perspective. The late twentieth century was an era of great, though insufficiently appreciated, accomplishment that intellectually and morally is still emerging from the shadow of an earlier era of depression and modern despotism. This is a work, then, that captures the historical distinctiveness of Europe in a way that transcends current party political debate.

John Gillingham is currently Professor of History at the University of Missouri, St. Louis. His previous book, *Coal, Steel, and the Rebirth of Europe, 1945–1955* (Cambridge, 1991), received the George Louis Beer Prize of the American Historical Association as the best book on the history of foreign relations published that year.

D0961740

European Integration, 1950–2003

Superstate or New Market Economy?

JOHN GILLINGHAM

University of Missouri, St. Louis

CAMBRIDGE
UNIVERSITY PRESS

PUBLISHED BY THE PRESS SYNDICATE OF THE UNIVERSITY OF CAMBRIDGE
The Pitt Building, Trumpington Street, Cambridge, United Kingdom

CAMBRIDGE UNIVERSITY PRESS
The Edinburgh Building, Cambridge CB2 2RU, UK
40 West 20th Street, New York, NY 10011-4211, USA
477 Williamstown Road, Port Melbourne, VIC 3207, Australia
Ruiz de Alarcón 13, 28014 Madrid, Spain
Dock House, The Waterfront, Cape Town 8001, South Africa

http://www.cambridge.org

First published 2003

Printed in the United States of America

Typeface Sabon 10/12 pt.   *System* AMS-T$_E$X   [FH]

A catalog record for this book is available from the British Library.

Library of Congress Cataloging in Publication data available

ISBN 0 521 81317 4 hardback
ISBN 0 521 01262 7 paperback

To Barbara

Contents

Preface

Economic and political integration has been a basic fact of European life for more than fifty years and will probably remain so in times to come. Its importance as a formative influence in the history of this period compares only to that of the Cold War and may loom even larger now that the Soviet Union has collapsed. The movement toward transnational regional cooperation in Europe has not only contributed to the revival, transformation, and rejuvenation of a battered civilization but remains as well a source of hope for the future. The integration process has not always been smooth, neat, pretty, or economically and politically costless, yet it has helped bring Europe to the cusp of a new era. The ancient but renewed civilization is leaving behind the slowly collapsing world system of the first half of the twentieth century, which it largely created – a system centering on national megastates and industrial economies wrenched into shape by the requirements and dislocations of total war. Europe is now advancing into a new, politically contested yet generally peaceful competitive world order whose broad contours are slowly becoming visible beneath the surface of events. The economic and political integration of this civilization has served as a mechanism for adjusting to international change and has also shaped global institutions and markets through a process of competitive emulation, reciprocal adjustment, and mutual adaptation. Europe has again become a force for world progress.

Three solid, specifically European historical accomplishments can be attributed in part to integration. One of them, palpable though difficult to quantify, is economic growth and welfare gains generally; another, impressive though imperfect in execution, is the extension and reinforcement of democratic government under law throughout much of the continent; and still another – immense, though hard to disentangle from a broader geopolitical, technological, and economic setting – is peace. The specter of war between the former European great powers has been banished and that of armed conflict between the smaller nations relegated to the periphery of events. This is the greatest single accomplishment to which European integration has contributed.

How integration has developed in Europe, or might develop, remains a source of confusion and controversy. Historical writing about the subject is in its infancy. No previous book examines the subject over its entire fifty-year history and within the broad contexts of its times.[1] A consensus is lacking for the meaning of the very term "integration," which can refer to either a process or an outcome according to the situation, describe an essentially political or economic phenomenon (as determined by the academic background of the discussant), and lead to something better or worse (or nowhere at all) depending on the mood of the editorialist. The misunderstanding that surrounds the subject stems at one level from the inscrutable operating methods of the European Union itself, at another from the shortcomings of the scholarly literature, and at still another from its polymorphous, mutable, and refractory character. But its causes are even deeper.

The trauma of the past still casts a shadow over a civilization deformed intellectually and morally by an era of wars, depression, and modern despotism. The events of the early twentieth century continue to shape perceptions of the past fifty years; whatever may have been accomplished since 1945 still appears trifling by comparison to the horrors and culminating tragedy of the three decades that began with the outbreak of the Great War and ended with Hitler's suicide in the *Führerbunker* and atomic bombings of Hiroshima and Nagasaki. The contours of the late twentieth century thus still lack historical definition. The effort to capture and define the essential character of these fifty years as a historical period is overdue. This book will argue that the previous half-century was an era of transition not only from material ruin to immense wealth and from institutions to markets, but also from bureaucratic thrall to a freedom within reach but not yet grasped. A new, still partly unsuspected realm of possibility is now unfolding, thanks to an invisible hand that is no longer lamed. The wonders and triumphs of the nineteenth century provide only pale intimations of what the future can hold.

The change that has taken place over the past fifty years of European history has resulted from a contest over policy making within a larger struggle between two principles of social, political, and economic organization: the state and the market. The West provided the setting for this struggle for the three decades after the war. Since the death of Mao, the "opening" of China, the collapse of the Soviet bloc, the beginnings of market reform in India, and the discrediting of state-led economic development in Latin America, it has become global. Within Europe, it has taken place at the level of ideas, institutions, and occasionally even hand-to-hand combat. Though sometimes constructive and beneficial, the tension between these two poles is responsible for the zigs and zags characteristic of the integration process – not to mention many sidesteps along the way. Europe has not always been at the forefront of progress; change has often originated abroad and its pace has often been faster elsewhere. Yet the overall trend is clear: The market principle has gradually supplanted that of the state in Europe's long march from the economy of war to that of peace. In *The Commanding Heights* (1998), Daniel Yergin and Joseph Stanislaw captured the better part of this fundamental truth but failed to appreciate the full significance of another part.[2] The shift has entailed more than the displacement of one power by another. The market does not so much occupy the "commanding heights" (described by Marx) as erode and level them by allowing a logic to operate that diffuses power, modifies institutions, generates new values, and sustains itself when allowed or enabled to work properly. The market process is slowly, even grudgingly, giving rise to a different kind of civilization in Europe and in the world generally.

There have been four stages in the history of European integration. The first one featured the founding of the European Economic Community (EEC) in the 1950s within the framework of American globalism and against the background of German economic revival, as well as the arrested development of these new institutions owing to the incompatibility of federalism with the mixed-economy welfare state. The second one brought about a "regime change" – the 1970s shakeout of the world monetary order inherited from the era of statism and warfare – which, by decade's end, witnessed the emergence of a liberal substitute wherein the state was unharnessed from the economy, nationally and internationally, and the mutually reinforcing bonds between the two levels weakened. Regime change set the stage for a quantum jump in the integration process. At the third stage, the 1980s, a new market system – though contested by socialists and "corporatists" – took root in individual countries worldwide and in Europe thanks to the force of globalization, the revival of economic liberalism as a doctrine, and the "spontaneous order" resulting from the exchange process. In the fourth stage – during the final decade of the century – the integration process suffered a series of eventually correctable setbacks that, however, still imperil the Community. These reversals result from misguided policy, malfunctioning Community governance machinery, and a breakdown of cooperation between the member-states (intergovernmentalism) that is itself partly the consequence of the European public's growing alienation from the Brussels institutions.

Since 1950, the integration process has advanced on three levels: as the result of interplay of forces nationally and internationally as well as regionally in Europe. One can term this phenomenon an "asymmetrical three-level interdependence game" if it is understood that the process is always in flux, that neither origins nor outcomes can be predicted, and that human agency and random events are inescapable variables. A cycle of change can start or end with events in the marketplace, competitive emulations of them, institutional adaptations to them, or preemptive anticipations of them. The notion of a three-level game has explanatory but not predictive value; in it, economics is bound inextricably to politics. Yet the process is at the same time fundamentally economic in character. This book will argue on the basis of economic logic and historical example that, in the absence of a *demos* – a sense of (European) nationhood – only one integrative approach can work: "negative integration," which takes place either through markets or institutions created to make markets operate properly (*Marktkonform*). Although other prerequisites may be necessary for the success of this "negative" approach, its alternative – "positive integration," the organization of Europe by means of bureaucracy and regulation in order to compensate for market failure – has never succeeded and cannot do so under present circumstances.

Yet there is no need to assume either that the conditions that have dictated such outcomes are necessarily permanent or that the integration phenomenon cannot undergo future metamorphoses. The development of a *demos* through successful transnational economic cooperation and problem solving is by no means impossible in the future. The integration process has indeed been *mutable, polymorphous,* and *refractory* over the past half-century: it has changed substantially over time, can take different forms, yet is also stubborn and resistant to change. This maddening (indeed, seemingly perverse) combination of features rules out prediction and generally has made fools of those who have tried to map out the future.

The priorities of European institutions have shifted, their size and responsibilities have grown, and the machinery of governance itself has developed in ways not foreseen or laid out in either the Treaty of Rome or antecedent and subsequent treaties. The process of integration cannot be identified with a specific set of institutions such as those headquartered in Brussels; neither can it be understood apart from the particular national political cultures that constitute Europe (and changes within them) or from broad international trends. The tradition of divorcing studies of the European Union from these surrounding contexts not only makes for arid texts; it can by default exaggerate the importance of official policy making and lead to unrealistic assessments of what the authorities in Brussels can or should do. Such estimates should be made in light of alternative lines of development, national and international contexts, and the possibility of exogenous shocks – and with the awareness that ideas can and do change.

There is no precast model for a historical study like the present one, which features the market as principal actor and is international in scope. This work has nonetheless drawn heavily from two important literatures that play vital supporting roles in the story. The dominant school of political economy, the neoliberal institutionalist approach of political science, focuses on the systemic level of interstate relations – on "what governments do" in the international system, especially with regard to finance and commerce – and centers on the creation and operation of global regulatory mechanisms. Its normative concern is with how, by means of "negotiated cooperation," governments and organizations adapt to change in the market. The analysis of such institutions is an important feature of the story that will unfold in these pages. Neoliberal institutionalists are, however, only secondarily interested in the workings of the market mechanism.

This is the concern of mainstream neoclassical economics, which combines rational utility maximization and general equilibrium–based perfect competition as a measurement standard. It arms the historian with powerful methods and valuable insights, but its applicability is limited. The static approach is ill equipped to deal with temporal change and compares idealized, modeled, stylized, or fictional conditions to real-life "imperfections." These, however, are givens in historical analysis, which must examine not hyperrational actors with perfect foresight but rather fallible human beings – men and women living in difficult, troubled, or otherwise "suboptimal" circumstances and limited to decisions made on the basis of imperfect knowledge.

The starring role in the present account goes to another camp of economists, a more heterogeneous group of "classical liberals" whose research and writing, though not the work of specialists in the international field, is replete with implications for it. "Classical liberals" are not, as the term suggests, purebreds – although they trace their pedigree back to Adam Smith – but rather mixed breeds of the tough, friendly, and occasionally vicious garden variety of mutt familiar to most people in most times and places. Those in this group posit an "interdependence of orders": the interpenetration and mutual reinforcement of the economic, the political, and the legal. This venturesomeness into new neighborhoods can produce unlikely combinations of features, but its offspring remain, nonetheless, all dogs. Stronger or better breeds may well develop from the muddy gene pool in the future. Although "classical liberals" move in many different directions – and some are surely headed in the right ones – economics remains the core discipline in their thinking. *Homo œconomicus* has not disappeared from their accounts but merely retreated from view because it is not yet fully developed. Classical liberal economists like Friedrich Hayek have roamed far and wide and into fields as remote as neurobiology in order to understand the workings of the human mind. Raising imperfect man from the primeval slime of ignorance into the impeccable, orderly, and antiseptic laboratory of perfect rationality is what ultimately drives the classical liberal agenda.

Classical liberalism has produced no overarching historical theory of its own but instead hypothesizes a process of market-generated change (spontaneous order) that provides an analytical starting point. From this seed have grown offshoots that have, in turn, led to breakthroughs in the understanding of how markets and institutions interact: ORDO-liberalism, public choice theory, and the new institutionalism. These schools have, for their part, provided the theoretical basis for a promising new political science approach – historical institutionalism – that has begun to influence European integration scholarship. The present account can be regarded as a preliminary attempt to demonstrate the utility of classical liberal–based theories to historical study on a macro scale, one that runs across a long stretch of time as well as a broad swath of circumstance and deals with an issue of cardinal importance to Europe's past, present, and future.

The book is shaped like a funnel. Its scope broadens, deepens, and goes more thoroughly into national cases as it moves toward the present and traces the rise of integration – resulting from the contest between market and state – as it has developed from the realm of pure thought into a force that both influences the lives of Europe's peoples and is influenced by them. Part I describes the origins of European integration at the levels of ideas (Hayek versus Monnet), institutions (those market-conforming ones created to promote free trade and currency convertibility, as opposed to those market-correcting ones built on the *dirigiste* model of the French Plan) – as well as the institutionalization of integration – against a backdrop of the German "economic miracle." Part I concludes with the twenty gridlock years that ensued from the failure of "positive integration."

Part II centers on the watershed event of the era, the regime change. This change resulted from the collapse of the international monetary regime that was designed at the wartime Bretton Woods conference and of the embedded liberal postwar system that supported the mixed-economy welfare state and its sequel.

The replacement of this system by a new market-based substitute enabled the integration process to descend from the realm of abstract ideas into the sphere of action; transformed the Brussels institutions from talk shops into agents of economic, social, and political transformation in individual nations; kept Europe abreast of world change; and set the stage for its development as an economic and (in a remote future) political union. Part II also provides a theoretical account of why the progress of integration required regime change.

Part III describes the most dynamic period in the history of European integration. The 1980s was a decade of liberalization that featured catalytic interaction of change at the international, national, and European levels as well as the struggle over the future of Europe between M. Delors and Mrs. Thatcher, as waged within both the European Union and individual nations. The contest pitted the ascendant market principle against an entrenched corporatism and socialism and – within the Community – set liberalizers who advocated geographical expansion ("widening") against market correctors ("deepeners") committed to institution building.

Part IV is concerned with the uneasy standoff reached in the 1990s between globalization and European protectionism, the crippling leadership problems that spread through the Community, the rising tide of public discontent with governance from on high, the policy errors of the EU – as well as the hazards its present state of disarray poses to the progress of integration, Europe's fitness for the challenges of tomorrow, and its ability to meet the promise of the future. The chapters of Part IV successively examine the development of Community institutions, the relationship between member-states and Brussels, eastern expansion (Enlargement), and the present economic challenges facing the EU.

A few words about language are especially relevant to this study. The subject of integration has a distinctly postmodern flavor; for much of its fifty-year history, the argument that only words have meaning is often persuasive. Language capture has been an important part of the European story. For nearly thirty years "integration" – to the extent that it implied more than the existence of a farm subsidy program (the Common Agricultural Policy) and the existence of a customs union – was only a verbal reality, as was the vocabulary invented to describe and analyze it. Thanks to the coinages of political experts and the customary usages of bureaucrats, such words (and the ideas behind them) have taken on a life of their own: they have shaped perceptions, guided discourse and discussion, defined future agendas, and, under the right conditions, been incorporated into laws, policies, institutions, and even constitutional principles. As with the use of any jargon, meaning can easily be lost in Brussels-Volapük. Euro-words may imply either more or less than evident, mean different things to different people, or simply mean nothing at all. It is thus necessary to cast official language aside whenever possible and use standard terms and common measurements in order to demystify ideas, events, and deeds as well as provide bases for comparison.

Another language issue arises from the need to use words that mean different things to different audiences, beginning with "liberal." As employed here, it should not be confused with the American synonym for "socially and politically progressive." The term should be understood broadly in the traditional European sense as an ideology of open markets and small government under law and responsible for the provision of public goods. The meaning of the term should be understood with reference to ends rather than means; it does not necessarily imply the adoption of specific policies. The term "embedded liberalism" refers in the text to the specific coinage of John Ruggie to describe a state-based, mixed-economy system designed to protect liberal values. "Neoliberal" is the most easily misunderstood member of this word family. In this book the term refers strictly to those politicians of the 1980s and 1990s who adopted liberal policies opportunistically and without openly identifying with the ideology behind them.

A final word on language is that this book will use many of them, even at the risk of alienating each of its specialized readerships along the way. Historians may be bored by political or economic theory, and social scientists may feel weighted down or distracted by excessive factual detail. This is an interdisciplinary study, one purpose of which is to demonstrate the relevance of different social science literatures to the overall concerns animating each of them, but especially to historians. Its author, as a member of their guild, has also felt obliged not to omit or otherwise "model" any aspect of the subject that might abstract it from reality. He has further tried hard to cast his net broadly – providing anecdote and example to illustrate the complexity and diversity of the subject matter – and to provide accurate descriptions of institutions and procedures even at the risk of burdening the text. He can only express regret that the EU governance machinery is excessively complicated and often operationally opaque – and promise to do the utmost possible to explain matters simply. In return for the reader's patience, he will (even while suffering from stage fright) also try to entertain. The journey is long. Let's make it pleasant.

The author has a number of apologies. He cannot for reasons of space present an overall survey of *national* developments as they relate to Europe's economic and political unification, federation, or coordination but must instead deal with specific cases that are broadly representative of trends and traditions within the European Union, provide insight into the diversity of Europe's national political cultures, expose particular problems facing the Community, or are fundamental to its overall development. Such judgments are somewhat invidious. The big countries – Germany, France, Great Britain, Italy, Spain, and Poland – necessarily get a disproportionate amount of play. A concern with length has likewise dictated selectivity regarding the treatment of EU-related topics. Exclusions are necessary. The author deeply regrets not being able to discuss any of the following important topics in sufficient detail: trade and Mediterranean policy; the special problems of Turkey, Cyprus, and the "second tier" of accession nations; cultural, internal security, public health, environmental and bio-tech policy; foreign aid and assistance; fisheries; and gender issues.

Few historians write about the present. The integration story cannot, however, be properly told as if broken off thirty years ago – the lapse of time normally required before archives are unsealed and made accessible to research. The restriction on access has heretofore prevented the historical literature from advancing beyond the 1960s. Although the source base for the first twenty years of the present study is largely archival, that for the next three decades cannot be. The author has drawn material for these years from a warehouse-bursting profusion of official and semi-official publications; financial and business newsletters and printed material falling under the general rubric "trade press"; scholarly and semi-scholarly books, articles, and papers; the writings of journalists, commentators, and other experts; and numerous autobiographies and other firsthand accounts. Although much of this evidence was retrieved as "hard copy," large additional amounts have been downloaded from electronic data bases (EDBs). Without access to such sources, it would have been impossible – for reasons of both time and money – to write a book of this scope. Certain EDBs provide hard-copy pagination, but others do not. Here it has been necessary to make approximations.

The book owes its genesis to research done as a Fellow of the Woodrow Wilson Center in 1991–1992. My apologies for the delay. I hope to have produced something that trumpets like an elephant rather than squeaks like a mouse. The academic year 2000–2001 that I spent as a visiting scholar at the Minda de Gunzburg Center for European Studies at Harvard University was the most stimulating intellectual experience of my life. Though none of their owners can be counted on to agree with more than a single word of the text, voices from Harvard echo throughout this book. It is unfair to mention only a few names – my debt to so many is so great – but I'll do it anyway. Andrew Moravcsik, Paul Pierson, George Ross, and Charles Maier have all taught me more than they realize. My apologies to the dozens of Harvard people who are not mentioned here. Tim Josling gave the project a big boost by inviting me to Stanford University for two summers as a Visiting Fellow of the European Forum. The excellent staffs of both the libraries and archives of the Hoover Institution were unfailingly helpful in enabling me to retrieve critical material quickly, and Helen Solanum was especially kind to me personally. I owe a profound personal and professional debt to my dear friend, Peter Acsay, who discussed the progress of this project with me every day during the year it took to write and also commented on the entire manuscript. A number of others have also done so. The two anonymous readers for Cambridge University Press provided insightful and, in one case, exceptionally meticulous and detailed comments. My thanks to each of you. A number of others commented on portions of the manuscript; thanks, too, to Philip Booth, Bruce Caldwell, Victoria Curzon Price, Fred Fransen, Michele Rutledge, Razeen Sally, and Larry White. The usual disclaimer applies: None of the aforementioned indiduals is responsible for any shortcomings that remain in the text. My thanks, finally, to the Research Board of the University of Missouri for enabling me financially to spend ten to twelve hours a day, seven days a week for 52 weeks at the monitor in my home dungeon.

Abbreviations

3G	third generation
Amcham	American Chamber of Commerce
APP	Approved Personal Pension
ASI	Adam Smith Institute
BFI	British Federation of Industry
BNOC	British National Oil Company
BuBa	Bundesbank
CAP	Common Agricultural Policy
CDU	Christian Democratic Union
CPI	Communist Party of Italy
CPS	Centre for Policy Studies
CSFP	Common Security and Foreign Policy
DG	Directorates General
DM	Deutsche mark
EC	European Community
ECB	European Central Bank
ECHO	European Community Humanitarian Aid Office
ECJ	European Court of Justice
ECSC	European Coal and Steel Community
EDC	European Defense Community
EEC	European Economic Community
EFTA	European Free Trade Association
EMF	European Monetary Fund
EMS	European Monetary System
EMU	European Monetary Union
EP	European Parliament
EPC	European Political Community
EPU	European Payments Union
ERM	European Rate Mechanism
ERP	European Recovery Plan
ERT	European Roundtable of Industrialists
ESPRIT	European Program for R & D in Information Technology
ETUC	European Trade Union Confederation
EU	European Union
EURATOM	European Atomic Energy Commission
EUREKA	European Research Coordinating Agency
FDI	foreign direct investment
FP	Framework Program
FSAP	Financial Services Action Plan
FU	Freedom Union

FUBAR	f***ed up beyond all recognition
GATT	General Agreement on Tariffs and Trade
GDP	gross domestic product
GM	grant maintained
GNP	gross national product
HDTV	high-definition television
HI	historical institutionalism
ICU	International Clearing Union
IEA	Institute of Economic Affairs
IGC	intergovernmental conference
IMF	International Monetary Fund
INI	Instituto Nacional de Industria
IRI	Institute for Industrial Reconstruction
IT	information technology
ITO	International Trade Organization
LO	*Landesorganisationen*
MAD	mutually assured destruction
MEDEF	*Mouvement des Enterprises Françaises*
MFA	Multi Fiber Agreement
MFN	most-favored nation
MLF	Multilateral Force
MTEP	Medium-Term Economic Policy
MTFS	medium-term financial strategy
NBER	National Bureau of Economic Research
NEB	National Enterprise Board
NEP	New Economic Policy
NHS	National Health Service
NIDC	National Industrial Development Council
NTB	nontariff barrier
NTMA	New Transatlantic Marketplace Agreement
OECD	Organization for Economic Cooperation and Development
OEEC	Organization of European Economic Cooperation
OMA	Orderly Marketing Arrangement
PDB	preliminary draft budget
PTT	government postal service
QMV	qualified majority voting
R&D	research and development
RTT	*réduction du terme de travail*
SAGE	Software Action Group for Europe
SAP	*Svenska Arbeider Parti*
SEA	Single European Act
SERPS	State Earnings Retirement Pension Scheme
SFM	single financial market
SPD	Social Democratic Party
TEA	Trade Expansion Act
TENS	R&D and infrastructure construction
TEU	Treaty of European Union
UMTS	Universal Mobile Telecommunications System
VER	Voluntary Export Restraint
WAP	wireless application protocol
WC	Washington Consensus
WTO	World Trade Organization

Part I

A German Solution to Europe's Problems?
The Early History of the
European Communities, 1950–1965

Introduction to Part I

A New Global Setting

THE MOST formidable of the many great challenges facing statesmen of the West after V-E Day was to tie Germany into Europe and Europe into Germany, both economically and politically. Most of them knew from the outset that this must take place as part of a larger recovery process that would eventually restore a Europe wrecked by two world wars to economic conditions like those that had obtained in the nineteenth century – with open borders, convertible currencies, competition, and the free interchange of ideas, a place where re-knit commercial and financial ties between nations would create essential networks of prosperity and so prevent war. This was the aim of all liberals, including men like John Maynard Keynes, who (at least for the medium term) thought state intervention necessary in order to restore the social and economic conditions under which market recovery could take hold.[1] There was, as he understood, a disjunction between means and ends. Sound ideas and effective action did not often go hand in hand in the ravaged Europe of 1945. Hope that self-sustaining growth could be set in motion through the market would remain only a dream until governments had been stabilized, institutions rebuilt, and laws enforced. Cooperation was called for between industry and commerce on the one hand and government on the other.

The situation at the end of the war gave rise to the state of mind, financial and commercial policies, and economic regulatory agencies for which the Columbia University political scientist John Ruggie coined the term "embedded" liberalism; they would provide a global institutional setting with interpenetration and interweaving of state power and market economy that would last for the next 25 years.[2] This regime was not all-powerful; nor did it always function as intended, and often it worked at cross-purposes. Rigid though not inflexible, the embedded liberal regime could, up to a point, be reformed in order to accommodate change. Within this regime cohabitated uneasily two distinct approaches to integration policy: one favoring the working of the market, the other the intervention of the state. An unstable amalgam, embedded liberalism would provide a bridge to a revived liberalism *sans phrase*.

Jean Monnet, a master of the interventionist approach, was even a Great Power in his own right. Without this immense standing, which he uniquely possessed, the diplomatic breakthrough upon which the subsequent integration of Europe would rest might never have occurred. The breakthrough – the Schuman

Plan announcement of 9 May 1950, which led to the founding a year later of the European Coal and Steel Community (ECSC) – brought about the reconciliation of France and Germany, the axis of political integration. Yet this accomplishment left an ambiguous legacy. Monnet's methods were elitest, undemocratic, and intended to provide definitive, irreversible solutions. The institutions he created (or tried to create) in order to advance the political and economic union of Europe did not operate properly, were unstable, or did not work at all. Monnet was initially the indispensable man, but both he and his legacy have thwarted as much as advanced the integration process.

The perpetuation of Monnet's legacy owes much to his German disciple, Walter Hallstein, the first president of the European Commission (the executive office of the European Economic Community). Hallstein laid the foundation stones of the Brussels Eurocracy, where his own presidency ended in tatters but in which the spirit of Monnet continues to dwell. The downfall of the German president would usher in a new period in which the states – rather than any single person, idea, or institution – took the lead in integrating Europe. The "Monnet myth" survived in the form of concepts, policy rationales, and a terminology that to this day influences thinking about the integration process.

Jean Monnet did not, however, "found Europe," as related in his memoirs, after a moment of divine inspiration. Integration grew out of post–World War II liberalization. Progress was, to be sure, slow. The return to peacetime conditions did not bring "normalcy" but merely a gradual shift from warfare state to welfare state. Although this course would later be partly reversed with the onset of the Cold War, the success of the Marshall Plan and its offshoots – OEEC/EPU and GATT – made it possible to dismantle the regime of controls inherited from the war, open up markets, and restore the competition principle to operation. The results were still a far cry from anything that might have existed midway through the nineteenth century. They did not, however, point in the direction of a "neomercantilist" restoration, as Alan Milward has argued – this would be bowing the wrong way toward Mecca – but toward a re-founded liberal order.[3]

In the early 1950s the former Reich became motor and model of the new Europe. Minister of Economics Ludwig Erhard's policies triggered a boom in the German economy and created durable trading relationships between the Federal Republic and its European neighbors that disciplined their markets as well. The fundamental purpose of the 1958 Treaty of Rome was to strengthen and perpetuate the new economic and political relationship that had developed between the German nation and its former victims in Western Europe. Though of necessity it included side deals, the treaty created a customs union and established the rules needed to make the competition mechanism work properly.

The German-fired European boom was both cause and effect of the formation of the new customs union known as the European Economic Community (EEC). Yet all was not well in the organization of Europe. Only the members of the coal and steel community ("The Six": Belgium, France, Italy, Luxembourg, the Netherlands, and West Germany) joined the EEC. Seven of the remaining nations belonging to the Organization of European Economic Cooperation (OEEC – an offshoot of the Marshall Plan) did not join the EEC but instead formed an alternative body, the European Free Trade Association (EFTA). As the name implies, the EFTA was a free-trade area as opposed to a customs union with a common external tariff and a political agenda. The EFTA was less formal and more easy-going than the EEC and was also remarkably successful, so it constituted a dangerous competitor and a possible alternative institution upon which European integration might have been constructed. In the meantime, the audacious bid of President Hallstein to turn his little office in Brussels, the Commission, into a kind of capital for Europe antagonized and alienated the EEC member-states. In July 1965 the French delegation, upon order of General de Gaulle, walked out of the Council of Ministers. It agreed to return seven months later only upon the express condition that France, and each of the remaining "Five," receive veto power. Blocked by the Council and immobilized in the face of impending economic turmoil, the Commission would remain on the sidelines for the next twenty years. The future of integration would hinge not on the initiatives of the Brussels Eurocracy but rather on developments within the member-states – developments that were both cause and effect of economic change.

1

The Liberal Project for an Integrated Europe

THERE *was* a liberal project for an integrated Europe, even one *avant la lettre*. Its author was the Austrian economist Friedrich A. Hayek.[1] He ranks alongside Jean Monnet and many others as one of the founding fathers of the new era. Hayek's work inspired both Ludwig Erhard, who turned West Germany into the engine and model of European economic growth, and Margaret Thatcher, the moving force behind the Single European Act, which restarted the integration process in the late 1980s, as well as many others who have followed their footsteps. Hayek discovered the logic underlying the integration process. It is as relevant now as ever. Hayek postulated that the competition principle, if allowed to operate, sets in motion a mutually reinforcing reciprocal process in which the market and self-government together reduce interstate conflict and promote economic growth. It is not only Hayek's devotees and admirers who hold that integration can proceed on the basis of such "negative integration." The argument has been restated and confirmed by many specialists and practitioners, some of whose work will be discussed in these pages. The result may, however, simply reflect the diffuse and pervasive nature of Hayek's influence. Not just economists but also political scientists, sociologists, and legal and constitutional scholars are all slowly becoming at least partly Hayekian, just as by the third quarter of the past century even President Nixon, as he famously announced, was a Keynesian.

THE LEGACY OF FRIEDRICH VON HAYEK

Friedrich von Hayek was born at the turn of the century and lived long enough to witness the fall of communism. His active career, begun after World War I, ended with the onset of senility in the mid-1980s. Hayek impressed people when still in his 20s as being serious beyond his years and, at 80, as being remarkably spry and alert. The sixty intermediate, grayish years of middle age were the most productive period of his life. Hayek was tall and slightly stooped, reserved, somewhat courtly, unmistakably donnish, and spoke English as a second language with accents that varied according to the time and place of his residence. The placid and unremarkable demeanor masked a personal life not always consistent with the image. Such matters are trifling by comparison to Hayek's ideas. Hayek never held public office but operated instead on (or close to) the intellectual plane. A great economist and social scientist, he was also a brilliant promoter of think tanks dedicated both to reviving the tradition of classical liberalism internationally and providing guidance to policy makers who shared his views. Hayek's influence has been both pervasive and enduring – not merely as a technical economist but as a political visionary with a deep understanding of the historical process. His gifts as a publicist and intellectual entrepreneur should not be overlooked in any assessment of his importance in the history of integration.

The Mont Pèlerin Society, which he co-founded in 1947, has served as a central point of diffusion not only for his own views but also for those of related schools influenced by them, such as monetarism, public choice theory, and the new institutional economics.[2] In addition, Hayek and other eminent members of the association have founded colonies of classical liberal intellectuals in the United States, throughout Europe, and, above all, in Great Britain. The Institute of Economic Affairs, despite its bland name, became a hotbed of policy formulation for the government of Margaret Thatcher, who – as has since been nearly forgotten – set in motion a new wave of liberal reform into the European Community in the early 1980s. The competition directorate (DG IV), the most influential branch of the eventually labyrinthine Commission bureaucracy, became its locus. Hayek also imprinted the thinking of the Freiburg School of so-called ORDO-liberals who devised the famous *Soziale Marktwirtschaft* (social market economy) associated with Ludwig Erhard and the German economic miracle of the 1950s. He thus played an important background role in turning the Federal Republic into the economic hub of the new Europe.

Friedrich A. *von* Hayek, as he was baptized, entered life in 1899 as the eldest son of a wealthy Viennese family of administrators and university professors ennobled, on both sides, in the late eighteenth and mid-nineteenth centuries. In 1919, the supposedly all-important three-letter particle disappeared by decree of the young Austrian Republic, to Hayek's apparent indifference. It should not be forgotten that Hayek spent a privileged youth as subject of the multinational and economically liberal Habsburg monarchy and belonged to the milieu of Karl Popper, the Polanyis, Ludwig Wittgenstein, the von Mises brothers, Hans Kelsen, Arthur Koestler, and Peter Drucker. Except for service as a lieutenant on the Italian front, where he received a minor head wound, Hayek never strayed far from the academy. The academies in question were located not only in Austria but also in Great Britain (London School of Economics), the United States (University of Chicago), and West Germany (University of Freiburg). Each of these great centers of learning had an impact on Hayek's intellectual development but was also, in turn, influenced by him. No thumbnail sketch can do justice to the complexity of the relationship between the man and the institutions, not to mention the individuals associated with each of them. The interplay of ideas was what bound them all together. Hayek's life centered on a continuous and immensely productive debate with other respected great minds – with none of whom he fully agreed and with many of whom, in certain respects, he fundamentally disagreed. Hayek's views also changed over time (as did those of many of his remarkably long-lived interlocutors), a welcome consequence of broadened inquiry. Hayek must be judged primarily on the basis of his importance as a thinker, but he was also a networker *par excellence* and both colleague and pupil of many prominent figures: from Vienna of the 1920s, Fritz Machlup, Gottfried Haberler, Josef Schumpeter, and his mentor Ludwig von Mises; from London of the 1930s, Edwin Canaan, Lionel Robbins, John Hicks, and Ronald Coase; from post–World War II Chicago, Frank Knight, Milton Friedman, and James Buchanan; and from Freiburg – both at the end of the war and in the last two decades of his life – Wilhelm Röpke, Walter Eucken, Alfred Müller-Armack, and Ludwig Erhard.[3]

Hayek's career witnessed plenty of ups and downs. His research arguing that business cycles stemmed from malinvestments due to the only partial liquidity of capital were hotly disputed at the time but, after his 1926 predictions of a coming financial crash, won him recognition as an economist of international stature by 1930. The following year he accepted a chair at the London School of Economics. Professor Lionel Robbins recruited Hayek for the specific purpose of counteracting the growing influence of John Maynard Keynes. Here he was a disappointment. The Austrian was bested during the Depression years, or so it seemed at the time, in successive and widely reported intellectual jousts – fought through the pages of academic journals – with his well-connected, better-known, and (since Hayek's English was not yet quite up to speed) far more articulate opponent. He was further denied any role in British wartime policy making because of his "suspect" origins. Hayek was drifting into obscurity until the sensational popular success of *The Road to Serfdom,* published in 1944 and excerpted the following year in the *Reader's Digest.*[4] The impact of this powerful and disturbing political tract – a warning that the mixed-economy welfare states of the Western democracies were headed down the same route taken earlier by Stalin and Hitler – made him many lifetime enemies. It also turned him into a celebrity, figured in his decision to leave Britain and accept a position at the University of Chicago, and marked a turning point in his career. Henceforth the technical economist in Hayek would give way to the political philosopher, the legal theorist, and the historian.

A Hayek revival began in the late 1970s as the economic and political consensus that had characterized the Western world disintegrated. The idea was no longer credible that economic growth, full employment, and a more or less stable price level could be achieved by macroeconomic management without fundamentally damaging both the micro-structure of a basically private enterprise system and the impersonal rule of law on which free economic transactions depend. The existence of the new consensus signaled the end of ideological disputes between advocates of collectivist and individualist forms of social and economic organization. The Austrian had won his battles of the 1930s with Keynes. Since the fall of communism, Hayek's reputation has continued to soar. According to the inevitably hyped-up blurb on a recent biography, "many of his ideas have been vindicated ... and Hayek's vision of a renewed classical liberalism – of free markets and free ideas in free societies – has taken hold in much of the world."[5] The findings of the present study, an investigation of a subject that cuts across only a portion of his life's work, adds to the weight and measure of his reputation.

An ambition to develop a universal science of society drove Hayek's intellectual inquiry, as it had done that of Max Weber, to whom the Austrian is often compared and with whom he had at one time hoped to study. Hayek's thinking also had important antecedents in the special traditions of the Austrian school of economics, in which he and Ludwig von Mises were recognized as leading figures. The Austrian notion of the market process provided Hayek with a precious insight into social and political development over time, a heuristic device for understanding the mechanisms of – to use an emotive word he would have avoided – *progress*. By any name, that is the end to which the Austrian concept of the market process points, a fact fundamental to it power and appeal.

The Austrian (as opposed to the classical or Walrasian) economist conceives of the market process as dynamic rather than static, as analogous to evolutionary biology rather than Newtonian physics, and as something that grows out of a discovery process. General equilibrium can never actually be reached in the Austrian view, as there is no such thing as pre-reconciling economic plans or "objective knowledge" of the market but instead only the personal and "subjective" competitive strivings of individuals entering into transactions. Transmitted through markets, price signals translate otherwise inexplicable and indigestible masses of data into the information needed to coordinate trade and production in a decentralized manner that then produces the greatest good for the greatest number and maximizes social adaptability. Markets create "spontaneous order" yielding sustained growth and optimizing positive welfare impact while embedding knowledge in institutions that in turn modify social behavior. Markets and institutions can thus be said to be both co-evolutionary and co-dependent, though the specific relationship between them in any given situation depends on the context.[6]

The Austrian theory has powerful implications. It posits that constructive economic and political change can be self-sustaining if allowed to operate within the framework of its own laws and if unimpeded by government (or other) interventions that supplant or otherwise distort it. The contention makes epistemological presuppositions that can be neither proved nor disproved empirically and that hence must rest on hypotheses about how institutions can and should function. "History," even a slice of it, does not offer acceptable evidence of its validity. But is it not more important to use history in order to understand economics than vice versa? Hayek's mentor, von Mises, made the point most eloquently: "Economics is not about goods and services, [but] about the actions of living men. Its goal is not to dwell on imaginary constructions such as equilibrium. These constructions are only the tools of reasoning. The sole task of economics is analysis of the actions of men, is the analysis of processes."[7] The question at hand is whether the Austrian theory of the market provides valuable insight into the historical process. European integration can be regarded as a test case.

The integration of Europe is not an overarching theme in Hayek's lifework. Yet it is a recurrent source of intellectual and moral concern raised by the problems of his age, which he tackled (at several different times in his career) with the formidable set of analytical tools at his command. Hayek developed the theory that is at the very core of the liberal project for Europe, but he remained vague about how the process of European integration could be set in motion. He did not delve deeply into specifics of implementation. Instead, one finds among the leading figures (ORDO-liberals) of the Freiburg School – men influenced by yet distinct from the "Austrians" – the clearest understanding of the fact that, in order to operate satisfactorily, the damaged economy of the war-torn continent had to be nested in a new set of "market-conforming" (*Marktkonform*) institutions that (a) guaranteed respect for property and contract, (b) was anchored in monetary stability, and (c) was designed to protect the competition principle. Such an institutional emphasis can be said to typify even liberal German economic thinking. ORDO-liberalism is also characterized by a profound moral revulsion to national socialism, deep ethical concerns and commitments, and a quite specific engagement with the problems of economic reconstruction in the remnants of the broken and occupied German nation. On the German issue, Hayek's Freiburg associates would "pick up the ball and run with it."

Hayek nonetheless first delineated the liberal integration project. In "The Economic Conditions of Interstate Federalism," which appeared in print on 1 September 1939 (a surely unintended accompaniment to Hitler's invasion of Poland), Hayek presents a compelling and, within his terms of reference, irrefutable explanation of why open markets and political union go hand in hand – that is to say, are both co-dependent and co-evolutionary. The logic of his explanation influences thinking up to the present.[8] He opens with a verifiable hypothesis – that no instances can be found of successful political federations without counterpart arrangements for the unimpeded movement of labor, goods, and capital – and then posits that the absence of trade barriers stands in the way of an identification of economic and political interests and so limits the pursuit of independent policies by member-states of a federation. Consequently, it is difficult for any such state to manipulate prices, adopt independent monetary policies, "discriminate" against one producer in favor of another, levy harmful taxes, or impose social or regional policies having differential impacts. It would, moreover, be even harder for a federation than for member-states to make invidious distinctions between producer groups; economic planning at a higher level would likewise be more difficult. Rather than legislate poorly, he suggests, a federation should limit itself to the proscription of antimarket policies. The weakening of federal and state power in a market-based union, he concludes, would result in the devolution of functions to the regional or local level, where they can be carried out more efficiently. Competition between these small units would, in turn, provide a salutary check on excessive growth and also encourage innovation.

Hayek's article describes a set of interdependent relationships that – if allowed to work themselves out – would reduce the threat of war, open up markets, stimulate innovation, bring about the devolution of political power to the level of government closest to the individual citizen, and in all these respects advance the human condition. But how should the process be initiated that would lead to such results? Here Hayek offered little more than a concluding plea for the abrogation of the "sovereignty principle" and the creation of an "international order of law" as "necessary complements and logical consummations" of his project. However, these preconditions for future integration are simply starting places.

THE CLASSICAL LIBERAL SOLUTION
TO THE GERMAN PROBLEM

The "German Problem" was of immense concern to Hayek during the war. His thinking about it reflects an otherworldliness like that of the most widely read scholarly book on the subject, *The German Catastrophe,* by the great Berlin historian Friedrich Meinecke.[9] Hayek was an early advocate of political union as a solution to the German Problem.[10] "The future of England," Hayek told a King's College (Cambridge) audience of historians in a speech delivered on 28 February 1944, "is tied up with the future of Europe and, whether we like it or not, the future of Europe will be largely decided by what will happen in Germany." A federation would be needed. The war, he said, had shattered many worthy German intellectual traditions even as others, too deep-seated to perish, had contributed to the rise of Hitler. German historical consciousness must therefore be revived, and even re-created, so as to enforce the acceptance of moral standards prevailing elsewhere in Europe. Since it would be difficult to arrive at a single policy among nations, Hayek proposed adopting a "flag under which men who agree could unite."[11]

The "figure who fits the bill as perfectly as if he had been created for the purpose," he discovered, was the late nineteenth-century Anglo-German liberal Catholic grandee, Lord Acton, a man "half German by education and more than half German in his training as a historian [whom] the Germans almost regard as one of themselves ... [and who] unites, as perhaps no other recent figure, the great English tradition with the best there is in the Liberal tradition of the Continent." Hayek proposed to organize an "'Acton Society' ... to assist in the task [of re-education faced by] historians of this country and of Germany and perhaps of other countries."[12] Unable to agree on whether to put the name of Acton, de Tocqueville, or some other hallowed figure on the masthead, the would-be founders of the proposed entity, something supposed to be "half-way between a scholarly institution and a political society," a kind of "International Academy of Political Philosophy," agreed to call it simply "The Mont Pèlerin Society" after the name of the site near Geneva where the first meeting was to be held.[13] The German Problem prompted Hayek's decision to create it.

Contrary to Hayek's intentions, neither historians nor political philosophers would have a major voice in the new discussion club. The policies and programs it generated would thus be almost exclusively the work of economists. Hayek himself set the unofficial discussion parameters for policy toward Germany: "The Allies [first of all] should make Germany a free trade territory ... [in order] to prevent a close re-integration of the [national] economic structure ... which would be the precursor of a future political re-integration." Germany should, Hayek thought, "become as closely as possible economically entangled with the surrounding world, the whole [being] as little self-sufficient [and] centralized as possible." The permanent solution to the German Problem would depend above all "on the development of some Western European federal framework into which the German states are individually received as they are emancipated from Allied control.... [T]he next step ... should not be complete independence and sovereignty, but ... partnership with the full rights of a minority in a larger European enterprise."[14]

Not Hayek but Wilhelm Röpke deserves to be remembered as the most serious liberal student of the German question. Nowadays almost forgotten as an economist save in the rarified atmosphere of the Freiburg School, this nostalgic, often despairing, impassioned, deeply principled, and profoundly insightful son of a Lutheran pastor resigned his chair at the University of Marburg only a week after Hitler came to power and left Germany – soon to be joined by Gerhard Kessler, Alfred Isaac, Richard von Mises, Ernst Reuter, Paul Hindemith, and the ORDO economist Alexander Rüstow as guests of Kemal Atatürk on the Bosphorus. In 1937 he accepted the offer of a chair at the Institute des Hautes Études Internationales in Geneva and remained there for the next thirty years.[15] Röpke's 1946 *The Solution of the German Problem,* which lives up to its title's promise, calls for "the application of a principle that in the world today surpasses every other in boldness and novelty."[16] It was, he announced,

the principle of absolute and even, if necessary, one-sided free trade.... The Allies [should] impose on Germany virtually nothing more than a single measure of economic intercourse with foreign countries and ... [also] bring this German free trade into effect the moment the settlement of the most urgent currency and financial issues permits.... Germans will [thus be compelled] to bring into play exceptional resourcefulness, adaptability, and abstinence.

This free-trade policy will, Röpke continued, break down the excessive industrial concentration of heavy industry and so

West Germany would be brought into entire dependence on international trade ... and converted ... into a region uniting an intense, highly developed agriculture dependent on the imports of foodstuffs, with a highly specialized industry, dependent on exports. It would become a sort of enlarged Belgium, and with its extreme dependence on foreign trade would have to abandon any idea of building up an "autarchic" war industry.

The solution would not entail the impoverishment of Germany, as envisaged in the more drastic of Allied occupation plans, but a return to "a prosperity that stands or falls with the interweaving of German industry with international trade."[17] Röpke emphasized that Germany should, in its own economic and political interests, eliminate tariffs regardless of what its neighbors did.

Röpke knew, contrary to public belief, that – in the absence of extreme forms of discrimination – mutual benefit can be expected to flow even from one-sided free trade. His conviction that German (and European) revival depended upon a unilateral initiative appears to be as deeply rooted in patriotic and religious conviction as in economic analysis, and it seems to stem from a belief that renewal must come from within and that economic and political federation must develop from the bottom up. According to Röpke's biographer, Razeen Sally, "national governments, not international organizations or international cartels are responsible for setting appropriate framework conditions for national order, out of which international order emerges as a by-product."[18] Röpke fervently hoped that a cleansed and reformed German nation would provide a beacon of light that "other governments would follow through competitive emulation."

Liberal economists could generate little in the way of illumination in those dank places the British publisher Victor Gollancz visited during a memorable 1945 inspection tour of what he called "darkest Germany."[19] Whether exiled like Wilhelm Röpke or marginalized within Germany like Ludwig Erhard, free marketeers had remained outsiders fully at odds with the fascist politics and the industrial and financial controls of the Third Reich. Its collapse did not bring them back into favor. Support for open markets was absent in both of the main parties that had been organized in the Western zones of occupation, the Social Democratic Party (SPD) and the Christian Democratic Union (CDU). Nor were the military governors prepared to relinquish authority over the economy unless absolutely necessary. Thick new layers of Allied regulation were superimposed over old networks of Nazi controls, which remained legally in effect. Orders and directives of the military governments regulated the collection and exportation of reparations goods but otherwise had little force in an economy whose miseries conjure up memories of *Trümmerfrauen, Kohlenklau, Zigarettenwirtschaft, Schwarze Markt,* and *Inflation* and whose population struggled to avert starvation by providing personal services to GIs and by securing emergency delivery of American foodstuffs.

Ludwig Erhard was the author of the June 1948 currency reform. It would both spark recovery and symbolically end the suffering of Germans who can remember the Occupation but would still prefer to forget. Erhard owed his unlikely rise, which started in January 1948, to an unexpected and unpredictable forced resignation, the inability of contentious German political factions to strike compromises, an apparent lack of any other suitable candidates for the position of director of the Economic Administration attached to the so-called Economic Council, and chance.[20] A politically unaffiliated, protestant Bavarian and consulting economist to an association of retailers, Erhard was a political outsider without support. He was indeed a man who had his moment in history and grabbed it.[21]

The Economic Council had been designed by the Anglo-American military governors of Bizonia to provide a depoliticized proto-government for a future West German state. Until Erhard arrived, the only reform its members envisioned was an updating and improvement of the rationing system and the elimination of "excess money" (*Kaufkraftüberhang*) as a first step toward the restoration of a future planned economy. After nearly fifteen years of Nazi and wartime overregulation, almost no German policy maker other than Erhard could contemplate "a jump into the cold water" of the marketplace. In the heated policy debates of early 1948, Erhard gained the upper hand as well as a token of valuable Allied support for a truly far-reaching currency reform plan, which would not only wipe out the internal debt and drastically curtail the money supply but also de-control prices.

There was simply no feasible alternative to what he recommended. The "steering mechanisms" inherited from the Nazis had broken down irreversibly and the existing price structure was meaningless. Only the restoration of open competition could send necessary and appropriate signals to buyers and sellers.[22] The currency reform of 18 June 1948 met with angry opposition from SPD economists and spokesmen for the labor unions, caused an increase in unemployment to over a million in 1949, reduced the forced equality of the hardship years, and at points even threatened to be inflationary. Yet it was the greatest success of any European economic policy of the twentieth century in both economic and political terms. Erhard became too popular for Chancellor Adenauer to fire – though he despised the chubby Bavarian and objected on moral grounds to the competition principle.

Adenauer first assumed office as chancellor of the new German Federal Republic in fall 1949, when hopes for integration in Europe in the form of a customs union appeared dim if not (in the words of the great Austrian Harvard economist, Gottfried Haberler) "utterly impossible." Haberler thought that, in an age of drastic government interference in the economic process, "a group of countries that wanted to create a free trade area would have to agree not only on a common tariff but also on all major phases of economic policy such as price policy and rationing, credit and development policies, monetary and fiscal policies and several others." Because such agreement was inconceivable, he concluded that "in a democratic Europe ... there will be either planning and no economic and political unification or ... unification [and] no comprehensive economic planning."[23] Equally skeptical was the celebrated Swedish economist and social theorist, Gunnar Myrdal (who, to his great displeasure, had to share the 1974 Nobel Prize with Hayek). In his 1954 book, *The International Economy,* Myrdal concluded after relentless analysis that "advanced welfare states" would, and in their own self-interest probably should, refuse to restore the mobility of capital, labor, and goods needed for integration. To promote something so "self-evidently desirable and economically necessary" as the growth of world (and intra-European) trade, he called for a heroic measure: transplanting the Scandinavian model to less fortunate parts of the world.[24] For his part, Haberler called for "a return to more liberal trading methods and a gradual elimination to the worst impediments to trade."[25] Both agreed that the embedded liberal postwar settlement, which rested on the interweaving of state and economy, constituted an immovable barrier to the integration of Europe. But neither had reckoned with Jean Monnet.

2

The Rise and Decline of Monnetism

JEAN MONNET has a strong claim to be called the Father of Europe. Monnet deserves almost single-handed credit for creating in 1951 the first of Europe's epochal institutions for integration, the European Coal and Steel Community (ECSC). He was also the power behind the grandiose but ill-fated European Defense Community (EDC), a scheme for an integrated armed force composed of multinational units and tied into the NATO command structure that was rejected by France in the summer of 1954. Jean Monnet was, in addition, the moving force behind EURATOM (European Atomic Energy Commission) – a proposal for a continental nuclear power industry – which he put forth in conjunction with the "re-launching" of Europe in 1955. Unlike EDC, EURATOM would not be dead on arrival; instead, along with the ECSC, it would develop into an organ (though only an appendage) of the European Economic Community (EEC). As president from 1954 to 1975 of the Action Committee for the United States of Europe, a lobby for the integration cause, Monnet would be an inexhaustible font of unification and federation initiatives. Yet after the mid-1950s he was reduced to the status of an outsider and could influence the integration process only indirectly through allies in Washington, Bonn, Brussels, and other capitals.[1] Thereafter, many initiatives associated with Monnet stemmed from self-anointed disciples – "monnetists" – acting (sometimes without specific authorization) on his behalf in a manner thought to be consistent with his "spirit." The spectacular flame-out known as the Multilateral Force (MLF), the Kennedy administration's project for a Euro-navy, was a memorable example of a misconceived monnetism in action. Dr. Walter Hallstein's controversial first presidency of the EEC was another debacle for the monnetist cause. In fact, the Frenchman's great achievements belong to the years immediately after World War II – when Europe was still recovering; the United States was supreme; power was held in relatively few hands; socialist, quasi-socialist, state corporatist, and organized capitalist systems were in vogue; and planning was *de rigeur*. They could not have taken place in any other setting.[2]

Jean Monnet thought of himself as an institution builder and has often been so regarded by posterity, but his greatest gift, like Hayek's, was in devising and circulating important ideas and putting words into action. He created, and to a considerable extent still shapes, the rhetoric of integration. To highlight this fact is not to denigrate Monnet's accomplishments but to underscore the inability of any other politician, technocrat, social scientist, or sloganeer to come up with comparable formulations: the big ideas that move the minds of men; concepts that can be organized, marshaled, and made to move in orderly fashion; terms that capture realities that otherwise elude definition; and words that morph into policies, programs, and institutions when nurtured in bureaucratic hothouses. Monnet's idiomatic language has taken on a life of its own and captured the minds of many. Key analytical concepts – the big words used even today to describe the integration process in textbooks, in political discourse, and in public relations campaigns – are Monnet's words: terms that he and his associates coined or that other students of his work invented to give meaning to what he was doing. *Supranationalism, sectoral integration,* and *functionalism* are perhaps the most important examples of such interpretive concepts that still shape academic and professional research. Countless other terms have entered legal, administrative, and economic vocabularies, and out of them has oozed modern Eurospeak. The apparent inescapability of this linguistic legacy makes Monnet an avatar of integration, albeit less owing to his powers as a pure thinker than to his uncanny knack – in an age of science and technology, mass production, and instant communication – to harness the powerful and fertile minds of others to his goals and policies. One might well call him a modern prophet.

Jean Monnet was preeminently a man of his times, one whose unsurpassed knack for getting things done derived from experience gathered over a long and extraordinary career. Monnet was driven by a stirring and powerful *idée fixe*: that the economic modernization and very political survival of both France as a nation and Europe as a civilization depended upon the creation of a federal union. Monnet was a go-getter and a deal maker *extraordinaire,* a man educated not so much formally or academically as on the job and in war management. As a remarkably young senior administrator responsible for France's overseas supply during the Great War, he soon understood the meaning of global interdependence and learned how to use the power of the state to strengthen the national economy. While serving in Washington in the unusual capacity of a French citizen on the British Lend-Lease mission during World War II, Monnet concluded from the miracle of American armaments production that the future would belong economically to the big battalions. Massive state intervention, huge markets, and central control were the order of the day.

Jean Monnet had plenty of additional experience. He had been deputy director of economic affairs for the League of Nations. He had made (and lost) a fortune between the wars as a financier and roving policy entrepreneur operating internationally in the realms of central banking, public finance, and project development. He had connections with powerful friends and policy makers on Wall Street, along the Potomac, and throughout Europe who would prove invaluable after 1945. Monnet's contacts, knowledge, indefatigability, and practicality opened doors to the movers and shakers of his age. But such political savvy would have counted for little without his intense commitment to European union. His determination to unite the continent deeply impressed the many brilliant and strong-willed individuals whose energies he channeled into the task of "building Europe." To them, quite simply, he was *l'Inspirateur* – The Inspiration.[3]

MONNET AND THE CONDITION OF POSTWAR EUROPE

Could anyone else have done what he did? Conditions in post-1945 Europe made classical liberal solutions, if nothing else, politically impossible. Apart from the fact that Germany was occupied – its fate unknown and at the mercy of Cold War conflicts – and that the Soviets were believed to be at the gates, the material and moral conditions prevailing on the devastated continent dictated that the prevention of famine, unrest, and revolution be the sole priority of economic policy. The only alternative to massive American emergency intervention was chaos. At war's end, however, the U.S. public – along with its elected representatives – was wary of such involvement as a costly waste, an attitude that could be changed only over time or by an abrupt shift of circumstance. Thanks in part to a public relations campaign on a scale unprecedented in peacetime, the turning point came with the adoption of the Marshall Plan.[4]

In light of conditions prevailing in continental Europe, the lack of pressure for market-based solutions should come as no surprise. Intellectual entrepreneurship was in this respect conspicuously *pianissimo*; approval of the government-inspired and -directed Marshall Plan was overwhelming even at Mont Pèlerin. Nor did the New York Federal Reserve or the big banks on Wall Street lobby for a policy of "letting the market work," since any destruction – even of the creative and ultimately constructive Schumpeterian type – was too risky to contemplate.[5] There was no substantial flow of private capital into postwar Europe; nor, in fact, could there have been. The embedded liberal regime in place, both nationally and internationally, had been built for the specific purpose of protecting state-directed economies from exposure to world markets. Its capstone, the set of institutions designed at the famous July 1944 conference in Bretton Woods, New Hampshire, was the product of a Keynesian epistemic community of British Liberals and Labourites and American New Dealers representing their two governments.[6]

Distinctions must be made between how they, as well as a broader set of surrounding institutions, operated in theory and in practice. The International Monetary Fund (IMF) was to be the centerpiece of the financial new order. The IMF did not effectively begin operation until 1958, after the period of postwar adjustment was over. It then set as the parameters of both national and international monetary policy an asymmetric, dollar-based system that precluded development of a single European monetary policy and put the nations of the continent at the mercy of Washington. Operation of the IMF required a degree of policy coordination between the Western nations and close ties between economy and state. The Bretton Woods system was conceived as necessary for transition to an open economy, but the length of its presumed lifespan was also to have depended upon the successful attainment and maintenance of full employment. If it came on-line late, the IMF also went off-line early – when the dollar-based system broke down in the 1970s. Later developing as a "work-out specialist" for countries faced with financial crises, the IMF functioned as intended for fewer than fifteen years.

John Maynard Keynes was the real father of the Bretton Woods system. Keynes drafted the proposal for an International Clearing Union (ICU) that provided its key mechanism. The adoption of these plans as the template of U.S. and British Treasury postwar reconstruction policy involved an explicit repudiation of a "Schachtian" Economic New Order model like that adopted by the Nazis after the Fall of France. Rejected was an overall economic strategy relying on the use of a hub-and-spoke network of bilateral, barter-based clearing agreements (though one centering on London rather than Berlin) set up to maintain the Commonwealth as a preferential tariff area, an approach consistent with trends of the 1930s.

Keynes knew that Britain would have to be tied to overall American postwar policy, but he hoped to modify it enough to protect essential British national interests. Article VII of the master Lend-Lease Agreement of December 1941 made U.S. aid and assistance conditional upon British acceptance of nondiscrimination and multilateralism as principles of trade policy, thereby shifting the burden of any "adjustment" to payments. Ruled out was any return to either the pre–World War I gold standard or the partial version of it reintroduced to the "pegged" currencies of the 1920s, which had broken down irretrievably in the Depression decade. Keynes's plans envisaged the survival of the sterling area within a global exchange system anchored in fixed parities and to a dollar gold standard. Successful operation of the system required that creditor nations provide loans to debtors. Without such liquidity, Keynes could argue, deflation would result; at the same time, without such loans, Britain would lose its privileged relationship to the Commonwealth as well as essential protective armor from marketplace competition. By turning a problem of power politics into a context of economic discourse, the brilliant Treasury representative achieved a minor diplomatic miracle. It was never altogether clear whether Keynes's proposals were meant to be medium-term or more or less permanent, but he set U.K. and U.S. policy on paths that, though never smooth, at least converged.[7]

Although extensively modified by British economists and senior civil servants as well as by American policy makers, Keynes's proposal eventually established the dollar – notionally backed by gold at the price of $35 per ounce – as the world monetary standard and fixed the parities between it and other national currencies. Revaluation could occur only in situations of extreme imbalance of payments, which an automatic lending facility was set up to prevent. A country running a deficit in one currency could count on receiving an offsetting amount, up to a certain point, from creditor balances. In the postwar world this involved provision of dollars by countries in surplus (meaning the United States) to those with deficits – chiefly Britain, the Commonwealth, Europe, and the rest of the world outside the Western Hemisphere – and, contrariwise, the acceptance of sterling (or other) balances in return.

The operation of the system depended less on such formal arrangements than on the effectiveness of national capital controls. In place almost universally, these were actually more extensive after World War II than during it. However, such controls were not strong enough to prevent the recurrent bouts of inflation and devaluation that wracked the economies of most European countries.[8] The Bretton Woods system did not, and could not, work until the Marshall Plan–created European Payments Union (EPU) and German liberalization created conditions for a European foreign trade increase that enabled eventual currency alignment.

A similar kind of distinction between plans and realities must be made with regard to trade policy, although in this respect a parallel to the Bretton Woods agreement is missing because the instrument that might have created it was never ratified. The International Trade Organization (ITO), negotiated at Havana in 1944, is a great might-have-been. Calling for tariff reduction and defining acceptable and unacceptable commercial practices, ITO was initially the darling of the traditional free-trade wing of the Democratic Party represented by Secretary of State Cordell Hull and his deputy, Will Clayton. It had long contended for influence in international economic policy with a more radical, socialist-minded group in the Treasury Department. The ITO bill became overloaded with bells and whistles in the ratification process. Its original purpose being defeated, it was allowed to die in Congress. The General Agreement on Tariffs and Trade (GATT), which today thrives as the World Trade Organization, was set up in 1947. The GATT did yeoman's work over the next four years in reducing duties but then lapsed into somnolence until the 1960s.[9] It has been a powerful engine of trade liberalization since the 1970s.

Experience gained internationally along the interface of economics and politics, management experience, connections, drive, and (above all) the intangible referred to as vision combined to develop in Monnet a special aptitude for success in navigating the strange and treacherous waters of postwar European statecraft. His experience in wartime Washington was crucial to his later success. Although officially attached to a British mission, Monnet had a large hand in devising the so-called Victory Program.[10] Adapted from a model developed in the United Kingdom, this program set production targets on the basis of military and economic requirements and factor availability; missed program targets indicated deficiencies. The existence of such an apparently well-planned scheme provided a welcome and surprising opportunity for a propaganda windfall and was of great assistance in mobilizing public opinion, but it had little operational importance. Thought at the time to be unrealistically high, the program's targets were soon wildly exceeded.[11]

Monnet learned from the Victory Program that a technocratic mystique enveloped the word "planning." Although his grasp of economics was weak, he learned enough of planning methodology to export some of it to France. Appointed (after Liberation) head of the new French national development program, the *Plan de Modernisation et d'Équippement,* Monnet hired Robert Nathan as economic consultant. Nathan had been a student of and staff assistant to Simon Kuznets at the War Production Board, one of the sprawling alphabet agencies that sprang out of the ground after Pearl Harbor.[12] During the war, Kuznets developed national income accounting to measure aggregate effective demand (or total output as defined by the sum of all business and consumer spending). He became known as "the man who discovered GNP" (gross national product), a central tool of Keynesian demand management.[13]

Monnet was also familiar with the input–output calculus being devised by another Russian-born Nobel prize–winning Harvard economist, Wassily Leontief. Using the classic notion that all producers are at the same time consumers and with the help of matrix algebra, Leontief devised tables of horizontal columns divided into eighty or ninety sectors (depending on the model) for inputs and vertical lines for outputs. By applying coefficients developed for the consumption of raw materials, he could then determine the effect of changes in inputs on overall output by end-product. Such tables made it possible (in theory) to optimize allocation decisions in a closed system. In 1943, Leontief presented a complete table – based on a model of the 1938 American economy – to the wartime raw material control board. Although the immense number of complicated calculations needed to make practical use of Leontief's tables would require an improvement in computer design, they appeared to represent another new and promising instrument for regulating national economies.[14]

The main source of Jean Monnet's postwar power was his special role as flow regulator along the American aid pipeline. Monnet could justly claim to be "The Frenchman that Washington trusted most!" – at least when it came to spending money. He served as the human conduit through which passed the subsidies that supported the French Provisional Government in Algiers and the armed forces of Free France, and he channeled them as long as possible in the direction of General Henri Giraud, whom President Roosevelt much preferred to the imperious and temperamental General Charles de Gaulle as head of the French provisional government. In early 1946 Monnet again turned up in Washington, this time as behind-the-scenes negotiator of the critical Blum Loan. He managed to earmark no less than half of its proceeds for the industrial development projects of the French Plan, which he controlled. President of that *dirigiste* policy directorate, the peripatetic Frenchman also became a top-level unofficial advisor and policy maker for the Marshall Plan.[15]

The European Recovery Program (ERP), the agency administering the Marshall Plan, faced management problems of unprecedented size and scope. How indeed should the largesse provided by the American taxpayer be allocated? Monnet came up with what sounded like a solution: each recipient nation should establish an equivalent to the French Plan. These could then be set into the ground as foundation stones in a veritable European pyramid of economic control. Monnet sold the idea to the American advisors, who then tried it at the embryonic Marshall Plan assembly of states known as the Organization of European

Economic Cooperation (OEEC). The idea would not fly. The ERP eventually doled out money using its own criteria. Actual expenditure of it would, however, by determined by intranational bargaining.[16] The OEEC would become a valuable piece in the free-trade game and the chief forum through which the removal of nontariff barriers (chiefly import and export quotas) was negotiated. Renamed the OECD (Organization for Economic Cooperation and Development) in 1959, it would transform itself into a high-level discussion forum for – and benchmarker of – global liberalization.[17]

MONNET AND THE ORIGINS OF EUROPEAN INSTITUTIONS

The failure of such visionary schemes as Monnet's at the OEEC by no means undermined or discredited him and may even have raised his profile as Idea Man. The Schuman Plan was even more grandiose than previous proposals. On 9 May 1950, French Foreign Minister Robert Schuman, reading from a speech prepared for him by Monnet, interrupted a regularly scheduled national radio program to make a historic announcement: in order to end the long struggle over west European coal and steel, France proposed joining hands with the ancient enemy across the Rhein in order to form a partnership, open to others, in a future heavy industry community that would make war politically unthinkable and economically impossible. Negotiations toward that end began five weeks later. Entered into by the three Benelux countries and Italy in addition to France and Germany, but with Great Britain remaining on the sidelines, they would continue for eleven months and conclude with initialing on 18 April 1951 of the Treaty of Paris, creating the European Coal and Steel Community. Providing for a powerless representative assembly and a rubber-stamp court, its main feature was a distant and forbidding "High Authority" (HA). Monnet would be the first president. His office was vested with the necessary power to administer the heavy industry of the region as a single unit and specifically to create a common market for coal and steel distribution. The HA controlled vast and far-reaching levers of intervention: it could regulate prices, direct investment, break up cartels or other trade-distorting industrial associations, set common external tariffs for heavy industry products, and involve itself in various different ways in issues of taxation, transportation, and labor. The treaty was to be binding for fifty years and reflected Monnet's own ideas.[18]

The European Coal and Steel Community never operated as intended or, for that matter, even satisfactorily. Yet it cannot be written off as a failure. The founding of the ECSC was a necessary first step to Franco-German reconciliation, which would have been difficult to achieve in any other way. Credit is due to Monnet's vision and deft combination of showmanship and backstage hard dealing. Success also required a unique set of circumstances in West Germany. One was the "lock" of Konrad Adenauer (an extreme Francophile) on the chancellorship. Another was Ludwig Erhard, who was almost as securely fastened into office at the Ministry of Economics. This equally unlikely figure was so supremely confident of the strength of the market economy that he could stomach a deviation from its principles even as sharp as that of the ECSC if it held forth a least some hope of reducing national trade barriers.[19]

The ECSC – though important in the long run as a source of European reconciliation – cannot take much credit for preventing war in Europe, the first sweeping promise made in the Schuman Plan announcement, but it has since served as the opening line in the integration mantra. The parameters of conflict had shifted in response to the events of 1939–1945. Underwritten by American money and power, NATO is responsible for having bound western Europe in a straightjacket that has tied the hands of any would-be mischief-makers and even, perhaps, for having helped contain the Red Army. The doctrine of massive retaliation adopted in 1953, as well as the later variant perversely and quite properly called mutually assured destruction (MAD) – together with the annihilating power of the American nuclear arsenal that lent credibility to them – is what really kept the peace during the Cold War. Developments in western European heavy industry were trifling by comparison.[20]

Moreover, the coal and steel sector was not (as the Schuman announcement implied) a "historic problem" and had seldom been a bone of Franco-German contention since World War I. After 1926, the coal mines and iron and steel factories in the neighboring countries were linked together in a dense, sturdy network of private and quasi-public agreements that regulated relationships between them in a mutually satisfactory manner and provided the underpinning of the International Steel Cartel (ISC) that survived until 1939.[21] The wartime relationship between the heavy industries of the Reich and occupied Europe involved more collaboration than conflict.[22] The revival of such conveniently forgotten traditions was featured as evidence of a "new spirit" in the heavy industry of western Europe.

The strategic importance of European coal and steel, particularly that of the landlocked Ruhr, turned out to be slight and diminishing in the 1950s. Changes in technology and a reduction of shipping costs unleashed a flood of American coal onto European markets; new steel plants were built in coastal regions, close to supplies of cheap combustibles from overseas. Oil from the Middle East flooded energy markets, and Asian and Latin American steel producers kept pressure on prices. Rates of growth were, in fact, slow in the "old" branches of European production as compared to the expanding new ones of the consumer economy. The tied-in, heavy industry–dominated trusts belonged to the past rather than the future. Conflicts over coal and steel were quickly being relegated to history's old curio chest. Monnet could score his diplomatic victory in the Schuman Plan negotiations because less was at stake than met the eye. In politics, non-problems are easily solved.[23]

Coal–steel conflict had nonetheless been severe in the five immediate postwar years and did stand in the way of Franco-German reconciliation. Supplies were short because of productivity declines not only on the war-torn continent but also in an exhausted Great Britain – no less important than Germany as exporter to a coal-deficient France. The result was cold winters and bottlenecks that limited industrial production. Who was to bear the cost? In an aggressive strategy designed to offset the lack of wartime investment and, indeed, to achieve European steel supremacy, the French *Plan de Modernisation et d'Équippement* – the "Monnet Plan," as it came to be known – embarked upon a crash building program to modernize the foundry industry. The defeated Germans would have to provide the precious coal.

Because falling productivity made it difficult to raise outputs, restrictions had to be placed on German steel production even if it meant delaying recovery. This was the object of French and Allied policy. A specially created International Ruhr Authority had the task of squeezing out as much coal as possible for exportation. "Level of industry" agreements set output maxima for steel, which in fact could never be attained and cast a shadow over the future. The same was true of the trusteeships that were set up to manage both the coal and steel industries: they clouded the ownership question and seemed to point to eventual socialization. Many senior managers found themselves relegated to months in the so-called Dustbin, an interrogation camp worthy of its name. Given the destruction of purchasing power, the extreme scarcity of raw material, and the virtual disappearance of wage incentives, it was clear that German heavy industry – like every other sector – could only limp along on handouts from the occupation authorities. More ominous still, the British began a dismantlement campaign in late 1948. The coal and steel industries were apparently not allowed to run at normal operational levels and in fact were to be at least partly destroyed, whether to create an artificial coal surplus (one explanation) or to reduce the threat of future competition (another). Work parties armed with wrench and blowtorch were still busily taking factories apart in the Ruhr on the day of the Schuman Plan announcement.[24]

Negotiation of the Schuman Plan was the turning point in Adenauer's *Westpolitik* and thus also the most important event in West German foreign policy – until collapse of the Berlin Wall in November 1989 made it no longer necessary to speak of a *West* Germany. *Westpolitik* was simplicity itself: the German nation would win its way back into the good graces of Europe by whatever means necessary, including the forfeiture of sovereign power, in order to end the Occupation. It is easy to forget that Adenauer won election as chancellor in 1949 with only the slimmest of margins against a candidate, Kurt Schumacher of the SPD, who had managed to antagonize each of the Big Four occupation powers by his unwavering commitment to restoring a national Germany. It is even more difficult to remember that, prior to the Schuman Plan, the biggest breakthrough in Adenauer's foreign policy had come in the area of *Teppichpolitik* (carpet policy). That is, in October 1945 the newly installed chancellor managed to be photographed standing on the same oriental rug with, and in the viceregal presence of, American High Commissioner John J. McCloy – a symbolic victory. He was now, it appeared, to be treated like a head of state. The fledgling German democracy was not only disarmed; it lacked diplomatic representation above the level of counselor service.[25] For the chancellor of the young Federal Republic to be treated on a basis of equality with the French premier at the opening of the coal–steel negotiations in Paris was itself a precedent of huge importance, even though appearances can mislead. In fact, Monnet had vetoed Adenauer's first two candidates to head the German delegation to the talks (the second of whom was Wilhelm Röpke!) and then handpicked the third, an obscure professor of law at the University of Frankfurt named Walter Hallstein.[26]

The Schuman Plan negotiations can easily be sentimentalized as the crucible of a new European spirit. They were, in reality, often tough and even brutal. Monnet played ringmaster. He set the agenda, chaired the conference, headed the French delegation, and behind the scenes coordinated his own policy with that of the U.S. embassy in Paris and the Allied High Commission in Bonn, both of which were headed by friends and disciples. The bitterest battles were over the future of the Ruhr. Monnet's policy was to "decartelize" coal and steel production – not so much to encourage competition, which could only strengthen the German economy over the long run, but to break up a potential concentration of monopoly. He meant to hogtie the Germans until they could be trusted or until France had gotten mean enough to handle them. The as yet unreconstructed and politically incorrect smokestack barons of the Ruhr thought this unfair and raged for months.[27]

The negotiations might have broken down at any point between late September 1950 and January of the following year. This was the critical period, following the outbreak of the Korean War, in which President Truman decided to build up NATO. It would no longer be just a cadre with color guard and a ceremonial headquarters in Paris but instead would become a tough fighting force of forty U.S. divisions operating as part of an integrated strategy and supported by another twenty European ones to be either built up from existing units or, in the German case, organized from scratch. The aid of a crystal ball was not necessary to prophesy that, as a result of events in a remote corner of the world, a momentous power shift to Germany's advantage would occur in Europe. Monnet grasped the point immediately after the first North Korean troops crossed the 38th parallel. To prevent the collapse of the Schuman Plan negotiations, Monnet cooked up plans for a second, even bolder supranational venture – the European Defense Community – and soon put the latter into play diplomatically. In the end, it was less the force of this initiative than the lack of strong allies that prevented the German forge-masters from sweeping the board at the Schuman Plan negotiations, becoming instead sweepings themselves. Chancellor Adenauer was willing to sacrifice the interests of the Ruhr to the greater good of reconciliation with France; Minister of Economics Erhard, though resentful at being pushed around, was prepared to accept almost any measure (regardless of intent) that would step up the pace of competition. Backed by the threat of American reprisal, Monnet forced the big German industrialists to accept treaty provisions and deals negotiated by McCloy that set tough preconditions for ending foreign control and restoring sovereignty. The novel feature of the deal was that control would no longer be exercised at the national but at the "supranational" level, by the High Authority of the European Coal and Steel Community. The mines and factories of the Ruhr would pass seamlessly from an Allied regulatory regime to the oversight of the High Authority of the new ECSC. This coal–steel settlement was to be part of the timetable governing German political restoration.[28]

The provisions for "deconcentration and decartelization" did not turn out to be of great operational importance. In spite of angry protests, the traditional marketing machinery for heavy industry products continued to operate much as before beneath a thicket of new names, rules, and regulations. This was because the coal and steel producers in the rest of the ECSC were only slightly less eager than the Germans to preserve the industrial status quo. A revived version of the old international steel cartel actually re-appeared in 1953. The partly dictated slimming down of the trusts was, for its part, a blessing in disguise and for competitive reasons was practically inevitable. One cannot speak of "business as usual" being the rule in Luxembourg, where the coal–steel community had its headquarters. Prices, marketing arrangements, licensing, transport costs, tax issues, and a host of other business matters were sources of bitter contention and endless wrangling between producers and the High Authority. *Dirigisme* (state-directed planning), like *la collaboration,* became a dirty word in several languages.

The High Authority could claim a short list of miscellaneous precedents and accomplishments. One was purely technical in character. Invited by Monnet to act as consultant, Jan Tinbergen (later a Nobel Prize winner in economics) produced pioneering analyses of inequities in both taxation and shipping costs. On the financial side, the HA imposed a special levy on steel output to cover operating expenses, the first Euro-tax. With the help of his close friend, John Foster Dulles, Monnet also raised a huge American loan whose proceeds were too large to spend; it served as his personal slush fund. Monnet plowed the money into high-visibility projects like worker housing. In a somewhat more exotic area, the HA organized a crisis cartel in scrap, which alleviated immediate shortages. The High Authority also administered an expensive scheme of income transfers from the productive collieries of the Ruhr, where pay was low and levels of investment high, to the worn-out producing districts of Belgium, where wages were high and investment low – a bad precedent and the kind of inequitable measure that would have a sequel in the Common Agricultural Policy (CAP).

The opening of the two common markets in coal and steel in 1953 counts only as a partial credit for the ECSC, since tariffs did not exist in coal and were low in steel and since markets continued to be distorted by a wide variety of nontariff barriers. Some importance must be assigned the public relations impact of the opening of the two markets, whatever the economic realities, because common markets and integration became linked in the public mind. The deficit side includes a lack of noteworthy progress in discharging statutory commitments to increasing labor mobility or in otherwise expanding and filling out the "social dimension." These, too, would be harbingers of things to come and not to come.

What came to be called the *sectoral* approach toward integration – placing a single branch of industry or economic activity in a new international regime with a view to renovating or expanding it, or at least creating some new tradition of cooperation within it – was, as demonstrated by the ECSC example, a flop. It neither accelerated industrial growth nor stimulated technological or organizational change; the long-term decline of heavy industry would continue inexorably. The consumer had to bear the costs of financial transfers and cross-subsidization. Morale suffered at the HA from the lack of progress, Euroenthusiasm went limp, and over cocktails bureaucrats talked less about business and more about perks. Unable to conceal his dismay at the detumescence in Luxembourg, Monnet spent as little time as possible there and immersed himself in other issues.[29]

The supranationalism of the ECSC nonetheless requires comment. It survived the dismal performance of the coal–steel pool. Owing to the aura of novelty and purposefulness surrounding the idea, it would remain a fixture of policy making and integration discourse. Momentous was the fact that governments of non-occupied countries (Italy, the Benelux nations, and above all France), which were not under duress, agreed to transfer sovereign power to an international body. What Monnet held forth nevertheless went far beyond the setting of a mere precedent. He claimed to have devised a new method for resolving conflicts between states. The supranational principle, as he envisaged it, required an international form of organization far more robust than a mere confederation or deliberative body like a League of Nations, which was capable of reaching agreement only by means of compromise and consensus. Monnet claimed that a strong and remote executive could act quickly and decisively – make big changes fast – and propagate the kind of economic cooperation that would ultimately lead to political federation and secure peace.

Supranationalism met with a varied reception. To the British it was an abomination, to the French a flag of convenience, to the Italians it was preferable (by definition) to government by Rome, to the Germans a welcome escape route, and to the Benelux nations a better choice than domination by powerful neighbors. To all of them, the transfer of sovereign power was a negotiable matter. No European nation (with the possible exception of Germany under Adenauer) would accept substantial material or political sacrifice for the sake of supranationalism, which was not considered – except perhaps in the case of the small countries bound in a narrow union of The Six – a necessary part of any integration scenario.

To locate deep and abiding enthusiasm for the supranational principle, one must turn to the United States. Perhaps because of the powerful grip of the American state-building tradition on the national imagination, the founding of the ECSC gave hope to the idea that, like the thirteen colonies, the nations of Europe could form a political union of their own. "Functionalism" grew out of this

belief. The seductive appeal of this theory has stimulated and guided what remains the most influential tradition of American academic integration research
to date; it still often lurks in the background of debates. As first argued by a
brilliant Berkeley political scientist named Ernst Haas – who, with the support
and cooperation of Monnet himself, developed the theory in a case study of the
ECSC – functionalism holds that the creation of new institutions at the supranational level will have effects that "spill over" into the national arena and so
generate counterpressures at the supranational level. Thus, a process of change
is set in motion that strengthens the authority of the state at all levels, increases
power supranationally, and binds states more closely together. In spite of the
theory's lack of predictive power, not to mention Haas's many disclaimers, its
reign continues.[30]

Of more immediate concern to the issues at hand is that the doctrine of supranationalism became "hot gospel" in the State Department under Secretary of
State John Foster Dulles in the 1950s. The notion that Europe could only be organized as a political federation headed by a strong supranational directorate was
for Dulles an article of faith – an idol, even, to which he was prepared to sacrifice
other American foreign policy objectives (like free trade) as well as important economic interests and large amounts of money. Dulles was an immensely wealthy
international lawyer and had been Monnet's close personal friend for many years.
The two men met at the Versailles Peace Conference in 1919. Dulles stood in
awe of the charismatic Frenchman and even bailed him out financially in the late
1930s, no questions asked. Monnet had many other allies as well. In the course
of the Schuman Plan and related negotiations he had enlisted an assortment of
friends, business associates, and government contacts into a tightly organized
though informal international "team" set up to promote, develop, and implement
his proposals. A few of the American members were acquaintances from before
the war, but many others had risen to positions of responsibility in the course of
U.S. engagement in Europe after 1945. These were no longer the quiet-spoken
gentlemen – with combed-down hair and wearing rimless spectacles, frock coats,
and shirts with detachable collars – whom one might have encountered in the
corridors of power between the wars. These were smart, buttoned-down, hard-
fisted, gum-chewing guys who could speak out of the corners of their mouths
when on the telephone while puffing on cigarettes at the same time. From their
ranks would come a hard core of dedicated monnetist disciples in the State and
Treasury departments, at the Pentagon and the CIA, and even in the White House
under Eisenhower and Kennedy. Their influence – which in fact extended to only
one corner of American policy, though it happened to be the often vital one of
European integration – outweighed their numbers. Colleagues who either did
not share their views or lacked their zeal mocked them as Theologians. Special
circumstances had to obtain in order for this team of monnetists to project their
visions broadly across policy making, and with the disappearance of such circumstances their influence soon evaporated as well. This group of true-believing
ideologues revitalized monnetism even as it was petering out in Europe.[31]

The European Defense Community was the climacteric of monnetism and a bad idea in both theory and practice – unnecessary both politically and militarily as well as antidemocratic from start to finish. Although Monnet's original purpose in devising the Euro-army proposal was tactical (i.e., to stall German rearmament), it soon took on a life of its own as sequel to the ESCS in the functionalist integration dialectic. Like the Schuman Plan, the EDC initiative bore the name of someone other than its author. René Pleven, the French *premier du jour,* had served as Monnet's deputy during one of the currency stabilization missions that he headed in the 1920s and as Monnet's assistant during his brief stint in London after the German invasion of France. Pleven had few qualms about serving as his mouthpiece.

The Pleven Plan was a clarion call for the creation of a European army composed of multinational units that would enshrine the spirit of the new Europe. Like the ECSC, however, it was structured in such a way as to provide guarantees of French security and to project French power. The allocation of authority within the organization was keyed into the size of military budgets. France had the largest armed force on the continent, and Britain predictably refused to participate in the scheme. French officers were thus to be placed in command of a force composed largely of German troops, at least over a period of no less than several years and until the occupation formally ended and sufficient time had elapsed for the Federal Republic to raise an army of equal size. Even then, it would probably take another decade before national parity could be reached. At stake were largely matters of gold braid and money, as well as the intangible of political clout. Although the issue was not discussed publicly, the EDC was intended not to operate independently of NATO but instead to have defensive responsibilities along the central perimeter, execute them according to NATO plans, and remain under the command of Supreme Headquarters, Allied Powers in Europe (SHAPE). It could engage in combat only by order of the American president. Hence EDC was a case of old wine in new bottles: a policy conceived in the French national interest, dressed up in European language, and from a military standpoint having little other than symbolic significance. With the adoption of massive retaliation as strategic doctrine before the treaty had been ratified, ground forces in Europe (no matter how organized) became bit players – mere tripwires to general nuclear war.[32]

There was considerably more to the EDC proposal than first met the eye. A commissariat, inspired by Monnet, was to have oversight power over the multinational armed force like that of the High Authority of the ECSC over the western European coal and steel industry. "More than a defense ministry," according to a West German military historian, "it [resembled] a European government with four ministries, with the *military* commissariat being like a ministry of defense." He adds that "the contractually guaranteed independence of the commissioners from their governments, the huge [planned] budgets, and the immense defense administrations which practically nullified national boundaries ... would surely have given the commissariat vast powers."[33] They were to include an "iron budget" that it would set and to which member states would be obliged to contribute. Also foreseen was the organization of a new Europe-wide armaments industry. American aid administrators, troubled by the immense waste involved in "unnecessary" duplication of the national programs of weapons manufacture then running, welcomed the introduction of centralized procurement. One senior U.S. military assistance official even suggested setting up a European Production Fund that would "combine elements of the programs previously administered separately as offshore procurement and defense support," putting American money into a common pot with the Europeans so as to facilitate order placement on a still greater scale, thereby providing an additional spur to industrial modernization.[34]

The foreign ministers of the six ECSC member-nations initialed the EDC treaty in May of 1952. At the insistence of French socialists (whose votes were needed for treaty ratification) that a political control mechanism be established to oversee the EDC, a new round of negotiations for a European Political Community (EPC) began soon thereafter. The document that arose from these discussions made provision for a council of ministers either identical or similar to that of the ECSC – the matter was deliberately left ambiguous – as well as a popularly elected assembly (whose relationship to the ECSC also remained unclear). A codicil to one EDC treaty proposed fusing it, along with the ECSC, into a federal union for Europe.[35]

Over two years of intermittent (though heated) public discussion and hard-fought behind-the-scenes struggles over the EDC treaty ensued in France and elsewhere until July 1954, when the French Chamber of Deputies finally let it die. No one but the Germans really liked the proposed Euro-force, and they had a special reason for feeling as they did: according to the May 1952 *Generalvertrag* (general treaty), approval of the EDC treaty by The Six ECSC nations would lead straight to the end of occupation and thus to re-armament. In the other five ECSC nations, the EDC met with varying degrees of disapproval, distaste, suspicion, and hostility. Only with greatest difficulty could it be ratified anywhere. The proposal remained in play for two reasons. One was a dependence upon American military aid. In the twelve months after the outbreak of the Korean War, European defense expenditures doubled from \$5 billion to \$9 billion, straining budgets and rekindling barely repressed inflation. At this point American military assistance had to re-enter the picture. From 1951 to 1954, which coincides roughly with the period during which the EDC was under discussion, annual aid provided under the Mutual Security Program approximated that of the Marshall Plan. In the not unrepresentative French case, this aid amounted to half of total defense outlays or about a quarter of the French national budget. Even after recovery, Europe remained precariously dependent upon Washington.[36]

Without increasingly harsh and eventually unremitting pressure from Washington, the EDC proposal could not have been kept alive for three-and-a-half long years. It would almost surely have been tactfully dropped had the Democrats won the 1952 presidential election. Though no great enthusiast for a Euro-force, President Truman was reluctant to go against the advice of Secretary of State Dean Acheson on the issue. Acheson thought integration a good idea but was no fanatic on the subject. In early 1952 he recalled David Bruce, one of Monnet's most ardent admirers, from the Paris embassy for overzealous integrationism. With more pressing issues (e.g., the Korean war) to deal with and for much of the time a lame duck, Acheson preferred to waffle. Like virtually all military men, President Eisenhower first reacted to the EDC proposal with astonishment that one would actually *want* to field an army in which officers might not understand the language of their men or of each other. However, he soon came to stand behind the proposal when convinced by The Inspiration of the overriding importance of the political goals animating the project.[37]

The changing of the guard in Washington made a big difference indeed for the Euro-army proposal. The new Secretary of State, John Foster Dulles, pressed home the point from the outset. Dulles's first tour of European diplomatic posts was

notable for the sheer intensity of will-power ... applied to [discussing] the discouraging prospects for the EDC. Gathering all the mission chiefs or their deputies at a meeting in the embassy in Paris, and after rather curtly paraphrasing his expectation of "positive loyalty," he stressed the absolute necessity for full ratification of the [treaty] within six months and ordered those present not to tolerate any discussion of alternatives within their embassies, nor to admit in their dealings with European officials and the press that alternatives even existed.[38]

To enforce the policy, and to browbeat the Europeans, Dulles took the unusual step of appointing the recently recalled David Bruce as special representative in Paris. The campaign on behalf of the EDC culminated in Dulles's notorious "agonizing reappraisal" speech of December 1953, in which he sullenly threatened to pull the rug out from under Europe – giving the ungrateful citizens of that sorry continent an opportunity to defend themselves against the Soviets – if the treaty were rejected. After the defeat at Dien Bien Phu and the decision to abandon Viet Nam, the French cabinet was finally in a position to risk the U.S. aid cutback. Six weeks later, the EDC was dead.[39]

"The rejection of the EDC," Bruce confided in his diary, would amount to

the greatest diplomatic triumph ever achieved by the USSR. In Russia, as well as in the Iron Curtain countries and amongst the Communist parties of other nations, including the Soviet-controlled Communist delegation in the French National Assembly, the cardinal policy of Soviet policy has been, for some years, to prevent the coming into being of the European Defense Community. The men of the Kremlin ... realize that the EDC has become the symbol of unity of the free world.[40]

Dulles went into an even deeper funk. The defeat of the Euro-army plans had precipitated, he warned, "a crisis of almost terrifying proportions."[41] Even Monnet was non-plussed. To Bruce he intimated a decision to resign as president of the ECSC, where in any case he had already been badly disappointed. For whatever reason, Monnet abruptly changed his mind and, convinced that the EDC was not "dead but only wounded," decided not to step down. In November he actually did resign, then rescinded the offer and eventually had to be forced ignominiously out of office in June 1955.[42] None of the predicted dread consequences of EDC rejection actually occurred. Within two months, Great Britain, France, and the United States had agreed to shift to the NATO alternative for German rearmament: the *Bundeswehr* would be organized into national contingents and be treated like any other member of the alliance. The Allied Commission thereupon cleared out its drawers, emptied its files, and shut its doors; the Occupation of West Germany was ended.

There is no reason to rue the failure of the EDC. The proposal would have (1) created an analogue to the military–industrial complex then developing in the United States, (2) excluded the possibility of democratic oversight or public accountability, and (3) tied the integration of Europe to the politics of the Cold War and to American hegemony. It was unnecessary. The NATO solution to German rearmament could have been adopted at any time. Only the Germans, whose economy was unburdened by the heavy military outlays of NATO members, benefited from the delay.[43] The Euro-force debacle was a setback for integration only in the sense that a better approach might otherwise have been followed earlier. The "re-launching" of Europe would begin within months of German re-armament. Its pre-history had less to do with Monnetist tradition than with the politics of liberalization.[44]

It is nevertheless hard to devise an alternative to the integration scenario actually followed at the inception of the process. Only the French government, or someone speaking on its behalf, could have set the politics of reconciliation with Germany on course. The matter could not have been discussed before the public, opened to debate in the National Assembly, or navigated through the relevant ministries. War and collaboration were bitter memories, and critical resources like coal were still scarce. Monnet had a policy for dealing with the immediate problem of the Ruhr in addition to a medium-term plan that, although in many ways unsound, at least provided mechanisms for a transition. He was also, thanks to his Washington connection, uniquely well placed to enlist the support of the (apparently all-powerful) United States for his policies and leadership. Adenauer immediately recognized the opportunity presented by the Schuman Plan and did everything within his power, including overriding both the Ministry of Economics and the leaders of Ruhr industry, to facilitate its acceptance. The politics of conciliation yielded large dividends. The Schuman Plan was the bridge that West Germany crossed back to Europe.

The ECSC was a boon to the Federal Republic precisely because the High Authority could not effectively exercise the vast powers conferred upon it by the Treaty of Paris. The ECSC could annoy, harass, and threaten, but it lacked the enforcement machinery to inflict much real pain. Supranationalism in practice was a paper tiger. The attempt to administer a single sector of industry from the top down was outrun by overseas competition. Though disappointment with the ECSC was general and though the level of discouragement was rising at the High Authority, Monnet (and the monnetists) drew the wrong lesson from the ECSC. Not more but rather less in the way of *dirigisme* – especially when steered or charted by Washington – was called for. Yet the EDC debacle failed to drive home the point. The blind alley of EURATOM would follow in the mid-1950s, and the dead end of the multilateral force proposal would be reached still another five years later.

At least in theory, however, supranationalism was something new under the sun. The founding of the ECSC did result in the transfer of sovereignty, the setup of a parliamentary assembly, court, and executive, and the assertion of a right to make European law. The coal–steel community further secured for itself the authority to conduct tariff negotiations within GATT on behalf of western European coal and steel producers. The uses to which such institutional shells and theoretical claims would be put were vague at best. Although the "re-launchers" of Europe – men painfully aware of the shortcomings of the Monnet approach – assiduously avoided all mention of supranationalism in the negotiations that would lead to the formation of the EEC, the proposal for a European customs union emerged from within the membership of The Six coal–steel pool partners and would take place within the conceptual framework of ECSC institutions. The persuasiveness of Monnet's ideas (more than their effectiveness) explains why the European Economic Community, organized for a different set of reasons, would bear a family resemblance to the ECSC, contain at least part of its genetic makeup, and retain the potential to develop along monnetist lines. The man Monnet handpicked as chief of the German delegation to the Schuman Plan negotiations, Walter Hallstein, would also be named the first president of the new EEC executive, the European Commission. Hallstein would prove to be faithful to the legacy.

3

More or Less Liberal Europe:
The Institutional Origins of Integration

"RE-LAUNCHING of Europe" is the phrase coined to capture the spirit of the lengthy round of diplomacy that began at Messina, Sicily, on 1 June 1955. It opened less than a year after the EDC fiasco and concluded, after the initialing of the Treaty of Rome on 25 March 1957, with the establishment of the machinery for a future customs union – the European Economic Community, or Common Market – on 1 January 1958. The term "re-launching," or "re-launch" as it is sometimes translated from the French *rélance,* is no misnomer: The first ship to embark, with *Schuman Plan* on its prow, had gone aground and so a second one of improved design, the *Messina,* set out five years later, heading off in another direction – toward market liberalization. No one knew how to find the destination, whether the vessel in question would be sturdy enough to get there, or whether a still stouter tub, following a somewhat better tack, might arrive first. The fog of uncertainty would not soon lift. Europe was becoming liberal, more or less, but the course was not set. Doubt would remain the rule even after 1960, when a competitive yet cooperative European Free Trade Association (EFTA) came into being as a potential rival, co-partner, or merger candidate of the EEC. Outcomes would be determined by economic trends, the continuation of the boom under way; by high politics, the European states' relationships with each other and with the United States; and by the personalities and policies of officeholders in Washington, Paris, London, Bonn, and Brussels.

The impressive economic growth of the 1950s sustained both re-armament and the expansion of the welfare state, and by the end of the decade it was beginning to produce a modern consumer society in western Europe. It rested on a steady (though far from complete) deregulation of the industrial economies, the restoration of currency convertibility, and the reduction of tariff and non-tariff barriers to trade. Growth within Europe depended upon the continuation of a "virtuous cycle" of trade in which expanding West German exports on world markets stimulated demand for the foodstuffs, raw materials, semifinished goods, and specialized manufactures of its neighbors, ECSC and non-ECSC alike. Open-market competition both from and within the Federal Republic exercised downward pressure on prices, kept inflation in check (except in France prior to 1958), and provided an early example of what Röpke termed "competitive emulation." Two unknowns stood in the way of forming a customs area around a German nucleus. One was France; the other, Great Britain.

The United Kingdom had refused to enter into the Schuman Plan negotiations or join the ECSC, reluctant either to break ties with the Commonwealth or weaken its special relationship with the United States; the conservative Eden government was similarly standoffish in 1955. Britain chose to be a spectator at the re-launch, hopeful that whatever went out would eventually sink. Only The Six ECSC member states would climb on board the *Messina*. Belatedly awakening to possible exclusion from European markets, in June 1956 the United Kingdom embarked uncertainly in a craft of its own, christened *Free Trade Area,* initiating a round of negotiations at the OEEC that would begin a year later and end in October 1958 with the enunciation of President de Gaulle's first memorable *Non* on the integration question. At stake in the rivalry between The Six and the others was not only the size of the future trade area – all nineteen nations would have been included under the British plan – but also its character. Be it customs union or free-trade area, a larger entity would be not only looser but, *nolens volens,* more open and competitive than a smaller one. Since support for a free-trade area was widespread in much of Europe outside of France, the lack of either British leadership or American encouragement – combined with Chancellor Adenauer's firm opposition to any attenuation of the new relationship with France – sealed the fate of the initiative. Seven of the countries left out of the EEC nonetheless revived the proposal, though excluding agriculture from their remit. Negotiations resumed outside the OEEC framework. Agreement soon followed to form the European Free Trade Association, thereby putting Europe – as repeated ad nauseam over the next several years – at sixes and sevens.[1]

Those in the vanguard of the French economic and administrative elite (as well as those governments of the Fourth Republic keened into industrial renewal) recognized that modernizing required access to large markets and, like their British counterparts, dreaded being left odd man out in a European association dominated by Germany. They wanted to enter a customs union with the powerful neighbor but faced two unpleasant realities: the entrenched and pervasive protectionism of industry, labor, and agriculture; and the existence of a "game preserve" (*chasse gardée*) in the form of the French Union. Even though this empire was being lost, neither big business nor senior officialdom would willingly give it up. Torn between the need for economic reform and the pain involved in the process, French treaty negotiators needed agricultural and industrial concessions from their European partners in order to avert repudiation. The fate of the customs union project would turn largely on whether France could be granted special favors without flagrantly violating the principles of free trade. Obfuscation was called for.

Here the sidelight known as the European Atomic Community entered the picture. Once again backed strongly by the U.S. State Department, Monnet injected this proposal for a European atomic energy authority into the customs union negotiations in order to advance integration along supranationalist and *planiste* lines. Thus EURATOM was to have organized and directed the development of a European nuclear power industry by controlling allocation of the fissile material needed to fuel reactors. The United States was the most important source of such material.[2] The governments of both Edgar Faure and Guy Mollet, which directed policy making during the re-launch, championed the Monnet proposal as the preferred approach to integration because it provided not only a convenient "smoke screen" (as Faure described it) behind which France could protect its interests but also a bargaining chip that could be traded for economic concessions needed to make French entrance into a future customs union politically acceptable.[3]

The ploy was effective. There was, as they knew perfectly well, no hope for EURATOM. France had pursued a coordinated program of civil and military nuclear development since 1946,[4] and the chance that it would be sacrificed in the name of Europe was nil. For its part angry about ECSC-type *dirigisme* and expecting to receive more equitable treatment from American business partners than from a Euro-nuclear power authority, German industry adamantly opposed the EURATOM initiative from start to finish. French negotiators must also have realized that the U.S. Atomic Energy Commission, under the direction of Lewis Strauss, would veto the assistance upon which the scheme depended. French negotiators might from time to time have tweaked the EURATOM proposal in the off chance of gaining technical advantage or some other form of support for their nuclear program, but they did not take it seriously. As a driver of integration, EURATOM was stillborn.

The customs unions negotiations were a huge triumph for France. In addition to special provisions protecting agriculture and the French Union, the Treaty of Rome would contain numerous carefully drafted escape and safeguard clauses. Thanks to the Rueff–Pinay reform of 1958, such hard-earned concessions became superfluous: the emergency packet of measures represented a belated but successful attempt to catch up with the liberalization process at work elsewhere in Europe. The bundle devalued the franc, brought the deficit under control and inflation to a standstill, helped produce a Gallic economic miracle, goaded the anxiety-ridden and lethargic producers of France into action, and proved that fears of uncompetitiveness lacked substance. The French could once again play a leading role in the integration process.

Britain would become the nucleus of the European Free Trade Association. It eliminated tariffs among its seven members (Austria, Britain, Denmark, Norway, Portugal, Sweden, and Switzerland) but did not provide for a common external tariff. The EFTA was explicitly non-supranational and apolitical, and its tiny headquarters in Geneva had only one real task: to organize the annual membership meetings where technical trade issues were, quite amicably, thrashed out. However, EFTA lost much of its *raison d'etre* after Britain joined the European Economic Community in 1972 and after the remaining members (through association agreements) also entered the customs union. The EFTA received little attention either during or since its heyday. Cooperation within the framework of this modest organization nevertheless wove the economies of the quite disparate organization together and promoted growth effectively – without much ado, at little cost, and to the mutual benefit and general satisfaction of its members. The European Free Trade Association remained the weaker of the two trade organizations cohabiting in Europe because West Germany did not join it. Though often treated as a captive of British policy or as a pale second best to the EEC, and though mistrusted and undermined by the State Department as divisive, EFTA actually represented a serious alternative model to the young Common Market.[5] The lessons that can be learned from it grow in relevance as membership in the EEC has increased.

World trade increased about threefold in the 1950s; intra-European exports and imports quadrupled while West Germany's exports and imports nearly quintupled during this decade. At the same time, the value of European foreign trade grew twice as rapidly as GNP, and German foreign trade expanded at nearly four times the growth of European GNP.[6] During these years the European economy was being internationalized – and the German economy "Europeanized" – in a virtuous circle that, if interrupted, would exact heavy penalties. The beneficial development of this set of reciprocal relationships presupposed a framework of international institutions that would set rules and provide the continuity needed for market exchange and expansion, the liberalization of the European economy, and the adoption of appropriate policies in Germany and eventually the other European nations as well.

FROM *PAX AMERICANA* TO *PAX UNIVERSALIA*

The *Pax Britannica* of the mid-nineteenth century developed directly through the market and was capped by a *système des traités,* a network of bilateral agreements to abstain from interference with the exchange process. To restore a liberal trading area, market-oriented World War II American peacetime planners (and their heirs) had to renovate what remained of ruined institutions or build new ones to replace them. Only then could a process of liberalization be set in motion. The machinery of embedded liberalism worked well but could have performed still better if markets had been opened up sooner. European sentiment in favor of such a forward policy was diffuse, but pressure for it came chiefly from the one remaining bastion of liberal theory, West Germany. There was little dissatisfaction elsewhere with the existing embedded liberal system, and there was a reluctance to change horses midstream. The system, in fact, produced satisfactory results – increased competition, expanded markets, and convertibility. Support for liberalizing institutions rested implicitly on the conviction that power and responsibility for the conduct of the international economic system should be shared. As recovery and prosperity took hold, Europe gradually emerged from tutelage. The economic *Pax Americana* was not set, poured, cast, and hardened into a rigid structure determined by the postwar distribution of power but rather resembled a nascent *Pax Universalia* of shared authority and responsibility that would grow, over time, out of deep commitment to common principle.

The liberalization process was long and complicated. Although GATT, the forum created for negotiating tariff reductions, launched three rounds of discussions between 1947 and 1951, only the first of them (which took place in Geneva) was of great importance. Progress on further reductions would not resume until the opening of the Dillon Round of 1961–1962. In order to avoid the free-rider problem inherent in the most-favored nation (MFN) principle, the Geneva talks adopted the "principal supplier" rule by which a country negotiates with its major suppliers only. The Geneva talks thus produced a multiplicity of bilateral agreements rather than reciprocal reductions across the board. The negotiations nonetheless yielded 123 such deals covering 45,000 items corresponding to approximately half of world trade; the result was an average reduction in the American tariff of 35 percent and lesser cuts elsewhere. The most important accomplishment of the subsequent rounds was to renew the initial agreement. This achievement falls under the nebulous heading of credibility and commitment: "Individuals and firms may be more willing," according to a recent student of the subject, "to engage in trade if they suspect that governments are committed to certain tariff rates – a stable trading environment – and the outlook promises further, if uneven, progress on trade liberalization."[7] The maintenance of reduced tariff levels also prevented backsliding and thus provided conditions under which the effects of eliminating quantitative restrictions could come into play over the medium term. Although matters like these are difficult to quantify, the steady removal of such quotas during the 1950s probably stimulated trade growth more than did tariff reduction.[8]

The Organization of European Economic Cooperation undertook responsibility for eliminating quantitative restrictions as part of its trade liberalization program. Established by the Marshall Plan as a mechanism to distribute aid money, the OEEC – after rejecting Monnet's proposals to organize itself as an international planning authority based on the French model – would develop along the lines of a British proposal. Decision-making power would rest with a council of ministers in which each member held veto power.[9] The OEEC took no account of European cooperation or "integration" as an objective. By opening markets rather than (as under Monnet's scheme) attempting to regulate them, it was a success.[10]

The OEEC was godfather to the European Payments Union (EPU), which served as a temporal and functional link between the Marshall Plan on one side and the EEC and the EFTA on the other. Was it optimum? In a famous memorandum written in late 1950, "The Case for Flexible Exchange Rates," Milton Friedman argued the contrary. The liquidity problem (or "dollar gap") in Europe would correct itself, he maintained, if relative prices for money could reflect demand for the commodity; lower exchange rates would make Europe attractive to foreign investors, and the resulting inflow of capital would hasten recovery. At the same time, a higher dollar would subject the U.S. economy to the brace of competition, and productivity would increase on both sides of the Atlantic. Friedman convinced almost no one. His commonsense recommendations, however sound in theory, sounded too radical in light of the prevalent embedded liberalism and also too risky in light of political uncertainty and the healthy recovery already under way.[11]

The EPU has had few detractors and is remembered today as the most successful of the postwar embedded liberal economic institutions. In a manner not dissimilar to Keynes's design for the IMF, it provided an automatic mechanism for the multilateral settlement of bilateral clearing balances between members – in this case, the countries belonging to the OEEC. Each nation joining the EPU initially received a global quota equal to 15 percent of its total foreign trade. A country in deficit beyond this sum would owe amounts credited against it in varying proportions of "hard" and "soft" currencies, the ratio of the latter to the former increasing percentagewise according to the size of the deficit; a country in surplus over the 15-percent threshold would be credited with a 50 : 50 balance of "hard" to "soft" currencies. The scheme, in other words, built in stronger disincentives to running a deficit than it provided incentives to building up a surplus, which would accrue to the balance sheet of the EPU itself. Settlements were in the form of bookkeeping entries rather than actual cash distributions, which – because the EPU functioned satisfactorily – were never demanded. Europe more than doubled its dollar holdings between 1949 and 1956.[12]

The system required capital controls in order to enforce currency parities, and a $350 million loan was provided by the Marshall Plan to cover capital requirements and offset the dollar gap of the EPU area. The European Payments Union was designed to operate within the framework of recovery policy, and the union would become superfluous once Europe had been put on its feet. Experts disagree as to when such a point was reached. It might have been as early as 1953; planning for the return to "normalcy" began in that year with the Dutch initiative called the Beyen Plan, a precursor to the EEC. It could in any case not have been later than 1958; in that year, the EPU ceased to operate and convertibility was restored with surprising ease. The statesmen who re-launched Europe in the mid-1950s fully understood that the transition from recovery to sustained prosperity was well under way, and they were determined to build on this postwar achievement, consolidate political gains, and sustain prosperity.

The EPU was more than a qualified success. Overall OEEC exports increased approximately 1.7 times between 1948 and 1955, and intra-OEEC trade grew 2.3 times over the same period. The expansion contributed to growth and structural change within Europe as well as to attaining the more specific objective of reducing Europe's need for American dollars. The boom in Germany surely deserves most of the credit for this result, but, according to Barry Eichengreen, EPU should get at least some of it.[13] To understand how the payments union operated, one must first bear in mind that trade discrimination against the United States was presumed to be necessary for the reduction of the dollar gap, given the maintenance of fixed parities required under the gold dollar standard of Bretton Woods. Distortions of trade and capital flows are the expected consequences of such preferences, but for special reasons this was not the case here, according to

Eichengreen. There was, first of all, almost no capital flow to distort: as a result of defaults between the wars, political uncertainty, and low per-capita GNP in Europe (on the one hand) and the prospect of decent returns with minimal risk in the United States (on the other), incentives for foreign investment in the OEEC nations were very weak. Whether dollar appreciation (*à la* Friedman) might, by restoring inflows, have changed the situation is theoretically possible but impractical to test.

Trade flows are a slightly more complicated matter. The lack of distortion may have resulted less from the smooth operation of a financial adjustment mechanism (like EPU) than from a specific requirement: acceptance of a Code of Liberalization, which was the "price" that the Marshall Plan administrators exacted for the dollar loan. By February 1951, all participants were required to reduce existing tariff levels (including those already lowered as a result of the Geneva GATT round) by half, and later by 60 and 75 percent; in addition, by 1955 quantitative restrictions (import quotas) had been lifted on 90 percent of importations. The EPU membership forced OEEC to develop into a preferential trade area. This relative openness, the existence of many low-cost producers in an area as large as that of the OEEC, and price pressure exercised by low-cost American imports account, in Eichengreen's view, for the relative lack of trade distortion.[14] Larger capital inflows and clearer price signals might have diminished it still further.

The economic rationale for the EPU is strong but still weaker than the political one. It might well have been possible to obtain the same (or even larger) increases in both international and European trade – and to lure capital as well – by moving earlier to convertibility or by not having created an adjustment mechanism like EPU in the first place and instead merely enforcing a Code of Liberalization. Nevertheless, as a bank the EPU could use its lending power to force compliance and as an institution it could encourage long-term thinking and thereby strengthen the credibility of Marshall Plan liberalization policy.[15] Thanks to the payments union and the development of the OEEC into a viable free-trade area, Europe was well along the way to currency convertibility by 1955. Having done its job, EPU could leave the scene – but not without a polite thank-you for helping span the transition from postwar to peacetime conditions.

Within five years of the EPU's ceasing operations and the restoration of convertible European currencies, the economist Gottfried Haberler pointed out that something truly significant was occurring in the world economy. After a break of nearly a hundred years, a long-term secular trend had resumed: the growth in foreign trade (6 percent annually since 1948) had, for the first ten-year period since the mid-nineteenth century, outpaced that of gross domestic product (GDP). A new cycle of liberalization had thus begun, successor to two previous ones: the opening of national markets in the mid-eighteenth century, followed by that of the world economy nearly ten decades later. Although Haberler remained distressingly vague about mechanisms – in particular, about the relative importance of markets and market-conforming institutions as contributing factors – he (like

Röpke) attributed developments at both the international and regional levels primarily to change at the national one.

Of particular importance, in Haberler's view, was the German-led incremental removal "of the jungle of internal and external direct controls that had grown up during the Depression and in war" – over prices, consumer rationing, raw materials, and so on. The elimination of such restraints on the market, Haberler added, released energies that (1) led to spectacular increases in output and consumer satisfaction and (2) carried over into world trade and finance, where the replacement of direct controls had been slower. He argued further that lifting exchange controls, eliminating quotas, and reducing tariffs "preceded and overlapped the regional reduction of trade barriers and regional integration in the European Common Market ... [and thus] the quantitative effects on trade of worldwide integration and liberalization have been much greater than those of the ... much advertised regional scheme."[16] To maintain the contrary, he concluded, was to put the cart before the horse.

Subsequent history has validated Haberler's first basic insight. Even in recessions, world trade growth has continued to increase relative to GDP, as has (at still greater rates) the growth of foreign direct investment (FDI) and capital mobility. The cycle of liberalization continues. Events have also lent force to his second significant observation – that European integration results in large part from the interplay of national and international economic influences – and even to an implicit third one: that such results presuppose the existence of an appropriate institutional framework. The international agencies created during and after World War II to regulate world finance and commerce may not have been optimal, but they were at least serviceable, eventually proved to be adaptable as well, and over the long run have fulfilled their mission. The *Pax Americana* has over the past fifty years advanced toward the *Pax Universalia*.

MIRACLES CAN SOMETIMES HAPPEN: ERHARD'S REFORMS

The high degree to which European prosperity depended upon West Germany in the 1950s is easily demonstrated. German GDP grew (1950 = 100) to 162 by 1958. Industrial output nearly doubled between 1950 and 1955. Total foreign trade more than tripled between 1950 and 1959, with exports rising from about a quarter to 40 percent of total output.[17] Closer to home, the rise of the Federal Republic's intra-European trade was even more dramatic, and within it the share of imports rose steadily over the 1950s. The importance of the West German market for imports from neighboring western Europe grew in both relative and absolute terms.[18] The Federal Republic was the largest market for the exports of France, Sweden, Austria, the Netherlands, Italy, Belgium, and Denmark. It also enjoyed exceptionally high increases in productivity as well as low (and falling) rates of inflation, which dampened price increases elsewhere. As Alan Milward first pointed out, the geographical pattern of western Europe's foreign trade was actually established before the creation of the European Economic Community.[19]

"The most spectacular feature of the postwar miracle and perhaps the key to understanding why it could happen," according to Herbert Giersch, "was the country's rapid emergence as one of the major trading nations of the world."[20] Critics of Economics Minister Ludwig Erhard often point out that many economic conditions in postwar Germany were highly propitious to growth. Some of them doubtless were: a stock of capital goods that had actually increased since before the war; an influx of well-trained labor; a national system of bargaining that restrained wages; rising demand on world markets; strong incentives to investment; and the encouragement of entrepreneurship. Such givens may indeed be necessary but are surely not sufficient conditions for the sustained growth of the 1950s and early 1960s.[21] The critical mechanism, according to Giersch, was the overriding priority in trade and payments policy of maintaining inflows in order to prevent the threat to monetary stability posed by export surpluses. Because revaluation was difficult (if not impossible) under the existing system of fixed parities, the only feasible approach to prevent rising prices was to relax import restrictions and allow competition to discipline the market. West Germany turned into a pioneer of European liberalization: "from 1953 onwards it took unilateral steps ahead in times of cyclical upswings" and, unlike countries with payment deficits, did not have to introduce temporary emergency restrictions. Rates of inflation actually declined.[22]

German liberalization was by no means a smooth or simple process. Prices were still regulated in entire sectors, such as energy and housing. Agriculture was under a tightly controlled marketing regime. The powerful industrial associations (*Verbände*) discouraged entrepreneurship. Protectionism remained a force to contend with in branches of trade and manufacturing that were oriented to sales on domestic markets. Unilateral moves (favored by Erhard) toward across-the-board tariff cutting and quota elimination could expect to encounter heavy resistance, as evident in the adoption of numerous safeguards and exceptions in many trade agreements. Such opposition was more than offset by the mounting pressure for unilateral liberalization exerted by both GATT and OEEC from 1953 onward as German surpluses mounted – even though, as Giersch points out, the tariff and quota cuts had the perverse effect under fixed exchange rates of stimulating export growth by reducing prices, enhancing productivity, and exerting downward pressure on wages.[23]

Moves toward Deutsche mark (DM) convertibility paralleled progress toward free trade, both within EPU and outside it. By 1955 the EPU had become a "bilateral affair," with accumulating German surpluses covering deficits in much of the remaining union and especially in France, where raging inflation aggravated the problem. There were limits to German willingness to accept such imbalances, particularly since they required the forfeiture of dollar earnings. Erhard wanted to dismantle EPU and restore DM convertibility as early as 1955. It eventually happened after two forced devaluations of the French franc and the adoption of the Rueff–Pinay reform in 1958. With insignificant exceptions, European currencies thereafter became convertible into dollars for current transactions. West Germany went even further and lifted restrictions on capital movements, a difficult operation in light of the inflationary impact that could be expected to result from large inflows.[24] Ten years after the Marshall Plan had put liberalization at the top of the policy agenda, the continent had returned to more or less liberal trade and payments arrangements and accepted the competition principle. At the head of the European policy agenda was the simple question of how best to strengthen this new set of economic relationships.

ALL HANDS ON BOARD: THE RE-LAUNCHING

The "re-launching of Europe" accompanied this return to the market. It was a lengthy, tedious, confusing, imperfect, but ultimately rewarding process. The main purpose behind this negotiating marathon was to set up a customs union, even though it disappeared from time to time under a heavy political fog.[25] The Treaty of Rome (1958) makes this clear. Two chief issues were at stake in the negotiations. One was the fate of monnetism, the other the compatibility of French *dirigisme* with the free-trade principle. A related issue was the desirability of a small as opposed to a large union. The re-launching process cannot be pegged to a single date, according to Andrew Moravcsik, because "trade liberalization had been discussed almost continuously since 1948 and during the eighteen months following the defeat of the EDC over a dozen new proposals appeared."[26] They seemed to be, as the Dutch Foreign Minister Willem Beyen put it, "springing up like mushrooms."[27]

The most important of them bears his name. Introduced into the intergovernmental discussions for a European Political Community (EPC), which accompanied the ill-fated EDC, the Beyen Plan recommended that a customs union be formed to advance European integration to the next stage. Beyen's proposal would be revived as the core of the "Benelux memorandum." This, in turn, would serve as *text du base* for discussions at the committee chaired by the Belgian Foreign Minister Paul-Henri Spaak at Messina, which marked the formal beginning of the re-launching in May 1955 by The Six ECSC states. A customs union was once again the central feature of the communiqué issued after the Messina meeting and also the main topic of discussion in the expert sessions convening over the following twelve months. The so-called Spaak Report of April 1956 distilled these findings into specific recommendations and advised that negotiations proceed. They began a month later at the Venice foreign ministers' meeting and concluded after nearly a year of expert discussions in March 1957. The only real bone of contention was that concessions had to be made in order to keep France on board. Three weeks after the matter was settled the treaty was finally initialed.[28]

Shortly after the French National Assembly's rejection of the European Defense Community in August 1954, Spaak contacted Jean Monnet in an effort to come up with new ideas about how to set the integration process back in motion. Monnet and his team at the coal–steel pool examined no fewer than fifty possible approaches over the next several months, including the introduction of direct elections to a European assembly and the formation of an armaments consortium. They eventually settled on three highly regulated sectors – transport, energy, and atomic power – as the most promising fields. The third one looked the best.[29] Monnet knew little about this highly technical and strategically critical sector. Its place in the integration story results from a suggestion made by an American attaché to the Paris embassy, who relayed it to Louis Armand (president of the French national railways), who then rang up Monnet. Monnet would depend throughout the negotiations upon Armand's technical expertise.

Monnet's interest in the nuclear industry extended only to the subject of integration. What drew him to atomic energy, according to Moravcsik, was a conviction that "successful political integration was possible only where there was central economic planning by strong supranational authority [and] where strong government intervention already existed."[30] Though drained of vitality, Monnet's EURATOM proposal would ultimately survive. Thanks also to the concessions exacted by France at the treaty negotiations and to the subsequent intervention of EC President Walter Hallstein, elements of supranationalism would be incorporated into the machinery of the EEC itself. This result was unintentional. "Political poison" in Paris and all but unmentionable in German industrial circles, Jean Monnet would be deliberately excluded from the talks that led to the formation of the customs union. The representative he insisted upon sending to Messina was treated "like a pariah." The reception should have been predictable. "A number of *idées-forces*," according to Monnet's occasional critic and sometime associate, Robert Marjolin,

which in previous years had ruled the thinking of those who regarded themselves as "Europeans," were totally discredited, even for many of their advocates. One could no longer mention the subject of European defense, nor that of supranationality, European constitution, relinquishment or delegation of sovereignty, or even European institutions, without in most cases eliciting from the listener a wry smile of disappointment, skepticism, or irony, and sometimes even a [hostile] reaction, as though one had suggested an abdication on the part of France, a renunciation of national independence, a total submission to a foreign will.[31]

The January 1955 replacement of the "anti-European" French Prime Minister Pierre Mendès-France by a new man known to be sympathetic to integration, Edgar Faure, was the touchstone to events that set the re-launch in motion. His successor, Guy Mollet, was well disposed to advancing integration, but found himself being drawn ever more deeply into the troubles brewing in North Africa and was otherwise preoccupied with the chronic battle against inflation.[32] To all but a handful of "Europeans" in Paris, the re-launching came as an unwelcome diversion. Indifference was not the main problem. "Fear," according to Marjolin, the chief of staff to the French delegation at the lengthy expert discussions, "had seized French business and especially government officialdom at the idea that the wall of protection ... built up during the prewar, war, and postwar years might one day come down and that French industry would then have to face foreign competition without customs duties, quotas, or state subsidies."[33] Marjolin's initial "positive but guarded" presentation of the prospects for a European community met with a frosty reception from all but one of the directors of all the economics ministries present.

The upshot of the meeting was a memorandum stressing that France could not compete on equal terms with the other prospective members of the customs union. High social insurance costs (including wages) thus had to be "equalized" before the lowering of customs barriers could be considered. Planning on a European scale would also be necessary, and special intervention would be required to protect agriculture. "Consideration" had to be given to the interests of the French empire as well. Currency devaluation must further be ruled out as detrimental to living standards; "harmonization" of wages and benefits would be necessary; and any arrangements would have to be reconsidered and, if necessary, renegotiated after a four-year trial period.[34] The gist of the memorandum, in other words, was that the costs of adjustment were to be shifted to the European partners.

France was to be made the exception to the rules. The concerns of the other parties were minor. Neither Germany nor Italy nor the three Benelux countries (Belgium, the Netherlands, and Luxembourg) needed to be converted to the customs union idea; the Low Countries were "natural allies" of the Federal Republic economically, had kept pace with it in quota elimination, and – because of the importance of transshipping in their economies – had maintained even lower tariffs. Since 1950 the three had been partners in the Benelux Union, a successful common customs area.[35] Fearing great-power domination, they wanted a central executive with the authority to mediate between the member states. Italy's preoccupation throughout the negotiations was to secure guarantees of unrestricted freedom of movement for labor in order to reduce chronic unemployment.[36] Convinced that government from any European capital had to be better than that from Rome, the Italian delegation welcomed the idea of European political federation and otherwise focused on securing waivers and safeguards for particular economic interests. France thus set the tone at the post-Messina proceedings, and "the issues raised by the creation of an economically united Europe [therefore] had to be settled in Paris, in a series of clashes between the adherents of liberalism and those who consciously or unconsciously, overtly or covertly, advocated a France closed to Europe and the world."[37]

France was indeed the odd man out. Not only senior officialdom but organized groups representing economic interests, the political parties, and the French public were all overwhelmingly opposed to membership in a customs area. It is true that France was steeped in *planisme* and *dirigisme* – though an exaggeration that French men and women could not imagine a world without it. Opposition to a customs union, though deep and pervasive, was less a matter of principle than of sheer demoralization; it could be overcome by a sound bargaining strategy, concessions, and good luck. Chief of staff to the French delegation, Robert Marjolin, was a rare bird, or as he himself put it, "the odd man out in France." His profile was unique. An American-trained economist from a working-class background who had served both with de Gaulle in London and with Monnet in the *Plan de Modernisation et d'Équippement,* he was a socialist by temperament, an economic liberal by conviction, and – while intensely pro-American and ardently pro-European – still French to the core. Marjolin had been the director general of OEEC for more than four years when the re-launch got under way.[38]

Marjolin wisely avoided abstract discussions, made durable bargains with concerned interests, and kept unresolved issues open. Success depended upon the cooperation of the negotiating partners in Brussels as well as good political timing. Marjolin was wise enough not to raise the issue of "harmonization," about whose specific meaning no two parties could agree and the need for which seemed dubious, and he doubted that French social outlays were substantially greater than those elsewhere. Their importance as a cost factor was, in any case, a more appropriate subject for economists' debates than as a premise for a negotiating position. The indispensable first step toward overcoming France's lack of industrial competitiveness was, moreover, not "harmonization" but devaluation. Another issue Marjolin deliberately avoided was capital mobility, a necessary and arguably inevitable concomitant of a customs union, which nonetheless conjured up public fears of the alleged bankers' ramp of the Popular Front era. He thus focused on two issues: the special needs of French agriculture and the role of the French empire in the future customs union. In resolving them he helped save the negotiations, but at high cost.[39]

Although often criticized for selfishness, French farmers were in a bind at the midpoint of the 1950s because of the Monnet Plan (*Plan de Modernisation et d'Équippement*) and could quite properly consider themselves victims of circumstance. The 1948 revision of the plan had raised agriculture to a priority sector for investment and allocation with the understanding that, if surpluses resulted, the government would support prices by subsidizing exports. When wheat production mounted and prices fell in 1953, the plan plowed aggressively ahead and actually targeted a 20-percent increase in commodities output. The decision turned on several national rather than farm-specific considerations. The experts had determined that (1) agriculture was the sector of production with the most underutilized resources as well as the one whose development could contribute most to closing the trade deficit; (2) output declines would force excessive migration into urban areas; and (3) without additional investment, the gap in living standards between country and city would expand. Whereas in 1948 France had been a net food importer, by 1954 the pumping of farm subsidies had produced large and mounting surpluses of high-cost output that required high-powered export promotion.[40]

French agricultural organizations launched a number of international marketing schemes in the early 1950s, but they were export novices who sought practical solutions for the pressing problems of overproduction and falling prices.[41] The

farm lobby initially insisted upon "tariff preference" at the customs union negotiations, but the term was an anathema. Well aware that Germany, Italy, and
the Benelux countries also subsidized the farm sector, Marjolin thought it only
necessary "to combine [national] protective measures into community protection, while at the same time establishing free movement of [foodstuffs] within
the Community ... [so a] common agricultural policy could see the light of day."
The argument used to justify this proposal was, as Marjolin fully recognized,
disingenuous: "in a market where the industrial products of the various member
countries circulated freely and naturally at much the same prices, it was unthinkable that governments, or official agricultural bodies, should pay different prices
to the producers of farm goods according to their nationality."[42] What Marjolin actually meant was that a Community-wide subsidy scheme that produced
price convergence could be fobbed off to the public as consistent with the competition principle. To avoid the negative connotations of the word "preference,"
Marjolin thus adopted the more innocuous term "non-discrimination," meaning that

in each country there would be only one system of prices regardless of product origin ....
It was impossible not to accept the term "non-discrimination," which had a free market
connotation and yet, given the systems of agricultural protection in force in the different
countries that were to form the Community, the end result was practically the same. But
such is the power of words![43]

The treaty provided for a common organization of agricultural markets but offered few specifics. These matters would be settled in successive conferences
taking place in the late 1950s and early 1960s.

The inclusion of the French empire (or French Union, to use the more politically acceptable name adopted for it in 1945) was an even shabbier – though
perhaps equally necessary, and better – deal for the other five negotiating states
if only because it had fewer adverse effects. Elements of luck and timing figured prominently in the French success. The French empire was not a customs
union but a network of bilateral treaties binding the colonies and dependencies
to France, which – by means of quotas and exchange controls rather than politically more visible tariffs – provided for reciprocal protection. Such restrictive
arrangements ultimately helped neither party. The so-called franc area provided
sheltered markets for high-cost goods at both center and periphery and fenced
out foreign overseas investment. By supporting the Monnet Plan, the European
Recovery Program had actually helped fund this ramshackle contraption. Currency convertibility and liberalization, which metropolitan France had managed
to limit prior to 1955, would have washed it away. In a 1955 background study,
Monnet's planners admitted as much. They concluded that bringing the empire
into a customs union would benefit the colonies (by opening markets to competition from France's partners) but would hurt France itself. The partners should,
the experts argued, therefore donate to the development of the colonies in order
to create markets for French exports. The matter was urgent, since "the French

government could no longer cope with the burden of financing investment in the overseas territories ... and was failing to mobilize private investment."[44]

The French employers' association, the *Patronat,* knew that "it would be technically impossible to develop a franc area customs union separately from a European Common Market in which France was a party without absurd anomalies arising."[45] Along with the "harmonization" of social benefits, special treatment of the franc area thereupon became one of the two supposedly nonnegotiable preconditions of employer support for a customs union. Since the very meaning of "harmonization" was obscure, winning over the *Patronat* required concessions to be exacted on the French Union. But it was necessary to keep "the question [of the empire] in abeyance during the long studies of the experts in Brussels [following Messina], knowing that it raised such fundamental problems for France that, once it came up, finalization of a common market treaty would be delayed almost indefinitely."[46]

Foreign Minister Pineau raised the sensitive issue in the opening statement at the first session of the Venice conference on 30 May 1956, but to ill effect. Of the French reservations committed to the record – concerning timetables, harmonization, and the inclusion of additional negotiating parties – the "most important one [was] that regarding ... the overseas territories." French employers insisted that

the other countries cannot expect to ... skim off the cream ... without at the same time contributing their share to the overhead cost .... Germany ... should no longer buy food and raw materials in whatever happens at the moment to be the cheapest market [but should instead be required to] absorb surplus products from the franc area before buying elsewhere.... Markets for such products will have to be "organized" on a basis that includes the entire community. There will [also] have to be a financial contribution by the other participating countries to the cost of developing the franc area territories ... for productive investments, public works, and other less profitable infrastructures.

Such retrograde ideas were not encouraging to free marketers. One American diplomatic observer opined that the franc-area issue could only be played as a trump card.[47]

And so it was. Prime Minister Guy Mollet sprung it on Chancellor Adenauer at the last minute, in February 1957. Adenauer went along. He had, in fact, already signaled to Mollet his readiness to save the negotiations at any cost during a highly secret Paris meeting with Mollet on 7 November 1956 by administering a humiliating rebuke to the German delegation for refusing to make progress on "harmonization." This startling gesture could have been prompted by his angry reaction to the U.S. condemnation of the Anglo-French Suez landing or by the more recent British decision to withdraw from the operation.[48] Adenauer's immediate objective was, however, to crush the free-trade initiative just launched by the British via the OEEC and vigorously championed by Erhard.[49] Mollet knew he could raise the ante at the right time. Adenauer was ready to deal generously once the French prime minister disinterred the knotty problem of the franc area. Adenauer agreed not only that goods from it could enter the future customs union duty free but also that a measure of tariff protection should be provided for its infant industries. A $580-million development package would further be provided into which France would divert $200 million from existing appropriations, the Federal Republic would add another $200 million of new money, and the remainder of The Six would contribute the rest. The *Patronat* had been appeased, and the preference zone called EURAFRICA was born.[50]

Top-level interventions like those of November 1956 and February 1957 were the exceptions, according to the cagey Marjolin, who boasted in his memoirs that "to come up with answers to ... reassure the French without unduly disquieting the other partners ... a real complicity developed in Brussels between the French delegation and others." Such "constructive collusion" rested on a consensus re-garding institutions, a determination to avoid notions like "supranationality" or "pretentious designations like 'High Authority'," and an agreement to "define concretely and simply the respective powers of the Commission and the Council of Ministers in such a way as not to arouse the hostility of all those who in 1950–1954 had opposed the first efforts to construct Europe."[51] Regarding one last concern, the transitional period, the French accepted a draft treaty clause con-taining a four-year timetable for tariff reductions to take place simultaneously with the erection of a common external customs border and the development of a common agricultural policy. The essential framework of the Community was now in place.

Or was it? Before the EEC could be launched it had to deal with the free-trade proposal designed by the British and officially sponsored by the OEEC, negoti-ations for which began in fall 1956. "From the outset," according to Marjolin, "the Community had to face a great danger, of more or less being sucked into a vast European free-trade area ... which might have prevented it from fully es-tablishing itself according to the terms of the Treaty of Rome."[52] The collapse of talks on the free-trade area was another colossal French diplomatic victory. Once again, the "outside man in Europe" managed to derail a proposal – sup-ported in some measure by virtually every OEEC nation – that would, if adopted, not only have eclipsed the EEC but also have dramatically diminished the French voice in Europe. The triumph was President de Gaulle's. On 23 May 1958 he had declared the existence of the Fifth Republic. His *Non!* was the first great service that de Gaulle would perform on behalf of the EEC; the next one would be the Rueff–Pinay reform. Had the Fourth Republic survived a year longer, the EEC might never have seen the light of day.

The British are responsible for the failure of the free-trade area negotiations. To them, a free-trade area was in the end only a way to weaken The Six as the nucleus of a new continental power. The negotiations had little to do with either trade strategy or a plan to reform the economy. Neither Harold Macmillan – whether as chancellor of the exchequer at the time of Messina or as prime minis-ter after 1956 – nor Reginald Maudling, who chaired the free-trade negotiations, were advocates of free trade.[53] They both thought comfortably "inside the box" and championed the corporate capitalism favored at the time by most of the Conservative Party. In this respect they lagged behind even the leaders of British industry, where demands for change were beginning to be heard.[54] Britain simply backed into the initiative for the free-trade area. The relevant cabinet memorandum of May 1956 argued limply that, because a year had elapsed since the Messina meeting, Britain had no chance to join The Six in a customs union and that exclusion from Europe would be prohibitively costly in the future. The only remaining option was to "re-direct the initiative [of The Six] into the orbit of the OEEC."[55] Well over a year would pass until negotiations began in autumn of 1956. Before their conclusion the Fourth Republic had been replaced by the Fifth. Maudling complained that it was at first much too hard for the French to make decisions and then, suddenly, far too easy.[56]

The free-trade area proposal could have been more than a stalking horse for Great Britain; it had real merit and, as an extension of the OEEC, would have been fully compatible with both it and GATT. A union of nineteen nations rather than six, a free-trade area would also have been far larger than the EEC. Created only to promote free trade and explicitly nonpolitical, interference with the market at the European level would have been ruled out. Competition would have promoted the principle of comparative advantage and reduced distortions to trade and investment at the national level. The lack of a political component simplified negotiations and made it easier to reach agreement.

The free-trade proposal enjoyed considerable support not only from Europe outside The Six but within it as well – indeed, almost everywhere but in France. Motivations varied. The non-Sixers disliked the Euro-federalist implications of the narrower union and, as small nations whose economies depended on the exportation of specialized products overseas, favored open markets. Within The Six, the traditionally pro-British Belgians and Dutch were world traders with low tariff histories; their preferences for the U.K. proposal were unmistakable.[57] Germany was by no means ill-disposed to it, either. According to Herbert Giersch,

neither trade unions nor industry in general favored the "little Europe" which finally materialized. Despite their differences with regard to integration concepts both supported free-ish trade, at least within the OEEC area and subject to escape clauses .... Arguments of political economy cannot alone explain why Germany finally consented to the "little European" solution.[58]

The German decision to let the free-trade area die was Adenauer's, and the motivation was purely political.

The free-trade area negotiators wanted an agreement that could take effect simultaneously with the Treaty of Rome, but the talks dragged on for two wearying years. At issue was the tedious but vital subject of low U.K. agricultural tariffs – the cornerstone of the preferential trade relationship with the Commonwealth – which Britain was not ready to sacrifice but which also touched on the most sensitive spot in French trade policy, the preferential export of surplus foodstuffs. This issue was never resolved. French delegates dominated the conference proceedings by presenting a host of proposals for sectoral integration intended to lead to the capstone of a European planning authority, and they interspersed these blind leads with increasingly nasty insinuations that Britain, as the guiding force in a free-trade area, would be a Trojan Horse for an American takeover of the continent. This was uncalled for. Though divided, the State Department tilted toward the EEC, kept "hands off" the proceedings at the OEEC as a European organization, and openly hoped that no agreement reached there would stand in the way of Franco-German reconciliation and the future organization of a federal Europe. The question was: How long could France hold out against the others?

By working through the summer of 1958, The Six finally obtained the French delegation's consent to a common EEC position as laid out in the so-called Ockrent Memorandum. It re-confirmed a commitment to conclude an agreement "allowing the association, on a multinational basis, of the member states of the OEEC with the Community."[59] Before the document could be submitted to the OEEC for discussion, General de Gaulle vetoed the proposal using press conference shock tactics for which he would later become famous. In December the British chairman of the OEEC intergovernmental committee, Reginald Maudling, accepted the French *fait accompli*. Adenauer did likewise, without comment. The free-trade proposal would later be partly salvaged: the EFTA, founded in 1960, would provide a healthy challenge to the EEC.[60]

De Gaulle's veto of the free-trade area may have enabled the EEC to survive, but without his support for the Rueff–Pinay reforms the customs union could not have been brought to life. The general's economic ideas were sketchy. A forceful advocate of a return to the gold standard, de Gaulle seems to have been blissfully unaware that exposing the controlled French economy to competitive currents would be like testing a Christmas tree in a wind tunnel. He was nonetheless deeply committed to economic modernization, if only to support a strong state and powerful armed forces. Like many military men, General de Gaulle thought that sound economic policy was largely a matter of delegating authority down the chain of command and of placing responsibility in the right hands. Results were what counted with him, not how they were obtained.[61] The appointment of Jacques Rueff to head a committee vested with plenipotentiary powers to overcome the severe financial crisis facing France in summer 1958 vindicated such an odd approach.

A member of the Mont Pèlerin Society and a prominent figure in central banking since the 1920s, Rueff was the most outspoken economic liberal in the *Corps de Finance*. Rueff's pills could not have been taken by any government of the Fourth Republic. Even under the forceful leadership of de Gaulle, they could only be swallowed in the face of threatened catastrophe. By mid-summer 1958 it was obvious that raging inflation, soaring budget deficits, mounting payment imbalances, and heavy government borrowing were accelerating the rate of inflation and rapidly draining foreign exchange out of the system; at current rates, France's reserves would have been reduced to nothing by January 1959. Rueff cut the budget sharply, eliminated quotas, reduced tariffs by 90 percent, ended indexation, and took the dreaded decision to devalue. His purgative did the job. Within a year, price inflation had been checked; wages had increased by about 1 percent in real terms; industrial production had expanded by 12 percent; the trade balance had shifted from the perilously negative 116 billion francs to a positive 259 billion francs, the healthiest since the war; and foreign exchange reserves had been built up from a negative $100 million to a positive $2 billion. France was on a trajectory that would raise GNP by over a third over the next ten years. The safeguards, escapes, and transitional arrangements painstakingly negotiated into the Treaty of Rome would be largely unnecessary. The Rueff–Pinay reform proved that the French could compete if the franc were set at the right level and allowed to float. With economic health restored, France would no longer be the odd man out but, under the leadership of General de Gaulle, would become the odd man in.[62]

4

All or Nothing? The Founding of the EEC and the End of an Era, 1958–1966

In 1958 the European Economic Community "hit the blocks running," exploded off the mark and then stumbled, not once or even twice but repeatedly – which might have been expected of someone who, having barely learned to walk, tried to sprint. By 1965 it was staggering and never reached the finish, because no one could find the line. Broken off by confused referees, the event would be scheduled to resume once the runner had better command of his feet and knew better what he was doing. The initial phase of the Community's history opened with a burst of energy and idealism, almost immediately encountered unexpected problems that tripped it up, and ended with a change in rules whose significance was at first not completely clear to anyone but that was necessary for integration to resume. The strange tale makes sense only in retrospect.

The founding of the EEC was to have launched a new era of impressive accomplishments, but in fact it occurred at the end of an old era and failed to meet expectations. Even so, the first period in its history was not devoid of results. Its greatest single achievement was the accelerated elimination of tariffs and quotas and the application of a common schedule of external duties over a period of nine instead of twelve years. A customs union thus came into existence earlier than scheduled.[1] The market opening that followed brought changes in business and finance, contributed to economic growth, and created fresh opportunities for the EEC. These were tracks left by first steps but not necessarily the beginnings of a long-term trend. Nothing like a common market, in which complete factor mobility exists, came into being during the early years of the Community. An economic union, with unified monetary and fiscal policies, was not even on the radar screen.

The reduction and elimination of tariffs and quotas were actually part of a larger project that included players like GATT and EFTA; the ECC's decision to cut and abolish them earlier than scheduled was as much reactive as proactive.[2] By the middle of the 1960s, monetary stresses and strains began to be felt. Economic growth slowed in 1962. Wages and prices rose sharply in France and spiked in Italy. By the third quarter of 1963, both countries were running large deficits while Germany had a large surplus. The following year saw the first of many future "runs," in this case against the lira, that would be symptomatic of the gradual breakdown in the world monetary system.[3] Instability set in before the EEC was even up and on its feet.

At work was the "Triffin dilemma," named after a Belgian-born Yale economist, Robert Triffin. Triffin discovered that the very dollars Europe needed for growth – by causing American payments deficits – undermined the fixed parity system of Bretton Woods. The result was an unacceptable policy choice between instability on the one hand and stagnation on the other.[4] The European economy flourished even as the very foundations upon which it was built were being eaten away. The dilemma might have been solved by breaking with the fixed parities of Bretton Woods and allowing currencies to float against one another, but this would have meant modifying or even breaking with a "given" of the postwar settlement and sacrificing a powerful American policy-making lever. The Kennedy administration's failure to deal with the deficit aggravated the problem. Rather than attend to such mundane matters, it turbocharged policy: spinning foreign-policy plans of breathtaking scope and ambitiousness that were expensive, intrusive, and entangling. American overstretch encountered European underreach. Europe needed to build strong economic institutions in order to accommodate the powerful influences in play. Dollar dependence was partly the consequence of thin and underdeveloped national capital markets. Large dollar inflows also resulted from a lagging entrepreneurialism. Such considerations had little more influence on policies made in Brussels than the payments problem had on policies crafted in Washington.

Walter Hallstein, the first Commission president, may not yet rank as a "great European" but he was undoubtedly an influential one. This somewhat neglected figure not only revived monnetism after its earlier eclipse but set the imprint of his ideas and personality on the European Commission, the EEC executive. The agenda he set for it was only tangentially related to the Rome treaty. A professor of constitutional law at the University of Frankfurt, Hallstein was the most rigorous and systematic thinker in the circle of *l'Inspirateur*. He developed an integration teleology, a legal doctrine, and an armament of policy rationales pointing to the inevitability and irreversibility of the integration process. This integration ideology cannot be dismissed as mere propaganda; it was more like an article of faith. In the apocalyptic spirit of the early Church, Hallstein fervently believed that Europe's redemption – in the form of federation – could take place within in a matter of years rather than decades. He fully expected to be installed as spiritual head, as president of Europe.

He nonetheless faced what can be termed the "Hallstein dilemma." While Hallstein appears to have believed that History itself conferred and consecrated his office, he found it nearly powerless. Unable to seize, grasp, wrest, or otherwise get his hands on the economic decision-making authority of the member-states, he could only pretend to rule and make maximum use of the few powers available to him. This took the form of building paper bureaucracies on the one hand and the pursuit of flamboyant diplomacy on the other. This rampant empire building assured his eventual downfall. It was also inconsistent with much of the treaty.

The Treaty of Rome vested only "negative" powers in the Commission: the authority to set and enforce the rules necessary to maintain competition in the new customs area. The most significant "positive" responsibilities specified in the treaty are in the special area of the Common Agricultural Policy, but they belonged to (and were tightly held by) the Council of Ministers representing the member-states.[5] Provision was also made for the formation of common energy and transport policies, but here the Commission had to contend with national bureaucracies. The remaining powers assigned the Commission defined the authority to eliminate specific competitive distortions.[6]

Hallstein fully understood that if the Commission's power were not bolstered then the EEC could dissolve into a free-trade area. To become the nucleus of a future European government, it had to take over economic management authority from the member-states and subject entrenched national bureaucracies – as well as public or quasi-public organizations and authorities – to Euro-*dirigisme*. This was not a matter of economic or social preference but of European necessity, in Hallstein's view. He continued to think of himself as a liberal. A powerful Brussels *apparat* was, however, only the stuff of dreams. Hallstein could only grubstake in the name of a higher cause, that is, engage in a doctrinally sanctioned scramble for new claims that might someday yield precious metal. Such a mission search could stretch policy-making "competence" into areas unforeseen by the Rome treaty. However, the short-run impact of Hallstein's frenzied power grasp was to unite the member-states against him. His downfall came after the refusal of France, backed by other member-states, to grant the Commission new authority to act independently of the Council of Ministers, which represented their interests. To underscore the seriousness of the situation, the French walked out, leaving behind "empty chairs."

WALTER HALLSTEIN'S COMMISSION

It is still not clear what to make of the elusive Walter Hallstein, a man who gave the impression of being a stiff, cloistered, colorless, humorless and almost faceless yet utterly selfless servant of the European cause. The sum of the known parts does not equal the whole. In official photos he often looks like an oversized doll stuffed into a bad suit, his featureless demeanor fronted by thick-rimmed black plastic glasses. Profile shots indicate that he had a bony face and a hawk nose. Robert Marjolin, Hallstein's deputy at the Commission, doubted that he ever had a social life of any kind or even any urge to have one.[7] Reginald Maudling, who worked with him at the free-trade talks, recalls being told by Hallstein "that he should be grateful if you would refer to me on all occasions as Professor." "It was," adds the congenial but perplexed Maudling, "a reasonable request but it did make me feel that there was a certain gap in temperament between us."[8]

The president of the Commission was in fact a bureaucrat run mad, or at least half-mad. Like the man who had found the philosopher's stone, Walter Hallstein burned with the zeal of one in possession of the absolute truth. His political testament, best translated into English as "The Incomplete Federal Union" (*Der unvollendete Bundesstaat*), reads like a Euroskeptic's worst nightmare. In the name of an ineluctable process of history it presents an integration dogma providing intellectual cover for a far-reaching interventionism that, as part of a grand scheme set in motion from on high and embedded in institutions responsible only to those who direct them, overruns the principle of self-determination and overrules common sense. Of greater interest than Hallstein's analysis of the "inner logic" purportedly driving Europe to a political federation of integration, a warmed-over version of functionalism, is the new doctrine of constitutional law that he advances both to justify and accelerate the process. It is the basis of his claim staking and an important legacy as well.[9]

Hallstein erroneously asserts that, in transferring sovereign power to a European authority, the founders of the EEC intended to create a federation: "The law of the Community therefore should take precedence over the law of the individual member-countries."[10] The European Court of Justice has ruled, he adds, that in ceding sovereignty the member-states embarked upon an irreversible course and that its writ applies uniformly and extends throughout the length and breadth of the community, thereby making the national courts responsible for the enforcement of a European law that legislatures cannot override. "The European Court," he concludes, "is performing a truly constructive, not to say creative, task of law-giving, interpretation, and guidance." The attainment of federal union will require taking a step beyond the development of a European constitutional law; it calls, he argues, for a constitution that specifies powers and responsibilities. Hallstein admits that such a proposal "will leave many lawyers breathless" and may well be "revolutionary" but confidently predicts that the legal path to integration will in the future be regarded as "the most creative achievement in the evolution of jurisprudence in our age."[11]

As for the Euro-constitution, Hallstein is vague about its specific powers but takes the expansive view that "integration is a *création continue* .... Every step we take creates new situations, new problems, new needs which in turn demand yet another step, another solution to be worked out on a European basis."[12] He meant by this that "integration in the field of economic and social policy should eventually be extended to defense and foreign policy, [as] inside the Common Market no sphere of economic and social policy ... lies outside the competence of the Community.... There can be no restrictive interpretation as regards the outside world."[13] The authority to make social and economic policy would and should, he adds, spill over into the fields of culture and internal security. Hallstein does not define limits to the exercise of this sweeping power, and even claimed that "the lack of precision in ... the treaty ... is in part a pledge of its signatories' confidence in its mechanism and in the gradual, ineluctable process of economic integration."[14]

The job of filling the empty spaces in this vast construction was to fall to the Commission. Hallstein's conception of it was Platonic. In *The Republic,* the Rulers or Guardians comprising the governing caste are men trained for leadership by a rigorous and austere education and who possess the special intellectual skill and vision required to produce a "creation myth," the foundation upon which every new polity must be based. They are utterly unselfish servants of "the community and never are prepared to act against it ... [they] alone have the chance to bring [the state] good government and prosperity." Such men cannot be allowed to accumulate wealth, according to Plato, but should be cared for by the community and not be granted more pleasure than the average member of it. They must live for the joy of service.[15]

As envisaged by Hallstein, the Commission should be no mere appendage of the Council of Ministers, which (according to the treaty) had to approve legislation; nor was its authority necessarily to be restricted to the power of initiative in drafting proposals, as a "narrow" reading of that document might suggest. It was also "the guardian of the Treaty of Rome," an "honest broker that stands outside national interests," and the very conscience of the Community. It should also serve as its brains, since "politics, the art of governing, has become more rational, more detailed, more 'technical,' in short more exact and more professional."[16] In his farewell speech to the European Parliament, Hallstein described the commissioner's office as sacred, requiring quasi-monastic self-abnegation. No commissioner, he warned, dare "regard himself as guardian of the interests of his own country .... The necessity to think and act ... 'European' ... makes the highest demands on ... moral integrity .... On this point ... the survival of the Community depends."[17]

Hallstein left little doubt that what he had in mind was a future EEC headed by the Commission and led by a president who, with the assent of a popularly elected (though powerless) parliament, governs with the advice of a Council of Ministers acting as an upper house. He was insistent that "the Commission should eventually be empowered to take all measures necessary for the implementation of the treaty on its own authority, without having to rely on the special and specific approval of the Council of Ministers," adding – in order to eliminate any remaining doubt or ambiguity – that "such reserve powers of the Council of Ministers as may be required during a period of transition should be gradually reduced, and the executive authority and competence of the Commission should be limited only where the Council of Ministers and the European Parliament jointly so decree." This dogma put the Commission on a collision course with the Council. Hallstein had nonetheless recruited his virtuous circle of superior young men, imbued them with an *esprit de corps,* defined their mission, and could personally attest that they were governing in the right spirit. Hallstein himself had invented the creation story that Plato thought indispensable to the formation of every new polity, and he made it the founding myth of the EEC. Upon it he built a legal doctrine that would eventually become, as he had hoped, a force for integration in its own right.

One task President Hallstein faced was to meet the American challenge, which was partly economic. The surge of American capital that accompanied the opening of the Common Market, and that was also required for growth, did not result in the takeover of Europe by American "multis" (multinational corporations) as described in Jean-Jacques Servan-Schreiber's best-selling tract, *Le défi Americain.*[18] It did, however, increase Europe's economic exposure to world markets, initiate structural change, and prompt defensive measures on the part of the Commission. Hallstein also had to deal with the threats and opportunities created by an ambitious new team in the White House. The Washington connection was a welcome foreign prop for the shaky new structures of Europe.

On the other side of the water, the hypergonadal Kennedy men replaced the weary Eisenhower administration in 1961. Imperial ambitions clothed in neo-Kiplingesque rhetoric were the order of the day. A deep commitment to setting the world in order and putting the Reds to rout cost big bucks. American payments had to bear the burden. The trade balance remained proudly in surplus until 1967, but financial transfers for NATO and military assistance and aid to developing countries tilted overall payments sharply into deficit beginning in 1959. The Treasury Department and the Bureau of the Budget issued repeated warnings that the result of such profligacy would be to undermine confidence in the dollar – or even induce a run away from it and toward the gold by which it was backed at the rate of $35/ounce.[19] The telephone admonitions that Jack received from old Joe Kennedy in Florida were also wasted. The juggernaut was hard to stop, especially once the turbo-Keynesians on the president's council of economic advisers discovered that one could use deficit spending to goose the economy without inflicting pain. The growing budget deficits of the late 1960s would compound the problem of instability.

Between 1963 and 1966 nearly $1.4 billion flowed annually into Europe, $837 million of it into the EEC countries.[20] The money went largely into direct investment but not (as was widely believed) into the fearsome mega-enterprises conjured up by Servan-Schreiber that captured imaginations and could realize the economies of scale created by the opening of the Common Market.[21] The findings of Harvard's Multinational Enterprise Project indicated that

> the three apparent causes for the distinctive behavior of industrial firms in the EEC were nontariff barriers, acquisition attempts to maintain national market divisions, and oligopoly duels resulting [from efforts] to shut out competitors [or] keep a foot in the door.... This picture ... seems to have little to do with the Common Market [and] much more to do with national government and oligopolistic ... efforts to protect existing patterns of activity and investment.[22]

Cutthroat Americanistic market-share struggles had yet to displace the cartelized old-world gentility of European business.

Evidence from the realm of finance also seems to suggest that structural weaknesses in Europe exercised a strong demand "pull" on dollars in concert with the "push" resulting from widening American deficits. Prior to the early 1960s, no real European capital market can be said to have existed but only national ones – each operating according to different rules and traditions, but all restricted to domestic borrowers. They were also all quite thin. Spreads (in many cases set by law) were wide, and rates were generally high. The ease with which large amounts of dollars could be borrowed offset much of the growing foreign exchange risk. Thus Euro-bond and Euro-currency markets filled the gap. The terms are misleading. The markets involved private placements, did not occur over an exchange or at any single location, and did not even need to be denominated in a European currency. Nor were they subject to any regulation or oversight, European or otherwise.[23]

The new monetary inflows had important consequences. Participation in consortia with Americans gave European bankers new experience in underwriting and marketing bonds and in the private placement of medium- and long-term paper with institutional investors, yielded increased competition between national markets, and encouraged the development of common disclosure standards.[24] The new offshore money also added to inflationary pressure. Central banks were hesitant to raise rates and thereby risk creating unemployment. The increased mobility of capital compounded the difficulty of defending national currencies, especially against a background of liberalizing but only partly open economies with differing rates of growth and inflation. The Commission's firmly held belief that coordinated cyclical policies (*Konjunkturpolitik*) could offset such instability was misplaced for the obvious reason that "harmonizing levels of economic activity between various economies does not call for identical policies, but for actions of a compensatory nature, just as walking in step calls for some to hurry and for others to slow down."[25] Brussels' *Konjunkturpolitik* never descended from the lofty realms of academic discussion to the down-to-earth level of policy implementation.[26]

Even though the essential machinery for Commission monetary policy was lacking, both Hallstein's office and Monnet's Action Committee spawned proposals for coping with inflation and instability. Robert Triffin penned the most serious of them. Triffin knew that the elimination of restrictions on trade and payments, the adoption of a common external tariff, and the enforcement of the competition principle would subject the EEC to market discipline and undermine the effectiveness of controls built into European economies. He disagreed, however, with "Rueffian" advocates of a single European currency, the adoption of which would administer a powerful one-time exogenous shock to the economy and melt rigid structures down into flexible markets. Triffin instead proposed a gradualist scenario in which a European unit of account would be created and then be made convertible into national monetary units, allowing circulation of national currencies at par within the Community. A new European monetary authority would take over the assets and liabilities of the national banks, and a single currency could then be introduced.[27] Unfortunately, the plan could not have worked. According to the Mundell–Fleming axiom, an open economy can maintain unrestricted capital mobility and fixed exchange rates only by sacrificing monetary autonomy.[28] The only theoretical choices – to reimpose restrictions on capital mobility or to break with the Bretton Woods system – were not contemplated as alternatives at the time. The collapse of the dollar gold standard would be required in order to clear the way for a monetary union.

Medium-term economic planning appeared to present fewer difficulties at the European level than either *Konjunkturpolitik* or monetary policy, and it also seemed to provide a way for Hallstein to break out of his dilemma. There was a precedent for such an effort in Monnet's short-lived attempt to turn the OECD into an economic directorate. A committee set up in 1964 and chaired by Robert Marjolin, vice-president of the Commission, picked up where Monnet had left off. Although this planning body would meet under Commission auspices, the member-states took the initiative to form the Marjolin group, which represented their interests. Few linkages existed between Brussels and the capitals of The Six. Although specific concerns about the effects of opening markets and a general anxiety about the new multis improved the prospects for coordinating policy at the European level, the national administrative bureaucracies dragged their feet and the Commission lacked the strength to push them forward.[29]

Fearing that competition in open markets would undermine their efforts to regulate the national economy, French planners sought from an early date to encourage intervention at the European level. Foreign trade was the least predictable part of the French Plan. To protect the payments balance in light of the scheduled January 1967 tariff reductions to 20 percent of 1957 levels, the Fourth Plan (1961–1965) adopted a scheme of subsidizing industrial exports by means of credit allocation and "quasi-contracts" guaranteeing profit levels to producers. An incomes policy was devised to enforce wage restraint. Unauthorized private-sector borrowing was made prohibitively expensive.[30] Such heroic measures by no means guaranteed success, according to Pierre Mendès-France, because

it is difficult to see how a national planning system could be integrated into a Common Market based on strictly liberal principles in which all intervention by public authorities is forbidden and economic development left to the working of the market.... The forecasts, calculations, and directives of the planners will quickly become useless if the member countries do not take ... certain measures which constitute the first steps towards supranational action, towards communal planning.[31]

Monnet personally opened the campaign to persuade the Commission to adopt the French planning model. "The large market," he wrote in the inaugural issue of the *Journal of Common Market Studies,* "does not prejudge the future economic systems of Europe. Most of The Six have a nationalized sector as large as the British and some have planning procedures. These are just as compatible with private enterprise in the large markets as they are in a single nation."[32] His close associate, Étienne Hirsch, was more candid in the next issue of the journal. "It would," Hirsch stated, "be infinitely desirable to see effective planning begun on the scale of the Common Market as a whole."[33]

The failure of the 1964 Medium-Term Economic Policy (MTEP) ended any real chance that the Commission would develop as a European economic executive or as the focal point of an effort to organize a mixed-economy welfare state at the European level. The awkward title of this ill-fated endeavor to set up planning machinery was chosen, according to the distinguished Labour Party economist Andrew Shonfield, "in deference to the ideologues of the marketplace, particularly in Germany" and to downplay the project's potentially far-reaching implications. The program

> set out the broad outlines of the economic policy intended to be implemented and to se-
> cure its coordination.... The Committee [of MTEP] was to examine the medium-term
> policies of the member-states and their compatibility with the program ... work out points
> of view on its own initiatives and submit them to the Council of Ministers.

The member-states collaborated actively in the Committee's work, Shonfield added, and "high national officials responsible for preparing economic policy in their respective member-states were dispatched to sit in on the meetings of the Committees and its subcommittees." The planning effort concluded that "public services are what people really want more than private consumption," that the competition rules (Article 85 of the treaty) should be changed in order "to improve the industrial structure of the community," and that merger and "cooperative" agreements between firms should be actively encouraged.[34]

The MTEP remained a paper project. Predicting that there would remain in the near future "a dangerous interval between the shedding of some of the old authority at the periphery and the consolidation of the new at the center," Schonfield left little doubt that, within the space of a few years, the construction of a mixed-economy welfare state for Europe would be possible.[35] Such hopes would never be realized. The committee, Stuart Holland complained, "became a [mere] talk shop for macroeconomic forecasting and [for making] statements of good intentions in structural and regional policy."[36]

Unable to influence events in the present, Hallstein turned to setting an agenda for the future. The Treaty of Rome left plenty of room for policy entrepreneurship. Andrew Moravcsik calls it a liberal framework document, albeit one with big loopholes for the Common Agricultural Policy (CAP) and the franc zone. It is *liberal* in positing as a goal the creation of a customs union, stipulating that competition should provide its mechanism, and forbidding specific practices that distort trade and investment. It is a *framework document* in enumerating specific powers that can be used to "eliminate tariffs and quotas, create an external tariff, establish common agricultural and transport policies, and coordinate many monetary and regulatory policies."[37] The treaty also makes provision for a set of quasi-institutional bodies unique among international organizations to house this framework: a European Commission, a European Council of Ministers, a European Court of Justice, and a parliamentary assembly. It left partly open both the means that could be taken in pursuit of the liberal values it embodied as well as the relationships between its different organs. Certain articles resulted from side deals arrived at in order to secure ratification. Agriculture constituted an important exception to the general spirit of the treaty.

Policies for market freedom nonetheless predominate over those for planning and control. W. R. Lewis points out that

The EEC treaty contains 248 clauses. 112 concern the institutions and the internal admin-istrative rules and financial obligations of members. The first eight articles on principles are essentially a treaty synopsis. Of the remaining 128 clauses, 29 apply to free movement of goods, 26 to the free movement of persons, capital, and services, and 18 to common rules ... concerned with eliminating distortions to competition, i.e. 73 *in toto*. As against this there are 10 dealing with agriculture, 11 with transport, 14 with common economic policies, 12 with social policy, two with the European Investment Bank, and six with the association of overseas territories.[38]

"The choice for the future," he adds, "is between Rome and Brussels: between the law of a Community constitution establishing and reinforcing personal eco-nomic freedoms on the one hand, and a new European-scale version of the bu-reaucratic, national, corporatist, over-centralized style on the other."[39]

Hallstein staked out his claims quickly in order to preempt such a choice and move Europe in the direction of superstate. "Before the opponents of the Euro-pean idea ... understood what was really happening," the Commission president moved opportunistically and by stealth along a line of advance – as indicated by the treaty whenever possible but extending far beyond it wherever a new mis-sion might be found – building new constituencies along the way and making shrewd tactical use of language and agenda setting. Hallstein grounded his ac-tions in his "broad" view of Commission powers, but he also developed a slew of original policy rationales in order to stake out claims.[40] Connections between them and either the treaty or the "inner logic" of integration ran the gamut from the intellectually plausible to the tenuous and simply preposterous. Some forays had impacts but most of them failed. Like proximity fuses, some lay dormant and others detonated at once. All of the programs, plans, and schemes would be inventoried and stored in the Commission's intellectual warehouse for use as necessary.

Their recognizable style reflects an ideology, developed during the Hallstein years, that raises integration to metaphysical dialectic. The process was not, however, the work of History but rather bore the stamp of a tight group of tech-nocratic zealots installed in office by Hallstein himself. No single logic, design, or philosophy guided Hallstein's policy except perhaps opportunism, and even this is no predictor of outcomes. As Paul Pierson has eloquently argued in re-cent years, institutions take on a life of their own, do not necessarily fulfill the purposes for which they were initially created, and become resistant to exoge-nous change.[41] The circumstances of origins and early childhood do matter, but growth vectors move off in directions of their own. Surviving institutions may or may not fulfill the purposes for which they were created or even any useful function, and they can resist the discipline of the market as well as public ac-countability. Still, Hallstein planted the seeds for the bureaucratic monster into which the Community executive would develop.

Energy and transport policy were big disappointments. The Commission could not make headway in the face of national bureaucratic opposition. Both fields were written into the treaty as prospective objects of integration, as each was thought to be "a classic sphere of activity where public authority has to intervene." Even after the consumption of hundreds of man-years of labor and thousands of reams of paper, it was impossible to arrive at agreement on a common energy policy because "the state has made its presence strongly felt in both semi-public enterprises and fully nationalized undertakings. In this sector of the economy the Community does not have to introduce new methods of *dirigisme.*"[42] The situation was no better in transport. It "remained in a state of pastoral seclusion ... since transport ... is in nearly all countries regarded, not as an element of the economy, which ought to be efficient and pay its own way, but as a 'public service' ... [making] it difficult to view in an unprejudiced way."[43]

Hallstein's interventions were certainly not all ineffective. He did manage to give a wholly unconstitutional twist to competition policy by setting up a market-correcting industrial policy and creating a rationale for a variant thereof: research and development policy. Articles 52 to 58 of the treaty define competition policy as the core competency of the Commission and require it to make and enforce rules to prevent unfair trade practices. Hallstein maintained that the effective discharge of this responsibility also requires far-reaching interventions into social policy and "positive measures" in the fields of taxation, monetary and fiscal policy, company law, and "market order" – none of which are specified in the treaty. Forays into such fields would seldom lead to satisfactory outcomes. The treaty-based competition directorate and the Hallstein-inspired industrial policy would often work at cross-purposes.

Outcomes in other fields follow no clear-cut pattern. In the area of research and development, Hallstein hoped to "plan" innovation, and a bureaucracy was set up to institutionalize this contradiction in terms. It repeatedly failed to deliver as promised. In the field of defense, Hallstein claimed a "competence" that Jacques Delors would later try to actualize. It remained a chimera. Virtually a blank page in the treaty, social policy would become, under Hallstein, a favorite playground of policy activism, but its legacy has been one of words rather than deeds. In the field of regional policy, however, mission creep was consequential. A peripheral concern in the treaty, it was used by Hallstein as a springboard for Commission influence. Interventions into the field of foreign policy, as we shall see, led to Hallstein's downfall.

As if by parthogenesis, Hallstein's version of competition policy begat its diametrical opposite: industrial policy. The need for the new policy arose, Hallstein argued, whenever "industry could no longer cope with the general philosophy and operation of a free market economy, and stood in special need of help from the public authorities." Such situations had become more frequent, he added, "as a result of the integration process ... itself"; indeed, industrial policy was a necessary adaptation mechanism over "the long-term process known as the Second Industrial Revolution."[44] Such expansive ideas figure in the rationale of the Colonna Memorandum, drafted in 1970 on the basis of preliminary studies done during Hallstein's presidency. Hallstein created a portfolio for industrial policy (DG III) without a mandate of any kind and before a need for it existed.

This DG III lacked a specific mission, and Hallstein's sole justification for creating the new bureaucracy was that his view of modern history warranted taking such a step. The crisis of the 1970s later galvanized it into action.

Might not the sunrise industries need a research and development (R&D) policy to meet the "American challenge"? Would it not also provide a nice pendant for the industrial policy if needed by the sunset industries? Hallstein moved less confidently in R&D. Although he demanded in *Der unvollendete Bundestaat* the creation of a "common market in innovation," he admitted uncertainty as to how to proceed and, in the attempt to encourage originality and creativity, discovered to his disappointment that "the trouble was that these improvisations lacked uniformity"![45] Though lacking expertise and with the flimsiest of rationales, the Commission would enter the pre-cooked innovation business with the adoption of the Framework Programs of the early 1980s. Defense policy should also fit into the Commission's brief, Hallstein figured, if only because it "has incalculably close links with technology." His case was not strengthened by admitting that "armaments are just as much a question for defense policy as for economic policy."[46] Who but an economic bureaucrat would think otherwise? Hallstein nevertheless managed to place security issues on the Commission agenda, and Jacques Delors would prove a worthy successor to Hallstein as defense dilettante.

Concerning social policy, the treaty said little. The six clauses covering the European Social Fund deal primarily with improving the efficiency of the labor market. Hallstein argued that this shortcoming was the result of a necessary deal with the French, whose demand for "social assimilation" stemmed purely from fear that high labor costs would "put it at a disadvantage in competing with member states."[47] Hallstein proposed to fill the gap in the treaty by creating a European social policy out of whole cloth, at least along the plane of ideas. Words being the only thing at his disposal, he initiated a round of discussions in order to bring about "a common usage of terms, a common language which would be bound to lead ... to a common basis for reaching decisions and taking actions ... an institutionalizing ... that could not fail to bring fruitful results."[48] Like Monnet – who had actively enlisted labor union representation at the French Plan, in the ECSC, and on the Action Committee for the United States of Europe – Hallstein brought them into the new Economic and Social Committee, a yak-yak forum.

The annual report of the Commission would henceforth contain a section devoted to social questions and deal not only with the specific issue of labor mobility, as provided for in the treaty, but with economic trends affecting social development, such as "structural" issues concerning employment, education, retraining, job creation, labor mobility, and social policy. This was conceived as a long-term investment. Hallstein was confident that the need to create a common market for labor would eventually lead to the creation of a single European welfare state and common citizenship. Though the Commission could not act on wage agreements, rates of pay, and the like, a small Social Fund had been provided for re-adaptation. In Hallstein's last days, the Commission prepared a major policy statement, issued in 1971, whose *leitmotives* – the need to end wage disparities and provide for convergence in social benefits – pointed over the hills to vast acreage for future plowing.[49] They still have not been reached. Commission social policy has been endlessly discussed and debated, but it remains just talk.

By comparison, mission creep has had far-reaching consequences for regional policy, which (since the days of Commission President Jacques Delors) has become the Community's second most important area of intervention. Provision for it in the treaty is sketchy. Article 226 allows the Commission to intervene in specific instances where an Act of God or the integration process inflicts damage on a locality. It provided a necessary policy wedge, but Hallstein's far-fetched argument stretches the rubber band to the snapping point. He maintains that the article's scope must be expanded because, in opening markets, Commission policies may inadvertently have divergent consequences from one place to another and so require authority to redress the balance between them. This calls for more than the occasional involvement because, as he clumsily expatiates:

In the final analysis we are in all spheres … concerned with the problems of adaptation.… Regional policy is development policy. It is therefore entirely legitimate for the Community to intervene, and such intervention is likely to continue. We are here concerned not with a problem of transition from a pre-Community to a Community period, but something of longer duration than a trade cycle.

Only once, he adds with customary expansiveness, "the true nature and magnitude of the 'New World' we have to face" have been recognized "will it become possible to take appropriate technical, administrative and political action."[50] In late 1963 the Commission and the European Parliament agreed that they must "assume a central element of responsibility for laying down guidelines for a common regional policy." Hallstein concluded long-windedly that there was "no longer any difference of opinion on the proposition that regional policy must be pursued in the perspective of the new, European dimension."[51] Such turgid musings would take on meaning as a result of successive enlargements. Trade-offs made in the name of regional policy would eventually supply much of the political glue that held the community together.

Foreign policy triggered Hallstein's downfall. During his presidency the EEC secured the right to negotiate economic agreements within the framework of international organizations, the power to discharge certain responsibilities in connection with EURAFRICA, and the authority to build a web of association agreements with neighboring nations. It could legitimately vaunt a solid record of accomplishment. This counted for little to Hallstein, who labored under the illusion that foreign policy would provide the quickest and surest route to political union: "a community foreign policy … is no more difficult to organize," Hallstein chugs on inexhaustibly through the pages of his memoirs, "than economic integration, which … involves a vast mass of complicated questions."[52]

He did not doubt for a moment that "every legitimate regional economic interest will be taken into account in defining the interest of the Community as a whole."[53] Hallstein severely censured Gaullist attempts to "re-invest national diplomatic services with authority in spheres in which the Community was to act on behalf of all [as] contrary to the ... letter and spirit ... of a treaty ... based on the principle that it is within and through the institutions of the Community that external policy is formed."[54] One must be reminded in light of such extraordinary pretensions that the EEC had neither an army, a diplomatic corps, nor even representation above the level of the single Washington legation. It lacked the authority to negotiate exclusively on behalf of members in trade forums. It did not even have its own sources of revenue but was, as Hallstein bitterly complained, "a pensioner of the member-states."

INDEPENDENCE, INTERDEPENDENCE, OR DEPENDENCE? PRESIDENT KENNEDY AND EUROPE

The success of Hallstein's venture would depend less on what happened in Brussels than in Washington. The State Department Theologians contemplated recognizing him as president of Europe, or such at least was implied in the Grand Design. The notion was inspired by Monnet and introduced by President Kennedy in one of his most memorable speeches. Not by chance, it was delivered on the Fourth of July (1962) to a select audience of dignitaries gathered in Independence Hall in Philadelphia. Nor was mention of a Declaration of *Inter*dependence coincidental. Kennedy contemplated heroic measures for combatting the EEC's present weakness and for tackling two other pressing diplomatic problems. One was Britain's future world role; the other, sharing nuclear power with France and West Germany. What the U.S. president seemed to have in mind sounded to the uninitiated like a partnership between two equals, the United States and a reinforced European Economic Community, that would be brought up to strength by adding the British as members and by having placed at its command a new Euro-military force – armed with nuclear weapons – that would operate as a full partner within the framework of NATO. The strengthened relationship would be preceded by a fresh round of tariff reductions, which would advance liberalization as well as improve the American payments balance. The stage would then be set for the formation of a European federal union. The Grand Design was evidently meant to be the grand slam of American policy; it promised to overcome past differences between the United States and Europe, tie Europe together, and interlock the United States and Europe in such a way that escape would become virtually impossible.[55] That it would also amount to a European Declaration of Independence, in the form of an American-type liberation from an unhappy past, was implicit in the language.

The policy devised in pursuit of these objectives was complicated not to say tortuous, fundamentally dishonest, and predestined to fail. Sweeping in scope, messianic in tone, breathtakingly arrogant in concept, and wildly irresponsible in potential consequence, the Grand Design exemplifies much that is not praise-worthy in an American policy toward Europe, the traditional and overarching aim of which had been to help a broken civilization recover so that it could, on the basis of common values, find its own way to a better future. Now it was to be handed a techno-strategic *Diktat,* tarted up in the fustian of the day, that would bind it indefinitely to American leadership and Cold War politics. Kennedy's proposal provides compelling evidence of the seductive power of fixed ideas as well as the folly of pursuing them blindly. It also supplies an inadvertent warning of the dangers that can ensue, even in a good cause, when theology gets con-fused with politics – especially nuclear politics. The Grand Design was a worthy successor to EDC and EURATOM. Like them, it failed. Kennedy's initiative brought to a head a complex of festering problems, triggered de Gaulle's veto of Britain's application for membership in the EEC and confirmed the general's determination not to cooperate with either NATO or the EEC, and marked the definitive end of American entanglement in the process of European integration. Even before Viet Nam had turned into a Washington obsession and relegated policy in other parts of the world to the back seat, monnetism had become the victim of its own inanition.

The attempt to maneuver the Trade Expansion Act (TEA) through Congress was the opening move of a policy in which commercial issues were to serve more far-reaching geopolitical aims: the encouragement of European unity and, be-yond this, the strengthening of the Atlantic alliance. The TEA was to have given the president broad authority to negotiate by category rather than item by item as under the Reciprocal Trade Agreement Act in effect since the 1930s. Tucked into the bill was a passage that stipulated that such powers could be exercised only in cases where the United States and the EEC together controlled 80 per-cent of world exports, which would in most instances not obtain unless Britain were to join the Community. The inclusion of the 80-percent provision in the draft bill was meant to force the two parties, then at an early stage in the ne-gotiations over British membership, to fish or cut bait.[56] The bill passed, but it became a dead letter as a result of what transpired at the December 1962 Nassau Conference.[57]

To that pleasant island Prime Minister Macmillan came begging Kennedy for a substitute for the abruptly cancelled U.S.-made Skybolt missile. The weapons system had been promised the United Kingdom as a means of extending the life of the so-called V-bombers that then provided the sole means of deliver-ing atomic warheads; without Skybolt, the heavy expenditure Britain had made in order to remain a nuclear "player" would go down the drain and the Con-servative government, more likely than not, would soon follow behind it. The "compromise" arrived at was to supply Britain with a few of the first-generation nuclear submarines armed with solid-fueled Polaris missiles, then in service for little more than a year. Britain would thus have its "own" system, in fact, a bet-ter one than before. What the public did not know (because such matters were closely guarded secrets) was that two keys had to be turned to fire the weapons in question, and one was to remain firmly held in American hands. The British had not achieved nuclear independence; they had fallen into complete dependence.

De Gaulle now had the pretext he needed to administer, at a regal press conference of 14 January 1963, another humiliating *Non!* to the despised Anglo-Saxons. The Brits would have to wait another ten years to get into the EEC. To make matters worse, two weeks later a by then slightly senile Chancellor Adenauer flew off to Paris for a weekend tryst in order to conclude with the elderly French president the notorious (and by the *Bundestag* later effectively repudiated) Franco-German Treaty of Friendship, which – as countless sniggering political cartoons suggested – all but put the German Michel and the French Marianne between the same sheets. If a Grand Design of any kind were to be realized, it would be de Gaulle's.[58]

The new trans-Rhenanian intimacy caused to surface a spectacular submarine-based deal that until then had been obscured somewhere in the fathomless depths of the Pentagon. The brainchild of one of Monnet's most devout disciples, Robert Bowie (at the time a member of the National Security Council), it was christened the Multilateral Force. Like its EDC forebear, the MLF had a purely political purpose; here it was to make a demonstrative display of nuclear parity. In the full flower of its blushing innocence, the proposal called for a surface navy composed of crews from different nationalities manning ships armed with snappy new Polaris missiles. The officers and men of this polyglot maritime force could inspect, admire, display – polish, fuel, feed, bathe, swaddle, and comfort – their babies. They just couldn't fire them. The authority to unleash the missiles, along with the all-important second key, was to remain in the hands of SACEUR, an American general under orders to the president. This power would be relinquished, or so it was intimated, once Europe was united.[59]

As soon became evident almost everywhere except in parts of Foggy Bottom, the proposal was a con job.[60] Neither the French nor the British would allow themselves to be tricked into forfeiting their costly war toys in the name of a political "Europe" – which both found distasteful – in order to foot the bill for a weapons system of negligible strategic value that neither could control. At the time facing the Berlin Crisis, West Germany reluctantly went along with MLF, as did nations like Belgium and Luxembourg, which had little hope of becoming nuclear powers on their own. Intense American lobbying kept the proposal afloat for nearly three more years until President Johnson, finally pulling the plug, sank it.[61] The MLF is remembered chiefly for having been, as de Gaulle once dubbed it, the Multilateral Farce.

EMPTY CHAIRS AND HALLSTEIN'S END

The "empty chairs" crisis that effectively ended the Hallstein presidency broke out in July 1965. It would be settled seven months later with the Luxembourg Compromise. The power struggle was only in the second instance between the Commission and the French along with the other member-states. In the first instance it was a struggle for order, a way to prevent the Commission from slipping irreversibly out of control. The target date of 1 July 1967, when both the Common Market and the Common Agricultural Policy would come into effect, set the stage for the struggle. It had been agreed that upon the same date the Commission would shift from dependence on the member-state contributions as a revenue source to its "own resources," meaning the duties levied on both foodstuffs imports (called "rebates" in Eurospeak) and everything else (customs duties). The sticking point came in the form of a sharp little hook slipped into a January 1965 Commission omnibus proposal, wrapped into thick folds of a complicated take-it-or-leave-it package, to change the procedures for approving the annual budget. Whereas until then the Council could authorize it by qualified majority vote, in the new version the Assembly (or parliament, as it was often misleadingly referred to by specialists in the public information section of the EEC) could amend the budget and then refer it back to both the Council and the Commission. If the Commission accepted the Assembly's version, a five-sixths majority would be necessary for a Council override. If, however, the Commission proposed changes, the Council could endorse the latter version by a four-sixths majority. Either way, the Council's power would be curtailed, but since it would be easier for it to authorize the Commission's version than that of the Assembly (a larger body and thus harder to work through), the Commission would also gain increased power over the Assembly. When acting in tandem, the Assembly and the Commission could make it nearly impossible for the Council to control the Commission by the purse strings. If the Commission had been getting out of control when still "a pensioner of the member-states" then what dread results might the future bring? By introducing the measure publicly before the parliamentary Assembly in March – rather than, as customary, privately to the Council – Hallstein threw down the gauntlet: he would go over the states and appeal directly to the European public.[62]

The Council deeply resented both the proposed changes in ratification procedure and the significance of Hallstein's gesture. Yet because *engrenage* – another masterful coinage of Eurospeak – was in play, nothing happened. This mystical term purportedly describes the process by which, according to an immanent integration logic, member-states become tied ever more closely together and so create a *solidarité de faits* (another unavoidable term) or "de facto unity." The matter was not so complicated: because the omnibus bill contained carefully balanced but generous political payoffs to every member-state, each of them hesitated to act alone and it was even more difficult to organize a common front in opposition to the Commission. The Council was already immobilized.[63]

The crisis was touched off when, after months of barren discussion in Brussels, the French delegation refused to extend, as was then customary, a negotiating deadline for the Commission's proposal – in this case, beyond 1 July. It soon became evident after "the clock had not been stopped" that a boycott was in effect; France's chair at the Council would be left empty. Why? De Gaulle was outraged by the Assembly's proposed new budgetary power, which threatened to undo the painstakingly negotiated Common Agricultural Policy.[64] To gain a majority in that forum for a policy so evidently weighted in France's favor would have been like herding cats. For the Commission to threaten such a complicated settlement, which involved not only a key sector of French production but also a critical component in long-term national planning, struck him as the epitome of irresponsibility. De Gaulle did not walk out to save the CAP under pressure from either French farmers or the *Patronat,* both of which feared that his action might wreck arrangements from which both had profited handsomely. *Engrenage* was indeed at work in the sense that it had already bound powerful interest groups to Brussels.

President de Gaulle explained himself in the press conference of 9 September 1965. His target, of course, was the Commission, "this embryonic technocracy, for the most part foreign." Ridiculing those who "dreamt" of a European federation, "a project devoid of all realism," he proposed instead returning to "a path of organized cooperation."[65] The speech was understood everywhere, according to Miriam Camps, "as a fundamental attack on the Community method, on those innovations that set it apart most sharply from traditional international organizations, and as a warning that there would be no resumption of French participation in the Community until these key features of the treaty had been changed."[66] To eliminate any remaining doubt on the score, on 20 October Foreign Minister Maurice de Couve de Murville called explicitly for a *revision d'ensemble* – a total overhaul of the treaty.[67]

Finding a replacement for it was not easy. General de Gaulle had all but officially dropped his proposals for setting up a confederal board of directors for the European states, the Fouchet Plans of 1960–1962. Although the EEC could still easily fuse with EFTA to form a large European trade or customs area devoid of "supranational" features, Great Britain would be included and France would have little voice in it; moreover, abandonment of CAP would be costly as well as ruinous politically. The only option was to reorganize the EEC by circumscribing the Commission's initiative powers, curbing its accretion of functions and responsibilities, and preventing it from behaving as if it represented the government of Europe.[68]

Such reforms were implicit in the "decalogue" of changes demanded by Foreign Minister Couve de Murville at the January 1966 Council of Ministers meeting in Luxembourg as conditions for a French return to business as usual at the EEC.[69] The paper contains an indictment of the Commission budget proposal, a litany of complaints about threats to CAP, and a surprisingly long and specific gripe list protesting Commission lobbying, demagogy, and public posturing. The latter was almost certainly related to the endorsement by Monnet of de Gaulle's relatively little-known opponent (Jean Lecanuet) in the forthcoming presidential election and to the open attempts to make "Europe: pro or con?" an issue in the electoral campaign.[70]

The settlement reached at Luxembourg came after six months of inaction had brought the EEC to a virtual standstill, figured prominently as an issue in the

French presidential campaign, left much of the public in The Six agape and confused, and in general bred ulcers and turned heads gray. It was settled in two characteristically awkward sentences, enveloped in layers of almost impenetrable prose. A unilateral French declaration stated that "when very important interests are at stake … discussion must be continued until unanimous agreement is reached [at the Council]." A statement read into the record merely acknowledged "a divergence of view [among The Six as to] what should be done in the event of a failure to reach complete agreement."[71] In non-Eurospeak, any member-state represented in the Council of Ministers could now veto any Commission proposal. Hallstein's hands were tied.

The implications of the Luxembourg Compromise would not become fully evident for several months, but in retrospect its significance is quite clear in several respects. Part of Hallstein's work would stand. His legacies would be the Eurocracy and, of transcendent and increasing importance, a new tradition of European constitutional law. The EEC had survived because no single member dared to pull out of it; the network of mutually interlocking agreements and arrangements made such a move almost too difficult to contemplate. This would change only if a substitute could be found for CAP. The customs union idea appealed both to organized economic interests and to the public, but for the time being it had to be limited to The Six lest the Brussels machinery be overburdened, EEC weakened, and liberalization then continue under different auspices. French *raison d'état* dictated British exclusion from the EEC because, in a wider union, the United Kingdom could compete for the German hand or otherwise dilute France's influence in Europe. The EEC survived, finally, from the lingering fear that Europe had to be organized from the center lest it fall apart and descend into war and chaos. It lost force, however, as memories of the war faded, as Cold War battlefronts hardened, and as partnership with Germany continued to yield dividends.

Supranationalism would be the main casualty of the empty chairs struggle. Monnet championed the creation of a federal union not as one among several but as the only guarantor of permanent peace and prosperity in Europe. He and his followers created the myth that such a union developed through the working of an irreversible historical process, could be set in motion and guided only by a single set of institutions – those of the Community – and could only be led by a right-thinking person deeply steeped in the integrationist faith. Verging on megalomania, Hallstein thought his work validated this theory. The early history of the EEC makes no sense in the absence of a monnetist belief structure. It guided and at the same time limited policy making. Coordination of economic planning was to have been the chief integration mechanism, but the Commission lacked the power to make state economic and welfare bureaucracies responsive to its demands. No European federal government could be created without their assent and cooperation, and public support for a political Europe was virtually nonexistent. The resolution of even simple issues caused endless discussion and debate in Brussels. It took no less than eight years of tiresome conferencing, for example, to fuse the moribund ECSC and the nominal EURATOM into the organizational framework of the EEC. The much-heralded "community method" was becoming synonymous with *immobilisme*.

Seen in light of the apocalyptic monnetist convictions that the end was nigh and the future European federation actually at hand, even the slightest gesture seemed imbued with cosmic significance. A grating, embarrassing, earnest intensity was often the result. Hallstein's notorious Blair House speech, in which he spoke as if representing a single European nation, was the last straw for de Gaulle and prompted the French walkout. Outside the confines of the Commission, the pair of ambiguous phrases that settled the empty chairs crisis effectively deflated monnetism as a philosophy of action. The myth nonetheless survived in scholarship and would continue to provide a context for integration studies and the essential vocabulary for the subject. But at the end of the decade, when the member-states restarted the integration process, it would advance without benefit of teleology, theology, ideology, or even heavy-duty propaganda. Practicality would return. The eight-year bid for papal supremacy having failed, a new era of conciliarism could begin.

Conclusion to Part I

Needed: A New Integration Scenario

EUROPEAN integration is an epiphenomenon of a larger process of change that grew out of the founder generation's deep and abiding commitment to surmount the horrors of the first half of the twentieth century and restore conditions akin to those that existed during the liberal age that spanned the middle decades of the prior, happier century. Liberalization, the term used to describe the means developed to reach this end, required the creation of new institutions to restore the market economy and the operation of the market mechanism itself. The specific mixture of the two required for optimal results has varied over time but remains subject to honest and perhaps irresolvable disagreement. After World War II, the creation of a viable framework for international trade and finance was the first order of the day. Yet once the economic reconstruction process had been completed and the promotion of growth became the overall aim of policy, the market mechanism could gradually take over. "Embedded" controls and restraints could be lifted and a purer form of liberalism allowed to develop.

Viewed in light of the liberalization process, the history of European integration does not resemble the familiar story told disciples faithful to the memory of Jean Monnet. To mention this fact is to state a scholarly commonplace. However, finding a substitute for the usual scenario has never been easy. It is impossible, first of all, to dispense with the figure of Monnet. His achievements of even a secondary order are immense. As the organizer of the French Plan he defined not only the contemporary French style of economic management but one that, precisely because it was the European exception, became a model for others. As a political thinker and actor of genius who operated outside of existing frameworks, he put major new political ideas into currency Europe-wide and indeed did "change the context" of politics – not merely in the case of a single nation or even several of them, but in all of them taken together and as a whole. To emphasize that Monnet's crowning achievement in the history of European integration is to have inspired, designed, and negotiated the Schuman Plan is neither to deny the man's undoubted greatness nor to "relativize" his accomplishments. Rather, it is to take a necessary first step in separating the process of integration, as it actually unfolded, from the encrustation of caked-on misrepresentation and misunderstanding that still obscures it.

It is easy to define Monnet's contribution as a historical actor but hard to disentangle the integration process from the myth he spun around it. The myth itself – its power to inspire and motivate, its durability as a theory of the integration process, its enduring importance as a teleology – will have to be the subject of someone's future book. One can only provide reminders at this point of certain indisputable facts about Monnet's contributions to the integration process. Monnet was, first of all, only on the fringes of the negotiations that led to the Treaty of Rome and the founding of the Common Market, and even then was included merely because the French needed his proposal, EURATOM, as a ploy. The Messina negotiations entailed a specific repudiation of organizational ideas that Monnet had built into both the coal and steel community (a disappointment) and the European Defense Community (a nonstarter) as well as the conscious abandonment of the notion animating them, supranationality. The most important thread of institutional continuity between the ECSC and the EEC was included in the former as an afterthought, and its subsequent importance was unsuspected by its designers. This was the European Court of Justice (ECJ), a body created not to arbitrate, mediate, or adjudicate but as an instrument to legitimate the exercise of transnational executive power and for the specific purpose of creating a new body of European constitutional law with the power to override national courts. However, the ECJ owed its rise not to provisions in the coal–steel treaty but to those in the Treaty of Rome, which empowered it to enforce rules necessary for the operation of the single market.

The new EEC was designed to be a customs union with open markets governed by the competition principle except when, as in the case of the Common Agricultural Policy, political concessions were necessary. The membership of the ECSC and EEC was the same, but the institutional and ideological resemblance was superficial. Monnetism survived at the EEC thanks chiefly to the Commission's first president, Walter Hallstein – once controversial but since largely forgotten. Hallstein violated the spirit of the Treaty of Rome by creating corporatist and centralizing bureaucracies outside its framework, and he overwrote the real history of the origins of the EEC with the mythological one based upon the ECSC. In his version, the Common Market became the New Testament version of ECSC: bigger, better, and accessible to all believers, but still part of the same great story. He also discovered an immanent logic at work in History, an integration process binding past to present and present to future through "spillovers" and related mechanisms that would lead, step by step, to the promised land of European federation. Hallstein's devotion to the idea of building Europe was evident in acts large and small, in word and in gesture; he shared this attitude in common with many other highly talented, energetic, prominent, and idealistic men and women devoted to *l'Inspirateur*.

There is little to "inspire" in Hallstein's tenure as first president of the Commission. He was forced to perform a conjuror's act in order to fashion an *apparat* out of the meager materials at hand. Ideological commitment, other than to the monnetist creed, counted little in this respect; its use was tactical – to establish the Commission's authority. Although adoption of the Medium-Term Economic Program as the centerpiece of the Commission policy might suggest a doctrinal predilection for French economic methods, or even for the kind of balanced and equitable society it was meant to produce, such a conclusion would be misplaced. Robert Marjolin, the chief designer, was skeptical of managed economies and normally an outspoken advocate of free-market approaches. His job as a Commission bureaucrat was nonetheless to build up the power of the Community, and – unless it were to limit itself to the role of rule-setter in an open competitive market economy, as intended in the treaty – it would have to become *dirigiste*. How *dirigiste*? Bruises sustained in early skirmishes with entrenched public interests in the fields of energy and transport would suggest "very *dirigiste* indeed." Yet the model was always French. Even in the post-Sputnik era of the early 1960s, when twaddle about economic convergence became *Salonfähig*, the Soviet model of a controlled economy appears never to have come up for discussion at Community roundtables.

Opportunism and bureaucratic entrepreneurship gave direction to Commission policy. The empire building left a lasting legacy even in cases when, in the near term, the Euro-executive could only plan and project. Social and regional policy provides one such example. More often such ambitions produced sheer silliness, as in the pompous insistence that the president of the Commission be accorded the honors due as Head of State, Federator, or Political Pope. It could also be reckless. EURATOM involved wading into the murky and radioactive waters of an advanced technology whose scary implications were barely understood. The European Defense Community proposal was a clear and present danger, as well as an evil omen of Kennedy's Grand Design, which ruled out self-determination as a future method of European integration and dictated a strategically determined and permanent subordination to American imperial domination. The unraveling of JFK's policy marked the end of direct, large-scale American intervention into the European integration process. The collapse of the Bretton Woods system and the dollar gold peg would eliminate the power of the White House to determine Europe's future.

Hallstein's presidency was not a complete failure. He cannot, however, take sole credit for its successes. Between 1958 and 1968, the year in which he formally resigned, the European economy grew at an annual rate of nearly 7 percent. Tariff reductions (part of a larger project) contributed to the outstanding results, but the specific importance of Commission policy making cannot be demonstrated. Though mass affluence was hardly yet the rule, by mid-decade nearly all western European households had radios, almost half had television sets, and up to 40 percent owned automobiles in most member-states. That this remarkable prosperity – a vast improvement on anything seen previously – should be associated in the public mind with the founding of the EEC should come as no surprise, even though economists have never found it easy to establish any significant correlation between the two (either in the 1960s or subsequently). The formation of small but influential and growing pro-European constituencies in European countries was likewise predictable. The German Social Democratic Party moved to a pro-European stance in 1959, and thereafter integration ceased to be a partisan issue in the Federal Republic. The future of the EEC also featured in the French presidential election of 1967 and would become a perennial of British politics after the first *Non*.

The outcome of the empty chairs crisis proved that the EEC was "here to stay" if only because abandonment of the CAP would have been too costly for farm interest groups and for France generally. Without this special arrangement for agriculture, and in the absence of a budding "pro-European" public opinion, the Community might nevertheless have drifted into merger with EFTA and formed a Europe-wide trading area or customs union. With Adenauer out and Erhard in as German chancellor in late 1963, this possibility was far from being confined to the realm of pure theory. And driving it was a powerful logic.

The integration story of the 1950s and 1960s has a couple of insufficiently appreciated chapters. One is the creation of an adaptable framework of institutions that would, over decades, make progress possible toward free trade, open markets, stable currencies, and liberal societies. Another chapter – even more significant for the near term – was the independent development of West Germany as motor and model for Europe: scripted by Röpke, directed by an Erhard who was faithful to the text, and shrewdly produced by Adenauer with an eye toward good reviews and maximum box-office returns. The result was indeed a different Germany-in-Europe. Hitler's Economic New Order, as planned by technocrats in the Reich's Ministry of Economics, was a giant Berlin clearinghouse, a hub-and-spoke network through which the finances and commerce of Europe passed bilaterally on dictated terms and which, by definition, could only have been exploitative. This payments system was the mechanism by which the defeated, occupied, humiliated, and murdered victims of German aggression could be made to bear the costs of their own enslavement and extermination. The Federal Republic's policies of unilateral tariff reduction, sound currency, open markets, and hard work promoted growth but also enforced rules of economic behavior that would advance reform elsewhere while allowing for shifts of power over time. The bottom line of interdependence is domination by no one.

It is hard to argue with success. The new Europe that began to take shape in the 1950s and 1960s was such an enormous improvement over the heap of rubble it replaced that it is difficult to subject the origins of European integration to critical examination without sounding persnickety. Yet the road taken was not always the right one. If it were, the detours would have been far fewer. Many of Monnet's initiatives were stillborn, otherwise unsound, and certainly not necessary parts of an inevitable historical process. Monnet's personal legacy was a fund of integrationist ideas like supranationalism, functionalism, and so on. The monnet*ist* legacy left by Hallstein consisted of the Commission, a tradition of European constitutional law, and ongoing pursuit of federal union as a goal.

If the empty chairs crisis closed the era of chiliastic monnetism, what brought its definitive end was the collapse of the embedded liberal regime in the early 1970s. The collapse of the Bretton Woods system pulled the props out from under the close state–economy relationship, without which it could not function. The next ten years would bring an interregnum in which broad progress on the integration front stopped. One heard little about "spillover" in this dry decade, even though the seeds then sown would restore life to the integration process in the distant future. The rebound would have little to do with the Commission's administrative centralizing and much to do with the original purposes of the Treaty of Rome.

Part II

From Embedded Liberalism to Liberalism,
A Step Forward: European Integration
and Regime Change in the 1970s

Introduction to Part II

A New European Situation

WHEN compared with the burst of enthusiasm that greeted the inauguration of the Community – or with the avalanche of progress ushered in by the Single European Act of 1986 – the turmoil, setbacks, and inertia of the 1970s seem devoid of accomplishment and even interest for the history of integration. It was an era of frustration, failure, and Euro-pessimism. Bad times and human weakness were not, however, the main problems. Their source was structural. Integration came to an impasse because the transference of decision-making power from the mixed-economy welfare states to the European level proved nearly impossible. The formation of a large customs union might have circumvented the problem and stimulated growth, but the market-based alternative was not in the cards. Britain had committed itself to joining the EC,[1] the United States faced severe domestic problems, and the Federal Republic was in transit from a social market economy (*Soziale Marktwirtschaft*) to a social state (*Sozialstaat*).

The open-market cause not only lacked a leader but was intellectually out of favor. State-based programs directed at correcting market failure were the fashion of the day, and by no means only on the political left. The market-centered alternative seldom received serious consideration in any quarter. The 1970s was the decade of Keynesian ascendancy. Planning remained the vogue in much of Europe. In most advanced countries, the government sector consumed half of GNP. Public–private partnerships sprouted up all over the industrialized world, and insidious new nontariff barriers (NTBs) reversed previous progress made in dismantling old-fashioned tariffs and quotas. A neomercantilist tendency was nearly everywhere on the rise, which bound state and economy more tightly together than before and complicated the enforcement of public accountability.

Trends in Europe mirrored the world situation. The European Community of the 1970s became deeply involved in sectoral policy. Agriculture was where the approach was first applied and would remain the most important example of it. About three quarters of the EC budget went into the giveaway program for farmers known as the Common Agricultural Policy. In the 1970s, the EC organized restrictive agreements in textiles, shipbuilding, and steel. The Commission's neomercantilist interventionism would soon extend into sunrise as well as sunset industries, providing a spearhead for the corporatist organization of Europe.

Yet the 1970s was not altogether barren as an integration decade. A period of soul-searching followed the impasse of the late 1960s. One result was a strong commitment among the member-states to put the process back on track. The Hague summit of December 1969, the first meeting of heads of states since the tenth anniversary of the Rome Treaty, laid much of the groundwork for future change. It settled the budget disagreement that had precipitated the empty chairs crisis, confirmed a decision to proceed with the enlargement of the Community (and specifically to admit Great Britain as a member), and established monetary union as the next goal in the creation of a single market. The Hague meeting also changed the integration context in four critical ways. First, the Community bound itself into an unholy fiscal settlement that, if not undone, will continue to limit reform, undermine legitimacy, and constrain political development: it removed CAP (i.e., the bulk of the budget) from the control of the Parliament and thus stunted the political growth of the Brussels policy-making machinery. Second, the summit also provided the model for the European Council, the extra-treaty body that would provide EC leadership in the 1980s. It took a third important step in deciding to consider British candidacy as a first move toward Community expansion. The United Kingdom's serious economic difficulties, the division of public opinion over the membership issue, and the nagging problem of its fiscal contribution to the EC reduced the immediate impact of its presence but not its long-run importance. Margaret Thatcher would briefly turn the United Kingdom into a major power within the Community. Fourth, the decision to advance toward monetary union within ten years would not only require the greatest relinquishment of sovereign power in European history, it would also set the member-states on a convergence course with Germany requiring fundamental structural reform.[2]

Though occasionally lost from sight amidst the chaotic events of the decade, certain positive long-term economic trends remained unbroken. The multinational corporation spread in spite of added governmental regulation and even nationalization. Cross-border capital flows increased substantially. Viewed as threats by national governments at the time, these developments were good for economic progress. Another, unrelated change had a similar effect: the development of a quasi-constitutional body of European law, which anchored the EC in legal principle, weakened national monopolies, and extended the authority of Brussels into the households of Europe.

"Regime change" was what really counted. It broke the logjam of interest conflict between Brussels and the mixed-economy welfare states that impeded the development of European institutions. The term "regime change," in recent years much abused, has a precise meaning as employed here. It denotes the fundamental shift in values, methods, and operating mechanisms that took place beginning in the late 1970s. In the West the shift came about as a result of developments in the monetary realm, where stability replaced full employment as the overriding policy objective. This change in emphasis had immense implications. Regime change displaced old loci of power and created new ones, imposed a different incentive structure, altered the scale of values, expanded opportunity, and gave a fresh start to European integration. Regime change also brought the integration process down from the realm of theoretical constructions – plans, projects, and imagined bureaucracies floating in the sky – to earth, where it could develop into a formative influence within European society. Without this decisive shift, and the new outlook resulting from it, European integration would have come to a halt.

Regime change started at the beginning of the decade with the collapse of the international buttress of the mixed-economy welfare state, the embedded liberal monetary systems of Bretton Woods. The downfall dethroned the dollar as *numéraire,* ended the fixed parity system, and weakened national monetary control. The layers of protection needed to buffer regulated economies from exogenous change were stripped away, and monetary chaos resulted. In lieu of wage and price adjustment through marketplace competition, stagflation set in. Recurrent crises broke out throughout Europe, which undermined the social consensus upon which the corporate state, in its various guises, rested. Such challenges called for new approaches. One of them was the difficult and only partly successful effort – made by the European Council with a view toward monetary union – to set the nations of the continent on a course of economic convergence with Germany and tie them to the Deutsche mark. An even more important trend was the liberal revival that took place in Great Britain under Margaret Thatcher at the close of the decade; it was both cause and consequence of the regime change.

Few EC policy intellectuals understood how the process of economic change worked in the 1970s. They knew that the integration formulas of the past had lost their magic, but their only remedy was more of the same sort of institution building that had led to frustration under Hallstein. Integration theory seemed to have reached a dead end. Yet two thinkers – the British economist Andrew Shonfield and the Anglo-German sociologist Ralf Dahrendorf – espied the light that could lead the Community out of political impasse. A single economist, the Dutchman Jacques Pelkmans, managed to explain theoretically why "positive integration" was destined to fail and why revival of the integration process would require a return to the all-but-forgotten "negative integration." Dahrendorf and Shonfield would survey new, alternate routes to a future constitutional Europe. Pelkmans would explain the operation of the only vehicle that could propel or draw Europe along such avenues; he would develop the core theory of European economic integration.

The founding of the European Council was essential to the restoration of forward movement. The influential new body shifted policy-making authority from a Commission that lacked the muscle to enforce its claims and restored it to the member-states, which had created the Community in the first place and where the real power had always reposed. Through the new Council, domestic reforms could be transmitted to Europe and vice versa. Thatcherism would provide the impetus to European integration during the 1980s. "Neoliberalism" would be the variant of it adapted for use on the continent, where free-market economics remained politically suspect.

From Realms of Theory to a Sphere of Action: Integration Revived

THE INTEGRATION process seemed to have run its course in the 1970s. Although the conflict between the institutional ambitions of Brussels and the entrenched national interests of the mixed-economy welfare states was the source of the problems facing the EEC, a failure of intellectual imagination compounded difficulties. Fresh ideas were rare, vision of the right kind in short supply. It was a time not unlike the present. There were exceptions: thinkers who understood that the problems facing the Community – that it was both undemocratic politically and immobilized economically – could not be solved by technocratic institution building. Their thoughts, relevant today, should be required reading for every delegate at the Convention on the Future of Europe, which has embarked upon the task of drafting a federal constitution by 2004.

In his famous 1972 BBC Reith Lectures, *Europe: Journey to an Unknown Destination,* Andrew Shonfield, the first such discerning thinker, took a distinctly British approach to European community building, an elevated kind of muddling through by means of which a history of successful problem solving in areas outside the reach of the nation-state leads, over time, to a viable tradition of transnational governance. Shonfield's integration scenario hardly grips the imagination, but it depicts a more realistic and sensible course of development for European institutions than anything envisaged prior to it and perhaps since. Although Shonfield's scheme lacks a serious economic counterpart, the political route he delineated has since been plotted more accurately and in greater detail by a heterogeneous collection of lawyers, economists, and political scientists who, having studied the European Union (EU) as a regulatory regime, contend that it can eventually acquire the properties of a representative government. For lack of a better term, they will be referred to henceforth as *institutional evolutionists.*

In *Plädoyer für die Europäische Union,* a compelling series of newspaper articles published under a *nom de plume* in 1973, Ralf Dahrendorf (at that point in his long and fascinating career an EC commissioner) drafted a more detailed and slightly different road map than Shonfield's. Like him, Dahrendorf rejected "First Europe" plans such as Hallstein's for building a political federation from Brussels. To advance the integration process, something self-evidently desirable to his mind, Dahrendorf called for the creation of a "Second Europe" in which a council of states would advance developments in a manner responsible to their citizens until conditions have become ripe for the emergence of a democratic

"Third Europe" with a real legislature and executive. Dahrendorf posited the existence of an open economy with competitive markets as a necessary (though not sufficient) condition of such an outcome. What Dahrendorf envisaged for the Second Europe resembles the European Council organized in the early 1980s – by French President Valéry Giscard d'Estaing and German Chancellor Helmut Schmidt – to re-ignite the integration process. Dahrendorf's scenario also fore-shadowed subsequent official and semi-official German plans for a European constitution. Those who think along the approach delineated in *Plädoyer* will be called *liberal federalists*.

The theoretical insights of the Dutch political economist, Jacques Pelkmans, buttress Dahrendorf's contention that the evolution of democratic institutions and the expansion of open markets go hand in hand. Although Pelkmans has never been identified with classical liberalism, a couple of pathbreaking articles he published in the early 1980s go directly to the heart of the school's case for integration. He added a powerful and persuasive public choice argument to Hayek's "The Economic Conditions of Interstate Federalism," contending that only "negative" (as opposed to "positive") integration can work and that such an approach is both cause and effect of transnational political development. The stipulation that open markets are the essential prerequisite to any permanent form of economic and political cooperation at the European level flatly contradicted the conventional wisdom of the decade, ran against the grain of Commission President Jacques Delors's subsequent policy in the late 1980s and early 1990s, and even today finds favor only among a small minority of integration practitioners and the academics who study them. Such views, then, have been far less important in advancing the integration process than the new context created by the regime change of the 1970s. The weakening of the linkage between state and economy, both nationally and internationally, that resulted from the collapse of the Bretton Woods system would unleash the power of the market as well as set the stage for the most constructive phase in the history of integration since the founding of the EEC itself. It would begin, politically, in Mrs. Thatcher's Great Britain.

TAKING STOCK IN A WHIRLWIND: RETHINKING INTEGRATION

The stalemate of the late 1960s shook the integration faith to the roots but also launched a search for new verities to fortify it. Such is the conclusion suggested by the writings of prominent influential policy intellectuals, some of whom wore (or had worn) the cloth of EC officialdom. Alone or foregathered in conventicles, they searched their very souls in order to find out why they had been forsaken, why the integration process had failed them, and how the old faith might be re-stored. From this body of scripture certain truths emerged: that Euro-enthusiasm was an elite phenomenon and not partaken of by the general public; that the EC, especially the Commission, was dogmatic and doctrinaire, out of touch with the world, antidemocratic, inefficient, and above all lacking in legitimacy; that functionalism and monnetist supranationalism explained little about the integration process; that progress toward the goal of European union would necessarily be gradual; and that anything other than a practical, empirical, and consensual approach to community building would fail.

The policy prescriptions that emerged from such contemplations were on the whole either vague or unrealistic. None of the doubters challenged the basic configuration of Community institutions – a reformation was not contemplated – but their estimates differed in regard to the extent and modalities of possible change. Such judgments depended in turn upon estimates of how and whether the Brussels *apparat* could be bolstered and built up into a stable amalgam of federal government and economic directorate. Securely cloistered, none of the prayerful fully understood that the storms raging outside were not simply inconvenient or disruptive but actually destructive of the very foundations upon which they hoped to build.

The seeking began in Brussels. The sophisticated public opinion polls then scrupulously conducted by Jacques-René Rabier on behalf of the Community pointed mercilessly to the hard truth that integration theory had far outrun reality:

pro-European sentiment was neither widely nor deeply felt among the mass populations of the Common Market countries in 1970, "committed Europeans" are only a minority, pervasive disinterestedness and almost numbness with regard to European matters is evident in most sectors of society and policy, and pro-Europeanism still remains largely an elite cult.[1]

Those repelled by "technocratic aloofness far outnumbered ... those inspired by the Common Market's symbolization of Europe." More troubling yet, the poll's findings suggested "a certain innate frailty in the whole supranational experiment [that suggests] monuments built in sand."[2] It recommended that an "elite ... point the continent toward a 'third force' posture in world affairs and begin accumulating the symbols and substance of great power status [because] ... traditional nationalists [would then] get the power and glory that their older nation states can no longer muster for themselves."[3] A dose of Euro-demagogy? A couple of graven images? Such temptations would be hard to resist.

For having raised excessive expectations of integration by overweening ambition, the sin of Pride, the functionalists did not have to be spanked. They flagellated themselves and each other with perverse pleasure, developing a countercritique to explain what had gone wrong with their theory. According to chastened grand master, Ernst Haas, it had failed because integration "spillovers" depended on the logic of liberalization and had thus neglected to consider both the Commission's penchant for interventionism and the rise to favor among the public of income transfers, quality-of-life issues such as environmentalism, and the mounting popularity of an antigrowth ethic.[4] One thoughtful leading disciple, the penitential University of Wisconsin political scientist Stuart Scheingold, confessed that the fathers of integration had mistakenly set the movement in motion with a view to solving pre–World War II rather than present problems and that, furthermore, the impact of the EC on economic growth was undocumented, evidence of a new entrepreneurial spirit scant, and a concern with political issues all but absent. Scheingold despairingly concluded that "the essentially nonpolitical, no-conflict, technocratic model does not explain the world around us in which political conflict coexists with affluence and in which the old problems of redistributing material welfare remain salient."[5] He recommended embarking upon "value-sensitive *empirical* research."[6] The word was good. After a decade, and with faith renewed by the integration breakthroughs of the 1980s, functionalism would beget a *neo*functionalist revival. Old disputes then resumed with newfound intensity.

The doubts and worries of the cloistered were little in evidence among a secular clergy content to expound dogma. It was the familiar statist litany, mouthed by some who appear to have believed little of it but simply lacked any other faith. To such worldly clerics, the Brussels *apparat* remained the alpha and omega of integration, the free market a Satanic threat to it. The Commission had to be strengthened in order to ward off evil. Euro-socialism meant redemption! Even those with doubts agreed because only heretics thought otherwise at the time. Such is the conclusion suggested by selected synopses of a representative sample of a few policy proposals then in circulation. It would require a powerful sign or omen – an earthquake, a parting of the skies, a regime change – to induce thinking outside of the box. These studies reveal the prevalent intellectual stagnation of the dark 1970s and also serve as a reminder of the intellectual distance traveled since then. They rely heavily on an unviable interventionism.

The Werner Plan for monetary union adopted after The Hague summit of 1969 was the special concern of the Federal Trust/UACES Study Group (composed of British government management experts) that met in the mid-1970s. Fearing it would fail because of inadequate administrative preparation, the group proposed several methods for bulking up the bureaucracy. The study group criticized the Treaty of Rome for containing a "management deficit" and blamed German liberals for opposing "economic coordination." The Werner Report's "principal requirement," according to the group's rapporteur, was a new "center of economic policy decision making ... with decisive influence over the general economic policy of the community" and with responsibilities extending to the economic and social spheres ("which will have to be transferred to the community level").[7] Lack of progress had been frustrating, however. A small but high-level Steering Committee to Coordinate Short-Term Economic Policy, set up in accordance with the Werner Report, accomplished little, as did repeated warnings and admonitions from the Council in 1972 and 1973. The problem of economic and monetary union, according to a May 1973 Commission investigation, had to be addressed "along a wide front, including not only a developed regional policy but also structural, industrial and social policies, [which require] ... an expanded community budget."[8]

Advocated was nothing less than "a Community with ... a common currency [in] a federal system like ... the U.S., with a central government wielding substantial economic control." To restrict the power of the member-states, the text recommended including tax harmonization within the scope of economic union. Large-scale transfer payments could then be made on the sly to subsidize an expanding bureaucracy. The words deserve to be quoted:

> The massive scale of resource transfers between different regions of the Community required under conditions of a common currency, and the political desirability of disguising their scale by drawing contributions from Community taxation rather from direct levies on national budgets, will also strengthen the argument for a substantial community budget ... [and] of course require a considerable administrative machine, even if execution of Community policies is decentralized to national governments.[9]

Envisaged was a thoroughgoing Euro-socialism, "a Community which will have to develop a clear set of central policies on prices, ... growth and income distribution, ... inflation, ... employment, ... social benefits, and incentives to industry ... that is to say ... many of the central questions of national politics,"[10] lest both it and the member-states lose powers of economic management. With trade as well as labor and capital mobility on the increase, the necessary means must be "developed for regaining control over the Community economy as a whole, which will [soon] be lost at the national level." Otherwise, European economies would be subject to "sharp and politically unacceptable disequilibria" requiring even more drastic centralization.[11]

A similar emphasis on the importance of the frontal approach to strengthening community institutions is even found in *Economic Policy for the European Community: The Way Forward,* a jointly authored work published in 1974 that summarizes the main conclusions reached by a panel of five highly distinguished economists (two of whom are still prominent in Community affairs): Sir Alec Cairncross, Herbert Giersch, Alexandre Lamfalussy, Giuseppe Petrelli, and Pierre Uri.[12] The group, presumably representing a national and political cross-section of advanced contemporary economic thinkers, included a prominent central banker as well as a leading figure associated with the ORDO-liberals. These two gentlemen must be assumed to have found themselves on the defensive. Only lip service is paid in the pages of this book to protecting open markets where they still can be found. Absent altogether from the analysis is any intimation of what subsequently would be called supply-side economics. Indeed, it treats business as an enemy of integration.

The panel's prescriptions for advancing integration could only have spread the ailments plaguing the state-centered national economies to the European level. The overriding, and characteristic, concern of the authors was that

> governments are more willing to allow market forces to play on the private sector than on the matters under their immediate control, [making] it necessary ... to move towards a distribution of power within the European Community which limits the authority of the national governments except in the domestic sphere and reserves matters of common interest for ... decision by the Community as a whole.[13]

To strengthen the cohesion of the Community in preparing for monetary union, its budget must be substantially expanded, thus permitting "a steady enlargement of [its] tasks."[14] Much more will be required, the book proceeds, than the mere coordination of national budgeting as provided for in the Werner Report; fine-tuning is needed for both social and economic reasons. "If progress is to be made towards fiscal integration," the authors state, "the composition and direction of public spending needs to be analyzed [in terms of] distortions of competition, the contribution to growth and equality, the regional allocation of resources, and the relief of inflationary pressures." Otherwise,

governments will continue to compete with each other in granting fiscal concessions in order to attract investment in industrial development. They will [also] continue to sacrifice public investment which generally contributes more to social amenities and the quality of life than does industrial competitiveness .... Harmonization in the proper sense is ... needed to forestall the unwanted consequences of competition left to itself.[15]

Far-reaching intervention was also thought to be necessary because the provision of comparable public services Community-wide would require massive transfers, the elimination of the principle of *juste retour,* consolidation of the Community budget, and reform of the Common Agricultural Policy. To raise the revenues needed for the new budget, a tax on the increase in land values was proposed.[16] The authors emphasized in their concluding remarks that monetary union must be delayed as long as necessary to prevent mobile capital from demolishing the control instruments of national economic policy and thus causing "anarchy" and weakening public authority; that fiscal policy must play a key role in influencing the distribution and formation of national incomes from nation to nation; that a "larger and larger" common budget must be provided in order to overcome the disparities of income and public service and to restrict migration from poor to rich areas; that a common industrial policy is needed "to establish a concerted approach to adjustment assistance"; and that megacorporations should be solicited to advance Europe to the forefront of technological development.[17]

Yet by 1980 the plans for such Euro-socialism had met with little success. In an article published in that year, Ulrich Everling (head of the European policy unit at the German Ministry of Economics) re-discovered the obvious problem: the member-states were still not about to relinquish their powers. He offered several explanations. The elimination of trade barriers as called for in the treaty required, he reminded the reader, the harmonization of national laws and common policies, but most important public policy issues remained responsibilities of the states; Brussels exercised only a power to "coordinate," which was actually being reduced by the increased power exercised by the member-states through the European Council and the Council of Ministers. A monetary union that rested on "automatism" would fail, he presciently asserted, and the existing "coordination" linkage was not strong enough to make it work. Although Everling admitted that economic thinking and structures appeared to be converging, the record of industrial and commercial policy did not suggest to him that "coordination" was getting any stronger. Underlying the problem, he proceeded, were disparities in economic philosophy, administrative methods, "structures," and regional standards of living. "Procedural tricks" such as majority voting or a two-track Europe would not make matters better until the missing "general consensus" could be created for the Community. Everling thought the Community was more than a simple administrative association (*Zweckverband*) and felt that increasing economic interdependence was inescapable, but he knew that an acceptable substitute for the Brussels machinery was not within view. He could offer no solution.[18]

More revealing than the recantations of political scientists or the dogma spouted by policy specialists was the appearance of two new integration gospels, efforts to recount and explain for the benefit of future generations the events and "good news" of the integration story. They can be read in texts attributed to a British economist with Labour affiliations, Andrew Shonfield, and a liberal German sociologist (at the time, a member of the European Commission) who subsequently became vice-chancellor at the London School of Economics and was later ennobled as Lord Ralf Dahrendorf.[19] In insisting upon the need to replace the monnetist–papal tradition of imposing change from the top down with a community of believers growing from the bottom up, each moved both morally and tactically in the general direction of democracy and representative government in what would be an integration reformation. The two men nevertheless had different ends in view and took separate approaches to get there. Integration made sense to Dahrendorf, a liberal federalist, only if aimed at eventual political union. To him the optimal (but by no means the only possible) way to reach the destination was through the market. To Shonfield, an institutional evolutionist, integration was little more than a shorthand method for coping with modern economic and political problems of a size and complexity too great to be handled by the nation-state. He argued that if such problems were tackled sensibly and successfully then suprastate cooperation would eventually provide necessary substructures for peace and prosperity, the desired end of the integration process. Neither writer related these different outcomes to the working of ineluctable economic laws or political processes. Their two scenarios were also essentially compatible. The differences in emphasis reflect political predilection as well as separate legal and constitutional tradition rather than fundamental disagreement.

In *Europe: Journey to an Unknown Destination,* Shonfield stressed that, for the EC as for any other political authority, *legitimacy* – standing out boldfaced in his account as the indispensable prerequisite and uppermost requirement of functional parliamentary government – can only be gained by an incremental, efficient, and successful solving of problems that cannot be managed better in any other way. In his view, satisfactory outcomes presuppose policy-making competition (rather than some imagined technocratic perfection), place a premium on practicality, and cannot be predicted.[20] Shonfield maintained that the market-based "compact of abstention" that framed the institutions of the Community was inadequate to deal with the problems arising from supranationality, something that he memorably – and quite distinctly from Monnet's usage – described as resembling "a bag of marbles ... soft on the surface and made of some sticky substance like putty, which keeps them clinging together as they are pushed around ... and make contact with one another."[21] He blamed the Commission in Brussels for having viewed itself "as guardian of an imaginary Ark of the Covenant" that had tried to re-invent Europe by a strategy of *la fuite en avance* but had yet to learn that community building expresses a set of common circumstances "continuously shaping the societies of all the member nations."[22]

Shonfield argued that legal fact should follow social practice and be based upon systematic compromises arrived at by the Council rather than imposed by the Commission. Above all, he insisted, a shift from technocracy to democracy must occur in order for the EC to be accepted by the public. Shonfield also warned presciently that monetary union, if effective, would put power in the hands of central bankers but otherwise would lead to recrimination and possibly disrupt the community. For "the second phase" of integration, he counseled gradualism and cooperation. The European Parliament (EP) should not, in his view, be directly elected but rather be composed of representatives from national parliaments who could coordinate policy and intermediate between the two bodies – an original idea that would have a long shelf life. The EP would in this scenario become a kind of committee of committees. He further recommended creation of new interstate boards to coordinate laws implementing European directives as well as reduction of the Commission to the status of an advisory body of political leaders rather than technocrats. His emphasis on the primacy of national courts within a common framework of principle is another suggestion that has been taken up by contemporary legal theorists.[23] Though unable to locate the future "destination" of Europe, Shonfield concluded that it can only be arrived at over an extended period and by problem solving that builds public trust and confidence.[24]

Ralf Dahrendorf's *Plädoyer für die Europäische Union* ("Plea for the European Union") presents a magisterial view of past, present, and future integration from the distinct angle of a German liberal navigating the angry seas of an antiliberal ocean. Although Dahrendorf (unlike Shonfield) felt confident that political union is the right "destiny" for Europe, he relegates such an event to a future era of a Third Europe. Yet he, too, had only a general idea about how or precisely when it would arrive. As for the Second Europe in which Dahrendorf found himself, the impasse reached by the First Europe had left it stunned, rudderless, without a map, and stranded in unknown waters; emergency repairs were needed quickly, and stellar navigation had to be mastered on the spot lest foundering set in.

According to Dahrendorf, Hallstein's methods had been overambitious, unrealistic, imbedded in rigid institutions, inflexible, and (in the case of agriculture) no good at all.[25] Europe should be made not by plan, Dahrendorf argued, but *à la carte,* so that "everyone does what he wants and ... no one must participate in everything," a situation that "though far from ideal is surely much better than avoiding anything that cannot be cooked in a single pot."[26] Preferring informal organizational methods, Dahrendorf advocated taking a variety of approaches in order to arrive at eventual union, which (as he envisaged it) would resemble a European version of a federal democratic state.

Dahrendorf insisted, though without much explanation, that such a federal construction would require economic reform. This was to include both monetary union and convergence of national fiscal policy that would deprive states of a key sovereign power and that would force economies to become competitive by eliminating devaluation and capital controls and by stripping away layers of the welfare state. The creation of such a union would serve, he thought, as the penultimate step – not only toward a democratic European federation but also toward an *economically liberal* European federation. Dahrendorf thought monetary union necessary for the single market, for economic growth and stability, and as a short cut to political federation – which, however, he did not think yet in sight. Until such a time, Dahrendorf recommended "flanking measures" like regional, structural, environmental, and education and research policy to keep integration moving forward, adding the stipulation that they must not be allowed to impede progress either by undermining market incentives or by creating new bureaucracies. Painfully aware that in the 1970s liberalism had fallen on hard times, Dahrendorf offered no immediate alternative to current policies, but he did express hope that the present cycle would run its course and pledged a determination to update and improve upon traditional liberal prescriptions for future application. Only against a broader pattern of change, he ventured, could a united Europe share responsibility with the United States as protector and promoter of the liberal world order.[27]

Dahrendorf presciently recognized the political danger posed by a monetary union – that it would require a vast transference of sovereign power to an international board of bankers – but also thought that such a union would set the stage for a liberal revival by disciplining monetary and fiscal policy, providing currency stability, and increasing competition. All three observations would subsequently be borne out. He did not, however, discuss various options for the future monetary regime; nor did he consider that – because the EC was a suboptimal currency area with restricted factor mobility – a "one size fits all" monetary policy would reduce growth, generate antiliberal political defenses, and generate counterpressures to reform. Two steps forward and one step back was still better than nothing at all. Dahrendorf's analysis was leagues ahead of the official Commission plan for monetary union, the Werner Report, which (as the Euro-socialist advocates also emphasized) left undiscussed the vital issue of whether the European economy was to be regulated by the competition principle or by *dirigisme*. The threat of the latter would have to be pushed by the wayside before real reform could begin.

The rigorous analyses of the political economist Jacques Pelkmans in the early 1980s provided the first convincing contemporary explanations as to why the very convergence of state and economy – upon which most contemporary experts relied for the construction of Europe – was itself the source of its weakness. He arrived at these conclusions at a time when, outside of Great Britain, traditional defenders of "negative integration" were conspicuously silent. One of a relative handful of expert economists specializing in the subject of European integration, Pelkmans is sharply critical of the failure of neoclassical economics to account adequately for the realities of "mixed economies of the capitalist variety" in examining the integration issue. Here he links arms with classical liberalism.

Pelkmans's 1980 "Economic Theories of Integration Revisited" opened with the brief but devastating observation that the theory of Béla Balassa – the reigning "economic" explanation of how, step by step, customs unions can come into being – was "twisted, if not simply false" because only the first three of the five stages Balassa posits take place in classical "*laissez-faire* economies where member governments initially do not intervene in markets except at their frontiers ... so as to obtain a truly free market over a larger economic space."[28] This Pelkmans termed *pure market integration*. In Balassa's final two stages, economic union and total economic integration, he detected a different mechanism at work: "The last two stages ... suddenly deal with policies that hitherto were considered nonexistent and harmonize or unify them." They constituted, in Pelkmans's words, "pure forms of *policy integration*" and were unrelated to the operation of the market process. Hence there existed a "*dichotomy of economic integration theory*."[29]

Pelkmans's comments on the "pure market" side, though neither immediately relevant to the issue at hand nor (strictly speaking) original, provide a necessary pendant to his remarks about the mixed economy and at the same time are representative of a general critique of classical theory made by policy economists who study integration from an institutional perspective. His treatment would raise the eyebrow of anyone looking to economics for a straightforward explanation of the integration phenomenon. Pelkmans noted straight away that neoclassical theory did not figure in the case made by the Spaak Report, the background document for the Treaty of Rome; rather, that report rested heavily on expectations raised by the American example, crudely identifying size with efficiency due to scale economies and also requiring large markets.[30] Existing trade theory provided no foundation for such assumptions. It should be noted that, in classical economic thought, a customs union is ipso facto a second-best solution because it interferes with the law of comparative advantage. The groundbreaking discovery in customs union theory was the demonstration that this need not always be the case: that under certain sets of circumstances a customs union could work to the advantages of those forming it. The proof derives from the famous distinction made by Jacob Viner between the trade-creating and trade-diverting effects of customs unions. It has nevertheless always been difficult to demonstrate which of the two effects would predominate in any particular situation.

As Pelkmans (along with many others) has argued, the theory has limitations. If Viner's assumption of constant costs is relaxed, then "the variability of production in the home country results in a welfare gain that can exceed the welfare loss due to the diversion of trade; hence a new gain can accrue to the home country as a result of a trade-diverting union even if fixed consumption coefficients are assumed."[31] Pelkmans additionally underscored the unsatisfactory outcomes in another main area of economic research, the attempt to measure the "dynamic effects" of economic integration – especially those unexplained residuals falling under the heading of "X-inefficiency" or the costs of producing under suboptimal conditions. He raised the additional troubling question of how non-effects can be assumed to be "dynamic."[32]

When one moves from customs union theory to economic analysis of the common market, in which the classical approach assumes perfect factor mobility, "the situation," according to Pelkmans,

is truly dreadful .... [Labor] mobility differs from goods mobility, and even more so in today's welfare states with national social security systems, national pension schemes and ... national diplomas. Also, goods have [few] language problems and no social ties, no attachments to national habits and customs, and no taste for food. [All] ... we have is an entirely incoherent set of notions about labor mobility, direct investments, regional imbalances, patents, and mobility of securities and other forms of financial capital."[33]

Pelkmans further insists that if market integration theory was weak then the theory of economic policy integration was all but nonexistent. In "The Assignment of Public Functions in Economic Integration" he tried to develop the latter by applying public choice theory,[34] which examines nonmarket decision making from the standpoint of economic logic. It rejects the assumption that the study of politics can be detached from self-interest. Though controversial, the approach provides a useful yardstick for measuring institutional failure and serves as a welcome counterpoint to the well-established Keynesian tradition of analyzing economies in terms of market failure. Pelkmans found public choice theory appropriate because, "even though in mixed, capitalist economies market signals are still of overriding importance, private economic agents do not have the sole prerogative in economic decision making."[35] The behavior of public agents must therefore be considered as well, he argued.

Why, he asked, should politicians in countries with mixed economies and representative governments – whom the theory assumes will act in a self-interested fashion – be willing to transfer domestic jurisdiction to a higher authority? The problem does not arise in acute form in the case of "economic cooperation," which in Pelkmans's usage correlates roughly with the economically liberal line of integration development. According to him, there is an initial "presumption to accept the primacy of negative policy integration [and] a reliance on thou-shalt-not rules [as] easier to tolerate politically ... [since] market processes are of course the prime mover of the economy and liberalization measures would amount to a recognition of this fact." Moreover, because the market mechanism is self-generating, "an initial reliance on negative policy integration will engender feedbacks since, by itself, it tends to alter the private/public 'mix' in the participating economies," thereby reducing the role of politicians. Since a national preference for such negative integration may be presumed to have deep roots, it is unlikely, Pelkmans proceeded, "that economic competences will ... be transferred to union [here, Community] public agents"; they will instead remain at the national level and thereby generate further resistance to positive integration.[36] Economic power, he might have added, will also tend to remain in private hands. Negative integration will probably lead to further negative integration and cannot be assumed to lead to positive integration.

Politicians in countries like those of the 1970s – with mixed economies and representative governments – must, Pelkmans argues, "minimize the number and confine the relevance of international commitments [as well as] maximize the number of escape clauses and loopholes in order to maintain the highest possible discretion.... Going beyond economic cooperation is rather daring [for them]."[37] The imperative need to protect authority and independence gets to the nub of the integration dilemma, since "the environment the government creates for commerce and competition is no longer that of 'laisser-faire,' but full of restrictions, prohibitions, minimum standards, and controls." Private economic decisions can "be 'freely' taken in such an environment, but are actually constrained."[38]

The only escape from this trap is for politicians to jump from the usual "constituency" or interest group–based politics to "electoral" or issue-based politics, but it requires special conditions (such as a vulnerability to exogenous influences, guarantees, and lack of exit) in addition to voter appeal, and it is especially difficult regarding regulated sectors of the economy. According to Pelkmans, "if the reasons for sector regulation are primarily income-redistributive the [European] *union* regime would have to be such that *national* politicians find sufficient room for their domestic constituency politics vis-à-vis the sector." The basic principle, he added, that "no one get hurt" by the transfer of authority was "prohibitive" and even paralytic.[39] Pelkmans doubted not only that negative integration could lead to positive integration but also, in light of the pressures faced by politicians and except under exceptional conditions, that positive integration could lead to further positive integration.

What might one realistically expect in the near future? In Pelkmans's judgment, a bid to "equalize" competitive conditions across the Community would have been overambitious and could only have taken place on a piecemeal basis. Financial market integration "would constrain domestic stabilization ... so much that its realization [would require] ... electoral politics changing themselves from being national to being federal," and currency integration "will come late in the economic integration process [and] require a strong political-will assumption ... in the form of hegemony." The gridlock was not likely to loosen, he added, because only under extremely integrationist assumptions can it be expected that ... politicians would permit the core of the mixed economy to be organized outside their electoral reach. Constraints accepted and transfers agreed to will be meticulously circumscribed so as to leave sufficient discretion or substantive instruments for domestic intervention.[40]

And for the next course? Since politicians cling to power, Pelkmans recommended reconsidering "more classic, least-interventionist economies [since] co-operative arrangements can be stable and credible as there is only a minimal probability that economic stabilization or a sectoral decline would lead to large-scale political intervention." Among mixed economies, in contrast, "the same functional outcome, resulting from mere cooperation in a classic world, requires extensive organization through rules and institutions before the venture is credible."[41] Pelkmans concluded that minimal interventionism, relying on the free play of the market and requiring only negative integration, has an "unassailable" logic but "necessarily [requires] a change in the economic order of the more interventionist country participants."[42]

The only conceivable alternative he could discern was "drastic" and called "for the equalization of ... conditions for private economic agents in as far as they purchase and produce." The domestic political implications of such a choice were far-reaching: "Once it is considered unacceptable to forgo interventionism, the subordination to rules and decisions at the [Community] level would largely prevent the national politician from creating an 'electoral profile'."[43] Even this choice was unrealistic and undesirable:

Since interventionism is a political response either to redistributive constituent pressures or to more fundamental "electoral" views on market failures and the desirable organization of society, it is political processes and [their] bureaucratic implementation that will determine [outcomes].... Efficient management of interventionism is already difficult enough on the national level; it is appreciably more problematic on the community level.... For any economic policy, the more interventionist the method, the more centralist the policy will have to be. To achieve the requisite uniformity in the face of divergent economic circumstances, a process of perpetual bargaining evolves wherein every element of the common regime will be translated into redistributive issues ... as a proof of good "constituency politics."[44]

Pelkmans cast a long shadow of doubt over both the feasibility and desirability of a large economic role for the state in the future integration process. It is an outcome, he concluded, that the relatively liberal countries did not want and that the interventionist ones could not (and should not) have.

Pelkmans's compelling logic is persuasive that integration under conditions prevailing in the 1970s had come to a dead end and could only be resumed in the form of "economic cooperation" along the alternative liberal line of development. The shift in the locus of integrating power from the Commission to the states had aggravated the plight of the Community and would continue to make things worse so long as the mixed-economy welfare states remained the norm in Europe; they were not assumed (except by liberals) to be the essential substructure of integration but rather the main obstacle to it. The fate of European integration would turn on the contest of economic systems; relegated to secondary importance were the dispute between de Gaulle and Hallstein that erupted into the empty chairs crisis, the policy argument that later emerged between the Brussels-centered and state-centered integration formulas, and the latter-day academic extension of it: the debate between political science advocates of functionalism and neofunctionalism on the one hand and of "intergovernmentalism" on the other.

The situation facing European integration was not altogether bleak. Pelkmans points to the inescapable conclusion that "positive integration" had reached a dead end. Yet he admits of no escape and is overly deterministic in taking no account of the exceptional individual, a shift in circumstance, the unpredictability of temporal change, or the law of unintended consequences. The two veritable antiheroes of European integration – the liberal federalist Dahrendorf and the institutional evolutionist Shonfield – tacitly understood the importance of such variables. The British economist's wise counsel to muddle doggedly through provided the approach needed to keep the integration process alive at a time when expert remedies were often worse than the malady they were supposed to cure. The rays of light – which the German sociologist had to squint in order to see as they shone through the thick and heavy structures of managed economies – would indeed shed more illumination once unnecessary beams and struts had been removed from the European structure and once stronger and more flexible girders had been fitted in their stead. But neither Dahrendorf nor any other contemporary observer could have been expected to predict precisely how such a renovation might take place. The regime change that would reopen the history of integration began with a slow but irreversible collapse and would take over ten years to form, develop, and mature to the point where its characteristics became identifiable. It would set the stage for liberalization and further transnational cooperation, be it by means of institutional evolution or liberal federalism.

REGIME CHANGE

The political-economic concept of regime change – as opposed to the current euphemism for overthrowing foreign governments – is indispensable to the historian of Europe and of the world. It is the watershed event in a somewhat featureless past half-century which, save for the fall of communism, lacks the eruptive large-scale cataclysms that often trigger decline or the infusions of new ideas or sources of wealth that can be prelude to progress. Missing from these five decades are big events – wars, depressions, famines, and plagues – as well as (until the 1990s) new discoveries, inventions, and ways of looking at the world. It has been an age without utopias.

The idea of regime change is at once abstract and variously understood and applied – and misapplied. It must be properly defined in order to be made serviceable as an organizing framework. The international monetary tumult of the 1970s was no less important in shaping the economic and institutional contexts for the most recent period of history than the chain of events that began with the October 1929 crash on the New York Stock Exchange had been in setting the stage for the Depression and the following four decades. Both created new sets of policy priorities that would alter profoundly the conduct of government, social and economic values, and even ways of life. This is the point of departure for the insightful but neglected recent work of Douglas Forsyth. In *Regime Changes: Macroeconomic Policy and Financial Regulation in Europe from the 1930s to the 1990s,* Forsyth and his co-author, Ton Notermans, maintain that there have been two recent instances of "changes" – of institution building and reorientation – and of new regimes that follow, the first of them from 1931 to 1947 (and the years thereafter until the early 1970s).[45] This period includes the years of embedded liberalism, as defined by John Ruggie. The second recent regime change occurred, according to Forsyth and Notermans, between 1973 and 1990, and its consequences continue to be felt up to the present. It defines the contours of the liberal era whose existence is posited in the present text. In macroeconomic terms, the change from the years before and after World War II was less important than the break of the 1970s. Where the former resulted in a shift from warfare state to welfare state, the latter shifted the balance between public and private power, reduced market-correcting interventionism, unleashed competition between governments as well as producers, and created a long-term tidal pull toward an open economy that could not easily be reversed.

Developments originating in the international monetary sphere have had far-reaching domestic repercussions, according to the co-authors. They emphasize that the notion of a monetary regime should not be confused with ideological politics because it overrides them and thus helps explain the similarities in economic policy between, for instance, Nazi Germany and parliamentary Great Britain in the 1930s as well as between Margaret Thatcher's free-market Great Britain and François Mitterrand's socialist France after 1982.[46] Peter Temin defines such a regime as "an abstraction from any single decision [and] the predictable part of all decisions, [a] thread that runs through the individual choices that governments and central banks have to make."[47] According to Forsyth and Notermans, the determining consideration governing the shift from one regime to another is neither the power of a great idea (though such could be used to great effect politically) nor a particular geopolitical or institutional configuration (though such things can determine the tempo and pattern of events) but rather the set of economic constraints governing policy making.[48]

What distinguishes the earlier and present monetary regimes, the argument proceeds, is that the former was a response to seemingly inexorable *deflation* and the latter to an apparently uncontrollable *inflation*. The guiding purposes of the policies devised in the 1930s (and in effect until the 1970s) were to promote growth, stability, and full employment. They involved the partial coupling of domestic and international economies, which, if expanding satisfactorily, permitted the modern welfare state to develop. This system in turn rested on a corporatist social consensus that kept wage increases in line with economic growth in return for social benefits. Inflation undermined this system in the 1970s, partly because of its deleterious economic consequences but more directly, according to Forsyth and Notermans, because it destroyed the effectiveness of the management tools that governments used to guide the state-dominated economies of the era. Ultimately, the only alternative was to discover substitutes for them. The shift to a new macroeconomic regime, they argue, should be thought of as "re-regulation" rather than deregulation. The shift weakens unions, threatens the welfare state, and moves the market back to center stage, but it does not necessarily entail shrinkage of the state.[49] The question of its size is increasingly subject to political choice.

According to David Henderson, regime change resulted in a partial but decisive shift – not from left to right but in the balance between openness and interventionism in economic systems.[50] Economic reform and liberalization are, in this sense, synonymous. The process has taken different forms at different times and in different places, but it picked up pace internationally and in Europe until the end of the 1990s, when the worldwide economic slowdown – and (within the EU countries) regulatory "teething problems," high unemployment, mounting labor union–led resistance, and governmental immobilization – reduced the pace of change to a crawl.[51] Liberalization is not, Henderson argues, a new phenomenon but a drama extending back to the late eighteenth century, when the process took hold after the removal of disintegrative elements in the economic and political system. In the absence of personal servitude, a new and open society emerged based upon legal equality and the exercise of personal freedom. Integration is thus an agent of liberty. In the liberal blueprint, the state protects this freedom by enforcing the rights of property and contract and also provides necessary public goods within the frameworks of law and self-government.[52]

In 1988, the Austro-American economist Gottfried Haberler planted the seed for a new historical interpretation of the present age. In a now nearly forgotten think piece, he put forth the suggestion that the main feature of the era commencing in 1945 was the rebound of "capitalism and free markets."[53] Ten years later, Daniel Yergin and Joseph Stanislaw went one step further. In a panoramic survey of world politics and economics in the 1980s, *The Commanding Heights,* they found evidence almost everywhere that a market revolution was sweeping out socialism and ushering in an economy of open markets and governments committed to economic growth. In their view, globalization and liberalization went hand in hand, revolutionary economic change had men and institutions in their grip, and the march of progress appeared to be unstoppable.[54] The powerful thesis predictably propagated numerous high-level critics who maintained that a new era was not within hailing distance but instead part of a long-term trend, that the nation-state was not faced with demise but merely with a change in its roles and responsibilities, and that the supposedly inexorable rising tide of the market might well soon ebb but in any event could be limited. Yergin and

Stanislaw's critics have doubtless enriched the literature,[55] and one cannot speak of a market revolution taking over the commanding heights of the world economy without attaching important qualifications. The Yergin–Stanislaw thesis nevertheless still stands in spite of contestation. Over the past twenty years, European politics have been stretched between "market opening" by economic liberals and "economic containment" by others who hope that a wealth-producing competitive economy can support the rising costs of the welfare state.

However, liberalization has advanced since the regime change of the late 1970s. The evidence upon which the contrary arguments are based – an increase in the ratio of public-sector spending to GDP since 1973 – is not persuasive. In fact, fully half of this growth occurred in 1974 and 1975; overall increases since then (within the OECD) have been insubstantial. More germane to the liberalization issue than relative size is the degree of intervention in the economy, which has decreased markedly. The state's industrial sector has been reduced by nearly half through privatization, to less than 4 percent of GDP. Deregulation has reduced barriers to entry, extended competition both sectorally and transnationally, and altered the structures of many industries and markets. Trade liberalization has likewise increased notably. Tax reform has also been disintegrative in the sense noted previously: reduced subsidies, lowered corporate and personal taxes, and limited social transfer payments. Public services have, through competition, been partly "marketized." Labor reform has taken hold in at least two OECD countries (other than the United States), the United Kingdom and New Zealand, and partially in two others, the Netherlands and Denmark.[56]

Post–regime change liberalization is evolutionary rather than revolutionary, but the pace of it has been stepped up as compared to previous decades. Foreign trade has continued to develop more rapidly than GNP growth, foreign direct investment (FDI) at a much faster clip, and capital mobility at a still more hectic pace. Barriers to the international movement of goods and services have also continued to fall. The Single European Act was, however, something genuinely new. The adoption of SEA reflected both dynamic international economic change and the popularity of new ideas and values, but it was also a work of Margaret Thatcher's statecraft.[57]

DOLLAR DETHRONEMENT AND COLLAPSE OF THE BRETTON WOODS SYSTEM

Bad U.S. policy – not OPEC, the international oil cartel – caused the world economic crisis of the 1970s and set in motion the regime change that would, after years of monetary turmoil, provide a new setting for European integration. The problem originated in the same Keynesian excesses that were causing the economic breakdown of the European welfare state in the 1970s. Coupled to it, however, was the special problem of imperial overstretch and the refusal of successive administrations to take sensible measures to reduce it. Failure to do so was a blessing in disguise for Europe, which in the 1980s could re-launch the integration process by itself (without Uncle Sam lurking close behind) and thus also develop in a manner consistent with the postwar aims of American policy rather than those bent and twisted by excesses of Cold War politics and diplomacy.

The maintenance of the dollar–gold parity standard established at Bretton Woods rested ultimately on the self-restraint of the hegemon; collapse resulted from the lack of it. The root of the problem was not a payments imbalance. "Dollar deficit" required the injection of liquidity into postwar Europe. The ambitious foreign policy of the Kennedy years turned deficit to glut – moved increasing amounts of American money offshore – and had inflationary consequences overseas. But as long as the U.S. domestic economy was sound and world economic growth continued, central banks lacked incentive to demand conversion of dollar reserves (for which they received interest) into gold (for which they did not). There was nothing really wrong with the American economy in the early 1960s. It grew at a healthy rate, the trade balance was positive, wage increases were moderate, and inflation (at 1 percent) was no problem at all. A coordinated realignment of currency parities would have been feasible economically, but it was neither pressing nor easy to achieve owing to various countries' different national priorities and strategies. A timely float could also have worked and spared the world serious subsequent problems. Knee-jerk invocations of "military security concerns" repeatedly derailed such proposals and likewise ruled out the many others of Jacques Rueff, de Gaulle's financial advisor, for a return to the international gold standard. The actual (as opposed to perceived) need to maintain the alliance system also militated against another option, the return to a closed system of trade and payments. The policy of the Kennedy and subsequent pre-Nixon administration of Lyndon Johnson amounted to little more than "ad hocery," a grasping for expedients concocted to defer dealing with, or to conceal, the shifting sands upon which the economy rested.[58]

Serious problems first began to develop with the 1964 "Kennedy" budget with its famous stimulative tax cut, so named because it was planned the previous year, the final one of his presidency. It was designed to produce a deficit on the assumption that – as expansion stepped up, employment increased and wages rose – higher marginal income-tax rates would generate revenues even faster then the rise in GNP, making it possible to run still larger deficits that would produce still more growth in the future and guarantee full employment. With the exception of a single year, budget deficits would henceforth be the rule until 1985. Inflation would reach 6 percent by 1970.[59]

These wretched results could not be placed entirely at the feet of neo-Keynesian economic advisers. In 1966, with Viet Nam–related defense expenditures for the first time weighing on the budget and with the economy growing rapidly, President Johnson's council of economic advisers unanimously recommended a tax increase. But LBJ feared that proposing it would cause Republicans and southern Democrats in Congress to maim the *vache sacreé* of Great Society programs.

The result of his inability to choose between the two was a sharp and immediate burst of inflation. This was followed by an impromptu emergency raising of the discount rate (by the badly browbeaten Fed chairman, William McChesney Martin), a sudden collapse of the housing market, and Martin's eventual agreement to lower rates in exchange for a Johnson promise of a 6-percent surtax on incomes. The President's refusal to cut back on either the scale of the war or his own ambitious social programs, according to David Calleo, spread "an inflationary psychology ... through the economy." Wages rose at excessive rates – 4.9 percent in 1967, 5.4 percent in 1968 – and the consumer price index followed at only a slight distance behind. Productivity growth slipped.[60]

The swelling American money supply – engendered by mounting deficits and rising inflation – did not reduce domestic demand and actually increased it abroad, spreading the inflationary virus as new dollar inflows (which the foreign central banks had to redeem in local currency) swelled reserves. The U.S. Fed, in turn, bought back the foreign central bank dollars with Treasury instruments, which added to the national debt. The survival of the Bretton Woods system depended on maintaining the willingness of central banks to hold increasingly overvalued greenbacks in lieu of gold, whose free-market price began to move rapidly upward in 1968 thanks partly to de Gaulle's repeated attacks on "dollar hegemony." It was the Reds who saved the dollar in spring 1968: "Danny the Red" Cohn-Bendit and his student comrades, who caused the Fifth Republic to buckle in May and thereby redirected speculative attacks to the franc; and the invading Red Army, which a month later ended the brief Czech flirtation with reform and triggered a flight of capital to the dollar safe haven.[61]

As the problems of the dollar mounted in the late 1960s, American policy became more aggressive toward its allies, trading partners, and foreign friends – now viewed increasingly as freeloaders. The Nixon administration bent over backward to shift responsibility for "adjustment" to the Germans, Japanese, Swiss, or any other nation that could still maintain a halfway respectable currency. To conclude that such a policy resulted from a calculated monetary strategy would be a mistake. The country was running scared, and at the head of the pack was former President Lyndon Baines Johnson himself. President Richard Milhouse Nixon fortuitously entered office after the semi-panic in Europe had reversed the dollar outflow, and the Fed – which had rediscovered virtue – was imposing rate increases that had begun to wring a few drops of inflation out of the economy. Paying a high price at the polls in 1970, Nixon decided not to shift course. By replacing the ramrod-straight Martin as president of the Fed's Board of Governors with the gracious but compliant Vienna-born Arthur Burns, he opened the floodgates to an endemic inflation that would be the chief source of the world's economic ailments until, at the end of the decade, Paul Volcker finally turned the situation around.[62]

Dick Nixon also ran scared, but unlike his cowboy predecessor, who high-tailed it off to his hacienda and hunkered down, he did the real Texas "thing":

threw out his chest and bragged. In the person of the new Secretary of the Treasury John Connally, Nixon put into service a tall Texan eager to boast and strut around on his behalf. The result was the proclamation of the "New Economic Policy" (NEP), which, name notwithstanding, did not derive from the inspiration of V. I. Lenin. The Treasury had known since 1970 that the dollar had to be cut loose from gold. The central bankers of Europe were no longer willing to back it because the inflation-spreading greenback engorgement was causing the breakdown of their own machinery for policy management. Nixon announced the 15 August 1971 decision to decouple the dollar from gold, which demonetized the one and devalued the other, as a triumph of "get-tough policy" – a way to force lazy, free-riding so-called allies to "get with the program" and start protecting civilization from the world communist menace. To eliminate any remaining doubt about his hard-line stance, he slapped a 10-percent surtax on imports. The dollar immediately fell sharply against the DM. New parities were negotiated in the December Smithsonian Agreement. Nixon's desperate NEP ploy turned out to be a success both politically and economically, early evidence that the "madman theories" about which he fantasized could actually work. The cheap dollar triggered an export boom and an inflow of foreign capital, put payments back into surplus, jammed the stock market up to new highs, caused unemployment to drop, and raised wages.

Dollar depreciation provided a quick fix, and was addictive to both Gerald Ford and Jimmy Carter (until the final months of his presidency, when he finally went cold turkey). In a chronic deficit country – especially one that, like the United States, faced social and political crises – a deflation-induced slowdown would have caused falling wages, unemployment, and business failures. It could exact a prohibitive political price and, given the "stickiness" of unionized wages and cartelized prices, might not have worked in any case. The safer course was to continue running large deficits and "go with" an indulgent and expansionary monetary policy in spite of inflation, relying on a growth-stimulating dollar depreciation to maintain an export advantage and encourage foreign investment. Inflation rose to a high of over 11 percent in 1974 and, after dropping briefly to below 6 percent in 1976, soon climbed back into double digits, eventually reaching 13.5 percent in 1980. Over the same period, the dollar dropped over 50 percent against the German mark. The sinking currency substituted for discipline on the domestic economy. By speeding up growth, the policy of "the downward-drifting buck" might have provided breathing space for a society licking its wounds. Whether such a growth increment offset the corrosive effects of inflation is a question that cannot be addressed here.

American exportation of monetary disorder was at the root of more easily perceived secondary symptoms of economic illness, beginning with the 50-percent rise of world food prices in 1972 and proceeding from there to the oil-price shocks of 1973 and 1979. It had important additional effects as well. While spurring European efforts to arrive at monetary stability on their own, it also doomed them in the short run. By both spreading inflation and slowing growth, it precipitated the breakdown of the mixed-economy welfare state. The turmoil and instability to which it gave rise damaged the world trading system and entrenched a neomercantilism that would have to be uprooted and cleared away before a combination of long-term international trends and domestic political reform could complete the process of regime change and so restart the integration process.

6

Better than Muddling Through:
The World Market, the European Community,
and the Member-States in the 1970s

HAVE IT as you will. In the 1970s, the Community was ground between the hither and nether millstones, stuck between a rock and a hard place, flattened between exogenous pressure from above and endogenous force from below. It was, so to speak, sandwiched. Pressed between the two thick slabs of bread were a thin slice of processed ham, a single soggy piece of lettuce, browning and curled at the edges, and a solitary smear of butter. Who could be blamed for not wanting a bite? Cast aversion and distaste aside. Lend an ear. The struggling Community was stuck between the world monetary disorder that bore down on it from above and the thickening mass of national protectionism that swelled up from below. The two left little wiggle room for the Commission, the Council, or the court stuck in between. The co-editor of the decade's standard work on the EC concluded that

the policy context of the European Economic Communities seems [close] to that identified by Lindblom in his "muddling through model" of public policy making ... [whose tendency is] to prefer maximizing security to radical and comprehensive innovation, [and] ... the policy process as a whole [is] characterized by incrementalism and a high degree of continuity.[1]

Is that a surprise? Is there anything to add to the elegant formulation of this eminent Yale political scientist?

The results were, under the harsh conditions of the era, actually a bit better than muddling through. The Community was pulled in a number of different directions. Britain joined the EC in 1972, opening the way to further expansion and new policies. An ad hoc body that soon became an institution, the European Council provided the leadership for which the Commission was unsuited. The new linkage between member-states and the Community lent credibility to an emerging, though controversial, body of quasi-constitutional European law. The attempt to build a European monetary entity encouraged a convergence in policy, national institutions, and economic practices without which integration progress would have been delayed. These steps led, albeit uncertainly, in a liberal direction. At the same time, the Community became entangled with neomercantilist and corporatist networks budding at the national level. Collusive and surreptitious policy making entrenched powerful economic interests, weakened oversight and governance, and shielded the Brussels *apparat* from public discussion, parliamentary responsibility, and market discipline. Left to its own devices, the Commission developed a new governance model as instigator and mediator of public–private collaboration, sponsor of Euro-champions, and promoter of the European social model. This neocorporatist (or neomercantilist) tradition would vie with that of the open market when the integration process resumed in the 1980s.

The broad trends of the 1970s influenced the development of core European institutions already in place: the Commission, the Common Agricultural Policy, and the peculiar, restrictive, and nearly opaque fiscal settlement that grew out of it and largely defined and limited the powers of the European Parliament. The effort to graft new institutions onto this stunted trunk was only partially successful. The tension and conflict between the Commission (and its "Community methods") and the member-states (and their intergovernmentalism) would persist in meeting after meeting and treaty after treaty down to the present.

International change would be transmitted to the European Community largely by the states after the failure (or only partial success) of national neocorporatist and neomercantilist policies. Except in Mrs. Thatcher's Britain, the result was not flight to a new standard, classical liberalism but rather a reluctant, step-by-step retreat from the mixed-economy welfare state on the part of neoliberal governments – a retreat resulting less from the turnabout directed by the new Great Helmswoman at 10 Downing Street than from the abject failure of President François Mitterrand's experiment with Socialism in One Country. Mitterrand's abrupt abandonment in 1983 of this ruinous course after little more than a year was timely but belated.

Five years earlier, after the death of the original Great Helmsman in Beijing, the plenum of the Chinese Communist Party – while specifically endorsing Marxism-Leninism-Maoism – adopted (in an extreme case of neoliberal adaptation) the program of "four modernizations." The targets were industry, agriculture, the military, and science; to set the program in motion, the plenum established the "principle of household responsibility," a restoration of peasant cultivation for the market. Here, then, was a Chinese analogue to Lenin's NEP as well as much more dramatic evidence of the lesson (learned subsequently in France) that, even in the absence of exogenous market pressure, Socialism in One Country cannot succeed over the long run.[2] Though not directly influenced by the regime change occurring in the West, China would – by re-entering the world trading system – become an ever stronger force for international economic change in the 1990s.

THE NEW PROTECTIONISM

The new protectionism of the 1970s was a defensive reaction to the ravages inflicted on the world trading system by international monetary disorder. Jan Tumlir was its most trenchant critic. Tumlir was one of a kind. A Czech "D.P."

(displaced person) who completed his education in the United States in the 1950s, he joined and then left the Yale economics department to become staff economist at GATT. He died unexpectedly in 1985 before completing his *magnum opus* on world trade. His *oeuvre* consists of a handful of brief articles about neoprotectionism written from the late 1970s to the month of his untimely death.

Like Jacques Pelkmans, Jan Tumlir applied the economics-based logic of public choice theory to explain the workings of economies dominated by the state sector. Unlike Pelkmans, he also identified himself with the classical liberal tradition. Tumlir was, it seems, at heart a political theorist who wrote in the guise of a trade economist. His emphasis on legal issues lent special character to his work. According to Razeen Sally, Tumlir placed a distinctive emphasis on the need to subordinate economic policy to general rules of conduct made as the product of legislative design in order to assure the appropriate operation of the market. The approach is consistent with Hayek's theory of the spontaneous order and its legal underpinning, and it posits the subjective, empirical, progressive, open-ended, and self-adjusting Austrian concept of market activity. Tumlir argues that "democratic constitutionalism" is the essential complement to the market order. It involves, according to Sally, "government by discussion, a collective effort on the part of the various branches of government, organized interests and the wider public to discuss thoroughly the means and ends of social action and to deliberate on necessarily collective choices."[3] The lack of such a deliberative process will send the wrong signals, resulting in policy error. Tumlir's demonstration of the interdependence of the economic and constitutional orders is highly relevant to the history of the EC, a malfunctioning embryonic entity with immature representative institutions. He provides a forceful reminder that effective parliamentary government and open markets must go hand in hand if either is to function properly – as well as a sharp warning that collusion is the enemy, especially when it occurs in international markets and in the absence of effective rule-making machinery. The institutional evolution of the EC underscores the importance of the warning, which is one that Jacques Delors might also later have heeded, and it remains relevant to present deliberations about the future of the Community.

The existence of an international market should not be taken for granted, Tumlir argues: only "when currency convertibility coexists with relative price-level stability in at least the core countries of the world economy and when all exporters have access to at least these largest markets" can it be said to exist.[4] In the absence of these conditions, the world trading system deteriorated in the 1970s. The implication of this fact was immense. Foreign trade connects national price structures to an international price system without whose signals "comparative advantage" is lost. To estimate the net costs of protection is never easy, according to Tumlir, but – contrary to popular belief – these costs fall on the importing as well as the exporting country. Protection raises prices to (and reduces the incomes of) consumers in the present and, by means of investment misallocation, leads to distortions that raise costs still further in the future.

The benefits it willingly hands one set of producers it must perforce take from another. Protection also inevitably involves redistribution and promotes rent seeking. It was all the more dangerous, Tumlir emphasized, because the 1970s featured increasing resort to surreptitious methods that are "artfully concealed, misrepresented, and ... misunderstood by the public."[5]

Between 1974 and 1979, the proportion of transactions subject to nontariff barriers increased from 40 to 48 percent of world trade. These barriers were far more formidable than the simple quantitative restrictions thrown up in the 1940s. They comprised, in Tumlir's precise formulation, "coherent systems of industrial protection, each with its increasingly pronounced and entrenched characteristics."[6] Thus, almost every "distinct area of trade (agriculture, clothing, steel, synthetic fibers, and petroleum)" had a "policy of its own."[7] General trade policy, a simple set of measures applying universally, could no longer be said to have existed. The "constituent elements" of the new protectionism were public subsidies and interfirm agreements or cartels. Tumlir shows that the rate of subsidization to GNP grew everywhere in the 1970s except in the United States; such subsidization did not replace protection but grew with it. Voluntary Export Restraints (VERs) and Orderly Marketing Arrangements (OMAs) were the forms taken by the revived cartels. Such arrangements had a shadow existence; they were private and not legally binding. Nonetheless, each required cooperation between government and either industrial associations or oligarchical producers.

Multilateral sectoral agreements such as VERs and OMAs are distinguished by relying on the export side for restraint. They exacted heavy economic and noneconomic systemic costs, Tumlir argues, by closing markets to new entrants, frustrating innovation, and distorting prices – not just in the importing country but worldwide, and not just in product lines but also in comprehensive networks.[8] They were hard to counteract because they were discriminatory rather than nondiscriminatory (like tariffs) and therefore divisive in effect; they were difficult to estimate in value because they were not readily auctionable like quotas; and they were beneficial to the parties on both sides of the bargain, who thus had incentives to conspire. Such agreements became the core, in Tumlir's elegant phraseology, of "an expanded system of protection [that] proceeds sectorally," involves far more than the mere restriction of imports, and indeed entails "the construction of industrial protection systems, each tailored to the specific needs of the industry in question, each administered by a highly specialized bureaucracy, often co-opted into public service from the respective industry association." The system coordinates the various instruments of protectionist policy but rests on negotiation and is, as Tumlir notes, "in a perverse way the result of international cooperation." Such arrangements have changed the nature of international trade policy, which in Tumlir's words has aspired to "a comprehensive management not only of transactions between countries but even of investment and production decisions between firms."[9]

In addition to the obvious economic dangers, multisectoral agreements posed political hazards for democracies. The negotiating process for VERs and OMAs invariably began, Tumlir argues, with a threat to impose an import quota (or other mechanism for protection) that the parties to the game understood as a bluff. The element critical to success in the arrangement was, as he points out counterintuitively, rewards received by the exporter, who could raise prices to the higher levels prevailing on the restricted market. Although this did not necessarily increase overall industry profits, it disproportionately benefited dominant firms in the export industries and provided government sanction against new entrants. The national administrations also gained from multisectoral arrangements. Discriminatory quantitative agreements are, as Tumlir could attest from firsthand experience as a trade negotiator, more complicated to manage than the nondiscriminatory variety and required many hands and consumed many long hours of continuous negotiation on both sides. In the exporting country, VERs and OMAs gave the national executive additional powers over the industry. On the import side, the bluffing legislator garnered new clients and strengthened existing relationships with the executive power, which could deal with him individually rather than with the legislative body as a whole and thus obtain policies for which a majority did not exist. Logrolling replaced discussion, representative government could then be bypassed, and special interests acquired valuable new relationships, anchored in mutual dependency, that profited them at the expense of the whole.[10] The erosion of the market and the corruption of government are, in Tumlir's account, of a piece.

According to Tumlir's most controversial argument, the problem did not originate in the markets (where price fixing and rent seeking have always been endemic) but in the law. It can be attributed to "a judicial doctrine drawing a distinction between the political and the property rights of citizens and considering the former to be more deserving of constitutional protection than the latter."[11] The doctrine took effect as a result of court decisions of the 1920s in most European countries and of the 1930s in the United States that exempt "economic regulatory legislation from ... rigorous scrutiny ... to which other statutes remained subject." The doctrine of "proper delegation of legislative power," requiring that specific standards guide the executive in the discharge of responsibility, suffered thereby. The abandonment of the need to secure majority support led, Tumlir argued, to a rapid buildup of executive authority and thereby also (1) increased the ability of individual legislators to serve constituency interests through the administrative process, (2) made rent seeking rewarding and secure, and (3) avoided the open discussion and debate needed to inform the public. Despairing of self-correction in the marketplace, Tumlir pleaded in a posthumously published article for the restoration of constitutional law as a first step toward the reinstatement of the most-favored-nation approach to tariff reduction, the revival of the international trade system, and, through it, the reform of the "redistributive state."[12]

Jan Tumlir's few brief articles convincingly demonstrate that an analysis of European integration cannot be considered complete if it fails to take full account of the mutual interdependence of the world trading system and the political,

economic, and constitutional structures of the major trading nations, as well as
the EC/EU. The reigning neoliberal institutionalist school of political science,
which focuses on how governments arrive at (and enforce) international agreements, might well bear in mind the need for constitutionally functional political
systems; without them, open markets will close, nationally and internationally.

Tumlir's explanation of the origins and consequences of multisectoral agreements such as VERs and OMAs sounds a cautionary note for Brussels, where
the power of the executive, weak though it seems, eclipses that of the parliament.
Impotent legislatures invite surreptitiousness and collusion, and they encourage
self-serving, self-perpetuating, and durable redistributionist political-economic
alliances (which, once in place, are hard to uproot). Laws that favor political
over property rights are corrupting. The ungainly structure and opaque operational methods of the Brussels institutions reflect the truth of these obvious
conclusions, as they also do the need for genuine constitutional reform – unlike
the sham efforts now under way at the Convention on the Future of Europe.

At the time of his death, Jan Tumlir no longer thought that reform could be
set in motion by a spontaneous (or any other kind of "bottom up") reinstatement of the market principle through change at the national level. He might have
thought otherwise had he lived long enough to see the first signs of light appear-
ing in the international economy. Though hampered by protectionism, trade
in fact continued to grow in the 1970s; dissatisfaction mounted (on the political left as well as the right) with the state-centered policy-making repertoires of
Keynesianism and *planification,* and the failings of corporatism and neomercantilism gave rise to a search for alternatives. Susan Strange's reminder is welcome
that while "anxiety for the consequences of market-sharing arrangements may
not be altogether misplaced ... the threshold to disaster is not quite as low as it
was thought to be."[13] Cartel-like relationships such as those Tumlir described
are inherently unstable and can be disrupted by recusants and fringe competitors
so long as the costs and benefits of market stabilization are not borne equally.
Competition is a powerful solvent. The neomercantilism 1970s would give rise
to corporatist policies and yet witness their progressive breakdown.

NEOMERCANTILISM AND CORPORATISM IN FRANCE, GERMANY, ITALY, AND GREAT BRITAIN

Neomercantilism, and the corporatism that often accompanied it in the 1970s,
can be evaluated in different ways: either in combination or alone, as components
of a functional system, as policy goals, political preferences, repackaging jobs,
political slogans, or demonstrable failures. The balance between the various elements in the package varied from country to country, as did the adjustments required to meet the economic and political challenges of the troublesome decade.
Outcomes differed substantially but on the whole were disappointing. Adopted
as policy for defensive reasons, neomercantilism and corporatism turned out to
be merely ways of clinging to the past. But might not Europe come to the rescue

of the nation-state? Failure of the neocorporatist class compromises and consensual incomes policies that underpinned Keynesianism led to a belief, according to Liesbet Hooghe and Gary Marks, that the "national state could no longer serve as the privileged architect of economic prosperity." This conclusion, they add, would provide "the point of departure for European integration in the 1980s and 1990s."[14] Better put: it would provide the *points* of departure, as underscored by even a brief survey of the relationship between state and economy in the larger European states. The differences between them rule out a one-size-fits-all European federal model.

It makes little sense to speak of *neo*mercantilism in the nation of Colbert, who invented the original version. In France the traditional industrial and financial system had (in the main) worked adequately, at least for the French, and the high barriers of custom and standard practice impeded institutional reform. Crisis containment by means of well-worked methods was the rule. Although shocks to the French system – like the events of 1968 and the inflation of 1974–1975 – triggered policy shifts, they involved reworking old methods and neither expanded nor reduced the large role of the state in the economy. The most salient change of the 1970s was the decision, made tacitly with the adoption of the so-called Barre Plan, to put the development of French society on a convergence course with Germany.

In the Federal Republic, the economic system worked satisfactorily and the political system was adequately responsive, though long-term problems had begun to set in. The efforts of successive social democratic governments under chancellors Brandt and Schmidt, which together spanned the decade, to defend and extend social gains and to maintain stability against an international backdrop of "stagflation" required maintaining both open markets and the value of the Deutsche mark. Nevertheless, the spread of protectionism within the economy, the persistence of stagflation, and the rise of a new activism – one that divided a society whose labor–management machinery operated on the basis of consensus and cooperation – weakened the very corporatist institutions whose perceived past successes had made them a model in many parts of Europe. Yet because the economy continued to perform relatively well, German influence in Europe increased over the decade. Chancellor Schmidt looked to the spread of financial orthodoxy to restore European growth and stability.

In Italy the political system was so decrepit, the economy (except for the large "unofficial" sector) so bureaucratized and politicized, social and regional inequities so pronounced and persistent, and the threat of violence so real and pervasive during the 1970s that almost any attempt to solve political problems at the national level would have been futile. A daring initiative launched in late 1973 by the Communist Party, an attempt to strike a "historic compromise" with the government party (the Democratic Christians) sadly failed. The aim of the bold proposal was to expand and update the ramshackle state-dominated but partial pseudo-corporatism inherited from fascism to include groups not privileged by it.

The British found a new cure for the persistent anemia from which their economy had long suffered in the mid-1970s: reconfiguring along continental lines. Having by then reached the point of exhaustion, the patient was indeed in dire need of a new remedy – but this was not the right one. Although the general adoption of neomercantilist or corporatist methods created a common basis for European policy making in the 1970s, the resumption of progress on integration required a truly fresh approach and something homegrown rather than a packaged import product.

"Steady as you go" was the rule under the right-center governments of France during this stormy decade. The one real exception to the rule had long since retreated into history. The Rueffian policy of devaluation, fiscal restraint, budgetary discipline, and tariff reduction – a lever with which to pry open the French economy – had produced high growth, reaped a huge export surplus, and filled the coffers of the Banque de France with precious gold. However, there were potentially inflationary consequences because, parities being fixed, the currency could not adjust upward. To stave off the threat of inflation, to serve the greater glory of Gaullist France, and to maintain a favorable payments position (the overriding goal of mercantilist policy), the Rueffian approach was sacrificed in 1963 to a *plan de stabilisation* developed by Minister of Finance Valéry Giscard d'Estaing. Giscard's policy featured a combination of budgetary austerity and the use of selective credit controls to promote exports and reduce domestic consumption. His replacement by the ultra-Gaullist Michel Debre meant a further tightening.[15]

The Giscard–Debre emphasis on exports reduced the importance of national planning but not the selective use of credit, profit guarantees, and subsidies. Only in a restricted sense can this policy be called liberal. The French state continued to dominate the commanding heights it had occupied since World War II. The electrical utility, natural gas and nuclear power industries, oil, coal and steel production, telecommunications and much of the electronics and information technology industries, defense and civil aviation, most of the automobile industry, and the better part of the financial sector – all remained within the public domain. Sectors of production and distribution not owned by the state operated within a constrained and cross-subsidized environment, were at the mercy of politics, and never got beyond the fallout range of administrative order, directive, and regulation. The 1970s would witness neither a reduction of the central role of the state in the economy, nor its influence throughout them, nor the politicization of the economic process, nor the use of the foreign policy to increase the economic power of the state.

The Giscard–Debre policy phase concluded with the upheavals of May 1968. The "Grenelle Agreements" of the following month, which ended the protests, raised the minimum wage by 35 percent, resulted in decreases of 10 to 25 percent across the board in the working week, and gave union cells special privileges in the factory. They also rekindled inflation, which – followed within months by a humiliating devaluation – then provided a "pick-me-up" to the export industries, which soon thrived on record profits and high rates of investment. In the hopes of gaining political capital, the government thereupon introduced undesirable changes into the system of indexing. Henceforth, wage raises would be linked to cost-of-living increases that did not take unemployment rates into account, and price setting would be based on cost-plus markups. Rising inflation, aggravated by the first oil shock, reached double digits and remained there for the rest of the decade. Unemployment more than doubled, reaching 5.9 percent by 1979. Growth fell by nearly a half, from 4.6 percent during 1969–1973 to 3.0 percent in the period 1973–1979.[16]

These slightly better-than-average numbers for the decade can be partly attributed to the Barre Plan of 1976.[17] The economic purpose behind it was pure and simple stability. It rejected both budgetary deficits and devaluations as instruments for stimulating growth, and it established the rule of thumb that the economy ought to expand only as fast as permitted by the medium-term payments equilibrium. It restricted growth in order to bring France into a companionable economic partnership with a strong and stable adjunct to French national power, Germany – an epochal change as well as a big step toward eventual monetary union.

At a time when France (and Europe) began to look to Germany as a new central power, and when the Federal Republic first recognized publicly the increased responsibility that it bore for the welfare of its neighbors, the spread of neomercantilism and the breakdown of corporatism began to tarnish the allure of "the German model" as a dynamic economy resting on social consensus and so reduced its potential to lead. German consensus rested heavily on the success of "Concerted Action," a policy formally in effect since the late 1960s. According to Herbert Giersch, this amounted to a "social compact between all major agents in the corporatist play of macroeconomics ... the government, the central bank and the so-called social partners, i.e. unions and employers' associations."[18] Its operation required wringing all inflationary expectations out of private contracts so that a gradual tightening of monetary and fiscal policy could take place without precipitating a stabilization crisis. The social partners were obliged to adopt cost-neutral policies limiting wage increases to productivity growth. Price stability could then be maintained without squeezing profits or lowering investment and reducing competitiveness.

The Bundesbank (BuBa) enforced stability by maintaining the discount rate at high levels (7 to 10 percent from 1970 to 1974) even as the dollar, franc, pound, and lira declined. The directors of the BuBa, who exercised de facto independence but constitutionally served at the pleasure of the government, diverged only reluctantly from this course. The central bank lowered rates in 1975 after the first oil shock stopped growth in its tracks and raised unemployment to the highest rates since 1950, and then once again in 1978 at a time when the economy was operating normally rather than at depressed levels. The reduction occurred only after much prodding by Chancellor Schmidt, who was himself goaded by the Carter White House to turn the Federal Republic into the "locomotive" of Europe. The move would rekindle inflation without stimulating growth.[19]

The decision to keep rates high during most of the decade protected the value of the DM but at the expense of an expanding economy. The lack of growth squeezed profits, lowered investment rates, and raised levels of subsidization and regulation that impeded structural change. A rising currency, stepped-up competition from the developing countries, and a lack of tariff protection all contributed to the spread of domestic quotas and VERs. By 1982, nearly 12 percent of German mining and manufacturing imports were subject to them and another 2.5 percent to antidumping duties and product standard inspections. Subsidies, including tax benefits, grew from 7 percent in 1973 to nearly 10 percent four years later. Such assistance benefited mainly ailing or sunset branches of industry rather than leading export sectors like investment goods. That the beneficiaries tended to be branches with political "clout" – those employing large numbers, dominated by few firms, and concentrated regionally – is consistent with a public choice explanation. Thanks to interventions by the Federation of German Industry and the German Federation of Trade Unions – as well as to a strong structure of national institutions committed to free trade – protectionist demands from particular branches of industry could be fended off in the name of the general welfare. Although employment during the 1970s continued to decline in the protected sectors, subsidies and nontariff barriers weakened defenses against new foreign competition and impeded adaptation to change in the marketplace.[20]

The breakdown of labor–management cooperation had a similar effect. In 1977, the trade union federation renounced Concerted Action as a result of a dispute over the co-determination (*Mitbestimmung*) bill enacted by the social democratic government. The bill extended the fifty–fifty employer–employee representation on boards of directors, previously limited to heavy industry, throughout the economy. As a result of a necessary concession made to the Free Democratic Party coalition partners in order to secure passage, the version of it that finally passed unexpectedly specified that one of the employee representatives was to be elected not by union members but by clerical staff, thus undercutting the principle of full parity. The employers, who opposed the bill in the first place, sued to block it. The unions not only left the roundtable for Concerted Action but would take a tougher stand in future wage negotiations and demand reductions of the work week, the right to bargain on quality-of-life-issues, guarantees of employment, and even the restriction of new laborsaving technologies. The growth consensus upon which shop-floor harmony depended had come to an end, and a new era of labor-market rigidity had begun. Restrictive labor practices, along with the rise of protectionism, lowered productivity and raised wage costs to among the highest in the world. The consequences of the developments made themselves felt in the low growth rates, high unemployment, and generally subpar German economic performance of the 1980s and thereafter.[21]

It is no less pointless to talk about *neo*corporatism in Italy during the 1970s than about *neo*mercantilism in the France of the same decade. Mussolini invented state corporatism. Not until the 1990s was the gaudy centerpiece of the fascist economic display removed. It consisted of an oversized, florid arrangement of giant, ill-run, state-owned holding companies intertwined with *Democrazia Christiana* (DC), the governing party in power since the war, and wrapped in and about with a sprawling, tentacular, and unreconstructed federal bureaucracy dominated by fascist-era appointees and packed with party faithful.[22] Clientage was the core principle. It linked the politics of Rome to the grass roots; tied parliament, the bureaucracy, and much of industry together in a single bundle; and gave almost every person with power or pelf a stake in the corrupt and inefficient status quo. The influence of this corporatist political-economic core pervaded much of industry and finance, a state of affairs deeply resented in the entrepreneurial sector of diverse, specialized, export-oriented family-run businesses that one finds in the various regions of the north.

The inefficient and corrupting mass at the center of the Italian economy was part of a larger immediate reality, the structural weakness of the Italian state, and a still greater historical one, the problematic character of Italian nationhood. Until these knotty issues could in some way be resolved, the dynamic people of a large and almost universally well-liked and admired nation would underpunch in the affairs of Europe. Embarrassment added to the mess. Fascism was supposed to have been dead, done in at the end of the war by the decent Italians of the Resistance. The heroic Resistance myth was the ideological bond that held together the diverse group of unprivileged, less privileged, or underprivileged voters who had faithfully supported the Communist Party during its 25 years in the political wilderness – during which time it refused to participate in government.

In November 1973, the improbable figure recently installed as head of the Communist Party of Italy (CPI), a minor Sardinian nobleman named Enrico Berlinguer, courageously proposed a "historic compromise" as a symbolic revival of the wartime and postwar coalition against fascism. Berlinguer held forth a personal vision of "an austere society, which will be more ... just and with greater equality, and enjoy more real freedom, more democracy and more humanity."[23] It was an appeal perhaps suitable to de Valera's postwar Irish Republic but one bound to meet with incomprehension almost anywhere in the sybaritic Seventies. What Berlinguer had in mind was, in most important respects, consistent with Catholic political doctrine. He wanted to expand the embrace of the state to include (as did the church's) those "left out." He wanted to bring them into a secure and sheltered area of civility and simple kindness, where – in familiar settings and guided by tradition and sound doctrine – ordinary people could, by cooperating with and working through networks of established authority, deal satisfactorily, successfully, and on a human scale with problems both large and small. It was a noble vision, though short on specifics.

The immediate purpose behind the "historic compromise" was quite simply to stave off a slide into civil war or the precipitation of a coup d'état launched to prevent one. At the beginning of the decade, Italy was wracked by a continuous, massive, and often vicious wave of left-wing protest as violent as that suffered by any large western European country since the immediate postwar era. It had a right-wing counterpart in a secret, well coordinated, and perhaps even police-orchestrated campaign of murder and provocation intended (or so the pattern of events seemed to indicate) to topple the incompetent and corrupt political system. In a vain attempt to appease the protestors, a succession of desperate governments made far-reaching and economically ruinous concessions to labor. This aggravated the plight of the country, brought political plans and projects almost inevitably to ruin, and created long-term problems that would take years to clear up.[24]

Between 1969 and 1973, wages rose 15 percent annually – nearly twice the rate of the previous six years – and the average work week fell 12 percent. A new *Statuto dei Lavoratore* made it nearly impossible to fire anyone, with the result that, contrary to trends elsewhere, employment actually increased in Italy during the 1970s. Productivity growth plummeted, however, while unit labor costs shot up 10 percent annually.[25] Consumer prices and inflation rates more than doubled, and the lira fell more than 40 percent against the Deutsche mark. Most sectors of industry operated at a loss. Private-sector capital investment stagnated while, in a frantic bid to stimulate the economy, public-sector investment increased 15 percent annually. A new public corporation, *Gestione e Partecipazioni Industriali,* was erected to take over failing companies. Fiscal deficits mounted to 9 percent of GDP as welfare costs ballooned. In 1975, the *scala mobile* for wage indexing was expanded and would be responsible for 60 percent of the overall wage increases for the next few years as well as for much of the continuing inflation.[26]

Berlinguer's initiative was well received. As a parallel to it, the new head of the producers' association *Confindustria,* Giovanni Agnelli, and the head of the labor federation, Luciano Lama, agreed to cooperate on a basis of a strategy like the German neocorporatist Concerted Action. The simultaneous deterioration of the latter did not auger well. In a speech of great courage and dignity, Lama came out "in favor of wage restraint, increased productivity, and labor mobility," asking in exchange only that unemployment be reduced and more assistance be given to the south.[27] In the appropriate setting of EUR, the modernistic city of the future built by Mussolini in the suburbs of Rome, "an event took place that had never before occurred in the Republic. Employers, labor unions, and government sat down to salvage the economy."[28]

It was already too late. Lacking a program of its own but pledged to support the DC government in power of Giulio Andreotti, the CPI found itself supporting an austerity program featuring higher taxes and an incomes policy, which – though undoubtedly necessary – inflicted hardship on the party's constituents. Between 1976 and 1979 wages increased only 2.6 percent annually, as opposed to 11.4 percent for the previous three years, and unemployment rose sharply. By 1977, wildcat striking had begun to break out in the big industrial cities of the north. Wage restraint came to an end the following year. The policy errors of the early 1970s would cause economic problems to rage into the 1980s and make a shambles of structural reform.

In May 1978, Aldo Moro, the man known as the "great weaver" for his skills as a political operative, was assassinated after prolonged incarceration and under despicable conditions. He had been the foremost DC proponent of the historical compromise. The communists left the cabinet the following January. In June they suffered a crushing defeat at the polls and returned to official isolation. The historic compromise had turned into an historic failure. A one-time opportunity for left–right reconciliation and systemic reform had been missed. What Patrick McCarthy terms "systemic clientelism" would soon enter its most exuberant phase.[29]

If in Italy neocorporatism was a misnomer, neomercantilism never had a chance. The breakdown of the state made it crucial that whatever survived of the functioning parts of the economy not be sacrificed. The depreciating lira made Italian goods cheap. The standout performance of the export sector, in which family-owned enterprises were prominent, was profitless but provided the leaven that enabled the bread to rise.[30] Thanks largely to exports, the Italian economy managed to grow at the annualized rate of 2.2 percent even during the years of turmoil. How this feat was achieved is difficult to document, since at least a quarter of the economy operated off the books, in the "black" area where markets still worked efficiently. Any serious attempt to manage this competitive sector would have been ruinous. The maintenance of Italy's welfare depended upon the success of entrepreneurs in reaching open markets beyond the range of the Italian state. For them, the neomercantilist temptation was easily brushed aside.

The strength of British political institutions offset national economic weakness, a paradoxical but not always desirable outcome because it made denial and deferral easy. Neomercantilism in practice amounted to little more than fudging. Britain "took it on the chin" in the 1970s: it had the worst economic record of any major industrial country and also far less influence in the European Community than expected.[31] Fundamental change eventually came at the end of the decade, and for the next ten years Britain would be Europe's pacesetter.

The neomercantilist era in the United Kingdom opened with fanfare in 1960 as a key part of a strategy devised by the cabinet of Harold Macmillan and enthusiastically backed by the Confederation of British Industry: the first serious Tory attempt since War II to make a new Britain.[32] It would prove to be merely another of the many panaceas sold to the public to cure industrial decline, which would continue in stop–go fashion until the 1980s. Sterling dropped 40 percent between 1972 and 1976, inflation averaged in the mid-teens over the decade, and unemployment hovered around 5 percent.[33] No single policy caused "Englanditis" but rather a combination of weak entrepreneurialism and bipartisan risk aversion that – until Britain became "ungovernable" in the late 1970s and the political consensus in both parties unraveled – reduced economic policy to an exercise in the pouring of old wine into new bottles. General timidity was the root cause of the British problem. The intervention of the International Monetary Fund was needed to jump-start the process that would eventually end it.

British neomercantilism featured the aping of continental policies. It made deep bows to the French tradition of state planning – with its reliance on selective controls over credit, taxes, investment, and incomes – as well as gracious genuflections to the German tradition of close cooperation between banking and industry, labor and capital.[34] The connection between the rise of neomercantilism as policy and Britain's first EC application was not coincidental; each was part of the long-overdue attempt to modernize.[35] Mercantilism tended to be associated in the public mind with the Tories, since Labour was officially committed to nationalization, but the change of government made little difference in this respect. The Conservative government of Edward Heath (1970–1974) broke with mercantilism for two years but then, in 1972, reversed back to a policy of public–private cooperation. The intervening Labour governments of Prime Minister Harold Wilson (1964–1970, 1974–1976) also lived comfortably with the policy, and that of James Callaghan (1976–1979) was too weak to break from it without foreign assistance. Thanks to the intervention of the IMF, the neomercantilist era flickered out amidst the economic and social disorders of the final years of the Labour government.[36] Margaret Thatcher crushed the remaining embers after taking office in 1979.

Neomercantilist business–state cooperation was tempting and even cozy when harsh economic winds blew outside. Governments could look to producers to provide cost-free enforcement of policy; and, in return for providing it, business could exact a rent instead of running the high risks of profit making.[37] The attractiveness of the arrangement may have been related to the distinct lack of zeal with which Labour approached nationalization; no profitable companies were taken by it. The Confederation of British Industry supported the attempts of both political parties to manage the economy, angering opinion on the far left as well as on the far right.[38]

Neomercantilism was ill-adapted to the British climate. The planning mechanism set up within the new National Industrial Development Council (NIDC) in 1962 was not a success. Its three annual growth targets were outrun by events, and the effort to set them was dropped in 1966. The use of NIDC to impose Gallic "planning agreements" between major companies and the government "covering prices, investment, technology, employment, exports, import-saving, industrial relations, product development, product quality and environmental protection" merely consumed paper.[39] State bartering of cash for policy compliance – whether through purchasing, credit policy, subsidization, or rents and charges for services – was no more effective in enforcing conformity than before.

Only in incomes policy did neomercantilism take hold, but there it fared badly indeed. The idea was itself unsound. To scale wages to previous performance rather than future promise is to destroy initiative and to perpetuate past injustice. To place the credit of the government on a policy that was certain to anger and dissatisfy when times were hard and that would be difficult to manage without the full support of the unions suggests a kind of death wish. To compromise the bargaining power of the unions was to open the door to radicalism. Both political parties recognized that wage increases had been inflationary, deleterious to the trade balance, and a prime source of repeated devaluations. Except during the first two "liberal" Heath years, the successive governments of the era thus tried to draw the labor unions into "social compacts" on the German model; they hoped to entice or coerce the labor unions into limiting wage increases to productivity gains in order to enforce sustainable noninflationary growth. The policy asked nothing less than the forfeiture of union power to bargain for wages as a free agent. No one took seriously the disclaimer that such a renunciation was meant to be only temporary.

The effort to impose an incomes policy brought down the governments of Ted Heath and, indirectly, of Jim Callaghan as well, and it set the stage for the rise of Margaret Thatcher. After two years of scrapping regulatory controls and moving closer to the market, Prime Minister Heath – in his fateful "U-turn" back to policies of economic management – in fact almost came "close to securing a comprehensive agreement with [the Trade Union Congress and] the Council of British Industry over the management of the economy and over the control of pay and prices." But when the talks finally broke down, the government imposed the most far-reaching statutory incomes policy in peacetime history."[40] The National Union miners went out on strike and stayed out. Heath called a general election, appealed for public rejection of lawlessness and disorder in the name of common sense, justice, and economic reason – and lost in so humiliating a fashion that he had to be deposed as head of what had become a bitterly divided party.[41] Margaret Thatcher replaced him.

Although the 1975 Industrial Relations Act of the new Wilson government improved the design of the tripartite machinery, it soon broke down under the weight of an orthodox policy of deflation dictated by the International Monetary Fund as condition for a loan requested in order to stave off yet another of many sterling crises.[42] Britain had to accept Third World treatment in order to qualify: agree to limit credit expansion and the money supply to the level appropriate to sustain the exchange rate. These restrictions on the so-called Public Sector Borrowing Requirement (PSBR) marked a beginning in the constructive phase of regime change, provided an instructive lesson, and set a memorable precedent. The IMF order, at a stroke, restricted monetary and fiscal expansion to operational requirements, subordinated fiscal to monetary policy, and curbed public inflation. Stability now overrode growth at the bottom line.[43]

Callaghan knew that an era had come to an end. His memorable speech to the 1976 Labour Party Conference is worth quoting at length. "For too long," he recognized, we have postponed facing up to fundamental choices and fundamental changes in our society and in our economy ... [and have] been too ready to settle for borrowing money abroad to maintain our standards of life instead of grappling with the fundamental problems of British industry.... The cozy world we were told would go on forever, where full employment would be guaranteed at the stroke of the Chancellor's pen, cutting taxes, deficit spending – that cozy world is gone.... [W]e used to think that you could just spend your way out of a recession to increase employment by cutting taxes and boosting government spending. I tell you in all candor that that option no longer exists. And insofar as it ever did it worked by injecting inflation into the economy.[44]

The belt tightening caused an abrupt slowdown of the economy, a sharp increase in unemployment, and a burst of inflation; it shred what was left of the social contract, collapsed incomes policy, and – amidst spontaneous work stoppages and the widespread breakdown of public services – led to electoral defeat and the resignation of the Callaghan government. It was Labour that had to suffer the consequences of adopting the tough but indispensable prerequisite to reform: a sound monetary policy. Margaret Thatcher could take it from there. And so she would – and to Europe as well.

A MOST IMPERFECT UNION: STRUCTURE AND POLICY PROCESS AT THE EC

Is the European Community (EC) a polity in the making? The question cannot be answered without first examining the institutions of the European Community themselves. The task is not a pleasant one. The EC is beset with crippling structural problems that pervert the governance process and must be eliminated if the Brussels institutions are to be worthy of serious consideration as a platform for a future European government. These problems derive from the fact that the Community is not sovereign and thus cannot tax but instead receives (on a treaty basis) subsidies from the member-states, the most important of which are for the Common Agricultural Policy – from first to last its most voracious ongoing program. It has, over the life of the Community, consumed between three quarters and one half of the annual budget. Neither the Parliament nor the Commission has any real control or authority over the distribution of these funds, which is determined each year on the basis of fixed and bewilderingly complex formulas. By restricting budgetary authority, CAP has warped the normal evolution of legislative institutions at the European level. What Tumlir warned about, or at least a large part of it, is reality in Brussels. The EEC/EC/EU is little more than a switch engine that has transferred public money from one hand to another in the self-aggrandizing manner confirmed by public choice theory. In the absence of a real legislature, deep-seated corruption is rife and entrenched inequity the norm.

These ills have become more serious over time. Prior to the 1970s, the EEC could adequately (though crudely) be defined as the CAP plus hot air emitted in the name of Europe; the neomercantilism of the 1970s enabled the Commission to extend its competence into the new field of industrial policy, which – by a perverse misinterpretation of the treaty articles pertaining to the internal market – put the Commission in the business of organizing producer cartels. The way was thus opened for a European homologue to replace failing national corporatist systems. President Jacques Delors would later follow this course, whose legacy is deeply embedded in the operating methods of the Commission.

Yet there remained an alternative line of Community development, one embodied in the Treaty of Rome itself: via the rule-making power of the competition directorate and the (to be sure, sometimes contested) authority of the European Court to make law. The use of such regulatory powers had contributed to the development of the single European market in the past. However, the main pressure for evolution along such lines does not – with the exception of the directorates for competition and the internal market – come from within European institutions but from the international market and the individual nations of Europe.

If budgetary allocations faithfully reflected the values, priorities, and interests of European civilization, as reflected in the policies of the Community, then cities would have to disappear, yodeling and bagpiping would drown out symphonic and techno music alike, and the care and feeding of farm animals would, as pastimes, crowd out the feeding and care of human faces. Yet not even with the present *Nostalgiewelle* have matters gone quite so far. The Common Agricultural Policy is (and always has been) at odds with the purposes and goals of European integration and thwarts its normal development. It occupies a secure and all but impregnable fortress that, even after years of effort, has not been breached in spite of overwhelming public opposition, governmental reluctance to foot the bill, the determination of the European Commission to move integration forward, and the existence of higher European priorities. It is a kind of monster. The unpopular regime for foodstuffs has been so often attacked, and from so many quarters, and has so few other than self-interested defenders that – notwithstanding its immense importance – only a brief consideration is needed.

The CAP represents sectoral policy in undiluted form. Though conceived with broad national strategies in mind – reducing income inequalities between farm and factory, smoothing out the movement from country to city, promoting economic modernization generally – its scope is limited to a single branch of enterprise. It takes no account of impacts on consumption, other branches of production, or the national or international economy generally.[45] Provision for a common agricultural policy was included in the treaty simply in order to win French support. The document itself provides few hints as to the mechanisms that might be used to achieve it, though mention is made of "stockpiling," a "common price policy," and "guarantee funds." From 1958 to 1960, the first agriculture commissioner (Sicco Mansholt) led the roundtable negotiations that hammered out the basic principles of the CAP. Two additional years were required to devise appropriate rules for various "commodity regimes": wheat, livestock, milk, and so forth. Twenty-three days of further nonstop haggling under Commission auspices ensued before the deal could be closed, "during which two heart attacks and one nervous breakdown among the participants took place" and an unpleasant precedent was set for future negotiations.[46]

Mansholt had hoped that ceilings could be placed on burgeoning levels of national protection, but this was sadly not to happen for over twenty years. De Gaulle insisted on farm subsidies as *contrepartie* to the opening of the common market for manufactures. Adenauer, who had cosseted German farmers for electoral reasons and refused to countenance any measure that might threaten the hard-won relationship with France, went along. The four basic principles guiding the new system, though by no means always respected, were: no barriers to intra-EEC trade in agricultural commodities; a common support system of farm prices; external protection and community preference to be operated by means of variable import levies; and common financial responsibility, as exercised through a guarantee fund administered as part of the Community budget.[47] Prices were pegged at the level of high-cost producers when the system eventually took effect in 1967. The die, as Richard Howarth glumly observes in his contribution to *The Cost of Europe,* had been cast.[48]

The consequences were devastating. The European consumer paid huge premiums above world food prices (1967 = 100), ranging from 131 for poultry to 483 for sugar, as per-capita output shot up to 5–8 percent per year in the 1960s and 1970s. Between 1960 and 1970, Community farm population dropped two thirds, to 5 million, and Europe shifted from being a net importer of foodstuffs to the world's second largest exporter. Total EC agricultural budget expenditures quadrupled between 1968 and 1977 and would increase another fivefold by 1990, finally pushing the finances of the Community over the brink.[49]

Levels of protection in most countries leapt far above their likely levels if left to their own devices. Based on "producer subsidy equivalent," a formula developed by the OECD to measure supports against world prices, EC farmers received "monetary transfers … from consumers … and taxpayers" equal to about 50 percent of income during the 1980s,[50] the amount increasing with declines in prices (and vice versa), or about 1.6 times as much as their U.S. counterparts.[51] The burden on consumers has been heavy. The 1980 report of the British Institute for Fiscal Studies estimated that the CAP amounted to a tax ranging from 5.6 percent on the poorest households to 2.9 percent on the richest, averaging 4.5 percent on all households. The CAP caused serious additional problems. It has beggared Third World farmers and contributed to the instability of world agricultural markets by subsidizing exports at times of surplus. It has provided a recurrent, maddening, and seriously disruptive source of conflict between Europe and the rest of the world in trade negotiations up to the present. By driving prices down, the subsidized exportation of surpluses has increased deadweight costs by 25 percent; it is thus, in part, self-defeating. The CAP has not proportionately helped average farmers, whose incomes have been bolstered less than the costs to consumers and taxpayers, so much as transferred resources to owners of farmland and farm administrators (who together consume 10 percent of the total budget).

The Common Agricultural Policy has not even worked as intended by its guiding principles. No genuinely common market exists in agriculture, even in the restrictive sense of having a uniformly administered price structure. The currency volatility of the 1970s brewed up something called monetary compensatory amounts (MCAs), which were retained until modified in 1999; these were a "green currency" created to offset shifts in exchange rates and maintain common pricing. Valued on the basis of a weighted average of community currencies, the funny-money provided windfalls to countries with a depreciating currency and had the contrary effect in those where values rose. To offset such unintended effects, national governments (especially the Federal Republic) reintroduced side payments. The result, according to Elmar Rieger, was a "renationalization of west European agriculture," one in which "countries retained considerable freedom to maintain the level of their domestic farm prices" while at the same time restricting intercountry transfers to "politically acceptable and economically reasonable" levels.[52] The introduction of MCAs, along with the side payments, thus had the effect of reimposing tariffs.

To dismiss the CAP as merely a regrettable diversion from the constructive purposes of integration – or to write it off as just a boondoggle – would be to overlook its destructive influence on the evolution of Community institutions. The Common Agricultural Policy has preempted the bulk of Community resources for a period of more than thirty years. The only significant reduction in its share of the budget, from roughly 70 to 50 percent, was the singular achievement of Jacques Delors. It resulted from a special (and in this case ironically welcome) challenge: the need, for overarching political reasons, to provide pork to the poor "Club Med" nations – Greece, Spain, and Portugal – that entered the Community in the mid-1980s (plus Ireland). Regional Policy had important institutional implications, but it did not necessarily imply revenue redistribution; money could end up in the same hands but for different reasons.[53]

The existence of CAP has nevertheless perverted the appropriations process so completely that the policy of foodstuffs subsidization must be junked – and responsibility for the agricultural sector be restored to the states – if Enlargement (the inclusion of countries of the former Soviet bloc into the EC) is to be conducted fairly and, beyond even this, if any form of parliamentary government worthy of the name is to be introduced at the European level. The CAP has drained the budget of funds that might have been better spent and has perverted the development of the Community; raised procedural thickets dense enough to discourage even the most intrepid inquiry into revenues and expenditures; introduced a paralytic rigidity into the planning process; triggered a succession of budgetary crises; nurtured fraud and spread corruption on a grand scale; made a travesty of attempts to enforce the principle of public accountability; and aroused the justifiable ire of a public fed up with having to pay a hidden tax.

The EC method of budgeting derives from agreements of 1970 and 1975 whose purpose was to provide the Community with its "own funds" and enable it to exercise a degree of autonomy from the states.[54] Such agreements were concluded between the member-states. The essentials of the revenue package were negotiated in anticipation of British entry and with a view toward favoring the beneficiaries of the Common Agricultural Policy, the French in particular. The bottom line was national inequity.[55] Only two nations were net payers up to 1987. The first of them was West Germany, in which atonement and self-interest had long since ceased to march in lockstep but upon whose continued beneficence, more than anything else, the survival of the Community depended. The other was Great Britain, at the time a relatively poor nation, whose largely vain efforts to impose the principle of fair shares, the *juste retour* – be it under the emollient Heath, the dyspepsic Wilson, the not-always-so-sunny Jim Callaghan, or the handbag-wielding Margaret Thatcher – brought discord and occasional pandemonium to European Council summitry in the 1970s and 1980s, harmed the United Kingdom's relationship with the rest of the Community, and soured a substantial segment of British opinion on the very idea of "Europe." Even as late as 1987, after years of wrangling, West Germany paid out 26.5 percent to the Community's "own resources" and received 14.7 percent in return; Great Britain provided 16.2 percent and got back only 10.7 percent.[56]

Repeated Community attempts to reform revenue raising and spending practices have nearly always failed. The traditional system of budgeting, though modified in the 1980s, remains essentially intact today. The amounts involved are surprisingly modest. As of 1990, the EC budget had been allowed to rise to only 1.2 percent of total member-state GDP, or 3.3 percent of total national budgets. Until the 1990s, two thirds of the budget was "compulsory" or nondiscretionary, and 80 percent of this amount was consumed by CAP. Limited by the terms of the treaty, restricted by the reluctance of the member-states to cede the power to tax, and hedged in by the special arrangements for agriculture, Community exercise of the "power of the purse" is tightly circumscribed. In fact, the EC has less taxing and spending authority than national governments, the states in federal unions, or even (in most countries) municipalities.[57]

The budgetary process has always been labyrinthine.[58] The incongruence between revenues and expenditure is one basic problem. It ipso facto induces the majority of recipients to spend too much and the minority of net payers to block reasonable expenditure increases.[59] On the revenue side, tax sharing is either restrictive or unpredictable, in spite of reforms. The first source, agricultural levies, depends upon world market crop conditions; the second one, tariffs, depends on the general state of the world economy and may also be affected by new international agreements; the third source, the value-added tax, falls on consumption and is thus regressive. Subsequent efforts to offset these serious deficiencies by assessing a GDP-based levy have had little effect. On the expenditure side, the roughly two thirds of the average "compulsory" budget devoted to price supports for foodstuffs (until the reduction in the late 1980s) was likewise subject to vagaries of climate and politics and, in practice, varied substantially from one year to the next; estimates made at the beginning of the budgetary cycle were often worthless in the end, thus throwing the entire process into disarray.[60] One should add that, according to the treaty, the Community budget must balance and that until 1988 the budget itself was limited by the member-states to 1 percent of GDP.

Furthermore, the budget ratification process was (and remains) cumbersome, protracted, and highly technical. It has commonly featured "power plays" on a scale and intensity far greater than the material stakes at hand, usually waged by the Council on behalf of the status quo and by the Commission and Parliament on behalf of change. None of the three parties involved in drafting even the "noncompulsory" remnant of the budget document (the non-CAP part) has enough authority to assume political responsibility for the final result and none, for that matter, has any real intention of doing so. The budgeting exercise involves more mummery than substance. The name of the game has been to jockey into position for the future exercise of power rather than to solve problems in the present.[61]

To delineate the ratification process is tedious but a necessary part of any book about the EC. It does not resemble anything like normal parliamentary procedure. The Commission sets it in motion in January of the coming fiscal year by presenting the preliminary draft budget (PDB), which technocratic experts have normally have begun preparing months earlier.[62] Commission efforts to establish new Community priorities by means of the PDB have normally met with little success. By May or June, the draft proposal normally reaches the Council for a First Reading (conducted in secret) and is then pored over by its chief bureaucrats, as represented on the Committee of Permanent Representatives (COREPER). In July, the modified draft is submitted on a privileged basis to leading figures in the Parliament for consultation – with a view toward producing a document that can win the approval of that body. The Council draft, according to Neill Nugent, almost always "proposes a tighter overall budget than that envisaged in the PDB ... and shifts from noncompulsory expenditure ... to agriculture."[63]

The draft then moves to the Parliament for a First Reading there, which invariably results in efforts to increase allowable noncompulsory outlays. Prior to the 1988 reform, disagreements then normally surrounded (1) the precise definition of the "annual rate of increase" (a restrictive technical formula based on inflation, growth of national budgets, and overall growth) that could be applied to noncompulsory expenditure, some of which is "privileged," and (2) the precise definition of this relatively favored sector as opposed to what remained, the nonprivileged remnant of the noncompulsory remnant of the budget. Assuming that such issues could be thrashed out, the Council would then, once again in secret and usually in mid-November, feverishly conduct a Second Reading – often as part of a "Trialog," to use the official designator, with the Council and the Parliament. Acting by qualified majority, the Council can then modify amendments to noncompulsory expenditure normally requested by the Parliament and accept or reject changes to compulsory expenditure. The Council then refers the budget back to the Parliament for a Second Reading, normally in December.

If the Parliament refuses to accept the Council revisions it may, after further "Trialoging," reject the budget by either a simple majority of the members of Parliament or by two thirds of the votes actually cast. If (as has often been the case) no agreement can be reached, the Community may fund itself monthly on the basis of the previous year's budget. It has not been established how long it can operate without a formal budget.

Accountability has always been very weak. Created in 1975 in order to monitor expenditures, the Court of Auditors over a decade later finally "went beyond the level of generalities about the level of fraud in the Community" and, for its 1987 annual report, investigated in four member-states (Britain, France, Germany, and Ireland) the export refunds paid in the "beefmeat sector."[64] Such payments amounted to 41 percent of overall farm subsidies. It might be noted that the sample did not investigate nations in which cheating the tax collector is regarded as a patriotic and familial responsibility and also excluded the "commodity groups" that thrive in such climes. The findings of the court were nevertheless "extremely critical." Claims for refunds were granted even though "product was not exported at all, the product exported was not beef, and the product was not exported to the destination intended."

Sniffing out an opportunity to add a *competence,* the Commission quickly produced a 47-point action program, proposing that 70 million ecus (European currency units) be immediately provided to fund it. The Court proceeded fatalistically, noting that "with refunds as high as they [were] it is highly unlikely that any system will make it possible to avoid the risk of fraud and the concomitant budgetary burden." No system, it figured, that applied a differentiated rate of refund could hope to frustrate determined attempts at fraud, especially since "the nomenclature for export refunds contains eighty different classifications for beef and rates of refund vary according to the country of final destination with the world divided into eleven zones, each of which has a significantly different rate."[65]

The inadequacy of EC fiscal machinery made a nonstarter of the most serious reform proposal of the 1970s. Anchored in comparative studies of political federations, the 1977 MacDougall Report correctly concluded that much had to be done in order to advance the Community from its "pre-federal" condition. The EC had to extend its authority into new industries and devise "structural and redistribution policies designed to bring about a greater convergence in economic performance and fortunes between member states and regions," in the absence of which "further integration of any fundamental kind would be unattainable." The report's recommendation of tripling the tax yield from 0.7 percent of GDP to 2.2 percent – although in line with many scholarly and other expert reform proposals made early in the decade – was unrealistic and, in light of the way the EC actually functioned, almost laughably so. The new money would never be necessary.[66]

The new ambitions of the European Commission were part and parcel of the neomercantilism of the 1970s. In the same years that systems organized along such lines were breaking down in most European nations, they took hold at the EEC in steel, textiles, shipbuilding, and, beyond that, into the sunrise industries where American and Japanese multinational producers seemed to be taking a commanding lead. The new *Interessengemeinschaften* formed at a Commission that was otherwise falling on hard times, according to Steven Warnecke: "It [was] neither a cabinet nor a national executive. The problem of representation is not resolved by resorting to a legal fiction about a European electorate, the technique of a direct election, and the construction of a parliamentary body."[67] And, he adds, "what the nation-state provides and the European Community cannot provide is the discipline of a legitimate system to deal with the antagonisms and centrifugal forces inherent in any political community."[68] The machinery with which to restart integration would in fact be organized beyond the framework of Community institutions and through the European Council – by the member-states rather than the Brussels *apparat*.

Meanwhile, in the Belgian capital, the Commission employed a corps of lawyers to ensure the faithful execution of the treaty, retained the right to initiate Community legislation, administered special funds, and supervised that portion of the local Eurocracy not subject to the Council of Ministers. In 1973 the Commission was a comfortable 7,000-person bureaucracy of handsomely paid, exceptionally well wined and dined, diplomatically privileged lifetime civil servants organized into nineteen "Directorates General" (*Directions Générales*) or DGs, to which each large member-state could (by informal agreement) appoint two commissioners and each small member-state designate a single one, for a total of thirteen. Appended to the Commission were ten services and agencies of various kinds. The power of the DGs varied greatly. In several cases – notably for environmental and consumer affairs, technology, and research – it was negligible. In others it was slight though growing. The DG for economic and monetary affairs had diverse responsibilities for policy coordination; the DG for commercial policy was responsible for working out a community negotiation position within GATT; the DG for competition policy had the authority to vet large-scale mergers but used it infrequently; the DG for regional policy administered a new but tiny regional fund, as was also the case in social policy. The DG for the internal market had begun to investigate, but not yet legally challenge, various nontariff barriers to trade.

The most powerful DGs were those that allocated foreign aid, managed the transfer payments system of the former coal and steel community, and administered CAP. The Common Agricultural Policy absorbed over 72 percent of the budget between 1968 and 1974 and employed over 60 percent of the staff. Coal and steel subsidies and foreign aid spent over 6 percent, while overhead ate up another 5 percent. The remaining sums were allocated to a number of tertiary activities.[69] Money was not always congruent with influence. The treaty and the courts assigned enforcement authority to the Commission in two specific areas – competition policy and internal market policy – the objective in both cases being to impose rules required for efficient market operation. Commercial policy was another exception. The GATT recognized the EEC as a negotiating authority. A network of association agreements granting duty-free entry had been drawn up with over twenty states from the Mediterranean, the Near East, and Latin America.[70]

Industrial policy was the first new source of Commission power since CAP and would be a growth axis in the future. The exercise of such "positive" and "market correcting" power was not treaty-based, except for the special cases of coal and steel.[71] Until the early 1970s, disagreement existed at the Commission about precisely what an industrial policy should do: Eliminate trade distortions? Iron out the adjustment problems of declining industries? Promote Euro-mergers and Euro-champions? Prevent takeovers by American or Japanese multis?[72] Declining industries provided the first opportunity. *Interessengemeinschaften* came into existence for the steel industry, which the Commission reorganized; in shipbuilding, for which it coordinated planning and worked out Orderly Marketing Arrangements; and in textiles, where it negotiated and enforced the Multi Fiber Agreement (MFA). Others would soon follow in automobiles, defense industries, and chemicals. By the mid-1980s, special relationships of one kind or another would extend throughout much of European industry, and plans for building new ones were top-agenda items. Such arrangements lent impetus to the creation of the Single European Market (SEM).

The 1976 collapse of the world steel market – long overburdened with excess capacity and badly distorted by the subsidized "national champions" found throughout Europe and elsewhere – triggered the first Community foray into managing industry. Plans for it had long been in the works. In 1975 the French steel industry declared a "manifest crisis," enabling it to form cartels under emergency provisions of the coal–steel treaty. Shortly thereafter, West German producers organized "rationalization groupings" created with a view toward coordinating investment and production cutbacks and included the Dutch and Luxembourgers; whereupon the French, to prevent German dominance, instigated the formation of the Community-wide EUROFER to lobby Brussels.[73] The Commission had in the meantime prepared an anti-crisis plan intended to provide a breathing space for European steel. It set minimum prices, included voluntary restraints on production, and provided for antidumping measures, which in 1978 turned into VERs negotiated with all exporters to the community.

The adoption of this Davignon Plan required the legal suppression of independent Italian minimill producers (the so-called Bresciani) as well as the imposition on modern Ruhr producers of a pricing system tailored to the least-efficient Belgians, state-sector Italians, and nationalized French and British.[74] The prevention of falling prices was only a stopgap. To promote long-run profitability, the Commission tried to restructure and rationalize the industry by means of carrot (investment, retraining, and reconversion assistance) and stick (suppression of state aids and subsidies). After markets weakened in 1979, quotas became mandatory, a new code enforcing strict limits on state aids was adopted, and a long-term phase-out of capacity entered into force. What had begun with "voluntary production quotas" had by 1980 evolved into a "full-scale compulsory system, armed with inspectors, reporting requirements and fines."[75] The Commission found itself the planning authority for the steel sector. Was the Davignon Plan useful, necessary, or wise? It reduced the competitive provision of state aids and brought about a permanent reduction of steel capacity, but at the expense of the efficient producer, the modernizer, and the consumer – and at greater cost and over a longer period of time than might otherwise have been the case.[76] The minimill revolution that swept the American steel industry by storm in the 1980s and 1990s would largely bypass Europe, where costs would remain unnecessarily high, production schedules rigid, and pollution a severe problem.[77]

As another aging industry and a big employer, textiles presented the Commission with a more difficult proposition than did steel. It was diffuse and decentralized, divided into artificial and natural fiber sectors, extended through many levels of production from thread making to clothing manufacture, produced at highly varying levels of efficiency, could not capture latecomer advantages, and lacked strong producer associations with which to negotiate. The essential prerequisites for a program of restructuring and modernization were missing. The most that could be done was to provide protection.[78]

The Multi Fiber Agreement had since 1974 set, allocated, and distributed national import quotas – including for Europe – albeit with disastrous results for inefficient British and French producers. Some 750,000 jobs would be lost over the decade. Working in cooperation with COMETEXIL, the producer association, the Commission negotiated bilateral VERs with thirty of the main exporting nations as a condition for the renewal of MFA in 1978. The arrangements took account of special relationships in eastern Europe, the Mediterranean, and overseas client nations. In the special area of synthetic fibers, where a handful of European producers controlled 80 percent of the market but where (owing to overinvestment) excess capacity was rated at 30 percent, the industry formed a cartel in clear violation of the rules for competition policy in the same year, but the Commission chose to look the other way.[79] Resort to such drastic expedients temporarily turned the situation around. Textile imports, which had increased 22.6 percent in 1976, fell 6.3 percent the following year.[80] Long-term change has been difficult, and next to agriculture the MFA remains the least fair and most divisive of international trade agreements.

The European shipbuilding industry was also plagued by excess capacity and high levels of subsidization. In this case, Commission-negotiated VERs aggravated an already bad situation. Faced with a rising yen on the one hand and an increasing level of Community subsidies on the other, in 1977 the Japanese hiked prices still another 5 percent and so enabled European shipyards to outbid their own. The costs to the European taxpayer were huge. Subsidies, an average of 5 percent in 1972, rose to between 20 and 30 percent in France, Italy, and Great Britain, and downsizing did not take place. The inefficient shipyards remained in operation.[81]

The new relationship between the Commission and industry was highly am-
bivalent. The interventions of Brussels, though often justified as an alternative to
national protectionism, could (as with shipbuilding) merely increase it. In steel,
the Commission brought about overdue capacity reductions but at high cost and
over a long period. In textiles it provided welcome bail-outs to producers of artificial fibers but otherwise merely prolonged a lingering death. The Commission
was a political convenience for hard-pressed producers and elected governments
loath to bear the onus of causing mass dismissals. By the 1970s, business had
begun to turn to the Commission and the Commission to business. A corporate
synthesis was beginning to form around the idea that Brussels should organize
a single market for the benefit of Europe's producers. Jacques Delors would become its champion.

TOWARD A LESS IMPERFECT UNION: EUROPEAN LAW, THE EUROPEAN COUNCIL, MONETARY CONVERGENCE, AND THE RECOVERY OF INTERNATIONAL TRADE

But all was not ill at the EC. A quasi-constitutional European law liberated captive national markets. A new European Council unbarred the door to Dahrendorf's Second Europe. The occasionally lapsetudinarian French moved toward
monetary and fiscal convergence with the sober-minded Germans. The long-
term expansion of international trade was not reversed in spite of neomercantilist barriers. All such developments were encouraging, though they hardly
constituted persuasive evidence that Europe was parting from one economic era
and moving into a new one. A symbol was needed to catalyze such impressions
into insight. This symbol took an unlikely form, and not only because it appeared in the guise of a female. Who could possibly have imagined at the time
that she would be an economic Amazon, spear at the ready, dressed in the armor
of nineteenth-century classical liberalism?

The importance of the quasi-constitutional law created by the European Court
of Justice is easy to underrate. The court itself was a treaty afterthought, and
the purpose for which it was created – the promotion of the European cause –
was obviously self-serving. Yet in the years when the Community seemed to be
dormant, the ECJ almost unobtrusively extended its reach deep into the national
laws of the member-states. Its jurisdictional claims, still largely unchallenged,
stand and are enforceable. Their impact is, for better or worse, at every hearth
and in every home within the Community. Whether this will be the case tomorrow hinges on the future institutional structure of the European Union and
the willingness of member-state courts to enforce its writ. It would therefore
be premature to speak as if a body of purely "constitutional" law analogous to
that of nation-states already existed within the EU.[82] The treaty does not assign
the court the power to act as federator. It has become one only by means of a
successful judicial activism that in recent years has frequently been called into
question.[83]

In a series of landmark decisions in the 1960s and 1970s, the ECJ established four doctrines that provide the cornerstones of a theory of legal intervention into the relationship between the Community and the states. The court held in the 1963 case of Van Gend en Loos, that provisions of the treaty could have *direct effect*. National governments could, in other words, be sued by individual citizens in their own national courts for nonenforcement of the treaty. The case of Costa v. ENEL established the *supremacy doctrine,* in which the court determined that state transfers of legal powers were irreversible and a permanent limitation on sovereign rights. The *preemption doctrine,* developed in a line of cases, is an extension of the previous one; it holds that "when Community law substantially regulates an area, it preempts national legislation in that area except where EC law provides otherwise." Finally the *judicial review* doctrine, once again established in a line of cases running through the 1970s, enables the court to determine the constitutionality of executive and legislative acts of government and to define their respective rights and powers.[84]

Legal scholars agree that the "constitutionalization" of treaty law is unprecedented, lacks unambiguous justification in the treaty, and may even be contrary to the intention of the contracting parties. They also disagree as to how the situation came about and whether it is desirable.[85] Although the balance between them remains controversial, several general explanations have been advanced concerning the origins of the present situation: tacit public acceptance existed of the idea that some form of European law was required for the discharge of Community responsibilities; elite opinion endorsed the notion that courts were called upon to act since other organs of the Community were immobilized, as well as to offset the rising power of the states in the integration process; national courts promoted the development of European law to gain leverage over legislatures and executives as well in the corporate interests of bench and bar; and the public was at the time ignorant of the consequences of judicial action at the European level.[86] The ability of the ECJ to enforce its writ has varied, and varies, substantially from place to place and time to time. "Law abiding" northern Protestant nations consistently, though often grudgingly, outpoint the others as reliable executors of orders from Brussels. What keeps the "good guys" in line is the deal-based *engrenage* that exacts prohibitive political prices for deviance.

Judicial activism reached the high-water mark in the late 1970s. Opposition to it has since been growing because, complained the University of Copenhagen law professor Hjalte Rasmussen,

in the attempt to "make Europe" the European Court went too far too often [and] in defiance of much European tradition ... engaged in a teleological crusade, the banner of which featured a deep involvement [that] led it to give primacy to pro-integrationist public policies over competing ones that were often even outside of the ring of losing litigants, considered as meriting some protection.[87]

Both the French *Conseil d'État* and the German *Bundesfinanzhof* have objected to extension of the direct effect doctrine to Commission directives, and Italian

and German courts have attacked the supremacy doctrine as a threat to constitutional guarantees of fundamental rights.

The most frequent objections, political and judicial, to further court activism
have arisen from national implementation of the Commission interventions
grounded in the "quasi-constitutional" development of European law. According to a report of the *Conseil d'État*, by 1992 this legal corpus included 22,445
EU regulations, 1,675 directives, 1,198 agreements and protocols, 185 recommendations of the Commission or the Council, 291 Council resolutions, and
678 communications. The Community had in fact become the largest source
of new French law, "with 54 percent of all ... laws originating in Brussels."[88]
Such enactments had far-reaching impacts on the societies and polities of the
member-states, inevitably helped some interests and hurt others, and had many
domestic repercussions.

The 1992 Treaty of European Union (TEU) drafted at Maastricht placed limits on the EJC. Since then, the Commission has devoted great attention to
simplifying the process of national implementation of Brussels-made policy.[89]
In spite of the threats, costs, annoyances, and inequities that result from the
Euro-law now developing, a powerful statement can be made in defense of it:
The EU law provides writs and devices to enforce fundamental rights and principles as norms for democratic government in places where earlier they may have
been abused, suppressed, extinguished, or not even known. According to Fritz
Scharpf, it has also served as a powerful instrument of liberalization. By reducing
the authority of national governments "to impose market-correcting regulations
on increasingly mobile capital," national polities find themselves competing as
market-strengthening rather than market-correcting regulatory systems.[90]

In the 1970s a new policy-making body, the European Council, supplied the
missing leadership for the integration cause. The Council provided a permanent
forum in which the member-states could negotiate binding settlements to outstanding problems that could then be acted upon collectively. It institutionalized
the process of informal diplomatic bargaining by which the member-states had
created the Community in the first place, and it provided the missing mechanism for integrating Europe "intergovernmentally," to use the term of Andrew
Moravcsik. An extra-treaty body composed of heads of state or government
representing the member-nations of the Community, the European Council met
three and later two times a year under a rotating chairmanship. Foreign ministers were responsible for maintaining continuity between meetings.[91]

The new Council was unencumbered by teleology and, though operating with
an eye to the long run, advanced the integration process one step at a time. The
Council bore a structural resemblance to the Gaullist Fouchet Plans of the early
1960s for collectively run management of a confederal Europe. The new body
sprang into existence for purposes of damage control and in particular to shield
Europe from world monetary disorder. Its activity extended to Europe as a region and thus beyond the membership of the EC; its methods were those of
traditional diplomacy and were not restricted by a particular set of institutions.

There were limits to what the European Council could accomplish. Repeated attempts over the decade to develop a common European energy policy went nowhere, and though the machinery for foreign policy consultation and discussion was in place, the attempt to coordinate it would remain largely futile without political and economic convergence. The Council's main accomplishments were monetary. Guiding it was the commitment, reaffirmed at the Paris summit of 1972, to achieve a currency union by the end of the decade.[92]

French President Georges Pompidou, who died in 1974, first proposed the creation of a European Council as part of the deal that brought Britain – as suspicious, even under the Europhilic Ted Heath, of supranationalism as France – into the Community. (The other critical part of the package was to lock CAP into an "iron budget.") Pompidou's successor, Valéry Giscard d'Estaing, developed with Chancellor Helmut Schmidt (who replaced Willi Brandt in the same year) a relationship of mutual trust that was needed to make the European Council effective. The agreement to form the so-called Snake was an unsuccessful initial joint foray into EU monetary policy.

The Snake was a pure exchange-rate agreement between central bankers to limit currency deviations to 2.25 percent above or below a dollar peg; when the latter began to float, this became a moving peg. Five non-EEC members (Sweden, Norway, Denmark, Britain, and Ireland) also joined the agreement, which was brokered by the Bank for International Settlements in Basel. The one large "strong currency nation" in Europe, West Germany, insisted that provision of a reserve fund be made contingent upon apolitically unrealistic policy convergence.

Within six weeks, speculation forced both pound and punt out of the permitted range and, by 1973, the lira as well. The remaining bits of the Snake then pulled apart in different directions – the "strong currency countries" (the Netherlands, Norway, and Germany) moving one way, the weak ones (France, Sweden, Belgium, and Denmark) going the other until, with elections approaching and the franc under attack, France devalued and withdrew in April 1974. The Snake somehow managed to wriggle on for another two years, with the Belgians and Danes joining the other "strong currency countries" and, for good measure, with the Norwegians and Swedes as associates. The experiment with the monetary agreement failed in two respects: it had neither influenced decisions to devalue nor produced a common policy toward the dollar.[93]

The adoption by the Giscard government of the strict, austere, and avowedly anti-Keynesian *Plan Barre* in 1976 set the stage for closer cooperation. The Barre Plan came on the heels of cycles featuring devaluations followed by increases in wages and government spending, inflation, and the failures of capital controls and restrictive credit schemes to limit still further devaluations. It thus represented a fundamental turning point in French establishment economic thinking.[94] In the future, only left-wing socialists and communists would oppose the policy of the *franc fort*, which by removing the advantages of a depreciating currency would force French producers to compete, keep wages in line, and put the lid on inflation.

Giscard and Schmidt want to extraordinary lengths to forge, shape, and fit the European Monetary System (EMS) into a shell hard enough to protect the still soft and vulnerable French economy. In January and February 1978, the two secretly worked out the terms of a joint proposal that the German Chancellor would present at the forthcoming Copenhagen summit. Its main feature was a European Monetary Fund (EMF) to support the Snake. It earmarked 15 to 20 percent of central bank reserves as coverage for a new unit of account, the European currency unit (ecu). The EMF did not come up for discussion at Copenhagen, but Schmidt and Giscard – though occasionally bringing in Britain's Callaghan – continued confidential discussions through "back channels." The central bankers and finance ministers of the other EMS nations were kept in complete ignorance of the project, as were ECOFIN (the EU's Economic and Financial Council), the rest of the Commission, and the Bundesbank, which would with dead certainty have objected to the Schmidt–Giscard scheme. The EMF proposal won approval at the October 1978 Bremen summit. Details were worked out under the auspices of the European Commission. Its engagement provided ideological legitimation and, by generating a measure of public support, helped overcome the opposition of the Bundesbank. Euro-rhetoric also provided welcome cover for the difficult technical negotiations, which turned on the issue of how the burden of maintaining parities should be shared between the "strong" and "weak" countries."[95]

The new EMS was ahead of its time. Like the Snake, it soon broke apart on the shoals of macroeconomic divergence. It thus cannot be deemed the first successful experiment in integrating by means of "variable geometry" – that is, by dint of a special Franco-German relationship enabling the two of them to march in the vanguard of a process that others would then follow at their own speed. It nonetheless revealed a new German willingness to make political sacrifices in order to build a monetary system for disciplining neighboring economies once the nations in question adopted disinflation as the preeminent goal of policy.[96] France under Giscard did, but under Mitterrand would not. Britain under Callaghan was curious and at the same time immobilized, but under Thatcher was like-minded and independent. Italy was still too weak for anything but free-riding. The regime change would have to be completed before monetary union would be realistic.

The continued rise of the multinational corporation – in spite of monetary disorder, the growing threat of government takeover, and the even more rapid acceleration of international capital flows – generated strong pressures for regime change. According to Helen Milner, the growing interdependence of firms operating across borders created trade preferences, conditioned by their position in the international economy as well as in the state, that offset to a considerable extent the trend to neomercantilism in the 1970s.[97] In a comparison of similar firms from the same industry engaging in business in the United States (a relatively open economy) with those assumed to be operating in the relatively closed economy of France, Milner detected similar preferences and consequences. French industrial exports as a share of overall output rose from 12 percent in 1958 to about 20 percent in 1968 and to almost 33 percent by 1981. In case after case she found that, contrary to conventional wisdom, "firms' preferences shaped the state's activity [and] initiated policy for the sector."[98] They neither sought nor accepted state help. Even national champions, when forced to compete, tended to slip their tutelage and support "freer" trade. She found additional supporting evidence that the new export sectors grew without large-scale state assistance; although the provision of aid for restructuring was common, exports credits amounted to only 2 percent of total foreign sales.

According to Peter Hall, state planning is what ironically began "to erode the 'étatism' of the French state."[99] Being forced to ally with industry in order to promote competition, the state itself "fostered the growth of large, dynamic multinational French firms who were much less dependent on [it]."[100] To contain the independent new multinationals, state building would have to take place increasingly at the regional or transnational level. Those who would engage in it would have to deal with the multis' global orientation as well as the pressures for liberalization generated by them. As aptly put by Werner Feld, this entailed "the pursuit of political objectives aimed at the elimination of [such] government-related obstacles to the optimal functioning of ... collaborative ventures ... as divergent national laws, regulations and policies."[101] Multinational firms might indeed enter "neomercantilist" bargains with the EC, but it would be difficult to restrict the range of their activity or influence.[102]

Between the late 1970s and the early 1990s, the development of the first truly postwar international private financial markets washed away capital controls and opened up the private banking sector. Even during the sorry 1970s, capital flows increased at a phenomenal 21 percent annual compounded rate (1972–1985), as opposed to 10.9 percent for world GDP over the period and 12.7 percent for world trade. Daily turnover in world financial markets, some $3 billion in May 1973, had swollen to an average of around $100 billion by the early 1980s. The Committee of Twenty IMF governors – set up in 1972 to recommend rules and procedures in the aftermath of the Smithsonian Agreement (which officially decoupled dollars from gold) and to smooth the transition to flexible exchange rates – was unfavorable in principle to the idea of capital controls but still recommended using them in order to limit disruptions and monetary shocks.

The West German abandonment of controls was particularly important. Having earlier eliminated restrictions on DM outflows, the Federal Republic's decision to lift limits on inflows in 1980 implied a decision, according to Louis Pauly and John Goodman, to allow at least partial use of the DM as a reserve currency because "financial openness was seen to promise benefits" – particularly to German private banks, whose international exposure had increased from $6.7 billion in 1973 to $73.3 billion in 1980.[103] The growth of such sums partly tracked the rise of the Federal Republic's overseas industrial investments (from $3.2 billion in 1970 to $7.6 billion in 1980) as well as its increase in industrial exports. To keep up with this business, German financial institutions needed better access to sources of dollar borrowing. The Deutsche Bank's acquisition of a 5-percent share of the British merchant bank Morgan-Grenfell was partly intended as a warning shot to German banking authorities that, if markets were not kept open, future export financing would take place overseas. The shot was heeded. The Bundesbank had begun to recognize that developments in the international sphere were changing the rules under which it had to operate.[104] Regime change had begun to shift the sands.

MARGARET THATCHER: FOUNDING MOTHER OF THE NEW EUROPE

Precipitated by world monetary disorder – and impelled forward by the expansion of world trade, the rise of the multis, and the explosive growth of international financial markets – the regime change that began in the 1970s would also develop "from the bottom up" as nation after nation found itself forced into confronting stagflation and the failure of Keynesian pump-priming to invigorate tired economies. Under Mrs. Thatcher, Britain would find itself in the unaccustomed role of model for domestic reform and provide the stimulus to change at the regional level. The fact that "from the bottom up" change first took hold in the United Kingdom has something to do with both the residual strength of the nineteenth-century liberal tradition and the vast expenditure of intellectual energy in the effort to overcome industrial decline. The Thatcher revolution can be attributed more directly to the vitality in Britain of a classical liberal intellectual revival as well as to the personal leadership of the prime minister. In the last analysis, it depended simply upon the fact that policies like hers provided the best available solutions to the problems facing Europe. The French would be among the first to get the point.

Thanks to the Institute of Economic Affairs, in whose establishment Hayek had a direct hand – as well as ancillary classical liberal think tanks that dealt more specifically with policy issues, like the Center for Policy Studies and the Adam Smith Institute – Margaret Thatcher entered office in 1979 powerfully armed with a well-formulated array of fresh initiatives that had been previously "unthinkable" politically. She also had the backing of the right wing of the Conservative Party.[105] The initial phase of Mrs. Thatcher's "liberal counterrevolution" would last three tense, angry, embattled years of touch-and-go politics that would end with a dramatic electoral victory in 1983. It gave the Tories the commanding majority that enabled Mrs. Thatcher to put her agenda for Britain's new enterprise culture into overdrive.[106]

Her three overarching and interrelated objectives in the early phase were to break the power of the unions, reduce the size of the state sector, and restore confidence in the currency. To build public support and intimidate the opposition, Mrs. Thatcher took a no-nonsense stand on law and order and a hard line in foreign affairs. The cosmic gullibility and even world-historical stupidity of the junta ruling in Argentina handed Mrs. Thatcher on a plate a war – of just the right scale, in just the right place, and at just the right time.[107] It brought patriotism to the rescue. The economic pain inflicted by the "liberal counter-revolution," necessary though it may have been, would almost surely have forced her out of office had not victory in the Falklands rallied public opinion behind the previously much derided (and often intensely disliked) schoolmarm–Prime Ministress – who, it seemed, had miraculously morphed into a living female incarnation of Winston Churchill.[108] The first three years of the Thatcher government were even rougher than the 1970s. Inflation raged, unemployment rose, growth halted, and disorder and unrest turned really ugly. Yet Britain turned a corner during the years between 1979 and 1983, putting the brakes on inflation while returning to growth. The policies then put in place would lead, over the remainder of the decade, to a halting yet irreversible "Thatcher Revolution." In addition to providing a model for states facing similar problems, the British example would inspire the Single European Act. If in the future Margaret Thatcher is remembered as a Founding Mother of the New Europe, then the misguided military plotters of Patagonia have at least a ragged claim to be regarded as its midwives.

In the same months that Mrs. Thatcher was struggling to launch the liberal counterrevolution, President François Mitterrand of France was conducting an even more ambitious (though diametrically opposed) experiment: building Socialism in One Country. Inspired by a uniquely French school of left-wing thought then in vogue, which supplied the common policy of the united left – including the communists, who (with the formation of the Mitterrand cabinet in May 1981) re-entered government for the first time since 1947 – it aimed at quasi-revolutionary reform of French society. Mitterrand and his allies spoke euphorically about a "rupture with the past" and dumping bourgeois capitalism with all its evil works. Instead, planning was to be restored, whole new sectors of industry and finance nationalized, unemployment conquered, wealth and political power redistributed from the top down, worker self-management (*autogestion*) introduced, and the bureaucracy strengthened as a political mechanism. With power thus shifted away from the private sector and toward the state, the really good stuff could begin. *Autogestion* would revive politics at the grass roots. Guided by enlightened leadership and supported by sound collective thinking, democracy could be organized from the ground up; heavy-handed Stalinist rule from above could be avoided and wire-pulling capitalists be put to rout. Keynesian deficit spending would be used to stimulate initial growth, and a predicted buoyant upsurge in world demand would sustain export expansion.[109]

This utopian policy, still another in a long series of vain searches for a Third Way between Soviet economics and the market, soon proved ruinous. The next two years would leave lasting memories of an economy careening out of control, capital flight, runaway inflation, the rise of unemployment, negative economic growth, three devaluations, and repeal of the social gains that had provided original justification for the "rupture."[110] Facing an IMF ultimatum and a refusal of the German government to contemplate further bailouts of the franc, Mitterrand dropped the policy with a vengeance, returning to a strict financial orthodoxy from which no French government (of either left or right) has since dared to deviate.

Defenders of Mitterrand have variously attributed the failure of his delusional policy to bad luck, to miscalculation and an inability to buck trends on world markets, or even to a devious but necessary strategy of discrediting challengers from the left simply by putting their otherworldly recipes into practice. Whatever the explanation, the economic disaster that ensued had this effect. It shattered the Communists (who withdrew from the cabinet in March 1983) and deeply demoralized the "Jacobins" and "Regulators" of the noncommunist intellectual left, whose quirky views had inspired the policy in the first place. Though down, they would – thanks to one of them, Minister of Finance Jacques Delors – never be quite out. Delors would put to the test the notion that – with hard money, clearer vision, and the compliance of Germany – what had failed in France could be made to work for Europe.

The conscientious intellectual spadework of the Institute of Economic Affairs (IEA) betokened a happier fate for Mrs. Thatcher's experiment. After contacting Hayek in 1947, a commercial farmer named Antony Fisher (the first successful U.K. mass merchandizer of battery hens) founded and organized the IEA in 1955. The Austrian had long advocated the creation of an intellectual counterpart to the Fabian Society. Fisher tailored the Institute of Economic Affairs to fit the bill. Its target group was the "second-hand dealers in ideas," policy intellectuals in universities, schools, journalism, and broadcasting like those who had earlier "tilted the political debate in favor of growing government intervention with all that followed."[111] The IEA faced the task of fighting and winning "the intellectual battle over the course of twenty or more years without regard to the short-term political situation."[112] Once the political climate had changed, it was believed, "the politicians would come around as well."

According to Richard Cockett,

if there is one central idea that the IEA can be credited with placing at the center of British politics, it is the doctrine of monetarism, which started life in the late 1960s as a highly technical economic technique for achieving monetary stability but later became the highly politicized motivating principle of Mrs. Thatcher's economic reforms of the early 1980s ... the "big idea" that was to dominate debate.[113]

Mrs. Thatcher's closest economic adviser, Professor Alan Walters, was a student of Milton Friedman, who also acted as informal counselor to the prime minister. Yet, as both Walters and Friedman readily acknowledged, the increasing acceptance of monetarist arguments had less to do with their persuasiveness than the natural response of policy makers to turn to new ideas at a time "when the old economic policies of the Keynesian postwar consensus seemed to bring only more inflation and less economic growth – the baleful condition known as stagflation."[114] The Adam Smith Institute (ASI) also had a big hand in waging the policy wars. Where IEA dealt in the "pure science" of political and economic theory, the ASI housed "policy engineers" who "made the machines which made events [and devised] the ways and means in which the ideas of pure theory could be turned into technical devices to alter reality."[115] By the mid-1970s, the Institute of Economic Affairs had

developed a coherent body of free-market ideas applicable to all areas of the economy [and] articulated a coherent set of principles of economic liberalism applicable to a modern economy, thus fulfilling Hayek's 1947 hope that the economic liberals would refine and develop liberalism into a modern, vibrant philosophy, [and had produced] a modern program of economic liberalism unrivaled anywhere else in the world.[116]

In 1974 Sir Keith Joseph (Baronet) founded the Centre for Policy Studies (CPS), a think tank set up to hard-sell Tories on economic liberalism. Joseph "emerged ... as the leading critic inside the party of the policy errors of the Heath government" and soon became Thatcher's mentor and closest political ally.[117] He had for years run a one-man road show on behalf of free-market economics, along the way making important converts at leading British universities. In 1978, one of them recalled as an Oxford undergraduate going

to a packed lecture hall to hear Sir Keith ... talk about free markets, about monetarism, about the perils of corporatism. Such ideas were in the air, but they were not understood ... and the sort of thing that a rather respectable parent would warn his son against; the sort of thing that an ambitious tutor would be worried about if his students started flirting with. Sir Keith's courageous visits ... changed all that.[118]

Joseph was particularly insistent about the need for trade-union reform. In the 1976 tract *Monetarism Is Not Enough!* he argued that Conservatives (still licking their wounds from the 1974 miners' strike) must recognize that – without a decrease in the power of "union barons" to dictate wages and conditions at arbitrary levels – the benefits of the market economy could not be realized. Attainment of the first three of the four objectives set out in the 1978 "Stepping Stones" strategy document, drafted to guide an incoming Conservative government, implied trade-union reform: currency stabilization (requiring "sustained monetary discipline, balanced budgets, public-sector wage restraint"); a shift of personal tax from income to expenditure; deregulation of the private sector (creating the "enterprise culture"); and using North Sea oil revenues to cut public-sector borrowing requirements, keep interest rates low, and encourage investment. At the depth of the Winter of Discontent in March 1979, the Tory shadow cabinet accepted the Stepping Stones document.[119]

From the outset, the Thatcher government acted decisively and in a manner consistent with its policy objectives: quietly avoiding battles it might risk losing and carefully preparing for those it was determined to win, while confidently counting on the White House to do (what from its standpoint would be) the right thing. The first budget, announced by Sir Geoffrey Howe in June 1979, had the dual purpose of (1) reducing inflation by imposing a monetary and fiscal squeeze and (2) redistributing income and restoring the work incentive by shifting the tax burden. Thus, income tax was reduced from an overall rate of 33 percent to 30 percent, the top bracket was dropped from 83 percent to 60 percent while personal exemptions were increased, the indirect value-added tax rose from 8 percent to 15 percent, and higher charges for health services were imposed. Public-sector borrowing shrank 1.25 billion pounds (to 8.25 billion pounds) and the minimum lending rate rose from 12 to 14 percent in concert with the incentive-based changes. In July and October, all remaining currency exchange restrictions disappeared. In order to underscore the permanence of change and regain the confidence of the markets, the government announced a medium-term financial strategy (MTFS) in March 1980 that set requirements for both monetary targets and borrowing. Though not strictly monetarist in the Friedmanite sense, this MTFS sharply reduced the government's powers of discretionary management. Market reaction to it was highly favorable.[120]

Fundamental structural changes ran parallel to those in the fiscal and monetary field. In stating that "public expenditure is at the heart of our current difficulties," the November 1979 Paper on Public Expenditures got right to the point. The bipartisan consensus on the desirability of maintaining high levels of government spending had come to an end. Any doubt that this document might have left about the matter was eliminated by a lengthy appended list of proposed benefit cuts. Over the next eighteen months, many specifically Labour government institutions were pole-axed – including 57 semi-autonomous agencies and boards ("quangos"), among them the price commission and the National Enterprise Board (NEB).[121]

The privatization program began in June 1979 with the sale of the 1,000 million pounds worth of assets held by the NEB. In October the British National Oil Company (BNOC) received the order to put a large number of its North Sea exploration blocks up for auction. In November, the Corby plant of British Steel Corporation was put up for sale; at British Leyland, a new management was installed to clean up the organizational mess and crack down on shop-floor labor agitation. Over the next year the government would sell its stakes in ICL (a computer company), Fairey Holdings, and Ferranti, as well as part of its holding in British Petroleum, British Aerospace, British Sugar Corporation, and Cable & Wireless. The sale of huge public companies like British Telecom, British Gas, and British Airways would begin in 1982 and would continue over the next several years.[122]

The Thatcher government was careful to avoid the sort of direct confrontation with labor that might rally opinion around a "cause," but it backed the management of British Steel when the first strike in fifty years broke out in January 1980. The strikers went down to defeat in four months.[123] When the coal miners threatened to walk out in February 1981, the government backed off and began accumulating stocks in anticipation of a future slowdown. Ruling out a more confrontational approach was a new wave of murderous IRA outrages – the assassinations of Thatcher's adviser Airey Neave and of Lord Mountbatten,

which were followed by months-long hunger strikes by the imprisoned terror-
ists. Following these foul deeds, the outbreak of race riots in Bristol (St.
Paul's), London (Brixton), and Liverpool (Toxteth) seemed the harbinger of still further
unrest.[124]

Yet by the beginning of 1982, the worst of the recession was over and calm
had returned. Unemployment gradually began to level off, inflation fell, and industrial growth resumed – thanks in part to the export boom sparked by high
American interest rates and an overvalued dollar. Rust-belt industry was ravaged in much of Britain, but growth had been restored without rekindling inflation. Though in retrospect this can be seen as a turning point, it set the United
Kingdom on a course that might subsequently have been reversed without the
fortuitous intervention of a "crisis" in a long-neglected island outpost of sheep-
farming off the South Atlantic. However, it would have taken more than victory
in a bully little war over St. Pierre and Miquelon to save the French experiment
with Socialism in One Country.

Its failure, more striking to contemporaries than Thatcherite success, led immediately to regime change in France and drove home to the rest of Europe the
unmistakable lesson that the economic tide could not easily be bucked. The
common policy of the left was supposed to have taught something different: the
commanding heights of industry were to be taken over by the state, income redistributed to stimulate demand, and a "self-management" regime installed at the
factory level to boost morale and productivity and to encourage democratic decision making "from the bottom up." French economic and political leadership
could then take Europe by storm. Instead, breakdown began almost immediately, starting with the ill-conceived buildup of the state industrial and financial
sector. In 1982, the sweeping program nationalized 36 private banks, two investment banks, and eleven industrial firms. Thereafter, the public sector of industry
employed nearly a quarter of the work force and produced nearly a third of total
output.[125] Three motives figured in the nationalization process: a need to support ailing branches of manufacturing, a wish to have a laboratory for social
experimentation, and a desire to build up a core of vertical trusts and national
champions (*fer de lance*) to lead the economy. Subsidies were lavish and by no
means limited to "modern" or "leading" branches of industry; they were spread
across the economy. Failure was glaring. In 1982 and 1983, losses offset the vast
subsidies and as a result, according to Jonah Levy, company "investment levels
increased not by fifty percent, but by a mere five percent."[126] Performance in the
neglected and capital-starved private sector was substantially worse. As costs –
and especially wage costs – rose, the French share of world industrial exports
dropped from 10.4 percent in 1980 to 9 percent in 1985.[127]

Runaway inflation was the real bugbear. To reflate the economy, the minimum wage was raised 10.6 percent in 1981–1982 (as opposed to an average of
3.3 percent the previous year), the workday was reduced, and 110,000 new civil-
service jobs were created. The economy barely grew, however, and the public
debt rose. The budget, which had previously been balanced, went into the red by

2.2 percent in 1982 and by 3.3 percent the following year. The payments balance also turned sharply negative, and unemployment increased beyond 2 million in 1983. Double-digit inflation forced two devaluations and, as a third one approached, the IMF put France under scrutiny similar to Britain after the failures of 1974–1976. The economy was out of control.[128]

The severe setbacks suffered by the Socialists in the March 1983 municipal elections catalyzed a week of intense secret discussions as to how to handle the breaking financial crisis. Voices from the left called for autarchy and a reign of socialist virtue. The decision to end the experiment and replace it with a new policy of "competitive disinflation" amounted to nothing less, according to Frederic London, than

the acceptance of the rules of the game of an opened up and internationalized economy. The spectacular alignment with the international economic policy standard simultaneously indicated the renouncing of a heterodox policy in a single country, and full insertion in a world economy, the disciplines and constraints of which were acknowledged and accepted.[129]

In other words:

The competitive disinflation turnabout was not simply an ordinary adjustment to a local crisis situation, [but] stemmed from a kind of revolution in the principles underlying a whole vision of the world. [It was] a revolution the effects of which were to become perceptible far outside the narrow field of policy-mix, in all aspects of economic life, and in particular in the new conceptions of profit and entrepreneurship which were paradoxically to be popularized mostly by ... socialists .... Crowding out the old Keynesian social-democratic referential [i.e., approach], the choice [led] ... to ... adoption of a neoliberal referential supposed to be in accordance with the new rules of the game.[130]

There would be backsliding as well as vociferous ideological opposition to nefarious capitalism, but the fact remains that – since the Mitterrand "U-turn," the French left has done as much to open the French economy as the French right.

Like it or not, the French left had to bend to regime change. Reversing the Keynesian budgetary and monetary priorities, competitive disinflation was tantamount to recognition that conducting an isolated expansionary policy by stimulating consumption and increasing public expenditures was a recipe for disaster. To assure full employment, growth had to be led by exports, and export success dictated maintaining competitiveness. Competitive disinflation required exposing the economy to price pressure, accepting German leadership of the European Rate Mechanism (ERM), establishing "credible commitments" (to reduce borrowing costs), lowering interest rates, creating an environment favorable to investors, shifting incomes from households to firms, and cutting deficits. Finally, competitive disinflation was a warning to the nationalized sphere to become profitable or else. The new emphasis on the need for a *franc fort,* for gaining competitive advantage through the market, and for ending social experimentation cast the socialists into "doctrinal disarray," the only escape from which was the policy of *ni, ni* – neither market nor state.[131] Was there an escape from the vise grip?

According to the socialist public banker and economist Jacques Attali, by 1982 Mitterrand was torn between two contradictory ambitions: European construction and social justice. The two-year experiment had proved to the French president that he had seriously overestimated the power of the state in a world of opening markets. Recognition of their strength by no means implied capitulation to it but merely strategic withdrawal. "Only Europe," Mitterrand stated when wheeling his nation around the sharp U-turn to competitive disinflation, "allows politics to restore its power."[132] Having failed in France, socialism would have to be built on a larger scale. The regime change accepted reluctantly, though definitively, at home by Mitterrand would be contested at the level of Europe. Delors would see to that. The presence of Mrs. Thatcher would assure that he did not have the field to himself.

Conclusion to Part II

Needed: A New Integration Theory

MIGHT one claim that the 1970s was the most decisive decade in the history of European integration? Prior to these otherwise dismal years integration had been a draftsman's project, though an admirable one. It was hard to get the design off the board. Progress was slow, difficult, and at times imperceptible. Euro-pessimism prevailed. Did the difficulties boil down to lack of zeal, as true-believing monnetists insisted? – or, more realistically, to bad policy? Once the EEC was up and running, and after the remarkable ease with which the customs union was set up, it became clear that monnetism, functionalism, and Commission-led integration had – by whatever name and for whatever reason – produced an almost unbroken record of nonaccomplishment, and worse. The Community governance machinery was malformed and faulty in operation. The ruinous Common Agricultural Policy, its controlling mechanism, drove a budget process whose strange modalities contorted the development of European parliamentary government. The only endogenous growth path open for the EEC/EC, given its lack of power and resources, was to become organizer-in-chief of corporatist Europe. The first steps in this direction were taken in the 1970s. There were, however, also exogenous development paths.

The revival of intergovernmentalism by means of the new European Council restored power to the states. The Giscard–Schmidt duopoly put France on a convergence course with Germany that much of the rest of Europe would eventually follow. A successful Snake pointed toward eventual monetary union. However, the German model (which France emulated) had begun to show signs of wear and tear. Changes in the international sphere corroded its basic structures. Globalization did not conflict with intergovernmentalism as a force for integration, but it did require accommodation. Globalization would also have a differential effect within the national economies of Europe. It remains to be seen whether intergovernmentalism can continue to function in a large multi-polar Europe unlike the small one run jointly by the French and Germans. The problems faced by the Community in the 1990s provide grounds for skepticism.

A more important growth path ran through the market, which was anchored in rule making and advanced by the competition principle. This approach was a proven success, or at least it had been on a smaller-than-European scale. The policies of Ludwig Erhard set the stage for the first phase of integration. The regime change would set the stage for the second one. Regime change swept away market constraints worldwide, brought down the Bretton Woods system and dollar hegemony, thawed out frozen masses of immobilized capital, increased the volume and value of international trade, and opened and expanded markets on a vast scale. It created pressures that, if not irresistible, at least required better and more tenacious defenses, opened horizons beyond anything previously imaginable, yet also posed new regulatory challenges. Improved institutional design would be needed for the proper operation of the new economy, one also suited to the requirements of modern democracies.

Progress down the liberalization path was uneven during the 1970s but there were gains, some of them intellectual. Jacques Pelkmans's logic explained why "negative" integration worked while "positive" integration nearly always failed. Both the liberal federalist Ralf Dahrendorf and the institutional evolutionist Andrew Shonfield proposed future constitutional designs for the EEC and plotted courses that might lead to them. Such figures were the exceptions. Unswayed by evidence from the 1960s, nearly all expert proposals and projects for reviving the integration process called for bigger and better versions of the policies that had already failed. They entailed buildup of the Brussels bureaucracy and introduction of planning at the European level, with a view toward creating a centralized social democratic Europe resting on the foundation of the mixed-economy welfare state. National bureaucracies and public-sector economic interests posed one obstacle to change along such lines. Another was the disinclination of the public to pay more for "Europe." The MacDougall proposal for a Euro-tax to shift the EC from a "pre-federal" status to a federal one went nowhere.

The auguries for Europe's future were not all good. Although neocorporatist and neomercantilist policies broke down at the national level in the 1970s, they found a new home at the EC. The VERs and OMAs that strapped international trade over the decade thrived in the opaque atmosphere of policy making in Brussels, with its undeveloped democratic machinery and a Commission in need of powerful allies. New forms of protectionism, as Jan Tumlir demonstrated, interlocked producers and governments in mutually reinforcing and reciprocally beneficial arrangements that were difficult to detect or hold accountable, could easily be masked by rhetoric, and were hard for the public to understand. The Commission thus became caretaker for the ailing industries of steel, shipbuilding, and textiles, and it further planned to become the official sponsor of sunrise industry. The industrial policy of the 1970s was the first new "positive" policy competence acquired by the Commission, but others (like R&D) would become offshoots of it.

More positive international trends offset the flight into protectionism. The rise of the multis, the expansion of international trade, and the spectacular increase in capital mobility eroded barriers to growth and also, as demonstrated by Helen Milner, exerted pressure on relatively closed as well as open economies. French producers were no more immune to these trends than American producers. The transition from the old embedded liberal system to the new liberal system did not occur at once but instead would be protracted, uneven, and sometimes even reversed. Advance seldom happened through ideological conversion but rather by the compelling persuasiveness of superior economic performance.

Mrs. Thatcher's Britain supplied one test case, M. Mitterrand's France another. The failure of the French president's attempt to introduce Socialism in One Country probably turned more heads at the time than the British Prime Minister's early struggles with her experiment. Yet what she accomplished would count for more than the botched French effort. Mrs. Thatcher had been well prepared; she would execute brilliantly and (albeit with the help of a little luck) succeeded beyond expectations. Thatcher's triumph in Britain may have been gradual and its reception in other countries difficult, but her undoubted success in turning the United Kingdom around nevertheless commanded respect elsewhere. British methods would become part of a neoliberal policy-making consensus that crossed traditional ideological lines and provided a new basis for cooperation at the European level. The proof of its existence is the adoption of the Single European Act and the enshrinement of the competition principle as its regulatory mechanism. The SEA was largely Mrs. Thatcher's idea and remains perhaps the greatest single contribution ever made to the construction of Europe. It would hardly broaden the integration growth path into a superhighway of change, but at least it would set change off in the right direction.

Part III

Seeking the New Horizon:
Integration from the Single European Act
to the Maastricht Treaty

Introduction to Part III

A New Realm of Possibility

THOUGH hardly recognized as such at the time in a workaday world of men and women absorbed in the worthy task of simply getting by, the drive for European integration – after lying dormant for nearly two decades – revived in the early 1980s with what seems like explosive force. The burst of energy then unleashed would have immediate impact but would also drive change into the coming millennium, alter the context of political and economic development in Europe, and open the door to the new era whose contours are only now taking shape. It re-launched Europe for a second time. Such big events rarely have simple causes. The progress of integration required strong leadership and wise statesmanship as well as a setting propitious to development. The transformation of European institutions grew out of a process of reciprocal interaction with counterposed and complementary national and international events. Brussels became a dynamic agent of change in an ever more complicated three-level game.

Much happened in the nearly six years between adoption of the Single European Act (SEA) of 1986 and the conclusion of the Treaty of European Union (TEU) at Maastricht in December 1991. The EEC started off as a customs union – a market with a common external tariff but still fragmented by a host of nontariff barriers and with no common institutions except the Common Agricultural Policy. By the end of the 1990s the same organization – now confusingly referred to as either the European Community or the European Union – had developed into an embryonic economic and monetary union stripped of many such NTBs, had generated several powerful common institutions, was headed toward the adoption of a single currency, and had begun to wield certain state-like powers. After 1986, regulations drafted in Brussels had the force of law in the member-states. They shaped national legislation on matters large and small, defined the parameters of legislative debate and public discussion, and (after the Maastricht Treaty of European Union) could even determine the outcome of elections. The interventions of the Commission could no longer be simply dismissed as annoyances, distractions from serious business, or bogeymen conjured up by Europhobes. Amorphous and ungainly, the Maastricht document incorporated a plan and timetable for a new European Monetary Union (EMU) and a single currency, and it also contained the traces of a general plan for the central institutions of a European federal government. "Europe" would henceforth present a challenge and a threat to national democracies.

A change in nomenclature reflected a claim to new transnational authority. The Maastricht treaty superimposed over the European Community (EC) the more overtly political and more general descriptor "European Union" (EU). The term implied political as well as economic functions, and it was meant to be sufficiently inclusive to embrace future "competences" as set forth in provisions for the development of common foreign and defense policy as well as internal security policy. The same years also brought two notable geographical expansions. The first included Greece (1981) as well as Spain and Portugal (1986), economically and politically underdeveloped countries for which joining the "club" of Europe became the top national priority. Here the European Union reprised a worthy tradition embarked upon by the coal–steel community in the 1950s. The EU became a vehicle of modernization and democratic development. In the same year as the Iberians entered the Community, the process began that led to the incorporation of the wealthy, social democratic nations of EFTA – Sweden, Finland, and Austria (though neither Norway nor Switzerland, both of which rejected membership). The collapse of the Soviet Union would be prelude to future eastern expansion. Both the poor "southern" and the subsequent rich "northern" expansions fundamentally altered the politics and operation of European institutions. The same result can be anticipated from the future Enlargement.

The regime change that set in during the 1970s provided the necessary backdrop to the progress of the 1980s. The collapse of the Bretton Woods system, the fiscal crises facing the mixed-economy welfare states, and the ineffectiveness of Keynesian remedies – as manifest in the slow and inflationary recovery from the second oil shock of 1979 – dethroned the embedded liberal order that had prevailed since World War II, discredited the conventional economic and political wisdom, and weakened the powerful national bureaucracies and trade unions that had resisted the centralization of authority at the European level.

What would, should, or could replace the old order nationally, regionally, or internationally? The volatility of the world monetary system had been compounded by rapid increases in capital mobility. The situation was unstable, characterized by wide parity swings, and manageable (at least for the medium term) only by means of settlements like the Plaza and Louvre accords of 1985 and 1987 reached by the G-7 nations at summits. These top-level meetings established rules for coordinating central-bank intervention in order to re-align currency values. The international trading system, though formally liberalizing, was beset by networks of official, semi-official, and unofficial restraints that violated or circumvented the rules or undermined them by widespread cheating. Strategies for coping with such financial and commercial problems had to be worked out in theory as well as in practice over the 1980s. The label of "neoliberal" has often been attached to the policy making of that decade. It should be used cautiously. Neoliberalism was less often a preference than the only choice at hand. Many of its most prominent practitioners were professed socialists who – while recognizing its bankruptcy as an economic philosophy – had no new faith or political ideology to substitute for it. Margaret Thatcher's right-wing government was the exception in openly professing the virtues of capitalism.

Mrs. Thatcher reformed Britain as closely as possible along the lines of classical liberal theory. The British example provided lessons that could be learned and methods that could be applied both nationally and regionally on the European continent. By 1985, the success of the Thatcher experiment was widely recognized. Fiscal restraint had slowed inflation, the reduction of union power had begun to restore flexibility to labor markets, and deregulation and privatization had started to yield large and often unexpected dividends: they lowered costs, improved services, attenuated strains on the budget, and generated a new class of shareholders, to mention only a few proximate consequences. The British example was studied carefully by reform-minded figures in governments from Sweden to Spain, in weary welfare states as well as eager modernizing nations. One size did not fit everyone; tailoring was needed.

The pace, extent, modalities, and results of renewal programs varied nationally, as did motivations. Common to each of them was the recognition that economic growth required empowering markets to operate in economic territory long dominated by the state. The process was often anything but straightforward. In most countries, liberal parties either did not exist or had little influence, a calculated outcome of welfare state institution building – be it in social democratic Scandinavia or Franco's Spain. Avowedly socialist (or corporatist) governments often had to take on the task of reducing powerful welfare states and weakening the labor movements that supported and benefited from them. The process could not be accomplished in a day.

It was hard to reconcile Adam Smith abroad with Karl Marx at home. In wealthy nations with well-established and durable political traditions, conflict between the two opposing schools of thought could be blunted by administrative reform. The "marketization" of public services, emulating developments within the private economy, could reduce administrative costs and energize bureaucracies. In countries with weak political traditions and high unemployment, rationalization of the public sector posed huge political challenges. Often liberal reform had to be introduced contrary to the wishes of frightened or ill-disposed electorates. The invocation of the magic word "Europe" could make such change politically palatable. In the absence of this transcendent justification, necessary reform might not have been possible in either Spain or Sweden, to mention only two exemplary cases.

Reform was by no means universal in Europe of the 1980s. Little of it took place in the two big countries run by purportedly business-friendly, right-centrist Christian democratic parties, the "loyal" and original EEC member-states of Germany and Italy. The former lacked a compelling need to rethink traditional approaches, at least until reunification; the latter faced a political mess that could be cleaned up only after collapse of the Soviet Union had reduced the risks of a long-overdue housekeeping. The traditional division between right and left would mean little in the new European "construction," which would be the product of intellectual design, political compromise, ideological consensus, international economic change, and dire necessity.

Forces of Change and Resistance
in 1980s Europe

THE FORCES of change not only welled up from within the Europe of the 1980s but swept in with exceptional force from abroad. The Community faced the escalating challenge of globalization, according to Wolfgang Streeck, in the form of the "regime competition" praised by economic liberals as optimizing welfare but decried by socialists as a race to the bottom.[1] It was precisely this trend that the incoming president of the Commission, Jacques Delors, would try to reverse by building a centralized, federal, and state-directed Europe dedicated to the protection of the "European social model." A man of exceptional energy, political talent, and ideological commitment, Delors was deeply immersed in the French administrative tradition. As president of the Commission, he could normally count on the support of France. He would also have the guile and good fortune to gain critical German support for his agenda. Jacques Delors, like Jean Monnet, was one of a kind, a man whose force of personality and combination of talents would produce otherwise unobtainable results. He, too, would leave a special imprint on the history of European integration. Yet Delors would have to buck powerful worldwide trends. The fate of his work would also depend upon events at the national level, including those within the United States.[2]

THE UNITED STATES AND GLOBALIZATION:
CHALLENGES TO EUROPE

The revolutionary changes that swept over the structure and operation of the European economy in the 1980s and 1990s were international in origin and have ideological, organizational, financial, and technological dimensions. The term "globalization" may through overuse have been deprived of precise meaning, but the development of Europe economic change since the 1980s cannot be understood without it. The influence of the new worldwide phenomenon did not make itself felt all at once but only gradually and unevenly. Lessons drawn from it could be learned only slowly. The tempo and character of its spread depended on decisions made both in Europe and elsewhere.

The expansion of world trade in the 1970s, in spite of stagflation and the proliferation of nontariff barriers to trade, must be attributed to new variables. One of them was a spectacular increase in cross-border capital flows. Another was a succession of dramatic advances in microprocessing that reduced manufacturing costs, improved design and performance, and stimulated product development in the booming fields of consumer electronics, communications, and information technology, as well as in manufacturing generally. Change on the American scene was the third critical ingredient in the making of globalization. It began almost spontaneously, had little to do with doctrine or ideology, and had only limited scope for application in the national political cultures of Europe, which were smaller, more tight-knit and homogenous, and less autonomous. What was occurring in the United States could not be overlooked or blocked; Europe had to accommodate it. In a restricted sense, the reign of TINA ("There Is No Alternative!") had begun. Unless and until Europe adapted from within, it would lose the luxury of choosing and become increasingly dependent upon the United States.

The dismantlement of the private American telephone monopoly AT&T, or "Ma Bell," and the deregulation of the huge airline and trucking industries in the final years of the Carter administration (1976–1980) were the first signs of what would become an immense force for change. The dissolution of such concentrations of market power produced huge cost savings as well as remarkable improvements in service. These breakthroughs owe much to the tireless missionary effort of a brilliant, self-effacing, and still inadequately recognized Cornell University economist, Alfred Kahn, who after appointment as chairman of the Federal Aviation Authority simply abolished the agency. Deregulation grew more broadly out of separate legal actions pursued through the courts and belongs to a special, bipartisan antitrust tradition of the United States. The approach was only loosely connected to any contemporary overall economic or political philosophy.[3]

The deregulation of *finance* was an especially powerful motor of economic progress. Developments in the field paralleled those in industry. The lifting in 1980 of the infamous Regulation Q was a beginning. By limiting interest on passbook accounts, Reg Q had for over a decade cheated widows and orphans out of their mites, had even longer subsidized country-club memberships for savings-and-loan bankers throughout the land, and had more importantly given the federal government access to a vast pool of discounted money. With Reg Q off the books, savers could benefit from market rates. Eliminated thereby was also the distinction between savings accounts and money market funds as well as between banks and other consumer finance institutions. Soon proliferating in number and variety, they would breed a spate of new financial instruments and also generate the markets for them.[4] Credit exploded. The return on and the costs of capital both sank. The velocity of transactions of all types accelerated rapidly. The deregulation of brokerage, the availability of new tax-deferred savings and pension plans, the creation of new investment vehicles, and the reduction of transactions costs across the board greatly increased the amplitude of the capital market and spread equity participation broadly through society. Securitization replaced banking at the center of finance.[5]

Appointed by President Carter in 1979 as chairman of the Federal Reserve Board, Paul Volcker was another surprising agent of change. By introducing the targeting of monetary aggregates, he hit upon a powerful new tool of economic management. Though a trained economist, the officially Democratic but essentially nonpartisan Volcker was often called a monetarist. The term must not be understood in the Friedmanite sense: Milton Friedman advocates restricting central bank independence by limiting expansion of the money supply to increases in productivity. Uninfluenced by any specific economic school, the new Fed chief broke inflationary expectations simply by impressing the markets with a come-what-may determination to limit expansion of the money supply to the long-term growth rate. Volcker demonstrated convincingly that a well-conducted monetary policy was more reliable than fiscal "fine tuning." Slowly but surely, power over macroeconomic policy would gravitate from the fiscal-minded Council of Economic Advisers and the Department of the Treasury to the monetary-minded Fed. Money gained a new measure of influence in government as well as in the economy.[6]

The American recovery from the 1980–1982 recession was rapid, disinflationary, and rested on a changed economic and political context. The upswing marked a turning point for the new pro-market dispensation. Reagan administration policies should not be confused with classical liberal prescriptions. Overall government spending increased sharply; budget deficits grew ominously; the trade balance titled sharply downward; industrial policy and protectionism were not discouraged; consumer protection fell into disrepute; and secrecy replaced openness in the process of government. The doctrine known as "Reaganomics" involved resort to an ad hoc and somewhat inchoate bundle of predilections and prescriptions. The key policy measures were largely uncoordinated, the work of influential figures in both parties and of Capitol Hill, as well as the Fed and the White House. Gut reaction trumped sound economic reasoning in the Cowboy Capitalism of the 1980s.[7]

Yet Reaganomics worked. Volcker's tight money policy cut down inflation from 16.9 percent in 1980 to 3.2 percent in 1983. It fell another 1.9 percent in 1986 after the economy had revived. The 1981 tax cut marked the beginning of the "seven fat years" of prosperity that followed. Growth – steady, though only slightly above average for a recovery cycle – was not accompanied by a resurgence of inflation. Wages grew, though not much. The number of jobs increased and everyone seemed to work harder. The pace of innovation stepped up. The development and application of new technologies brought wide-ranging change in social organization and values. The bedroom communities located between Stanford University and the undistinguished suburban city of San Jose turned into Silicon Valley, spread, and (in a manner of speaking) would engulf much of the San Francisco Bay Area over the coming decade. Something distinctly new and worthwhile, of large though ill-understood relevance to Europe, was now afoot. "Supply-side" economics got much of the credit for the results. What did it amount to?

It involved a self-conscious rejection of the Keynesian emphasis on stimulating aggregate demand by means of budget deficits and easy money, as well as a relearning of the obvious – like Molière's bourgeois gentleman, M. Jordain, discovering to his amazement that he had been speaking prose his entire life. "Indeed," according to Reagan's former director of the Council of Economic Advisors, Martin Feldstein,

much of our supply-side economics was a return to basic ideas about creating capacity and removing government impediments to individual initiative that were central in Adam Smith's *Wealth of Nations* and in the writings of the classical economists of the nineteenth century [that] has characterized most economic policy analysis during the past two hundred years.[8]

Yet the supply-side economics of the 1980s can be considered in two respects original. The emphasis in the bipartisan 1981 tax reform bill, the decade's most important single piece of legislation, was on "changing marginal tax rates to strengthen incentives for work, saving, investment, and risk taking." It brought a 25-percent reduction in across-the-board income-tax rates, breaks for the two-income family, cuts for long-term capital gains, new tax-deferred savings accounts, the indexation of tax brackets, and (for business but also, indirectly, to benefit the stock market) accelerated depreciation schedules and tax credits for research and development. The tax bill may not have made it possible to get rich quick, but it offered powerful incentives to innovation, promoted savings, and – by making credible commitments – reduced transactions costs and encouraged long-term investment. The tax incentives also offset a third of the projected increase in the budget deficit. The new revenue came almost entirely from the top brackets. The wealthy, whose tax rates dropped, actually paid a larger part of the bill out of new earned revenue. Over a period of eight years, the Reagan administration also reduced the nondefense share of the federal government from 9.3 percent of GNP to 7.4 percent, thus reversing a 30-year trend, freeing resources for tax reductions, and shrinking programs with adverse effects. Henceforth there would be less opportunity for security in the public sector and more chance for rewards in the private one.

Finally, one must consider the personality of Reagan himself, which through some strange chemistry built confidence. The former film star said little and wrote even less that sheds light on what he might have been thinking. The oft-peddled notion – that, because his economics education at Eureka College (in rural Illinois) ended in the 1920s, his mind was untainted by Keynesianism and when activated by a question would, as it were, "default" to the side of classical economics – may be emotionally reassuring but will not hold much water. It is by no means obvious that Reagan understood what his key policy makers were up to. A long string of angry resignations indicates that these figures disagreed vehemently among themselves over basic issues of policy. Mechanisms for coordination were weak. Volcker had little contact with anyone at the White House. Unhappy with the general situation and especially about the gaping budget deficit, he resigned in 1987 rather than accept another term.

There was no Reaganaut brain trust – except, perhaps, after hours on Fridays at a trendy watering hole named "Michael 1" in New York's financial district, where a thirsty group of Chicago-trained economists, business journalists, and men-about-town gathered for cocktails and discussion. Robert Mundell and Arthur Laffer were the leading lights among them. Alan Greenspan put in the occasional appearance. The steadies were the journalists Robert Bartley and Jude Wanninski. Two clear-cut conclusions emerged from the intense, invigorating, and slightly boozy intellectual debate: that the Philips curve, which predicated a trade-off between inflation and unemployment, did not work; and that the Laffer curve, which postulated that tax reductions would increase revenues, did. This became the favorite theme of the *Wall Street Journal* editorial page and, because experience seemed to confirm it, of the Reagan administration as well. Dead reckoning, seat-of-the-pants navigation worked. An "X-factor" also helps account for Reagan's success. His mind operated in a dimension normally unfamiliar to politicians, the celluloid plane. It enabled him to speak vividly of seeing dazed, living skeletons staring meaninglessly into space at the liberated concentration camp in Dachau – even though, having spent the war in Hollywood, the closest he had ever been to the place was East Los Angeles. Or to conjure up visions of an America protected from nuclear war by an impermeable prophylactic of a new generation of awesome space-age weapons powered by technologies of the future. Compared to such leaps of the imagination, a belief that unimpeded market forces would work as posited in classical economics was not much of a stretch. Thus he openly welcomed the Schumpeterian gale of creative destruction (which, in the first two years of his presidency, turned whole swaths of his native Midwest into a rust bowl) and publicly reveled in the destruction of the striking air controllers' union. One sensed that here was someone who could, for whatever reason, do what other politicians could not do, a man who could be counted upon to succeed where others were bound to fail. Margaret Thatcher was among the President's most rapt admirers.

The administration's openhanded pro-business approach and its unqualified support for "flexible labor markets" helped trigger a heavy influx of foreign industrial investment into the United States. Even in the pro-market late 1980s, when American capital poured into Europe, the flows remained strongly positive, putting upward pressure on the dollar. The European fear of American financial takeover, as things turned out, was wholly misplaced. The misperception was hardly unique. As shirtsleeve politicians on rural hustings fanned the paranoid delusion that inscrutable Japanese were secretly buying up (and somehow actually transshipping) Midwestern farmland to the foothills of Mt. Fuji, the European takeover of U.S. companies passed quietly unnoticed by the American public. The inflows of foreign capital set off a boom that would persist, with only a slight interruption in the early 1990s, for nearly another two decades. Rapid American growth – due in part to heavy investment by Europeans themselves – would present a daunting economic challenge to ancient ways. Retreat from change was impossible. Relentless, ongoing pressure for adaptation would be applied both nationally and regionally.[9]

The years between the Single Europen Act (1986) and Maastricht (1992) brought the dawn of a new era already opening elsewhere to Europe – a gradual backlighting of a distant horizon whose contours and features would only over time become visible, take shape, and acquire color. Impetus to reform derived from abroad: from the United States (and Japan) and, less remotely, from Great Britain; it arose from access to new money and the competition of transplanted foreign firms. The progressive elite of European technocrats, statesmen, politicians, and top-level CEOs were not a driving force for change. Nor did change stem from within the bowels of European finance or industry – which generally favored competition in principle but often sought protection in practice – or even from the public itself. Growth and adaptation *did* occur in a number of places: in emerging fields of service and manufacturing, in branches and firms subject to privatization and deregulation, in reformed sectors of public service, and in markets influenced by rules and regulations imposed at the European level. Innovation nevertheless remained weak.

Only Britain can be said to have turned a corner in the 1980s; elsewhere, accommodation to new world conditions – while often recognized as being necessary – encountered barriers or pitfalls and so remained partial. The 1980s were not tranquil. They opened with a paralyzing stagflation, and the worldwide stock market collapse of October 1987 nearly knocked the wind out of the international economy at the end of the decade. The period closed economically in 1992 and 1993 with wild speculative attacks on European currencies that threatened to wreck the EMS and introduce a new era of monetary disorder. The 1980s also brought the first in a series of large-scale waves of industrial and financial reorganization – as well as their unhappy accompaniment, massive unemployment. The nature and extent of underlying change, and the reforms needed to meet its challenges, would become clear only as the long day drew on.

MONSIEUR JACQUES DELORS MEETS EUROPE

The progress of integration over the years between the Single European Act and the Maastricht treaty will long be associated with the name of the high-strung, overbearing, rude, thin-skinned, dynamic, inexhaustible, creative, independent, deeply mystical, outwardly conventional, elusive, and maddening though irreplaceable loner who became president of the European Commission in 1985 and (thanks to reappointment in 1989) would remain in office until 1993, when reelected to a third term, of which he served two years. An undeniably great figure whose place in the Euro-pantheon is second only to Monnet's, Jacques Delors realized many of Walter Hallstein's dreams. He rescued the Commission from indolence and put the collective body of Euro-guardians in the front ranks of the drive to integrate Europe. Yet Delors was more than merely a successful bureaucrat. He intended to construct a powerful new, united "Europe" that was immune to globalization and strong enough to contest the international leadership of the United States. To do so, however, he had to rebuild and reconfigure at the European level a latter-day equivalent of the embedded liberal regime washed away in the 1970s. This was both unrealistic and unwise. In the futile attempt to realize his vaulting ambitions, he would be a catalyst to changes that (on the one hand) were more enduring and beneficial than anything he personally planned or directed but that (on the other) subverted the values he held and the policies he espoused.[10] The Europe he bequeathed his successors was both economically more liberal and politically weaker than the one he tried to build.

Community institutions were not in good shape when Delors arrived upon the scene. In the fallow years from 1972 to 1985, the growth of the EC budget had outpaced that of member-nation GDP by a factor of two and, as a percentage of budgetary outlays, had risen from 1.7 percent to 2.8 percent. The number of personnel had tripled.[11] Who, or what, was the new Brussels civil servant? "He is a bureaucrat without a country," a reporter for the *Wall Street Journal* snidely commented, and

for the past thirty years he has written rules that nobody had to follow. He has pronounced upon matters nobody particularly wanted him to pronounce upon. He has invented jargon nobody understood. He has been well paid, well fed, and universally mistrusted by the people who employed him. He was, and is, a Eurocrat.

What to do? The answer would not be easy:

the postwar founders of the European Community invented three cumbersome and mutually incompatible bureaucracies, spread them inconveniently around three capital cities, and spent much of the communal budget translating and trucking around nearly one million pages a year of rules, regulations, suggestions, and admonitions written in [various] languages – only to have each country's own bureaucrats ignore them. (The rest of the budget went into agriculture, including payments to farmers that the Eurocrats called 'monetary compensatory amounts.' That means 'cash.')

In fact, the indictment continues, "for a quarter of a century or so, the twelve nations agreed on nothing else but this: The pseudo-government they had created and set up in Brussels should have no real power."[12] Delors put an end to such contemptuous dismissals. He might not have made the Commission (or the Community) universally respected, but he did make it feared. According to the *Journal*'s reporter, he "put the Brussels bureaucrat in the driver's seat." Or so it seemed from the outside. Delors would retain his own tight grip on the wheel.

Jacques Delors had trained at the French *Plan de Modernisation et d'Équippement* and was a student of the "Monnet method." Impatient with customary bureaucratic procedures, Delors, like Monnet, formed an elite team loyal to him personally rather than to a particular institution or ideological tradition, and he vested team members with the authority needed to turn ideas into action. He relished cutting big deals with other power brokers. Delors lacked the time or inclination to operate in any other way. Within the Commission he dealt with key figures like Lord Arthur Cockfield (who drafted the Single European Act), Sir

Leon Brittan (the powerful competition commissioner), and Martin Bangemann (Brittan's counterpart for industrial policy) as a sultan might have handled powerful satraps. Ray MacSharry, the tough and skillful Irish commissioner for agriculture, was the exception; he and Delors could not abide each other. The Irishman ran what for all practical purposes was an independent operation. Delors largely ignored most other commissioners. On overall policy, the influence of the Commission as a college was slight. Delors relied on the members of his predominantly French and completely *francophone* cabinet to corral the directors general and various civil-service chiefs of the remaining 34 branches of the administration, most of whom resented being left "out of the loop." Jacques Delors could hardly have ended the Commission's long hibernation without arousing growls of anger and howls of protest. Blisters did arise on the tender feet of the sleepy, cosseted Euro-administrators he put through "forced marches"; the Delors experience was acutely painful for them. But the well-paid nerds – who earned (net) between 72 percent and 89 percent more than comparable German civil servants – had their revenge:[13] the Commission remained unreformed.

It was thus incapable of adequately discharging the new "competences" it claimed after 1986. Three of the five structural funds were lodged in different Directorates General (DGs), which ran them according to their own particular logic. The information DG was generally regarded as a disaster, and DG V, the social directorate, was not far behind. There was duplication of activity between the directorates for high technology ("a self-sustaining empire"), the internal market, competition, industrial policy, and information – as well as a proliferation of small directorates such as those for the Consumer Protection Service and the Task Force on Human Resources. In "framework policy areas" (research and development), "there had been an explosion of new tasks with which the services had not caught up. The large fisheries DG had copied its organigram [organizational chart] from another directorate and was in the process of hiring staff simply to fill the empty boxes."[14] No less than three separate entities dealt with foreign policy issues. There were on the one hand too many big fish – "generals," "colonels," and senior noncommissioned officers, all of whom needed jobs to match their titles – and on the other hand a spreading plankton mass of temps, part-timers, private contractors, vendors, and stringers.

The biggest problem of all was that it was impossible to penetrate much below the surface and explore the lower depths. Such was the conclusion of the "screening" or evaluation procedure conducted in 1985 by Jacques Delors's trusted deputy, Pascal Lamy. It was still unfinished when Delors stepped down nearly a decade later. Although he had galvanized the Commission into action as a political actor, he had not even attempted to strengthen it institutionally.[15] When Sir John Hoskins pointed to the existence of fraud at the Commission in the course of his annual speech as chairman of the British Institute of Directors, Delors threatened him with a lawsuit, even though the board of auditors estimated that CAP fraud ranged from between 8 percent and 25 percent of total Community income.[16]

Jacques Delors was no friend of economic or political liberalism.[17] He regarded it as a threat and – if his grander rhetorical flights are to be taken seriously – little more than a cloak for an Anglo-Saxon plot to undermine the European way of life. Delors danced to a drummer of his own. Like Monnet he was, within the French context, an original: a figure at the very apex of power who lacked customary academic credentials and whose exceptional talent was political and economic deal making at the transnational level. He would make his mark as a political operative. Unlike his role model, Delors did not fashion himself as a Doer, the purely practical man of action, but as a Doer who was also a Thinker. He harbored a grand design for Europe and was not ashamed to articulate it.

Clarity was not his strong point; "Delphic" is the description most often applied to his utterances. Nor was consistency. As Ralf Dahrendorf once put the matter, Delors's "prescriptions [are] an astonishing mixture of Keynes and Friedman – of demand- and supply-side economics, or as he [himself] puts it, a 'judicious blend of different instruments'."[18] It is often necessary to extract the meaning of his words from the rhetoric infusing and engulfing them in order to figure out what Delors is driving at. His ideal future Europe would be conservative rather than liberal in inspiration and would favor stability over growth, risk aversion over high returns, tradition over experimentation, the familiar over the exotic, the predictable over the potential, and a regulated over an open society. The ideal federation he had in mind would have resembled France (more precisely, his version of a humanized France) – partly Germanized and writ large.

Its essential characteristics boil down to the following. A Euro-elite at the center of power would rule, governing through a supercharged Commission. Though respecting such rituals, trappings, formalities, and procedures as needed to acquire "democratic legitimacy," the executive board would be the source of all important economic and political policy making. The reach of this new Euro-directorate would extend far beyond anything envisaged by the drafters of the American Constitution for the federal government and include extensive powers of intervention analogous to those exercised in contemporary mixed-economy welfare states. The macroeconomy would be steered, and at least partly planned; the competition principle would be nothing more than a guide to economic decision making. European priorities would be influenced by suppositions about how markets behave, but outcomes would not be determined by them. Instead, policy parameters would be set at the top and the scope of permissible market operation would be circumscribed on the basis of moral and ideological conviction. Implementation would be by means of industrial policy, research and development policy, regional policy, and (above all) labor market policy.

For Delors, the need for solidarity was of commanding importance. The existence of a "European social model" had to be safeguarded – whether through protection, income transfers, or intervention at the level of firm and shop floor.[19] It follows that disruptive change must be contained and that power must be concentrated at the center. "Subsidiarity," written into the Maastricht treaty as a guiding principle of Community policy, had a special meaning to the president of the Commission. Although generally understood as limiting the centralization of authority to those instances in which it could not be better exercised locally or nationally, Delors maintained that subsidiarity had to be authorized administratively at the European level before taking effect; in the absence of a strong central framework harmonizing rules and regulations, it would otherwise become divisive and undermine the integrity of European institutions.[20] He would apply the subsidiarity principle only in this convoluted sense.

As the hapless minister of finance during the early months of the misbegotten Mitterrand experiment, Jacques Delors learned the hard way about the difficulties of introducing Socialism in One Country. It is an exaggeration to say that he expected to introduce it at the European level merely by the exercise of political power. He also viscerally understood that deficit spending could lead to inflation and loss of control; he was always for hard money. He stood in awe of technological systems, recognized the need for marketplace competition (if only with circumscribed markets), and appreciated the importance of financial incentives. Delors's purpose was not to topple business but to enlist it into partnership under central political direction.

Delors has often been described as a Euro-Colbertist, but he has identified himself as a disciple of the corporatist Catholic "personalism" of Emmanuel Mounier. However, his many attempts to explain the linkage between the philosopher's ideas and his own policies tend to get snarled up in wooly opacity or to dissipate entirely.[21] Delors's personal political and economic viewpoint would seem to coincide closely with that lucidly presented in the economic tract *du jour*, Michel Albert's *Capitalism versus Capitalism: How America's Obsession with Individual Achievement and Short-Term Profit Has Led It to the Brink of Collapse*, an exaltation of the superiority of German corporate capitalism over the "Anglo-Saxon" variant.[22] Albert vaunts the "Rhenish" approach as a model for Europe. His message has been the mantra of the non-Marxist left, especially the French "Second Left." Its simple message – that socialism is about worker control, not about state ownership of the means of production – has been a recurrent theme for twenty years. Its distinctive method – the use of state power to promote decentralization and social enfranchisement at the local level – as well as its specific injunctions are deeply imbedded in Delors's thinking.

Whether one chooses to characterize his views as personalist, liberal associationalist, or Second Leftish, Delors envisaged a stronger and more humane France, with a state-directed modern industry but run along cozy, corporatist German lines. Among the prominent leaders of the era, he felt really comfortable only with Helmut Kohl.[23] Nor was anti-Americanism a chance companion of Delors's campaign to instill Euro-patriotism; it was at the heart of the endeavor. He was certainly an odd "neoliberal."

Delors's presidency divides into three chapters that, if examined separately, appear to lack coherence. It is nonetheless important to look at them one at a time, as the impact of each was different. The Single European Act (1986) was the first great accomplishment of the Delors presidency. It rested heavily on the work of others and was Thatcherite in inspiration. The Big Idea behind the SEA was the elimination by 1992 of all nontariff barriers to trade. It also contained provisions pointing the way to an economic and monetary union as well as further institutional reform. A wave of free-market enthusiasm buoyed the policy. Delors viewed the Single European Act as a vehicle for advancing his agenda: valuable for promoting economic growth (and, he hoped, for building high-tech Euro-champions) but also for bolstering the powers of his office. Coupled to the SEA were provisions replacing the Luxembourg Compromise with new procedures introducing qualified majority voting.

The second chapter of the Delors presidency opened with a campaign to strengthen the Commission. It resulted in the adoption of the "Delors Packet," a bundle of linked measures he deftly navigated through the Council. It brought about the greatest single reform of the Brussels administrative machinery ever undertaken, a 1988 deal that re-directed a portion of community revenue from the ill-starred Common Agricultural Policy into new Structural Funds. The packet thus represented the boldest attempt ever to deal with the rot at the core of "Europe." At the same time it introduced a new politics of patronage into the Community that would both corrupt and create a set of new entitlements no better than the old ones it replaced – and so provide enough "pork" to turn the Club Med nations of the southern enlargement into clients of the Commission. The Delors Packet also raised the overall Community budget and set up a planning procedure that increased Commission autonomy.

The third main chapter concerned the Maastricht treaty. The legacy of this project, the most ambitious since the Treaty of Rome, would be even more ambiguous. It provided for the creation of a new monetary union and a single currency – which were intended to serve as the substructure of a future European state – but also for two new "pillars" to complement that of the "economic one" already in existence. One was to be for foreign and defense policy, the other for domestic security policy. The treaty also included new "competencies" as well as an optional social charter. Even though the Maastricht document was obviously meant to serve the purpose of European state building, the relationship between the two new pillars and the monetary union was obscure. Most confusing of all, the treaty erected two separate but related entities: an economic community and a larger political union, the relationships between which were not properly articulated.

Delors's attempt to organize a federal Europe from the center was probably doomed from the outset. It had become apparent by the 1970s, according to Wolfgang Streeck, that an integrated international market economy did not require the creation of a supranational state, and economic integration thus became ipso facto identical with liberalization: the "elective affinity" between nationalism and liberalism could then come into play, the specter of supranational interventionism be banished, and the national state receive a new lease on life. Apart from the fact that the diversity of national interests and traditions stood in the way of Euro-state building, Streeck adds, the governments of the era were keen to shift responsibility for tough decision making back into the private sphere. Thus the prevailing trend was not a transfer of power to the Brussels institutions but to supranational agencies "operating in the mode of technocratic regulatory authorities." The result was the creation of a

multilevel political economy where politics is decentralized in national institutions located in, and constrained by, integrated competitive markets extending far beyond their territorial reach and [supported by] supranationally centralized institutions ... dedicated to implementing and maintaining those markets.[24]

A regional organization like the EC/EU was caught betwixt and between.

Yet the scenario had to play itself out. Delors would try to build Europe against a background of Thatcherite reform as well as in the face of continental efforts to modernize the welfare state. The 1980s would be the scene of struggle between market and institution, both nationally and at the level of Europe. It would intensify in the 1990s – paralyzing the reform of the Community and setting policy on a potentially ruinous course – but still not derail the long-term trends spotted by Streeck. Delors's attempt to reverse the tide would in the end merely discredit the EU and jeopardize European integration.

8

Mrs. Thatcher, Europe, and the Reform of Britain

MRS. THATCHER's Britain was the pacemaker of adaptation to regime change in the 1980s and a model for Europe. She in fact reformed the British economy and public administration more thoroughly than has yet been possible anywhere on the continent. At the same time, the Single European Act of 1986 provided the first impetus to liberalization since the creation of the Common Market. The SEA had vast implications. It opened Europe to the competition not only of private and public markets but of private and public regimes as well. The single market project thereby not only contributed to growth and stability; in addition, it served as an agent of change in modernizing nations and gave a new lease on life to the besieged welfare state. Taken together, the U.K. example and the SEA program set a wave of reform in motion that, though dikes have been built to contain it, continues to exert a tidal pull.

Two sharp spurs prodded free-market reform in Europe in the 1980s and 1990s. One of them, a fiscal crisis, cut sharply into muscle after the second oil price shock of 1979. The pain was felt by small, wealthy, democratic nations with open borders, highly regulated economies, and generous social protection like the Nordic welfare states. In such countries, runaway government spending had produced ballooning budget deficits that – instead of stimulating the use of idle productive resources in a Keynesian manner – accelerated inflation, raised the costs of wages and imported raw material, eroded productivity, impeded both export and overall growth, and accelerated the velocity of the stagflationary maelstrom. At stake was national competitiveness. To restore it required the reform if not the transformation of the welfare state. Part of the remedy was to join the European Community.

The other spur cut even deeper but set modernization off on a gallop in countries needing to catch up with the rest of Europe – Greece as well as the two Iberian nations, which later entered the Community in the mid-1980s. Called for was not so much the reform of existing institutions as the creation of new ones. Needed was not just structural change but a process of modern nation building. Sought was membership in the Community, not only for aid but for help in imposing needed rules and regulations to substitute for laws that could be made democratically only in more mature political systems. An EC-driven economic opening accompanied reform on the domestic front.

For a brief, exceptional, and decisive period of policy making, the Community set itself on an evolutionary course heading toward the formation of the kind of large, minimally regulated, decentralized, market-driven interstate federal union that might have met with the approval of Friedrich Hayek. The Single European Act of 1986, designed and drafted by Lord Arthur Cockfield (a close associate of the British prime minister), pointed in that direction and sometimes still does even now. The SEA is an elaborate enactment containing provisions that open the European Community to several different possible lines of development, but at its core is the stipulation that some 300 nontariff trade barriers (NTBs) were to be removed by 1992 in order to transform the EC, up to then little more than a partial and backsliding customs union, into a single market.

The remit of the act covered the public as well as the private sphere and included state aids, public contracting and service provision, public norms, standards and regulations (both public and private), agreements in restraint of trade, and the competition principle. "For those of us who believe in markets," commented one enthusiastic classical liberal economist, "the single market based on the White Paper and the Single European Act is a fantastic dream, a pure exercise in deregulation, the devolution of power to the market and economic federalism [and] one of the best ... blueprints for economic cooperation that has ever been devised."[1] The enormous upside potential of the SEA was cumulative rather than one-time, capturing static efficiency gains, the dynamic effects of increased competition, and economies of scale. Such a wealth-creating policy implied social as well as economic benefits – that is, not only fatter bank accounts but more and better hospitals. A more efficient and productive Europe would, economic liberals hoped, also be happier and more self-confident.

One special circumstance boded well for the SEA. In the landmark *Cassis de Dijon* decision of 1979, the European Court of Justice established the principle of mutual recognition – thanks to which the Commission lost the authority to set single binding standards for the Community as a whole. Henceforth, the norms of any member-state would have to be recognized throughout the EC unless they failed to meet certain minima. Recognizing the legitimacy of a variety of means for arriving at the same end, *Cassis* constituted a triumph for the federalizing as opposed to the centralizing approach. By subjecting regulatory standards to competition, the court's ruling also empowered the consumer to make decisions that had previously been made on his or her behalf by producers or governmental authorities and thus also reduced the need for bureaucratic decision making.[2]

The Single European Act, which required open bidding for public contracts regardless of nationality, extended the *Cassis* principle into whole regulatory systems – no trivial matter, since government purchasing amounted to 15 percent of GDP. The SEA further entailed the free movement of services across frontiers, deregulation of national financial systems, and the eventual creation of a real European capital market. Still more broadly (and assuming governmental responsiveness), it set the stage for competition between preference regimes: trade-offs between stability and opportunity, risk and reward, income and leisure, savings and consumption, and so on. Citizens would then "be free to choose between all sorts of possible environments, from a combination of low income, low social security but a quiet life, low taxes and a good climate, all the way to the high-income, high tax, high blood-pressure rat race that one tends to find in the cold and rainy north of Europe."[3]

MRS. THATCHER AND EUROPE

But who was ready for this free-market paradise? Massive structural adjustment would be required, meaning the rearrangement of ownership and control, plant shutdowns, and unemployment or reemployment. Opposition could be counted upon from workers, managers, government officials, elected representatives, trade unionists and (at the EU) from advocates of regional, industrial, and social policy as well as Jacques Delors. Forward progress was bound to be slow – marked by zigs and zags as well as protracted stretches of inactivity. There were, furthermore, limits to Britain's missionary ability.

Consider, first of all, how little Britain's influence was felt even after ten years of Community membership. Ted Heath, the uniquely Euro-enthusiastic prime minister who negotiated British entrance into the EEC in 1973, remained in office only a year thereafter. The government of his Labour successor Harold Wilson, whose initial membership feelers had been rebuffed by General de Gaulle nearly a decade earlier, rested on a divided party that faced far more pressing concerns, such as an apparently irreversible economic decline. Desperate to catch the right political wind, Wilson resorted to the unprecedented expedient in 1975 of calling for a public referendum on Europe. Although resoundingly endorsing British membership, the referendum was too loosely conducted to provide a clear mandate. James Callaghan – who assumed office after Wilson's unexpected resignation a year later – lacked a majority, had a cabinet packed with anti-Europeans, was cautious by nature, and faced a grueling IMF "work-out." He bypassed the opportunity to join the European Monetary System in 1978.[4]

Consider, second, the lady herself. Culturally and temperamentally, Mrs. Thatcher was an unabashed and unapologetic British patriot with little attachment to continental tradition – especially political tradition, for which she had a pronounced distaste. The same was not always true of European politicians. Some she liked, especially those who behaved like Englishmen. The transfer of British sovereignty to any continental capital city was unthinkable to her, which is to say that she refused to recognize how and why it had already begun to happen. This limited the exercise of European statecraft.[5] She was withal, in the British context, a masterful politician: endowed with superb gifts of language, an uncanny knack for timing, a highly developed sense of the possible, and an almost instinctive understanding of the great underlying strengths and occasional weaknesses of the traditions within which she operated. She was a commanding leader in public as well as an effective one behind the scenes. She had the intellectual vision and depth to earn the respect and win the devotion of an exceptionally capable – though independent-minded and extraordinarily contentious – group of men and women who came to be known as Thatcherites.

A certain parochialism marred her greatness. It was almost as if, to Mrs. Thatcher, not even most Englishmen behaved like Englishmen. Included among the many fallen angels "who had let me down" were one-time allies in the cabinet as well as others dispatched as missionaries to Brussels but who "went native." A stubborn refusal to compromise even with supporters and admirers triggered the party revolt that toppled her.[6] The changes she introduced seem irreversible. Mrs. Thatcher triggered reform from the top down, but it soon also bubbled from the bottom up.

Mrs. Thatcher made British cooperation in the European Community contingent upon a reduced net contribution, a policy to which her Labour predecessors had also been committed. The settlement of this divisive issue at the 1984 meeting of the European Council at Fontainebleau opened the door to full British participation in the EC. The honeymoon soon ended with a nasty public spat between the British prime minister and the man she had supported to succeed Gaston Thorn as president of the European Commission, Jacques Delors. The contretemps occurred at a press conference following the London Council in December 1986.[7] Although the circumstances surrounding the affair are confusing, underlying the dispute was profound disagreement over the future direction of the European Community.

As a third limitation on Britain's influence within the Community, consider that no government on the continent would have dared, as she did, to smash the labor movement – in the United Kingdom as elsewhere, the chief obstacle to reform. Doing so would have inflicted unacceptable damage to the democratic process in some countries and in others might have threatened civil war. Clashes like the titanic Miners' Strike of 1984–1985, the watershed event in Margaret Thatcher's domestic policy, had to be avoided on the European continent; over time, "big labor" had to be co-opted into fictitious partnership with capital or otherwise gradually finessed or marginalized out of power.[8] Whether and how this was and remains possible vary according to circumstance.

For Britain, the results of confrontation with labor have been quite unequivocal. According to the Stanford economist John Pencavel:

It was as if at a relatively brief moment of the electorate's disenchantment with unionism the government seized the opportunity to curb collective bargaining over the next fifteen years ... and to subject it to discipline that has left it debilitated .... By the year 2000, unionization's role in private society looks precarious in light of its difficulty in organizing in new establishments .... Nothing in the writings on unions and industrial relations in the 1970s forecast this change in fortunes.[9]

Margaret Thatcher's European legacy should be less sought in pursuits that involved "disarming the left" than in those directed towards "re-arming the right." One should examine her success in building new institutions whose sound operation has changed mentalities by the exercise of reason, the use of persuasion, and the demonstration of utility and effectiveness. Mrs. Thatcher's fresh approaches did not always achieve the desired goals, nor were they necessarily optimum for the purposes envisaged; nor, when effective, were their consequences necessarily apparent: many impacts were long-term ones. Still, the U.K. experiment merits more than cursory treatment in a history of European integration. According to Andrew Gamble, the Thatcherites were "the first group to grapple with the problems of turning their criticisms of postwar social democracy into practical programs and policies."[10] More important still, the intellectual bankruptcy of European socialism in the face of globalization eliminated any alternative to market-based reform. To protect the welfare state the left, too, would need to draw arrows from Mrs. Thatcher's quiver. The British reform experiment has thus occupied center stage in European integration since the 1980s.

MRS. THATCHER AND THE REFORM OF BRITAIN

While in office, Mrs. Thatcher failed to reshape the Conservative Party in the image of her ideas but did profoundly change the context of British politics. By 1992, Labour leader Neil Kinnock had not only reformed his party but had also accepted the irreversibility of fundamental reforms introduced by the opposition since 1979. The changes included

the sale of council homes and the spread of share ownership, the denationalization of public sector industry, the abolition of exchange controls, and the international integration of financial markets and production; the permanent contraction of manufacturing employment, and the reorganization of work and industrial relations .... [Labour was] in particular forced to recognize that there could be no return to national economic management and welfare programs based on the Fordism of the postwar boom.[11]

The present Blair government built upon what Mrs. Thatcher set out to accomplish, and the Tories have since swung to the right on the question of Britain and Europe.

Margaret Thatcher entered office intellectually well prepared.[12] The most significant confrontation resulting from the Thatcher experiment was not across the picket lines but along the plane of ideas. The policy discourse of the years from 1979 to 1990 brought to light fresh thinking about how modern societies can and should be organized. "The strategy of the Thatcher government," to quote again from Gamble,

identified the national interest and the general interest of capital with furthering the integration of the British economy into the world economy ... [and] obliged all other sectors to prove themselves internationally competitive or go to the wall.... The future of the British economy was tied not to a major revival of domestic manufacturing but to remittances from foreign investment, the growth of internationally tradable services, and the continuation of inward investment flows. Thatcher's policies indeed cost Britain "any coherence it still possessed as a national economic space," but at the same time they made the United Kingdom "the first of Europe's former great powers to relinquish an illusory national economic sovereignty, maintained at great expense, in favor of an unprecedented acceptance of transnational financial and commercial integration."[13]

Mrs. Thatcher's economic policies can only be discussed selectively and with a view to their general European relevance. Common themes run through each of the three main sectors of policy: reduction and reform of the state; privatization and deregulation; and supply-side, especially labor-market, reform. The same is true of the means used to achieve them: creation of cost savings; activation of markets as engines of wealth creation and economic growth; and economic and political enfranchisement of the individual. The main reform fields were labor, home ownership, education reform, medical care and pensions, industry, and finance.

After 1979, the new Tory government's chief policy aims were to reduce the budget deficit, control public expenditure, and slow down inflation. The large majorities produced by the elections of 1983 and 1987 enabled the Prime Minister to proceed with her agenda for what she called the "enterprise culture." Her main concerns in these and following years were to reform labor unions, introduce privatization, and overhaul the public sector. Impressive change had come over Britain by the time Mrs. Thatcher left office. The state-owned sector of the economy had been reduced by 60 percent, over a quarter of the public owned shares of stock, and 600,000 jobs had migrated from the public to the private sector. "Taken together," according to Madsen Pirie, "the privatization program probably marked the largest transfer of power and property [in Britain] since the dissolution of the monasteries under Henry VIII."[14] The foreign impact of Mrs. Thatcher's policies can be attributed partly to their impressive results. The heretofore laggard British economy grew faster in the late 1980s than any in Europe other than Spain; business investment grew more rapidly than in any other industrial economy whatsoever, as did productivity; and profitability also improved nicely. Employment increased by over 3.3 million between March 1983 and March 1990.[15] Many Europeans started to wonder whether the medicine taken by weary Britain might also work for them.

Strike-busting was only one (albeit the least attractive) of the labor components of Mrs. Thatcher's supply-side policy. Another was to reduce the special privileges and coercive power of the trade unions. In successive measures, secondary boycotting was restricted, the closed shop pried substantially open, officials' unlimited immunity from liability for damages circumscribed, the use of the secret ballot increased, and the exaction of political levies made more difficult. The percentage of employees covered by collective agreements declined from 70 percent in 1984 to 54 percent in 1990 and to 48 percent in 1998.[16] The market-opening initiatives of the Thatcher government can be grouped under four main headings, which correspond in a general way with the range and scope of their overall impacts: human resources, where change is diffuse and can only be evaluated over the long term; government services, where institutional lags restrict or impede the operation of the market; the field of production, where hard data provides an acceptable basis for comparison; and finance, where market response can be instantaneous.

The Right to Buy apartments and houses rented from the local government-owned county councils was the only privatization initiative specifically announced in the Tories' 1979 election manifesto. Its overall purpose was social rather than economic: to lift the earthy "prole" into the sensible middle class. This Right to Buy included a spate of measures designed to serve different purposes: increase private home ownership; improve labor mobility; promote economic empowerment and discourage welfare dependency; raise morale; and enhance the condition of, as well as add to, the housing stock while creating a large and liquid market in residential property. Specific measures eliminated rent control, repealed the council housing system, rolled back entrenched local governments, broke up blocs of captive subsidized tenant voters, and stanched the hemorrhaging of public funds. The policy elicited angry protests from tenants upset by rent increases as well as stubborn resistance from Labour-controlled local authorities who could recognize a threat when they saw one. Nevertheless, some 80,000 housing units annually shifted from public into private possession during the Thatcher years, during which the rate of home ownership rose from 57 percent to 68 percent.[17] The policy has been an unquestionable success.

The same cannot be said of educational reform. In this always controversial field, the effort to introduce change met with predictable amounts of resistance from diverse quarters. Though impeded by a division of responsibility and authority between an ambitious national government and entrenched county councils, progress in Britain has nevertheless been marked. The education policy of the Thatcher government turned on the usual concerns about standards, curriculum, and the distribution of decision-making power. Its novel feature was to introduce the concept of parental choice in order to break the monopoly of the education establishment. The idea is often packaged politically in the name of a "voucher system" that assigns parents an entitlement, a rough analogue to the ballot, conferring a right to determine where to enroll their children. The "voucher" in this case was to have been a check made out by the government in the name of a child's parent and made payable to the school of choice. The 1988 Education Reform Act implemented a compromised version of the scheme, which included open enrollment in a wide range of schools and budgeting according to the number of pupils registered. Supplementing this scheme was another one for "grant maintained" (GM) schools, which could opt out of county council funding and administration in favor of direct state support and greater operational autonomy. The GM schools scheme included a wide selection of denominational, traditional private (public in the British sense), specialized technical, and other institutions. While structural reform has been well received and appears to have raised standards, the attempt to define educational content and to impose a standard national curriculum has encountered heated objections, met with little acceptance anywhere, and remains divisive.[18]

University reform has been even more controversial than that of the schools, and its implications are perhaps even more far-reaching. Mrs. Thatcher's policies outraged most academics but also deeply divided the cabinet; any outsider who ventures into the subject area is asking to be skewered. Even the normally intrepid Mrs. Thatcher is loath to discuss the matter in her memoirs. Yet she introduced sweeping changes. Tenure was modified and a student grants system partly replaced with a loan program; universities received the authority to raise money privately and maintain endowments; and national evaluation standards were introduced that encouraged closer contact between the academy and the economy.[19] Business schools became respectable. The tremors from such tectonic shifts still reverberate.

In reforming the public sector, the Thatcher government drew on the "new public management," a set of approaches that involve such devices as the development of internal markets, outsourcing, tendering, and special financial incentives. All found application in the medical field. In Britain, the National Health Service (NHS) was a welfare state icon that even the critical Mrs. Thatcher had to revere publicly. But NHS had a longer payroll than any bureaucracy except the Indian National Railways and the former Red Army, and only slightly better cost control. It also faced unlimited demand for its services. Investigators soon discovered to their surprise that the British health service was in no more of a pickle than other public medical systems of comparable size but of a different design – from which, it had been hoped, the right lessons might be learned. Reform of the NHS began from scratch. Adopted as a first step toward the creation of a genuine internal market for health care, the *provisioning* function was separated from those of *finance* and *purchasing*. Cost and supply could then be linked to specific cases rather than, as previously, merely estimated and allocated globally. Operations thereby became more transparent and open to competition, and services could be delivered more cheaply and efficiently.

One welcome immediate result was to reduce delays in treatment: hitherto the Health Authority had allocated a fixed budget to each hospital and the efficient ones would understandably refuse patients who would involve additional costs but bring in no revenue; under the new system, the hospitals could afford to admit them. Another change, one roughly analogous to the "grant maintained" schools, was the introduction of "trust hospitals." Medical facilities opting for the plan received funding from general tax revenues but became free to set their own pay and staff conditions as well as to sell their services to other health authorities or even to the private sector. In a further move toward the market, general practitioners with large practices gained the authority to contract for patient health care (including nonemergency services) with a view toward cost effectiveness. British reform of the medical system, though hardly an overnight success, was at least a bold attempt to reduce cost without sacrificing service, a challenge faced by health care in all advanced industrial countries.[20]

The reform of unfunded "paygo" (pay as you go) pensions was another common problem, though especially severe in countries with generous social security systems. Prompted by concern with future costs, Thatcher's Britain again took the lead by turning a so-called two-pillar scheme into a three-pillar one. To the first pillar (traditional social security, paid at a comparatively low level) and the second pillar (the State Earnings Retirement Pension Scheme, or SERPS, a state-supplemented income-based contribution scheme), a 1988 act added a third: a voluntary private alternative to SERPS, known as APPs (Approved Personal Pension schemes), along the lines of the American 403(b) and 401(k) defined contribution plans. The creation of private pensions was another application of the "contracting out" mechanism. Thanks to favorable tax treatment, a small state supplement provided as an incentive, and better growth prospects than SERPS, over half of those eligible opted for APPs by the early 1990s, reducing the budgetary burden and providing rich fields in which financial managers could graze. By the mid-1990s, Britain's private pension fund sector accounted for half the European total. The Labour government augmented the private scheme by shifting it from a voluntary to a compulsory basis, requiring employer participation (though not contribution). According to a recent economic study, the private plans have increased household savings, encouraged labor mobility, and – in sharp contrast to every other major industrial nation – ensured that liabilities will be met without an increase in tax rates, which are likely to fall in the future.[21]

Privatization did not figure prominently in the manifesto for the 1979 election. The ground had nonetheless been well prepared for it. Budgetary crises usually prompted action. The popularity of the policy, the savings generated by it (and without which the annual budget deficit could not have been contained), as well as its apparent success in reducing cost and increasing productivity produced a snowball effect. Privatization was a policy whose time had come. It would end only when there was nothing left to de-nationalize. By 1992, two thirds of state-owned institutions had been transferred into the private sector, or 46 enterprises employing 900,000; the only two that remained public, the British Coal Mining Board and British Rail, have also since disappeared.[22] These nationalized companies were failures. They had not brought labor peace but instead had merely shifted union disputes with employers or management to the government, diverting problems that might have been settled through bargaining in the marketplace to the plane of political confrontation. Although a lack of market accountability made it difficult to fathom the full extent of their problems, none of the nationalized companies was competitive.

Although not originally so conceived, privatization turned into a "long-term program for promoting the widest possible participation by the people in the ownership of British industry."[23] Budgetary gains from the sale of public assets had to be balanced against the desirability of creating as many new shareholders as possible. Although in certain cases a small portion of share ownership (for presumed strategic or actual electoral-political reasons) remained with the state, the privileging of beneficiaries, beneficiary groups, or coalitions and alliances of them was specifically disavowed and faithfully enforced as policy.

Privatization had never been attempted before. It required much on-the-job training. No one knew how far it should go; only a small true-believing minority among even Thatcherites initially imagined that the process could extend to "natural monopolies" such as utilities. Since the market for public corporations had never been tested, appropriate offering prices and terms at first had to be divined, guessed at, or in some other manner approximated until trial-and-error learning provided guidance. Privatized entities often had to be restructured before going to market in order to survive or encourage competition. Institutions for re-regulation had to be devised in order to prevent public monopolies from turning into private ones and to handle externalities such as environmental protection. Lack of knowledge and intellectual disagreement on technical issues often forced open new lines of inquiry but also led to serious errors of implementation.[24]

The sorry state of British Leyland, which had been organized in the Wilson years as national champion in the car industry and kept alive on a bipartisan basis since 1975 thanks to 2.9 billion pounds of public money, made the company a tempting candidate for early privatization. By dispatching the dinosaur, the Thatcher government parted with the policy of promoting national champions. In the 1950s and 1960s, the consensus view was that a thriving car industry was vital to national economic health. It was also the hub of a manufacturing complex; its disappearance meant that a network of dependent suppliers would be driven to the wall if necessary to improve British competitiveness on world markets. As elsewhere in manufacturing, the decision to reform set in motion a long-term process. British Leyland turned out to be even more dilapidated than feared. Problems within the once-booming world automobile industry became chronic. The Thatcher cabinet fell before privatization of the hospitalized car producer could be completed.[25] The process would continue through successive waves of reorganization in which component companies have either merged or disappeared. Its end is not yet in sight.

The British National Oil Company (BNOC) was the largest and, from the standpoint of share issuance and marketing, the most challenging case confronted in the first wave of privatizations. The BNOC had been set up by the Labour government in 1976 to explore, produce, refine, and distribute North Sea oil. Although accounting for only 7 percent of total output, BNOC held the right to buy and sell 51 percent of it and enjoyed other privileges which, according to the energy minister Nigel Lawson, discouraged private exploration and development. Conversion raised big problems. Lawson's first task was to turn a "Morrisonian public corporation" into "a straightforward company" under the Companies Act, which first of all required equipping "Britoil" (as BNOC was renamed) with an appropriate balance sheet. Both the Bank of England and Warburgs (the energy ministry's advisors) doubted that the market was large enough to absorb the new issue. After turning back proposals for a share giveaway to all citizens along the line of subsequent Czech or Russian schemes, Lawson went ahead with the disposal of an initial tranche of 51 percent. Rather than sell at a pre-set price as had been done (with mixed results) in earlier offerings, he adopted the method of an underwritten tender – with initial payment preset and the balance due depending on the strike price – a procedure open to criticism as a "payoff" to City (i.e., London financial) interests. On the eve of the flotation, a gloomy offhand prediction made by the all-powerful Saudi energy minister that a fall in oil prices was imminent caused the Britoil issue to tank, leaving 70 percent of the undersubscribed shares in the scorched hands of underwriters. The remainder was successfully floated in August 1985.[26]

Although much smaller than BNOC, British Airways had also been an early candidate for privatization. Its sorry financial state dictated postponement. Hard hit by the 1979 recession, it consumed too much cash to be brought to market in London, where no airline shares had ever been quoted. Taken over in 1981 (while still public) by a management with a reform mandate, British Airways was transformed in three years from among the least to the most efficient world carrier. Peripheral businesses were disposed of, unprofitable routes discontinued, advertising and marketing were upgraded, and productivity improved in every aspect of the business. Threatened with an ultimatum to become competitive or disappear, the labor force – which remained fully unionized – granted larger concessions than anything previously imaginable. Although antitrust violations (which helped bring down the first real aviation discounter, Laker Air) delayed going public until 1987, the issue was eleven times oversubscribed when eventually floated. Over 90 percent of the British Air labor force purchased shares in the company.[27]

In need of more new investment than the government could provide under restrictive public-sector borrowing requirements, British Telecommunications had to be put under the hammer and would set the key precedent for privatization. Although too large for public flotation and with a high public profile that increased political risks should things go wrong, the company could not be vivisected in the manner of "Ma Bell" owing to labor and management resistance. A regulatory regime had to be designed in order to prevent the exercise of monopoly power by the future privatized company. The Office of Telecommunications (OFTEL) was the result; it would limit future rate increases to the rate of inflation, minus a factor that was to be based on gains in efficiency. (This formula pleased the public but might have deprived it of still further efficiency gains.) The flotation of British Telecommunications was a whopping success, as it turned out. Comfortably oversubscribed, it doubled the actual number of shareholders in Britain. " 'Popular capitalism'," according to Nigel Lawson, "became part of the stock-in-trade of Conservative speech making from that moment on."[28] All future privatization issues would be heavily oversubscribed.[29]

No single overriding consideration led to the privatization of the other utilities – gas, water, and electricity – each of which involved different problems and approaches. Results were by no means always satisfactory. British Gas was an easy target. The recently opened North Sea oil beds provided the nationalized company with unlimited access to cheap gas, of which it was the monopoly distributor. It could easily underprice the "town gas" generated as a by-product of coal consumption (of which it had also previously been the monopoly distributor) and still leave ample margin for profit. The result of this pricing windfall was an expansion binge: acquisition of Britain's one producing onshore oilfield, as well as offshore deposits of both oil and gas; and creation of a useless network of retail outlets throughout Britain. Nigel Lawson, the minister of energy at the time and a vigorous advocate of pro-market policies, packed the British Gas board with like-minded members and forced management to dispose of noncore properties. Although unable to lobby support for breaking up the monopoly, he managed to float an issue for a big single company in December 1986. It was a relatively simple operation that netted the Treasury 5.4 billion pounds, even more than Telecom. However, the gas industry was not restructured and the pipeline grid remained under the firm's control.[30]

The de-nationalization of water presented special problems, not the least of them due to the popular belief that the resource should be provided for free, "like air," or that supplies should at least remain in the public domain. A well-intentioned but careless remark made by Lawson during an interview in an ill-advised attempt to win support for his plans – to the effect that, in France, no less a figure than Colbert had privatized the supply of water and still the French had the only world-scale distribution companies – did little to persuade a wary public of the merits of his cause. Mrs. Thatcher's more pithy reminder – that while God might have produced the rain, He certainly did not provide the pipes – probably converted at best only a few souls.

A dire need for an infusion of government money for long-overdue maintenance and upgrading put water privatization on the agenda in February 1985. The principle of "integrated river basin management" governed the most recent reorganization of the utility, one undertaken in 1973 by the Heath government, which divided it into ten regional units. The authorities were also responsible for settling environmental and riparian questions, competencies which (if the distribution companies were to be made marketable) had to be hived off. Somewhat ignominiously for the Office of Water (OFWAT), a new semi-autonomous public corporation (or quango) had to be set up for regulatory supervision before the ten new regional water suppliers could be successfully brought to market. Although the issues were once again all oversubscribed, public opinion surveys continued to register strong objections to privatization of the supposed public good.[31]

Electrical power proved to be the really difficult nut to crack. The problem was political. Under the nationalized *ancien régime*, British Electricity monopolized both the generation and distribution of power. Separating the two functions was not difficult in principle, and twelve regional boards were created to purchase current from the national grid. The problem was that one enterprise, CEGB (the

Central Electricity Generating Board), controlled 95 percent of the power and could crowd out competition from independent suppliers. It could not be broken up because Mrs. Thatcher, an ardent supporter of the British nuclear power industry, was grateful for the help lent her by its management during the Miners' Strike. She was also confident of the technology's merits and convinced that reactor development was necessary for Britain's long-term strategic interests.

By the mid-1980s, the financial markets had become suspicious of atomic power. A purely nuclear generating company could not have been floated. Given the way the industry was configured, the only realistic option was to create two mixed companies, National Power and PowerGen (in addition to the twelve distributors). Unfortunately, the industry had seriously underestimated both the risks of nuclear power and the costs of decommissioning the plants. A debacle ensued. Construction had to be halted, reactors shut down, and plant management (and operating losses) "socialized." A second reorganization straightened out the mess. The industry was divided into a single transmission company and three generating companies; surviving nuclear plants were privatized in 1996; 30 percent of supply was now derived from the new low-cost, gas-fired generators whose introduction had been encouraged by regulators. They kept prices down and forced closure of uneconomical suppliers.[32]

Privatization has not proved to be a panacea, only a resounding success. Costs have fallen overall, though not perhaps quite as dramatically as possible. In special cases like water, where heavy investment was necessary, costs have risen less than they might otherwise have. General quality of service has obviously improved in telecommunications – and at least has not declined in gas, electricity, and water – though estimates of such things are difficult. Both total factor productivity and labor productivity have increased faster in the United Kingdom than elsewhere, partly because of "improvements in working practices on the shop floor."[33] While it may be true that competition rather than privatization accounts for most of the productivity gains, it is difficult to imagine one without the other – at least in the Britain of the 1980s. If companies like British Air made big gains while still public, they did so in the course of preparing to be privatized. Involved also was a degree of "downsizing," to use the then-current euphemism for labor shedding, that no one but Mrs. Thatcher would dare have attempted. Nor were the gains from privatization merely a "one-off event." The characteristic pattern of decline in the rate of industrial growth that followed a sharp initial spurt after the shift in ownership was evidence that rates of increase diminish as idle resources are put to work.[34] The British experience pointed unmistakably to the lesson that incumbent managements resist restructuring where sunk costs are high and so regulation (or re-regulation) is necessary to promote competition. This can occasionally require the heavy hand. "It was not," according to a recent study, "until the early 1990s, when British Gas negotiated specific (and rapidly declining) targets for market share and took several steps to help rival suppliers, that competition really took off."[35] Privatization offered no guarantee of competitive success, as the situation of British Leyland underscores. Those firms that did survive nevertheless pulled abreast of their compeers in the private economy. As employment in the manufacturing industry – some 200,000 in 1980, half of it in the state sector – dropped to less than 75,000 by 1992, with less than a third then employed in the newly privatized firms, "productivity growth in [once] public plants caught up to private plants."[36] Privatization salvaged at least something of the decrepit public sector.

The evidence concerning "contracting out" and more generally the "new public management" based on the creation of internal markets is at best fragmentary. The data suggest that large savings in government operations were made in the 1980s, but also that bigger ones were possible. A large-scale study of trash collection at 305 local authorities demonstrated that costs fell 22 percent when contracts were awarded to private bidders as opposed to 17 percent when awarded on an in-house but competitive basis and that hospitals, when contracting out for domestic services, saved about 20 percent. Compulsory competitive tendering, begun in 1988 at the *national* level, saved 2 billion pounds on the provision of white-collar services. Still further savings resulted from better management, more flexible working practices, more efficient use of capital, and greater innovation spurred by competition. Compulsory tendering at the *local* level produced savings of 10 to 20 percent over previous in-house contractors, which suggests the prior existence of political favoritism. One remove from "contracting out" was Mrs. Thatcher's introduction of private finance initiatives, which involve investing private capital in the provision of services previously supplied by public institutions, like prisons. Private finance initiatives have several advantages: removing investment from the budget allows greater spending as well as risk transference and, if competition is open, offers better value for the money. By reducing both costs and risk, such methods liberate assets freed for better purposes in both the public and the private sphere.[37]

Far-reaching financial reform paralleled changes in government and the economy in Britain during the 1980s. A joint public–private effort with American antecedents, it complemented (and was complemented by) developments in both industry and government and had immediate repercussions both far and wide. The Thatcher government's first move toward financial liberalization was to end foreign exchange control. The importance of the move, according to Nigel Lawson,

is difficult to overstate.... [I]t marked the start of a process of deregulation which embraced the world in general and the European community in particular and ... enabled U.K. firms to invest where they liked,... ensured that investment in the U.K. would yield a worthwhile return, and without [which] The City would have been hard put to remain a world-class financial center.[38]

Allowed to float, the pound actually rose slightly once controls were lifted, providing a plausible short-term argument that they had been superfluous. Still, the external value of the pound would not be stable in the 1980s, and policy would swing between a managed float and pegging to the Deutsche mark. The relationship of exchange-rate considerations to those of domestic policy would become a bitter source of contention within the Thatcher cabinet. The issue of British membership in the European Monetary Union still divides both parties.

The lifting of foreign exchange controls was the first step toward the Big Bang of 1986, the long-overdue reform of the London Stock Exchange. The second such step was the elimination of credit cartels in Britain – especially that of the Building Societies Association as monopoly lender for home loans. The association had adopted the practice of rationing in order to keep rates down, but in the process produced a "mortgage queue" that created much ill will and de-layed construction. In the brave new world without credit controls, competitive mortgage lenders (including the banks) soon entered the markets, lowering rates, improving service, eliminating barriers between markets, and thereby setting a healthy precedent.[39] A third step was the encouragement of equity investment and stock ownership through pension and tax reform, as already noted.

The decisive breakthrough came with the settlement of an antitrust suit in 1983 that required the London Stock Exchange to shift, as had been done ear-lier in New York, from fixed to variable brokerage commissions within three years. It ended the comfortable 200-year reign of so-called jobbers and brokers over the trading floor and set preparations for the Big Bang in motion. Within days of this noisy event, the Bank of England set forth new rules re-regulating capitalization requirements, establishing penalties for crimes against the mar-ketplace, and clarifying the duties and obligations of market participants. Free after 1986 to acquire direct stakes on the exchange, banks and other financials jumped in – triggering a wave of mergers, consolidations, and reorganizations that greatly strengthened The City's power, especially in Europe. The value of market capitalization for companies traded on the London exchange had long been a mainspring of British power. It amounted to 88 percent of GNP as op-posed to about 50 percent in the United States, only 29 percent on the Paris *Bourse,* and lesser values elsewhere.

In the five years after the Big Bang, the leadership gap would widen: London equity trading would more than triple, with approximately half of all trans-actions involving non-U.K. securities. About half the business in large French and German issues would henceforth also go over London. Reform of the ex-change chiefly benefited financial institutions as more liquid markets facilitated portfolio management, but by lowering borrowing costs it helped corporations as well.[40] The overall result has been, according to Roy Smith "an increase in capital market usage, new market technology, greatly enhanced competition, various new forms of securitization, and drawing of London into transactions in international equity and other securities."[41] In the 1980s, The City successfully managed the big British privatizations, largely (though not always successfully) restructured itself, financed huge new two-way trans-Atlantic flows of capital and credit, and helped guide (though often also frustrate) industrial mergers and acquisitions as well as various other forms of buyout, which – having become commonplace in Mrs. Thatcher's Great Britain – were also beginning to take place across the Channel.

Mrs. Thatcher's reforms were absolutely necessary. She had first of all to lift the dead hand of inefficient and politically troublesome nationalized companies and reintroduce competition into the economy. The coal, steel, and automobile industries were each in dire need of reorganization. The overall effort was an undoubted success. She also had to create a new electoral constituency to support the enterprise society. Here, too, she came off well. Home purchasing was universally popular and long overdue. A new class of shareholders also sprang into existence. Education reform was more of a mixed bag, yet she did manage to enfranchise parents and increase school accountability. At the university level, she did more than any previous government to eliminate barriers between the academy and the economy and to raise the status of research as a national priority.

Reform of the state was also at the top of Mrs. Thatcher's agenda. The "new public management" was an administrative breakthrough. Its practitioners treated the citizen for the first time as a consumer and demonstrated how service delivery could be made responsive to demand. Marketized provisioning of purported public goods eroded the boundaries separating the public and private sectors, undermined the notion that "natural monopolies" restricted the applicability of the competition principle, and produced huge cost savings at the same time. Mrs. Thatcher also applied the market principle to pension reform. Among EC nations, only Britain's scheme was (and remains) fully funded. The mobilization of savings, in both pensions and mutual funds, furthermore created vast new pools of capital that reduced borrowing costs and added to the power and influence of The City, where concomitant reforms were already under way.

Hence, the Big Bang put Britain at the forefront of the financial revolution of the 1980s. New capital mobility would be a powerful and almost instant agent of change, although other economic sectors would prove to be more resistant. Deregulation and re-regulation of the network industries, though beneficial on the whole, raised a host of practical questions for which simple answers were not (and are still not) adequate. As with the marketization of public services, however, huge potential savings in cost and improved service remain largely untapped. The creation of a new regulatory "architecture" continues to pose a challenge to the EU, international agencies, and the individual nations of Europe.

9

The Crisis of the Welfare State and the
Challenge of Modernization in 1980s Europe

THATCHERISM would not prove to be quite the exception it sometimes appears to be from the continental vantage point. Herman Schwartz was among the first political scientists to grasp that heavy international market pressures – which in Mrs. Thatcher's Britain had brought about "not only a shift toward 'less state' but also a shift toward a different kind of state" – were also being felt elsewhere with varying degrees of force.[1] The need to accommodate regime change would eventually prove to be universal. Geopolitics, size and international exposure, the state of the domestic economic and political systems, and the intentions, ideas, and abilities of national leaders would all influence outcomes.

Such outcomes varied. A tradition-conscious France would regroup in order to rebound; a modernization-minded Spain would rally the left politically in order to reform from the right; and a complacent Germany would try to rule quietly in order to let Europe relax. There would be other national combinations as well, each motivated in part by a need to reform the welfare state or a desire to modernize. Member-states both new and old would try to use the Community in order to introduce hard-to-impose change – sometimes as excuse, other times as agent, often as both. The relationship between the EC and the individual nations varied from country to country and thus must be examined on a case-by-case basis. Adjustment could be hard, easy, or seemingly impossible, fast or slow, short or long, and could start early or late. It could follow a pattern or logic of its own, be at the mercy of events, and succeed, fail, or be postponed. The reform process that came over Mrs. Thatcher's Britain in the 1980s would remain unfinished on the continent even twenty years later. Although great progress occurred, especially in the modernizing nations, the cost of delays continues to mount.

Schwartz, a political scientist at the University of Virginia, observed in particular that exposure to the market had brought about especially "sweeping changes ... in small countries governed or influenced by parties of the Left," namely Australia, New Zealand, Denmark, and Sweden.[2] Although not all welfare states with internationally exposed economies were immediately responsive to such pressures – one might cite Finland, the Netherlands, Belgium, and Austria as latecomers – that it happened at all was in one respect remarkable. Public choice theories and theories of collective action would have predicted, or at least suggested, that the "dense networks of interest groups built up in and around

discrete parts of the welfare state, along with the broad public support generated by the universal provision of welfare, would make reform of the welfare
state impossible."³ Almost but not quite: if such structures did not prevent market reform, they at least impeded it. A process that took fewer than five years to
complete in New Zealand and later (under emergency conditions) took even less
time in Finland is still under way in Sweden – the most important test case of
welfare-state survivability. Small-country cases are interesting in and of themselves but also because they are, at bottom, simpler than those of large countries.
Close examination of them exposes fundamental truths that the more complicated realities of large and diverse nations sometimes obscure.

The crisis that brought about reform in the small welfare states had a common
cause in the failure of 1970s-style Keynesian "bridging" or recovery strategies,
which by the early 1980s had produced little growth but much inflation while
expanding public and foreign debt to unsustainable levels. "Sheltering" (i.e.,
protection) added to wage pressures, raised unit costs, and increased deficits on
current account. Centralized wage bargaining spread pay hikes throughout the
economy (including the nontradable sector), aggravated inflation, and added to
payments deficits. Job creation in the public sector, together with high levels of
unemployment compensation, strained fiscal resources.⁴ Between 1982 and 1984,
political demoralization and occasionally violent public protest forced changes
of government in Austrialia, New Zealand, Denmark, and Sweden; of the four
countries, three were socialist. In the remaining case, Denmark, a despairing
socialist cabinet resigned and was replaced by a four-party, minority bourgeois
coalition.

The ineffectiveness of Keynesian remedies in curing the economic and political ailments of the 1970s was also painfully evident in the large continental EC
member-states and seldom contested. In at least two instances, their failures
gave rise to ambitious reform programs. Results varied. The French tradition of
statism proved to be remarkably flexible: under governments of both the left and
the right, the nation's elites – their power shaken by M. Mitterrand's experiment –
re-established their traditional economic and political authority on a new basis.
In Italy, the technocracy (which was far less influential than in France) made a
bold attempt to curtail the mounting systemic abuses that had spread corruption,
undermined political morale, and vitiated national strength. The implosion of
the entrenched party-political system in the early 1990s provided what appeared
to be a unique opportunity to introduce long-overdue change, but in seizing it
the reformers would soon collide with an unpleasant yet fundamental reality:
on the one hand, those who clamored for change (most Italians) were, on the
other hand, also to some extent beneficiaries of the inequitable, inefficient, and
morally tainted status quo. The third main EC member-state, Germany, had
also been the most successful and surely was also the most complacent. Few
Bundesbürger doubted that *Modell Deutschland* would continue as de facto European leader. Indeed, under Chancellor Helmut Kohl the power of the Federal
Republic reached an apogee. It would not long remain there.

One large EC member-nation, a new one, requires special mention. Spain not only managed to adapt successfully to the economic and political changes of the 1980s; over the decade it became, thanks in part to the EC, a new nation. The change was less a matter of economics than politics, and it involved not only the alteration of governmental structures but also the creation of a new civic spirit – an activism and sense of engagement (long repressed by authoritarian rule) that provided the essential fiber of democracy. The path that led to this accomplishment nevertheless took numerous odd twists and turns. The destination was seldom in sight.

NEW ZEALAND EXPERIMENTS

Distant New Zealand would become a benchmark of European progress in the 1980s. Isolated, unconstrained geopolitically, for the most part homogenous socially, egalitarian in spirit, democratic, nonideological, very *British,* and to all intents and purposes content, the island nation was ideally endowed to serve as a laboratory for the Thatcherite reform that continental Europe would later import; thus it will better (than its larger and more diverse antipodean neighbor) serve as a model in this account. The Kiwi reform wave launched in 1984 represents, in the words of an experienced OECD observer, "one of the most notable episodes of liberalization that history has to offer."[5] New Zealand was long overdue for change. The need for it was glaring, undisputed, and universally recognized within the business community as well as by leading financial officials and their economic advisers. Heir to a bipartisan tradition of "cradle to grave protection," the N.Z. economy was crippled by overregulation. Controls extended to wages, imports, foreign currency, many commodity prices, and exports. Government ownership was widespread in banking, insurance, health, education, transport, energy, and utilities.

New Zealand's economic performance had long been dismal and was deteriorating. Per-capita GNP, 92 percent of the U.S. level in 1938, fell to 70 percent in 1950; from there it dropped by the mid-1980s to about 50 percent. Between 1974 and 1985, public and private debt rose from 11 percent to 95 percent of GDP, and net public debt increased from 5 percent to 32 percent. Inflation remained in double digits for the entire period. Current account deficits reached 8.7 percent in 1984, while the budget deficit rose to 6.5 percent. Unemployment stood at 4.8 percent in June 1984, up from 1.7 percent in March 1980 and 0.2 percent in March 1974.[6] In June 1984, the likelihood that a change in government would bring a devaluation of the N.Z. dollar started a run on the currency. Convertibility was suspended. The country entered a constitutional crisis. The stage was set for reform.

A resounding socialist electoral victory over a divided, demoralized, and clueless opposition provided a one-time chance to press for change. For six years the party would rule the roost in the country's British-style "elected dictatorship." This apparently powerful grip on office enabled the government to risk voter disaffection in order to introduce necessary economic reform and rebuild constituent support on a new basis.[7] The scope of action was breathtaking. It included phasing out import licensing, reducing the tariffs over a five-year period, eliminating agricultural protection (tax breaks as well as price supports), and wiping out marketing boards. In addition, exchange controls were lifted and rates allowed to float in 1985. A liberal competition policy was adopted in 1986. Tax and market incentives were eliminated between 1984 and 1998. State aids to industry ended between 1984 and 1990, and free trade with Australia was phased in over the same years.[8] State-owned enterprises (SOEs) were privatized, the tax system was thoroughly overhauled (to make it the "least distortive" of OECD nations), monetary policy was re-directed solely to the purpose of controlling inflation, fiscal policy was reformed to limit debt and enforce transparency, and labor market restrictions were eventually lifted to the extent that "New Zealand's ... was one of the most liberal [regimes] in the OECD area ... accelerating the decline in union membership and making wage determination and employment conditions markedly more flexible."[9]

Sequencing was important. First came deregulation, especially of the financial sector, and the creation of a new legal and administrative framework to guide monetary, fiscal, and competition policy; those interests directly affected were close to power and therefore "locked in." Following soon thereafter were privatization of state-owned companies and marketization of the government services, "costless" reforms that foreign lenders could be counted on to approve. The simultaneity of change in different areas obfuscated consequences, and losers were soon compensated elsewhere. Constituencies stripped of protection could be counted on to demand that the same policies be applied to their suppliers, thereby impelling the liberalization process forward. Labor reform was the last item on the agenda. Only in 1990 – once recovery had taken hold and the benefits enjoyed by the public – did any N.Z. government (in this case, the National Party) feel strong enough to tackle an issue that, at least from an economic standpoint, would better have been confronted earlier.[10] The challenge to union power brought the brief reform era to a close. The changes introduced during it have, however, been lasting.

Writing five years later, a group of senior economic advisors active in the reform effort concluded that many valuable lessons applicable to Europe could be learned from New Zealand's experience. By imposing open financial markets, formidable disclosure requirements, and formal contractual relations with respect to monetary and fiscal policy, the reforms set constraints that future governments could not easily lift. The experts might also have added that the beneficiaries of these new arrangements – a successful class of entrepreneurs – could provide a new basis for electoral support. The reforms also demonstrably improved upon past policies of heavy regulation, import protection, and the attendant high deficits and inflation, revealing that "the potential for market solutions appears to be larger than commonly believed." Previously protected groups like farmers welcomed the changes; learning and adaptation were rapid.

Furthermore, privatization – particularly of telecommunications – yielded immediate and unsuspected large payoffs. Finally, fiscal consolidation took place more quickly than expected, and a deficit of 9 percent was turned into a surplus within ten years.

The authors of the study were pleasantly surprised that apparent intangibles like "credible commitments" and " transparency" can – if respected as operating principles – produce immediate, demonstrable, and widely recognized benefits.[11] To conclude as they did that an electorate will necessarily reward reformers seems dubious. So too does the finding of the distinguished panel: that there is no distinction between private and public enterprise in the production of savings and efficiencies and that marketization of public services can substitute for privatization. The timeliness and effectiveness of the economic reform in New Zealand did not, to their shock and amazement, win the socialists another term in office. In 1990 a resurrected National Party swept them out as thoroughly as they had blown away the Nationals only four years earlier. Even in New Zealand, pain outweighed gain at the polls.

DENMARK CONSERVES

A fascinating study in its own right, the case of Denmark also sheds light on the problems and challenges that have faced its Swedish neighbor since the 1980s – in particular, the latter's decision to join the European Community. The Danes would strike a satisfactory, tradition-based accommodation to the challenge of regime change. To understand the nature of this adaptation, one must first refute an influential theoretical explanation of how it came about that has also been applied to other welfare states. As first pointed out in a stimulating article by Torben Iversen and Anne Wren, advanced welfare economies face a "trilemma" and must make specific trade-offs between budgetary restraint, earnings equality, and employment growth. In a post-Keynesian, post–regime change world in which financial stability has replaced full employment as the paramount goal of economic policy, the choice boils down to promoting either earnings equality (which creates unemployment) or employment growth (which reduces wages). Neither is an attractive option.[12] According to Iversen, "the question for Scandinavian social democracy is whether it wants to deepen class divisions by accepting greater inequalities, or whether it wants to create a marginalized class of people, excluded from full participation in the economy."[13] Where is the escape route? In a subsequent solely authored article, Iversen tried to locate it.[14]

He argues that two adaptations to the "trilemma" are possible: one is "neo-liberal" and *in*egalitarian, in which decentralized wage bargaining promotes private-sector employment; the other is "Christian-democratic" and "solidaristic," which creates unemployment. Rejecting the first course in favor of the second, Iversen argues for the restoration of centralized wage bargaining. This mechanism was the keystone in the arch known as the Rehn–Meidner model, a master plan for Swedish (and, more broadly, Scandinavian) social democracy. "When unions," he argues, are sufficiently large for their agreements to affect the general price level, and when monetary responses are predictable, a nonaccommodating monetary policy [that rules out devaluation] gives bargainers an incentive to moderate demands because they know that moderation will raise the real money supply, and hence demand and employment.[15]

This formula, a form of incomes policy, was the very approach that had been badly fraying in West Germany back in the mid-1970s, got ripped to pieces in Callaghan's Britain, would be shredded a few years later in Scandinavia, and today is failing in the European Monetary Union.

The Danish scenario ran opposite to Iversen's prediction.[16] Electing (at the time of the Snake) to forfeit monetary sovereignty and peg to the Deutsche mark, thereby eliminating the quick fix of devaluation, Danes placed the burden of adjustment to competitive conditions on regulated labor markets. The adoption of this nonaccommodating stance brought about the early breakdown of centralized wage bargaining. Denmark thus "sequenced" reform differently from New Zealand. The Danish case featured confrontation with labor, a less decisive outcome than in Great Britain, and a truncated course of neoliberal reform. A similar scenario would play out in Sweden after that country also adopted a nonaccommodating policy. Denmark liberalized only partially in the 1980s. A new mood nevertheless affected the development of the welfare state, albeit in subtle and nationally specific ways. Traditional institutions remained largely intact, and political contexts evolved only slowly. The battles of the 1980s would carry into the next decade important implications not only for the small Nordic nations but for the construction of Europe as well.

The Danes entered the Snake in 1973 and subsequently joined the European Monetary System, a policy strongly favored by the central bank and the financial community. Membership was neither costless nor, at least to union wage negotiators, ever "credible" enough to make it worthwhile to forsake wage gains. Since devaluation was incompatible with the nonaccommodating policy, Denmark's payments soon ran into deficit during the 1970s – especially with Sweden, where resort to the easy way out of currency depreciation was recurrent and necessary in light of chronic wage inflation. In spite of steadfast Danish commitment to pegging their krone to the Deutsche mark, excessive wage increases – arrived at through centralized bargaining and due to "drift" – elevated inflation above German levels and thus also raised Danish borrowing costs. At the end of the 1970s, real interest rates were so high that construction came virtually to a halt. Unwilling to break with DM pegging but unable to control wage inflation, the social democratic government simply gave up and resigned.[17]

The new bourgeois government of Poul Schluter had several reasons for initiating the reform of the Danish welfare state. One was a mounting concern in various portions of the electorate with its purportedly corrosive moral effects; somewhat less cosmic was the issue of global competitiveness; and the most immediate was a determination to remain linked to the German currency and economy. This policy required bringing inflation under control. The effort started with the wage bargaining system. Reform also extended to the partial decentralization of government services and the gradual replacement of an entitlement system with one based more closely on need. Although resting on a coalition of four small parties, the Schluter cabinet acted decisively and to considerable effect. It adopted a policy of "austerity" that won credibility in the capital markets, eliminated the budget deficit, and brought Danish interest rates down from 10.9 percent to 5.5 percent, in line with Germany's.[18] The reduction of borrowing costs generated huge gains in asset values, which more than offset the contractionary effects of smaller government expenditures and tax increases. Wages went down, unemployment remained high but declined, and growth resumed. Without it, reform would have come to naught.

Unlike the socialists in New Zealand, the Schluter government confronted labor directly. It ended price indexation of wages, curtailed many social transfers, and implemented far-reaching stabilization policies. The struggle would be continuous. The unions vehemently objected to the new course, and conflict with management escalated. Because of "drift" (the capture of wage gains by the noncompetitive sector), government wage ceilings were regularly exceeded. Over the next couple of years, producers in exposed sectors – reasserting control over the national employers' organization – managed effectively to decentralize wage bargaining.[19] Since the late 1980s wages have been set at the sectoral level, "drift" has declined, and earnings growth has decreased. In 1988, the unions accepted decentralized negotiations and also agreed not to demand raises above German levels. It was not the strengthening but rather the weakening of central wage bargaining that led to the restraint needed for growth in employment.

Though belonging to the same process as labor union reform, changes in the welfare state grew out of worries about runaway cost as well as moral concerns about the rights and duties of citizenship. A subtle shift in the operation of the welfare state resulted from these preoccupations. The expansion of the Danish welfare state ended in the 1980s. Its already very high costs were thereafter contained better than those of comparable states. More importantly, according to R. H. Cox, its rationale changed from providing the "socially optimum" to guaranteeing only a "social minimum."[20] The distinction, though not obvious in aggregate spending, emerges from analyses of both changes in coverage and discussions surrounding reform. Such investigation reveals a pervasive fear that the welfare state was corrupting tradition, giving rise to entitlement-based rent seeking, encouraging illegal profiteering, and contributing to irresponsible and impersonal administration from above. In addition to bringing costs under control, the purpose behind the changes was to restore what must be called (for lack of a better term) a sense of civic virtue.

In health care, prudential criteria substituted for universal entitlement. Coverage was declared to be no longer unconditional but restricted to need in order to curtail goldbricking and absenteeism. To discourage employees from making frivolous use of sickness benefits, a two-day waiting period was introduced before they would be paid. The tax reforms of 1987 and 1994 limited deductions on unearned income (which had favored upper brackets) while simultaneously broadening the tax base, an austerity measure opposed by the pro-rich Conservative party but supported by the have-not left.[21] In pension reform, a limited means test was applied to the flat-rate social security benefit (*Folkepension*) to encourage older citizens (aged 67 to 70) to retire in favor of young people; it was later also extended to tax-sheltered investments in order to "claw back" unearned income from affluent retirees. Reflecting the needs-based preference, another provision provided eligible elderly poor with supplementary payments.[22]

An additional set of measures based on earned income reveals the new policy importance assigned to the achievement principle, a shift that indicates a breakdown of the "solidaristic" ethic. Along with decentralized wage bargaining, skilled workers demanded and received separate private pension schemes that reflected the greater value of their labor relative to that of unskilled workers. Employers supported the effort. Concern that the welfare state was undermining a sense of civic responsibility also played an important role in the new attempt to reward merit rather than confer privileges. A slew of studies corroborated evidence of self-seeking behavior among the young. High rates of absenteeism elicited frequent complaint that those who benefited from the welfare state had forgotten that it was built for those who needed it. An active press provided reminders that many publicly funded state activities – such as higher education, museums, operas, and home mortgage subsidies – rewarded mainly the well-to-do.[23] The existence of a lively shadow economy provided additional ammunition "for those who wish to believe that the Danish welfare state promotes the wrong type of behavior," since high levels of taxation encouraged working "off the books."[24] "Workfare" policies were adopted to cure idleness, prevent those receiving assistance from providing untaxed services, and discourage drunkenness.

Coupled to the new emphasis on traditional values was a demand for return of administrative authority to local control. Cost savings provided some of the motivation, but it was also thought that "an efficient, decentralized system of administration would be more democratic and responsive to the concerns of citizens" than distant bureaucracies. This devolution occurred amidst a long-term consolidation of the patchwork of local government jurisdictions that dated from the Middle Ages. Intended to strengthen traditional local autonomy, the reform gave municipal governments new competence in the welfare field. In addition to their traditional power to raise and collect taxes – itself unusual in a unitary state – towns and cities acquired the authority to develop and fund policies for providing assistance to the unemployed. Terms and conditions varied widely between "workfare," retraining, cash payments, and some combination of the three. In addition, the government adopted a large-scale program of grants incentives to stimulate official entrepreneurship and improve service delivery at the municipal level.[25] Hard to measure, the impact of the new approach marked only a beginning of the marketization process then under way in the United Kingdom. Liberalization in Denmark less resembles a coordinated full-scale policy of reform like New Zealand's than an adjustment made with a view to protecting traditional interests and values – but requiring fundamental reduction in the power of organized labor and at least a partial reconfiguration of the welfare state. Denmark's story is a successful one of how a vibrant democracy can shape up an overweight welfare state.

SWEDEN'S BEACON GOES OUT

The reform of Sweden, the leader in theory and practice of the Third Way and a beacon of hope for progressive intellectuals worldwide, required no less than a change in mentalities. Only with considerable reluctance did the Swedish political establishment eventually conclude that EU membership was a necessary step in the adaptation process. The citizens themselves are still not sure this is true. To many of them, the welfare state defines the very essence and identity of modern Sweden. Yet the "Swedish model," according to Assar Lindbeck, can be said to have existed as a distinct economic and political system for only about a generation.[26] It dates from (and worked best during) the still golden years of the 1960s, buckled in the 1970s, and collapsed economically when exposed to world markets in the 1980s. Although economists generally understood that the Swedish model was wearing out, the public did not soon catch on to the implications of this fact. A catalytic crisis – like the impending currency collapse in New Zealand or the abject resignation of the social democratic government in Denmark – did not occur in Sweden until the 1990s. The process of change started with a bursting asset bubble followed by a run on the banks, a severe financial crisis, a wrenching economic slowdown, and a painful rise in unemployment. A breakdown of centralized wage bargaining was the medium-term cause of the financial collapse. Without the linchpin of this core institution, the wheels of the Swedish cart careened wildly off in different directions, the thing screeched to an inglorious halt, and those who had thought they were getting somewhere had to dust themselves off and go home by foot. Unable to weather competition, the regulated economy broke up and no one knew what – in the confusion that followed – would replace it. The long-term cause of both immediate crises and medium-term breakdown was the faulty economic design of the welfare state itself. It hindered productivity, reduced competitiveness, and prevented the rise of incomes. Whether the Swedish vehicle can be fixed up and again set rolling remains to be seen.

Before 1960 and prior to the excessive growth of the welfare state, Sweden was a wealthy industrial state whose public sector was about the same size as similar nations, about 35 to 40 percent of GNP. Thereafter, the costs of government grew rapidly. By the mid-1970s they had expanded to 65 to 70 percent of GNP, the highest in the OECD. At the same time, the long-prominent union movement *Landesorganisationen* (LO), to which 85 percent of the labor force belonged, began to dominate the country. Its power was unparalleled in any modern industrial democracy. Control over central wage bargaining, the source of this extraordinary state of affairs, enabled LO to make overall economic and social policy, shape Sweden's fundamental institutions, and guide its

future development.[27] The main features of *economic* policy were the replacement of market participation by a structured kind of collective decision making;
strengthening the central institutions and, in particular, the employers' association as bargaining partner and contract enforcer; use of selective credit controls
to stimulate industrial growth; adoption of punitive tax laws to level incomes;
imposition of restrictive capital controls to seal off the domestic economy; development of a regulatory system that established rules of conduct and also authorized direct government intervention into firm decision making; and political
manipulation of transfer payments. Intersectoral, interclass, intergenerational,
and interinstitutional income and asset re-allocation were in the Swedish case
disproportionately prominent.[28] One mechanism of redistribution was a special pension scheme whose provisions placed 5 percent of Swedish industrial
shares under control of the union. In effect, LO determined how transfers were
allocated – who got what. Income redistribution was its main lever of political
power.

Economic policy was guided by LO theory, and the Rehn–Meidner model was
the master plan that grew out of it.[29] This model rested on the government's use
of fiscal and monetary manipulation to restrain aggregate demand below the full
employment level in order to reduce wage-cost pressures that would otherwise
make themselves felt in the market. Retraining would then eliminate unemployment, and reskilled labor could be shifted from less to more productive use. A
"solidaristic" wage policy would assure that those doing the same work received
equal pay, a goal reinforced by "wage compression" – the reduction of pay differentials between skilled and unskilled workers. Having benefited from wage
restraint, employers would be required to consign "excess profits" to the public
via the transfer mechanisms of the state and the labor movement. Although the
Swedish socialist party (*Svenska Arbeider Parti*, or SAP) never officially adopted
the Rehn–Meidner model, it was in fact the template for national policy.

The power of LO was well entrenched.[30] Most Swedes worked directly for
the state or were dependent upon it. The economy was pocketed with privilege, and about three quarters of its activity took place within the confines of a
protected nontradable sector. The modern Swedish export industry was also a
recipient of special handouts from the state; it could take advantage of relatively
low corporate tax rates, generous provisions for depreciating investment, access
to subsidized credit, and tolerance of cartel relationships.[31] Market-distorting
policies put producers at the mercy of government decision makers, caused
competition to atrophy, and restricted all but favored new entrants. The interventionism constricted the development of Swedish small business and stifled
entrepreneurship.[32]

Almost everyone relied fully or in part on transfer payments for income. The
LO exercised what amounted to statutory control over the dominant political
party, the socialist SAP, and held the electorate in thrall: nearly everyone could
take advantage of the generous welfare state in some way.[33] And why would anyone want to be the first to relinquish his privileges? It was the prisoner's dilemma

on a grand scale. The appeal of the welfare state was no less genuine than the fear aroused in a dependent population of what might happen in its absence. The political opposition in Sweden, which represented diverse nonlabor interests entrenched in the system, was no less bound to it. The other parties were less an alternative to the dominant socialists than a corrective to them. Public acceptance of *social* policy thus set the parameters of acceptable political change. In short: as long as growth continued, Sweden was stable.

Unilateral devaluation was the dirty secret that enabled the "Swedish model" to work, the grease that oiled the wheel that allowed the cart to roll forward. Not union restraint but devaluation, according to Lindbeck, was what caused real earnings to decline.[34] In recovery phases, wages outstripped growth. In both slowdowns of the 1970s (each the aftermath of an oil shock), devaluations got the economy moving again: once in 1975/1976 and again in 1980/1981. In each successive round, however, the medicine was less effective. In order to overcome unemployment and maintain family incomes, the public payroll had to be padded by making new, low-paid jobs available for women in the field of daycare and eldercare. This form of work creation did not provide new services but simply displaced traditional ones; it involved "cross-haulage" in which mothers would care for each other's children and daughters for each other's parents – a screwball socialization of the family.[35]

In 1982, a socialist government returned to office after a hiatus of six years during which a "bourgeois" government had been " 'forced' to socialize corporations to an extent that the previous socialist government had never dreamt of doing during forty-four years of rule."[36] The incoming cabinet contained at least a few men like Finance Minister Kjell-Olaf Feldt, who recognized the pressing need for reform. Feldt sought to change the rules of the game rather than merely seek their preferred outcome in the context of extant laws and regulations.[37] He had an uphill battle to wage against the entrenched powers of unions, a central bank in which Keynesianism still reigned, and representatives of consumer and ecological interest groups.

Yet change began. The government cut spending as a percentage of GNP, directed state enterprises to make profitability their goal, and even privatized some of them. More importantly, it soon lifted all restrictions on the movement of capital, including restraints on foreign investment. A long-overdue consolidation of the banking sector set in immediately, forcing borrowers to become creditworthy – a powerful incentive to corporate change. In 1988, the government reduced marginal income-tax rates from 85 to 50 percent, eliminated taxes on dividends, and shifted the tax burden toward a value-added tax. By the early 1990s, Swedish corporate taxes were the lowest of any OECD nation. The beginnings of liberalization and the partial restoration of competition combined with the lingering effects of the devaluations to spark an export and investment miniboom at the middle of the decade. At the same time, the regulatory system and the apparent social and political consensus began to break down at the point of centralized wage bargaining. As the 1980s drew to an end, the government planned for further change.[38] Sweden would nevertheless have to suffer a severe financial crisis before it could be swept politically by a new broom. Even then, much was left unturned.

The Swedish economic record – though once a beacon of hope for the Third Way – is not worth boasting about. In the OECD tables, Sweden's per-capita consumption dropped from fifth in 1970 to twelfth in 1990, the worst performance of any member-nation. Low productivity growth was at the heart of the problem. Assar Lindbeck attributes it to the large size of the public sector, to low returns on capital, and (more directly) to profit squeezing by the Rehn–Meidner model.[39] Offsetting the weak productivity were credit subsidies, generous depreciation allowances, and foreign exchange controls forbidding the movement of funds abroad. These misplaced incentives force-fed investment into industry. The growth inducement was more effective under the parade-ground conditions of Fordist *Spartakiad* than it could be against the open-field individual acrobatics of the new economy.

The bottom-line source of the Swedish productivity problem was the wide tax and benefit wedge, or spread, between employer costs and employee wages. In the 1980s it ranged between 70 and 80 percent and reduced marginal pay rates by between 10 and 20 percent.[40] High benefits also had secondary effects that, though difficult to quantify, further adversely impacted labor productivity. They include the usual suspects: poverty traps, moral hazard, and cheating. Among their manifestations were high and rising rates of absenteeism (26 days/year vs. 14 in 1955), an increase in the receipt of social assistance (from 4 percent of the public in 1950–1965 to 10 percent in the 1990s), and a huge jump in early retirements at times of full employment.[41] Whatever the precise reason, the lagging labor productivity cannot be unrelated to the fact that real after-tax wage earnings, adjusted for inflation, remained flat from 1970 to 1990.

The culprit, according to an IMF expert, was "wage drift" brought about by centralized bargaining and "solidaristic" tradition. By the 1980s, Swedish earnings differentials were substantially the least of any industrial nation, 34 percent between the highest and lowest deciles, versus 45 percent in the United Kingdom (and 490 percent in the United States).[42] Although unconnected to the adoption of a Danish-type nonaccommodative monetary policy, Swedish centralized wage bargaining broke down for largely endogenous reasons. Wage restraint was absent after 1980, according to Ramana Ramaswamy, because low productivity growth and high employment made it hard to impose on the tradable sector; at the same time, the tax and benefits wedge would have to widen in order to cover increased transfers to support public-sector employment.[43] Thus, as LO tried to maintain "solidarism," skilled workers broke away to negotiate higher wages. After the initial breach, the union movement continued to fragment. Public employees replaced metalworkers as the largest affiliate, LO split into several main blocs, and employers managed to foster competition between them. Wage differentials, and thus labor incentives, began to widen by the mid-1980s. In 1990 the emboldened employers' federation closed down its bargaining division, refused to compile the earnings statistics needed to administer solidarism, and in the following year abandoned the tripartite boards that had been the "iron triangles" of Swedish corporatism. It was a declaration of independence. Finally, Volvo shut down the celebrated "new factories" where workstations and multifunctional robots had been brought in to humanize assembly-line production. The enlightened labor practices did not meet the profitability test.[44]

Industry's gain was labor's loss of the controls and powers acquired in the 1970s and early 1980s. The rollbacks included such areas as job security and promotion, health and safety, gender equality, educational leave, powers of co-determination, and the right to sit on company boards. Another result was severance of the organic connection between LO and SAP, the socialist party. The practice of "collective affiliation," whereby members of LO automatically became members of SAP, officially ended in 1990, by which time support of union members for the party had declined to only 50 percent. The most important development of the 1980s was the uncoupling of the LO from government and industry.

Swedish repudiation of union domination was by no means tantamount to a rejection of the welfare state.[45] It took a major financial crisis to galvanize a Swedish government into ideological confrontation with the problem presented by it.[46] The right-center cabinet formed under Carl Bildt rose to the occasion, and even the socialists were moving in the same direction. In a late 1989 think-piece written for the party magazine, Finance Minister Feldt stated baldly that the market economy's facility for change and development – and thus for economic growth – had done more to eliminate poverty and "the exploitation of the working class" than any political intervention in the allocative system. It was time, he insisted, "to stop knocking the market economy; and ... accept private ownership, the profit motive and differences of income and wealth."[47] Feldt accordingly planned to introduce a far-reaching bill for fiscal reform that would reduce the basic income-tax rate from 50 to 30 percent and the top marginal one from 77 to 60 percent. He expected the marketization of public services to generate the necessary cost reductions. Feldt threatened to resign if the proposal failed to meet with cabinet approval, but deep-seated differences within the cabinet between economizers and job creators caused the project to stall.[48]

There were further intimations of changes to come. In May 1991, Prime Minister Ingvar Carlsson planted – in an obscure footnote attached to an emergency budget announcement – the momentous news that Sweden, in a departure from the quasi-sacred policy of neutrality and autonomy, would seek membership in the European Community.[49] The decision came after nearly a decade of systemic economic breakdown as well as on the heels of intense lobbying by the financial community, especially by Volvo president Pehr Gyllenhammar. Gyllenhammar was founder of the powerful European Roundtable, a pro-integration idea mill for the business elite of the continent.

Sweden's cherished policy of neutrality and autonomy was in any case something of a myth. The Swedes respected the U.S.-imposed COCOM restriction on trade with the Soviet bloc and had long coordinated security policy secretly and unofficially with NATO staff planning. Moreover, Sweden had been prominent in EFTA, and its multinationals were heavy investors (as well as important buyers and sellers) in the EC, to which it was linked by long-standing bilateral tariff agreements. In July 1991, Prime Minister Carlsson formally filed for Swedish membership in the Community.[50] The decision was born of the hope that the Danish approach, in which a nonaccommodating exchange policy and competition rules disciplined both labor and the economy, might also do Sweden some good. The public was apparently not to be trusted with the truth that "Europe" was to be called in to help rescue the country from itself.

The financial crisis that swept the Moderate Party candidate Carl Bildt into power unfortunately soon became too severe for his boldly proclaimed New Start to get under way. Upon taking office, Bildt had pronounced the "age of collectivism" dead and proclaimed that Sweden would soon be put on a path leading to dynamic free enterprise. He promised to shut down union-controlled wage-earner investment funds; launch privatizations, beginning with the pharmaceutical firm Pharmacia; introduce the principle of choice into competitive future public services; overhaul tax laws; and introduce a hard currency, like the Danish krone. The days of unilateral devaluation were declared to be a thing of the past.[51]

The origins of the financial crisis that broke at the end of the 1980s trace back to the half-liberalized condition of the Swedish economy. It was an unfortunate mix of the old and the new: on the one hand, an unreformed tax system with punitive marginal income brackets but generous deductions for home ownership and consumer interest charges; and, on the other, recently liberalized capitalized markets and inflationary expectations. The combination triggered a borrowing spree and a boom in home purchasing and construction. This produced a perilous condition of net household dis-saving. The retrospectively inevitable credit crunch hit with devastating effect. Between 1990 and 1993, one fifth of industrial jobs disappeared, official unemployment (which does not include equal numbers of persons engaged in make-work schemes) rose from 2 to 8 percent, and GDP shrank at a horrific 5 percent annually. Sweden found itself in the throes of the deepest recession since the 1930s. One early casualty was the peg of the krona to the European Monetary System; in September 1992, the markets drove the currency down over 20 percent. It had to be de-linked, thereby threatening to restart another vicious round of inflation, which soon set in. Sweden in 1993 won the European record for budget deficits, a new high of 13 percent of GDP. The public debt reached nearly 100 percent of GDP, almost – but not quite – a prizewinner. In the 1993–1994 special event of public expenditures and transfer payments as share of GDP, the Bildt government won back the Swedish Cup from the previous socialist administration with a whopping 73.2-percent performance.[52]

Bildt's legislative program was in tatters long before he was put out of office in 1993. Sadly, not even the *pièce de résistance* of his administration's record – the tax reform bill of 1991, which in fact had been largely drafted by Feldt and

eventually passed with socialist support – had an opportunity to take constructive effect. Patterned on the Reagan tax reform of 1986 and regarded by tax
experts as "the most far-reaching reform in any industrialized country in the
postwar period," the necessary but complicated measure aimed to end differential treatment of various types of income, eliminate deduction and amortization
loopholes, reduce marginal income brackets, broaden the tax base, and shift
from direct to indirect sources of income without reducing overall yield. The
bill was a crisis measure, but it was conceived with a view to restoring work incentives and promoting competitiveness over the long run. It foresaw efficiency
savings and tinkered at the margins of coverage and entitlement, but it called
neither for liposuction nor radical surgery – nor, for that matter, any other of
the sharp cutbacks in the public sector needed to displace the outsized welfare
state from the hub of the economy. Under better conditions the new tax bill
might have stimulated the growth required for necessary structural change over
the medium term.[53]

Sweden preferred to postpone confronting the legacy of a welfare state losing
its luster. The thing had become so deeply ingrained in thought and habit, and
was so intimately wrapped up with the modern Swedish sense of national identity, that living without it (or even with somewhat less of it) was hard for many
and remained unimaginable for more than a few. A political solution would be
required for Sweden's economic reform, or so concluded a blue-ribbon committee of economists empaneled by the government. They closed their investigation
with the "hope that ... Swedish democracy is able to change the institutions and
rules of the game that have so far made it difficult to carry out a successful economic policy."[54]

FRANCE REGROUPS

Sweden found it hard to file for divorce from a *dirigiste* "model." After the
wretched eighteen months of the Mitterrand government's ruinous experimentation with Socialism in One Country, France found it easy. Yet filing turned out
to be one thing whereas, in actual practice, breaking up after such a long marriage to the state was quite another. Property had to be distributed and rights
and obligations agreed upon; old relationships with children, family, and friends
had to be reworked while new ones of another kind were allowed to develop before the liberated ex-spouse could embark upon a different kind of existence.
Such matters always take time.

The French government acted quickly and firmly once the decision had been
made in March 1983 to take the U-turn from home-baked radical economics to
the strong franc, productivity, and Europe. The government pumped huge subsidies into modern sectors of industry and let lame ducks die, eased the rules
governing employee dismissals, restored managerial autonomy, encouraged nationalized companies to sell off subsidiaries, and embarked upon a vast project
of financial reform.[55] If the socialists had remained in office after 1986 they might

also have launched the next great wave of reform, the privatizations – whether with a similar outcome can only be guessed. The surge in the sale of state-owned companies began after the formation of the self-proclaimed neoliberal center-right government of Jacques Chirac.

It remained in office for two years. The short-lived French Thermidore accelerated the reduction of the public sphere but did not displace it. Nor did Chirac's policies have anything like the far-reaching impacts on French society that Mrs. Thatcher's reforms had in Britain. The neoliberal episode nonetheless made it harder for a future government of the left to buck the long-term trend toward liberalization. The 1986 electoral victory of the two allied parties (RPR and UDF) of the right-center testified to the distaste in the public for excessive state interventionism. Although their campaign rhetoric echoed Mrs. Thatcher's and President Reagan's broad appeals, and must have sounded exotic indeed to French ears, the predominant emphasis in the platform was on reducing the power of an over-mighty state: the government's share in GDP was to be trimmed from 45 to 35 percent of GDP; price controls, exchange controls, restrictions on hiring, firing, and pay all were to be lifted; and the number of civil servants was to be reduced systematically, year by year. Although these goals were overambitious, budgets (especially for the many economic planning agencies) were actually slashed; financial markets were opened and mobilized; and much of the labor legislation was repealed that maddened managers by creating interference on the shop floor.[56] The conduct of privatization guaranteed that French society would nevertheless move only with measured step toward liberalization.

In France as in Britain, the primary purpose of privatization was to restore national competitiveness. The French version entailed something more, however, than the sale and release of burdensome companies. It involved de-amalgamating not only ailing but healthy firms, many of which had previously been amalgamated or otherwise organized by successive governments as national champions. These fattened-up companies were intended to play an even larger role in the future. The structures, internal operations, and profitability of such new creations had resulted from – and to a great extent depended upon – direct interventions of the state.[57] The size, shape, leadership, and ownership of such companies, as well as the timetables and modalities that regulated their creation, would likewise be determined less in markets than by ministerial fiat. Lip service notwithstanding, the goal of French reforms was not, as in Britain, to create a "popular capitalism" aimed at the widest possible distribution of shares and the eventual creation of a mass political party of enterprise-minded property owners. The French purpose was to restore and rejuvenate the technocratic elites sired by the French educational system.

Here they succeeded almost too well. By the beginning of Mitterrand's second septennat, traditional managements – having been helped back into the saddle – faced less interference than before. The successful among the restored companies, once able to compete internationally, started to slip out of the state tutelage they no longer needed and exhibit some of the dynamism they had long been accused of lacking.[58] A process of accommodation on a new basis then began under the new prime minister, the socialist Michel Rocard, associated with the words *ni, ni*. The slogan appealed to the avoidance of the extremes of both statism and economic liberalism, now feared by a public worried about benefits reductions. The new mood provided an opening for corporatist reform along Rhenish lines of the kind sought by the Second Left – admired by Jacques Delors, zealously championed by the prime minister himself, and devoutly hoped for by progressive thinkers generally. The main upshot of Rocard's efforts was to create new French versions of the Deutsche Bank to serve as capstones to the networks of "hard core" interest groups organized in the course of privatization in the French mode.[59]

Economic reform in the post–U-turn France of the 1980s took place against a backdrop of solid if slightly lackluster economic accomplishment. Leading indicators reveal that the decline which began during the 1970s had been reversed. Growth was slightly above the European average, inflation had been tamed, industrial investment was healthy (though still less impressive than the even greater spurt in productivity), and trade was in balance by 1992. Although unemployment (at 9.3 percent) was slightly below the European average over the decade, it remained unacceptably high. Per-capita income was flat.[60] The situation would remain tolerable only until memories of the 1981–1983 debacle faded.

At least for a time, however, they remained vivid. The first eighteen months of the Mitterrand presidency had produced a counterrevolution in sentiment and, according to Suzanne Berger, remedied a malady in French life associated with a "refusal to accept the legitimacy of the exercise of authority within private firms or acknowledge the public goods that result from an economy based on the market and private enterprise."[61] Sensing the mood swing, organized business moved from a defensive crouch to an attack position: its spokesmen no longer talked about the rights of property but about the virtues of entrepreneurship. Employers exalted "the creation of a company as an act of adventure and independence calling forth a superhuman dynamism and energy" as well as, especially in socialist rhetoric, "enterprise as the source of national wealth." Producers appeared ready to go over the top.

The *Patronat* dared not openly proclaim that "the last days of trade unions are within view" and yet, according to Berger, "the notion [was] clearly in the air."[62] The *Confédération Général du Travail* (CGT) in fact lost over a quarter of its members between 1980 and 1983, and organizing campaigns routinely failed. To replace CGT, the *Patronat* encouraged the formation of company proto-unions around the factory councils and committees set up only a few years earlier under the Auroux law in order to promote the worker self-management (*autogestion*) so adored by the Second Left. A semipopular literature sprang up attacking unionism as corporatist, archaic, and destructive of good relations between labor and management. The beginnings of a national movement toward "enterprise-based trade unionism" were also detectable at the time. The new market enthusiasm swept Jacques Chirac into office and enabled producers to carve out a larger sphere from the state, win a new measure of respect from the public, and instill dread in the remnant of industrial workers still loyal to unionism.[63] Economic liberalism would nonetheless have difficulty descending from the boardroom down to the shop floor and extending from the factory out into the market.

Progress came most easily in the financial field, the reform of which was a top priority. After the third devaluation and the decision to restore and maintain the *franc fort,* the creation of functional financial markets that could send the appropriate price signals throughout the economy was the essential step toward making it competitive. The year 1984 witnessed a spate of new measures reducing unnecessary red tape, loosening controls over exchange rates, eliminating most price controls, and cutting down on various business taxes. The following year brought the creation of a commercial paper market that enabled companies to raise money directly from the public and, shortly thereafter, a futures market. These and other measures reduced the dependence of industry on the banks. The share of nonbank financing nearly doubled, from 30.7 to 60.6 percent, between 1978 and 1985.[64]

Chirac's neoliberals picked up where the socialists left off. The policy of selective lending to industry (*encadrement du credit*) ended in 1987. No longer under the thumb of the Treasury, the Banque de France acquired the powers of counterparts elsewhere to use interest rates as levers of macroeconomic policy. Laws were passed to facilitate leveraged buyouts, create employee stock ownership plans, and provide incentives for employees to acquire shares in the firms for which they worked. Finally a "Little Bang" reformed the Paris *Bourse* along the lines taken earlier in London.[65]

Market enfranchisement played only a secondary role in privatization. Gathering momentum in 1986, the process largely mirrored the previous nationalizations. Industry was not consulted, a handful of technocrats dictated timetables, and ministerial interventions into the sphere of management decision making were accepted as routine practice. Although firm autonomy increased after 1981 as profitability came back into fashion, top-level civil servants routinely ordered or forbade both mergers and acquisitions on the one hand and divestitures on the other, appointed and dismissed CEOs, made investment decisions over the heads of management, and controlled the flow of credit and subsidies.[66]

The principle guiding privatization was the creation of *noyaux durs,* "hard cores" of interests integrally locked together and keyed into broader industrial and financial structures, in which the state – though one degree removed from management – still retained the last word.[67] Foreign owners were vital as sources of capital and technology, but they were to be brought in only as junior partners in French-led enterprises. The lucky "hard core" beneficiaries acquired shares in large lots sold directly by the state at a slight "management premium" to market prices, far less than the value conferred by control. The result was a giveaway of titanic proportions.[68] For cosmetic purposes, a portion of each issue was set aside for company employees. The remainder seems to have ended up in relatively few hands, at least compared with Britain.[69] The new private firms were intended to be large and strong enough to become Euro-champions and compete worldwide with the despised Anglo-American multis. Money considerations were ever-present in the background to privatization. The divestitures relieved the budget of a huge subsidy burden. The infusion of tax and credit resources into the big firms, along with the restructuring that followed, pumped up wimpy weaklings into market musclemen. The state reaped the windfall. Most companies sold for three times the acquisition price.[70]

How privatization was done, or not done, is hard to discern in individual cases. The interviews of senior managers and civil servants conducted by Vivien Schmidt (for use in *From State to Market?*) provide rare insights into their conduct. The minister of finance made all the key decisions, which depended, however, on different sets of considerations in every instance. St. Gobain was an early candidate for privatization because it had a strong balance sheet, a clear company profile, and a management eager to be de-nationalized. AGF, on the contrary, lacked reserves and was not. Crédit Agricole was forced to privatize against the will of its management. Dassault, a military contractor, wanted to go private but for national security reasons could not.

The minister of finance normally had the final say in determining which interests would constitute the "hard core." In the case of the Société Générale (a large bank), the finance minister simply advertised for all interested parties to appear at a particular office at the Bureau of the Treasury and made a list of everyone present. Although the bank's president objected to one name on the list, the Banco de Santander, he was overruled. In the case of CGCT, a telephone switching manufacturer, no less a figure than Prime Minister Chirac decided that "in the European interest" the company should be sold neither to AT&T (which was technologically superior and which CGCT's management wanted) nor to Siemens (which would have made the Germans happy) but to the Franco-Swedish Matra-Ericsson.[71] Privatization, Schmidt concludes, "was a heroic affair [that] involved minimal consultation on the choice of firms to be privatized and only somewhat more on the hard-core memberships, [but] generally satisfied the participants and was not seen as a highly *dirigiste* as a result" – even though that was, in fact, very much the case.[72] The wave of mergers and acquisitions that would ensue in the aftermath of privatization featured resort to similar (but less frequently applied) interventionist methods. Although the new giants – many genuinely international in operational scope – would be more independent of national control than all but a relatively few French multis of the previous era, they, too, would be run mainly by members of the technocratic elite whose power (nearly all commentators agree) grew during the Mitterrand era. Traditional French statism, strengthened by a dose of liberal reform, emerged from it as secure as ever.[73]

The hopes of many on the Second Left that M. Rocard would revive what remained of its policies after the embarrassments of 1981–1983 had little substance. Between *ni* and *ni* it was hard to find The Third Way. *Autogestion,* although

now championed as essential to productivity rather than to social justice and political progress, was relegated to the realm of café chatter. Other cherished ideas
met similar fates. Decentralization and the revival of self-government could not
be ordered into existence by edict of Paris or of Brussels but rather had (or so it
seemed) to well up somehow from below. Nor could small and medium businessmen be turned into entrepreneurial adventurers merely by sitting around
conference tables and being "serviced" by mid-level bureaucrats from government agencies; they needed a product to sell at a market-clearing price.[74] The
solutions called for were reduction and simplification of burdensome taxes and
massive cuts in social spending.

Nor could much progress be made by riding the favorite new hobbyhorse of
the late 1980s, *modernisation negociée*. Many, including Jacques Delors, viewed
the approach as a vital component of an overall plan to navigate the narrows between hard-eyed Stalinism and gunslinging Reaganism. The idea represented a
new "take" on labor market policies, the panacea of the French left. Such updated
training schemes were to be called in to rescue centralized wage bargaining, keep
social democratic governments in power, and restore a humanized economic system. The notion behind the program – something sensible enough if conducted
on a small-scale, as-needed basis but fatal as macro policy – was that employees had to be retrained in order to anticipate economic innovation. Thus the
hire-and-fire methods of "savage capitalism" ("external labor markets") could
be supplanted with the "internal" flexibility of workers in possession of new
skills acquired in advance of technological and economic change.[75] Advocates of
the proposal did not explain whether introduction of new processes at the plant
should be made contingent upon establishment of the administrative machinery
needed to implement the training program or possibly even upon the availability of an adequate stock of upgraded workers. Nor was it evident why it should
be easier to plan for future labor requirements in the present than it had been to
plan for present ones in the past, where failure had been the norm.

Those steeped in the faith looked to *Modell Deutschland* for validation, as the
fabled place where active labor market policy combined with centralized wage
bargaining had won the "trifecta" of growth, stability, and full employment.[76]
However, according to Jonah Levy, the only "model" imported from across the
Rhein during the Rocard years was the universal bank.[77] In Germany, a well-
established tradition of stock swapping had tightened the interdependence of
German finance and industry to form a rocklike hard-core network of allied economic interests. It seemed to trouble no one in France that serious economic
thinkers in places like Frankfurt and Munich were wracking their brains in an effort to overhaul *Modell Deutschland* before it stultified growth and immobilized
the nation, or that management at the Deutsche Bank (and elsewhere in German finance) had already concluded that the traditional German business model
was outmoded and needed updating. The final episode in French liberalization
during the 1980s would strengthen a version of corporatism already undergoing
stress and strain within Germany itself.

GERMANY RESTS

All was not well in the Federal Republic, yet it was an exemplar of monetary rec-
titude and an anchor of financial stability for Europe in the 1980s. Consumer
price inflation declined from 6.2 percent in 1983 to 0.6 percent within six years.
Growth was fairly steady, though at only a moderate 2 percent.[78] The slowdown
may be traced back to the loss of latecomer advantage in that Germany had
"caught up" to the American pacesetter and, in lieu of some new impetus to
change, would henceforth have to move in convoy. Comparison with the United
States suggests even more strongly, according to Herbert Giersch, that supply-
side constraints stood in the way of better performance. He locates them in the
usual places: a high level of subsidies to ailing industry that misdirected resource
allocation; excess regulation (e.g., in the classic case of shop opening hours); an
incentive-destroying income-tax bracket creep; a broadening tax wedge caused
by increases in the cost of social security, health, and unemployment benefits;
and high wage rigidity, whose effect was evident in the persistent coexistence
of high unemployment and large numbers of unfilled jobs.[79] In Giersch's view,
these considerations – combined with a "tax reform gap" – largely account for
the profitability differential between American and German firms as well as the
low rate of investment in the latter.

"Labor market rigidity" has meant two things in Germany: employees cannot
be fired; and all who work an eight-hour day are paid full benefits. The result
is that no one is ever hired. This situation, according to Giersch, explains at
least part of the problem of high and persistent unemployment. Aggravating the
situation is the rigidity of the wage structure. Intersectoral American wage dispersion had no counterpart in the Germany of the 1980s; as a result, 24.8 million
new jobs were created in the U.S. service sector while only 1.6 million developed
in the Federal Republic – too few to offset losses in the manufacturing industry. "A structural wage gap combined with a fairly rigid wage structure between
sectors may well explain," Giersch concludes, "a good part of the persistent
unemployment in West Germany."[80] The solution of the problem would have
required eliminating contracted wage minima arrived at in centralized collective
bargaining and therefore also "overhauling the tightly knit social net," as well as
breaking with a deeply entrenched policy of equalizing incomes regionally. The
much-touted active labor market policy had little effect on reducing unemployment, he adds, because the real obstacles to placement in new jobs were financial
disincentives, lack of mobility, old age, ill health, and poor morale – not inadequate skill sets.[81]

The stolid Kohl government had little incentive to risk introducing change
on a broad scale and still less inclination to do so. Germany did not face an
acute crisis in the 1980s, so the need for reform was less obvious than elsewhere.
The lack of it may presage the onset of Eurosclerosis, but the malady is not easily diagnosed. Partly as a result of political decisions governing reunification

that themselves reflect electoral predilections, the German market reform leader during the golden era would become the laggard of the next decade. The Federal Republic's performance during the 1980s nonetheless had an upside, and thanks to it inflation could be wrung out of neighboring economies as well as its own. The West German record was, in fact, good – just not quite good enough to keep abreast of more rapid change being generated elsewhere. The wheezing of the German locomotive would supply another reason for looking to "Europe" for a new impetus to economic change and development.

ITALY RESURRECTS ITSELF

The economic performance of Italy during the 1980s resembled that of its neighbors to the north and west, when viewed at a distance. It featured the stabilization of the currency (a very difficult feat) and slow but fairly steady growth – accompanied, however, by rises in unemployment that derived from supply-side weaknesses, rigid labor markets, and an oversized public sector. Economic stability and the relative absence of social conflict could even leave one with an impression of "rosy prosperity," at least until the onset of recession and the forced devaluation of the lira in 1992.[82] The appearance of health was only superficial. The warm skin glow masked serious maladies, requiring more aggressive treatment than anything needed in Europe north of the Alps – nothing less than a fourth re-founding of the Italian state. Although less dramatic than the earlier political transitions in Iberia or the later velvet revolutions in eastern Europe, the reforms that swept swiftly across Italy between 1992 and 1994 would still be remarkable in scope. Pulling movement forward was the perceived imperative of making Italy fit, politically as well as economically, for the new Europe. Pushing it even more powerfully from behind was a deep and pervasive sense of grievance within Italian society, a resentment of systemic political and economic injustice that would cut across customary lines, fissures, and divisions of class, region, and ideology. Although giving rise to chronic public complaint as well as a high level of intellectual criticism, the mounting wave of anger and frustration found little organized political expression until the end of the 1980s.

Battle fatigue from the violent 1970s partly explains the lack of political activism; so too does social and generational change. None of the old parties, ideologies, and rallying cries meant much to the increasing numbers of new middle-class voters too young to have memories of Mussolini, the war, or its bitter aftermath. Something further must be said about reform in Italy. Almost anyone who might have been part of the solution was also part of the problem, a beneficiary of unearned or undeserved privilege for which merit-based substitutes were either unsought or unattainable. The vast, impenetrable, and unfair system of entitlements had turned Italy into a community of guilt. The collapse of the USSR would open the floodgates of long-overdue and much-desired reform. What rushed through them was unexpected, sudden, dramatic, and unpredictable. At the head of the flow was an odd new movement, populist in character, that cannot be easily subsumed under customary political rubrics. It was the by-product of clientage run amuck.

"Clientelism," as Patrick McCarthy terms the system that until quite recently reigned in Italy, had several central features. The system derived from Mussolini's corporatism, which even the mighty efforts of Luigi Einaudi, Italy's liberal post-war minister of finance, failed to unroot. A huge state-sponsored manufacturing complex remained at the dead center of industry.[83] Post-1954 clientelism rested politically on vote bartering. Clientelism originated in local and regional traditions of hostility (and even criminal opposition) to the national state; it rested upon the effective monopoly of a single ruling party, the Christian Democrats, as well as the existence of a semi-official and quasi-permanent opposition, the Communist Party of Italy. Each party could, in turn, count upon bases of support in the United States and the Soviet Union, respectively. Clientelism developed into a neocorporatist governing philosophy in the Amintore Fanfani years of the late 1950s. Cabinets of the 1980s – dominated by the unholy alliance of the coarse, Mussolini-like socialist Bettino Craxi from Milan and the consummately cynical, mafia-associated Christian Democrat Giulio Andreotti of Sicily – sculpted control by corruption into an art form.[84]

Clientelism ravaged the political system, made a mockery of political discourse, and frustrated attempts at reform and modernization. In Italy as elsewhere, the decade of the 1980s was a heyday of "model building." Could Italy learn from the development of the French state and modernize by instigating change from the center? Or rather by adopting corporatist "concertation" as directed by organized labor in Sweden or as practiced in the Netherlands and Austria, where it seemed to be more successful? Or from German or British (or even American) examples of capitalism? Aside from the fact – less obvious then than now – that many such "models" were at the time either obsolete or breaking down, they were essentially irrelevant to the problems facing Italy, where programmatic political experiments routinely failed. The events from 1992 to 1994 drove home the simple lesson that Italy – a political culture that was ancient, tough, complex, evolving, and unpredictable – cannot be fitted into a single political reform model as easily as a perfectly proportioned human model can slip into a ready-made suit of clothes. As a practical matter, the Italian state lacked – and, in the main, still lacks – the necessary infrastructure to implement prescriptive national policies.[85]

One avenue of change was open, though where it would lead was then clear to only a few among the *technocrazia* that advised the directors of the single fully uncorrupted central institution in the country, the Banca d'Italia. The example is instructive. Pessimistic about Italy's ability to reform itself politically, the central bank's highly intellectual policy-making elite looked to membership in the European Monetary System to impose discipline. Its members hoped that pegging lira to Deutsche mark would force the economy to become competitive in an open European trading area. The financial experts were committed to convergence theory. Like the Danes, they also understood that the decision would place the burden of adjustment on labor markets and hoped that it would force them to become flexible.[86] Fundamental institutional reform was needed before such a policy could really take effect.

The 1981 "divorce" of the central bank from the Treasury was a first step. Up to that point, the bank was obliged by law to put onto its books all government notes. The debt was all short-term because the Italian state was not creditworthy enough for a bond market to develop. The Treasury could not, in other words, sell into the market. The arrangement gave the government a license to print money and made it impossible for the bank either to control money supply or influence interest rates on its own. The central bank–Treasury divorce came with strings attached, Italian style: the government could still set official rates and thus also influence market rates. The budget, too, remained beyond central-bank control. The bank went along with the policy of maintaining high real yields on government notes in order to support the external value of the lira. By the late 1980s this consequential stance shifted investment away from industry, feathered the nests of millions of middle-class Italian families, and contributed to short-term political stability while weakening the economy over the longer run.

From the viewpoint of the bank *technocrazia,* the policy was a necessary evil in the fight for independence.[87] "By the late 1980s," according to Bernard Connolly, "the Banca d'Italia found that it could push against the open door of 'Europe' in the pursuit of its ambitions for greater economic policy power, even if that power would have to be shared with other bankers in a European Central Bank."[88] At the European level, Italian bank technocrats aggressively sought to enter international agreements that would restrict spending in the name of a sound currency in order that "Italian governments would be the servant, not the master of a powerful central bank."[89] Such a hope was remote from the political realities of the 1980s. A blue-ribbon committee of economic experts – headed by the subsequent EU competition commissioner, Mario Monti – first proposed liberalization of Italian capital markets in 1982. At first the Treasury blocked the proposal, but then it came around in 1986. Two additional years were required to prepare the necessary decree law. Deregulation did not begin to affect state–industry relations until the following decade.[90] Italy would remain a follower, even compared to Spain, until the onset of political upheaval in the early 1990s.

Clientelism ravaged the economic as well as the political system. Bribes paid for public contracts, McCarthy reminds readers in *The Crisis of the Italian State,* were not just a tax on consumption but subverted entrepreneurial values as well. Since efficiency had become useless, it vanished (along with honesty) in favor of "connections." As political influence replaced market competitiveness, the private sector produced a "state bourgeoisie."[91] By the 1970s, according to a central banker, "we [had] taken responsibility from the entrepreneur but ... not done away with him, ... opened the door to state intervention but ... not planned it, [and] ... corrupted socialism and capitalism alike."[92]

If one hand of the bargain reached out for bribes, the other reached into the public purse for subsidies and free credit. Control of the banking sector was an essential part of the operation, not only as a source of sweetheart loans but as a fabricator of monumental financial fictions invented to divert public money into private pockets. The security services and the mafia were available for hire whenever the ramshackle system needed propping up. A list of the collapses, scandals, feuds, threats, and acts of violence associated with Italy in the 1980s would be too lengthy to record here. Suffice it to say that the country lacked even the ground rules needed for the proper operation of market institutions; they appear to have been respected only in the export-oriented sphere of small family enterprises that remained effectively beyond reach of the government. The banking structure was archaic and highly politicized; the Milan stock exchange was itself a scandal and not merely the scene of many of them; tax law was impenetrable and not respected; cost structures were hopelessly skewed, markets rigged, and incentives grotesquely warped.

The major economic indices for Italy were by no means all bad. Annual growth over the decade was an acceptable 2.2 percent but, for the first time since World War II, below the European average. The nonaccommodative monetary policy in effect after 1979, when Italy joined the EMS, drove inflation down from a perilous 20 percent to below 6 percent by 1986. Interest rates remained very high, with rises into the low twenties in the early 1980s. Large-scale labor "shedding" took place in the manufacturing sphere. A generous income maintenance scheme partially disguised an unemployment increase. Public spending went up by 9 percent of GDP in the same years. By 1986 these relationships were well fixed except for a rise in inflation, which was partly offset by the commodity price reductions of the late 1980s. Public-sector wage gains were the big problem. They showed up in the deterioration of the trade balance – particularly in a sharp increase in import penetration, which occurred in spite of substantial improvement in industrial productivity. Productivity in the public sector fell, largely because of the re-employment of those shed earlier by industry.[93]

Why, ask the economists Stefano Micossi and Pier Carlo Padoan, did prices continue to rise in Italy during the 1980s in spite of a nonaccommodating monetary policy that should also – either by lowering wages or increasing unemployment – have reduced demand? Instead, unemployment increased, wages rose, and demand invariably exceeded supply. The finger of guilt for this market distortion points to the public sector, where the deflator was steadily high compared to manufacturing, wages rose the most and productivity the least, and in which loose budget constraints, inefficiency, overstaffing, and excessive remuneration were the norm. Studies indicated that – often because of bribery – the government habitually overpaid for services and supplies, which lowered technical standards and attenuated market pressures. Extensive government intervention also altered relative prices, income distribution, and the structure of production and employment. Tax increases further skewed structures. The budget deficit reached 13 percent in 1986 and declined only slowly thereafter.[94]

The unhealthy rise in spending went largely into interest payments, personnel costs, pensions, and other vehicles of government by welfare. The burden was unevenly distributed, partly because of widespread cheating. Farmers, small enterprises, the liberal professions, and southerners were net beneficiaries. In general, taxes hurt productive workers, particularly in the north, and benefited the less productive ones, who were disproportionately from the south. The number of benefit recipients (as well as their overall cost) increased; they accounted for 41 percent of the rise in disposable income over the decade. Tax and benefit wedges also spread. An ominous gap opened between the north–south productivity/income ratio, which presumably helps explain why increases in welfare spending led rather than trailed those in unemployment.[95]

In light of such anomalies, it is difficult to explain why the lira did not come under stronger attack during the 1980s. The aggregate data do conceal countless absurdities and injustices that eventually brought about the breakdown of the old regime in the early years of the following decade. At the same time, they also partly account for its institutional "stickiness." Between 1985 and 1987, the Italian National Research Council subjected the system to close scrutiny as part of the "First Targeted Project on the Economy." According to project leader Fiorella P. S. Kostiris, the evidence pointed unequivocally to a "unanimous awareness [among the researchers] ... irrespective of ... value premises and ideological convictions" that the time had come to apply the formula 'more market and less state,' as well as a different kind of state."[96]

The public sector, she argued, was indeed the heart of the problem. The cleanup of the bureaucracy was essential if inflation were to be pulled down, the deficit reduced over time, and growth stimulated – something compatible with improving services and benefits. Dr. Kostiris's team found, to cite just one overdue reform, that governmental utilities monopolies should be broken up where markets could be made contestable or where institutional failure exceeded market failure. Increases to scale should no longer be invoked mechanically as a rationale for public ownership, and strategic rescue should be abandoned as an excuse for government takeover. Why in the name of common sense should the state continue to be a baker of *panettone*?

The researchers encountered a host of additional evils. Pensions and salary benefits were inflationary and often had no connection to either contributions or productivity. Subsidies to industry distorted supply, encouraged speculation, and led to firm overcapitalization. High marginal income-tax rates discouraged productivity, reduced employment, and lowered savings. Tax collection was too often an exercise in harassment.[97] The differential application of taxes to various forms of investment income created "opportunities for arbitrage that [led] to revenue losses and distortions in resource allocation."[98] But the indictment went further. The standard of public service had declined markedly in education, social security, health, and power supply in spite of growth in the budget to 45 percent of GDP – which, including the public sector as a whole, amounted to substantially more than half of total outlays.[99] Finally, unemployment benefits were either paltry or nonexistent for young people in search of jobs yet extremely generous for persons able to benefit from the Wage Supplementation Fund, which brought unearned benefits up to 80 percent of previous gross wages and included a built-in cost-of-living adjustment.[100]

The ill-functioning machinery of the welfare state created the public-sector problem. Benefits drained away over half of total government expenditure, a quarter of which went into education, health, housing, culture, and recreation while another third went into income support. Service delivery was woefully inadequate in all areas. Old age, survivor, and disability pensions did not amount to even 40 percent of the average wage. The shift away from merit-based selection in the schools had created nightmarish difficulties without ending class bias. Health care was so poor that those who could afford to do so – some 15 percent of the population – shelled out for private insurance.[101]

The provision of universal benefits, in theory the operational principle of the welfare system, was in reality fraudulent and self-defeating. Those who profited from it had to be well positioned to operate along the private–public interface – people with the time, income, and guile needed for intelligent finagling. The unfunded "paygo" pension system penalized those in the fastest-growing age brackets (i.e., younger workers) regardless of their income level rather than those with high incomes. The removal of the merit principle in school selection undermined the prestige and effectiveness of institutions that would have increased opportunities for social mobility, and it placed responsibility for education back into the family and other informal private networks that had been traditional breeding grounds of inequality. The surfeit of dirigistic regulations enacted in the name of social protection took no account of the market, could be easily circumvented, provided false incentives, and sent faulty price signals. Utility charges set without any regard to allocative efficiency, kept low to protect (in theory) the needy, actually raised costs and caused huge losses. Centralized wage bargaining had the undesirable yet totally predictable effect of increasing the cost of employing those one wanted to help. Tax concessions and credit subsidies interfered with factor prices and actually delayed the restructuring process.[102]

These and many other problems came home to roost in the *Mezzogiorno,* which (thanks to massive subsidization) had not fallen further behind the north in terms of per-capita income. Incremental growth nevertheless exacted a high price. Transfer policy aimed at raising household purchasing power had a low multiplier effect because it failed to increase outputs locally. The increased public investment normally called for would have provided the mafia with access to illegal sources of revenue, facilitated underbidding for public tenders, and intimidated potential competitors. While the dishonesty and incompetence of southern bureaucrats made resort to discretionary procedures risky in the first place, according to Kostiris, the lack of adequate accountability requirements for project completion increased the likelihood that either speculation or the "build-up of excessive liquidity" would result from additional public investment. In other words, the crooks would simply take the money and run. The low cost of (illegal) capital – idle money or sweetheart loans set aside in political deals – had the unintended further consequence of stimulating investment in technologies or sectors with a high capital/output ratio – in machines rather than jobs. Taken as a whole, according to Dr. Kostiris, the market-distorting incentives caused net wages to rise faster in the south than in the north, outran gains in productivity, and created a situation that could only be remedied by infrastructural improvement.[103] How this could have been done under the given circumstances is a question that the research project did not attempt to answer. At a minimum, major political changes, stronger institutions, and more efficient markets were necessary.

Such reforms would not be easy to introduce. One fifth of the labor force, according to the calculations of economist Mario Baldassari, supported the other four fifths – which, he cynically remarks, included "ten million pensioners ... to whom thirteen million pensions [were] paid."[104] (He did not mention the names of the lucky three million.) The remaining 80 percent of "nonpenalized" Italians who benefited from the perverse distribution mechanisms could, Baldassari continues, "be counted upon to resist changes since, macroeconomically speaking, it is impossible for anyone to admit being a beneficiary of a distorted national budget or a status quo that he or she has an interest in maintaining."[105] The chances were therefore trifling of putting together a political majority "dedicated to true economic reform which obviously embraces the entire political spectrum, as true affiliation is not to parties, but to corporative lobbies, which [were] to be found in all parties."[106] Baldassari expected that, in the absence of reform, the international financial markets would eventually catch on to the hollowness of the Ponzi-like scheme of buying social peace by expanding a pricey public debt – especially debt incurred to support a system that operated in the name of social justice, equal opportunity, and universal coverage but that nonetheless punished the productive few for supporting the idle many. It was, at the same time, a scheme ridded internally with both niggling and nontrivial differential privileges and inequities that were difficult to sort out, divisive politically, and resistant to change.

Bettino Craxi – the socialist prime minister from 1983 to 1987 and, along with *éminence grise* Guilio Andreotti, the leading political figure of the decade – was far from being a reformer as often claimed. He gave clientelism a new dimension. Craxi had nevertheless fashioned his image to please the expanding group of prosperous young middle-class voters who found the Christian democrats stodgy and distrusted the communists. His profile was of someone secular, pro-abortion and pro-divorce, who was both a good European and an effective and forceful representative of Italian interests in the world. From one hopeful angle, Craxi even looked a little like the long-sought leader of the absent Italian liberal party. He was lucky in presiding during a period of economic growth and social peace, to which he modestly contributed. His much greater legacy would be the growth in public indebtedness: from 55 percent of GDP in 1981 to 92 percent in 1987.[107]

Craxi's real political success was not electoral at all but rather as the rough-and-tumble spoilsman who grappled for control of the national petroleum company, bit off a chunk of state television, and put a hammerlock on local and government agencies. A succession of scandals inevitably ensued. When the imprisoned Roberto Calvi (who organized the secret masonic "P-2" lodge at which top representatives of leading Italian elites plotted coup and countercoup) divulged that he had lavishly bribed the Socialist Party, Craxi stepped hard on the toes of the Milan magistrature in order to secure Calvi's quick release and to ensure his silence. It was unwise of Craxi to make enemies on the bench, however. The judges knew that Milan was rapidly mutating into *tangentopolis* – bribe city – and that its socialist boss definitely did not have clean hands (*mani pulite*).[108] The scandal of scandals was about to unfold. By the end of the decade Craxi was exacting enormous tribute. A brother-in-law was mayor of Milan; his son was party secretary and a board member of Silvio Berlusconi's AC Milan, an Italian equivalent of the New York Yankees. Clan members ran things from behind the scenes in Salerno, Naples, Pomicino, and Bari.[109]

No one was prepared when the end came. It began most improbably, with clamorous demands ringing from the middle-sized cities of Lombardy for the restoration of medieval communal rights, a break with Rome, and the destruction of the Italian state itself. Sweeping through the prosperous northern centers of small, high-quality manufacturing at the end of the 1980s, the Lombard League (*Lega*) barbarians would even besiege Fortress Milan and eventually put its inhabitants to rout. Beneath the display of quirky pageantry and the rise of the shrewd but erratic (even slightly unhinged) leader of the movement, Umberto Bossi, there simmered a tax revolt whose depth and breadth would become evident once it began to boil over in parts of Italy far removed from the tidy cities of the Po Valley. Rotten to the core, the system of clientelism would not be overthrown. When the impending and then actual fall of the USSR removed the buttress supporting it on one side, the party-political system merely collapsed on itself.[110] Reform could begin.

SPAIN MODERNIZES

Spain ranks second only to its peninsular coinhabitant Portugal as the greatest western European national success story of the final quarter of the past century – one for which the European Community deserves much credit. The choice between the two nations is not easy. Although each of them has been a champion modernizer, the edge goes to Portugal for four main reasons: it was the first of the two to break with authoritarianism and the only one that faced and successfully banished the prospect of imminent civil war – the most serious such threat anywhere in postwar western Europe; the Lusitanians had also labored longer under authoritarian government than the Spaniards; in addition, they had to make a difficult transition from an imperial to a continental orientation; and finally, since "the turn" Portugal has grown economically without suffering from the Spanish pox, the scourge of chronic severe unemployment.

Compared with Spain, Portugal is a small, compact, relatively homogenous nation and *ceteris paribus* easier to reform, in a better position to take advantage of special situations, able to profit from the experience of larger pacesetters, and not costly to cut in on a deal. Upon second thought, the Iberian contest should be considered a draw. Flip a coin. Though the transition process is still under way, both countries have evolved into modern civil societies under law; both feature functional parliamentary governments, open economies, and commitments in principle to peace and social justice. Each national case is instructive, but this chapter will delve into the larger Spanish one, which is more significant for European politics.

When Felipe Gonzales took office, Spain was only seven years removed from the authoritarian, quasi-fascist, corporatist, yet nonideological and eventually even forward-gazing regency of Generalissimo Francisco Franco. It had lasted for over forty years. Traditional Spanish deference to the powerful state – as governor not *through*, according to Victor Pérez-Diaz, but *of* law – grew in strength over this period.[111] Respect for the state as impersonal rule-keeper had never been much in evidence in Spain and would not develop at once. The Spanish people received a new democratic constitution after Franco's death but still lacked many of the strong institutions needed to govern the country effectively. Political parties were weak, their commitment to ideology or programmatic statements of any kind was questionable, and loyalty to them was often temporary.[112] The party in power in the early transition years, the *Union de Centro Democratico*, split and disappeared altogether in 1982. Its successor would remain in power for the next fourteen years: the *Partido Socialista Obrero Español* (PSOE), which was officially Marxist until 1982; then it became, not as it profiled itself ideologically at the time, a "social democratic party organized along west European lines," but a de facto neoliberal bloc held together by a distinctly Spanish variety of clientelism. For its part, the PSOE government was followed in power by a conservative party that re-invented itself as populist.[113]

Regardless of ideology, these political associations all faced two imperatives.[114] They had to respect democratic conventions, and they needed to make life better for their supporters. Hypocrisy resulted. A highly permeable barrier separated the public and private spheres. The inability to resist demands for patronage and other favors encouraged corruption and gave the state sector a tendency to grow quite independently of either ideology or policy. There is no great need to make careful distinctions between parties that might have been heir to Franco and those that might not; all of them were. The same could also be said of every other major Spanish institution at the outset of the Gonzales era. When he stepped down, the situation would begin to change in ways that were not necessarily sought or desired but that brought about a turn for the good. Whether it happened because or in spite of the man in power remains a subject of great contention in Spain.

The Spanish modernization process took place against a backdrop of the worldwide regime change of the 1970s. The government applied the usual formulas in adjusting to it, but the special circumstances of Spain determined how they worked. Europe and the market were the drivers of change. Those that would fall victim to the modernization process were, in the end, the very institutions that the government relied upon to guide it. Spanish modernization has not always been pretty, even if for many years its chief guide had the looks of a matinee idol.

The Felipe Gonzales era (1982–1996) was by no means, however, the only crucial episode in Spain's transition. The difficult but smooth political turnabout piloted by Adolfo Suarez in the immediate post-Franco period may well loom as more significant historically and more important in the future.[115] Complicating the Suarez years was an economic crisis – perhaps the gravest to confront any nation in Europe in the generally dismal late 1970s, and one so severe that the impact of the second oil shock (which hit with such devastating effect in much of the rest of Europe) barely registered in Spain. What the neighbors did in these years nonetheless significantly influenced events in Iberia. Suarez acted like a Keynesian and a corporatist. Yet his battles were defensive, and he thus left a less memorable legacy than Gonzales.

Pepe Gonzales, a man of the left, set Spanish liberalization in motion; it was during his long term of office that the character of the new Spain would emerge. A commitment to Europe was basic to the Gonzales package, indeed to that of all post-Franco governments. The EU influence was not felt at once but over many years. Spain had long been on a glide path to the Community. The Spanish would have entered before 1986 had Mitterrand not blocked them in order to prevent dilution of French power.[116] A seven-year transition period followed accession in order to minimize the shock of tariff reduction. By the time that Spain had passed through it, the Single European Act, which directed the removal of nontariff barriers, had been enacted. The liberalization process thus moved seamlessly from one phase into the next. Expectations influenced economic decision making substantially, sometimes inducing change ex ante after the long period of Spanish adjustment to Europe and the market. In the realm of political and economic policy, Spain was a market taker rather than a market maker. Ideas tried elsewhere affected Spain differentially. Tradition impeded "convergence." Standards, norms, and expectations guided the overall integration process even when they could not be met.

A commitment to social democracy was another part of the Gonzales package. That, however, was the rub. Although an eloquent and much-sought spokesman for the cause – indeed the poster boy for the Socialist International – Pepe Gonzales did more to dig its grave than any figure of the era with the possible exception of François Mitterrand or Margaret Thatcher (who, incidentally, "liked Sr. Gonzales personally, however much I disagreed with his socialism").[117] She had nothing to worry about. Pepe's heart may have been on the left, but he wore his wallet on the right. Gonzales has often received bitter criticism as a result.[118] There was much in his record to attack – deep-seated and outrageous social injustice as well as seething moral corruption, to which a parade of political crimes and economic scandals lavishly attests. The common origin of these problems was the corporatist state inherited from Franco.

The way to solve them was not to build it up. Yet Franco's system could not have been torn down without jeopardizing support from the large portion of the electorate that, in numberless ways, still depended upon it for life's essentials. Good manners (as well as political expediency) prompted Gonzales to preserve the pleasant fiction that those who had drawn upon the Franco system had all become good social democrats – and then, when the right moment arrived, to ease them out of their privileges and bring in new interests. That is what he tried to do. Upon assuming office he confirmed a "deal" with the unions that looked like a power-sharing arrangement but was not. The so-called Moncloa Pact had been concluded by the Suarez government in 1977 in order to secure worker acquiescence during the difficult post-Franco transition, but it turned out to be a bad bargain from the economic standpoint. It overpaid the few at the expense of the many, creating high levels of official unemployment. In 1986, once the critical transition period had been traversed, Gonzales let the pseudo-pact lapse.[119] He did not, however, invite confrontation like Mrs. Thatcher but pursued monetary policies that would predictably weaken the labor movement in ways the public could be counted upon not to understand.

Beginning in 1985, the Gonzales government kept interest rates extraordinarily high in order to overvalue the peseta. The result was to force the shutdown of uncompetitive industry, channel investment into new sectors, and drastically increase the value of financial assets. His was a daring, even ruthless policy of induced creative destruction. It basically worked, though with foreseeable devastating consequences that would reverberate into the early 1990s, when Spain had to devalue. This brought down high inflation at the cost of a crippling unemployment.[120] Gonzales exacted such sacrifice, which was arguably necessary for modernization, as a necessary prerequisite of admission into the European Community. Gonzales's demagogy was, in short, a critical variable for Spain. Without both the guile and charisma of the man in office, events might have taken a different turn or none at all.

Psst! Franco was not all that bad. The message, though still only whispered in public, comes through loud and clear for anyone with the time and patience to plow through the already thick and still growing scholarly literature on contemporary Spain. This least ideological of purported fascist heads of state set his nation on a long, looping course of accommodation with the West after 1945, which was neither always sought by the other party nor for many years very successful. Until the 1960s, Europe moved forward too fast for Spain to catch. At the end of the 1950s, however, Franco started to reform from the top down by promoting technocrats from the secretive and elite Catholic *Opus Dei* movement into key positions in government ministries. These exceptionally privileged and powerful men, many of whom became prominent after 1974, were equipped as economists with the intellectual tools (both Keynesian and otherwise) needed to play the catch-up game.[121] They did it well. By actively canvassing foreign investment and cutting apertures into the walled-off economy, they turned Spain into a growth dynamo during the last fifteen years of Franco's reign.[122] Success came at a price: the exercise of a type of central control over the entire banking system that was not consistent with either good practice or the opening of financial markets.

For those Spaniards bunching together near the bottom of the social pyramid, Franco had built up one of the most lavish job protection systems ever devised under corporatism. By exposing Spain to the first blushes of prosperity during the fifteen years of economic growth, the *generalissimo* created real loyalties to the system as well as a reluctance to change horses. During the Franco years, according to one scholarly observer, "the working class was able for the first time to participate in consumerism, thus occasioning a kind of *embourgeoisement* of the masses [as well as] a partial erosion of class barriers that strongly favored the establishment of political democracy."[123] The entrenched position of organized labor would be crucial to the Moncloa Pact, a none-too-distant echo of arrangements prevailing in the fascist-era *Organizacion Sindical Española,* which in the clear but stilted language of Omar Encarnacion "encased meaningful participation of workers in management" in a system that "stands alone among essentially exclusionary, repressive, authoritarian regimes for the extent of democratic worker participation and representation allowed within the official union structure."[124]

The Suarez government, along with the smiling representatives of business and finance, shook hands with labor over the pact. The toilers were actually represented by two unions: the first a revived affiliate of the Socialist Party, the *Union Centro Democratico*; the second, the *Comisiones Obreras*, inherited from the fascist era but revived and linked to the Communist Party. Together they represented only between 10 and 15 percent of the labor force. Both had to establish credibility. How seriously did anyone take the high-minded purposes of the Moncloa arrangement? Its subtext was the important thing: all parties would, at least under Suarez, respect the rule that forbade tampering with what Franco had done to protect the jobs and better the lives of loyal Spanish workers. The old order would remain intact under the new dispensation as long as necessary to smooth the transition.

The Moncloa Pact system produced labor peace and political stability. It provided "rituals of concertation to the process of democratic consolidation," which made it possible to prevent strikes, impose wage reductions, and bring down inflation – from 27 percent in 1977 to 8.8 percent in 1986.[125] Gonzales was the concertmaster. The public enjoyed the music. Few played out of tune, though not everyone always played well. In 1984, at the beginning of the kind of strong recovery that normally makes union representatives upbeat, the government let the deal lapse. A promised tripartite chamber never materialized. Unemploy-ment had increased from 5.7 percent in 1977, when the first pact was concluded, to 20.5 percent when the last one expired in 1986. The protected workers none-theless remained quiescent.[126]

Sensing a vague malaise in the population, the unions declared a general strike on 14 December 1988. Their demands did not include revision or redesign of the pact machinery but merely an acceleration in the tempo of government spend-ing in order to mop up unemployment, then running at the decade's horrendous near-low of 16.4 percent. Taken by surprise, the government capitulated. Com-ing during an upswing, the stimulus was bad medicine. A new surge of inflation ensued and unemployment increased.[127] The inequities of the Moncloa Pact sys-tem would get even worse.

The first of these evils was a bifurcated labor market. On one side was to be found a pleasantly sheltered sector with high wages, blankets of protection, and iron-clad security. On the other was located an expanding but officially unrecog-nized oil slick of disadvantaged, displaced, or discouraged work seekers exposed to the market and obliged to accept part-time, low-wage, disposable, and often illegal jobs without benefits. Between 1977 and 1985, permanent employment fell from 6.52 to 5.91 million while the number of those in temporary work rose from 1.61 to 3.01 million.[128] A tacit understanding to overlook the inequitable split labor market enabled the Spanish economy to absorb nearly a million farm workers "rationalized" out of livelihoods in the countryside – as well as another 500,000 put out of work in the uncompetitive industrial sector – by turning them into the kind of underpaid labor force that foreign investors find appealing.[129] They were, in fact, Spain's main source of comparative advantage. Thanks to them, the share of wage earnings in total national income declined steadily over the period.

The *Partido Socialista Obrero Español* was essentially a post-Franco invention re-packaged largely by Gonzales in the aftermath of the Mitterrand experiment with Socialism in One Country.[130] Pepe and his comrades were deeply troubled by the French train wreck. The PSOE came to power in 1982 committed not only to consolidating democracy but to rejecting outright any independent course like the one France had previously embarked upon. The objective was to raise Spain to European standards of competitiveness. The PSOE was nonetheless oriented to the market and economically orthodox. Its policies focused on combating inflation and earning credibility internationally through the enforcement of re-strictive monetary policy and wage moderation. It was also nationalistic and catered to the needs of domestic interests as a matter of choice. These policy preferences would be permanent.

Contexts would change. Following a quick devaluation after taking office, the socialist government brought down inflation over the next three years by reduc-ing the money supply and raising interest rates. Wage increases trailed rises in productivity. Capital flowed in and investment boomed after 1985. The econ-omy grew at the annual rate of 4 percent for five years. Easy money was much in evidence, perhaps too much. Scandals resulted. Spain would nevertheless be an OECD darling for the rest of the decade. But, by the end of it, the once stable peseta had become 40-percent overvalued as a result of the high–interest rate policy. The stage was set for the economic turmoil of the 1990s and for the tumble of the currency in 1992.[131]

Gonzales was in a position that would have turned any Italian prime minister green with envy. His Spanish equivalent, according to Paul Heywood, was not simply *primus inter pares* within the cabinet "but ... the unambiguous [director] of a strong executive ... empowered to monopolize the most important decisions over national policy."[132] As in Germany, the Spanish prime minister cannot be voted out of office except by a "constructive vote of no confidence," which requires that a majority in parliament can agree on a designated successor. The head of government in Spain can also appoint or dismiss cabinet ministers. Thanks to big PSOE majorities between 1982 and 1993 – and to the implosion and virtual disappearance of the opposition party – Gonzales did not have to share real power with the legislature, which nonetheless gave the impression of being suitably rumbustuous and contentious.[133] Like his counterpart in New Zealand, Pepe was a legal dictator.

The structure of the economy and the availability of policy tools limited Gonzales's scope of action. "Not a leaf can be turned," one heard in Madrid, without the permission of the Ministry of Economy and Finance, which set the parameters for policy throughout the administration (including the budget) and was responsible for monetary and fiscal affairs, overall economic planning, and domestic as well as foreign trade. The technocrats and technopols of this superministry, along with a group of outstanding economists from the Banco de España, managed the economic modernization process. Central to its history in the 1980s was the displacement of Keynesians within the *Opus Dei* elite at the beginning of the decade.[134] The congruence of views between prime minister and policy-making elite was either a fortunate coincidence or an operational necessity. Whether in Franco's Spain or in post-Franco Spanish democracy, orderly reform and economic modernization would have been impossible to direct from any other center of power.

As with their compeers in Italy, the tiny group of Spanish technocrats sought above all to maintain and even strengthen their grip on the levers of power. If the Italians' main task was to pry authority away from a corrupt network of politicians, high officials, and favored business interests in order to promote reform, the Spaniards' primary goal was to carve out a still larger zone of influence within the framework of the existing system in order to strengthen the status quo. Both groups cast their lot with Europe and, with eyes wide open to threats as well as challenges, plumped for restrictive hard-money policies that would predictably accelerate a modernization process in which there would be losers as well as winners. Spain's technocrats and technopols fully expected to belong to the latter.[135]

Spanish modernization policy confronted both a deeper legacy of corporatist economics and more severe structural problems than Italy. Spain had plenty of small producers but no equivalent to the dynamic sector of niche-filling, family-firm entrepreneurs that had rescued Italy time and again; the Spanish situation would in this respect be more like what eastern Europe would soon encounter.[136] It dictated industrial triage on the one hand and dependence on foreign capital on the other. Opportunities to restructure and regroup finance and industry in the manner and scale of the French approach were few and far between. "People's capitalism" à la Thatcher was only a remote possibility. Spanish industrial policy was mainly a rescue operation.

The Franco-era Instituto Nacional de Industria (INI), a vast holding company, dominated the Spanish economy. INI included monopolies like railways, electrical utilities, television and broadcast networks, gas distribution, toll roads and highway concessions, tobacco, and oil refining and distribution; it also controlled a miscellaneous group of companies in banking and finance as well as various specialized engineering and high-tech fields deemed to be in the national interest. Finally, there was INI's long list of rust-belt companies: big steel mills, coal mines and shipyards, defense industries, and many other loss makers. They provided 70,000 jobs, most of them in the politically sensitive industrial north. The chance of bringing such zombies effectively to market was nil until they could be brought back to life. The de-nationalization of industry was just getting under way when Gonzales left office.[137]

The private sphere in Spain was industrially underdeveloped. The biggest private firms were to be found in the retail, construction, and utilities sectors rather than in manufacturing, in several branches of which the country was unrepresented. Although the U.S. Department of Commerce representative in Madrid detected an improvement in Spanish entrepreneurship, the real action was located, she concluded, in fields entered by multinational corporations. Between the state (with 35 percent) and foreign investors (with an equal share), comparatively little of Spanish industry was actually owned by Spaniards.[138] Gonzales was stuck with the rust-belt turkeys, to which he had to throw corn; starved (at least initially) for foreign capital, which he had to lure; and committed by political instinct to healing and nurturing the economy's walking wounded, for whom he had to find crutches.

His only means of handling this thicket of problems was with the help of the financial community: via the central bank and the economics ministry and, through their close relationships with private banking, with the rest of the economy. In a remarkable case study that may well shed light on other still unexamined national adaptations to change, *Banking on Privilege: The Politics of Spanish Banking Reform*, Sophia Pérez provides a rare glimpse into a cartelized financial system in the course of transition to a market economy. Pérez shows that, in Franco and post-Franco Spain, the thinness of national capital markets limited government financing operations to direct dealing with the private banks. The relationship had certain advantages. It freed the government from the uncertainties of the credit market and gave the banks a handsome guaranteed profit margin. For them it was simple, secure, and lucrative. The arrangement had more than offsetting disadvantages for others. It was costly, bred complacency, restricted the availability of scarce credit to vital growth sectors, and stood in the way of adaptation, accommodation, and reform. New entrants were discouraged, which in the 1980s included not only other bigger and better banks but novel fast-breaking methods of "disintermediated" financing over markets.[139] Pérez blames the banking structure rather than inflexible labor markets for Spain's economic ailments. Both were obstacles to change, but neither was impervious to it. Indisputably, bank clubbiness promoted the corruption that surfaced in the late 1980s.

The Spanish financial community blocked change along "Anglo-Saxon" lines, something front and center on the reform agenda in 1977, until 1988. Even then it happened only as a result of a directive from the European Commission. The gaping budget deficits of the 1980s strengthened the banks' hands in dealing with a cash-hungry government. The banks succeeded fairly well, according to Pérez, in maintaining oligopolistic control while deregulating credit – pressures from Brussels and world financial markets notwithstanding.[140] Their determination is not in question. In 1983 RUMASA, a publicly owned company as well as the only major bank not a member of the dominant "Big Seven" cartel, got in trouble. Instead of rescuing the enterprise, Minister of Economics Miguel Boyer broke it up and sold off the "privatized" pieces to the privileged banks.

In the accession agreement to the European Community, according to Pérez, "Spanish negotiators negotiated a special seven-year interim period in which the authorities could invoke an 'economic necessity' clause to limit ... the entry of foreign banks while maintaining the existing limitations on foreign banks already in Spain until the end of 1992."[141] Abutting this arrangement was a "gentlemen's agreement" negotiated by the Banco de España in which the Big Seven relinquished the sale of ailing subsidiaries to the foreign interests then eagerly seeking footholds in the Spanish economy. At the end of the 1980s, the central bank launched a drive to consolidate the Big Seven. Reversing a ten-year trend, the big financials resumed investing directly in industry.[142] The parallel to France under Premier Rocard immediately comes to mind. The idea was that Spain (like France) was to become another Germany, with an economy regulated by universal banks.

Change came, according to Pérez, "in spite of ... the Bank of Spain and Ministry of Finance officials' ... almost single-minded concern with safeguarding the national character of the banking sector."[143] In 1988 the long-overdue "belated bang" in Madrid, an echo of those in London and Paris, transformed the *Bolsa* almost overnight. Prior to it, only 300 issues were listed on Spanish exchanges. The big banks, along with a couple of utilities, held over 70 percent of capitalization; industry, only 30 percent. As undervalued share prices – which had fallen 90 percent between 1974 and 1983 – sucked capital into the market in the late 1980s, Madrid became the go-go bourse of the day, and plenty of easy money was made and changed hands. Even Spanish bankers "swiftly caught on to the fact if they were to profit from the boom in foreign investments, they would have to offer a wider range of stock market services." They did not, however, renounce insider advantage.[144] The bankers managed to delay until 1991 the introduction of mutual funds, which then became an overnight sensation; but by foot-dragging, traditional interests held on to nearly 60 percent of the new market.[145] One particular innovation weakened and changed Spanish bank cartelism. The Treasury managed to launch its first note issue and thereby cut the lead strings to banks, which thereupon re-directed their attention from the captive government to the new El Dorado: the long-cheated consumer.

The Banco de España's campaign to reorganize the Big Seven into national champions did not bring about the desired results. An arranged marriage between the Banco de Bilbao and BANESTA turned into a knock-down drag-out battle and was never consummated. BANESTA was eventually taken over by Banco de Santander, which then began to offer interest on deposit accounts in emulation of new foreign-owned competitors. The war for the Spanish depositor had begun. Even though many restrictive practices continued, especially in the emergent field of consumer finance, the banking cartel formally dissolved at the beginning of the new decade. Two new public banks were organized in the early 1990s, and the Big Seven gradually boiled down to a still Bigger Four. None of the traditional finance leaders succumbed to foreign takeover in spite of abnormally high profits. Even so, their hold on the commanding heights of the Spanish economy remained vulnerable, in light of the much-sought but much-feared influx of foreign capital. The biggest of The Four ranked only in the mid-sixties on world tables. Between 1985 and 1990, the foreign ownership share in Spanish industry rose from 17.1 percent to 31.5 percent. Half-helped though surely no less seriously hindered by the private banks, competitive pressures brought capital market reform willy-nilly to Spain.[146]

Such forces were beginning to change the structure of industry as well, though here developments would continue to lag behind even those in the financial sector. This should not be a surprise: in the post-Fordist era, manufacturing was not the growth engine it had been in the 1950s and 1960s. The industrial question was not, as in France, central to the nation's status as a great power; it was for Gonzales a worry, a cost, and a matter of catch-up – a problem that had to be solved before Spain could converge economically with the rest of Europe. Industrial employment declined only slightly between 1975 and 1995, from 30.8 to 29.8 percent of the total working population. Over the same years, service employment increased from 53.0 to 55.2 percent, a trend generally in line with European norms but attributable in Spain almost entirely to public-sector growth. Small firms contributed about two thirds of GNP, but "they did not, on the whole, adapt to the changed circumstances of competition in the large market."[147] Some 12,000 firms disappeared between 1978 and 1990. Firms employing more than 500 workers still accounted for less than a quarter of the total number employed in Spain. In virtually all modern branches of industry, levels of concentration were low and, concluded Mary Farrell, "the Spanish ... industrial structure seemed ill-prepared for the demands of European integration."[148] The merger movement remained on a small scale.

The real action stemmed from multinational corporations trying to capture the many economies of scale and scope available in Spain. There were plenty of opening consumer markets to tap and much available cheap (and comparatively productive) labor upon which to build export platforms for catapulting goods and services into the European Union. Net foreign direct investment nearly tripled from 67.6 billion pesetas in 1980 to 156.1 billion in 1984 and ballooned from there into 1,073.1 billion pesetas in 1990.[149] Although "spillover effects" are difficult to quantify, the European Commission "warmly endorsed the contribution of the foreign direct investment in Spain ... to the quality level of human skills, technological advances and the productivity of firms receiving investment."[150] The Commission's study indicated that some of the new money went into the export industry – above all, the automobile industry, which by the early 1990s accounted for a quarter of Spanish foreign sales.

Trade flows would eventually become as important to Spain's competitiveness as foreign direct investment. Yet the full impact of EU membership was not felt until 1994, because the accession agreement allowed a seven-year period for the reduction of high Spanish tariffs. Volumes of both exports and imports nevertheless rose rapidly as a percentage of GNP. The "openness coefficient" increased from 37.5 percent in 1986 to 64.9 percent in 1996 (as measured in constant prices). On the export side, a significant shift occurred away from labor-intensive, low-skilled production in favor of "high-skilled labor and with greater product differentiation," but the high-tech field remained virtually unrepresented.[151] A chronic trade imbalance indicated a continuing lack of industrial competitiveness even after the 1992 devaluation. Fundamental change in this respect remains unlikely. By the mid-1990s, net financial flows had reversed. The new money made in the Spain of the late 1980s understood neither stickiness nor loyalty. Much of it apparently migrated elsewhere.[152]

The most striking change to come over Spain in the Gonzales years was public-sector bloat. It was certainly not the intended result of neoliberal policy. The horrendous unemployment was the main source of the problem, but the heavy subsidization of industry – something economically unwelcome though (because of northern regionalism) politically necessary – also played a role. Finally, the importance of patronage cannot be discounted. Party control of officeholding grew from 67 percent of government positions in 1991 to 72 percent in 1994.[153] The austere, remote, and relatively small state of Franco gave way to a large and diffuse administration that pushed down to the grass roots. Partly because of the new "associationalism" – the proliferation of lobbies and interest groups (economic, professional, consumerist, hobbyist, etc.) in these years – it was hard to detect where the boundary of the public sphere ended and the private one began. There was plenty of negotiable terrain along the public–private interface.

The scandals that after fourteen years finally ended Gonzales's long reign brought the shortcomings of the system to the surface yet were also a back-handed testimony to change. Too much power had become concentrated in too few hands. Though Spain boomed in the late 1980s and rapid social change was palpable, the political system was immobilized and the government either could not or would not do anything to alleviate the crippling unemployment problem. The sharp downturn of the early 1990s added a sense of grievance to accumu-lated suffering. Although the bugs in the system may not have been much worse than before, they had become less tolerable. Amidst it all, as Victor Pérez-Diaz eloquently explains in *Spain at the Crossroads,* the great, long-troubled nation was becoming a modern society.[154] What prompted a sense of outrage in the new setting might well, a few years earlier, have occasioned nothing more than a resigned shrug of the shoulders from a public that did not expect anything bet-ter from its government. The scandals that rocked Spain in the early 1990s were evidence of a new civic spirit.

There was nothing either particularly spectacular or notably awful about the economic scandals, except of course from the Spanish point of view. They paled in comparison to the sophistication of the Byzantine schemes pervading Italian society, to the arrogance of Colbertist thefts brazenly launched by the French *État* before the very eyes of its victimized citizens, or to the amplitude (not to mention range and variety) of the fraud, malpractice, and dirty dealing encoun-tered at every governmental level in that great republican experiment, the United States. For relative novices in democratic politics, however, the PSOE did not do badly. The RUMASA affair of 1983 was the only big scandal to involve privatiza-tion. Although never investigated by the parliament, at issue were the modalities of compensation. RUMASA was an isolated event and soon forgotten.[155]

The succession of major affairs that broke out at the end of the decade was a more serious matter. No less then twenty investigations ran concurrently that involved abuse of office. Though all parties were besmirched, most of the mud landed on the one in power. In an affair redolent of cronyism, Juan Guerra – Gonzales's deputy and head of the progressive faction of PSOE – had to resign because of his brother's shady real-estate deals cut from a luxurious rent-free gov-ernment office. At the regional level "corrupt practices ... came up everywhere," in Andulasia (Ollero), Navarre (Urralburu), even in supposedly lily-white Cat-alonia. They involved dirty politics-as-usual: insider real-estate deals, payoffs, bribes, general palm greasing, and mutual back-scratching. Local journalists detected great reader interest in coverage of the remarkable lifestyle improve-ments enjoyed by familiar political figures. Scandal-mongering articles became daily fare in the tabloids.[156]

Dirty party financing along the lines of the "Gallic model" was another wide-spread practice. Pressed for money in 1986, PSOE "set up a network of illegal financing shells in imitation of the French Socialist Party ... and established inter-mediary societies which, under the cover of producing technical reports to busi-ness companies, channeled illegal funds to the party." The FILESA consulting firm received a billion pesetas from big companies and banks for xeroxing copies of draft laws. It seemed a lot to pay. Two politicians would do hard time for failure to prove otherwise.[157]

Not all Spanish cheats were unimaginative. Carmen Salanueva owned the official gazette, the publisher of record for the laws of parliament; she was nabbed for false invoicing, which – without kickbacks to co-conspirators among the lawmakers – would have been an act of sheer stupidity. It may well have been, anyway. In a later case involving an attempt to swindle precious paintings, she was sentenced for impersonating the Queen of Spain on one occasion and Carmen Romero on another (Ms. Romero was Pepe Gonzales's wife).[158] In 1991, the World Economic Forum awarded Spain the silver medal for corruption (European division). Italy took the gold.[159]

Even more damaging to government credibility were affairs that – though not, strictly speaking, actionable – suggested widespread and habitual abuse of power in high places. Miguel Boyer was an arch-technocrat with close PSOE connections. Minister of economics from 1983 to 1986, married to a knockout ex-model, and with a life style as glittering as his wife, he was also emblematic of *los beautiful,* the jet-setters of the day who filled the pages of weekly glossies like *¡Hola!.* Public fascination with the glamorous Boyer only increased when, shortly upon leaving office, he rose to become chief executive of a couple of holding companies controlled by two fabulously wealthy sisters born with eastern European names but in possession of proud and ancient Spanish titles, each married to men named Alberto, who were cousins. Daily news articles about newly discovered variations on four-way hanky-panky kept reader interest steaming. When the economy turned sharply south at the end of the decade, it soon became apparent that the two Albertos had badly overreached in an ambitious bid to expand their financial empires. Down came the cousins Alberto, down with them the sisters Koplowitz, and shortly behind them tumbled Miguel Boyer and his unforgettable bride.[160]

Boyer took seriously the infamous boast of his successor as minister of economics, Carlos Solchaga, that Spain was the European country in which one could get rich the quickest. In 1992 he and his wife would be implicated in an even bigger (though disappointingly less colorful) scandal, IBERCORP, named after a failed bank holding company bailed out by the government. This time the hard-loving glitterati couple would be in even better company. The investigation led to insider trading and stock manipulation by several well-known wheeler-dealers prominent among *los beautiful,* one of them the former president of the Madrid stock exchange. Others involved in their deals, in addition to the glamorous Boyers, were Mariano Rubio, the governor of the Bank of Spain since 1992 and a minister of economics from the previous government, and Carlos Solchaga, at the time PSOE's parliamentary secretary. Solchaga apparently wanted to put his theory into practice.[161]

The era of Spanish socialism started well and ended ill. It is easy to apportion blame. The two-tier labor system hypocritically institutionalized and perpetuated social injustice. The buildup of power at the center distorted policy making and, abetted by inadequate firewalls between the private and public domains, led to sleaze and corruption. It is hard to argue, however, that Gonzales made the wrong political choices. He could not have attacked union privilege within a decade of Franco's death. The PSOE might have collapsed had he been less inclined to coddle it. Nor could he have replaced the financial elite that directed modernization policy: there was no other center of economic leadership. Perhaps Gonzales should have broken openly with both the Moncloa Pact and the technocrats once the economy began to boom in the late 1980s, allowing the currency to find its own levels in foreign exchange markets. Exports might then have flourished, unemployment have declined, growth been smooth, the economy have become more stable, and income have been distributed more fairly. But the peseta would then have tumbled out of the EMS and Spain would have found itself dumped unceremoniously off the glide path to Europe, which would have had severe consequences. Membership meant more to Spain than participation in song contests, ownership of BMWs, and easy access to tall, buxom blondes. If "Europe" represented to Mrs. Thatcher a chance to build a market economy on the neighboring continent and to Mitterrand an opportunity to consolidate the power of the state and project French influence and to Kohl the best available solution to the German problem, for Gonzales it offered an escape from the strictures that national tradition had placed on economic modernization.

How else could he have bootstrapped Spain than by opening his country up to competition in the European marketplace? That such a policy would generate new wealth involved an act of faith on his part. Spanish industry was still unreformed, ailing, and sometimes in need of life support. The activation of trade was promising, but the full impact of the new flows would not be felt until the end of the transitional period. Only in the financial sector had structural change begun to take hold by the early 1990s. Once forced to compete, even on a limited basis, the big banks faced a hard choice between reforming and regrouping or facing eventual extinction. They could no longer be joined at the hip to the Spanish state. The breaking of this close bond hardly meant that Spain had "liberalized," merely that a process had been set in motion that would be hard to stop. By breaking the stranglehold of the economic policy-making elite, his old allies, Gonzales had gained a new measure of political independence for the Spanish people as well as his office. No longer merely nominally free to choose, they would in the future have real choices to make between market and state. Spain could now turn democratic pretense into democratic opportunity.

REFORMING THE WELFARE STATE

The success of the Thatcher experiment in Great Britain, along with the failure of Mitterrand's in France, set the parameters of national economic policy in Europe during the 1980s. It made little difference what they called themselves or to which ideology they nominally subscribed: all political parties, once in power, tried to stabilize currencies, bring spending under control, curtail excesses in the state sector, open markets, and restore industrial competitiveness. The policy shifts that occurred when new governments formed, an infrequent event in the 1980s, stemmed largely from changing conditions and requirements rather than different ideological or political preferences. Most governments of the decade recognized that the trend toward world market opening was worldwide, impelled by deep-seated forces beyond the control of any political authority (national or European) and over the long term probably irresistible. Necessity rather than principle made neoliberals of those holding office, be they nominally socialist as in Spain or nominally right-centrist as in France. Adaptation and accommodation to the inevitable were the order of the day. The process would not be easy.

Was there an alternative? Not on the far left. Mitterrand's failure was the last big experiment ever undertaken from that quarter. Even the post-Mao Chinese communists had given up on Socialism in One Country. In the 1980s, nonmarket economies were on the defensive. Attempts to shore them up were ineffective – especially in small, wealthy countries with mixed-economy welfare states. Huge national labor unions dominated government in Scandinavia. Their authority derived from a monopoly over wage bargaining and the power to re-allocate national income. Such regulated economies, unless reformed as in New Zealand, broke down over the decade and were increasingly hard to patch up. In corporatist systems like the German one, where labor and management shared power, the ailment was more long-term and the symptoms harder to detect. The gravity of the situation would become increasingly apparent in the future. Modernizing economies faced more complicated problems. In post-Franco Spain, corporatism was eroded economically even as it became necessary to string it back together politically. In still partly modern Italy, clientelism had produced an almost unreformable tangle of interests whose cure would require a sharp break with the past.

Few alternative ideas then in currency had much to offer. The decade's newfound champions of building "socialism" by means of worker self-management – as opposed to the already badly discredited method of state ownership – learned little from either the post-Mitterrand lifeboat experience or the failure of the Swedish model. In Sweden, an undiluted Third Way policy had been pursued since the 1960s. The result was not grass-roots control of the economic and political system but instead a trade-union dictatorship that destroyed the productivity of industry, agriculture, and commerce, created a dependent public, and left a legacy that has been perniciously hard to overcome even long after being discredited. The collapse of the Swedish model originated from within. It was triggered by the rejection of "solidarism" by the most productive segment of the industrial labor force, the skilled workers. The same thing happened in Denmark. The Swedish system broke down on its own. Once deprived of the easy out of devaluation, it could not stand up to competition.

Can a properly conceived and executed labor market policy restore growth, overcome unemployment, invigorate central wage bargaining, and bring governments into power that are committed to income redistribution and maintenance of the welfare state? Although arousing more interest in academic circles than in places closer to earth, the dream of reinstating a refurbished Rehn–Meidner dies hard. However implausibly, it remains a part of scholarly discourse. For those thinkers on the French Second Left who survived the sinking of the early 1980s, Michel Albert's version of *Modell Deutschland* provided a stylized example of how things could and should work. The notion that the German system could simply be transplanted was fanciful; it was not an export product. The only feature that France took over from the German corporatist–capitalist model during the Rocard years had little to do with worker self-determination, social equality, or benevolent intellectual oversight; it was the capital tie-in at the commanding heights between the universal banks and industry. This bond had been a distinguishing characteristic of the German economy since Hitler. In spite of a concerted effort to disentangle the tie during Allied occupation – and to loosen it during the Erhard years – it held together into the early 1990s. The big bankers, with the help of the government, have by now long been desperately trying to reform. While the intellectual left in Paris was clamoring for the "Rhenish" model, the leaders of German finance had for sound economic reasons quietly begun to go "Anglo-Saxon." To point out the essential irrelevance of arguments like Albert's, which he himself later rejected, is not to deny their force. They would remain influential in the years between (and even after) the Single European Act and Maastricht.

An alternative to Thatcherism, or an appropriate adaptation of it, would have to be found separately in each of the national political cultures of Europe. The application of prescriptive "models" to the reform of any country is perilous. Disproving conclusively the Aussie jibe – that they are nothing more than "Pommies without brai-ins!" – not even the pristine, Anglophile, and quite thoroughly overhauled New Zealanders elected to follow Mrs. Thatcher in locking horns with the powerful unions until *after* the liberalization of finance, foreign trade, and the restrictive regulatory system was well under way. The application of the same direct methods that worked for Britain was neither necessarily desirable nor even possible elsewhere. Neoliberal policies consequently varied from place to place.

It is hard to quibble with outcomes – which, given the proximity of events, can only be considered provisional. There is also little reason to do so, because in retrospect the results seem to have been nearly optimal from the various national standpoints. The Gonzales era hardly ended in a blaze of glory, but the Spanish prime minister did break sharply with the legacy of corporatism, directing his country on a course of liberalization that would be difficult to reverse and that would, in fact, be successfully continued by his conservative successor, Jose-Maria Aznar.

Spain embarked on liberalization well ahead of Portugal, where events took a slightly different course. There, a financial technocracy and an allied banking cartel ironically supported Mrs. Thatcher in opposition to the curtailment of monetary independence by means of the European Monetary System. Portugal would continue to operate within the framework of an IMF adjustment strategy that delayed liberalization until the 1990s. The gradualist policy set back structural reform but at the same time helped spare Portugal the high unemployment suffered by Spain. A special circumstance had a similarly beneficent effect: Portuguese wages remained very low because, although benefits were generally high, the lack of unemployment compensation provided a strong disincentive to bargaining. In any case, Portugal has had little choice but to follow the course led by its increasingly competitive neighbor. It joined the European Rate Mechanism in 1992.[162] Concomitantly, a wave of corruption – similar in both cause and effect to Spain's – afflicted Portugal.[163]

The Italian situation seemed hopeless. Yet within only a few years, and then over a period of mere months, peaceful reform on a previously unimaginable scale would sweep through the country with breathtaking ease. The corrupt system seemed to come down; already in collapse, it would, at any rate, long be on the defensive. The Danes, for their part, managed to start modestly reforming the welfare state at the cost of high unemployment but without sacrifice to either their own distinct traditions or one of the highest living standards in Europe. The Swedish adaptation to regime change has been the most difficult to date. Reform would have to be far-reaching. The close association of national identity with "the model" nonetheless posed a big obstacle to faster and smoother adaptation. By opting for Europe, the Swedes began to turn a corner. The German nut could, in the end, be the hardest to crack for the paradoxical reason that the mixed-economy welfare-state system has worked better there than anyplace else. The costs of the Federal Republic's corporatism are, however, becoming increasingly apparent in the long term, as year follows year of laggard growth.

The reform process began with recognition of the ineluctability and desirability of global change, an acknowledgment that "Europe" was and would be an important part of it, the adoption of regulatory and then financial reform needed to promote competition, the sponsorship of privatization, the reduction in the size and scope of the state, and the overhaul of governmental administrative machinery. The next stage, the late 1990s, would bring the spread of market institutions from which, slowly and tentatively, is developing a distinctly different and probably better kind of society.

In the 1980s, Europe entered stage one. Mrs. Thatcher led the way and took Britain further along the road than anyone else could travel. Only in the United Kingdom could one detect the inklings of what the future might bring. The British experiment involved trial-and-error learning and thus also a number of instructive mistakes. Mrs. Thatcher and her people made plenty of them but learned much in the process. The first lesson was that the power of organized labor was the central obstacle to reform. Her solution, brutal confrontation, was not applicable elsewhere. Another was the speed and ease with which financial reform could be introduced as well as the immediacy of its consequences. Thus "bangs" of one sort or another soon reverberated on Europe's national bourses, and new capital markets developed almost spontaneously. Financial reform lowered borrowing costs, expanded markets, put wealth in new hands, and increased money power. Capital mobility soon became a powerful force for change but also met with the resistance of entrenched interests, which have slowed down the subsequent progress of reform but have never been able to prevent or repeal it.

Privatization taught several important additional lessons of its own. As quickly became obvious, privatization had no hard-and-fast boundaries: it could extend throughout the economy and even include services previously thought to belong in the government domain. The success of the program changed the concept of a public good. Supposed "natural monopolies" like electric power were no longer sacrosanct. Privatization thus served as a catalyst to administrative reform. In public services, "marketization" became a byword. At the same time, the de-nationalization of state-owned companies also required considerable governmental intervention: they often had to be healed in order to be made saleable, required infusions of capital or credit or even needed to be reorganized, merged, or broken up and resold. Re-regulation in some new form was also often necessary in order to prevent the substitution of private monopolies for public ones. It became swiftly evident that the sale of public assets could have diverse consequences: provide a cash-hungry government with a welcome source of revenue; serve as a mechanism for shoring up wobbly economic institutions; be an engine of wealth redistribution; or provide the means for changing political mentalities.

The reduction, reorganization, and redefinition of the state's role in the economy was yet another facet of Thatcherite change, but its lessons were less evident. The theoretical substitutability of private for public service providers was not at issue, but the specifics of implementation were. The extent to which marketized public agencies could be made competitive with private companies attuned to the market remained a subject of serious controversy. A further thorny matter was the desirability of substituting private for public control; it could not simply be thrashed out at the level of theory but had to be decided individually in different political contexts. In the stable democracies of northern Europe its results were likely to be efficiencies and cost reductions, whereas in the modernizing nations of the south its consequences were more likely to be the creation of private monopolies or, in certain cases, the reinforcement of corrupt or criminal associations. The potential value of aggregate savings from the reform of government services remains largely undetermined. Rising costs for medical services and pensions will force the welfare state to locate and exploit such economies.

The British learned above all that Mrs. Thatcher's quest was not neatly laid out on a map; it followed a course that widened almost imperceptibly into a long and unpredictably twisting road that would follow the topography of politics as well as economics but whose end was not in sight. The fate of Thatcherism on the continent would be determined separately in each national political culture; so, too, would the future of the European Community. The French made their own satisfactory (though still partial) accommodation to regime change and only flirted with neoliberalism, which provided a welcome diversion from a long, often wearying, and much too serious marriage to the state. The fling did them some good: in the end, it even strengthened the long-term relationship or at least made it bearable. The French re-constitution of elites was an extraordinary feat of seigniorage and statecraft but not an option open to others. Would any other European electorate have acquiesced in a policy at once so nationalistic, so undemocratic, and so inequitable? Or could it have worked anywhere else?

Spanish technocrats must have been overawed by the French accomplishment. Although their system was also highly centralized, Spain lacked the other pre-requisites to a French solution, those needed for formation of new communities-of-interest (*Interessengemeinschaften*). Spain's elites were thin, and its industry was weak and dependent upon subsidies. The banks at the commanding heights were formidable only within a local context. Unemployment was a crippling phe-nomenon that, in addition to inflicting great injustice, drained scarce resources out of the economy while vitiating both the state and government. Clientelist Italy also lacked the necessary prerequisites for a French-type policy. Any at-tempt to reweave the dense networks of public–private collusion permeating the Boot was something best avoided. In egalitarian and neutralist Scandinavia, the open pursuit of a French-style policy of top-down control by elites was politi-cally unthinkable. There remained as alternative to the new British approach only the German corporatist model. Although breaking down slowly in the 1980s, it would remain the favorite of Mrs. Thatcher's European critics for an-other decade.

The European Community impelled the opening of markets throughout the continent in the years between the Single European Act and Maastricht, but not always in ways easily measured by economists. Its most important impact was felt through the European Monetary System, which – by forcing currencies to peg to the stable Deutsche mark – reduced inflation, stabilized and opened markets, expanded trade flows, and increased foreign investment. The EMS has never received great press and has often been dismissed as a second-best or interim so-lution. Yet it deserves much credit for moving the nations of Europe away from the monetary and fiscal disorder of the 1970s.

The Community also exercised influence politically and morally. Subsequent to the Single European Act, its neoliberal posture influenced the planning of gov-ernments no less than it changed conditions in the marketplace. Not only actual competition but expectations dictated investment and marketing decisions. The instinctive reaction of most governments to foreign competition was often to seek cover. Only Mrs. Thatcher (and, of course, President Reagan) enjoyed the political luxury of being able to contemplate the disappearance of whole sectors of industry with apparent equanimity and without fear of social upheaval. The EC's authority derived in part from an ability to overcome resistance by captur-ing or satisfying the needs, hopes, and imaginations of national political leaders as well as of the informed, influential, and interested European public.

Neoliberalism did not quite do the trick ideologically. Although it brought about necessary economic results and got governments re-elected, its appeal was only pragmatic. The virtues of Hayek's "spontaneous order" remained unap-preciated. The governments of the era nevertheless recognized that marketplace competition stepped up the pace of economic change. Integration would enter its most constructive phase after 1986. At the same time, the Commission would soon set countercurrents in motion that would put unexpected bends and detours in Mrs. Thatcher's road to the future. They lead back to the horrible press conference after the London summit in December 1986 and to the disagreement behind the angry standoff between the two great Europeans of the decade. Mrs. Thatcher assumed that the opening of markets would lead to a cascade of self-generating market development that would modify institutions, increase the economic and political sovereignty of individual human beings, and produce a society based on merit as earned through competition. Jacques Delors had a different idea. He intended to remove obstacles to the formation of mega-strength corporations that could hold their own on a world scale in order to produce the economic growth needed to support a European federal government with the strength to reorder societies across the continent – in a manner consistent with notions of the just and the good that were held by intellectuals like himself.

10

Maastricht Ho! (by Air, Land, or SEA?): The Parameters of Change

THREE routes led from the Single European Act (SEA) to the Maastricht treaty. The functionalist approach went by Air. The theory holds that – once put into currency and institutionalized – the integration idea has reverberating, reciprocal, and dynamic spillovers that drive the process onward. This approach, the way of Monnet, Hallstein, and Delors, went through both the European Coal and Steel Community and the European Commission and would (if Delors had his druthers) debouch into a "European social and economic space." Another approach, liberal intergovernmentalism, was by Land and passed milestones at the European Economic Community, the European Council, and the European Monetary System, each of them a Grand Bargain sealed by heads of state that advanced the integration process from one stage to the next. Finally, one might travel by SEA, promoting competition and eliminating barriers to the movement of goods and factors of production. The Common Market and the Single European Market marked this course, a hard one to chart, even though the route it followed – liberalization – was widely agreed to be the proudest achievement of the integration process prior to the great changes that swept Europe in the 1980s.

The economics of integration are not well understood. The static models of neoclassical economics cannot account for change over time. Nor do the conditions they posit exist in a Europe of welfare states. No integration variable has yet been isolated, and no existing purely economic theory of endogenous change can explain how integration advances from one step to the next.[1] The heterogeneous schools of classical economics inspired by Adam Smith and in which Hayek is the central figure – but which also include various strains of *Ordoliberalismus,* monetarism, public choice theory, and the new institutional economics associated with Douglass North – each help to explain in some way how change occurs through markets and institutions. None of them, however, provides an overarching analytical framework. Their insights must be verified empirically when applied to the study of history.

The events of the years from 1986 to 1992 would put the various means of locomotion to the test. As champion of institutions built on Euro-ideas, Jacques Delors would create a durable framework of discourse that qualifies him for recognition as lead Airman. The heads of state and government – convening in various venues and forums – built solid, well-piered institutional structures for reliable mass terrestrial conveyance; their feet planted firmly in the ground, these sound bargainers opened new areas to competition, reduced inflation, and disciplined budgets. The European Monetary Union is a product of intergovernmentalism. Markets would be the wild card, the spoilers of plots, the twisters of schemes, the upsetters of plans, the shifters of circumstance, the shortcutters of change, and the engines of the learning process. The route by SEA passed through uncharted realms, could not be plotted in advance, and – as a creation of spontaneous order – could only be discovered on the spot by trial and error.

Which of the contending political science theories takes one farthest and fastest? A new one perhaps? "Historical institutionalism" (HI), a young and promising approach, has assumed the task (according to advocate Paul Pierson, professor of government at Harvard) of closing gaps left unexplained by either functionalism or liberal intergovernmentalism, both of which are still assumed to tell essential parts of the integration story. Doubtless *functionalist* spillovers occur, he agrees, but just when, where, and how cannot be predicted. *Intergovernmentalist* Grand Bargains, he continues, should be regarded as context-shifting events that have unintended, as opposed to optimal, consequences: institutions are path-dependent, self-serving, anchored in short-run considerations, influenced by feedback loops, lacking in oversight machinery sufficient for "dense" policy issues, and unable to foresee possible spillovers. EU institutions are, Pierson adds, "sticky" – designed to be resistant to change, unlikely to face direct attack (because of "opt out" provisions in Maastricht), and still less likely to be challenged owing to the high sunk costs of the contracting parties in longstanding bargains.[2]

In attempting to provide an improved theory of causation, HI tries to demonstrate how temporal processes embedded in institutions – and producing only partly intended results – manage to advance, inhibit, and shape change over time. The school's interdisciplinary and integrative approach to developing a new logic of institutions draws selectively on the classical liberal tradition. By assuming that change takes place in a unique and distinct setting that cannot be reproduced, HI is also partly historical; by recognizing the existence of markets as agents of change, it is partly economic as well. Historical institutionalism may provide the theoretical foothold needed to scale the heights commanding a view of the whole.[3]

The HI theory of institutional causation has advanced rapidly, but the research program is still in an early phase. To date it has produced only "snapshot" examples of institution–market interaction over the course of European integration. These micro studies can nonetheless be suggestive. In trying to provide an institutional explanation of the gap between intent and outcome in Community social policy, Stephan Leibfried and Paul Pierson show that – by opening the provision of health-care services to competition – the Commission and the European Court have inadvertently restricted state policy options, changed the economics of health delivery systems, and influenced the quality of medical treatment.[4] They have thereby removed responsibilities from the national health services that the

EU executive cannot handle, inadvertently placing them in invisible hands. A policy of re-regulation has turned new powers over to the marketplace.

What Liebfried and Pierson present is not evidence of institutional failure or random change but of market success within the established legal framework of the treaty. Their data supports the ORDO-liberal notion that the European Union has a kind of default drive – is endowed with an "economic constitution" with formative power. The corollary is that integration can take hold and develop only in a manner consistent with the ideas of those who originally designed it: as a free-trade area regulated by laws and institutions designed to allow markets to function properly.[5] The mysterious SEA thus provides the only sure route to integration. The other approaches, by Air and Land, can partly determine how and when the integration process unfolds but can also thwart it.

The route that began with the Single European Act and led to Maastricht was paved with ambiguity. The problem, according to Herbert Giersch, originated in the conflict of two paradigms of EU development.[6] The first, which Hayek calls "constructivist rationalism," focuses on institution building, bureaucratic integration, political unification, centralism, and some version of planning. Since the "p-word" lost favor in the 1970s (as did the attenuated version of it, economic coordination), variations have taken the form of regulation as well as the harmonization of institutions, taxes, and norms. The alternative view holds that markets are wiser than bureaucrats, that productivity arises from diversity rather than uniformity, and that "harmonization" takes place by means of evolutionary competition via the discovery process. Such an optimal decision-making approach vests ultimate power in the consumer. Delors was a force for "constructivist rationalism": his goals were to strengthen the power of the Commission, build corporate alliances at the European level like those forming in contemporary France, and set an agenda for the future advancement of integration that included the creation of a "European social and economic space." Mrs. Thatcher took the other point of view, but she supported M. Delors's centralization initiative out of a conviction that the removal of national nontariff barriers would ipso facto promote a liberalization that would override and nullify corporatist and *dirigiste* tendencies. Delors's economic plans went down the drain. So, too, did Thatcher's hopes that market reforms would sweep away the detritus of socialism and corporatism. Both leaders eventually parted the scene in anger, convinced that the other had won.[7]

Each was at least partly right. In the years between SEA and Maastricht, the budget of the Commission grew in real terms by about 50 percent, to nearly 50 billion euros and nearly 30,000 employees. Even more impressive, the population of lobbyists, intellectual service providers, and assorted camp followers surrounding the Euro-*apparat* increased to a lush 10,000 over the same years.[8] The change reflected the rise in Community expenditures as well as its added power, its inability to discharge increased responsibilities by itself, and the existence of a flourishing new symbiotic relationship that had sprouted up between organized economic and social interests and the Eurocracy. At the same time,

Brussels-initiated liberalization – enforced through the SEA and competition policy – took hold. Interacting with, promoting, influencing and being influenced by parallel changes at both the domestic and international level, the market-opening process modified the structure and operation of the economy and thus changed the context of politics. Liberalization also met resistance along the way. The struggle between Delors and Thatcher did not resemble a gladiatorial contest; it was fought by different creatures, like cobra and mongoose in a pit enclosed on two sides by the Single European Act and on the two others by the Treaty of the European Union.

THE SEA AND THE MAASTRICHT TREATY: NEGOTIATING FRAMEWORKS

The Single European Act of 1986 was a complicated piece of legislation with a convoluted history that pointed in several directions. Yet at bottom it remained Mrs. Thatcher's baby.[9] The SEA had three parts, the most important of which provided for liberalization. Containing 279 proposals made by a Commission White Paper drafted by Lord Arthur Cockfield a year earlier, it aimed at the creation of an area "without internal frontiers in which the free movement of goods, peoples, services, and capital is assured." This was supposed to happen by 1992. The elimination of nontariff barriers called for a comprehensive opening of trade in services and the removal of domestic regulation that impeded competition; required a reform of the state as well as the economy; and implied far-reaching changes in the relationship between the two. Included in the proposed package were the elimination of customs procedures, harmonization or coordination of industrial standards and regulations, liberalization of trade and investment, abolition of discriminatory taxation, and elimination of both preferential public procurement and provision of state aids.[10]

The SEA also introduced three institutional changes of substantial but varying importance. It partly restored the method of *qualified majority voting* (QMV), which had become all but null and void as a result of the 1966 Luxembourg Compromise; QMV now applied to matters needed to ensure the development of the internal market. Thus the *liberum veto* that had hung over the Commission's head since the compromise of 1966 was partly lifted, so terminating an arrangement that had made further enlargement of the Community difficult if not impossible. The way was opened for Iberian membership. The SEA also endorsed the principle of *mutual recognition*, thereby reinforcing the famous *Cassis de Dijon* decision of the European Court of Justice. Henceforth one could dispense with the cumbersome, time-consuming, vexatious, and even niggling Commission requirements applying a single standard for products and processes; it now became possible to meet the lowest acceptable one prevailing in the Community. The resulting savings in paperwork were immense. Finally, a new *cooperation procedure* provided an opening that increased the European Parliament's closely circumscribed lawmaking power; it gained the authority to propose amendments that, if accepted by the Commission, could then be referred back to the Council for consideration. A step in the right direction, representative government at the EU level would nonetheless remain in the realm of *Zukunftsmusik* and be important only with reference to the future. The same thing, it would appear, was true concerning the third part of the SEA, which adumbrated lines of future development: assigning the Commission new "competencies" in the areas of environmental, social, regional, and monetary policy.[11] Yet in remarkably short order, Delors would with considerable effect assert his authority in those fields.

The Single European Act was not Delors's idea. Between 1980 and 1984, Commission officials – led by the commissioner for industry, Karl-Heinz Narjes – developed a comprehensive plan to overcome nontariff barriers. Starting with the harmonization agenda of 1968, Narjes added the reduction of customs formalities and a schedule for deregulation of services and transport, the latter endorsed by the European Council in December 1982. The next year, with strong approval from Kohl, Narjes and officials from the member-states secured agreement on a special Council of Ministers meeting for internal market matters.[12] Shortly thereafter, he gained approval of a directive calling for prior Commission notification of any changes in new product and process standards. Interest in developing the internal market was likewise alive at the European Parliament, where in 1981 – following a comic precedent of naming factions after exotic beasts – a "kangaroo group" formed in order to lobby for market liberalization and Thatcherite policy that could jump across national borders.[13] The Copenhagen summit of 1982 made the definitive decision to assign top priority to development of the internal market. Key pieces of the puzzle had begun to come together in Brussels well before the arrival in 1985 of M. Delors as European commissioner or even of Lord Cockfield, who had signed on the previous year as commissioner for the internal market and was actually assembling the economic part of the "1992 package" when Delors moved into his new offices.[14]

The ascendant spirit of neoliberalism was important to the background of the SEA. Writing close to the events in question, the Harvard Business School professor Malcolm Salter found during a quick *tour d' Europe* that the ancient civilization was all but "awash in political change." In France, he reported, privatization was well under way and advancing rapidly. He admitted that the new German Kohl government was moving slowly, but it had promised to slash budgets, open up capital markets, cut the state's holdings in Volkswagen, and privatize Lufthansa. The socialist prime minister of Austria, Franz Vranitsky, planned to dismantle Österreichische Holding (which owned the state's shares in much of industry), reduce subsidies, and "make people know where their balance sheet lies" – but here, too, the professor found more talk than action. He was nevertheless very much impressed by the spectacle of normally retiring and understated Swedish businessmen demonstrating in bowler hats to protest profit squeezing, as well as by the government's commitment to sell off 1.5 billion kronen in state assets. At the same time, he noted that the decision may have been unavoidable in light of the huge subsidies provided for industrial life support, some 2.8 percent of GNP. Each job in both the steel and carbon steel sectors cost $64,000. The governments of both Spain and Italy also made formal commitments to privatize, Salter noted; and even in profligate, regulation-choked, chronically demoralized Belgium, whose per-capita public indebtedness was (by a wide margin) the greatest in Europe, the young Liberal Prime Minister Guy Verhofstadt declared as his top policy priority the introduction of "a genuine liberal policy ... [to] reduce the impact of government in the real life of people, fight against the enormous pressure of the fiscal system,... and cut back on overregulation [and] the number of enterprises ... managed by the state." These laudable ambitions soon ran afoul of entrenched interests. Elected politicians, no less than big businessmen, welcomed the opportunity for buck-passing.[15]

Britain was indeed, as Mrs. Thatcher stated in *Statecraft: Strategies for a Changing World,* "the originator of and the driving force behind" the Single European Act. The single market was to be "the foundation upon which everything was to be built ... and to house the competition policy that was to be the furniture."[16] Lord Cockfield – who until then had owed his reputation to success as CEO of Boots, the drugstore chain – was "personally and professionally" very close to Margaret Thatcher and had previously served as "her self-styled hatchet man" while chancellor of the Duchy of Lancaster. He was sent to Brussels for the specific purpose – and no other – of working up internal market proposals.[17] In an understanding similar to those Delors reached later with the successive competition czars Peter Sutherland and Leon Brittan, Cockfield received a free hand from the president to make internal market policy. He was thus spared the need to coordinate his moves with the other members of the Commission. Though careful both not to overstep his mandate and to avoid proposals that might have met with Delors's disfavor, he counted on the new boss to maneuver his White Paper through the collective body. In fact, it was discussed only once before the Commission – when a minor amendment was made to a single provision.

The June 1985 Milan summit of the European Council, where the Single European Act was negotiated, left British foreign minister Geoffrey Howe with the "characteristically Italian impression of having been thrown together like some scene-stealing film set."[18] Prime Minister Bettino Craxi made no effort as chairman to seek consensus, relishing conflicts that would enable him to step in and overshadow his foreign minister, Giulio Andreotti, as "good European." The meeting was "ill-tempered on all sides." Mrs. Thatcher was with good reason unusually "techy."[19] Instead of replying to her recently circulated proposal "Europe: The Future" – the most pro-Community statement she would ever make – Chancellor Kohl had forwarded it to Mitterrand as the basis for a joint statement that, without acknowledging its authorship, reiterated the essentials of the British paper. There was unanimity at Milan to proceed with the single market agenda but disagreement as to whether this required overturning the Luxembourg Compromise. The British led like-minded Danes and opportunistic Greeks in opposing the majority on the grounds that such a change involved an undesirable shift in power from the member-states and the Council to the

Commission; for precisely the same reason, it was the keystone of Delors's reform program.

In a move coordinated in advance with Emile Noel (head of the Commission's civil service), Craxi called a for a surprise and arguably improper majority vote to convene an intergovernmental conference (IGC) under Article 236. Isolated, outmaneuvered, caught unprepared, and powerless to oppose this first-ever majority vote by the European Council, an enraged Mrs. Thatcher walked out. After carefully reviewing the pros and cons, Foreign Secretary Howe later persuaded the prime minister that Britain should participate in the IGC convened to work out the details of the treaty. The intergovernmental conference introduced qualified majority voting under Article 100 as needed to promote its development in the field of transport, external tariffs, capital movements, and the rights of corporate establishment. In an important concession to supply-side Britain, fiscal harmonization remained subject to unanimity. Delors's effort to attach provisions for new Commission "competences" (in the fields of technology, culture, and the environment) met with little success. Reference to monetary policy was limited to a rhetorical reference to "progressive realization" – which Mrs. Thatcher unwisely did not take seriously – but gave Britain a de facto veto over entry and opened up the possibility of a "two-track Europe." Delors was successful chiefly in adding a treaty provision for an unspecified amount of "structural funds." The need for them was unconnected to liberalization except in Commission propaganda. Delors argued persuasively that, without the support of Greece and Ireland and later Spain and Portugal, SEA ratification might have been threatened. Although an engine of liberalization, the Single European Act emerging from the summit was a compromised and contradictory document that would be invoked to justify Delors's policy of state building in addition to the creation of the internal market.[20]

The road to Maastricht and the Treaty of European Union was beset with confusion, contradiction, and (retrospectively) predictable but largely unintended consequences. In spite of the good face put on events, none of the main contacting parties was happy with the results. The French state, backed strongly by Delors as Commission president, was the driving force behind the creation of the European Monetary Union. Behind France's determination to organize an EMU was a powerful urge to have a voice in monetary policy (instead of, as heretofore, being kited by the Bundesbank) and also a deep-seated need to "stand up to the Americans." As expressed by a member of the monetary council of the Banque de France, the idea was that a "single currency would suck capital out of the U.S., force U.S. interest rates up, create unemployment in the U.S., and force the U.S. to accept global exchange rate management. The U.S. would then have to sit down and negotiate the shape of the world economic order."[21] The French seldom disagreed with the BuBa's "sound money" policies; indeed, since the days of *Plan Barre* and apart from the early Mitterrand interlude, France had been prepared for sacrifices if necessary to remain on a convergence course with Germany, the Bundesbank, and the Deutsche mark.[22] At issue in the monetary negotiations were less differences in Franco-German policy than considerations of Gallic prestige.

The shift to monetary union was replete with irony. Unable to generate an alternative to the policy of strong franc and competitive disinflation, the French became captive of the Germans; meant to increase French independence, the shift to monetary union restricted it. German outcomes were no less ironic. The man in the street hated the idea of a single European currency, as did the Bundesbank. But Chancellor Kohl wanted the EMU in order to reduce German visibility in Europe after reunification and the future northern and eastern extensions, each of which was expected to increase German political power but did not. The stability and convergence criteria needed for the viability of the currency union produced a Bundesbank-like policy for Europe, which the BuBa did not want, and also increased German monetary power within Europe, which Kohl had not intended. Both German and European economic growth suffered from the austerity policies required for the glide path to monetary union. The expenses of German economic reunification were partly to blame for the slowdown. Disappointing economic performance actually reduced European power compared with that of the United States. The German Problem in the 1990s would be one not of too much but rather too little in the way of authority. It has never been necessary to brake the economic locomotive.

In spite of a disinclination to relinquish the beloved Deutsche mark in favor of an unattractively named currency – the euro, whose pronunciation in English suggests micturition – the Germans got their way in the negotiations that led to monetary union. Its organization, methods, and rules reflect the preferences of a Bundesbank that would have preferred to remain freestanding. The convergence that the so-called economists had demanded in discussions of the Werner Plan of the 1970s had become a reality in both France and among Germany's small neighbors, and it had become at least an aspiration of the financial elites in Italy, Spain, and elsewhere. The Germans had a clear march route. An epistemic community of financial officials and economists controlled policy making. As a legacy of Erhard's ORDO-liberalism, the group's characteristic formulas for integration included market-induced change from the bottom up, free trade, conservative monetary and fiscal policy, and the need for frameworks of binding rules enforced by strong institutions.[23] This was the gist of the German economic policy. Given the monetary and fiscal incontinence prevailing elsewhere, there may have been no short-term alternative to it. The big unanswered questions were whether monetary union required a single circulating medium and, if it did, whether the EU was an optimal currency area or one in which a one-size-fits-all policy would slow growth and become politically destabilizing.

The Maastricht treaty (the Treaty of European Union) also worked at cross-purposes with Delors's policy preferences. The policy within the European Monetary System of pegging to the DM – though it improved monetary stability – had required labor markets to bear the costs of adjustment to competition, either by wage reductions or unemployment increases. The EMU offered more of the same but on a permanent basis. The only escape from the dilemma was to make wages, benefits, and working conditions responsive to markets, which was an anathema to "solidarists." The superimposition (over the bankers' directorate) of a political board vested with power to loosen monetary policy, something for which Delors lobbied, was not a realistic alternative; it would have whipsawed the EMU apart. The French negotiators demanded such a thing out of a vague longing to "capture" German power, but not even they wanted to risk loosening fiscal policy and opening the floodgates to inflation after having made such a long and costly effort to wring it out of the domestic economy. A deflation-biased directorate like the European Monetary Union, which Delors labored to so hard to negotiate, could only make a travesty of his attempt to organize a "European model of society." Fundamental contradiction beset his policy.

Only two matters were seriously at issue in the long negotiations that led to the EMU. Could the BuBa be given adequate assurance that a panel composed of central bankers from the member-nations would be able to exercise powers at the European level comparable to those that it had wielded at the German one? And could a college of such bankers also be bound by rules to policies like those favored in the Federal Republic? Although the Bundesbank was not happy to forfeit its independence, its loss would be bearable if a Euro-bankers' club could be counted upon to make decisions on behalf of the EU like those BuBa would have made for Germany – assuming that its actions could have binding force in the other member-nations. Accumulated knowledge would thus have been embedded in a broader set of institutions similar to those in the Federal Republic and then, under appropriate circumstances, progress could take place.[24]

The struggle over policy toward monetary union did not occur among central bankers. The monetary economist Adam Posen, though "loath to let people in on the key finding of his twenty years of research," revealed nonetheless that "today almost all central banks behave the same way. If one were to take out 1973–1982 in the OECD economies, and a couple of hyperinflations in the developing world, one could say that most central banks have behaved much like the Bundesbank for most of the postwar era."[25] Hence the only issues at the negotiations were between the bankers and the representatives of national political interests, who – though reluctant to cede power to an irresponsible European authority – with the single important exception of the British lacked any feasible alternative approach to creating one. The central bankers won the bargaining process in 1988 when, as precondition for entrance into the proposed organization, those who did not already enjoy the privilege gained Bundesbank-like independence from national governments. The biggest changes occurred in France and Italy.[26] The rules adopted for stability and convergence also meant that the values and views embodied in the new European central bank would henceforth drive domestic policy making throughout the future monetary union. These rules provided a set of constraints directed primarily at disciplining governments and only secondarily at promoting liberalization.

Whether (and to what extent) the stringent rules would force – or have already forced – governments to shape up are topics that have divided scholars, policy makers, and the Thatcher and subsequent British governments. The squabbles in London originated over theoretical disagreements regarding monetary policy between "fixers" and "floaters." The monetary approach does not dictate a choice between them. If currency cross-rates could be truly fixed – for example, by interlocking currency boards bound to provide full coverage in a single standard (gold, dollar, commodity basket) – then the world would have what amounted to a single currency with different names, and correct price signals could be transmitted through all economies. If currencies truly floated then exchange rates would bear the burden of adjustment, either by increasing or decreasing the money supply as productivity changes occurred within the real economy. Eminent voices made themselves heard on both sides of the sometimes arcane but nevertheless fundamental dispute.

Mrs. Thatcher's cabinet was divided between "fixers" and "floaters." Chancellor of the Exchequer Nigel Lawson, backed by Foreign Secretary Geoffrey Howe and the pro-European faction of the party, was on one side. Lawson wanted to peg the pound to the DM with a view toward creating a single currency standard for the Community and in the belief that such an approach would accelerate the development of the Single European Market. Echoes from Hayek resounded at the other extreme. Hayek advocated the de-nationalization of currencies, whereafter (he predicted, reversing Gresham's law) good money would drive bad money out of circulation, thus forcing market-conforming policy on recalcitrant decision makers. Influenced by such thinking, Margaret Thatcher's personal economic adviser, Sir Alan Walters, advocated floating an ecu (European currency unit) in a loose grid against member-state currencies within the EMS context. Competition from a floating ecu would then constrain the fiscal and monetary policies of the member-states. Mrs. Thatcher would have preferred having nothing whatsoever to do the European Monetary System, but rather than turn her back altogether on the project she pressed for Walters's approach over the head of Lawson, who used the authority of his office to undercut the policy of Mrs. Thatcher's "economic guru." The British disagreement over EMS – which began with honest intellectual differences between otherwise like-minded political figures – grew into a bitter personal dispute, brought down the Thatcher cabinet, and split the Tory party. It has deprived Europe of its most powerful and principled voice for liberalization policy, leaving the cause leaderless and without any alternative to the institutional arrangement now in place. This, too, was an unintended outcome.[27]

BIG BUSINESS AND THE COMMISSION: HIGH-TECH NEOCORPORATISM IN ACTION

"Business activism" was relatively new on the Brussels scene. Industrialists and financiers had taken comparatively little interest in the European Economic Community prior to the early 1980s. Monnet had trampled on the coal and steel producers of Germany and France, as well as in the other four founding members of the heavy industry pool. Industry was unrepresented and all but overlooked in the negotiations that led to the Treaty of Rome, and it was seldom consulted – or even seriously taken into account – in Community policy making during the 1960s and 1970s. Instead, the main emphasis in Brussels was either punitive or (through competition policy) corrective.

The Commission's so-called Vredeling directive of 1980 temporarily slammed the door on cooperation with big business. The directive required multinational enterprises to consult with employees on general strategy; moreover, it applied not only to relations between the parent company and foreign subsidiaries but to those between parent companies and domestic components, as well as to parent companies headquartered outside of the Community. "Vredeling" was meant to be – and was understood by business as – a Trojan Horse for *autogestion*. This unenforceable, counterproductive, and gratuitous political gesture stupidly cut the Commission temporarily off from its natural allies: the minority of big European companies not comfortably nested in the thick regulatory networks of domestic economies – those intent upon growth.[28] Given the near impotence and limited resources of the Community at the time, it is not surprising that the big national producers of Europe channeled their energies into acquiring political influence at home. With few exceptions, the only advocate for European firms in Brussels was a weak employers' association, UNICE, representing national industrial associations. Foreign firms were the first to set up lobbying shops in the European capital. American and other multis threatened directly by Vredeling made serious efforts to peddle influence at an early date. The campaign soon took on a positive spin, as both consultant–advisers and Brussels officialdom learned to appreciate the common interest that both shared in the replacement of national systems of regulation with uniform standards and laws.

Industry Commissioner Viscount Étienne Davignon was the first to welcome big business to Brussels with open arms.[29] The formation of something called the European Enterprise Group (EEG) was the first sign of serious new producer interest in the Community. The group – representing firms like British Petroleum, Fiat, Ford, Hoechst, IBM, ICI, Shell, Solvay, and Unilever – first brought about the reform of UNICE. Its ungainly overgrowth of committees was trimmed away, allowances were made to represent individual firms and for branches of industry on the surviving committees. A tough, new senior executive came over from Shell as secretary general to take charge of the re-organized umbrella organization. Having shaped up UNICE, the Enterprise Group also served as progenitor to the less euphonious ERT, the European Roundtable of Industrialists. Davignon coordinated the effort.

The Roundtable would seem to validate conspiracy theory. An exclusive club of a handful of the most powerful CEOs in Europe, it was founded to function as a nerve center for integration policy. Early members included Umberto Agnelli (FIAT), Carlo de Benedetti (Olivetti), Wisse Dekker (Philips), Roger Faroux (St. Gobain), John Harvey-Jones (ICI), Olivier Lecerf (Lafarge Coppée), Hans Merkle (Bosch), Wolfgang Seelin (Siemens), and Dieter Spethmann (Thyssen). These men wanted to build an overall regulatory framework for a single market at the European level in order to capture scale economies, particularly in the emerging markets for new technologies and products. Underlying this concern was diminishing profitability during the 1970s in the face of powerful competition in growth sectors from the United States and Japan. The problem was blamed on the need to set up production on a national basis in order to sell in regulated domestic markets; the days of such small-scale operations were thought to have passed. Far-reaching rationalization raised serious political issues, as Maria Green Cowles points out: "restructuring would require paring down budgets, closing factories, combining R&D facilities, and laying off workers" – politically speaking "no-no's," especially in social democratic welfare states. Resort to buck-passing would be necessary. "Europe" was also needed, Cowles adds, because "in the area of high technology... no single European firm was financially capable of undertaking ... new R&D developments" in such fields as computer chips and high-speed switching gear. Public procurement would have to be centralized on the European level in order to create the vast new markets needed to cover the fixed costs of launching expensive new high-tech systems in fields like telecommunications.[30]

These preferences were only partly congruent with the single market proposal. If, on the one hand, they included the elimination of protected national markets and the NTBs that maintained them, on the other they required future subsidization and the formation of privileged European-scale monopolies. The CEO of Philips, Wisse Dekker, put the matter delicately. Can Europe afford, he asked rhetorically, "for the technology of the future ... to be too dependent on non-European suppliers? It is high time that a European industrial policy came into force which took account of a number of undesirable consequences of such a scenario."[31] How the two incompatible policy aims of open markets and protectionism fit together would become clearer in actual practice than it ever was in theory. "Europe 1990" – a proposal drafted by Dekker, who became the unofficial spokesman for ERT – laid out what the group was supposed to stand for. The document closely resembled the White Paper penned by Lord Cockfield, which was the template for the liberalization portion of the Single European Act.

Debate about who "really" authored SEA has raged ever since. To Cockfield, Dekker was a "John the Baptist who had been howling away in the wilderness for years" and "had been campaigning in general and uncoordinated fashion." The "Brit" did not want it assumed that he was Dekker's handmaiden or carrying out his program which, Cockfield maintained, was still "piecemeal, partial, and with too short a time frame."[32] The Dekker proposal focused on market liberalization, divided reform tasks by category (fiscal, commercial, technical, and government procurement), and emphasized the importance of scale economies. Dekker linked commercial liberalization and tax harmonization, and his proposal set 1990 for the completion date of the program. However, it neither specified targets for reform (as Cockfield's White Paper did) nor adopted 1992 as the terminal date for realization of the single market.[33] The latter was Delors's contribution – 1992 was the year his term of office ended.

The similarity of the ERT and Commission plans was not circumstantial. It reflected shared views that would become the basis of a partnership in which

Europe's business leaders helped the Brussels bureaucrats organize and manage programs that would put money in the pockets of their companies and also leverage Commission power. To Delors, the Single European Act and its competition policy complement were welcome as an engine of wealth creation, a money pump working tirelessly to cover the costs of "structural" policy, and as a leveler of national obstructions to the creation of Euro-champions. He let the relevant DGs "run" with the single market program, confident that in the end he could assert control over the economy just as surely as was being done in contemporary France. "At one end of the range of concepts," he pontificated to a captive university audience in Florence,

are those states that favor institutional or indeed political projects designed to ensure the qualitative leaps dear to the hearts of all staunch Europeans, including I am bound to confess, myself. At the other are all those who, whether out of realism or for ideological reasons hold to a purely libertarian vision of Europe – to what is customarily called "economic integration" …. Our task, modest though it may be, must be to overcome and go beyond this underlying contradiction by advocating perseverance and tenacious action, continued with political construction.[34]

Even before the ink on the SEA had dried, Delors began to apply himself to the task of creating a "European technological community" as the first big step toward a "European social and economic space." The policy, a species of so-called industrial policy, simply violated EU competition policy. Definitions of industrial policy unfortunately range from "a wide-ranging, ill-assorted collection of micro-based supply initiatives which are designed to improve market performance in a variety of occasionally mutually inconsistent ways" (P. A. Geroski) to "the initiation and coordination of governmental activities to leverage upward the productivity and competitiveness of the whole economy and of particular industries in it" (Paul Johnson). Gilberto Sarfati concludes that, by any name, both the EC and the national states run unofficial but active industrial policies that distort the international and external evolution of competition.[35] One manifestation of such policies was the proliferation of technical directives and regulations. It took the EC 35 years to produce the first 315 as opposed to 1,136 in 1992–1994 alone. Sarfati also detects the workings of a "substitution effect, in which the member-states tried to cheat their way out of the single market." State aids totaled 42 billion ecus in 1994, but they were less important than EU-level nontariff barriers such as "new standards, environment and anti-dumping rules, and expenditures of Community funds and, further, Voluntary Export Restraints (VERs), unfair public procurement practices, and limitations on ownership." It was R&D that spearheaded an otherwise diffuse industrial policy, whose challenge as an alternative to competition policy stood or fell with it.[36]

This success of R&D policy required a hat trick. Since the Commission lacked the necessary financial resources and expertise to direct such a project on its own, big corporations would have to be lured in to do the job. To the presidents of Europe's leading high-tech firms, the Commission President thus proposed a lavish subsidy program for research and development that they could plan themselves, free of both oversight and competition. Organized labor was excluded. Competitors and consumers were kept in the dark, and other interested parties were not consulted. The program was a real giveaway. Dekker's company, Philips of Eindhoven, had already sunk big money in long-term capital investment programs. Commission largesse provided a hedge, an opportunity to become a Euro-champion, in case the firm's other strategies came up short. The offer was too sweet to decline.

Delors had set the Community on a morally and materially dangerous course, which runs continuously into the present: a course of subordination to outside interests, government from behind the scenes, and fiduciary irresponsibility; involving bad science, bad economics, and bad politics. The easy money also changed the Brussels scene, where a Washington-type inner-Beltway lobbying industry soon materialized. "Policy networking" became the political buzzword of the day and indeed was even discussed as a new "governance model."[37] Delors's economic plans were unworkable and eventually petered out. The worst did not happen. The effort to build a "European technological community" nevertheless was, and is, costly and has squelched entrepreneurship and suppressed innovation while squandering billions in taxpayer ecus and euros. Delors's R&D program survives even after having helped bring the Community to the lowest moment in its history – the forced resignation of the entire Commission in 1999. The trigger was the discovery of a contract inexplicably awarded by the science commissioner, Edith Cresson, to her hometown dentist in order to study the spread of AIDs. The banal incident of petty graft, the tip of a vast iceberg of misappropriation, was emblematic of a deep-seated official irresponsibility and lack of public accountability that have made a mockery of the EU's democratic pretensions and provided Euroskeptics with a field day.[38]

The failure of Delors's plans should have been recognized many years earlier. The effort to compress scientific research into the confines of a special European industrial policy was fundamentally misguided. Knowledge is universal and science no more "European" than German, Black, or Patagonian. Like that of economic growth, its development is path-dependent. Any effort to level the "playing field" and provide equal shares regionally or socially is bound to be wasteful. Intellectual breakthrough, when it occurs, cannot often be predicted. Nor can the pace or consequences of change. "Picking winners" is never easy but, in basic science, those best equipped to do so are other scientists – not bureaucrats or businessmen with vested interests. American scientists pressured Roosevelt to build the A-bomb. Their counterparts got nowhere with Hitler. Although in Japan the MITI has made occasional commercial strikes, determination of product viability requires testing in the marketplace – not rigging the rules to prevent its efficient operation.

Such basic objections to the Delors's research and development scheme, which are supported by a rich history of science and economics literature, had not stood in the way of previous Commission failures; his policy built upon the unfortunate precedents of his less ambitious predecessors.[39] "The record of intra-European cooperation during the 1970s was ... a poor one," according to Stephen Woolcock, "with the exceptions of the European Space Agency and Airbus, which were intergovernmental as opposed to European Community projects."[40] Nor did failure result in abandonment. Instead, Delors's policy mutated. There have now been six multi-year Framework Programs for R&D, each with a different emphasis from the previous one. Like the steam-engine airplane, none of them has ever gotten off the ground. The basic design – which conflates science, economics, and politics – is flawed.

The demand for a European technological community arose, both explicitly and implicitly, from *Le défi Americain*. Monnet's brainchild, EURATOM (created by the Rome Treaty) was a great disappointment. Its sequel, the Colonna Memorandum of 1970, was a dry run for state capitalism. This charter for Community industrial policy proposed horizontal and vertical mergers on the basis of a common European company law. A French "Memorandum on Community Industrial Policy" spelled out its main points in detail and – in themes later replayed in Brussels – called for the creation of European enterprises for joint research and development, European preferences in public procurement, control of European inward investment by an advisory panel, and joint funding of investment projects. Harbingers of Delors's subsequent scheme, the French Plan, came to naught because the Germans, industrial leaders of the day, refused to dilute their strength for the sake of Europe. Ad hoc attempts at transnational industrial cooperation in advanced fields like ELDO and Concorde failed over the short or long run.[41]

Ronald Reagan's attempt to entice European companies into participation in the Strategic Defense Initiative or "Star Wars" project (albeit only as junior partners and subcontractors) – along with the fear that "Europe" was losing the high-tech battle to the MITI-directed Japanese and the Pentagon-steered Americans – set in motion the next great wave of dependence anxiety in France. Deftly surfing across over an ocean of domestic economic worries, President Mitterrand came up with EUREKA (European Research Coordinating Agency) as an alternative to Reagan's fanciful project. "Amid much fanfare," according to John Peterson, "Siemens, Philips, GEC and Thomson signed a 'declaration of common intent' to cooperate within EUREKA on the development of strategic components .... The agreement brought together four Big Twelve firms from four different countries. Their collective weight gave EUREKA ... a critical endorsement from European industry."[42]

EUREKA was not a Community scheme but rather an intergovernmental facilitator of bilateral or multilateral projects funded nationally on an individual basis. The program's emphasis was on shortcutting delays in bringing product to market. EUREKA's largest investment would be to develop a high-definition television (HDTV) broadcasting network, an effort spearheaded by Philips as leader of a consortium of big European electronics firms. The Community's European Program for Research and Development in Information Technology (ESPRIT), launched in 1982 by Viscount Davignon, was closely associated with it and provided co-funding for HDTV. ESPRIT was the biggest component of the Commission's own broader Framework Program (FP), championed by Delors, which dated back to 1986. The Japanese central planning agency and "intellectual cartel," MITI, was its inspiration and model. The FP would develop (it was hoped) the organs, muscle, and limbs to enable it to perform in Europe the production miracles without which it was difficult – for most European thinkers of the day – to understand Asian penetration in cutting-edge markets. Though centering in the field of information technology, the FP was broadly conceived. It included such branches as RACE (components), JESSI (semiconductors), BRIDGE (biotechnology), FLAIR (energy), and ECLAIR (environment), not to mention BRITE (manufacturing technology), SPRINT (technology transfer), STRIDE (regional technology initiatives), COMMETT (training programs), and other offshoots that would apparently continue to proliferate until the supply of clever acronyms ran dry. The Commission programs did not, like EUREKA, encourage the formation of consortia to market specific products – which would have violated the Rome treaty – but concentrated instead on promoting research and development in the "pre-competitive" sphere, an invented category. The distinction had little meaning in practice.

The Framework Program, set up primarily to aid industry, was legitimized to the public in terms of cultural affinity. According to one former DG for research, Antonio Ruberti, "European cooperative programs involve countries that in spite of their distinctive cultures share an economic and political viewpoint as well as an interwoven history that joins them in what has been called a 'common destiny'."[43] Professionals like the Swedish molecular biologist C. G. Kurland were not gulled by such bunk. "Academic scientists," he pointedly noted in a 1992 article published in the research journal *Science,*

must apply to [the Commission] ... to recover support that was reassigned from national budgets. But a funny thing happened on the way to Brussels: Money taken from national budgets re-appears earmarked for the train of the future, the car of the future, and the toilet-seat of the future. Not surprisingly, corporate groups that produce trains, cars and toilet seats, rather than academic groups, get the lion's share of these funds. The net effect is that money ... cut out from basic research programs emerges as industrial subsidy.[44]

If Brussels had its way, he conjectured, peer review and bottom-up planning would give way to a system not unlike the one in the former Soviet Union, in which "research missions were identified centrally and these, together with matching resources, were apportioned downward through the national academies to individual academic institutes," unchecked and unmediated by intellectual competition. The secrecy of such proprietary industrial and state research is, as he underscored, "contrary to the openness ... and the free exchange of ideas, [which] is not a simple conversational luxury [but] the very basis of the heuristic skepticism that is the hallmark of Western science."[45] Had the Eurocrats forgotten this fact, he asked sarcastically, now that the Soviet Union had disappeared?

Complaints about the conduct of the Framework Program were legion within the scientific community. And why not? Science spending had become, as Deborah MacKenzie reported in *New Science,* a pawn in Europe's politics. As a result of a dispute between the Council and the Parliament, to cite a single noteworthy example, funding for Framework II – originally scheduled to begin in 1990 and run to 1994 – was set back by more than two years. The disagreement occurred amidst squabbling over legal and administrative technicalities on the one hand and high principle on the other, bringing tears of frustration to Mrs. Thatcher and having like effects on anyone intent upon actually getting an experiment off the ground. In this case, the European Parliament wanted to change the type of committee managing two of the five programs, assign more authority to the Commission, and exclude participation of non-European companies. Delors agreed that the member-states had ignored the rights of the EP, a critical matter since an intergovernmental conference was "currently deciding how power in a future, politically united Community will be shared out between Parliament, Commission, and the future governments."[46] The Council threatened to sue in the European Court of Justice.

Administration of the politically fraught program caused severe headaches. Eighteen months were required between the time of application and the award of a grant. The paperwork was bewildering and peer group evaluation so badly conducted that, in some fields, only 10 percent of the proposals could be funded. Success too often depended upon "working the system." According to the British contact man for grant applications, "The EU's biotechnology work plan alone runs to fifty pages. There's a lot of ambiguity in determining what research is eligible, so it is hard to advise people, and the result is too many bids."[47] Scientists also found it difficult to find suitable "partners" in countries like Portugal, Greece, and Belgium; resented high overhead charges; and could only wonder about the sort of laboratory miracles that might now occur at Ispra, Italy, or any of the other EU regional research centers – none of which were located near scientific capitals like Cambridge, Paris, or Berlin.[48]

The Davignon committee of 1997 reached a similar verdict on the Framework Program. It concluded that the FP lacked "focus and [was] underachieving," had been "blocked by a flawed consultation process and a requirement that the Council of Ministers approve the program by unanimous vote," that pork-barrel politics too often overruled pure science, that "the program [supported] too wide a range of projects," and that "as conceived and managed it [was not] flexible enough to respond to new challenges and opportunities."[49] The vast size, bewildering complexity, and number of organizational permutations through which the six Framework Programs have passed make overall evaluation difficult. Even the Commission's own attempt to introduce self-evaluation in the targeted research fields had to be given up.[50]

A couple of tentative conclusions can nonetheless be advanced. The FPs sunk far too much money into the chimera of cold fusion, missed the boat altogether on genome sequencing – the most important scientific breakthrough since splitting the atom – and to date cannot boast about anything more than having sponsored development of the ARM processor for Apple's Newton handheld computer.[51] It also failed utterly in its overall aim of closing the Amero-Japanese lead in the industrial technology race. The issue, according to the *Economist,* was not lack of brains. Europe's 580,000 produced three times as many scientific papers as Japan's 453,000, though far less than the United States (about 1 million). Nor was lack of investment – 2 percent as compared to 2.8 percent and 2.9 percent for the United States and Japan, respectively – responsible for the weak European showing. The EU's share of European total R&D outlays, at about 5 percent, was arguably too little to be decisive in accounting for the difference, even considering that the sums had to be matched. The root of the problem was that American and Japanese firms were better able to use the fruits of scientific research.[52]

A chemical industry spokesman blamed not "a simple lack of money but ... poorly defined or misdirected policies." Rather than more funding from the Commission, which amounted to only a single percentage point of what the industry itself spent, Europe's producers needed "a better climate for innovation, more support for education and basic science, and a new set of priorities for publicly funded research."[53] A study by the American business consultants McKinsey and Company, echoing the need for innovation, emphasized that this required getting closer to the consumer and breaking away from high-margin official markets: "Europe cannot blame its poor showing on the sluggish economy, industry cycles or higher factor costs. The problem stems from missed opportunities to cope early on with the superior approaches and faster pace of world-class competitors" as well as from the fact that

European electronics manufacturers have traditionally focused their strategies on the high end of each [market] segment, where they could extract premium prices. Rather than seeking to capture as large as possible a share of the world market they ... turned out complex and over-engineered products ... and [avoided] competition in standardized, high-volume products .... Companies that neither continuously increase productivity nor constantly review and re-direct the way they deploy their capital, people and management resources wrap themselves into stable patterns of behavior that lower their performance even further.... Achieving sustained success [requires] adaptation of business processes, organization, and *especially* cost structures.[54]

The administrative flab, the requirements for political correctness, the lengthy application procedure, the sluicing of money to sluggish incumbents rather than nimble challengers, and the nonmarket orientation boded ill for the development of a "European" technology-based consumer product with high capital requirements. This would soon become apparent in the HDTV debacle. High-definition television involved not merely a product but an entire broadcasting system and distribution network, and it was to drive an overall industrial policy that would include restructuring the defense, automotive, and textile industries.[55] The failure in 1993 of the HDTV program, the largest and most critical program in both EUREKA and ESPRIT, definitively ended Delors's bid to create a "technological community" as a first step to filling Europe's "social and economic space." Delors was bitter about the matter, according to his biographer Charles Grant, because "his enthusiasm for this *grand projet* transcended economics." He thought HDTV necessary not only for competitiveness but "in the name of cultural defense .... The Community refuses to leave the monopoly of audiovisual techniques to the Japanese and that of programs to the Americans."[56]

In early 1993, Delors sacked research commissioner Filippo Maria Pandolfi, split up the Framework Program, assigned computer and telecommunications research to the tough German industrial policy commissioner, Martin Bangemann, and left the "soft science" residual to the Italian, Antonio Ruberti.[57] It would be only the first of successive reshufflings, repackagings, and reorientations in the direction of product development on the one hand and pop science on the other. That even a mutant Framework Program has long survived the demise of Delors's lofty initial ambitions raises deeper questions about the functioning of bureaucracies than about the scientific merits of the scheme. A 12 May 2001 comment in *Lancet,* the prestigious British medical journal, might well have been written a decade earlier:

Previous Framework Programs (FPs) have been criticized for lack of coherence and continuity. FP 5 (1998–2002) in particular is not highly regarded by scientists because of its tortuous application procedure, the lack of transparency in evaluation of the applications, and the lack of opportunity for open-ended creative research.[58]

The strongest argument in the FP's favor is that, at an annual rate of roughly 4 percent of annual overall European outlays for research and development, it has wasted too little to count for much.

The EC's HDTV policy was an exercise in pure protectionism. The story is not lacking in irony. A 1984 Green Paper, "Television Without Frontiers," first lured the Commission into the information technology field. The Green Paper advanced the view that television and related services fell under treaty provisions providing for the free movement of goods, the freedom to provide service, and freedom of establishment. Included among the latter was the right of any EC company to set up in any market, a blow to national broadcasting monopolies that opened the door to cable and satellite transmission. Faced with rapid technological change, government objections weakened.[59] After this overture to the market, the Commission abruptly shifted key in 1986, when the French government managed to prevent the adoption of the Japanese MUSE transmission system, the first market-ready HDTV technology, as the world standard at the Consultative Committee for International Radio conference in Dubrovnik.[60]

The stakes in the matter were huge. HDTV technology replaced the bulky cathode ray screen with a flat panel that could be hung on a wall. It provided high resolution, color enhancement, undistorted "real world images," and great digital sound. HDTV was more than the focus of an improved home entertainment center. It was a venue in which market competition would erase customary divisions between the consumer electronics industry, the computer industry, and the telecommunications industry as well as blur the traditional distinction between such producers of hardware and the owners or designers of intellectual property and software.[61]

High-definition television became the scene of an ongoing struggle between the market and the Commission industrial policy after it launched the "MAC directives." D2-MAC was the proprietary satellite transmission technology of Philips as well as the standard for such other European big firms as Bosch, Thomson, and Thorn-EMI. Without so much as consulting with other interests involved, Delors came in 100 percent behind the manufacturers. The Commission set up a "HDTV Directorate" dominated by the big firms to run the program; sponsored the "EUTV 95" program, which soon became the second-most expensive public works project under way in Europe after the Chunnel; and launched the "Vision 1250 EEIG" campaign to promote the D2-MAC standard throughout the world.[62]

The MAC technology had two big glitches: one a serious threat to Commission policy, the other crippling. The first of them was that, technologically, it had become obsolete even prior to being put in place. After the Europeans torpedoed MUSE, in which American companies had a secondary role by dint of "strategic alliances," the U.S. Federal Trade Commission wisely threw open to competition the development of a new transmission system before deciding which horse to back. General Instruments won the race by inventing, in surprisingly little time, a new compression technology that would make digital systems marketable within a decade and thus also shorten the life cycle of analog systems like MAC, which was to have been up and running in 1986, to only a few years.[63] The other problem was that the large bandwidth needed for analog transmission required the use of satellites rather than cable. Conversion costs to the new MAC standard would have put the owners of such systems out of business. Rupert Murdoch – the Australian-American media mogul who owned the BskyB network – balked, insisting that "the markets decide which rights of way and what technology is used." There was, he added, "no reason to stop broadcasters from choosing among a growing family of technologies instead of insisting on one."[64] The president of Philips anathematized Murdoch, but the British government stood behind him.

While a frenzied Commission struggled to raise the necessary hundreds of millions of dollars needed to put the new Euro-standard into operation, Philips backed out, announcing that it had given up on D2-MAC though not necessarily on HDTV. According to the careful study by Xiudian Dai, the strategy of the Dutch giant had been one of "multi-commitment" that involved R&D activities for a fully digital system in the United States while actively employing MAC in Europe.[65] Concluding that the EC's policy led to distortion between alternative technologies, Dai adds that – even from the Commission's standpoint – the program may not have been necessary because "Philips and Thomson have become two of the few leading HDTV manufacturers in the United States even without [having received] any government help ... [and so] they may not have been as weak as the EC thought."[66] Philips had indeed already set plans in motion for VADIS, a digital compression system. As a EUREKA project (not a Community one), "its partners would be the big TV makers, the BBC and other broadcasters, and universities from most western European countries."[67]

The Commission got snookered. Judgments on its HDTV policy were withering. The *Financial Times* editorialized that it was "dictated largely by the defensive self-interests of Philips and Thomson, [which] lobbied for European standards not as a way to promote demand and the supply of new services, but to erect barriers to competition from Japanese manufacturers." The Commission had furthermore "failed to consult broadcasters, consumer organizations and television viewers."[68] The result was a bit like the ill-fated Delorean car of the same era: "Expensive and exclusive, developed with a good deal of taxpayer assistance, and with no clear market demand" – and, one might have added, placed in poor stewardship.[69] The administrative ineptitude characteristic of both HDTV and the general Framework Program need not be embroidered. As a result, the science directorate has been the graveyard for the reputations of three commissioners: Filippo Pandolfi, Antonio Ruberti, and Edith Cresson.

The failure of HDTV in 1992 sapped the strength of Delors's high-tech policy, but funding for Framework Programs has continued to increase even as successive permutations of them have veered off in the direction of "softer" targets like environmental issues, health-related science, and social matters. In terms of administrative cost alone it was poor value for the money – 7 percent of total outlays as opposed to the 3 percent of the British research councils. The larger question, according to the *Economist,* was "whether there should be a 'European' science policy at all" as distinct from cooperative arrangements like CERN, used to fund big projects like linear accelerator construction and maintenance. The fifth Framework Program, FP 5 (1998–2003), ominously described by its bureaucratic sponsors as a "great leap forward," was the most expensive to date and the third-largest source of EU expenditure. Once again "reformed and simplified," FP 5 was clearly out of control. According to Sir Leon Brittan, the Framework Programs "had to subcontract much [R&D] work to outside agencies which ... could not be fully controlled or monitored .... Financial irregularities and, occasionally, downright corruption had arisen .... I suggested that we ... review our programs ... [but] it did not happen."[70] The incongruence between ends and means would be the source of disorder that brought about the forced resignation of the Commission in 1999.

Delors's hope that a European industrial policy could buck globalization was futile. Europe's trade balance in information technology, about equal in 1978, fell to a deficit of $40 billion by 1991. Its share of the ultracritical semiconductor market shrank from 17 to 10 percent between 1978 and 1990. The immediate problem was not, as a review committee chaired by Wisse Dekker argued in 1992, that the Framework Program was too diffuse and theoretical. Nor was it even, as researchers maintained, overpoliticized and administratively inept. It was simply too far removed from the market. The solution was to shift toward it, but that would take time. As the importance of the Commission's industrial policy waned, that of its competition policy grew. Its success prevented the domination of the single market by oligopolies and super-cartels.

COMPETITION POLICY AND THE SINGLE MARKET

Competition policy (laid out in Articles 85–94) is at the core of the Treaty of Rome and reflects the thinking of ORDO-liberalism. In many respects similar to American antitrust law, the tradition developed as an intellectual subcurrent in turn-of-the-century Germany as an offshoot of the Austrian School associated with Karl Menger, to which Hayek was heir, and in opposition to the dominant historicist approach then prevailing in the Wilhelmenian Reich. Menger turned Adam Smith around in one important respect. Instead of focusing on the division of labor as the engine of growth, his starting point was on the consumption side. Growth, in his view, had no other meaning or significance than the satisfaction of consumer demand. Reasoning backwards, Menger concluded that – to fulfill its primary purpose of meeting human needs – the macroeconomic system required a competition policy in order to enforce rules for preventing the misuse of public and private power.[71]

The Weimar government adopted an antitrust law in 1923, but it could not be enforced in the legal, administrative, and political system prevailing in the 1920s and 1930s – an era hostile to market-based (rather than historical-institutional) economics, during which courts enforced the cartelist practices associated with "organized capitalism." The modern German belief in the desirability of competition did not, as in Britain, grow out of experience gained in the marketplace but rather from a painful effort to learn from the mistakes of the past. It developed self-consciously as an alternative to prevailing legal theory and derived from economics and political philosophy – not (as in nineteenth-century Great Britain) mainly from a customary, sensible, and fair way of getting things done. German competition law derives from the Freiburg School (ORDO) and dates as legal doctrine from the founding of the Federal Republic in 1949. ORDO principles are enshrined in the antitrust law of 1957, which states that competition provides an essential guarantee of individual rights vis-à-vis the exercise of both public and private power. The cornerstone of much subsequent legal interpretation, this basic liberal idea is a lodestar to the future as well.[72]

David J. Gerber's *Law and Competition in Twentieth Century Europe: Protecting Prometheus* traces the relevant articles in the Treaty of Rome back to ORDO-liberalism. These provisions set out precise rules for competition; specifically forbid abuse of dominant position, whether by trusts or public undertakings or through state aids; and provide standards for determining both anticompetitive conduct and permissible exemptions to it. Competition policy, according to Francis MacGowan, is "deeply-rooted in the treaty,... has driven policy ever since,... has had a strong legal basis," and is deeply intertwined with European law.[73] Regulation 17/1962 denoting Commission powers includes investigation, fining, consulting with governments, and even conducting "dawn raids." The anti-cartelizers can enter premises, examine company documents and accounts, and take affidavits and depositions. A string of ECJ decisions has sanctioned and broadened the exercise of this authority. Yet until the "re-launch" of the mid-1980s they were rarely used.[74] Delors encouraged the exercise of these powers in order to expand the authority of the Commission and was confident of being able (eventually) to put them in the service of his own causes. Competition policy thus became

> unique [and] represents the first truly supranational policy of the EU in so far as it is the Commission and not the Council of Ministers or ... the European Parliament that acts as the EU policymaker .... This policy is actually bringing "federal" implications for the future administrative and governmental structure of Europe.[75]

Among the commissioners, only the one for competition has real "clout" – can make and enforce independent judgments without regard to the interests concerned. Even the president of the Commission lacks the power to stand in the way of such judgments.

The rise of competition law within the Community is inextricably bound up with the 1980s process of globalization, the institution of domestic competition regimes, and the spread of neoliberalism. It has an antecedent in the antitrust provisions written into the original International Trade Organization agreement of 1944, transnational counterparts in the "competition law and policy" committee set up by the OECD and (more recently) a parallel body at GATT/WTO organized in order to make competition regimes compatible with one another. Producer assistance has been actively solicited and received. An "international competition policy community" exists as a potential framework for the development of an appropriate body of commercial law.[76] Globalization raises a host of theoretical questions about how antitrust laws, designed to operate within closed national economies, can be reconfigured to create efficient markets in open economies.[77] The European Union's role in the development of international competition law is critical and of increasing importance. The EU's antitrust powers have grown to an extent unimaginable twenty years ago, and the competition directorate's authority within the Community is now even greater than its American counterparts in the U.S. administration because it extends to abuses of state as well as private power. Competition policy is the one sphere in which the EU's legitimacy is universally recognized, even though it can inflict high costs on those subject to its judgments. The respect it enjoys is due in no small part to the determination of the most recent DG IV commissioners, Mario Monti and Carlo van Miert; but it also owes much to their predecessors, Leon Brittan and Peter Sutherland, who (like Monti and van Miert) are committed economic liberals. Brittan and Sutherland headed off many of Jacques Delors's wilder initiatives and carved out the autonomous policy space that the competition directorate occupies today.

Peter Sutherland, commissioner from 1984 to 1988, asked Delors for the competition job because, in his reading of the treaty, the Commission had more power in that field than in any other. He "saw the law as a way of promoting federalism and the Court of Justice as the most important Community institution."[78] A nationally ranked rugby player as well as a successful lawyer, the Irishman eagerly flung himself into the scrum. Using the Commission's power to ban state aids – which fueled industrial policy, then amounting to about 3 percent of Community GNP – he brought a skein of suits against the member-states to the European Court of Justice. To end price fixing, Sutherland conducted dawn raids, threatened and exacted punishment, and inspired fear in potential miscreants. Delors called him "the sheriff," though he really acted more like an ambitious reforming New York State attorney general. In 1988 he resorted to the draconian powers available under Article 90 of the treaty to liberalize the market for telecommunications equipment.[79] Stretching the authority of the Commission under Article 85 (which bans anticompetitive agreements) into the power to regulate mergers and acquisitions, Sutherland forced British Airways in the same year to sacrifice routes acquired after taking over British Caledonian.[80]

Leon Brittan ran the ball downfield. Brittan was another lawyer (Yale-schooled, in fact) who thrived on civilized forms of combat, especially of the intellectual variety. Mrs. Thatcher dispatched him to colonize Brussels, as she had Lord Cockfield. But he, too, went at least partly native.[81] Competition commissioner from 1988 to 1994, Brittan ranks as the most articulate and influential pro-European among the economically liberal wing of the Conservative Party. His position reflects those often represented in the *Financial Times,* which is surely not coincidental. The byline of his influential brother – Sir Samuel, a senior assistant editor – featured prominently in its distinctive orange pages for many years. Like Sutherland (who moved from the Community to become general director of the World Trade Organization), Sir Leon, when later EU trade commissioner, viewed the process of European integration as a response to globalization. He described it as "a highly sophisticated attempt on the part of European countries to have the maximum possible influence over the future in a world of globalized economic activity."[82] Integration had a dual significance for Brittan, providing a practical method of protecting de facto sovereignty in a world in which the nation-state was losing power as well as the means whereby a "common business culture," geared to the fulfillment of consumer demand, would develop. It would rest on the existence of common producer attitudes toward each other and the state, the mutual trust of governments not to subsidize or engage in other unfair activities, and their willingness to respect and enforce their own competition rules.[83] To bring about such a state of affairs was a tall order.

Notably suspicious of anything that "that might lead [the EC] down a blind alley of overprotected, introverted, and closed arrangements between governments,"[84] Brittan was especially wary of any "European social model in which the state provides the protection of welfare benefits and health care from cradle to grave and in which economic decisions in industry … are taken wherever possible on the basis of a consensus hammered out between the social partners, i.e. the employers and trade unions."[85] Though he looked to globalization to liberalize Europe, he also expected the principle of subsidiarity to "stop the Union from legislating for the sake of it" and to encourage the

ebb of some powers away back to the European governments … and the flow of others to the center … [resulting in] a more moderate, flexible, and pragmatic Union, able to respond to the task at hand without tilting Europe toward any particular ideology …, reassuring those who fear that [the EU] is a one-way street towards a U.S.-style Euro-government with power gravitating inexorably towards the center.[86]

This view was heuristically and normatively consistent with Hayek's integration scenario as developed on the eve of World War II in "The Economic Conditions of Interstate Federalism." This fundamental statement of the liberal position on integration posited that increased competition in expanding markets would stimulate economic competition between states, liberalize society, erode historic divisions that had given rise to nationalism, and produce the growth that would frustrate future appeals to it. The rosy scenario did not, however, unfold quite as planned. Delors twisted "subsidiarity" into a cloak for market interventionism.[87] Even without the self-serving grasps of the Commission, the concept was difficult to apply: the optimal line between local control and the need for common rules was hard to draw.

The future European Monetary Union presented a problem of another sort. The EMU did not, as many reformers hoped, create flexible labor markets.[88] The powerful forces supporting organized labor, social corporatism, and the welfare state cannot be expected to roll over and play dead.[89] The introduction of "flexibility" has met with intense resistance. The goals of Brittan and his successors would encounter far more headwind than expected. If competition policy were to fail or be discredited, the EU would lose much of its potential as a force for liberalization. Economic liberals like Brittan might then cease to back EU membership and try, as Mrs. Thatcher advocated in *Statecraft: Strategies for a Changing World,* to reduce the importance of the regional organization by subordinating it in a broader framework of trans-Atlantic and global institutions.[90]

Yet Brittan could claim victory in most of the scrimmages surrounding competition policy: he did manage to preside over the natural death of Deloronomics. It must have been a pleasure: "There is a conception of competition," pronounced M. *le président* in his inimitably perplexing combination of abstraction and bureaucratese, "which aims to privilege only consumption, which can be destructive of production …. That's what Leon Brittan and I disagree about."[91] Delors made no secret about his suspicions of both consumerism and the consumer movement. He had no qualms, when defending tight restrictions on the use of "marks of origin" to a group of farmers, about letting them know that "we have to resist this tendency we find in Europe, according to which the consumer is king and so intelligent that he can himself choose between different products."[92]

The 1990 proposal of commissioner Martin Bangemann for a new industrial policy initiative – the replacement of a purely sectoral approach by a new "horizontal" one that directed aid to training, research, and infrastructure – revived Delors's hope that something could still be done to turn the liberal tide, and he was heard to exclaim: "Whatever some may say, I say long live Euro-champions!"[93] His offer of a $5 billion grant to help Bull, Olivetti, Philips, and Siemens create an Airbus-type venture for semiconductor production nevertheless met with a negative response, according to a friendly biography, because "in the long run they preferred to make global alliances with Japanese and American firms."[94] Although language permitting the continuation of industrial policy was written, at Delors's insistence, into the Maastricht treaty, the 1992 Edinburgh summit scotched his final bid to direct Community funds into "improving industrial competitiveness."

Brittan fought at least part of the way toward the goalpost. Competition policy became the axis of advance for the 1992 program. Two powerful forces worked in his favor. The big corporations preferred "one-stop shopping" to endless litigation in different jurisdictions. Setting an important precedent, they lent their support to Brittan's successful campaign to secure a European merger act, which he in fact soon used. This would be an important step for a broader and lengthier campaign, in which the competition commissioner would later figure as a key leader, to create single sets of trans-Atlantic and even global standards for finance, accounting, and production.

In building up the authority of his office as "cartel cop," Brittan could also count on increasing support from the member-states, several of which (like Italy and the United Kingdom) adopted new – or (like Germany) revised old – competition laws. Courts in these and other countries began to deal with antitrust matters under national as well as EU statutes. Competition policy requirements were also included in the renewal of the many bilateral association agreements through which the EU traded with much of the outside world. They would comprise a critical section of the *acquis communautaire* – the EU's regulatory machinery – that candidates for the EU would be required to accept as condition for membership. By 1996, seventy countries – which together were responsible for 79 percent of world output and 86 percent of world trade – would have their own competition laws.[95]

There were plenty of scraps that Brittan did not feel strong enough to enter and other skirmishes in which his nose got twisted. Undeniably, as he noted in a political tract written shortly after he stepped down in 1994, 62 billion ecus of public money had been plowed into the European steel industry since 1975, and many sectors (including textiles, footwear, coal, shipbuilding, consumer electronics, chemicals, parts of the automobile industry, agriculture, and fisheries) still lived partly off of some form of subsidy, were protected by external trade barriers and artificial pricing schemes, or had their bottom lines strengthened by "strategic" research spending.[96] Liberalization remained far from complete. Foot-dragging rather then ideological opposition was the problem. "Industrial policy," as a 1993 study concluded, "is increasingly being made by the selective application of competition policy."[97] The angry French could do little about it.

Brittan accomplished a good deal. In the matter of state aids or subsidies, the Commission steered clear of blatant cases such as the airlines (Air France, Alitalia, Iberia, Olympic, Aer Lingus, and Sabena), coal (the German and Spanish industries), and banking (Crédit Lyonnaise). To the horror of President Delors, Brittan did order Renault to pay back subsidies to the French state. To Delors's immense credit (and own political discomfiture in France), he backed the competition commissioner. The dispute was settled by a judicious compromise. Overall, state aids declined from 40.6 billion ecus in 1986 to 34 billion ecus in 1990.[98]

The new Merger Regulation (4064/1989) enabled the Commission to tackle a wider range of cases than before and gave it the power to vet all fusions involving companies with global turnover of more than 5 billion ecus or EC turnover in any nation of greater than 250 million ecus. The regulation brought good results, thanks in part to an early precedent set in the commuter aircraft market: Brittan blocked plans of the Italian firm Alenia and the French firm Aerospatiale from taking over the Canadian manufacturer de Havilland. The planned merger would have created either a monopoly or a Euro-champion, the choice of terms indicating one's side in a bitter dispute that broke out within the Commission but soon spilled over into the public domain. The well-drafted de Havilland settlement set guidelines for future mergers, any plans for which would soon, as a rule, be presented for Commission scrutiny during the negotiating process. Though the competition directorate's workload increased, its interventions became less frequent.[99]

The competition directorate also achieved important breakthroughs in deregulating the so-called networking industries. This effort faced powerful constraints: the legacy of monopoly control; widespread public ownership and state aids; political and institutional diversity; public service requirements; and the existence of natural monopolies. In the networking industries, the need to interconnect imposed cooperation between rival firms and could give rise to incumbent abuse of position. Thus the deregulation process normally passed through three distinct phases: monopoly; monopoly and competition; and competition – each of which had to be accompanied by a new form of re-regulation. The process turned on such issues as high sunk capital costs, "systems markets" (the need for a standard interface), universal service requirements, and assurance of uninterrupted operation. For legal and administrative reasons alone, the shift to market competition could easily last a decade.

The breakup of public and quasi-public government-regulated monopolies would nevertheless inaugurate a far-reaching market-driven reform process. Not only could one form of ownership replace another or one kind of service provider substitute for another, but something altogether new might materialize – a different type of service or industry, a better product, or perhaps an improved technology. The reform process could also change relationships between sectors or blur boundaries between them to the point at which they disappeared.[100] Not all of this happened at once, of course.

Dynamic change was at work in the telecommunications field by the 1990s. Legally, deregulation had been completed by 1 January 1988 and, according to Brittan,

already in November of that year, the Commission could announce substantial gains for the consumer. There was an explosion of new players ... and no fewer than 284 companies offered international telephone services, 218 companies [provided] comprehensive national telephone services of the kind previously only offered by public monopolies, and 77 new mobile operations had been licensed.[101]

New entrants appeared, and the forms of organization, products, technologies, economic settings, and even habits and social relationships changed.[102]

In the air transport field, Brittan used the new merger law to impose U.S./U.K.-type deregulation. When Air France, UTA (a private overseas French airline) and Air Inter (a domestic carrier) tried to fuse, he required French aviation authorities to open major routes to competition and give new entrants access to takeoff and landing slots. The Commission also directed the lifting of route restrictions and the introduction of fare competition. By 1995, 71 percent of scheduled passengers flew at reduced rates, a figure that rose to 85–90 percent if charter flights are included. The total number of routes increased sharply between 1990 and 1996 – for instance, by 36 percent in France, the largest national market. Results in electricity and natural gas were paltry by comparison, however.[103] Although Great Britain and the Scandinavian countries were well ahead of the pack, electricity and gas directives could not be issued until the end of the 1990s. As often had occurred in the United Kingdom, prices nevertheless began to drop in anticipation of future competition. Employing 1.4 million persons EU-wide, the postal service was the last bastion of organized resistance to change in the networking industries. Competition from private carriers and e-mail had nevertheless begun to erode obstacles to change by the beginning of the new millennium.[104] The process Brittan helped unleash would be hard to stop.

Concurrent changes in the financial field also moved it along. Though cited in the Treaty of Rome as the *sine qua non* of the Common Market, capital mobility would remain an empty concept until the removal of national controls in the 1980s. The 1989 Brussels banking directives laid the basis for a single financial market. One directive set solvency ratios. A second one established a unified licensing procedure that enabled any bank chartered in one member-state to set up branches in another. A third adopted a broad institutional bank model in order to avoid fragmentation. Mergers and consolidations began at the national level, universal banks acquired merchant banks, and the barrier between national markets began to fall. The Commission seldom intervened directly into the banking sector but instead let the financial community set its own rules on the basis of mutual recognition. In fewer than five years, the rudiments of a single financial market were in place.[105]

But did the liberalization policy associated with the 1992 Single European Market program produce real economic benefits? The quick and dirty answer is that they are difficult to detect in the short run. The SEM program targeted four types of trade barriers for elimination: fiscal barriers such as taxes and subsidies; quantitative and qualitative import and export restrictions; market access restrictions directed against other members of the Community, especially in the realm of public procurement; and border controls, technical regulations, and other trade costs. The famous Cecchini Report on the costs of "non-Europe," the official Community study of the impact of the SEA, pointed to benefits in addition to direct savings in trade costs: greater production efficiency achieved through market enlargement, better resource allocation, and the reduction of monopoly power. It estimated gains of from 4.3 to 6.4 percent of GDP. Although 90 percent of the Cockfield targets had been met by 1992, according to the survey conducted by Harry Flam, measurable gains were quite small.[106] A study by Gasiorek and colleagues determined that GDP had increased only 1.5 percent by 1992, of which three quarters was due to increased competition and economies of scale and the remainder to savings in trade costs. Another study, by Haaland and Norman, set the gains at a mere 0.5 percent. In the end, Flam finds hard evidence only that " '1992' will save on resources in intra-Community trade and inject a considerable and healthy dose of competitive pressure into many product markets."[107] The Commission's own conclusions were not much more positive. A summary of 38 sponsored studies done by outside consultants indicated that the Single Market Program had raised Community GDP by 1.1 percent over the previous six years, generated 300,000 to 900,000 jobs, and reduced inflation by 1.1 points – worthwhile but hardly revolutionary results.[108] Whether these studies capture the dynamic character of the process remains unanswered. Nontrivial structural change indeed occurred.

Alexis Jacquemin and Andre Sapir attribute such commercial and financial development to the "reinforced constraint" of increased import competition within European markets, especially in high-tech or "ailing" branches of industry. They also found that "corporate strategies [had] largely anticipated the conditions of the post-1992 single market through various forms of restructuring, including a growing concentration on the main product lines, an extension of geographic coverage, and a multiplication of cooperative arrangements, mergers, and acquisitions."[109] While economic growth rose from 2.8 to nearly 4 percent from 1985 to 1990, Community industrial output increased at an average rate of 3.8 percent and profits and investments reached an all-time high. Consumers were relatively disadvantaged compared to producers – especially those of capital goods, who benefited most. The latter enjoyed average annual output increases of 4.4 percent.

Sectoral output growth correlates with that of direct American and Japanese investment. In fact, Europeans cooperated more frequently with foreign partners, especially in high-tech fields, than with other Europeans. As for mergers, increasing numbers of the horizontal (as opposed to the conglomerate) type occurred, though rarely on an inter-European basis. Consolidation of national market position seems to have been the most important motivation. In a semi-official report, Jacquemin and Wright cautiously concluded from this evidence that "the business community has been the main engine of the integration process through its internal and external restructuring and its cross-border cooperative agreements, mergers and acquisitions."[110] To an extent impossible to disentangle, these results can also be attributed to the real or anticipated impact of globalization, especially the diffusion of new technologies; the establishment of international production and cooperation networks; and huge increases in international capital flow, a multiple of the trade in goods.

Deregulation did not mean no regulation. Still, a lot had been accomplished in ten years. The 290 Cockburn directives superceded fifteen sets of national laws. The competition commissioner's whistle-blowing had deterred far more miscreants than the 168 actually punished. Several new areas had been brought within the Commission's purview, among them telecoms, transport, airlines, energy, and the postal services. Gosplan-like industrial policy dreamt of in the 1970s had been laid to rest. The liberation of markets had assumed a momentum of its own. The effort went further than most states were willing to go by themselves. Public procurement and state aids to industry were two fields crying out for reform. Here one could only hope that governments under pressure to meet the convergence and stability criteria for the EMU would have to sell off state assets and that business leaders faced with increased foreign competition would rationalize across frontiers. Although the tempo of progress could not be foretold, it could reasonably be claimed that – thanks to Sutherland and Brittan, and to successors van Miert and Monti – the EU is lending a strong hand in the creation of a single international competition law.[111]

The Single European Market also held vast implications for the relationship between state and economy. Shortly after the conclusion of the "1992" program, Jacques Pelkmans – admitting to being "perplexed" by the lack of reflection being given so serious a subject – tried to describe the kind of Community that one might find in 1993. He was close to the money. Pelkmans was fully aware of the program's incompleteness, the vigorous lobbying for industrial policy, the complexity of deregulation, and the large variation in national adaptations that it would require. He predicted that completion of the internal market would deprive member-states of many policy instruments, significantly heighten the exposure of sheltered economic activities to continentwide competition, and (for a number of reasons) also reduce the effectiveness of national economic policies. Capital mobility and the free movement of financial service, as well as limitations on the ability to tax, would require ex ante macroeconomic policy coordination between states – especially in the monetary field.

Pelkmans made a number of predictions. Aids to industry would be restricted, the cost of public services brought down, and competition introduced into delivery systems. Technical regulations, standards, and patents would be harmonized by means of mutual recognition. Financial services would be marketed, freight transport subject to Community competition, and professional mobility increased. Knowledge requirements for exporting would be reduced to familiarity with conditions in local markets, and price dispersion would diminish. The attenuation of state power would, finally, shift the center of political power from national capitals to Brussels, where one would expect to witness "greater reliance on positive integration, much less autonomy for domestic indirect tax policies and a commitment to faithfully coordinate macroeconomic policies." "*Can one really believe that this will happen,*" he queried rhetorically in italics, "*without alterations in the political machinery at the Community level?*" "No matter what the Single [European] Act says," he emphatically added, "IF the internal market program will be truly successful, *it MUST surpass the institutional 'evasiveness' of the Single Act.*"[112] Really? The development of Community "political machinery" has in fact fallen increasingly farther behind the advancing marketplace.

Stumbling toward Superstate:
The Delorean Agenda

WAS IT really worth the price of a Jaguar? The Delorean automobile looked pretty nice. It was burnished silver and had gull-wing doors like the ritzy Mercedes SL coupe of the late 1950s, but beneath the sleek skin was only a Renault – a sturdy little French design – or so the world belatedly discovered. It was hard to explain why no one had realized this earlier. Delorean had, after all, taken tens of millions of dollars from the government of Northern Ireland in order to manufacture a dream car and at the same time provide hundreds of new jobs. Why had it gone unnoticed that his factory was empty and that no one had been hired? And where, after all, had all the money gone? Please excuse a bit of word play you might find unbefitting the earnestness of the European endeavor. It *does* suit the case at hand.

Delors's sympathetic biographer, Charles Grant, coined the term "Deloronomics" to describe the weird conflation of cloudy theory and *cris de coeur* that steered his economic agenda. "Deloropolitics," though no less accurate, is a little awkward for the other bookend. So why not use the euphonious "Deloreanism" to describe the whole kit and caboodle? No one would seriously suggest that Jacques Delors was a mere fraud like John Delorean, even though his scheme was every bit as unworkable as the scam of the fast-talking auto man. Take the European Monetary Union, the work of the "Delors Committee." One of the primary purposes of the banker-dominated negotiating forum was to undermine the centralized wage bargaining central to his political faith. The EMU would have no such consequence. Or consider research and development policy, which was anything but pure science. It warped free inquiry, was the plaything of political and economic interests, and diverted money into an entrenched and noninnovative business community, which wasted it. Or think about the ceaselessly reiterated and idealized European "social and economic space." If central Brussels provides an intimation of it, the zone in question would be filled by lobbyists rather than "solidaristic" workers or virtuous peasants bound "organically" to the soil. The policy networking that took hold at the Commission during the 1980s would serve only special interests; the tax-paying public had no influence over it.

The intense Parisian had more in common with the hotshot from Motor City than adherence to a failure-prone agenda. Although Delors often sounded like a mere doctrinaire French socialist, the man had many dimensions and could be many things to many people. Like Delorean, he was something of a flim-flam man – the tricky con artist who "baits" quarry with one thing and then "switches" to another. The secret of the successful flimflam man is total self-confidence, no matter how misplaced; he must always remain a step ahead of the victim, who then, half-wittingly, does his bidding. Delors did indeed harbor a secret plan for creating a "European model of society." Only as it unfolded and was revealed would it be possible to determine what it contained and what it was worth. By then, however, it would be too late to act upon – one would have been both baited and hooked (*engrenage*).

According to George Ross, a brilliant American sociologist who in 1992 had the unique experience of serving as Boswell to the Commission president, Delors plotted a strategy to advance his agenda virtually upon arrival at the Commission and then followed it from start to finish. It was referred to, within the intimate confines of Delors's cabinet, as the strategy of the Russian Doll. In the manner of that intriguing wooden plaything, the plan was to be exposed only one level at a time. Each hollow form, when pulled apart, revealed a new previously concealed character, quite unlike the one seen before. M. Delors designed the Russian Doll; determined how the mysterious expressions on its various faces should be painted; and made sure that it was carved properly, fit together neatly, could be unscrewed smoothly and easily at the right time, and that the opening of each successive layer would present a new surprise. Only the president of the Commission knew what the solid little figure at the end of the process – the long-awaited "European Model of Society" – would look like. It was, after all, his toy.[1]

Jacques Delors's confidence that, at the right time, he could spring his trap and catch his prey is not surprising. Delors had won many times before. His multi-dimensional policy was intricate, sometimes opaque, dealt with the unfamiliar, required complicated compromises, and could produce surprising outcomes – and was in any case hard to follow because concealed. His first priority was to guard Commission turf and, whenever possible, expand it. This objective re-quired entering pacts with more powerful parties. The French could be counted on to be sympathetic (Delors was, after all, Mitterrand's man); the smaller nations had traditionally sought Commission protection from large, powerful neighbors; the British could easily be marginalized; and the Italians could be counted upon to follow the rest of the pack.

This left the Germans – the most important player – and the Club Med na-tions. Chancellor Kohl was the most pro-European Chancellor since Adenauer and also, once the reunification process began, the one most in need of allies. Delors could generally count upon him to be well-disposed. Finally, there were the recent arrivals from the southern enlargement. Delors brought their loyalty with two generous aid packages, the regional and cohesion funds. These sub-sidy deals involved complicated bargains with the positive result of the first (and last) significant reduction in the CAP and the negative result of a clientage re-lationship between the Commission and the new entrants. Delors also pursued a social policy largely of his own devising, which was stronger in word than in deed; it was undermined by the opening of markets that resulted from the Single European Act. The outcome was not the other extreme – an Arcadia of competitive welfare optimizers – but of across-the-board, dynamic conflict between challengers and incumbents, cross-pressures from Brussels directives and innovative change in the market, and struggles for influence between new voices and entrenched interests.

Eventual settlement of such matters depended upon the resolution of two others. The first and most consequential was the monetary union. In this field, Delors was not the master of all he surveyed. Real authority rested with the bankers. These experts themselves did not fully understand the economics of the task facing them – and to explain it will require digression into the technical literature. Nor did either the bankers or Delors entirely grasp the full political implications of their creation. Delors was intent upon building a Europe strong enough to stand toe-to-toe with the big guy across the water. The bankers wanted to tie the hands of fiscally irresponsible governments. They never seem to have appreciated that the European central bank they meant to found would threaten the principle of self-government and even jeopardize the "European construction."

The second unresolved issue was institutional in character. To deal with the lack of a political counterpart to the EMU, Delors engaged in frantic state building. The unsatisfactory result of these efforts is evident in the formless, badly written, almost indefensible political sections of the Maastricht treaty; how they can (or should) relate to the monetary union is unclear. The unresolved problems in the text – and, more broadly, on the political side – would provide endless opportunities for misunderstanding and argumentation among member-states and between them and the Commission, and they would also lead to premature, inappropriate, and reckless constitution-building ventures in the future. Delors stepped down amidst the wreckage left in the wake of the financial cyclone that hit Europe in 1992 – his work unfinished, his legacy powerful but perhaps not enduring. He, too, would be surprised by the figure at the core of the Russian Doll.

The Single European Act was the first Russian Doll, and five additional ones would subsequently open. The next doll would be a financial package, and following it would be others for social policy and monetary (and political) union. Topping off the process would be a second, even more ambitious financial package and, finally, a White Paper redolent of the Mitterrand experiment. The successive (though temporally overlapping) policy episodes, which would prove to be of varying importance, played themselves out against the dramatic backdrop of Soviet collapse, German reunification, and the financial and economic upheaval that followed. Such events actually facilitated the realization of Delors's plans, but they did not change them. The struggle for the future of Europe would continue to be waged within the parameters of EU discourse – with Margaret at one pole and Jacques at the other.

THE DELORS PACKET AND REGIONAL POLICY

If the Single European Act was the first Russian Doll, the second one was the "Delors Packet," which Ross, the president's amanuensis, calls "the most under-discussed major event in Europe's post-1985 renewal."[2] Delors aimed to end the recurrent budgetary crises, stanch the CAP hemorrhage, and raise new money for structural funds. He also put forward a new "five-year financial perspective" for budgeting. Its main feature, a mechanism for advance agreement on "fair shares," was meant to end the rancor dividing the Commission and the Parliament from the Council of Ministers, which had immobilized the Community over the previous several years. The proposal granted the European Parliament an increase in "noncompulsory expenditure" to include the structural funds for disadvantaged regions. Access to such money tightened the EP's tie to the Commission while at the same time increasing the support Delors could muster from the Club Med nations in the European Council. The deal required an angel willing to bear the costs. Helmut Kohl, self-styled as Adenauer's last great disciple, turned out to be the man with the wings. In an unprecedented and almost self-sacrificial act of good-Europeanism, the German agreed to bear the entire cost of the transfers. He thereby handed Delors his greatest single triumph.

The budgetary agreement arrived at in February 1988 increased overall Community funding to 1.2 percent by 1992 in real terms; added a fourth new source of revenue based on per-capita GNP; extended the British rebate; "capped" agricultural price supports at 74 percent of the growth in Community GNP; and, above all, doubled the transfer of financial resources to have-nots by 1993. The big increase in structural funds – which after five years were to comprise 25 percent of the budget – was, Ross correctly states, "the first really substantial European-level commitment to planned redistribution among member-states."[3]

Redistribution should not be confused with a regional development policy. The funds, according to David Allen, were meant by the Council to be allocated for the short and medium term as side payments in order to facilitate the negotiation of "general packages" and compensate incumbents for future enlargements. Their purpose was to ease accommodation to the single market, not substitute for it. Things hardly worked out as planned. The recipients rebuffed attempts by the Commission to assert control over allocation and expenditure, and "renationalization" soon began. The "rot," according to Allen, then set in. None of the four Commission "principles for implementing structural funds" was ever respected. They were not *concentrated* around priority objectives, did not involve *partnership* between Commission and regional authorities, failed to respect *additionality* (meaning, in non-Eurospeak, that the funds should complement rather than replace national project expenditures), and were not *programmed*. Instead, old-fashioned pork-barrel politics were served up generously on a larger platter.[4]

The situation got even further out of hand after the post-Maastricht Edinburgh European Council in early 1992.[5] The Council then agreed to nearly double allocations of structural funds, from 18.6 billion ecus to 30 billion ecus by 1999,

but the Commission bid to win Council support for specifying investment categories for the funds broke on the shoals of recipient-state resistance. Instead, a
"cohesion fund" would for the following four years be divided up into national
shares. Spain was to receive between 52 and 58 percent, Greece and Portugal each
between 16 and 20 percent, and Ireland between 7 and 10 percent. Guidelines
for expenditure were to have been agreed upon later. The largesse represented
a huge cash infusion into the economies of three small countries. Accordingly,
in the words of Alvaro de Vasconcelos, "unlike other areas of European integration, the [Portuguese] national consensus regarding cohesion and the ... priority
attached to it was as wide-ranging as could possibly be, uniting supporters and
opponents of Europe, federalists and intergovernmentalists alike."[6] The appeal
of the freebie was almost irresistible.

THE SOCIAL CHARTER, IMAGINED SPACE, AND POLICY NETWORKING IN BRUSSELS

The regional doll opened to a social doll. The big decision makers, who represented the member-states in Council, were not particularly attracted by its
impassive blandishments. Basking in the success of "1992," Delors unveiled new
plans for what would later become the Social Charter at the 1988 Stockholm Conference of the European Trade Union Confederation (ETUC), a Commission-
subsidized poodle. The speech contained a pointed reminder that, in his view,
adoption of the SEA was "not a question of ... simply creating a free-trade zone,
but rather an organized space endowed with common rules to ensure economic
and social cohesion and equality of opportunity in the face of new opportunities."[7] The Social Charter of May 1989 represented a "solemn commitment"
on the part of its signatories – which did not include a furious Britain – to respect a set of "fundamental rights," in reality consisting mainly of specifics about
wage agreements. The charter was not legally binding and thus taken perhaps
too lightly by opponents, who at the time regarded it as merely an exercise in
"feel-good politics" – or, more cynically, as a bone to be tossed to organized
labor, which had been left out in the 1992 program and whose power was declining as a result. It was, according to Paul Pierson, "a saga of high aspirations and
modest results ... cheap talk."[8]

Delors did not take the charter lightly; instead, he determinedly launched an
Action Program to "operationalize" it. This program generated a slew of 47
different "hard" proposals involving living and working conditions, freedom of
movement, worker information, consultation, and broad social policy, as well as
"recommendations" for "a convergence of objectives in social protection" and
"minima in social assistance" directed to the poor and an "opinion" on appropriate minimum wage levels. Delors's "cheap talk" had a preeminently political
purpose. It was a bold and risky effort to reach out to the battered and discouraged unions and to give heart to the demoralized socialists – by a man who had,
despite his big words, few political weapons at his disposal.

Delors did have a single, though short, lever of power that might be extendable. Article 118b of the Single European Act empowered the Commission (in its own weasel-words) to "seek to encourage" labor–management dialog at the European level. Neither the union (ETUC) nor the employers' association (UNICE) had any real power. Each specifically lacked the authority to negotiate wages and working conditions, and the latter had resisted "dialoging" with labor on issues that its members considered the prerogative of management. Interchange between the two bodies held little promise of delivering results. Delors nonetheless used every opportunity to bring the term "social dialog" before the public, if only to convey the impression that it was something real.[9] He tirelessly jawboned UNICE in the hope of eventually wearing down opposition to the idea. Perhaps he expected (as public choice theory would indicate) that, in order not to lose its mission, the producer association would eventually be drawn to engage in "social dialog." If nothing else, Delors managed to keep the notion in play until something concrete could be done. Like Monnet before him, he minted a language that, though detached from the realities of European integration, has nonetheless influenced it.

The 25 square miles of 1000 Brussels in which the Eurocracy dwelt bore little resemblance to M. Delors's stylized "European economic and social space." The robust marching columns of confident, arm-locked, square-jawed workers of Stalinist realism put in few appearances. And rarely did one see secure, contented, and gracefully retired men of the soil waiting patiently in the manner of Spitzweg at the gentle banks of clean, fresh-flowing streams until the fat trout bit. Instead, one bumped into lobbyists scurrying about everywhere, many of them speaking Americanese. In the years between the SEA and the Maastricht treaty, policy networking became the established way of doing business in the capital of Europe. More than 10,000 professional lobbyists roamed the halls of the Commission, one to serve each 1.3 of its officials. More than 200 large corporations set up government affairs offices in Brussels, and another 500 corporate lobby groups surrounded them. In preparation for their enhanced role, "the world's first school for lobbyists has opened in Brussels, in this case focusing on how to deal effectively with European institutions, [the] European Institute for Public Affairs and Lobbying or Euro-lobby."[10]

American interests were overrepresented at the seat of Eurocracy for several reasons: U.S. companies lacked the cozy relationships of their European counterparts in their home countries and needed allies at the level of Europe; operating across borders, they required the existence of an agency with the exclusive authority to set single European standards in order to capture scale economies; and they were keenly attuned to cutting-edge political issues and likewise familiar with modern methods of public relations. In response to strong demand from European interests, lobbying expertise in fact became an important American export product on the Brussels market. Like their American counterparts, Community firms would also come to rely upon the sophisticated influence peddlers.

The new science of political packaging not only changed the *modus operandi* of the Commission: it forced organized business to become structurally and methodically more flexible, encouraged producers to enter into the public marketplace of merchandised ideas, and built new types of interest-group constituencies to influence the Euro-*apparat*.[11]

Lobbying in Brussels must be distinguished from its Washington cousin in one important respect. The U.S. Congress has traditionally been the primary focus of American interest peddling, a place where the name of the game is mobilization of grass-roots support behind organized economic interests. The "democratic deficit" existing in the Euro-capital meant ipso facto that the Commission was where decisions would be made and legislation shaped. There, insiders normally made their influence felt directly, with the encouragement of the Commission's president and by dint of privileged relationships; the public was not consulted. As Shirley Williams, former Labour minister of education (and subsequent founder of the British Social Democratic Party), put it: "Brussels ... is accessible to professional lobbyists – many incidentally from the United States and Japan – with company credit cards in their pockets ... but not to Greek peasants, Portuguese fishermen, Spanish factory workers, and Scottish bank clerks."[12] Unlike Washington, lobbying in Brussels was unrestricted: "the European Commission had no register of proposed regulations to solicit public comment, parliamentary hearings on draft legislation are rare, and virtually no formal advisory bodies exist in the EU public policy system."[13] The technical issues under discussion were often either intrinsically difficult to understand or made incomprehensible by the use of administrative gobbledygook, compounding problems of accountability. In the words of one expert, "the technical and regulatory nature of EU legislation ... contributes to the low public profile of European lobbying, as opposed to the more redistributive policy making in the U.S."[14] The issue at hand was typically not how to cut the pie but how to bake it. Jan Tumlir would not have been happy.

A breach began to open in this closed system at some point in the late 1980s. In response to pressures felt through the market or in anticipation of Commission decisions that would impact market outcomes, lobbyists organized new interest groups and created new "vertical constituencies" to compete for influence in policy making. The effort hardly eliminated the "democratic deficit," but it did at least begin to subject policy making to the influence of those Europeans who dwelt outside the charmed circle of official and quasi-official Brussels. The U.S. methods of lobbying and American public relations firms have served as valuable intermediaries in preventing regulatory capture – by which organized interests would become the dog that wags Europe as its tail.[15]

Far from causing alarm, the existence of a system based upon policy networking encounters little criticism from either academics or the public; indeed, both insiders and experts considered it "a perfectly respectable and necessary part of the policy process."[16] More specifically, as put in a laudatory management study,

[its] informality gives ... European public policy its vitality and flexibility, allowing as it does for the development of informal relationships, the apportioning of favors, and the establishment of trust. This creates a potential "win–win" game for the EU institutions and lobbying firms and it encourages long-run business–government relationships.[17]

The strongest justification that can be made for the existing situation is the lack of any feasible alternative. Faced with the daunting task of drafting the legislation needed to implement the single European market and, for both legal and practical reasons, bound to do so by applying the standard of "mutual recognition," the Commission (in this view) could not have proceeded without the cooperation of interested parties. "Accessibility" and "transparency" – to cite the two terms most widely abused to describe this clubby state of affairs – are thus necessary and desirable for the conduct of business.[18]

This purely technical explanation does not get to the heart of the matter. Two other main considerations dictate the need for access to Community policy makers. One is that 92 percent of the budget is subject to redistribution and thus to political pressure. (The remaining 8 percent is overhead.) The other is that, since the mid-1980s, the Commission has been able to make or break big mergers, police marketing arrangements, and impose standards with huge implications for both producers and other concerned parties. Such vast stakes require large-scale, multidimensional, and permanent operations. The process only starts with the provision of technical "input."[19]

The U.S. multinationals caught on early to the need for lobbying. The American Chamber of Commerce (Amcham), and the firms it represented, set the pace for the Europeans. Whereas UNICE represented national employer federations, themselves divided into sectoral associations, Amcham represented both firms and associations. It was also better geared than its clumsy European counterpart to meet the needs of the Commission:

By adapting the organizational structure around twelve specialized technical committees on issues such as competition, trade, social affairs, and the environment, Amcham was able to complement the European Commission's issue-based forums. It was not uncommon for the membership of both committees to be the same.

It helped that American firms were represented by prominent European nationals with close ties to the Commission.[20]

The European Roundtable of Industrialists might have represented a challenge to Amcham, but the new interest of Community producers in Brussels resulted in closer alliances and general linkage between European and non-European interests. UNICE copied American methods, allowing for direct firm membership and reorganizing on the basis of functional committees. American firms joined both UNICE and sectoral bodies like the European Automobile Producers Association, the European Chemical Industry Council, and the European Federation of Pharmaceuticals Producers.[21] The loosening of organizational structures as well as resort to ad hoc methods made it easier for outsiders to challenge the position of entrenched market incumbents.

This change worried the cozy. A 1991 article in the ERT-sponsored journal *European Affairs,* "Taking Care of Business," spells out some of the problems. The author, a "public affairs consultant in Amsterdam," was troubled that ESPRIT, the Community-sponsored telecommunications program, "has produced almost no technology that is commercially useful." She also fretted that Michael Porter's *The Competitive Advantages of Nations,* then becoming the business policy bible of the decade, required "governments to disallow mergers, acquisitions, and alliances among industry leaders" and to encourage competition. More to the point, the consultant was troubled that the Commission seemed no longer to be playing by well-established rules. Recently, a directive on "pesticides [had been] formulated by the Directorate-General for agriculture without prior consultation with producers."[22] This seemed almost inexplicable to her because "the agriculture DG sees its role as promoting the interests of the users of pesticides and writes directives from this point of view." Equally distressing was that, "in drafting the directive to liberalize public procurement markets in services, DG III [internal market and industry] did not consult ... DG VII [transport], which should operate as an advocate for the interests of all transport sectors." She concluded sadly that whereas

influencing the competition of the internal market used to be relatively easy ... industry has [now] got to put more effort ... into representing its interests in Brussels ... [because] as the [Community's] powers increase and more interest groups set up shop in Brussels, European industry is threatened with losing its exclusive relationship with European policy makers.[23]

What should be done? First of all, the subsidiarity principle should be used to maximum advantage whenever Brussels officialdom seemed recalcitrant. Otherwise, the consultant recommended that industry become "proactive instead of reactive," especially in order to head off future evils in the fields of environmental and social policy and product safety: "Environmental policy," for example, "offers European industry opportunities for self-regulation and representation during the decision-making process, [in which] active involvement is required to head off unworkable and drastic regulations."[24]

The Commission's publication in 1992 of the Postal Green Paper was the opening shot in a still inconclusive running skirmish in which new public relations weapons would be put to the test. The paper proposed extending the still limited competition between public delivery and private courier services to cover most letters as well as packages. The PTTs (government postal services), which employed several million persons Community-wide, initially resorted to intimidation: raided the offices of the couriers, slowed down customs processing, delayed licensing, planted hostile news articles, and launched a campaign of judicial harassment. Supported by the competition directorate, encouraged by American firms, and advised by specialists in "government relations," the challengers organized user interests in the member-states to exert pressure on the postal monopolies from behind the scenes. A new "Express Carrier Conference" coordinated the effort.[25]

The PTTs then raised the ante. In order to embarrass the Commission politically, they set up an organization to "widen the public debate to include a fundamental reassessment of EU postal and social policy." The couriers countered by organizing a new body to "build a wider political base ... through public workshops and seminars appealing to consumers." It may well be true, according to one expert, that the conferences and workshops actually helped the PTTs and the couriers to "find some technical common ground, ... encouraged joint ventures ... and [promoted] learning and innovation."[26] If nothing else, a decision that might have been made behind closed doors was brought before the public and a political dialog started that, over time, could help define new voter constituencies and broaden the decision-making process in Brussels.

On one important issue concerning intellectual property, the "new lobbying" changed outcomes. The May 1991 Commission directive for the legal protection of computer programs standardized the copyright law on software, banning re-engineering. A European Committee for Interoperable Systems – representing the interests of smallish European and Japanese firms – formed to oppose it. A Software Action Group for Europe (SAGE) thereupon sprang into existence to represent IBM, Philips, Siemens, Apple, Microsoft, and Lotus to curtail the "piracy of copyright theft" and protect consumers from "poor quality goods." The Commission split. Motivated by "research and development considerations," DG III (industrial policy) favored SAGE, the incumbents, and the Commission. DG IV (competition) and DG XIII (research) favored the pro–re-engineering challengers, who allied with the cyber-community's Computer Users of Europe. The Council reversed the Commission.[27]

The proliferation of issue-based, ad hoc groups and coalitions – especially in the high-tech, science-based fields like information technology and biotechnology – transcended traditional sectoral boundaries, brought new political constituencies into the policy process, and stepped up competition between firms providing public goods. The new activism has also strengthened the hand of the Commission by enabling it to sell to the highest rather than the only bidder. The large contribution of American businesses, Amcham, and U.S. public relations firms provides interesting anecdotal evidence from an unexpected source that supports the contention of the Cecchini Report (as well as the finding of economists Jacquemins and Sapir) that, under the Single European Act, foreign competition would be the main stimulus for growth and, it follows, structural change. New technology challenges and market opportunities were beginning to fill the void that M. Delors called Europe's "social and economic space." The unintended but predictable consequence of a corporatist policy resting on special relationships with a business community that itself was responding to market-induced change, the realities of this construction bore scant resemblance to the dreamy images of Delorean ideology.

THE EUROPEAN MONETARY UNION EXAMINED

The next Russian Doll was economic and monetary union, which upon closer inspection looks like something even more impressive: economic, monetary, and *political* union. Whether and to what extent it merits the inclusion of the third adjective remains the source of controversy. The political sections of the treaty are a mess. Their relationship to the key provisions for the European Monetary Union is obscure and far less important politically (not to mention economically) than creation of the EMU itself – the most momentous development in the history of European integration since the conclusion of the Rome treaty.

The economic rationale for the monetary union is anything but compelling. Nor is adoption of the euro for other than political reasons either necessary or desirable. There are a couple of obvious benefits, both small, to the use of a single currency. The value of the first such benefit – savings gained by eliminating foreign exchange transactions – can easily be exaggerated. Hedging in futures and spot markets reduces most of the risk of doing business in more than one currency, and the widespread use of electronic transfers and "e-currency" cuts down on cost and inconvenience. Second, the value of improved price transparency should also not be overstated; it is restricted largely to the retail consumer. Even at this market tier, the big change came with the elimination of nontariff barriers to trade. The reduction in currency conversion does save resources and increases trade among member countries, but even if it is "trade creating" rather than "trade diverting" the gains will be slight.[28]

Offsetting these two minor benefits of monetary union is one major cost. Europe is not an optimum currency area and will not be until four "Mundellian" prerequisites are satisfied: the economies of the union must be relatively homogenous; domestic wages and prices must be flexible; the labor force must be mobile; and fiscal transfers must be responsive. None of these conditions obtains. The relinquishment of monetary and fiscal policy independence places the burden of adjustment to exogenous change on labor markets, which are rigid. Until, at a minimum, this ceases to be the case and markets become flexible, a "one size fits all" monetary policy that cannot accommodate regional variations and lacks adequate mechanisms for fiscal transfers will impede rather than promote efficient operation of the internal market.[29] The plight Europe faces is simply this, according to the late Rudi Dornbusch: "If exchange rates are abandoned as an economic tool, something else must take their place. Maastricht's promoters have carefully avoided spelling out just what that might be. Competitive labor markets is the answer, but that is a dirty word in social welfare Europe."[30]

A quasi-economic rationale for what in 1999 would become the European Monetary Union turns on credible commitments.[31] The argument reflects the belief that a permanent institutional arrangement was needed to tie the hands of governments and bind them to monetary stability in order to stimulate invest-ment.[32] Proponents must, however, take account of the huge progress made by European governments in reducing inflation between 1975 and 1990, prior to EMU – as well as that made over the same years and subsequently by the United States and Great Britain, which have remained outside the framework of the agreement. Does Europe really need a chastity belt? Would it not be more com-fortable without one? Can such an arrangement ever be considered permanent? If not, how credible is it? How long can virtue remained unsullied? And, with virtue intact and "credible," might not the rusty, unsanitary, and surely un-comfortable appliance someday be safely removed? The potential advantage of government by rule must also be considered in light of its costs ("knowledge losses") to the process of government by choice.

One could further maintain that, without a single currency, Europe cannot de-velop its own capital market. But this claim will not withstand scrutiny. Controls over capital at the national level had for three decades hindered the formation of a large market denominated in the currency of any single European nation. A Euro-dollar market developed a single Euro-currency market. With the lifting of restraints on mobility in the 1980s, a Euro-capital market also began to grow through use of the ecu. Although at first merely a *numéraire* (unit of exchange) in settlements between the central banks of the European Monetary System, a private market for ecu-denominated bonds took root. The currency unit then became a store of value as well. The size of ecu capital markets would most likely have continued to increase. Competition with the dollar could only have lowered borrowing costs and increased market liquidity. The euro can follow a similar path. It would be rash to assume that any single new European currency will replace the dollar as a reserve currency. The dollar's incumbent advantage is huge: it is used on one side in 80 percent of all international transactions and on both sides in 60 percent of them. Europe also will require far-reaching struc-tural reform in order to make a single financial market possible.[33]

Nor did any agreement prior to Maastricht require that a future economic and monetary union adopt a single currency. If alternative approaches had been seriously considered at the top level of decision making, a distinctly different "European construction" might have resulted. The ecu could, for instance, have continued to circulate as a "parallel currency" alongside national monies. Such use of it would also have obviated the high cost of converting national curren-cies to the new euro standard. Nor is there any purely economic reason why a such a "floating ecu" could not have been accompanied by a "growth and stabil-ity pact" that imposed "convergence criteria" by binding governments to strict rules (governing budget deficits, size of the national debt, and rates of inflation) and that had the additional advantage, because not entailing a single unified monetary system, of being loosened when desirable.[34] Adoption of methods less formal than those of the EMU would also have prevented the founding of a pow-erful, unaccountable, antirepresentative "Euro-Fed" – or at least postponed its creation until if and when it became opportune to embark openly and democratically upon the drafting of a genuine constitution for the self-government of the European peoples.

Monetary union was implicit at the very origin of the European communities, according to the Italian central banker Tommaso Padoa-Schioppa: it is not mentioned anywhere in the Treaty of Rome, he mistakenly insists, because the permanence of the fixed but adjustable Bretton Woods system (which, in fact, had not yet begun to function) was simply taken for granted. A Community proposal for a monetary union actually first appears in the Segre Report of 1966, where it provides political wrapping for a policy aimed at eliminating national capital controls as a necessary first step toward the creation of a European capital market. The Commission study focused on capital investment, in other words, not consumer convenience.[35] The basic idea behind the monetary union is that it will make Europe strong and independent.

Concerns about the stability of the increasingly erratic dollar prompted the drafting of the famous Werner Report (1970), which was endorsed at The Hague summit. This report called for monetary union within ten years, to be achieved in three stages. Governments would first limit exchange-rate fluctuations and coordinate monetary and fiscal policy. Next, exchange-rate variability and price divergences were to be decreased. Finally, exchange rates would be irrevocably set, capital controls removed, and a "Euro-Fed" be set up to control the monetary policies of member-nations. The resemblance of the Werner scheme to the eventual EMU was superficial. It called not for a single currency but for a monetary federation, and it rested not on the enforcement of rules but on policy coordination, fiscal federalism in particular. It was a demand-side arrangement predicated on a big increase in the Community budget and a framework of *planiste* institutions of the sort that integrationists had vainly tried to build in the 1970s. Capital controls were to have been lifted only at the conclusion of the process. Liberalization would be the end rather than the means of policy.

Modest by comparison with the ambitions of the Werner Plan, the European Monetary System in effect after 1979 served as a bridge to the EMU. The EMS aimed to stabilize national currencies by pegging to the Deutsche mark but without fully eliminating policy divergence or imposing fiscal and monetary rules. The shift to the politics of stability in France and elsewhere made alignment to the DM feasible for most member-nations in the mid-1980s, but it failed to prevent sharp devaluations at the beginning of the decade and in 1992. The events of that year trace back to the mandatory phase-out of capital controls required by the Single European Act of 1986, which stripped central banks of means (other than by market intervention) with which to regulate or contain capital flows. A hybrid system like EMS would have been hard-pressed in the absence of serious economic reform and, in the short run, risked failure under conditions of unrestricted capital mobility.[36]

The Single European Act posed a clear choice: a fully floating regime or a single currency. A floating regime was not inconsistent with monetary union, whose definition is institutional, not economic. The defining characteristic of a monetary union is the existence of a single, indivisible, decision-making authority. One could in theory have worked with a plurality of competing currencies à la Hayek, as the history of nineteenth-century free banking demonstrates. Sir Alan Walters (Mrs. Thatcher's unofficial economic advisor) attempted with partial success to impress the point upon British negotiators serving on the Delors Committee. John Major, then chancellor of the exchequer in the Thatcher cabinet, briefly championed a modified version of the arrangement. As the preferred policy of the Treasury, Major proposed that a European Monetary Fund issue "hard" floating ecus that could be swapped for national currencies in the expectation that the stability of the Euro-money would discipline national monetary policies.[37]

The only convincing economic arguments against such a floating regime, according to Barry Eichengreen, are political.[38] Within a free-trade area, a rapidly devaluing currency may elicit protests of "exchange dumping" and thus stir up protectionism. In Europe there was, furthermore, the special consideration of the Common Agricultural Policy. Costly "green money" interventions would be required to prevent exporters in a country with a depreciating rate of exchange from driving supported CAP prices through the floor. The elimination of border controls and nontariff barriers by the SEA aggravated the problem. The generic (though contestable) argument in favor of the single currency was that, in a still partially controlled economy, it would be "less disruptive" than the competitive system. The British proposal was without influence on the Delors Committee.

The 1988 Hanover European Council, which set up the special committee charged with "studying and proposing concrete steps leading towards monetary union," did not specify what it meant by the term. Central bankers provided the definition. Meeting under Delors's chairmanship they decided that it had meant "three things" – the single market, fiscal and budgetary discipline, and the unification of monetary matters – and they addressed them in their order of importance.[39] The first "thing" was nearly an established fact. The 300 or so specific targets of the SEA were being met on time; most relevant, capital controls had been removed or, in a few minor instances, were slated for removal. The second priority was arguably the most pressing item on the agenda. Fiscal discipline was prerequisite to monetary union of any kind, but how best to enforce it was an issue upon which experts disagreed. There is, first of all, no economic reason for claiming that a monetary union cannot function in the absence of rules (or some other means) for imposing fiscal discipline; a profligate government will simply have to pay a high premium to borrow. If, however, a tradition of political intervention impedes the proper operation of the market, then something else must obviously substitute for it. Rules were necessary, according to Padoa-Schioppa, because "it was indispensable to present monetary union as being based on sound budgetary policies, since consensus on monetary union would not have materialized without reassuring public opinion that it would be built on solid fiscal foundations."[40] Thus the basic rules were laid down: fiscal deficits could not exceed 3 percent of GDP, public debt could not exceed 60 percent of GDP, and no currency can exceed the inflation rate of the Community mean by more then 1.5 percent. Such rules also provided a way to bind governments without having to mandate actions. Compliance would have to be enforced by making "exit" prohibitive, as part of a larger process of *engrenage*.

The third "thing" that monetary union meant, the Delors Committee decided, was a national currency for Europe. At issue was more than merely "the irrevocable locking of exchange rates," something that implied comparison to an international standard of value and the existence of linkage between currencies. Bretton Woods was in such a sense a fixed–exchange rate regime; so, too, was EMS. What came to be called the euro was conceived as "one immutable measure for the whole economy in which it is used" like the American dollar. Control of this new currency was to rest solely with the European Central Bank (ECB). According to Padoa-Schioppa:

In the preparation of the treaty on economic and monetary union a consensus was reached at an early stage that the single monetary policy of the Community should be conducted by the [ECB], which would be independent of both the Community institutions and of national authorities. The [central bank] will have as its overriding objectives price stability and, without prejudicing this aim, support for the general economic policy of the Community .... The political dimension of Community monetary policy will be relatively small.[41]

Put somewhat more bluntly by Richard Cooper, "the [ECB] will greatly widen the democratic gap. [It] is a ... powerful body of Platonic guardians, effectively accountable to no one, yet with strong influence on the course of economic affairs."[42] Or, as Barry Eichengreen chimes in, the ECB is "insulated from pressures at least as strong as the Bundesbank .... The drafters of the treaty responded to the worry that public support for price stability does not run as deeply in other [Community] countries [as in] Germany."[43] That was precisely the point. The bankers designed the monetary union for two explicit purposes: removing monetary and fiscal policy from the reach of vote-seeking politicians; and placing authority in the hands of disinterested experts committed single-mindedly to the goal of economic stability.

Having agreed at the outset to create a single currency and a Bundesbank for Europe, the Delors Committee focused on the transition to monetary union. The negotiations were highly technical and often wearying. The positions of the various parties were nevertheless fairly straightforward. The reluctant Germans were courted by the rest; the French pressed hard at least for the appearance of political oversight; the Italians, concerned about qualifying, fought hard concerning deadlines and conditions; the Spanish had similar worries and, anticipating a "cohesion reward," were especially eager for the project to succeed; and the wary though inventive British were brushed off by the others. The objectives of stage I of the process were to complete the elimination of capital controls, accelerate the convergence of inflation and interest rates, and stabilize exchange rates. In stage II, a new European Monetary Institute would coordinate monetary policies during the final phase of transition to the union, which would begin by 1999 *if* – in the judgment of the European Council – by 1997 a majority of countries met the entrance requirements. At the beginning of stage III, exchange rates would be irrevocably fixed, the European Central Bank founded, and the modalities for putting the new currency into circulation worked out and put into operation. The near-collapse of the EMS in 1992 almost wrecked the transition plan. Otherwise, the tightening of policy constraints previously imposed through the EMS provided stability, low inflation, and steady if unremarkable growth – though at the costs of persistent high unemployment – for the rest of the decade.[44] The deadlines would be met.

Verdicts on the economics of the Maastricht agreement have been generally harsh. Even the pro-integration *Economist* called it a "bungled design" that "ignored [a] copious literature ... and came up with three proposals that have nothing to do with optimum currency areas, at least one of which is likely to turn into a positive hindrance."[45] The biggest problem concerned the provisions for public finance, which – though they brought Italy and Spain into a "culture of stability" – were nonessential and unnecessarily rigid. The "excessive deficits" provisions had, in fact, required fudging by all parties (including the fiscally righteous Germans) in 1997 and 1998. The economic rationale for the tight collar is simply wrong, in the view of the *Economist*. The fear was that, once in the EMU, a country would borrow excessively because of moral hazard, raising rates for everyone. However, the *Economist* argued that, as indicated by the American example of the 1980s, high rates of debt do not necessarily undermine currencies if coupled to sound supply-side policies. The anti-bailout provision in the treaty will, moreover, cause markets to demand an interest-rate premium as a result of excessive borrowing, thereby curbing it.

The real problem, in this view, is that the stability provisions will interfere with the work of automatic stabilizers. Such can be the result if growth rates fall by a percentage point in countries running close to the 3-percent limit since, as estimated by the OECD, the percentage-point drop raises the deficit by half a point. The tight constraints on national deficits also send the wrong signal from the center: fear of eventual bailouts. They also raise the vexatious issue of fiscal transfers, which would require a commitment to federalizing far beyond anything acceptable to the public. The prognosis? – doubt that the EMU can work as intended and skepticism that it can work satisfactorily without relaxation of the stability criteria.[46]

If the economic case for monetary union is weak, the justification for EMU must come from elsewhere. The Maastricht negotiators decided to adopt a national (or territorial) currency for Europe largely as a matter of political choice. As explained by Tommaso Padoa-Schioppa, who represented Italy on the Delors Committee that hammered out the basic agreement, "[we] conceived [of] monetary union not as a rule for international cooperation, but as a 'national' monetary system. With this approach the logic on international agreements gave way to that of monetary constitutions. [It] inspired ... decisions that ... held unchanged right through to Maastricht."[47] These decisions included focusing on the final goal instead of how to reach it, emphasizing institutions rather than policy coordination, and insisting on the indivisibility of the money supply.

The identification of a currency with the modern state occurred after the 1648 Westphalian peace settlement. Yet it took over 150 years for territorial currencies gradually to crowd out a competing, more cosmopolitan monetary regime – a "free banking system" of private as well as publicly issued monies – whose values rested on market-determined pricing. The territorial system arose in order to meet the need for standardized units of account, provide a vehicle for compensating the poor (as well as introduce the disadvantaged into a monetized economy), prevent coin clipping, and reduce the cost of exchange transactions. Building trust in and loyalty to the state also figured strongly in the rise of territorial currencies. One goal served by the creation of an American national bank note after the Civil War was to "strengthen the bonds of union" and to inspire a "sentiment of nationality." The new money was meant to encourage individuals in a nation-state to feel themselves members of an "imagined community," to use the term of Benedict Anderson.[48] The practical concerns that gave rise to territorial currencies in the past have no present analogue. The chief reason for adopting the euro was to inculcate love of a European motherland.

The second one was to collar the politicians. The looping, elegant phrases of Padoa-Schioppa state the matter more delicately:

the rise ... of a political philosophy based on "minimum government" provided the ... combination of minimum harmonization and mutual recognition ... that unlocked the full implementation of the single market .... In western Europe the powerful world-wide movement towards the supply side ... took the form of a cooperative project to create a single market through the process of deregulation.[49]

Likewise, "the growing conviction that monetary policy should concentrate on the primary objective of price stability and that central-bank independence was a prerequisite [of it and] ... implied ... limited ... central bank discretion." The notion prompted the idea of organizing a European central bank "even before attempting complete political union."[50] Padoa-Schioppa adds that in the 1960s – when the challenge facing monetary policy was thought to be that of striking a suitable balance between inflation and unemployment, a political decision – it would have been impossible to entrust such authority to a committee of central bankers "placed outside the framework of a fully fledged political constitution."[51] Padoa-Schioppa also generously acknowledged that Margaret Thatcher contributed heavily to the EMU by "pointing the way to the single market and ... the doctrine of minimum government" and by "deflecting proposals to complement monetary union with fiscal union"[52] The central bankers and those who represented them on the Delors Committee seized upon a propitious moment to shift irreversibly the responsibility for making monetary and fiscal policy from national parliaments, elected by the public, to a European directorate beholden to nothing but a few basic rules and the principles of sound money. Self-determination gave way to the efficiency principle.

A third overriding political reason for having a monetary union was cosmetic. The disparity in size between the shambling, overproportioned chancellor of Germany and the stiff little president of France was an official portraitist's nightmare, not to mention a caricaturist's dream. The unexpected implosion of "real existing socialism" in the steroid-driven German Democratic Republic, which until then had been much admired by advanced thinkers of the western European left – as well as the rapid and bloodless reunification of the two Germanies that would soon follow, which further demoralized it – seemed to suggest that cartoons depicting the aspiring co-managers of Europe, Herr Kohl as Edgar Bergen and M. Mitterrand as Charlie McCarthy, were not really so funny after all. The embarrassed wooden puppet bolted, waving his hard little fist in anger. Kohl reached for his makeup kit, painted on the mascara, plucked an errant eyebrow, hit the powder puff, smeared on the rouge, primped his cheek, applied lip gloss, and practiced batting his eyelashes. No one need be scared away by a big bad Germany, he said to himself in the mirror. His country would even give up the mighty Deutsche mark in favor of the friendly euro, he mused; Germany, now more powerful than ever, would have to be *very* nice to everyone. Through a crack in the door, M. Delors observed the scene with a wry smile on his face. He recognized a friend in need when he saw one. Jacques cuddled up to the painted lady.

The collapse of the *Ostblock* would not only accelerate the Maastricht negotiations but also introduce irrelevancies, distractions, confusion, and plain bad ideas into the discourse. The unkempt Maastricht treaty provides plenty of snarled clauses and tangled-up articles that reflect the garbled outcome. The inclusion of some 18 million new Germans into the most economically and politically consequential European state nonetheless raised serious questions about the balance of power.

The eminent Harvard economist and director of the National Bureau of Economic Research, Martin Feldstein, criticized the proposed EMU and the Maastricht treaty forcefully from an early date. Feldstein discussed its political as well as economic components – a rarity. The outspoken economist had previously served as chairman of President Reagan's committee of economic advisors. His opinions convey authority. A 1997 article written for the quasi-official *Foreign Affairs,* a publication of the New York Council on Foreign Relations, warned in no uncertain terms that dire consequences would result from the dangerous and unstable combination of overreaching political ambition and bad economic fundamentals upon which the Maastricht agreement rested. Feldstein drafted, in other words, the "horror show scenario."[53]

The troubled economist feared that Europe's course had already been set in the run-up to Maastricht – that the shift toward a single currency would amount to a "dramatic and irreversible" step toward federal union, even in the absence of treaty language calling for evolution toward one. Feldstein paid little heed to the political "garbage can" provisions except in defense and security issues. His concerns were chiefly with the implications of monetary union in light of the gaps and omissions on the political side. The Harvard economist predicted alarmingly that the Maastricht-created union would increase rather than reduce the likelihood of future conflict both within Europe and between Europe and the United States. The only recourse, he thought, was for the United States to maintain strong bilateral ties with the individual nations of the EU in order to prevent the union from evolving into a superstate.[54]

Feldstein argued that no suitable political mechanism had been provided to contain the distributional conflicts arising from the pursuit of a single, Europe-wide monetary policy, which would inevitably help some regions while hurting others, and that the limited sums available for EU regional transfers were far too small to count in this respect. He also pointed out that member-state loss of direct control over monetary policy and of indirect control over fiscal policy would have unpredictable consequences. The EU's Economic and Financial Council (ECOFIN), which held a reserve power to override the policy of the European Central Bank's executive board, was not only untested but – if activated – would likely reflect national preferences in which "monetary stability" is only one of several policy criteria.[55] The results of such conflicting priorities could not be known in advance. More likely, he thought, unemployment would increase – and inflexible labor markets become even more rigid – as pressure for "harmonization" at the European level increased. Europe would then become less competitive, more protectionist in outlook, and more inwardly focused.[56]

"Incompatible expectations" would also create a variety of new problems, Feldstein added.[57] "Co-management" of an unequal Germany and France could neither last indefinitely nor be reconciled with the rising demands for "voice" of the other members in the expanding community. The machinery of governance would become still more unwieldy and immobilized. Nor could a successful defense be mounted against Commission encroachment into "bananas and beer"; not even the Tenth Amendment to the U.S. Constitution – which reserves to the states (or the people) all powers not specifically delegated to the federal government – has prevented the extension of its authority power into an enormous range of local issues. EU encroachment would continue, he predicted, to generate resentment, whose consequences are difficult to estimate; subsidiarity had proved, in any case, to be unenforceable and had become all but meaningless as a corrective to the centralization tendency.

Feldstein warned in particular of geopolitical hazards. He thought that the common defense and security policy envisaged in the Maastricht treaty, when supported by nationally integrated EU armed forces, would be divisive in a diverse community like Europe. A Euro-military would furthermore weaken NATO "and to that extent make Europe more vulnerable to attack." The lack of "exit" in the Maastricht agreement could lead to attempted secession and raised the threat of civil war. Such contingencies seem remote, even unrealistic, as

Feldstein freely admits. Nonetheless, the European decision to move toward political union would require "changes in U.S. policy, especially in light of French anti-Americanism."[58] America can no longer, according to Feldstein, count on Europe as an ally in its relations with third countries but must rather be prepared for "policies ... contrary to the interests of the United States."[59]

Feldstein's analysis was right in three important respects: the design of the EMU is flawed; the Community lacks adequate institutional machinery for handling the political fallout it would produce; and a foreign policy not subject to any form of democratic control is ipso facto dangerous. The distinguished economist nonetheless sounded the alarm too soon. If only for economic reasons, The House that Jacques Built (or at least tried to build) – a Euro-federation powerful enough to challenge the United States – has not really gotten off the drafting board and will not stand. The inability of exchange rates or wage rates to adjust through the market to exogenous shocks increases both unemployment and the cyclical instability of the economy; it also slows down growth and exacerbates existing social problems. The convergence course upon which the member-nations of the European Monetary System had embarked did reduce European inflation impressively but also widened the differential between U.S. and European growth rates while perpetuating high unemployment. Since 1980, the latter had fallen below 8 percent only for one quarter. By 1993–1994 it was again above 11 percent; by comparison, the U.S. rate briefly peaked at 7.6 percent then soon declined to below 6 percent.[60] Ratcheting Europe up from monetary convergence in the EMS to monetary identity in the EMU has kept it on a divergent course with the United States.

The EU's authority as an institution has also continued to decline. The gradual but steady spread of the market principle and the continuing retreat of the state at the "commanding heights" account for much of the weakness. Additional factors like the impending Enlargement and German reluctance to serve as paymaster also figure in the diminution. Differences in wealth, outlook, and institutions as well as the increase in sheer numbers have compounded EU governance problems and strengthened centripetal forces. The relative costs of "positive" (institutional) integration as opposed to "negative" (market-based) integration have increased. As "deepening" – that is, constructing new Eurocracies – has become more difficult, the era characterized by attempts to integrate Europe via Franco-German co-management (on the basis of French ideas) has begun to draw to an end. Condemned to failure in advance was what George Ross describes as the Delors "strategy [of accelerating] European integration of the existing Community beyond the point of no return by superimposing a state-building logic upon the underlying dynamic of the '1992 Program'."[61] The Delorean approach has, if anything, delayed realization of the European project.

POLITICAL MAASTRICHT

Unlike the monetary provisions pertaining to the EMU, the political sections of the treaty are of dubious value and read like an afterthought.[62] The word "grotesque" is often attached to them. They are the product of a collective effort, set in motion after the fall of the Berlin Wall and pushed vigorously by Delors, to add an institutional dimension to the treaty. The results left no one satisfied. Most member-states wanted a three-pillar configuration: a tall, stout one for the single market combined with shorter, less substantial frameworks for two more hypothetical pillars: Common Security and Foreign Policy, and Internal Security. Delors preferred a different model: a tree stout in trunk, with plenty of branches, and even buds in the spring. Somehow the two images fused. The result was not a triad of freestanding pillars but a temple, usually schematized in drawings that show three neat Doric columns surmounted by an entablature to hold the design together and prevent the columns from falling away in different directions. The strange tumbledown ruins of Stonehenge – a site of weird ancient worship whose meaningless rituals are today followed only by cultists – would make a more appropriate image for the Maastricht treaty than the classical perfection of the Parthenon. Serious worshippers in any case attend services at an unattractive but solid new temple in Frankfurt.

The terms of economic and monetary union had already been agreed upon and the decision to proceed with the negotiating process already made before the notorious *Schandemauer* (Wall of Shame) came down in Berlin. In April 1990 – a few weeks after the first free elections made it evident to disbelievers, skeptics, and Third Way socialist dreamers alike that reunification could be only a matter of months away – political union was added to the agenda of the planned intergovernmental conference (IGC) required in order to propose treaty amendments. This occurred at the insistence of Chancellor Helmut Kohl, a man long committed to political union, who was prepared for the moment to do almost anything required to see the delicate recoupling operation through to a happy conclusion.

Kohl had to pull off one of the great political balancing acts of the century. On the one hand he needed to assure a bloodless Soviet withdrawal; on the other, he had to defuse the angry resistance of President Mitterrand – and, regrettably, soon also Prime Minister Thatcher – to what at the time seemed like a Europe on the verge of falling under German domination. Delors exploited the opportunity to the hilt. Turning his back on the Anglo-French grumblers, he cast the Commission's lot with the compliant yet hardly inconspicuous German chancellor. Thanks largely to Kohl's backing, often provided in the form of money, the European grand master of policy entrepreneurship succeeded against great odds at having some of his pet projects written into the Maastricht treaty.

The IGC for *political* union was a sideshow. It should have taken place under the big tent, however, considering the far-reaching implications of the decision to create EMU. The European Central Bank "affects the state and its government," and its exercise of power is thus no less inescapably political than Community decision making. Elimination of trade barriers, setting of agricultural prices, deregulation of banking, framing of association treaties with third countries, harmonization of tax structures, and reduction of state aid to industry are all examples of governmental acts that, by economic means, impose choices between different and often conflicting interests. The EMU was a further step in this direction. The de facto failure of the political side of negotiations for union meant that the European public would have to depend utterly upon the powerful governing board of the ECB to make the right economic decisions on its behalf. As Rudi Dornbusch put it: "Good central banking is apolitical, and the more apolitical the better. That is what a European central bank is all about. And that is why EMU is not a transfer of sovereignty over money but a Europe-wide abdication."[63]

Where should one draw the line in assessing the political side of the Maastricht treaty? Its provisions do not synchronize with those on the economic side. The three uneven pillars upon which the "temple" rests do not include one for the EMU. Lacking structural integrity, the Maastricht treaty is a confused blur of fuzzy ideas, empty boxes, monetary transfers, and the politics of pals. It reveals traces, however, of the predilections of Jacques Delors for a European social model. A computer-scanned word count of the document would probably provide mathematical confirmation of the outlines, however sketchy, of his grand design. What the words actually mean is an open matter. The political IGC completely failed to meet the challenges raised by monetary union and provided no direction whatsoever.

Neither his friendly biographers nor Delors himself have kind words for his strategy at the political IGC.[64] He simply overreached. The Commission's draft treaty indicated the usual Delorean preferences for industrial, regional, and social policy as well as for extension of qualified majority voting. The draft also contained a new emphasis on political union that was far too "federalist" for the governments, "reflected his own, personal priorities," and indeed went over the edge. The proposal called for a new division of labor between the three federal organs: the Council and the Parliament would agree on "laws," whose implementation would be left to the Commission. The national governments would fill in the details in order "to promote subsidiarity." In external affairs, the Commission would be virtually the sole authority: it would represent the Community in international forums like the IMF, would (along with whoever happened to be holding the rotating presidency) run foreign policy, and would direct the preparation and implementation of common policies.[65] It seemed to the Spanish minister for Europe, Carlos Westendorp, that "the Commission's chief concern [was] to give themselves more power."[66]

The Luxembourg presidency rejected the Commission document as a basis for negotiation and substituted what amounted to a French three-pillar alternative. To the immense surprise and nearly unanimous disapproval of the other member-states, the Dutch delegation (which held the Council presidency for the second six months of 1991) revived Delors's proposal. The chief adviser to the Dutch delegation and minister for Europe – the chain-smoking socialist Piet Dankert, who happened to be a personal friend of Delors – saw to it that large portions of the Commission's original proposal found their way into the official Dutch negotiating document. Some of the stuff ended up in the Maastricht treaty.[67]

The Treaty's bold pronouncement of a Common Security and Foreign Policy (the second pillar) was a real no-brainer. Here talk was distinctly cheap; in fact, not much else was involved. Policy making bowed to traditional French demands for a European defense force not subject to NATO control. The proposal could be grounded in a European antecedent to the U.S.-dominated alliance, the Western European Union (created in 1948 and re-activated by Britain in 1954 after the failure of the European Defense Community). The notion reflected a common commitment to submerging a German defense identity into something larger and seemed in keeping with the changed power balance following Soviet collapse. Furthermore, and best of all, it changed nothing of substance. There was no Euro-armed force and there would not be anything worthy of the name for at least a decade, even in the highly unlikely event that any head of state or government (except the French) either wanted such a thing or would be prepared to shell out for it more than the pittance one might hand to Salvation Army bell ringers at Christmas time.[68]

President Delors's inaugural speech on defense matters was delivered in March 1991 at the Institute of Strategic Affairs in London. A resounding proclamation of the compelling need for a European defense identity, it raised a few eyebrows but scared nobody at the Pentagon.[69] President George Bush actually favored and encouraged the EU bid to assume increased regional responsibility, provide aid to eastern Europe, and take the initiative toward the self-dismantling Yugoslavia. Contrary to Delors's expectations, there was little risk that the United States would be overshadowed or crowded out of influence by a successful Common Security and Foreign Policy in the Balkans.

The publics of the member-states had been deeply divided over Operation Desert Shield, the late-1990 American mobilization for the Gulf War, which the Germans strongly opposed but the British and even the French favored. The split paralyzed EU policy making.[70] The independent initiatives of Mitterrand to head off war by compromise were rebuffed by both sides. When Shield became Storm and (in less than a week) U.S. and "coalition" forces had crushed Saddam Hussein's demoralized legions in memorably efficient fashion, the Europeans – quibbling amongst themselves – arrived too late at the victory banquet and had to be content with the crumbs. They were also stuck with a substantial part of the bill. A Belgian refusal to sell ammunition to British soldiers fighting in the Gulf was certainly not a high point of European defense cooperation.

If the Iraq campaign offered little reflected military glory in which the EU could bask, Yugoslavia offered nothing whatsoever to awaken a European sense of pride and accomplishment. A running diplomatic debacle for the Community, the successive policy failures outpaced even the rising tide of IGC Foreign and Security Policy ambitions. The French wanted to keep Yugoslavia together. Delors believed that, with enough aid, it would survive by grace of the ambitious economic reforms promised by prime minister Ante Markovic. When the Commission president went to Yugoslavia in May on his first actual visit to the country, he was dismayed to discover, in the deadpan language of his biographer, "that the leaders of the republic did not want to work with Markovic."[71] Four days after the Slovenes and Croatians seceded from the rump Yugoslav Union, which then prepared for military action, Kohl spoke out forcefully in favor of independence for the two peoples. Major and Gonzales backed the French.

The time had arrived for the EU to broker a peace plan. In July, a "troika" of ministers sent out from the IGC persuaded the various factions to accept an arrangement providing for a Croatian federation within the Yugoslav union, a withdrawal of Yugoslav troops, and the beginning of constitutional discussions. The Italian foreign minister snidely remarked that the Americans had been "informed but not consulted."[72] The "troikan" from Luxembourg, Jacques Poos, proudly declared: "This is the Hour of Europe, not of America!"[73] The EU sent 200 observers to monitor the peace, but none of the hostile parties respected the arrangements and hot war broke out in August. Persistent and profound disagreement ruled out any Community military commitment, the pace of peace conferencing stepped up, the Serb armies kept on marching and brutalizing civilian populations, and the Germans found themselves accused by the French of secretly lusting for a revived *Mitteleuropa*. Humiliation turned into outright shame as – amidst frenzied diplomatic fluttering in The Hague and other European capitals – traditional rough-and-ready Serbian butchery, rape, and pillage geared up over the following six months into the more purposeful and focused contemporary policy known as ethnic cleansing. "Europe" was powerless to do anything about a campaign of organized mass murder being conducted on its very doorstep. The Common Security and Foreign Policy was not a success in the Balkans. Call it a potential learning experience.

The Maastricht treaty provisions relating to legitimacy represent another grave case of policy failure; if anything, the "democratic deficit" widened – especially when measured against the powers of the planned European Central Bank. Involved was a war-within-a-war at the IGC in which Britain, opposed to any increase in the exercise of power at the federal level, entered into a marriage of convenience with M. Delors. Though pouting after member-state rejection of his grand institutional reform scheme, he remained, as ever, sensitive to the potential erosion of Commission authority. Together Delors and his unlikely Anglo-Saxon ally managed largely to deprive the European Parliament of new responsibilities.[74] It would remain almost impotent. Under German leadership, the small countries and the heavily-subsidized southerners eventually arrived at face-saving though tortuous compromises.[75]

The process of government at the EP is of such unnerving complexity that none but the brave would attempt to summarize it. The Maastricht treaty instituted complicated new co-decision procedures in which the elected chamber could influence the outcome of legislation by referring proposals back to either the Commission or the Council for revision in a number of specified fields: the free circulation of labor, the internal market, the Framework Programs for research and development, certain environmental and consumer protection programs, and the trans-European networks (for transportation and communication). For reasons that even the man-on-the-spot for the *Economist*'s "Intelligence Economic Unit" failed to understand, the SEA's convoluted "cooperation procedure" – different in each of five separate legislative fields – survived intact.[76] Only one new EP power would be used in a way that even the best-informed members of the public could be expected to appreciate. A new "double investment" process, which gave the body an opportunity to accept or reject a whole slate of proposed commissioners (though none individually), also applied to dismissals. A threat to invoke this apparent legislative afterthought brought down the Santer cabinet. This "horizontal chop" is the only noteworthy thing the Parliament has ever done.

Delors got his way on two important issues taken up at Maastricht. One was regional policy, the only deal that paid tangible dividends. With Delors's encouragement, the Spanish exacted a new protocol on economic and social cohesion, promising to take "greater account of the contributive capacity of individual member-states ... and correcting for the less prosperous member-states the regressive elements existing in the own resources system."[77] Decoded into English, this means: "the Spanish will get more money." The Commission president cared less about Spain than the opportunity to get a big new transfer mechanism into operation. Kohl, who paid the bill, was happy to have comparatively low-cost allies along Europe's southern rim (and in Ireland). Promised was a special new fund – only indirectly controlled by the Commission – to underwrite environmental costs, build new transportation networks, and redress inequities in CAP, which did in fact put Mediterranean farmers at a disadvantage. The formation of a new (though subsequently insignificant) Committee of Regions was provided to legitimize, or at least lend an air of plausibility to, the giveaways.[78] Cash amounts were apparently agreed upon but left unmentioned in the treaty in order not to jeopardize ratification. The huge payoff came at the Edinburgh summit in 1992.

The so-called Social Charter, appended to the treaty in the form of a protocol, was Delors's biggest coup at Maastricht. A tactical blunder by John Major helped him pull off this work of legerdemain. Delors's line of "negotiate or we'll legislate" had not endeared UNICE, the feeble European employer association, to the idea of entering into "constructive social dialog" with its designated partner, the fattened-up and Community-subsidized ETUC. In fact, no progress could be reported. After the rejection of their first draft for a social charter, the Dutch – ideologically committed to consensual policy making although, like the Germans and other "northerners," distinctly uncomfortable about more shackles on management decision making – proposed in the second draft a much diluted version of a social protocol presumed to be watery enough even for Thatcherites to swallow. Keen upon demonstrating "game, set, match for Britain!" and already disgusted by the "cohesion" deal, Major refused to sign any further amendments to the treaty and left for London.[79]

Delors thereupon arrived with the original, more forceful paper and inveigled it through the conference in a 31-hour negotiating marathon. The Club Med

nations, opposed to losing the competitive advantage of cheap labor but reluctant to jeopardize future income flows, found themselves beached by the British.
They were, in any case, all well-schooled adepts at the conduct of meaningless
"social dialog." The southerners went along with Delors. Britain "opted out,"
the remaining eleven signed on, and the employers – having been inadvertently
sold down the river – found themselves party to a deal that no one had ever
really wanted other than Delors, a handful of behind-the-scene supporters, and
his tame shadow union. In a debriefing session of the cabinet, Delors's second-
in-command Pascal Lamy boasted that "we were a good hour and a half ahead
of everyone else."[80] Although linking the Germans and Spanish on "cohesion"
was no small accomplishment, "the Commission's most successful intervention
was on the social protocol, a product of prior brainstorming and quick action
... and smart politics by Delors." As so often had been the case, "it was the
obliging Helmut Kohl ... who placed the proposal on the table."[81]

Political Maastricht – vague, unrealistic, contested, and insecurely linked to
the monetary side of the TEU, the SEA, and the Rome treaty – added substantially to the structural problems of the EC/EU. It was a species of constitutional
clutter that, in the even less substantial treaties of Amsterdam (1997) and Nice
(2000), would give rise to more of the same over the remainder of the decade. The
"Consolidated Treaties of the European Union" indeed fail virtually "every test
of clarity and brevity" and reveal "shortcomings in the way the Union works."
Their sheer unsuitability dictates replacement with a single document that "sets
out the EU's mission in simple language," clarifies "the role and responsibility
of EU institutions to befuddled voters," and draws clear distinctions between
"supranational and national competences."[82] Needed are not still more details
and ambitious treaties and enactments but, quite simply, a spring cleaning.

AMBITIONS AND REALITIES:
DELORS II AND RATIFICATION

As plans for Maastricht developed, the time had come to expose Russian Doll
number five, the "Delors Packet II." Preparation of the proposal began early in
1991 to coincide with the planned IGC. Delors II was, so to speak, the inside
negotiating channel, a complement to the more public one aimed at the treaty.
This proposal sheds considerable light on Delors's thinking. Like Delors I, this
"packet" was about the budget and provided for a five-year financial plan with
increased autonomy for the Commission, additional funding for "social and economic cohesion," substantially increased appropriations for "external funding"
(foreign policy and foreign aid), more money for R&D and infrastructure construction ("TENS"), and additional cash for surviving remnants of industrial policy. The rationale for the higher spending was Orwellian. The Community was
said to be "moving from specific to general competencies" in a "proto-federal"
and "evolutive" (translation from Eurospeak: implies gradual, natural, organic,
and necessary) manner.[83] The principle of subsidiarity was evoked to justify a

rate of Commission spending that increased twice as fast as spending at the national level. The convoluted justification for the extra money was the supposition that, to promote "subsidiarity" (a term implying devolution of authority), the Community would have to take over powers from the member-states. "Building the second Delors package around such arguments," according to George Ross, "was essential not only to portray a more grandiose post-Maastricht Community but also because the distribution of costs and benefits of new policies 'do not coincide in either the short or the long term'."[84] There would, in other words, be losers as well as winners among the member-states, but no one should catch on to the fact.

Delors wanted a Community budget equal to 2 percent of GDP by the year 2000, a breathtaking increase from the 1.2 percent of 1992. The Commission package, presumptuously entitled *From the Single European Act to Maastricht and Beyond: The Means to Match Our Ambitions,* appeared in February 1992. It proposed a staggering increase in funds for economic and social cohesion of 11 billion ecus over five years, twice the Spanish request, a tripling of the budget (to 3.5 billion ecus) for "external action," and a further 3.5 billion ecus "to promote a favorable environment for industrial competitiveness" (translation: industrial policy).[85] These targets were to be met by jacking the budget up to the maximum obtainable. Savings in the CAP were supposed to cover most of the difference; its share of the increased budget was to diminish, though outlays were to remain constant. CAP reform rested on the phase-in of income maintenance in place of price supports, which would gradually be allowed to fall to world levels. The success of Delors II would, in other words, depend partly upon the outcome of the Uruguay Round of GATT talks being led by the DG for agriculture, Ray MacSharry. If they fell through, then so would Delors II.

A storm front was nonetheless forming. Unemployment began to edge up in the final quarter of 1991. Neither an unleashing of "animal spirits" in the economy nor an outburst of public enthusiasm greeted the Maastricht treaty. The text, some 200-plus pages, read like a London bus schedule and was no easier to understand.[86] Gaffes and missteps ensued in the conference aftermath. Delors told a French television audience that the time had come for France to hand over control of its nuclear arsenal to "Europe." An uproar followed in Paris. A 4 May 1992 article in the London *Sunday Telegraph* titled "Delors Plans to Rule Europe" – based on inside information from an anonymous Commission informant – reported that Delors wanted to scrap the rotating EC presidency, centralize power in Brussels, strip the member-states of their veto rights, and have the European Parliament elect an EC president to replace the Commission president. Delors neither confirmed nor denied the story, merely remarking offhandedly that the plans were apparently for "ten or fifteen years hence."[87] The response was hardly reassuring.

Within days of the news article, sentiment in Denmark (one of only two countries that allowed its citizens to vote by referendum on the Maastricht treaty) shifted sharply against ratification. The pro-EC Danish government thereupon unwisely flooded the country with 300,000 copies of the document. Most found it unreadable; others, more skilled at deciphering, found it frightening. In spite of a huge organized campaign in its favor, ratification failed by a small but decisive margin of 50.7 percent to 49.3 percent.[88]

That should have buried the treaty, which could not become binding without the acceptance of all twelve members. This rule was simply chucked. The Danish government, which immediately requested renegotiation, was told by Brussels in so many words to "shove it." A top-level German official memorably remarked in a tone unfamiliar to post-1945 Europeans: "We are not going to let 45,000 oddballs stop Europe's momentum! Legal solutions can always be found!"[89] In a French television interview shortly thereafter, Delors said just as much: the Danes would be demoted from the Community to the European Economic Area – a holding tank for ex-EFTANs (European Free Trade Association nations) who had applied for EC membership – and lose benefit of the CAP. So much for Brussels' respect for the rights of small countries! Meeting on the margins of a NATO conclave in Oslo, the hastily assembled European Council, the body representing all the member-states, decided to brazen it out and proceed with the ratification procedure as a "matter of life and death" for the Community until arm-twisting persuaded the Danes to change their minds. Delors was to be effectively gagged until then.[90]

How could one explain what had gone wrong in Denmark? It enjoyed the second highest standard of living in the EC, was a substantial net beneficiary of its odd transfer flows, and in fact represented the closest living approximation (at least within the Community) of Delors's idealized "European social model." The Danes had a large but healthy welfare state. They were indeed a nation of progressive family farmers and virtuous skilled workers, if one can ever be said to have existed. The entire Danish political class (fringes excepted) was, moreover, in favor of ratification, as were all organized economic interests worth mentioning, the mainstream media, and well-educated people generally. The rest, whoever they might have been, were opposed. About the only sentiment this disorganized, anonymous mass had in common was a vague feeling of resentment at being pushed around by arrogant elites. Populism had surfaced.

Mitterrand did not get it. Well aware that there was no organized French opposition to ratification at the national level and apparently persuaded by favorable poll soundings, he decided on the spur of the moment, on the day after the Danish referendum, to call a similar popular vote for France in September – fully confident of winning the kind of ringing endorsement that would both strengthen his government and silence the Maastricht doubters Europe-wide. Such a step was quite unnecessary; ratification by the obedient National Assembly was already assured. Mitterrand soon discovered that he had made a catastrophic, perhaps fatal blunder. As in Denmark, opposition sprang up spontaneously and apparently out of nowhere.[91] The bitch-box overflowed with endless gripes, running the gamut from adulteration of Camembert cheese (recently subject to a Brussels directive) to the threat of Judeo-Masonic conspiracies (a perennial problem for at least 200 years). The political loyalties of the *"non"*-minded ran from Moscow to Rome, though surely not crossing by way of Brussels.

The people of France apparently resented having never been even consulted about Maastricht. As put delicately by George Ross, "perhaps more than any other large state, the various steps of the renewal of European integration had not been subjects of extended European debate. There was a profound thirst in France to talk about Europe."[92] It was not easy to persuade the aroused citizens to like what they heard, even after they had been granted an opportunity to blow off steam. The *"oui"* camp – the most united front presented by the French establishment since World War II – included not only the usual political figures, senior administrators, bankers, businessmen, and other "respect figures" but also leading academics, public intellectuals, actors, artists, designers, musicians, athletes, icons of pop culture, and the odd media priest. All warned that a *non* would derail European integration, shame France, wreck the economy, open the way to German revival and domination, and be a precursor to chaos. To eliminate any uncertainty concerning such dire consequences, at the last minute the massive bulk of Chancellor Kohl appeared on a canned live television discussion with the diminutive President Mitterrand to validate the awful outcome that rejection would assure. On 4 September the French people gave their *petit oui* of 51 percent to 49 percent.[93] It was a squeaker – enough to save both Mitterrand and the treaty, but nothing more.

The financial markets had already begun to get the point. They were (as always) potentially unstable, this time because of heavy engagement in "convergence plays." At the beginning of the year, confident that the glide path from EMS to EMU would work as scheduled at Maastricht, money had poured into lira- and peseta-denominated bonds in order to capture risk premiums expected to disappear as Italy, Spain, and other "weak currency" countries met the membership criteria of the monetary union.[94] The slowdown that began in 1992 was the first sign of economic strain. An unexpected (though predictable, in hindsight) Bundesbank decision in July to raise the Lombard rate seriously aggravated the situation. Although a downturn would normally prompt a cut, the Bundesbank concluded – correctly, from the standpoint of German national interests – that an unsettling expansion of the money supply due to the high costs of reunification called for deflation rather than reflation. The bankers, as always, feared losing control over the circulating medium.

The other EMS countries, forced to follow suit, reluctantly raised their rates. In the meantime, the dollar fell in response to cuts (in the prime lending rate) made in order to stimulate the U.S. economy, and the pound – in the EMS since 1990 – trailed it down. With the gap between U.S. and European interest rates approaching historic highs, and with the dollar cheap and EMS currencies expensive, the market had reason to anticipate future slowdowns in Europe and thus also to worry about the Italian and Spanish budget deficits. The Danish referendum rattled the vulnerable currencies but did not drive them through the bottom of their bands.

A remark by Mitterrand did. Desperate to win last-minute points with the electorate in the rigged pre-referendum telethon starring Chancellor Kohl as The Hulk, he stared straight out at the imagined living-room audience watching the tube by the millions and told it a bald-faced lie: the future European Central Bank would not be run by a board of nonelected central bankers in Frankfurt but instead would take orders from the European Council representing member-state governments like France. Caught by surprise, the markets freaked out. "Convergence plays" began to unwind like spinning tops. Lacking the necessary reserves to regain control over the situation, the Bundesbank used "triage": in short, they decided to save the threatened French franc (which remained steady) and let the other currencies die. Finland was first to devalue. Neighboring Sweden, which had also tried to shadow the DM, resisted with heroic measures but soon had to follow. Neither country was in the EMS. In September, the peseta quickly lost a quarter of its value against the DM and the lira soon lost over a third. Crashing through their floors, both had to be devalued. (The new and highly competitive parities would, however, remain fairly stable for the rest of the decade, giving Italy and Spain an export advantage particularly vis-à-vis France.) The EMS barely survived. Against backdrops of begging bankers on their knees in Rome and Madrid, the Germans agreed to grant temporary derogations for the two currencies. Italy and Spain would not be rolled off the glide path to Europe. They could stay on board.[95]

Britain *would* have to get off. It had actually only been "on" since 1990. Mrs. Thatcher, clothespin on nose, joined the EMS for party-political reasons: in order to prevent her disagreement with Foreign Minister Geoffrey Howe and Chancellor of the Exchequer Nigel Lawson from splitting the cabinet. Thatcher objected to EMS membership mainly for patriotic reasons, but Lawson, a former financial journalist, believed strongly in the importance of British participation in the single market project, was convinced of the economic wisdom of pegging sterling to DM, and felt quite confident about both the utility and the survivability of the EMS prior to Maastricht. On the eve of the 1988 Madrid Council, Mrs. Thatcher's two key ministers presented her with an ultimatum on EMS membership: either join or they would resign. She parried the low blow in the only way possible: sacked both of them; appointed John Major as Lawson's replacement as exchequer; and, in order to preempt a possible *fronde,* ordered Major to put Britain in the EMS.[96]

As prime minister, Major later found himself stuck with this unhappy compromise, but lacking Thatcher's prestige and as heir to a divided party he was too vulnerable to back away from it. Paradoxically, the British opt-out from monetary union at Maastricht supplied a plausible rationale for remaining in the EMS, if only as the best available vantage point from which to slow down the increasingly unpopular "conveyor belt to Europe." Compounding Major's problems, the pound was overvalued relative to the DM – as the Bundesbank had warned at the time of British entrance into the European Rate Mechanism, which set parities for the EMS. The EMS also throttled economic growth. Major's unexpected triumph in the April 1992 elections seemed all the more unlikely in light of the slowdown.

With the credibility of his new government at stake, Prime Minister Major stood hard and fast by ERM during the monetary *Sturm und Drang* of late summer 1992.[97] On 10 September he told an audience of Scottish industrialists, to his great subsequent regret: "I was under no illusion when I took sterling into the ERM. I said at the time membership was no soft option. The soft option, the devaluer's option, the inflationary option, would be a betrayal of our future."[98] Within a week, in spite of heavy intervention by the Bank of England but without benefit of any help whatsoever from the DM bloc, sterling broke through its feeble supports, tumbling Britain out of the EMS and shattering John Major's reputation.[99] The national humiliation of 16 September, Black Wednesday, was a blessing in disguise. Set free to float, the pound would soon recover. With a flexible monetary policy and orientation to the supply side, the British economy would by any criterion – growth, inflation, or unemployment – outperform its peers on the continent for the rest of the decade. The British distaste for monetary union nonetheless remains profound to this day.

GERMAN UNIFICATION AND THE CRISIS OF 1992

The most serious of 1992's storm signals was difficult to detect because it originated not where one would expect, in the weak currency countries, but from within the nation that anchored the European monetary system, the purportedly over-mighty Germany. Only the Bundesbank fully appreciated at the time what now seems self-evident: that the reunification policy – adopted by the Kohl government, endorsed by all organized German economic interests as well as the opposition political party, and supported overwhelmingly by the citizens of both halves of the formerly divided nation – was ruinous and, if left unchanged, would permanently weaken the Federal Republic's economy, undermine its leadership in Europe, and weaken Europe's power in the world. There was nothing inevitable about the outcome. It would have been theoretically possible to adopt the post-1948 Erhard policy of opening markets, welcoming new competition, preparing for the gale of creative destruction that would have obliterated the obsolete and the inefficient, accepting the rapid movement of people up and down the social ladder and throughout the land, and waiting until the political chips fell into new configurations of power and responsibility.

The appeal of "Rhenish capitalism" removed such an option from the political agenda. It held forth to *Ossis* the hope that they could become overnight *Bundesbürger,* enjoying the full rights and privileges of consumerism while being protected by a sturdy and comfortable safety net. Its appeal to *Wessis* was less evident but equally strong: they would not have to be bothered by *Ossis,* who would be allowed to develop con-socially into full Germans behind their own borders. No need for a Wall. The new Germans could be bound democratically to home, family, school, friends, job, village, town, city, and region by the same intricate network of official and unofficial institutions that had made *Modell Deutschland* such a shining example for its partners in Europe. Things in the West could then go on much as before, without any need for real sacrifice or risk taking. Just please be kind enough not to rock the boat! The only objection to such a managed solution was that it might be costly. Here the politicians prevaricated, and the public allowed itself to be persuaded. At the end of the day, German taxpayers would be prepared to pay hundreds of billions of DM to try to make the scheme work. The Federal Republic would be short of pocket change in the future; every pfennig would have to be counted. The days of Kohl's casual Maastricht munificence were over.[100]

The immediate problem facing the Bundesbank after Maastricht stemmed from Kohl's decision to convert the DDR mark to the Federal Republic's DM at a ratio of 1 : 1. Although the real value of East Germany's fiat funny-money could not be determined, on black markets it was worth no more than a quarter of the conversion rate. Even more alarming, labor productivity in the former workers' paradise was less than half of that in the Federal Republic. Bundesbank President Manfred Pöhl resigned in disgust over Kohl's decision. His successor, Helmut Schlesinger, would take an equally hard line but likewise to little effect.

The creation of new money was inflationary, but its consequences could have been contained if the former seat of "real existing socialism" had been able to capture its main source of competitive advantage, cheap labor. Instead, centralized wage bargaining quickly took hold. *Ossis* were promised 80 percent of wages prevailing in the West as well as wage equality within five years. The government went along with the insane policy. In the face of such a powerful disincentive to industrial investment, money either stayed put or flowed into neighboring countries through the porous eastern border. The *neue Bundesländer* – the old East, where the net value of industrial capital was negative and cleanup costs often prohibitive – turned into a factory graveyard. Unemployment would be chronic at somewhere between 20 and 30 percent. Rhenish capitalism had condemned *Ossi* civilization to the dole.[101]

The crisis of summer 1992 provided the first real indication that Europe had become hostage to misconceived German policy. The Bundesbank had also, in a way, been victimized. The strong, silent men of Frankfurt had not sought European leadership; the role was thrust upon them by ambitious politicians: Schmidt and Giscard in the case of the EMS, Kohl and Mitterrand in that of the EMU. In both cases, the express purpose of these men had been to tie elected though economically irresponsible governments to stabilization policy, a task such governments could not manage on their own. To be faithful to the mandate imposed upon it, the BuBa had to keep money tight and hope that deflationary pressure would induce the German government to enforce policy change from the top down. To have done otherwise – and loosen the money supply within the rigid (and now ossified) structures of German "organized capitalism" – would have opened the door to an unacceptable and irresponsible inflation. It would have violated the trust placed in the bank and could have broken the chain linking

Europe to its German anchor, an outcome dreaded by European citizens and governments alike. The member-states of the EMS (and, subsequently, the EMU) had no choice but to follow in the tracks of a tight German monetary policy that would destabilize their currencies and hurt their economies. The only way out of the dilemma would be for Germany to reform itself or for someone to devise a different monetary regime.

The failure of the Maastricht negotiators to take the public into account, the exchange crisis of summer 1992 (and the damage it did to the EMS and to the prospects of the EMU), the strains being felt by the German economy, and the shift of the European Council to a British presidency all contributed to reducing the size of Russian Doll number five, the Delors Packet II. The Edinburgh Council, which Major chaired, moved the EC at least one step in the direction of a free-trade zone. A formula was found for re-admitting the Danes by means of guaranteed opt-outs, a condition Major had in fact set before he would bring the treaty to Parliament for approval. A timetable was agreed upon for bringing in the Scandinavian and Austrian ex-EFTANs, whom Delors had meant to leave stranded in the purgatory of the European Economic Area until the Maastricht treaty was concluded.

An essential prerequisite of Packet II was also newly on hand, the phase-in of CAP price and subsidy reductions (along with a shift to income maintenance) negotiated by MacSharry at GATT in November 1992. This was a tough deal to come by, especially because campaigns for the impending presidential elections obliged the Americans to act mean in order to curry favor with the electorate. MacSharry amazingly arrived at an agreement one week before Clinton defeated Bush, only to be repudiated by a Delors newly attentive to the plaints of the majority of *non*voting French farmers. The DG for agriculture, his enormous accomplishment apparently in tatters, resigned in torrent of rage and was followed by the rest of the EC negotiating team. Delors groveled, MacSharry returned to office, and the Blair House accords were signed on 22 November. The GATT deal brought CAP another step toward reform, an agreement for gradual shift from commodity support to income maintenance.[102]

It was hard indeed to squeeze money out of the Germans at Edinburgh. Major arrived at the Council with a long reform agenda. It featured a thick packet of objectionable Community legislation in the "social dimension" that demonstrably violated the subsidiarity principle; a proposal for a seven-year (rather than five-year) scheme for increasing "own resources," which cut structural funds and excised industrial policy altogether; as well as an array of other counterinsurgency weapons to combat "creeping federalism." Major's talking points were not all well received. In a dramatic display of righteous indignation at the threatened cutback in transfer payments, the Spanish delegate stalked away from the table, gesturing that he was ready to depart, "but when it turned out that the financially strapped Germans favored something like the British, the Commission and the South had to split the difference." In the final version of Delors II, "own resources" would rise from 1.2 percent to only 1.27 percent by 1999, "structural fund" growth would be reduced (though supplemented by the new "cohesion fund" for infrastructures), funding for industrial policy disappeared altogether, and the principle that budget contributions should be progressive and linked to per-capita income received only nominal acknowledgment.

Delors II was a compromise document but surely more favorable than what he could have achieved later.[103] It showed, according to Charles Grant, that his "deal-making derring-do had not diminished with advancing years." He had managed to squeeze out from the reluctant Germans 156.5 billion DM in structural cohesion funds, two thirds of which were reserved for the poorest regions. Delors was tireless, "like a second-hand car salesman," recalled one ambassador, "like a Turkish carpet salesman," according to another, "applying rudeness, finesse, insight, and diplomatic skill at the same time, while promising more than there really was."[104]

By 1993, EC unemployment was up to 17 million and growing. In the French elections of March 1993, a landslide swept the center-right government of Edouard Balladur into power. Although in dire need to resuscitate the economy, Balladur knew that any French attempt to lower interest rates independently of the Germans could trigger an attack on the franc. It began in June, immediately after a pointed Bundesbank refusal to consider anything more than a nominal reduction in the Lombard rate. Not even massive interventions by the two central banks in July could hold back the floodwaters of speculation. Either the Germans had to revalue or the French had to devalue. The Dutch and the Belgians, the remaining hard-currency members of the ERM/EMS, vetoed the first course. No choice remained but to let the franc sink while expanding the allowable spread of the bands to 30 percent. The "dirty float" left a fetid, brownish residue of pessimism in its wake. Prospects for EMU looked dim.[105]

At this late stage, Delors opened still another nested shell: Russian Doll number six, the White Paper entitled "Growth, Competitiveness, and Employment." Presented before the Copenhagen Council of June 1993, this bulb of pure Deloreanism, having wintered over many months, sprouted spectacularly into full color yet soon withered and lost its petals. They apparently blew away. The "be all and end all" of the paper was the now chronic unemployment problem.[106] The document claimed, if not quite to have discovered a solution, at least to have found the right direction "forward into the twenty-first century." The White Paper promised to create 15 million new jobs. Old signposts had been taken down and new ones put up, but "Growth, Competitiveness, and Employment" led to a familiar dead end. The paper contained appeals to the usual incompatible mix of principles (competitiveness on the one hand and solidarity on the other), called for low deficits but also for "re-structured spending ... to promote sound investment," and praised openness to international markets but also "intelligently recognized global interdependence"; instead of simply leaving well enough alone, it discovered a need to grant administrative "space for local initiatives." A tarted-up industrial policy also put in a vulgar appearance. Small and medium-sized enterprises deserved to be "stimulated," TENS would lead to an information superhighway and bridge the divide of the Iron Curtain (actually a fresh emphasis!), and there would be a new "guiding light." More accurately, an old idea would be microwaved. As expressed in the clunky prose of an un-named Euro-visionary, "encouraging intercompany cooperation will gradually become a basic principle and not just one 'aspect' of Community research and development policy, targeted on new information technologies, and bio- and eco-technologies."[107]

"Redefined social solidarities," the document proclaims, would be at the heart of the plan. Although it is difficult to understand what this characteristically De-lorean construction might actually have been intended to mean, George Ross – ear close to ground – assures us that the critical phrase was that "the new model of European society calls for less passive and more active solidarity." And what might this entail? "A negotiated, decentralized, and rapidly evolving 'sort of Eu-ropean social pact'" in which "new gains in productivity would essentially be applied to forward-looking investments and to the creation of jobs .... Wage earners would be asked to accept annual raises pegged at one percent below productivity gains in the interests of job-creating investments."[108] This doll was indeed a surprise! The Rehn–Meidner model that had wrecked the Swedish economy in the 1970s and 1980s was now, in 1993, to be recommended for Europe-wide application. Lest anyone be left with doubts on this score, the text of "Growth, Competitiveness, and Employment" specifies how the pro-gram should be implemented; it takes one straight back to the 1981 program of François Mitterrand. Delors had come full circle. It was now time to step down.

Conclusion to Part III

Needed: A New Integration Direction

WHY, after remaining dormant for so long, did the European integration process suddenly revive, get moving, and then, just as mysteriously, stop in its tracks? The two extant general theories – intergovernmentalism and functionalism, both deriving from American political science – get only partly at the answer. Although the Big Bargains of intergovernmentalism did create the new diplomatic, political, and institutional contexts that define successive stages of integration, the theory says little about the nature of the choices made and even less about the outcomes arrived at. Both were quite different in each of the two Big Bargains of the Delors era. The adoption of the Single European Act was a choice for the market, a judgment on the part of the member-states to shift decision-making authority away from national political institutions as well as government-regulated economies and toward that abstraction, buyers and sellers. It represented an acknowledgment that the model of the national mixed-economy welfare state had had its day.

The adoption of the Maastricht treaty also involved the transfer of policy-making power away from the member-states, but this time to a different kind of entity: a central-bank directorate. It was as if the heads of government had placed the European patrimony in a trust in order to protect it from spendthrift heirs; the act acknowledged that they did not feel competent to serve as trustees for those who had elected them. Neither of the Big Bargains either increased the individual or collective influence of member-states or bolstered the power of Brussels, and both involved buck-passing. One enfranchised the consumer and the other created a new power center in Frankfurt of greater authority than Brussels itself. As acts of state, they involved more self-immolation than self-aggrandizement. The next Big Bargain would have to rest on a new political consensus strong enough to recover national economic powers forfeited earlier and to either reassign them back to the states or place them within the framework of a constitution-based European federation resting on popular consent. It would not soon happen.

What happened to functionalism? Delors's presence revived interest in the theory: on the scene was another "great animator," a can-do guy of European proportions, a second, possibly third (if one includes Hallstein) prominent, though increasingly generic, "monnet" – someone who knew how to switch on the integration dynamic. Much current flowed. But to what end? And why might it

294

have stopped? Jacques Delors had a grand design but neither a powerful organizing idea like the Schuman Plan nor a strong and expandable framework like the Treaty of Rome. Delors's design was ill-conceived and worked at cross-purposes to the ideals he professed. Nor did it suit the conditions of the emerging new Europe. No doubt the dynamic Frenchman made a difference: he presided over the initial and long-overdue reform of the Common Agricultural Policy and introduced Regional Policy, the first great program of income transfers since CAP. Delors was a symbol of strength and continuity at a time of Community expansion and deserves credit for bringing new and historically disadvantaged members into the community. He was also (and perhaps unintentionally) a convenient smoke screen for needed change, a man who preached democratic socialism while shifting power to oligarchs and central bankers. Without the rhetoric and bafflegab, resistance from the left might have doomed the Single European Act. The most impressive real accomplishments of the Commission during Jacques Delors's tenure were the work of others: Sutherland and Brittan at the competition directorate, and Ray MacSharray at agriculture. Delors deserves special recognition for not suppressing their efforts.

The Delorean legacy is otherwise unimpressive. The R&D *cum* industrial policy central to his scheme of things has been an expensive mistake and should be regarded, like any other deliberate attempt to politicize science, with embarrassment. Delors's encouragement of policy networking, which featured sweetheart deals for privileged incumbents, squandered vast amounts of public money and discouraged innovation. The failure of this supercharged industrial policy was welcome. It would, if successful, have given the giant corporations a stranglehold on Brussels' governance and pushed the "democratic deficit" into a bankruptcy of the democracies.

Deloronomics led nowhere. Nothing but annoyance, hassle, and the whir of spinning wheels came of his bizarre but tireless campaign to introduce industrial corporatism, "active labor market policy," centralized wage bargaining, and other favorite recipes from the dog-eared leftist cookbook. The effort only scared off capital. Delors made but a perfunctory attempt to overcome the "management deficit" by reforming the Commission itself. Was it not to be the seat of executive power in the government of a future federal Europe? Why bequeath a rag-bag? Delors's forays into foreign and security policy are best left undiscussed. The word "Bosnia" is enough to damn them. Jacques Delors was catalyst to change, by no means all of it desirable. Nothing much "spilled over" anywhere or into anything. Delors's policies did not trigger the operation of a functionalist servomechanism. The changes that came over Europe during his presidency do not bear the imprint of his ideas, which were largely unrealistic and unworkable. Where he excelled was in deal making.

Since Eurocrats and member-states can only partly regulate the integration process, a new general theory is needed to explain it. Historical institutionalism may be the launching pad of the future. Until then, a less elegant yet kindred historical empiricism will have to be relied upon to unearth the necessary evidence. Integration advanced in the 1980s as the result of a complicated, asymmetrical, interactive three-level game. In play were globalization from the top, Thatcherism and neoliberalism from the bottom, and European integration at the interface. The pressures for change in Europe originated in the United States, but not from some central "room of buttons" at the Pentagon or on Wall Street. An unplanned and all but unforeseen combination of new technologies, profound changes in social values and organization, the development of different kinds of markets and institutions, and an eclectic concoction of fresh "supply side" policies pulled the country out of the stagflationary slough of the 1970s and, over the following decade, set a new standard for low-inflation growth and economic competitiveness. Like the United States before it, Europe would have to brave the sweeping tide of change or be swept under by it.

Impressed by the successes of Reaganauts and Thatcherites – but also troubled by the failure of the French experiment with Socialism in One Country – the European governments of the decade adopted neoliberal reforms less out of conviction than for lack of anything better. More important than their political coloration, which more often than not was leftist, were the national settings in which the parties in power operated; they defined the parameters of the possible. Outcomes also varied substantially. In "economically decadent Britain," reform came with astonishing speed and thoroughness, thanks to Mrs. Thatcher's sound and careful policy making and to a strong parliamentary tradition. In France, the strength of the state enabled a phase-in of a more market-based economy without entailing any real shifts in power. In Spain, the weakness of the economy made it hard for even a powerful state to resist the inroads of markets into the institutional domain. In Sweden, public attachment to the tradition of the welfare state impeded the admittedly needed reform in what had become a weak economy. In Germany, the relative success of Rhenish capitalism made it possible to defer adaptation. In Italy, political immobilization prevented reform. Further examples would underscore the point that painting with the neoliberal brush may have partly modernized Europe but neither homogenized it nor appreciably reduced the strength of national traditions. If anything, the contrary was the case. The national variations of the reform process, which remains under way, assure that differences of outlook and interest will remain as marked in the future as they have been in the past. Any future European federation will have to respect such diversity.

Without far-reaching international and national change, European integration could not have become an independent force in its own right during the 1980s. The Single European Act was effective and extended Community-wide partly because the removal of nontariff barriers had already begun in individual countries – several of which, especially Britain, outpaced Brussels in liberalizing. Reform of financial markets, though a part of the Cockfield package, was already well under way elsewhere, and indeed appears almost inescapable in view of growing capital requirements. The increase in industrial scale and scope, the expansion of international trade, and the acceleration of capital mobility associated with globalization created the need for common rules, in the first instance for a single Community-wide competition policy but also in the fields of banking, insurance, stock exchanges, accountancy, patenting, and licensing. Brussels would acquire useful new "competences" in these and other business-related fields. Breakthroughs in telecommunications and information technology made the Commission a natural venue for policy making. Although less immediately consequential, the Commission also would take an active hand in the reorganization of "networking industries" like the utilities and transport. The need to maintain international competitiveness continued to force the pace of liberalization and prevented the Single European Act from becoming a dead letter.

The economic impact of the SEA is hard to measure, but anecdotal evidence suggests that it induced structural changes that first became visible in the 1990s. Reform came quickly in the financial sphere, driven more by markets than by governance models. Privatizations, scheduled in several European countries to begin at the start of the new decade, would hit a speed bump in 1992 and resume on a large scale only after stabilization in 1994; they would cover "lame ducks," the networking industries, and public services. Foreign competition, the most important impetus to growth cited in the Cecchini Report, affected mainly new product markets in addition to those for services. The rise of U.S. lobbying in Brussels thickened and spread networks of American service industries like consultancy, accounting, advertising, and law.

A time lag often stood between the removal of nontariff barriers and the creation or penetration of new markets in manufacturing. The knee-jerk producer response to planned or actual market opening was to seek defensive alliance, sometimes with non-EU competitors but more often with domestic counterparts. The bold takeover bid that might result in a real shake-out remained the exception. Many of the new arrangements were short-lived or broke down. In a number of traditional lines of production, market-sharing agreements of various kinds persisted, some sanctioned by industrial policy. Distinct and quite different national business traditions remained largely intact. An anonymous reporter for the *Economist* aptly commented that

in the second half of the 1980s, when America went through the most wrenching structural changes in fifty years, Europe tried to get away with doing nothing. Firms were holding on to old management hierarchies, ancient diversifications, and outdated working practices, stuck in national markets, and hemmed in by pervasive regulation. Europe seemed to be a fortress, designed not so much to keep out the Japanese and the Americans but to keep out change.[1]

The Single European Market presented each producer with a different challenge and entailed complex calculations of profit and loss as well as political and economic unknowns; adjustment was complicated and by no means easy to detect or understand. How the new challenges would be met would only gradually begin to become evident. That it would involve plenty of losers along with lucky winners was certain.

The SEA set in motion a process that is consistent with world trends and whose speed and amplitude are subject to overestimation – but whose overall impact clearly favors liberalization. Both EMS and its Maastricht-initialed successor, EMU, were meant to promote liberalization by stabilizing exchange rates, lowering inflation, reducing transactions costs, restricting the freedom of elected officeholders, disciplining labor unions and the welfare state, and promoting the competition principle. The EMU did not do so optimally; EMS was a better choice.

The EMS nearly broke down at the beginning of the decade and fell apart at the end of it, but between the two dates pegging to the DM helped wring inflation out of the French and Danish economies and set a standard that "weak currency countries" would later try to meet. Undeniably, unemployment resulted in uncompetitive economies unable to allow their currencies to find their own level. The European Monetary System was an arrangement of convenience with a built-in margin of flexibility that could, within limits, be loosened or tightened as required. Although viable over the long run only if the burden of adjustment to change could be borne by the economy, EMS could be reworked or even temporarily suspended when necessary. It could have evolved into a monetary union anchored to a "virtuous" European currency against which national note issues floated. This optimal arrangement never received the consideration it deserved because the designers of the European Monetary Union were less concerned with economics than with competing with the United States and restricting the fiscal autonomy of national governments.

The EMU, unlike the EMS, was meant to be permanent. The European Monetary Union provided for a single unit of currency rather than a currency regime and was anchored in rules stripping national governments of monetary (and, indirectly, fiscal) independence. Eight years would be needed for governments to adjust to its tight constraints, which even in boom conditions kept growth low and unemployment high. The tightening of the monetary tourniquet would, by weakening the economy, slow down "deepening" even without the "widening" of expansion. The EMU also posed huge political dangers for Europe. Vitiating national parliaments was the most important of them; another was the lack of coordinating mechanisms between EMU and any legitimate authority; the third was the unresolved constitutional problems to which this situation gave rise.

The two previous expansions had changed the Community significantly. The entrance of Britain (along with Denmark) reopened it to liberalization. The Mediterranean enlargement (along with the earlier Irish entrance) engaged the Community in a process of modern state building. The planned future Nordic (along with Austria) expansion would later move a host of new issues like environmentalism forward on the European agenda. Each additional member complicated the political process. The newly tightened German purse strings made grease for the creaking machinery hard to find. The unviable Delorean agenda would cause breakdown.

Even deeper problems stood in the way of another dramatic re-launching. Socialism was not dead but only dying. While globalization and competition shaped the new economy, political adaptation was slow. No new ideology accompanied the economic change except for Thatcherism, which was not readily exportable. Euro-ideology as concocted and pumped up in Brussels rang hollow. Except in Britain, economic reform came about either by indirection or by placing it "above politics." It encountered foot-dragging and organized interest-group protest but little principled opposition. A dull sense of resentment was palpable. No one much believed in "Europe" anymore. It would require a stretch of the imagination to describe the EU as a "polity in the making."

In a heroic attempt to revive the old dispensation, Delors launched a counter-Reformation – albeit from an energized Brussels rather than a reformed Rome, and over the heads of the squabbling and self-seeking member-states rather than those of corrupt bishops. Taking full advantage of darkness and cover, he and his spiritual commandos, the Guardians of Europe, stealthily discharged one successful mission after another, following the twists and turns of a lengthy integration scenario that Delors had scripted and whose outcome only he knew. It opened one phase at a time, each one quite different from the last. Within the Commission it was referred to as the strategy of the Russian Dolls, and it had always managed to keep potential adversaries off balance. Six of the nested hollow shells had been opened, each revealing a bigger surprise than the one before: the SEA, the Delors Packet (I), the "European economic and social space," the Economic and Monetary Union, the Delors Packet (II), and the White Paper "Growth, Competitiveness, and Employment." Only the solid little figure at the core, the "European social model," remained unrevealed. What would it look like? What would be the ultimate surprise?

M. Delors tenderly parted the two halves of the last shell, fondly lifting out the solid little figure and placing it in his left palm. With a finely manicured thumbnail he carefully scratched off thick accretions of dialog, discourse, jargon, and excess verbiage that had formed a crust around it. He could first detect the outlines of the hair: solid and golden, curved in immaculate waves, sculpted and immovable, held together by some invisible plastic. The brows, he saw, arched upward over the nose and slanted downward like a hip-roof over piercing, electric blue and perfectly round eyes, which stared forward intently like headlights. And the teeth: exposed across a broad expanse, they were newly capped, uniformly white, perfectly in line, good for biting. Encasing them was a remarkably large, bowed smile. Staring out was the grinning face of Margaret Thatcher.

Part IV

A False Dawn?
Challenge and Misdirection
in 1990s Europe

Introduction to Part IV

A New Global Framework

As a European era, with a distinct personality of its own, the decade of the Nineties actually opened late and in a foreign setting, on 15 April 1994 at Marrakesh, Morocco. There an agreement was signed concluding a GATT negotiating marathon that had begun eight years earlier in still another distant place, the sleepy beach resort of Punta del Este, Uruguay.[1] The big challenge facing the trade negotiators – globalization – would provide the main theme of the "short" decade. The trade representatives met it by producing a sweeping deal that reduced industrial tariffs to insignificance, heralded reform in agriculture, and created new rules for services, intellectual property, and investment. The conclusion of the so-called Uruguay Round provided an opportunity to transcend the currency turmoil of 1992, the haggling at Maastricht, and the paralytic cross-purposes at which the EU seemed to be working, as well as to kick-start an integration process that, if not derailed, would set parameters both for the internal development of Europe and for its future international role. The conclusion of the new trade agreement coincided with the beginning of an upswing in the international economy that would produce a powerful surge of prosperity, propel the world into the new millennium, expose Europe to the "new economy" taking root in the United States, and lead (both nationally and internationally) to serious efforts to meet the economic and political challenges of the coming era. The end of such a process – though since the first millennial downturn only occasionally within glimpse – would be a future regime of world economic governance in which Europe would play a featured role.

The 1990s witnessed the collapse of communism, the all but definitive discrediting of socialist economics, and the spread of representative democracy both worldwide and in eastern Europe. Improvements in living standards occurred nearly everywhere but especially in the developing countries. International economic cooperation grew impressively. The twin triumphs of political self-determination and free-market economics did not, however, result in "the end of history," as proclaimed by Francis Fukuyama in the decade's most widely discussed work of contemporary historical-philosophical analysis.[2] What began with such promise, and advanced so boldly, has not concluded on a high note. The economic downdraft set in motion by the bursting of the dot-com stock exchange bubble in spring 2000 exposed grave legal and institutional flaws. The "growth recession" that set in over the next several months and continued uninterrupted through 2002 called into question the permanence of the gains of the previous twenty years, generated powerful political countercurrents, and clouded the future. The disillusioning experience ended a decade of optimism and structural change. However, if Hayek's theory of the business cycle is sound, then this unhappy outcome should have been predictable and prosperity will resume after the inefficient are forced out of business and a new round of investment begins.

Whether Europe will be able to benefit proportionately from a global recovery remains to be seen. The downturn in that quarter has been more severe there than in the United States, and the upswing promises to be later and less rapid – according to economist Daniel Gros – because structural problems reduce long-term growth and because new investment and productivity increases are both lagging.[3] In 2002 the European economy grew at less than half the American rate of 2.4 percent. The challenge from Asia also continues to mount. Between 1985 and 1995, 33 developing countries – nearly half the total – swung from relatively closed to open trading regimes; 30 of them switched to allowing cross-border movements of capital; and nearly all of them to some extent liberalized trade and payments. This "bottom up" development, according to Razeen Sally, has been "the most dramatic episode of economic liberalization the world has ever seen."[4] It can only intensify competition in years to come.

As the new millennium began, it became painfully evident that basic European institutions needed to be overhauled. Rigid labor markets and bloated welfare states stifled growth, created cultures of dependence, frustrated innovation and creativity, bred unrest, and set the stage for larger problems in the future. For Europe, the 1990s were a decade of missed opportunity. In the attempt to advance the integration process, political leaders have inadvertently slowed down and impaired it. The shift to monetary union and the adoption of the euro would continue to reduce growth and increase unemployment until labor mobility, market-based wage determination, and other compensatory mechanisms provided an essential precondition for an optimum currency area; without such changes, competitiveness will continue to suffer, as it did during the run-up to the EMU in the 1990s. France, Germany, Italy, and even the Commission president, Romano Prodi, are now demanding a loosening of the convergence criteria required by the growth and stability pact. Such loosening, although perhaps needed to stimulate short-run growth, punishes fiscal "virtue" while rewarding fiscal "vice" and hence might whipsaw the young arrangement apart as asset or price inflation takes hold in economies operating at full employment. A rescue of the EMU could require replacing the single-currency system with a monetary regime of national monetary competition, a float, against a hard euro.

The European Monetary Union has also been also politically harmful. The transfer of monetary (and, in effect, fiscal) policy-making power to a directorate of central bankers disenfranchised those subject to their decisions – the citizens of the nations of Europe – and eviscerated the authority of national governments, contributing to a legitimacy crisis that became manifest at the end of the decade.

As the convergence criteria bit, electorates felt the pain, and elected political leaders lost the ability to relieve it. Their power and prestige suffered, strength turned into weakness, and governmental authority waned. Scope for independent action on the domestic front diminished. As a result, at the European level, summit after summit ended in discord, gridlock, or nothing at all. The word had to substitute for the deed, debasing political currencies on both sides of the former Iron Curtain and leading to disillusionment and division.

The undemocratic European Union faced an even more severe legitimacy problem than the member-states. The turnout for elections to the European Parliament dropped steadily from 63 percent in 1979 to 49 percent in 1999.[5] The problem was normally referred to as the "democratic deficit," but it involved more than a lack of self-government. In the absence of representative institutions, EU's moral and political credibility rested largely on the public belief in the adage "results count." In the 1990s the Community faced a painful dilemma. The policy-making machinery broke down at the very time that regulations and directives implementing the Single European Act began to register in the lives of ordinary people, leaving many of them disturbed, unhappy, and fearful. No one could doubt any longer that what went on in Brussels really mattered: passed down from on high, Commission rulings altered social, legal, and professional contexts, reshaped institutions, interfered with customary ways of doing things, and created losers as well as winners. Foot-dragging, noncooperation, or (particularly in the south) cheating often resulted. The EU seemed at once pompous and threatening yet meddlesome and impotent – but also, and especially after the adoption of the euro, permanent.

Scandals did little to improve its image. The Commission's often heavy-handed and manipulative effort to make things better only made them worse. When it should have been cleaning house, it called a phony Convention on the Future of Europe to draft a constitution for a federal government. Many merely wagged their heads in disbelief at such antics. Euro-hopefuls took the exercise seriously. Shocked and angered, still others became Euroskeptics. The constitutional convention was, however, more than mere eyewash. Conducted in the stealthy and opaque manner that has become customary at the EU, the exercise has so far skirted most of the fundamental problems facing the Union, will likely aggravate existing disagreements and increase tensions between member-states, and – if presented as a *fait accompli* – could split the EU or arrest its future development. The European Union, almost in spite of itself, continues to fan smoldering resentment into brushfires of popular insurgency.

The need to advance the integration process is not imaginary. To heal the wounds of the Cold War, modernize the economy, strengthen democracy in places where its roots are shallow, and qualify Europe for participation in the emerging global order, progress must be resumed toward the creation of what Timothy Garton Ash calls "the liberal order." Such a liberal order is one in which peoples pursuing different ends coexist peacefully and nonhegemonically, which eschews both the use of force and scapegoating "the other" in order to create loyalties, and legitimizes principled mutual interventions into the internal affairs of nations but does not require "a forced march to unity."[6] The liberalizing world economy of the 1990s provided plenty of intimations of a brighter future: more productive industry and agriculture, better ways of living, and a society with fewer invidious social distinctions, improved educational standards, increased opportunity, additional leisure, and more personal freedom. The Single European Act advanced the process of progressive change, yet the ill-conceived Maastricht agenda now impedes it. The effort to implement Maastricht has gridlocked policy making, threatens good government, and – by betraying the promise of Enlargement – imperils Europe's future. The EU is fast ceasing to be a problem solver and is itself becoming a problem.

The decade of the 1990s boded well for the progress of European integration. The Uruguay Round brought the regulation of world trade abreast of the globalization occurring over the previous two decades and established the agenda for "organizing liberalization" worldwide. The events set in motion at Punta del Este belonged to a larger process driven by changes in both technology and ideology and under way both nationally and regionally, through which Europe would have to pass. The Uruguay Round can be credited with several impressive specific achievements: cutting industrial tariffs to the point of near insignificance, strengthening some trade rules to prevent subsidization and to facilitate dispute settlement, and creating new ones that apply to services, intellectual property, and investment. The trade negotiators also eliminated a broad array of nontariff barriers in textiles, leather goods, and shipbuilding. The effort was more inclusive than in previous rounds. Resting heavily on the input of producer interests, it also enlisted participation from a wide variety of nongovernmental organizations representing the interests of consumers, the environment, and labor.[7]

The Uruguay Round also produced a built-in future agenda, including timetables for the reduction of agricultural subsidies and their phased-in replacement with income support schemes. The trade representatives set up continuous negotiating machinery for the expanding field of trade in services, and they established as future priorities the examination of government purchasing practices and the restriction of abusive national regulations in the fields of consumer health, product safety, environmental regulations, and certification – as well as for other fields in which a lack of transparency and predictability impeded "market-friendly access." Another important priority at the Uruguay meeting was the enlistment of private actors into greater responsibility for the smooth functioning of the multilateral trading system and to serve as participants in cooperative, self-regulatory arrangements between corporations and private groups. Self-regulation provided the mechanism that with luck would, in the future, balance the conflicting interests of animal rights, environmental protection, and child labor on the one hand and those of the world trading system on the other. Finally, GATT itself, which had been organized in 1948 as a provisional body, was re-constituted as a formal and permanent structure: the World Trade Organization (WTO), which was fitted out with a new dispute settlement mechanism and vested with enforcement authority and the power to create case law. It was well positioned to mediate between the interests of a broadening network of regional trade associations like the EU and bilateral commercial relationships.[8]

The rise of GATT was both cause and consequence of growth in world trade – a rising proportion of it in manufactures and high-technology production – as well as restoration of the international market economy, a process that went hand in hand with the development of regional economic and political institutions like the EU. It has been accompanied by a sometimes slow but steady growth in power and responsibility. In the 1950s and 1960s, GATT's sole aim, in a succession of negotiating rounds, was to reduce tariffs and other discriminatory trade barriers impeding trade between its 22 members, a fairly straightforward matter since tariff restrictiveness is easy to quantify. Each successive round has been more ambitious than its predecessor. Those of the 1950s transformed quotas into tariffs and then reduced the latter steadily. The Kennedy Round of the late 1960s sharply increased the extent of multilateral tariff cuts. The Tokyo Round of the following decade extended the GATT system to nontariff measures. Tariffs on manufactures declined from an average of 40 percent to 6 percent from 1948 to 1980. The Uruguay Round brought agriculture and textiles into the system. Over the next ten years, international trade in goods grew twice as fast as world income, trade in services grew even faster, and direct foreign investment (at 11 percent annually) increased at a higher rate yet. The composition of trade also shifted. Whereas the combined share of raw materials, minerals, and foodstuffs still equaled that of manufactures in 1960, by 1993 three quarters of world trade was in finished or semifinished goods. The roles of Europe and Japan have increased correspondingly.[9] China is now a member of WTO, and Russia has applied to become one. It is widely recognized that GATT/WTO has both accommodated and facilitated long-term shifts in global economic power.

The rise of GATT/WTO owes much to a healthy symbiosis of the EU and the world trading organization. "The postwar record," according to C. Fred Bergsten,

is an unbroken chain of positive interaction between the global system and its main regional subsystems .... [M]odest liberalization begets broader liberalization. By demonstrating its payoff and familiarizing domestic politics with the issues, regional deals can provide useful models for broader global agreements, and the adverse impacts of new preferential arrangements on outsiders induces the latter to seek new multilateral compacts.[10]

The creation of the EU thus led to the Kennedy Round of the early 1960s – both to prevent trade discrimination and to open the way for a new Atlantic partnership. The inclusion of Britain in the EEC led to American initiation of the Tokyo Round in the 1970s. The adoption of the single market strategy prompted the creation of the Uruguay Round. In each case, albeit with the significant exception of agriculture, the EU has reduced the external tariff. Both NAFTA (the North American Free Trade Agreement) and APEC (the Asian Pacific Economic Council) came into being when the Uruguay Round seemed to falter, helping restore its momentum. Like the EU, these bodies have multilateralized their liberalization on a fully reciprocal basis. In addition, WTO membership has grown to more than 140.[11]

The World Trade Organization has developed into something far greater than the U.S.-run club that its GATT predecessor once was, and in a manner that strikingly validates the purposes behind the American policy that originally gave rise to the latter. Today the European Union exercises co-leadership within the WTO. With an economy as large as the United States and more importance as a trading entity, it has been, according to Bergsten, "a fully equal partner ... on trade issues, ... can veto any global trade accord, and has been a necessary co-leader of all multilateral enterprises."[12] Not surprisingly, the most influential advocate for the launching of a future Millennial Round, now already under way, was the trade commissioner who represented the EU during the Uruguay negotiations, Sir Leon Brittan.[13]

The design for the new Millennial Round, according to Bergsten, is clear. The round would start at once, following the "bicycle principle," to prevent slipping backwards. The exercise must also be bigger in order to permit trade-offs over a broader front of issues and be coordinated with monetary policy in order to prevent widening of the American trade deficit. The United States and Europe will be required to act as joint stewards. The Millennial Round should plan to conclude, according to Bergsten, with the "elimination of all barriers" at some point between 2010 and 2020.

The backsliding that followed the Kennedy and Tokyo Rounds – and which featured the imposition of the U.S. import surcharge, the Multi Fiber Agreement, and a panoply of new Voluntary Export Restraints for autos, steel, and machine tools – did not occur after the Uruguay Round. Instead, the follow-up included new agreements in telecommunications services, financial services, and information technology products – each of them generating EU counterparts – as well as a new regional initiative in 1997, in this case from the Asian Pacific Economic Council. The round's ambitious goal, a major new initiative, was to replicate the information technology agreement in fifteen additional sectors.[14]

Only at the end of the decade did the bicycle start losing its chain. Sage minds are still pondering the world-historical significance of the antic attacks by the bare-breasted, face-painted, antler-crowned, hammer-wielding young harpies who smashed Starbucks' windows at the WTO meeting of 2000 in Seattle. The rise of demands for protection can now be heard on both sides of the Atlantic. In order to get "fast track" authority (to lower individual tariffs without threat of Congressional veto), President Bush felt obliged to invoke "safeguards" against steel imports – more a matter of political sound than economic fury, as it turns out. The United States will also increase commodity support prices by 80 percent – a retrograde step that raises domestic food costs, hurts Third World producers, and undermines reform of the CAP. It furthermore violates the free-trade principles upon which American policy has rested since World War II and can only retard the development of the new transgovernmental system now beginning to take shape globally.[15] The U.S. administration has subsequently described the measure as a tactical ploy aimed at reopening the entire problem of international agricultural price supports in the Doha Round.

Attempts to describe the contours of the emerging international order can amuse as much as enlighten. Anne-Marie Slaughter's version deserves to be taken seriously.[16] Slaughter does not posit a disappearance of the state in the face of globalization but rather a disaggregation of it into functionally distinct parts and their re-constitution into transnational networks by national representatives as needed to manage market-originating issues beyond the scope of state power. In this scheme of things the WTO could provide a capstone – not in the sense as a supreme arbiter in a hierarchical administrative structure, but as co-ordinator of informal, purpose-created, problem-solving networks. "Meetings between securities regulators, antitrust or environmental officials, judges or legislators" may lack the drama of high politics, she adds,

> but for the internationalists of the 1990s ... transnational government networks are a reality. Wall Street looks to the Basle Committee rather than the World Bank. Human rights lawyers are more likely to develop transnational litigation strategies for domestic courts ... than to petition the U.N. Committee on Human Rights.[17]

Transgovernmentalism avoids the creation of cumbersome, self-serving bureaucracies and leaves ultimate decision-making authority in the hands of governments responsible to their citizens.

Slaughter cites several important examples of transgovernmentalism in action. Networking by judges has contributed to the adoption nationally of "best practices" rulings and methods as well as to cooperation between national and supranational courts and regionally between chief justices. This interaction results, as she describes it, not in the creation of a unified legal structure topped by a supreme court but rather in a flexible system encompassing many rules of law, accommodating regional differences, yet reinforced by common values. The rise of this body of law connects to the development of the regulatory web, which is composed of strands of antitrust policy, securities regulation, environmental policy, criminal law enforcement, and banking and insurance supervision.[18]

Such transgovernmental cooperation can be conducted ad hoc, or by means of mutual and legal assistance treaties, or by memorandums of understanding between regulatory agencies. The latter is an example of "positive comity" that enables antitrust officials in the United States and European Union to share information, coordinate policy, and provide mutual encouragement. The adoption in 1988 of capital adequacy requirements for financial institutions is another important instance of transgovernmental cooperation. National securities commissioners and insurance regulators have arrived at similar arrangements. Such practical agreements do not imply a continuous or separate international existence independent from the purposes for which they were created. Their effect, according to Slaughter, is not to create a new international law but to internationalize national laws. The results are a healthy competition between the sound and the unsound, a learning process that can carry over into undemocratic or immature governmental systems, and the validation of state authority internationally. Transnational cooperation creates good-faith agreements that, if properly written, can be self-regulating but do not create binding law, which can take place only at the national level and is thus ultimately subject to public approval. A democratic rule-setting authority is indispensable not only to legitimize a market-based order but for its sound functioning. Transgovernmentalism may well provide the sinews of what Slaughter calls "the real new world order."[19]

The spread of the developing approach is a consequence of the liberalization process that has unfolded in Europe since the Single European Act.[20] The logic that gave rise to such change is not easily understood. According to Brian T. Hanson, a resurgence of protectionism should have been expected in the 1990s. The 1991–1994 recession cost 6 million jobs EU-wide, where average unemployment was 11 percent. Neither governments nor business nor the Commission viewed tariff reduction as a necessary concomitant of the SEA. The Cockfield report warned in a single sentence: "The commercial identity of the Community must be consolidated so that our trading partners will not be given the benefit of a wider market without themselves making similar concessions."[21] Trade protection was included in the recommendations put forward by the European Roundtable of Industrialists. Several early Commission proposals were blatantly protectionist. The Second Banking Directive, which restricted access to European markets to those financial institutions whose home countries provided reciprocal benefits to European banks, would have required the United States to provide more favorable treatment to European banks than to domestic ones. Trade Commissioner Willy De Clercq declared at the time that "we are not building a single market in order to turn it over to hungry foreigners."[22] Yet something like that has happened.

Since 1990, individual EU member-states have abolished over 6,300 qualitative restrictions against imports from outside countries; reduced the number of surveillance measures in such critical fields as machine tools, electrical components, and electronic products; and at least not increased the number of antidumping measures. In the Uruguay Round the EU agreed to cut tariffs 38 percent and eliminate them altogether for construction equipment, farm machinery, pharmaceuticals, and most categories of steel, paper products, and furniture. The Community also concluded 26 bilateral treaties providing market access, among them the Europe Agreements with nations of the former Soviet bloc.[23] There was no return to Fortress Europe.

Liberalization did not occur for the usual reasons cited in the political science literature: the erosion and disappearance of uncompetitive sectors, the internationalization of successful ones, or the increased power of interest groups that gained from economic openness or from ideological conversion in some form. Hanson's own argument – that EU voting rules made the reintroduction of protectionism difficult – also carries little weight. Hanson overlooks new types of industrial policy like the Framework Program for research and development. An explanation for the progress of liberalization must rather be sought in the realm of what Hayek called "spontaneous order," the ever-evolving, self-generating, utility-optimizing process through which information transmitted by price signals determines the relative price of goods and, by extension, shapes the overall structure of production.[24] This process is also behind the resumption of the long-term secular trend toward liberalization first noted by Gottfried Haberler.

Spontaneous order does not develop solely through the market but also – as Hayek argued in "The Economic Conditions of Interstate Federalism" and as subsequently elaborated upon by Jan Tumlir – through institutional, constitutional, and legal mechanisms of adaptation and change within it. Hayek's one stab at writing "conjunctural history," which concerned the emergence of international trade between 750 and 550 B.C.E., holds important implications for the present. Trade, Hayek argues, developed contrary to the preferences and predilections of rulers for autarchic order and through the spontaneous development of "international private law societies" for institutionalizing trust between traders – by means of marketplace competition and marketlike competitive emulation between states via an empirical "discovery procedure."[25]

The Treaty of Rome provides the essential framework for a common market as a self-organizing system. The treaty laid out the requirements for establishing a commons customs area and commercial policy, eliminating tariff and nontariff barriers, abolishing obstacles to the free movement of persons, services and capital, and preserving open competition; it furthermore endowed the European Court of Justice with the authority to enshrine this "economic constitution" into law.[26] By lifting the dead hand of national protectionism, the Single European Act enabled the invisible hand of the market to work on a far greater scale than previously, and with foreseeable economic consequences yet unintended political ones. The liberalization of markets, unleashed internationally at the same time, gave rise to a new competition not only between producers and consumers but also, as Hayek predicted, among institutions and between markets and institutions. The consequence was not the oft-stigmatized "race to the bottom" but the creation of wealth resulting from the unplanned efforts of myriad individual market participants to profit from previously obstructed opportunity freed by the lifting of institutional restraints to the effective operation of the competition principle. This intra-European event complemented, reinforced, and furthered the worldwide trend advanced politically by the Uruguay Round.

There was nothing automatic about its operation – even though, as Jeffrey Sachs put the matter in 1995, "the puzzle is not that capitalism triumphed but that it took so long."[27] The necessary precondition of the market revolution was the collapse of the Second and Third World models of state-led, autarkic development. Not only should the origins of the Soviet economic collapse have been evident by the mid-1980s, but appropriate lessons should have been drawn from the fact that by then virtually every Latin American government was in default. Included among the many international bankrupts were profligate oil exporters like Mexico and Nigeria, which amidst unprecedented booms went under as the result of the incredible waste, inefficiency, and corruption attendant upon state-led strategies of industrial development. To mention Europe in the same breath with such basket cases may not be in good taste. Sachs is nonetheless right to remind us that even greater risks to the creation of a world market system anchored in the international rule of law "come from Western Europe ... than the United States, [since] the EU labors under a much more extensive, rigid, and expensive social welfare system ... and [will] require much more downsizing."[28] Neither the prosperity of the 1990s, nor the opening of markets of which it was both cause and effect, were of sufficient strength or duration to overcome the lingering crisis of the mixed-economy welfare state.

The effort to shore up the tottering system at the European level has delayed and complicated a necessary adjustment process, impaired the effectiveness of the EU as regulator and rule setter, and even, at least for a time, turned the Union from a force of light into a force of darkness. Instead of providing a "common European home" for the former Soviet satellites of eastern Europe, the EU has issued them a second-class ticket on a first-class train. This sorry outcome was the unintended consequence of corporatist protectionism: a deplorable eleventh-hour bargain of 25 October 2002 – between a determined, chameleon-like French prime minister, Jacques Chirac, and the recently re-elected but weak German chancellor, Gerhard Schröder – to preserve the EU status quo. The deal prevented reform of the costly CAP, cheated the accession candidates, and locked in "structural fund" subsidies for the near rich instead of transferring them to the genuinely poor. Worse yet, labor mobility – a fundamental guarantee of the Treaty of Rome – would, with specific national exceptions, apply in the future only to citizens of the favored member-states of the West and not equally to all "citizens" of the Union, who can now plainly see (as on Orwell's *Animal Farm*) that some are "more equal" than others. The issue should be brought before the Convention on the Future of Europe.

12

Almost a Road to Nowhere:
The EU in Trouble

JACQUES Delors cast a long shadow over the development of Community institutions in the 1990s. The EU's agenda for the decade was his: the completion of the internal market, the attainment of monetary union, and, above all, the erection of the second and third Maastricht "pillars" – one for a Common Security and Foreign Policy (CSFP), the other for Justice and Home Affairs (JHA). A new commitment to widening the Union, the eastern Enlargement, dated from 1993. Until the very end of the decade, however, it received lower priority than "deepening" (i.e., building up) Community institutions. Delors's commitment to institution building was unwavering. The prospective addition of new member-states merely gave him a handy excuse for accelerating the program. The president was wary of anything that might dilute the authority of his office. The French felt likewise about their power within the Community. They, too, dragged their feet when it came to taking in new members. For Mitterrand as for Delors, Enlargement distracted from the real task ahead – the construction, bureaucratically, of a federal Europe. They would have tried to build "vertically" even if it had not become – owing to the collapse of the Soviet Union and the challenges of globalization – politically and economically necessary to expand "horizontally."

The historian of the EU during the 1990s should practice for the task of writing by playing arcade video games of the sort that feature a movable object – the driver of a racing car, for instance – faced with navigating successive and often quite unpredictable perils and pitfalls in order to arrive safely at a distant finishing line. The driver must possess certain arcane skills – be able to correct for faulty steering and bad brakes and, while doing so, heed advice selectively (something conveyed, presumably, through a wired helmet) from referees and other rule-enforcers, pit-crew chiefs, and expert mechanics as well as concerned spouses and significant others. Not many players can be expected to arrive "home."

The EU, like the imaginary race-car driver, would not have it easy through the 1990s. The Community's development would follow an unforeseeable and perilous course, guided by faulty mechanisms and surrounded by a cacophony of conflicting voices. Its history over the period cannot be traced along a single axis, does not echo a meaningful narrative, and indeed moved all over the map. Those who spoke confidently about where it would go (or should have gone) have often ended up disappointed. The game, moreover, has not yet ended and still remains in play – for how long is anyone's guess.

After 1992, top-level policy making concentrated on political issues. Economic matters put in only the occasional appearance prior to the so-called dot.com Lisbon summit in 2000. They soon slipped down the agenda. Both the courtly and conciliatory – though eventually discredited – centrist Luxembourger Jacques Santer (1995–1999) and his determined though ineffective successor, Romano Prodi (1999–present), remained bound by Delors's agenda, even though Prodi's inaugural address to the European Parliament would set Enlargement as the goal of his Commission presidency. Neither Santer nor Prodi could lead the member-states, none of which subscribed more than partially to the Commission viewpoint. Each country naturally tried to shape and direct Community policy according to national sets of preferences.

The member-states failed, however, to provide an alternative to Commission leadership. Consensus was absent in the European Council summits of the decade. The Franco-German couple, which previously had led, faced hard times. Other pairings tended to be transitory or opportunistic. None were enduring or could be built upon. Marriages of convenience, polygamy, polyandry, serial marriages in the American fashion, "temporary marriages" in the Islamic mode, open marriages, gay marriages – as well as every quasi-legal or institutionalized sort of "living arrangement" – seem to have been tried in the couplings, uncouplings, and recouplings of EU intergovernmental politics in the 1990s. In spite of promising beginnings, cooperation at successive European Council summits broke down amidst quarreling and mutual recrimination. These biannual events accomplished precious little. By the end of the decade, even the pretense of civility had been dropped at such gatherings. The reconciliation of disparate positions and the hammering out of joint policy had become all but impossible. Although certain experts claim that the 1990s were "polity creating," the opposite was actually the case.[1]

Failure could not be blamed entirely on the summiteers. External events also came into play – like the discovery of fraud at the Commission, the formation of a government in Austria resting on a purportedly post-fascist political party, and the outbreak of "mad cow disease." The public, since Maastricht for the first time really engaging with the politics of Brussels, did not like what it saw. Hostile constituents tied politicians' hands. Mounting domestic problems encouraged Euro-demagogy. And Germany had less grease for squeaky wheels. As sound compromise became more difficult, governance issues crowded substantive matters off the European agenda. This zero-sum game led to ferocious infighting. The Union nevertheless faced more than procedural problems: along with the member-state governments, it suffered the ill effects of a deflationary economic policy for which they jointly were responsible – and with which they were stuck.

The Commission faced problems of its own. The Guardians had grown long in the tooth. The good life held more attractions than did long hours, endless argumentation over the meaning of meaningless phrases, and the pointless filing of documents. Moreover, the Commission had to handle the Delorean agenda without Delors. The failure to replace him with a Thatcherite, in the end, fore-closed any other option. Though the Frenchman's two successors – Jacques San-ter of Luxembourg and Romano Prodi of Italy – were honorable men and though Prodi was an administrator, economist, and statesman of daunting attainments, neither president managed to put his stamp on the office or, in fact, accomplish much of anything. The odds against success were overwhelming. Delors's ideas were unrealistic and at times destructive. The member-states were crabby, and getting worse. Serious problems – in the states as well as at the Commission – disrupted progress and wrought havoc on what political scientists are wont to describe as the "governance process." It was often more like a spitting contest.

There were two stages in the 1990s Community "governance process," the first of which involved primarily the member-states. These were the successive summits where, as customary by the rota rules, the holder of the presidency could set at least part of the agenda and, secondly, the intergovernmental con-ferences convoked to revise the treaties. At the Amsterdam IGC (1996–1997), the Franco-German partnership broke down. The important "Agenda 2000" sum-mit in Berlin also fell apart, this time because of a scandal at the Commission that eventually brought about the resignation of Jacques Santer. This affair ex-posed the true condition of the Euro-executive and called into question its very right to exist. The resulting brouhaha wrecked Agenda 2000 – the best oppor-tunity ever presented for dealing with Enlargement.

The Lisbon summit would be another lost chance, but for a different reason. The main points on its agenda were modernization and liberalization. Lisbon might have been a kind of dot-com reprise of the Single European Act, an op-portunity to put the Community back on track. Nothing came of it, however, because the Austrian affair diverted attention from the program of the cheery techno- and market reformers and produced a host of new difficulties that for months diverted the Commission. Austria was, in fact, a non-problem: conjured up by cheap-shot politicians in an attempt to divert attention from threats on the home front and acquiesced in by a floundering Commission president, Prodi, desperate to be seen as "Mr. Good Guy."

The bullying of the Alpine republic made Brussels look threatening as well as ridiculous and provided a *Paradebeispeil* – a convincing demonstration – of Commission arrogance and disregard for member-state rights. Damage control would preoccupy the latter for months. The home-front problems centered on Belgium, where an unsolved string of pedophilic murders had triggered the worst political crisis in its post–World War II history. The story of how the Austrian crisis, with its Belgian antecedent, wrecked the Lisbon dot.com summit provides an insight into the bizarre situations that sometimes underlie the official politics of Brussels, an intimation of the damage that can result when a weak Commis-sion allows itself to become the plaything of local politics, and an opportunity to take a close look at the sources of public disaffection and resentment.

The run-up to the Nice IGC of December 2000 opened the second stage of the unfolding governance process. The long-planned event was supposed to have reformed Community institutions in preparation for Enlargement. The Commission and the member-states prepared for a leadership showdown at Nice that never actually happened. The Euro-*apparat* was simply shoved aside and instead, the member-states viciously did battle with one another. The appalling spectacle culminated the clamorous discord of the decade and disgusted delegates and publics alike, but at least it did not derail Enlargement. Total breakdown was narrowly averted. The upshot of Nice was not, as it should have been, a bit of R&R (GI lingo for "rest and recreation") but a *fuite en avance,* the projection of still more ambitious projects and programs.

The opening of the grandiose Convention on the Future of Europe in 2002 was an apt culmination to a decade in which EU departed further and further from political reality. It was a bad idea from the get-go. The process, advertised as similar to the Philadelphia Constitutional Convention of 1787, has little in common with it and was, in fact, conceived as a public relations ploy to quell worries about the "democratic deficit." The EU has not yet approached a level of political development sufficient to warrant discussion of a constitutional project; at this point it amounts to little more than a pretentious federal bureaucracy. By comparison to the American example, the European unification process has been topsy-turvy. The founding of the United States began at the grass roots – via self-government, through the town meeting, to the states, and from there to union. It did not originate at the apex of authority, in the authority realm of high politics, or as an elite project advanced by a centralizing executive authority at the expense of democratic institutions.

The prospect of a federal or even a "proto-federal" state is, according to the thoughtful remarks of one of Britain's most respected Europhiles, William Wallace, still very remote. Wallace calls the EU not a "provisional structure" (halfway between sovereignty and integration) or even an "intergovernmental regime" but rather a "collective political system" that is persistently "provisional," deliberately "ambiguous," and less structured, formal, and "sovereign" than even a German *Staatenbund* like the Confederation of 1815–1848 – or its precursor, the Holy Roman Empire. Change ("policy initiative") within this system (or anti-system) does not stem, he adds, from any one source; instead, the "fragmented" process rests on a "moving consensus" that in turn develops from within "epistemic communities" or "cartels of elites." Policy making is "opaque," lacks legitimacy (except perhaps post facto, in terms of results), and rests, in Wallace's view, on at best "passive popular consent." Furthermore, the issues with which technocrats are concerned are not those that interest or arouse the public, such as the outbreak of "mad cow disease"; and no political machinery either links or otherwise mediates between the two. A European *demos* does not exist. Wallace concluded that the approach best suited to explain the political evolution of the EU is historical institutionalism. The pace and direction of European integration has not been formulaic or teleological but determined in part by inertia, unintended consequence, "beliefs, paradigms, codes, cultures, and knowledge," the development of legal doctrine, and "different institutional configurations."[2]

At the June 1994 Corfu summit, when they selected a successor to Delors to serve as president of the Commission for the five-year term beginning in 1995, the EU heads of government had big decisions to make: whether to get on with the economic agenda or stand pat; and whether to "widen" or "deepen" or both. It was recognized at the time that the EU had never faced a more difficult period than after Maastricht. The governments disagreed on what the Union is for, and most ordinary people mistrusted Brussels. The decision was to play it safe, find a conductor who could hold the orchestra together – not a willful soloist – someone without a political program of his own and thus able to reconcile the disparate views within and between member-states.[3] Deliberately rejected was the Leon Brittan or Peter Sutherland, who might have lobbied heavily for the reduction or "repatriation" of CAP, cut down the bureaucracy and tightened accountability, pressed hard for completion of the single market, given priority to the establishment of a "trans-Atlantic dialog," restricted regulatory interventions to measures needed for the proper operation of markets, applied the subsidiarity principle as originally intended (to enforce the devolution of authority to the lowest practicable level of decision making), and press hard for Enlargement. It may be speculative to imagine that such a policy would have been better than the one actually followed – and surely unrealistic to expect that a Thatcherite candidate stood a chance of replacing Delors – but it is hard to conclude that the outcome would have been much worse. The EU would not meet the challenge of worldwide change of the 1990s or face up to the moral responsibility of healing the wound that ran across Europe. Policy making led nowhere. Instead, Deloreanism – with its high-flying institutional pretensions and its paltry yield – burned itself out in a succession of spectacular conflagrations touched off in an atmosphere of intellectual aridity and fueled by the availability of combustible material and an ample supply of hot air. Although the Enlargement process began in a positive vein, hard decisions would be deferred and a status quo protected that perpetuated injustice and impeded both economic and political reform.

SUMMITS AND SCANDALS

Even in the muddy ebbs and flows of policy and process in post-Delors Brussels, what had to be done was clear from the outset: reform was needed to ensure greater accountability, transparency, efficiency, and democracy. The prominent mainline European Policy Forum in London concluded that seven key changes were needed:

1. the EU should be made accessible to ordinary citizens;
2. the *acquis communautaire* should be amended so that new members could "opt in" rather than "opt out";

3. membership in the monetary union should be made elective;
4. the Council of Ministers should adopt a double voting system – one representing the interests of the member-states themselves and the other representing those of individual citizens on the basis of equality – in order to balance the interests of large and small nations;
5. for reasons of efficiency, the Commission should be reduced in size to a maximum of ten members approved by both the European Parliament and the Council; and
6. a senate should be created with representatives from national parliaments, as Shonfield had earlier suggested.

Certain obstacles impeded reform, the report added, and had to be reduced or removed. The Commission had too many and too diffuse responsibilities and was poorly organized, overworked, and underproductive; it often operated at cross-purposes and found itself chronically short of cash. Delors's reliance on his "kitchen cabinet" had undermined the authority of the directors general, the senior civil servants. National quotas, not merit, governed appointments. The Commission also lacked adequate policing powers, so fraud mounted. Although only 188 million pounds worth of malfeasance could be detected, CAP fraud alone probably amounted to 4 billion pounds. Expenditure of structural funds could not be accounted for. *Glasnost* was needed in Brussels.

Furthermore, the Council's own staff (COREPER, composed of national civil servants) had encroached upon Commission turf. Although more efficient than the Euro-*apparat,* COREPER operated extra-legally and in total secret. Enlargement, moreover, would require changes in both the voting system and the rotating presidency as well as reductions in the number of working languages. As for the rest, Maastricht had introduced minor judicial reforms, created a Committee of the Regions without any well-defined authority, provided the European Parliament with the trappings rather than the substance of new power, and done nothing to clarify the relationship between Brussels and the national legislatures – while at the same time sanctioning an "opting out" procedure that opened the possibility of a "multi-speed Europe."[4]

The reform plans of the 1990s would be buried under bad policy making, self-serving behavior, demagogy, corruption, and animosity. There was no simple explanation for the mess. Bad temper and bad luck both played a role, but at bottom the problem was intrinsic. The unworkable Delorean agenda overloaded the capacity of ill-designed Community institutions. Short of breaking with the former and reforming the latter, the best and most practical approach for the 1990s would have been to preserve what remained of the liberalization scenario of the 1980s, make Enlargement fair and feasible, and do nothing further. The activism of both Commission and member-states weakened institutions, aggravated existing problems, created altogether new ones, and pushed Europe itself toward crisis.

The Amsterdam IGC was the scene of the first serious flap. The specific task facing the intergovernmental conference of 1996–1997 was to build up the Common Security and Foreign Policy as provided for in the Maastricht treaty. It turned out to be a "crabby" meeting, according to the *Economist,* which made "embarrassingly clear" the fact that the Germans and French were no longer on the same wavelength. The long-forgiving Chancellor Kohl took strong exception to the new French Prime Minister Lionel Jospin's attempt to blame him personally – and the German-dictated convergence criteria for EMU membership indirectly – for France's 11-percent unemployment rate. The Franco-German relationship, now clearly unraveling, would never be the same again.

The Amsterdam sessions featured pontificating about the need to coordinate labor policies, but they brought no progress in either that area or with regard to the CSFP issue. The talks instead concluded with squabbles that failed to reconcile disparate views about reweighting representation in the Council and the Commission in order to reduce underrepresentation of the big countries. The CSFP would revive after the debacle of EU diplomacy in Bosnia; the rejiggering of votes would remain at the forefront of proceedings for the rest of the decade and be the subject of endless rows at the monumentally embarrassing Nice summit of December 2000. Amsterdam was not a complete dud. Apart from slightly increasing the "co-decision" powers of the European Parliament – hardly a matter substantial enough to justify a whole new treaty – the meeting confirmed a determination made three years earlier to proceed with Enlargement.[5] The "obvious vanity" of the heads of state, according to Andreas Middel of *Die Welt,* augured ill for the ambitious enterprise. How, he wondered, could a future thirty succeed where an existing fifteen had so ingloriously failed at cooperating – and in light of the fact that the economic problems of the decade were subjecting the Franco-German relationship to more stress than either side could bear?[6]

The Commission's Agenda 2000, a 1,300-page strategy paper for bringing the nations of central and eastern Europe into the EU by 2006, showed its best face and was an appropriate expression of the promise made by M. Santer to provide "less but better" policy making. Fair, sound, and politically feasible, Agenda 2000 coupled Enlargement with a reasonable reform program for the Community. Intended as a sequel to Delors II, the blueprint provided a framework for the cost savings needed to bring the new nations into the Community without having to increase "own resources" to more than 1.27 percent of GDP. The plan assumed a realistic 2.2 percent annual growth rate. The Enlargement process was to begin with the five "first wave" nations, which would be eligible for entry as early as 2002 but no later than 2004. The goal could be met, but just barely, by reducing the two programs that together consumed over 80 percent of the EU budget. CAP intervention prices would be phased down in the three largest commodity sectors (wheat, cattle, and milk) while income maintenance replaced the existing price-support regime. Regional funds would likewise be reduced by

administrative savings. The "cohesion funds" provided to help Club Med countries adjust to the single market would, however, remain sacrosanct.

Agenda 2000 also endorsed the very sensible membership criteria for new applicants adopted at the 1993 Copenhagen summit: the provision of stable democratic institutions based on law and the guarantee of human rights, especially the
rights of minorities; the existence of a functioning market economy able to cope
with the competitive pressures of the EU; and a willingness to assume the obligations of membership (including for EMU) as well as to incorporate the 80,000
pages of some 14,000 directives comprising the *acquis communautaire* into national law. The latter, though costly to the accession countries both directly and
indirectly, was also necessary considering the inadequacy of the administrative
systems inherited from communism. Agenda 2000 also called for the provision
of adaptation funds to cover the considerable expense incurred in adjusting to
the new rules.[7]

Several problems prevented the acceptance and implementation of Agenda
2000. Prime Minister Blair refused to allow any discussion of the British rebate.
The Club Med spearhead, Prime Minister Jose-Maria Aznar of Spain, would
brook no talk about reducing regional funds. Backed by the angry Community
farm lobby, the French opposed CAP reform and refused to consider "repatriation," the re-nationalization of farm policy.[8] The relatively inexperienced Chancellor Schröder of Germany, which held the presidency of the European Council
for the first six months of 1999, faced a couple of special domestic problems.[9]
On one hand, Schröder's troglodytic Minister of Economics Oskar Lafontaine
pushed a Big European Idea of his own – which the ex-Trotskyite French Prime
Minister Jospin was also believed to favor secretly – for a Europe-wide deficit-
stimulated employment policy complemented by a "leveling upward" of working
conditions.[10] On the other hand, former Chancellor Kohl's pledge to reduce the
overgenerous German contribution siphoned off winning public approval from
the new government. Schröder played the nationalist card, took a hard line on
financing, and left the apoplectic Lafontaine sputtering in the wind about labor
market policy.

Nothing came of Agenda 2000 – and the CAP again slipped through un-
scathed – because no one was prepared for what occurred next.[11] Several weeks
before the Berlin summit opened, a Committee of Wise Men – set up to investigate allegations of fraud made by an obscure Commission accountant –
made a surprise announcement. Edith Cresson (the French EU commissioner
for research and education) had, among other derelictions, awarded a substantial contract for the study of AIDS in Africa to her longtime dentist and political
ally in Chatellerault, where she had been mayor. For that matter, she had also
authorized his equally unqualified son to help himself to another big dollop of
Union money. The disclosure unleashed a scandal that would bring down the
entire Santer Commission.

Mme. Cresson was an interesting piece of work.[12] Well before the curious affair broke, she was a woman certain to be remembered by history – as the least

popular prime minister ever to hold the post in the Fifth Republic. President Mitterrand made the appointment on 15 May 1992 in a last-ditch attempt to revive the energy of his flagging Socialist regime, quell the gloom on the left that set in after the blitzkrieg success of Operation Desert Storm, and to end "his days *en famille* with his political daughter at the helm." The French public reveled at having a woman as prime minister but delighted even more in the persistent rumors that Mme. Cresson had been close to Mitterrand in more than just the political sense. *Oui* or *Non,* was she or wasn't she, had she or had she not been his mistress? The personal interest that the president had taken in the prime minister's career was a matter of record. The sniggering was infectious. Low comedy followed. Mme. Cresson's maiden speech was dubbed *le Flop.* Her suggestion of chartering aircraft for deporting illegal immigrants met with ridicule. She referred publicly to the Japanese as ants, maintained at her side a guru who acted as deputy prime minister, and had to be muzzled by the president. She also memorably observed – on the basis, presumably, of substantial firsthand experience – that a quarter of British men are queer. Her decision to move the incubator of the French elite, the *École Nationale d'Administration,* from Paris to half-Hunnish Strasbourg was hardly calculated to win her friends in high places. With her approval record plummeting to the historic low of 19 percent, perilously close to the pathetic 18.3 percent of the vote garnered by the Socialists in the regional elections of 22 March, Mme. Cresson was out as PM within a year and soon thereafter rusticated to the Belgian capital.[13]

There, scandal had been brewing since December 1998 when a lowly Commission bookkeeper, Paul van Buitenen, disclosed to a member of the European Parliament (a Dutch woman of the Green Party) that he possessed evidence of misappropriation, malfeasance, and general lack of oversight in a number of Commission programs. A 41-year-old assistant auditor in EU service for nine years, the father of two small children, and a born-again Christian, van Buitenen simply "could no longer stand it that the EU concealed its scandals."[14] After two vain years attempting to bring the incriminating evidence to the attention of his superiors, the junior official concluded that – unless he spoke out – the Commission would become incapable of reforming itself in the future. Van Buitenen acted not to embarrass the EU but to save it, salve his conscience, and, in the process, make his job endurable.

Attached to the whistle-blower's 34-page plea for the EP to take action were 700 pages of documentation exposing widespread graft in programs to promote tourism and for aid to Mediterranean states, the disappearance of millions in foreign aid, and (above all) vast accountability gaps in Mme. Cresson's research and education directorate – altogether, some hundred instances of corruption or outright theft.[15] Fearing for the worst, van Buitenen stuffed several trunkloads of additional evidence into his car and removed it beyond the reach of his employer. His fears were not misplaced. The high-strung young idealist, now a pariah in official Brussels, was immediately put on half pay and threatened with dismissal.[16] Denying that von Buitenen's charges contained anything new, Commission President Santer charged him with "trying to play judge and jury" and then stonewalled.[17] It was a partly excusable but fatal mistake. Santer had made an honest attempt to clean up the administrative mess he inherited from Delors. Most of the misappropriation was the work of fund recipients, the Club Med countries and developing nations, rather than the Commission itself. Several commissioners – especially those from the Protestant northern nations with clean hands – urged him to sack those without them. Fearing protests from Madrid and Paris, Santer decided it would have to be all or nothing.[18]

The Wise Men's 16 March report to Parliament was devastating. Focusing on selected areas of Commission activity – tourism, the Med programs, the Humanitarian Aid Office (ECHO), the "Leonardo da Vinci" vocational training program, nuclear safety, and the Commission Security Office – the sages found substantial evidence of administrative failure, financial irregularity, and nepotism everywhere they looked. Fully 31.5 million ecus of ECHO funds were "missing," and 317 million ecus of structural funds could not be accounted for because the Commission had lost the relevant records. The report grimly compiled a long list of derelictions:

a catalog of instances of fraudulently altered tender specifications and disregard for lower tenders, fictitious and double invoicing, and inflated fees; unjustified and illegal payments, nonexistent reports, simple fraud, clear cases of favoritism in employment, and evasion of tax and social security obligations [as well as] "ghost personnel," ... a low level of overall competence and a pervasive subculture of petty graft, favoritism, and criminality.[19]

It found particularly damning the fact that the Security Office had become a "state within a state ... a private club for former police officers from Brussels ... for whom special recruitment 'competitions' were arranged."[20] The Security Office even "wired" and "tailed" the Commission's own antifraud unit in order to block its investigations.[21]

The Wise Men were especially critical of Mme. Cresson's cronyism. Her lame reply was that it was "good for people, even if they were friends, to experience life in EU institutions."[22] She blamed the charges against her on an "Anglo-German conspiracy" and a "German-inspired bid to damage France," artlessly claiming that she was "guilty of no behavior that is not standard in the French administrative culture."[23] Cresson did not even try to defend her administration of the half-billion-dollar "Leonardo" youth program. Other commissioners also came under heavy fire: Monika Wulf-Mathies, the Green German commissioner in charge of regional policy; Manuel Marin of Spain, the vice-commissioner; and Joao de Deus Pinheiro of Portugal. Although none of them were charged with personal involvement in fraudulent activities, all bore responsibility for tolerating large-scale "instances of fraud, and irregularities or mismanagement in their services or areas of responsibility." The report criticized the functioning of the Commission up to the highest levels of command and could not "find anyone who has even the slightest sense of responsibility."[24] The entire Commission would have to go. Rather than wait for the European Parliament to exercise a "co-decision" power recently gained in the Amsterdam treaty – which in extreme cases enabled it to sack the Commission as a whole (though no single member of it) – Santer and his colleges resigned jointly. The censure might well not have passed. A first attempt of the Parliament to dump the Commission had failed in January, when the delegates from the Mediterranean unanimously opposed the measure "because there," complained Member of Parliament Ingo Friedrich, "a completely different idea of patronage (*Vetternwirtschaft*) prevailed."[25] Official acknowledgment of this north–south divide on public morals would be rare: the subject was taboo but at the same time, of course, an open secret.

What should be next "for the twenty-five officials who earn more than the president of the United States"? – so queried Barry James of the *International Herald Tribune*.[26] There were "no procedures for the resignation of all commissioners together." One official remarked: "We are into uncharted territory here .... We had to ensure that we acted with dignity."[27] The following day it was business as usual at the office. After the resignation of the most tainted members, a "caretaker cabinet" of the nonimplicated formed that would run the EU for the next six months. A special committee headed by Neil Kinnock, a British Labourite, was set up to fumigate the Commission. In April the vigorous and ambitious Romano Prodi was designated as Santer's successor, but an interregnum would ensue until his installation on 18 September. Several days later, the case against van Buitenen for "breaking confidentiality rules" was dropped, his lost pay reinstated, and only a "negative note" put into his files as sanction.

Though quasi-vindicated, van Buitenen can hardly be said to have won his one-man battle to save Europe's Guardians and integration vanguard. The Commission would not be reformed but, as a result of his disclosures, was perhaps fatally weakened. Prodi would wage a futile struggle to restore its prestige. Hopes encouraged by Agenda 2000 dissipated, and the issues it raised would remain unresolved. The attempt to join Enlargement and reform would be bucked up to the higher level of the European Council. The Commission, far from providing leadership, would strain its voice to shout over the din of contending, angry heads of state and government engaged in increasingly frantic and desperate bids to score points with electorates whose disaffection was becoming too troublesome to dismiss.

The Lisbon summit of June 2000 provided a welcome interlude of light relief from the problems facing the Commission. The agendas of such gatherings – which culminated the six-month rotating national presidencies, reflecting both the old and the new – included ongoing business as well as first-time items included to guide future developments. At the top of the Portuguese list of "old business" was the need to reform institutional structures – to reweight votes in the Council, rationalize Commission operations, and simplify voting procedures in preparation for Enlargement. Next came the perennial need to reform CAP, followed by consideration of regional policy. Attached to the latter was a potentially ugly new issue masked under the rubric of "immigration policy." In fact, it concerned how to restrict the fourth of the freedoms guaranteed in the Rome treaty – the movement of labor from the future accession states within the Community.[28]

Before the agenda would be fully deliberated, a "good governance" issue surfaced. It involved the de facto expulsion of a member-state because of its voting preferences. Austria was the EU's intended victim, but the EU would eventually become a victim of its own demagogy. By branding Austria with the scarlet letter ("A," appropriately) and trying to ride it out of the comity of respectable nations until its electorate recanted, the EU provided a demonstration of a willful, unprovoked, irresponsible, completely unnecessary, and illegal exercise of power that validated the criticisms of Euroskeptics and demonstrated the risks of investing any future, democratically irresponsible central authority with broad, ill-specified powers of enforcement and compliance. The message was particularly well understood in small states that could easily be pushed around. Substantial fallout resulted.

On 4 February 2000, the coalition that took office in Vienna included the far-right Freedom Party led by the telegenic young Jörg Haider. Haider did not, however, hold office in the new government and had even resigned as official party chief. Haider is hard to defend. His views reflect a half-curdled, sneering blend of *Heimatpolitik,* xenophobia, pointedly ill-concealed anti-Semitism, primitive economics, and an "up yours" antiestablishmentarianism. By flaunting his sympathies for various icons of right-wing German nationalism and by conspicuously refusing to disown Austria's Nazi past, Haider can only blame himself for being called a "post-fascist." He did not, in any case, seem to mind the association. The prominence of the junior demagogue owed less, however, to his unsavory ideas than to the fact that a vote for his wretched party was, and remains, the only feasible way an Austrian can register electoral protest to the stultifying and unfair system of *Proporz* – a mutually rewarding control over patronage – that has enabled the red–black cartel of the two dominant political parties to monopolize power since the war and to quietly suffocate any serious organized opposition.[29]

The EU decision to sanction Austria by "freezing all diplomatic contact" was unjustifiable on several grounds. Neofascists had participated in the Italian government without causing a ruckus or being censured; nor did anyone quibble about the participation in several member-state governments of former still-unreconstructed communists. The Austrian Prime Minister Wolfgang Schüssel was nontoxic and, upon taking office, specifically repudiated Austria's Nazi past in language stronger than used by any previous head of government. The new center-right coalition had, in fact, done nothing to cause offense. Most damning of all, the EU had no right or prior authority of any kind to interfere in the domestic politics of any state, member or otherwise. By asserting a power to determine "appropriate" electoral behavior and frustrate the outcome of national elections when it felt voters had made a choice outside an acceptable range of

European values, the EU set a precedent for drastic intervention into domestic politics. The EU was behaving, according to the *Economist,*

as though [it] were a single political space, as well as a single economic space. And in so doing, it is lurching, if prematurely and controversially, in what many Europeans consider a logical direction ... [toward] ... political harmonization .... They have set a precedent for drastic interference in a member's domestic policies.[30]

Austria was to serve as a guinea pig to test the waters of federalism.

Austria was also a convenient scapegoat for politicians trying to relieve pressure on the domestic front both in France and, more obviously, Belgium – like Austria, a small nation staggering under the weight of excess taxes and tightly controlled by political cartels.[31] Beset, like the Alpine republic, by historic regional and ideological divisions, Belgium also suffered chronically from the infamous language problem. The split between the Dutch-speaking Flemish majority and the Francophone minority had threatened to break up the country for over a generation. Many speculated that the government in power at the time the Haider crisis broke could be "the last chance" to hold the unhappy little nation together. Logrolling and pork-barrel politics served as the main bonds of Belgian unity. The separatist-nationalist *Vlaams Blok* (Flemish Block), a linear descendant of the collaborationist *Vlaams National Verbond* of the German occupation, had scored well in the previous election and was eager for a bust-up.

Heroic measures were needed in order to form the new government, the first one since the war in which the large Flemish-dominated Catholic party – now discredited by years of misrule – was absent. The new cabinet included no fewer than 58 ministers, secretaries of state, and special commissars, all of whom were entitled to six limousines apiece – each driven by a personal chauffeur paid $37,970 per year. The most serious office stacker was the Wallonian region, an industrial basket case. With a population of only 3 million, it had seventeen ministers including three for education. Headed by a well-oiled Socialist patronage machine operated by Elio di Rupo, Wallonia depended heavily upon handouts from the economically more dynamic Flemish-speaking regions.[32] Belgium faced more than structural problems, however. Public trust in government was virtually nonexistent.

The Belgian foreign minister, Louis Michel, drove the anti-Austrian bandwagon at the EU in a preposterous attempt to profile his thoroughly corrupt nation – one, incidentally, not remembered for humane and enlightened colonial administration in the Congo – as the conscience of Europe. To underscore the point, political spokespeople told Brussels taxi drivers and waiters to be rude to Austrian visitors, discouraged Austrian firms from participating in trade shows, and encouraged Belgian schoolchildren to cancel student exchanges and traditional ski holidays.[33] Michel's moralistic crusade was a real change of pace in a country that generally hit the news because of the breadth, depth, and lavishness of its political scandals.

The Dutroux affair would be the most serious in a succession of them. Others included the Brabant murders of twenty or so people, which took place in super-markets around the Brussels area and which were apparently acts of retaliation by a right-wing faction in the national gendarmerie; the unsolved murder in 1991 of the Liège socialist, Andre Cools, on the doorstep of his mistress, a case closed in 2001 owing to suicide of the leading suspect, a political rival and for-mer minister of education; the Agusta and Dessault affairs, routine political rake-offs from military contracts (which, however, brought about resignation of the former prime minister Willy Claes, who had also been secretary-general of NATO); the Inusop scandal, in which a public opinion research institute of the well-respected Free University of Brussels charged the government exorbitant fees for work never done; and another sordid affair in which two serving minis-ters, Vice-Premier Elio Di Rupo and Education Minister Jean-Pierre Grafe (both openly homosexual) were apprehended for having illicit relations with underage male prostitutes.[34] Such cases have rarely been settled in court. The Dutroux matter would be no exception.

Marc Dutroux was a well-known and convicted pedophile who raped children for several years in the 1980s but served time only briefly before being released with a $2,000 monthly disability pension. After his arrest in August 1996, Bel-gians recoiled in horror at the discovery of the bodies of four little girls at various homes he had owned. Two others, aged 12 and 14, were found half-starved and then freed from basement cells clinging to life. Two of the dead girls had been kidnaped fourteen months earlier, and the others were known to be missing. When questioned in 1995, Dutroux's wife admitted she had known that two small children were incarcerated in a home the couple owned in Charleroi but, though taking the trouble to feed dogs kept there, declared herself too "afraid" to help them. When eventually arrested five months later, Dutroux admitted to kidnapping but denied murdering the girls, whose whereabouts, he said, were unknown to him. The police detective who then investigated the Charleroi home later claimed that the cellar where their bodies were found was well concealed and that the childish voices he remembered hearing at the time appeared to come from somewhere outside the dwelling. He also confiscated films and a video but did not, he later testified, bother to look at them. Most of the stuff on film turned out to be ordinary kiddy porn, but the video actually showed Dutroux building the children's dungeon. At the time, the incompetence of the investigating offi-cers seemed staggering – if not beyond belief – and only confirmed suspicions of high-level collusion.[35]

The scope of the investigation widened, and public mistrust deepened, once it became clear that Dutroux – who in any case had no visible means for the purchase of his several homes – was no mere solo pervert but a well-established purveyor of little girls to a group of unsavory associates who arranged parties for wealthy patrons with a penchant for sadism and torture. In response to an Octo-ber 1996 plea from investigating magistrate Justice Robert Connerotte to victims of such practices to come forward and present evidence, a witness named Regina

Louf appeared. She would be the first of ten who could describe her harrowing experiences in sickening detail. Louf's story of the macabre sex-murder of one victim, Cristine van Hees, was later corroborated by police. The only public figure who had made any effort to advance the investigation, Connerotte, was thereupon dismissed on the flimsiest of pretexts. That did it. What happened next was nearly spontaneous. In response to a mother's appeal, 400,000 outraged Flemish and Francophone Belgian women – dressed in white, the color of purity – marched together on the Palais de Justice in Brussels to demand an end to chronic evasion, lies, and misgovernment. Belgium found itself in the throes of the biggest political crisis since World War II.[36]

The approval rating of the left-center government, triumphantly re-elected in May 1995, plummeted to 19 percent in December 1996. A respected poll indicated that only 15 percent of the electorate thought that the political, administrative, and judicial systems of the country were working well. More than three fourths of respondents attested to a complete lack of confidence that politicians would set things right, and nearly two thirds thought that "democracy was in danger."[37] With the government all but powerless, King Albert called for an investigation. Paddling desperately against the tide, Prime Minister Jean-Luc Dehaene promised to prosecute all adults identified in Dutroux's filthy videos to the fullest extent of the law, called for tough new laws protecting the rights of victims, announced an end to the political appointment of judges, and promised to open a new real-time missing persons bureau for children like the one recently organized in Washington, DC. His reeling government barely survived.[38] It would fall with the next scandal, one concerned with something nearly as disgusting as pedophilia to the food-conscious Belgians: tainted chickens.

The full truth of the Dutroux affair may never be uncovered. No fewer than twenty persons associated with it have died or been killed. Inaction has been the rule. The system is as suspect as ever. Albert II, King of the Belgians, is still obliged to issue public denials of alleged participation in pedophile sex orgies with Dutroux and his depraved accomplices.[39] Marc Dutroux himself remains in jail. By court order he cannot be tried for another year.[40]

The *Vlaams Blok* – similar in outlook to the Austrian Freedom Party and, until the "Haider crisis," the only Belgian party of any significance excluded from membership in the national political cartel – naturally stood to gain from scandals like the Dutroux affair. Foreign Minister Michel freely admitted that, in scapegoating Austria, he had "reacted quickly and violently" to prevent the right-wing, separatist Flemish party from forcing its way into the governing club. According to an *Economist* profile, Michel wanted to teach the "naive" and "simple" voters in the Alpine republic a lesson and thought it his right and duty to hector a fellow EU member, proclaiming "Austria is my business … France is my business! Great Britain is my business! I am a European!"[41]

The EU would have a price to pay when a loudmouthed politician like Michel kicked problems upstairs. The external threat rallied Austrian opinion behind its elected government. The representatives of other small EU countries quietly let it be known that the anti-Haider crusade was leaving a bad taste at home. Over the next several months, a half-chastened Prodi would have to grovel his way back to compromise with the embittered little country of ski instructors and eaters of strudel. Recognizing that the EU had made itself look stupid as well as reckless and tyrannical, the early 2000 EU presidency held by the Portuguese – historically unopposed to the Inquisition and the Atlantic slave trade – rapidly backpedaled from its prior denunciations of high-altitude fascism in landlocked rump republics and decided to conclude its brief period of Euro-prominence on a happier note.[42]

The result was that Lisbon became the "dot.com" summit – in the words of Tony Blair, the "least ... controversial he had attended since [becoming] prime minister three years" earlier.[43] The widely recognized need for détente felt in the aftermath of the Haider episode, along with the current wave of high-tech mania, set the scene for the unusual atmosphere prevailing in Portugal's lovely capital. It was evident going into the meeting that little headway could be made against the perennial problems of institutional reform, employment, and enlargement. As a result, Blair and Spanish Prime Minister Jose-Maria Aznar, an economic liberal, had what appeared to be a unique opportunity to revive the free-market agenda along the lines of the Single European Act. Europe was to adopt a precise timetable with the express purpose of overtaking A****** – the name was never mentioned in the official text – by 2010 in the field of high technology.

The intent behind the agenda was clearly to "move the focus of the EU away from the old industrial models of social control and *dirigisme* toward the more market-friendly Anglo-Saxon ... liberalized and deregulated new economy."[44] Although it was easy to ridicule the dot.com agenda as "politics by announcement," it did complement major programs under way, especially within the internal market directorate headed by Frits Bolkestein. Twenty or so of the fifty-plus recommendations adopted at the summit dealt directly or indirectly with the high-tech field and were at the core of the program, but others touched on financial markets as well as deregulation. One follow-up to the Lisbon strategy was the preparation of a new e-commerce directive, another the intensification of the attempt to deregulate energy and communications markets, a third the launching of a campaign to set pension reform in motion. These goals called for an Action Plan to be implemented by 2005, according to Bolkestein. Somehow the subject was dropped amidst the Austrian recriminations and in the run-up to the Nice summit.

Almost nothing was said about the liberalization agenda at the Stockholm summit two years later, in Spring 2002, which was to have measured progress toward the Lisbon goals. A row did take place at the Swedish capital, however, over the foot-dragging refusal of the French to allow foreign interests to compete with *Electricité de France* on domestic energy markets, a right reciprocated by all other member-nations – but Chancellor Schröder caved in and nothing was done. Silence prevailed concerning dot.com Europe.[45] In fact, the timing of the Lisbon summit could hardly have been worse. The NASDAQ tech index, which hit an all-time high of 5132.5 on 10 March 2000, fell to 3409 by 1 June and from there plummeted to 2470 by the end of the year. The bubble had burst and, after the lapse of about a year, hope faded that a revolutionary "new economy" was just around the corner. The dot.com summit turned out to be a case of too little and too late.

Even more troubling in the future would be those matters left undone during the Portuguese presidency of early 2000. The long list included reducing the size of the Commission; re-allocating Council votes; and broadening the use of qualified majority voting, "where proper negotiations have not yet begun." "Doubt and equivocation" also surrounded discussions on Enlargement. Several members revealed "mixed feelings" about "immigration," a euphemism for the free movement of labor from eastern Europe, and the Club Med nations indicated a persistent reluctance to share the Brussels cornucopia with their poor central European neighbors. Although bold new federalist ideas were being floated, "the discrepancy between aspiration and reality" had accentuated starkly over the first six months of the year. Due to begin in July, the French presidency was, according to the journalist Peter Hort, "already groaning under the growing burden of aspirations"; he warned that it would have to concentrate on reforming the EU's governance machinery lest "the 1997 Amsterdam debacle [be] repeated at Nice."[46]

PRODI, NICE, AND THE BREAKDOWN OF GOVERNANCE

Where, many asked, was President Prodi amidst the confusion?[47] Having fumbled the Austrian affair badly, Prodi was a mere shadow at Lisbon in spite of his commitment to economic reform. By then well into the first year of his presidency, he habitually shrugged off criticism with the self-deprecating remark that, like a diesel motor, he was slow to start but reliable over the long haul. Romano Prodi had one of the most remarkable backgrounds of anyone ever to serve as president of the European Commission. A professor of industrial organization at the University of Bologna and with a distinguished professional career that included associations with the departments of economics at Harvard and Stanford, he was the rare academic who had a chance to practice what he preached. After serving as minister of industry in 1981, Prodi became chairman of the vast government holding company, the Institute for Industrial Reconstruction (IRI), from 1982 to 1989 and then later from 1993 to 1994. In the course of reorganizing the Mussolini-era conglomerate, he turned a $2 billion (annually) loss maker into a company making $760 million in profit.

A devout Catholic and a member of the DC party with no previous experience in electoral politics, Prodi became a founding member of the center-left Olive Tree coalition in 1995 and entered parliament. Italian prime minister from 1996 to 1998, he introduced massive public-sector cuts and privatizations in order to beat the odds against Italian qualification for the European Monetary Union. The austerity measures contributed to a sharp rise in unemployment that eventually brought about the fall of his government. Not even a whiff of scandal ever touched *il professore,* an outwardly modest man whose integrity was above re-proach and whose hands were squeaky clean. Utterly without pretense, Prodi rode a bicycle, was devoted to his wife and two children, and even appeared to enjoy being called "old sausage face." He happily admitted "I am from Emilia-Romania. I am fat. Therefore I am an optimist."[48] It has been said of Prodi that he lacks charisma, a situation that – under the right circumstances, given his ob-vious decency and honesty – might have disarmed his many opponents and won over the public. The modesty card was a long shot but still perhaps the best chance he had to save his presidency. It would be downhill all the way.

Prodi's views were conventional, uncontroversial, and by no means out of line with the traditions of the Commission.[49] He was a federalist in the manner of Altiero Spinelli, a believer in the need for a constitutional government for Eu-rope. As a trained economist, Prodi understood what was necessary to make markets work properly.[50] His preferences were to eliminate the CAP, do away with industrial policy in its various guises, proceed more rapidly with the single market program, and make labor markets more flexible.[51] At the same time, as a "political realist" Prodi was loath to rush things "because we have not yet built a common philosophy [and] lack the strength of the United States."[52] Prodi sup-ported the EMU as a symbol of unity, not because of its purportedly beneficial economic effects. He knew that the "the first task is to reform the Commission" in order to make Enlargement possible before he left office in 2005. The in-coming Commission president also fully understood that the power of his office rested on the support of the Franco-German condominium and that, without it, he could do little. Finally, he recognized that he had to fight for his turf or risk becoming a pawn of the member-states.[53]

Prodi arrived like a White Knight and promised "cultural revolution." Endors-ing him unanimously, the European Council gave him a strong mandate both to clean up Commission sleaze and to rationalize, reform, and rejuvenate the administration.[54] Greeted like a "providential figure" and heralded in the press as the "First Prime Minister of Europe" when installed in office six months later, Prodi's presidency faltered almost from the outset.[55] He could not, as promised, choose the new commissioners but, as customary, had to accept member-state nominations as doled out among them according to their own rules. Pascal Lamy, the new trade commissioner, had been Delors's former "Exocet"; Guenter Ver-heugen, the Enlargement commissioner, had served as Schröder's "strong right arm"; Neil Kinnock, the corruption cop, ran his own show. These and other fig-ures, such as Mario Monti (competition commissioner) and the internal market chief Frits Bolkestein, would become individual powers in their own right rather than as members of a Prodi team.[56] Although Prodi wrested a promise from the commissioners to respect his authority to order individual dismissals, he could never exercise it.[57] The new Commission president did manage to replace the DG nomenclature for the branches of the Commission bureaucracy with functional names, but internal administrative reform effectively ended there. Stalling, foot-dragging, and outright disloyalty were much in evidence. Hostile press reports based on leaks abounded, as did gripes about his preference for "indirect rule," inattention to administrative detail, and disinterest in "working the system." The slayer of the IRI dragon would never be master of his own lair.[58]

By spring, Prodi's Commission was "floundering in a sea of troubles." Intrigue was rife, and plots were allegedly being hatched to dethrone him.[59] The media was unhappy and the German press unsparing in its attacks – perhaps because, according to an official of the Konrad Adenauer Foundation, "Germans feel that Germany is losing ground in the European Commission."[60] Anti-Prodi sentiment was not restricted to Germany. Even the journeyman EU-watcher Lionel Barber, writing in the official publication of the Commission's Washington office, noted condescendingly that Prodi had "found it hard to adjust to life in Brussels" and disparaged him as "a man of grand visions and flowing rhetoric ... who has had a habit of launching high-profile initiatives without assuring the full backing of the fifteen EU states ... and has had to retreat, lessening his authority."[61]

And then there was what George Bush, Sr., called "the vision thing" – or, more specifically, Prodi's utter lack of one. Europhiles found the situation galling. "Europe," railed Nikolaus Blome in *Die Welt,*

is embarking upon the greatest venture of recent decades – but no one is holding his breath. Expansion to the east, common army, internal reorganization, forever new competencies, guarantees of basic rights, and after that even a constitution: The European Union is re-inventing itself for the twenty-first century, but ... [do] voters yet know why or wherefore? The elites in the national capitals say that Europe will not "sell" to the public, but in truth they have never made the effort. They still advance as always. The fifteen member-states arrange *faits accomplis,* out of the limelight, then justify them after the fact, hewing to the line until the goal is reached. Such was the approach taken with the euro, and it worked. But it will not succeed again. Europe must be sold to the public, and Brussels must present itself like a national government, if it is to engage the people. That is the job of those who want to do something with power.[62]

Yet according to the French quotidian *Le Tribun,* Prodi was "already on the verge of disgrace. The advocates of the poor devil have run out of pleas, and critics are coming to regret the absence of Jacques Santer."[63]

In a bold attempt to set things right, Prodi delivered to the opening session of the European Parliament on 15 February 2000 a major speech in which he presented his proposals for dealing with the chief problems facing the Commission. The result was a serious embarrassment.[64] Notwithstanding his many virtues and accomplishments, this president of the Commission obviously lacked fresh ideas. The speech consisted of a winding string of banalities, clichés, and bromides interrupted only by bursts of empty rhetoric, restatements of the obvious, and outpourings of vapid techno-administrative jargon that visibly wearied an audience already suffering from chronic Euro-blather overload. It was as if he had tried to out-Delors Delors. The Commission president candidly admitted that the EU faced a big problem: "Europe's citizens are disenchanted and anxious ...

have lost faith in European institutions ... and are losing patience with our slow rate of progress in tackling unemployment" as well as "divided between hope and fear" on the Enlargement question.[65] What was to be done apart from – as Prodi recited the litany – restoring economic growth, providing security, giving Europe a sense of meaning and purpose, and projecting its "model of society into the wider world"?

Generalities would have to serve as answers. Although Prodi emphasized that Europe needed "a new, more democratic form of partnership between ... different levels of governance," he offered no specific suggestions and, in lieu of them, merely implored his audience "to radically rethink the way we do Europe. To reshape Europe. To devise a completely new form of governance for the world of tomorrow!"[66] Toward that end, he proposed the standard academic nostrum of a "no-holds-barred debate on [the] institutional question with all the players involved" and reminded his audience, as if for the first time discovering the fact, that "actions speak louder than words!" How was one to close the gap – now noticeably widened by his speech – between "rhetoric and reality in Europe," he wondered out loud.

As the answer to the question of the day was delivered from the speaker's chair, the sense of letdown must surely have been audible. There was not even the glimmer in Prodi's words of a new architecture but only the prospect of building Europe by screwdriver. The remedies were all purely technical. The Commission would "review its priorities and focus on its core business, shift from a procedure-oriented organization to a policy-oriented one, [and] concentrate on its real job and do it efficiently and well."[67] Structural reform, he announced with great gusto to his fidgeting audience, "is not an option but a necessity!" And if that applause line failed to raise the flagging spirits of the Euro-faithful, he promised still more: tidy up the Balkans; draft a charter of fundamental rights ("and keep a close watch on the situation in Austria!"); and "restore full employment," a job that he promised would be manfully tackled at the forthcoming Lisbon summit. In spite of present troubles, he concluded (for the benefit of those not already deep in slumber) on a note of hope – as it turns out, false hope: "The economic outlook is good, and the unique combination of sustained growth, the information society revolution, and the expanding European market offers us the 'virtuous circle' we need."[68] Dot-commers to the rescue!

Verdicts on Prodi's leadership during his first year in office were devastating, not least because the assemblage of commissioners, taken as a whole, had turned out to be perhaps the best ever.[69] Pascal Lamy, Frits Bolkestein, Mario Monti, Franz Fischler (agriculture), Günter Verheugen, and Chris Patten (foreign affairs) had all for varied reasons received glowing marks from the press as forceful, independent, and effective representatives of their offices. But Prodi's ratings were even lower than Santer's.[70] The "once jovial Italian," as *Die Welt* put unkindly, "has lost his smile."[71] Although Kinnock's janitorial team continued to roam with soap bucket and scrub brush in search of sleaze to clean up, the opportunity to reform the Commission, scant though it may have been, had been lost.

The Commission seemed even to have forgotten its mission. "Brussels," opined Hajo Friedrich of the *Frankfurter Allgemeine Zeitung,*

– or rather the Commission – is increasingly becoming a commonplace term of abuse across Europe, not only as it once was, on the street, but also among leading politicians and businessmen. Why do we need the Commission at all? Despite the disclosure of abuses and scandals, this question would have caused bewilderment a year ago. Now even long-serving EU officials and diplomats, disappointed by Mr. Prodi, would not be shocked by such questions .... In the policy visions of some national presidents and foreign ministers, it no longer has a role at all as a desirable or reformable institution.[72]

The 15 September 2000 summary of the Commission's first year of activity was very thin gruel. The Guardians could legitimately take some credit for keeping Enlargement on track, but the four other claims made on their behalf were weak. An internal reform effort had been launched, but results were not yet forthcoming. The attempt to widen the agenda of the coming intergovernmental conference would mean little if agreement could not be reached. The Commission rightly "identified food safety as one of the keys to restoring the popular confidence in the EU," but it required little insight to reach this conclusion amidst the panic over mad cow disease then sweeping over Europe. The claim that the Austrian policy was a success will not withstand even cursory examination. Left unmentioned in the upbeat report was the steady deterioration throughout the year in the relationship between the Commission and the member-states, France and Germany in particular.[73] Both German Foreign Minister Josef ("Joschka") Fischer and French President Jacques Chirac had presented constitutional drafts for the future government of Europe by early summer. In each of them, the Commission was reduced to a secretariat.

On 3 October, Prodi hit back in a forceful speech to the European Parliament that riveted his audience for precisely twenty-seven minutes and twenty-one seconds. Castigating the member-governments for trying to strip the Commission of its initiative powers, Prodi launched a flat-out attack on the intergovernmentalism that had enabled the states to bypass the Commission and arrange things between themselves. The practice, he warned, points

to only two possible outcomes, both of them undesirable. Either it will turn the Community into an international talking shop incapable of producing a real pooling of sovereignty around the common interest, or it will deceive people by constantly creating new bodies which are exempt from any form of democratic scrutiny – a real government of bureaucrats.[74]

Coming from the Commission, this final remark surely was surely a crowning insult.

Prodi demanded not only new powers for the Parliament ("democracy at every level") but also a new Commission "competence" as economic advisor to the central bank. Moreover, he specifically objected to efforts by the Council of Ministers to create a new office to perform that function – even though, according to the Maastricht treaty, the power to set exchange-rate policy ultimately

belonged to the Council. Prodi warned in conclusion that if "the extension of
the intergovernmental model corrupts the judicial and institutional mechanisms
of the Community ... [then] the achievements of the single market, the common policies, the solidarity mechanisms, and the strength Europe exercises by
speaking with a single voice will be in vain."[75] Prodi then set the Belgian former
commissioner Jean-Luc Dehaene to work on a draft of a constitution for a federal Europe with a reinforced Commission as its centerpiece, thereby enraging
the British, French, and Germans equally.[76]

Prodi had thus begun to set the stage for a showdown at the Nice summit
planned for December 2000.[77] On 11 November he went further, warning the
European Parliament that it had a "last chance" to make necessary reforms before
Enlargement took place. Immediately required, he enumerated, were a common
defense policy, majority voting for virtually all areas of EU activity, and a reduction of large-country votes in the Council of Ministers. This was close to an outright declaration of war. As the December event approached, Prodi maneuvered
into position. On 21 November he told Chancellor Schröder in no uncertain
terms that he would rally the small nations against any curtailment in Commission power that either Germany or France might be seeking.[78] On 1 December
he warned that the member-states had to give up the national veto or no future
progress could be made in the areas of taxation, social security, border controls,
or external trade – not to mention the still greater issue of Enlargement. "The
mathematics are beyond doubt," he argued, and the conclusion was inescapable
that "in a union of twenty-seven or more member-states, the unanimity requirement will quite simply paralyze progress in every area where it is maintained."[79]
Painfully aware that each big member-state insisted on retaining the veto in one
or more areas, he braced himself for confrontation. Careful preparation, the
ex-economist figured, would raise his chances of success to fifty–fifty.

But Ol' Sausage Face would never get a chance to unholster his pistol. The
shootout with the member-states did not take place. Instead, the once self-
described happy fat man from Emilia-Romagna found himself caught in a deaf-
ening cannonade between them. For four days they would bombard each other
unrelentingly around the clock using a vast stock of shells of various caliber and
explosive configuration, fired from different angles, lofted at high trajectories or
aimed flat and directly at the target, often apparently timed so that two or more
bursts would hit simultaneously – all for what, from the standpoint of a frightened bystander like the Commission president, must have seemed to no apparent
purpose. Impressions can mislead. The negotiators knew what they were doing.
The violence Prodi witnessed involved the playing out of a mutually destructive
bargaining process of such intricacy and complexity that – in order to remain in
the game – the principals had to be armed with high-speed computers, spread-
sheets, and a working knowledge of advanced statistics.

On the agenda were the "leftovers from Amsterdam," that is, the adjustment
of community institutions needed to accommodate the twelve candidate countries slated to enter the Union after Enlargement: reconfiguration of the European Commission; reweighting of votes at EU ministerial meetings; adoption

of new rules for qualified majority voting; and altering representation in the European Parliament.[80] The intense, nasty (sometimes even bitchy), and seemingly endless haggling over the Amsterdam "leftovers" crowded other important subjects off the agenda. At issue was the allocation of national power within Community institutions rather than strengthening them, a subject in which only the Commission was interested. The battle between "functionalists" and intergovernmentalists, between Commission and Council, had in fact been decided weeks before the summit opened. Except when being deliberately slighted by President Chirac, Prodi was generally ignored.[81]

The theoretical purpose of the negotiations was to make intergovernmentalism function properly under the new conditions of Enlargement. The practical issue was whether it could be revived and made to work at all. The Germans, who stood to gain the most by the inclusion of nations from eastern Europe, also had the most to lose by being stubborn. Their chief interest was to provide appropriate representation on the Council for the new entrants without sacrificing the traditional (though no longer vital) "French connection" while also making it difficult for any group of nations to pass measures that it opposed. The French, divided by the awkward Chirac (right-center)–Jospin (socialist) "condominium" and on the defensive, insisted on maintaining formal equality (parity in the Council) with the Germans and tried to secure a new Mediterranean alliance in order to offset the advantages accruing to their "partner" from eastern expansion. Whereas Prime Minister Jospin concealed his integration views behind the slogan "No to No!" for electoral reasons, President Chirac – the figure officially responsible for foreign policy – was distinctly Gaullist in outlook. His preference was for a "Europe of United States" rather than a "United States of Europe." The French thus preferred voting arrangements favoring the representation of the nation-state over that of population size as well as the preservation of the status quo whenever possible.

The British consistently opposed the "deepening" of the Community, wanted to retain veto power in critical policy areas, and sought to prevent the development of central institutions and the extension of competencies other than those required to implement the Single European Act. They had to remain sufficiently "in the game" to participate in issue-specific coalitions, reject unwanted initiatives, solve real problems expeditiously, and retain the wherewithal for trade-offs. The weighting of votes was less important to Britain than either Germany or France. The Spanish were above all intent upon preserving the right to veto any reduction in regional aid and upholding their standing as one of the Big Five, a policy that created a conflict of interest with Poland and its German electoral ally. Since the accommodation of new voting members almost necessarily had to come at the expense of the overweighted smaller nations, they found themselves on the defensive.

The necessary pain of re-allocating voting power, a zero-sum game, was not mitigated by the Commission's inability to serve as "honest broker." As president of the Council, Chirac chaired the meetings and was universally rebuked for high-handedness and magisterial disregard for non-French interests. His planned diplomatic triumph turned into a public relations disaster. The smudge stuck to almost everyone. The normally popular Blair, roundly scolded for his carping negativism, left the final session with a scowl.[82] Schröder seems to have come out the least scathed among the heavy hitters. He made what seemed like the only gracious concession of the conference, ceding parity with France in the Council.[83]

The small countries were exceptionally bitter. The Portuguese delegate called the Nice document "a profoundly negative treaty that cannot be accepted. It hands power to the big countries."[84] Elmar Brok – representing the Parliament, which was treated like a dustbin for cast-off problems – was little happier: "Individual interests ruled the day, and the winners were those able to trample all the others under foot. They were feted when they got home."[85] Prime Minister Jean-Claude Juncker of Luxembourg, putting the matter elegantly, observed "it's rare that I've had such a strong feeling that Europe is a fragile enterprise."[86] The *Nouvel Observateur* was less subtle: "The delegates all went to the Cote d'Azur not in order to make a baby but to despoil a corpse. Weakened by the departure of Jacques Delors ... Europe has lost all sense of direction. The meetings of the Council ... increasingly resemble the haggling of rug merchants."[87]

The only "hero" of the wretched spectacle was Guy Verhofstadt, the prime minister of Belgium – the most pro-European of member-states because it was the one that stood to lose the most by reduction or removal of the EU *apparat*. Verhofstadt made the concession that finally ended the proceedings. After hours of wearying debate that threatened to undo the elaborate structure of trade-offs worked out inch by inch over four miserable days, Verhofstadt finally gave in on the Belgian demand to preserve parity on the Council with the much larger Netherlands. In return, every other future summit would take place in the Belgian capital instead of that of the host country. The Brussels hoteliers were pleased. Without the last-hour deal, there would have been no treaty at all. In the words of Joachim Fritz-Vannahme of *Die Zeit,* Verhofstadt

has governed his country for a year and a half his own way and energetically, with great popular approval. He owed his victory to scandals, the rage over the child-rapist Dutroux and the dioxin [chicken feed] crisis. The Belgians are sick of the clientage of the Socialists and the Christian Democrats. The Flemish premier works with a six-party coalition – with Liberals, Socialists and Greens from Flanders and Wallonia. He is thus completely at home with what happened at Nice – all the spitefulness, petty selfishness and jostling of big interests, conducted in different languages, justified by iron-clad senses of identity.[88]

Would the EU become another Belgium? The day of the intergovernmental conference, by unanimous agreement of those who had survived nearly six days of it, had come to an end. Another debacle like Nice, or so it seemed in the aftermath, would leave the Union in tatters.

What, precisely, did the conference formally accomplish? The following description of the negotiating issues will read like the text of instructions written for the assembly of a grass-catching bag made to fit the specifications of a Japanese-manufactured lawnmower: it will be necessarily technical and un-avoidably dry. The Commission was, first of all, a fairly simple matter for negotiators to deal with. Each country had the privilege of naming one com-missioner, but the Big Five (France, Britain, Italy, Spain, and Germany) were entitled to two. It was agreed that each of the large nations would relinquish one of its appointments until 2005, when Enlargement to a union of 27 nations was scheduled for completion. The number of commissioners would then be reduced to twenty and be assigned on a rotating basis. The obvious disadvan-tage of the arrangement is that an already swollen *apparat* would expand still further.[89]

The weighting of votes in the Council was a much more complicated and con-tentious matter. Under the existing system, the four largest countries (Germany, Britain, France, and Italy) had ten votes each; Luxembourg, by far the small-est, had two votes – was grossly overweighted to prevent the large nations from dominating the small ones. After expansion, however, such a bias would enable the small nations to outvote Germany, with many more citizens than all of them put together. The compromise actually struck would better reflect the distribu-tion of the population, albeit with the proviso – insisted upon by France, and graciously conceded by Germany – that parity be preserved between the two. In return, Germany received additional votes in the Parliament. Qualified majority Council voting was extended to cover thirty policy areas, with the veto still ap-plying in those important to individual large big countries: the British insisted upon retaining veto power for taxation and social legislation, the Germans for immigration policy, the French for protection of national cultures, and the Span-ish for regional aid.[90]

Contrary to the "never again" threats made in disgust at the end of the Nice conference, the story would go on: the treaty, once ratified, would provide an "historical space-holder" until the next IGC planned for 2004. Nice at least did not derail Enlargement; the admission date for the first tranche of candidates remained 2004. If Nice was a triumph for eastern Europe, it was a disaster for the Commission. Guardian leadership clearly belonged to the past. Thus the German historian and press commentator Arnulf Baring posed the rhetorical question:

Should we really let ourselves be led around on many issues by an uncontrollable EU-bureaucracy, even though we Europeans are in many respects closer to the matter [at] hand, each on his own territory, as well as much more knowledgeable, and therefore able to act more effectively? What necessity, what justification is there for Brussels to in-tervene, whenever it chooses, into everything concerning the lives of its member-states, which, as always, are democracies and chiefly responsible for maintaining the law, public welfare, the tax system, culture, education, security and defense?

As Prodi had glumly conceded, "We have lost the thread .... The subtle proto-cols and the more and more complex formulae cannot conceal our differences."[91]

Both parties denied the fact, but the Franco-German relationship also reached a "notional turning point" at Nice. Already fraying, it would now have to be rewoven. Seven years had passed since the last important Franco-German integration initiative. The mistrust encountered by German constitutional proposals, French reticence on "Europe," and the inroads of Blair's opportunistic diplomacy all indicated that the marriage was all but over. After Nice, divorce would be openly discussed.[92] Notwithstanding Chancellor Schröder's graceful concession to the French on parity in the Council, neither Germany nor any other member-state accepted France's claim for permanent, historically consecrated preference. An assignment of additional parliamentary seats to Germany sent a subtle but powerful signal that the terms of the old partnership could no longer be maintained and that France's days as co-director of Europe were numbered.[93]

Chirac's pomposity and the sumptuousness of his staging ill concealed the truth at Nice that a weakening France had little to offer the other member-states, be it vision or hard cash. "Launched on a wave of national self-confidence," commented a British journalist, "France's six months at Europe's helm are ending in bathos as critics conclude that the country's leaders have no coherent vision about the continent's future."[94] *Libération* described the summit as "a political fiasco."[95] Policy responsibility was divided between the Euro-vague premier, Lionel Jospin, and the more easily profiled Gaullist president, Jacques Chirac. In summer 2002, Chirac achieved instant notoriety by proposing a European constitution that distinguished invidiously between a directing "pioneer group" and the others. All the member-states with the exception of Germany and Belgium rejected the "infamous document" out of hand. Jospin also distanced himself from it, and it was withdrawn from discussion.[96]

The Chirac proposal bears the characteristic imprint of the French right: a preference for a narrow union of European states without central direction and run by the states on the basis of military strength, where France was the only nuclear power. Britain was either left out or sidelined in such schemes. The document harks back to de Gaulle's various Fouchet Plans of the early 1960s and also resembles that of Chirac's former prime minister, Alain Juppé, whose own (more detailed) constitutional model eliminates the Commission and specifies the obligations of a future union to the member-states. M. Chirac is also close personally and intellectually to Jerôme Monod, whose recent "Manifesto for a Sovereign Europe" recommends replacing the EU with a "Sovereign Union of Europe's Republics and Monarchies" based on "historic nations." It would limit a future EU to a "critical mass" of activities. If there is little new about Chirac's plans, there is also little common ground between them and earlier German proposals like those of the Christian Democratic Union under Kohl (written by Karl Lamers and Wolfgang Schäuble) or those subsequently drafted in 2000 and 2001 by Foreign Minister Fischer and Chancellor Schröder for a federal democracy.[97] Jacques Juilliard of *Nouvel Observateur* concluded that, "despite the vague professions of goodwill, the secret model of Chirac and Jospin is Margaret Thatcher."[98]

This was surely taking matters too far. Prime Minister Blair may have found Nice to be a grueling ordeal, but for the United Kingdom it must be reckoned a success. Blair managed to retain the right to veto social and fiscal policy and to gain recognition of the nonbinding character of the so-called Charter of Fundamental Rights, which had been cobbled together after the Santer cabinet's disgraceful exit. The British preferred weakening the Commission. The fraying Franco-German bond opened the politics of the community to practical, limited type of working arrangements. A "space-holding" treaty was needed precisely to stave off "deepening" until the entrance of five to ten new members would choke off any such policy in the foreseeable future, increase the likelihood of "repatriating" CAP, and introduce an eventual "de-privileging" or phase-out of preferential arrangements. Sensible progress could then resume along evolutionary institutionalist lines. Time, numbers, and gridlock worked in Britain's favor. The only real alternative to the U.K. approach was the remote one of a liberal federalist Europe that would be both democratic and German-led.

Chances for progress of any kind seemed slim after Nice. The worst casualty of the botched summit was the intergovernmental approach to the integration process. Prodi could not be blamed; the fault lay with the member-states themselves. The fact could hardly be kept secret. The German press in this case provides a fairly representative sample of public reaction to Nice. Forwards, sideways, and from top to bottom, the criticism was relentless. The editorialist for the *Kölnische Rundschau* complained angrily that

old rivalries broke out in the struggle for power and influence. The negotiations got stuck in a struggle for prestige, lacking in common sense. In the daily political fracas it makes little difference whether or not a state has an extra vote in the Council of Ministers. Such jealous rivalries demonstrate how little heart the leading politicians have for Europe.

The *Handelsblatt* called the treaty "unworkable"; the *Berliner Kurier* characterized it "pettifogging, and hardly evidence of vision in the House of Europe"; and, in an odd mixed metaphor, the *Badische Neuesten Nachrichten* griped that the statesmen had produced "a shoddy piece of knitting, within a hand's breadth of going under." The *Frankfurter Rundschau* observed trenchantly that, "instead of dealing with strategically important subjects like trade, taxes, political asylum and immigration, and the shift to majority voting, the summit got lost in trivial details [*Petitessen*], out of which came sloppy compromises."[99]

The real blame for the Nice debacle rests less with shortcomings of the participants, who were caught in a no-win situation, than with the institutional monstrosity that the European Union had become. According to journalist Klaus-Dieter Frankenberger, "it signals the end of making European treaties that was occasionally characterized by political autism, that was ineffective, time-consuming and satisfactory," but which also worked. The process of "building Europe" intergovernmentally in the German manner can (in theory) be restarted at any time, but in order to get anywhere it will have to (1) occur outside the EU framework and (2) be democratic, expressing the wills of Europe's peoples rather than the views of their self-appointed spokesmen.[100]

Brussels did not catch on even after the Irish referendum. No one expected any member-state to reject the Nice treaty, in spite of its obvious flaws. The price to be paid for blocking Enlargement was simply thought to be way too high. Whatever the treaty's shortcomings, it was counted upon to produce a textbook example of *engrenage*. That Ireland – the single country required to ratify the treaty by referendum rather than by legislative majority – would vote down the treaty was not seriously considered. Why should the Irish behave like Danes? They had arguably benefited proportionally more than any other member-state and were, according to the polls, the most pro-European among them. Once again, the political establishment and the church – as well as the rich, the well-born and the able – strongly endorsed a "yes" vote. The opposition, as in Denmark, was disorganized: a poor, unfocused, odd coalition of greens, pacifists, IRA nationalists, archconservative Catholics, and free marketers. It nevertheless captured 54 percent of the (low-turnout) vote. Apparently even the Irish were tired of being told how to conduct their affairs by Brussels. But who cared a hoot about what they thought? Guenter Verheugen, the enlargement commissioner, said that "such a referendum in one country cannot block the biggest and most important project for the political and economic future of Europe."[101] Forget the rules! The EU simply disregarded the popular vote and proceeded without a treaty. In October 2002, after months of threats and cajolement from Europe's capital city and intense campaigning by both main political parties, the chastened Irish electorate approved the Nice document by a respectable margin.

PLANS, PROJECTS, AND THE CONVENTION ON THE FUTURE OF EUROPE

Planning for the Convention on the Future of Europe got under way shortly after the *Walpurgisnächte* at Nice. A flagrant example of *Flucht nach Vorne,* the convocation was a predictable sequel to the less spectacular gathering that convened in 2000 in order to slap together a Charter of Fundamental Rights as a confidence builder after the disgrace of the Santer Commission.[102] The Charter was endorsed at Nice but, under British pressure, only on a "nonbinding" basis. The banal document is now nearly forgotten.[103] Whatever emerges from the Euro-eloquence of the constitutional *grand projet* under way since 28 February 2002 will likely provide a fittingly undistinguished sequel.

Heralded by its promoters and planners as a parallel to the American gathering of 1787, the Convention on the Future of Europe now meeting in Brussels is nothing of the kind.[104] The official leading the charge on behalf of the Commission, Michel Barnier, misrepresents the conclave by suggesting that "the only [unresolved] question is whether the EU should be a federal state in the conventional sense, modeled on Germany or the United States, or whether it should pursue the end of political union through other means."[105] Little more than a fix-up job, the "Future of Europe" get-together differs in crucial respects from the American Constitutional Convention. The Philadelphia delegates represented sovereign states and were responsible to the citizens of those states, the people whose rights were held to be inviolate by natural law. The political system they created emerged from open debate between independent statesman-scholars elected or democratically appointed to represent them. The U.S. Constitution rests upon the application of a novel system of checks and balances that resulted from open debate at the convention and requires the consent of the states and their citizens, who retained the power to withdraw it. The Euro-conclave does not involve any such fresh start. Discussion takes place only within the parameters of nonrepresentative EU institutions, whose interests the delegates are both dependent upon and pledged to uphold. The elimination of Community institutions is not on the table. There is no Euro-analogue to the antifederalists of Philadelphia, and the existence of any substantial opposition party or parties is ruled out. The Brussels convention is an intramural affair run largely by old Community warhorses completely out of touch with the European public.

The real purposes of the Euro-delegates are to modify EU institutions in order to better accommodate the various interests in play, strengthen public loyalties, and display evidence of concern about the "democratic deficit." Overriding the principle of self-determination, the delegates can act merely as agents of a process that – although draped in the trappings of representative institutions and procedures – is initiated, directed, and controlled from on high. The Commission point man at the convention, Michael Barnier, thus finds it necessary to

maintain and carefully reform the methods we have followed to date, arrive at truly convergent economic policies, a harmonization of taxation and financial policy, more intensive cooperation in the Euro-zone, and common foreign and defense policies [since] *Gemeinschaftsmethoden* [are] the heart, method, motor of integration.

The EU Commission must, he adds, "preserve its right of initiative, but in the future enjoy more legitimacy in the eyes of its citizens."[106] Distilled and unrepentant monnetism is the governing philosophy at the Convention on the Future of Europe.

The former competition commissioner, Peter Sutherland, pointed out the folly of such a constitutional exercise in the 1977 William Rhys Williams Memorial Lecture. Monnet, he observed, "was not much concerned with public support or understanding" and never said "where he [thought] the journey would ultimately end." Europe cannot just "tinker," Sutherland said, if it is to meet the future challenge of Enlargement; should cease trying to "build Europe by stealth"; and should cure itself of the bad habits of producing "unintelligible texts" and "obfuscating." Such abuses have led, he added, to the result that, "whenever electorates of the member states are required actually to vote, they have shown that the generalized goodwill and enthusiasm displayed by the Eurobarometer surveys cannot be translated into support for the European Union." Sutherland warned that Maastricht treaty ratification shifted "debate over the governance of Europe, [which was formerly] the exclusive domain of national governments, European institutions and academics, to the wider public, national parliaments, constitutional courts, and political parties." Indirect legitimacy could no longer

maintain loyalties to the new Europe, he concluded, but will require the development of a still absent sense of "shared identity."[107]

The Commission first proposed the constitutional convention as a riposte to
a new German policy activism.[108] Signaling the change was Foreign Minister
Josef ("Joschka") Fischer's "private and personal" Humboldt University speech
of May 2000, "From Confederacy to Federation: A Comment on the European
Finality."[109] Supposedly launched only to stimulate discussion of EU reform, the
"democratic deficit," and federalism, the proposal of the head-stomping former
radical student leader indeed forced the pace. The elegant Chirac soon entered
the Euro-vision contest, then the quick-thinking Blair, followed by a long string
of minor artists and performers like the Belgian Verhofstadt and Toomas Ilves,
the Estonian foreign minister. A now gray-haired, reflective, and slimmed-down
Fischer called for a two- or three-stage process running for at least a decade in
which sovereignty would be divided between the EU and the states. Joschka did
not hesitate to use one "f-word," *federalism,* to describe the relationship and did
not flinch from the use of another "f-word," *finality.* His constitutional sketch included a two-house European Parliament – one representing the member-states,
the other elected by direct vote – as well as a president elected by the states and
with a Commission serving the executive branch. The proposal bore an apparent similarity to those of both Dahrendorf and Shonfield, but it was detached
from policy and made no other mention of the means by which the end ("finality") might be reached.

The German foreign minister's federal design was ill received outside of the
Federal Republic. Apparently written partly to influence the agenda of the forthcoming French EU presidency, it caught Foreign Minister Hubert Védrine – as
well as Chirac and Jospin – by surprise. Their reaction, while polite, was distinctly cool.[110] Blair and Aznar met jointly to underscore their resistance to any
movement toward federalism, the smaller nations registered objections to it, and
in Poland – by far the largest and most important of the accession nations – it
elicited both official and unofficial protest.[111] The Fischer proposal, a trial balloon, exposed a distinct uneasiness at the prospect of German leadership of the
Community and was quickly and quietly shelved.

Any doubt concerning Chancellor Schröder's determination to assert leadership disappeared after the Nice debacle. In a press conference of 24 January 2001
the chancellor delivered what amounted to an ultimatum, "an underlying message from the Germans ... that if the French cannot accept their vision, Berlin
will look for other partners and downgrade a relationship that has pushed the
European project forward for fifty years." "The German plan is clear," *Le Figaro*
editorialized, "it intends to make Berlin the linchpin of a Europe reoriented to the
east," and neither France nor the Commission was meant to lead it. Rather, the
French would be asked "to support a constitution and a strengthening of institutions, which would inevitably entail a gradual dilution of ... national sovereignty
in an expanded community."[112]

The new German policy activism actually burst into the open six months earlier than planned. For reasons that can only be surmised, a proposal for European

federation bearing Chancellor Schröder's signature and written for the SPD party congress in September 2001 was anonymously leaked to the weekly news magazine *Der Spiegel* in time to appear in the 4 May edition. It was due to arrive at the newsstand only three days before the opening of the fifth two-day congress of the Party of European Socialists in Berlin.[113] The Schröder document was admirable, constructive, and democratic in inspiration; though sketchy, the proposal was meant to mark a major turning point in policy. Since none of the EU partner states was informed of the draft in advance, it is assumed to have been written for internal consumption. The CDU endorsed the document at once but soon distanced itself from it.

Like the earlier Lamers and Fischer initiatives, Schröder's proposal was genuinely federal in inspiration and obviously influenced by the German national model. It strikingly reduced the power of the Council of Ministers, which would lose the last word on legislation and be transformed into an upper house representing the member-states. The existing Parliament would serve as the popularly elected lower house. The two would share the power to tax. The Commission was to answer to a strengthened and reinforced Parliament empowered to set budgets. The text established a clear line of demarcation between its responsibilities and those of the member-states and also called for "repatriating" CAP and phasing out regional funds.[114]

The Schröder plan, though generally consistent with both the Dahrendorf and Shonfield models, met with a frosty reception – in part because the manner of its disclosure suggested an attempt to force the hand of British and French socialists.[115] The proposal did in fact dominate the proceedings of their Berlin conclave. Tony Blair's opposition was predictable, not least of all because it interfered with a sedulous attempt to keep European issues out of the national debate taking place in conjunction with the British elections planned for 7 June. Blair was also irked that the matter came before the socialist conference when it happened to be chaired by Foreign Secretary Robin Cook, the most pro-European figure in the cabinet.[116] The French were angry about the Schröder initiative for a very special reason. According to the astute social scientist Anne-Marie Le Gloannac, "they want a strong Europe with weak institutions."[117] The bankruptcy of this approach was now exposed for all to view. Pierre Moscovici, the minister of European affairs who had close ties to Jospin, brusquely dismissed the Schröder proposal as "an idea that goes a long way down a German, that is to say a federalist road."[118] Chirac was angered by the threat to CAP, the Spanish by the blow to regional funds, and the Austrians, Danes, and Swedes by the incursions on sovereignty. Aware that being pro-European would cost votes, both Berlusconi and the leader of the Italian center-left, Francesco Rutelli, remained conspicuously silent on the subject of Schröder's European vision.[119] Only the cynical Belgians showed much enthusiasm for the German version of Euro-federalism, but they wanted to preserve CAP.[120]

The main objection to the German chancellor's proposal was fear of "superstate," even though (as Europhiles quickly pointed out) the EU employs fewer bureaucrats than does the city of Amsterdam. The importance of another, more sensitive issue also increased as "functionalist" and intergovernmental institutions weakened and a more direct form of representative government entered the European agenda. The matter can more tactfully be described as a preference for running one's own affairs rather than as an aversion to being governed by Germans. The conclusion is nonetheless unmistakable that Schröder's federal proposal, the most fair-minded and democratic of such constitutional plans to date, had outdistanced European public sentiment. No sequel would soon be forthcoming from the new capital of Berlin.

Meanwhile, Brussels was not idle. Prodi made good on his word to run hard like a diesel – indeed, his engine was racing – but he got no traction because no one took him seriously after the disastrous first year and the catastrophic Nice sequel to it. The Commission had ceased to count. As wheels spun to the stench of burning rubber, morale at his sleepy *apparat* slipped badly. The Council of Ministers' senior administrative staff, COREPER, was rapidly encroaching on Commission turf. The Guardians found themselves saddled with donkeys' jobs like reconstructing Kosovo and containing political aftershocks of the mad cow disease crisis. Administratively, the Commission was coming to resemble a "huge post office, where it takes twelve signatures to authorize a single grant to help small business."[121]

A foul odor continued to pollute the atmosphere at Commission headquarters. In 1999 the Guardians wasted 4 billion pounds of taxpayer money, according to an independent audit. The European Court of Auditors itself estimated that between 5.5 and 7 percent of the budget was squandered. The list of sins and sinners was long, even though only the surface could be scratched. Subsidy payments made to farmers across Europe were found to be error-ridden and chronically vulnerable to fraud. In Germany, Denmark, Spain, France, Italy, and Portugal, "aid recipients over-declared either surface area or the number of livestock," bogus payment was made for nonexistent storage costs, and farmers received premiums for slaughtering beef without having to provide any evidence that they had actually done so.[122] In Greece, 35 million pounds in farm subsidies were diverted to an insurance fund and to support of the farm workers' union; another 300,000 pounds went into refurnishing farm co-op offices. Aid expenditure in Bosnia was 20 percent greater than stipulated in contracts. The auditors called for 52 separate financial investigations.[123]

Differences in reporting and compliance made it difficult to get to the bottom of the fraud problem. The *European Report* of the Commission's European Information Service gingerly related that "member-states notified a total of 6,587 cases in 2000. The United Kingdom proved to be the most vigilant both in terms of the number of cases (406) and regarding the sums involved (euro 349 million), followed by Germany (482 cases involving euro 57 million). Greece didn't notify a single case."[124] Fraud actually increased sharply in 2000, in terms of both cases and sums. Other areas where it was present in 2000 include transit (11 percent of the total funds) and incorrect designation of goods (10.4 percent). The incidence of fraudulence in the farm sector grew 10 percent, but the total value of it jumped a whopping 104 percent because two cases of long-standing schemes were discovered in Italy. The structural funds also turned up an anomaly: the number of cases increased 74 percent since France and the Netherlands began reporting, but their total costs actually went down 5 percent from the previous year. The European Social Fund had the worst record of any program. The investigators opened 148 new inquiries in 2000, their total value estimated at 170 million euros.[125]

These figures underscore how little the Commission actually knows about the full extent of fraudulent practice. Complicating the effort to recover them is a requirement that

the final decision can only be taken on the conclusion of a multi-annual program [and] ... the visibility of the sum to be recovered suffers from a lack of communication on the part of the member-states, which should in the future transmit reports annually on sums to be recovered, without awaiting the conclusion of ongoing structural programs.[126]

Stripped of jargon, the report says that the states distribute EU money on their own and as they choose and that, once spent, it cannot be recovered.

The amount of fraud seems to correlate with the size of the state sector and the north–south divide on the one hand and with the strength of a good government tradition on the other. It is obvious to those unwilling to turn a blind eye that huge differences exist between essentially "clean" and definitely "dirty" member-states, as well as between those with small as opposed to large state sectors. Given the paucity of official information, OECD estimates of the shadow economies of its seventeen member-nations should provide at least some insight into the incidence of EU fraud. The OECD reported a noteworthy rise in the size of the shadow economy between 1994 and 1998 except in the United States and the Netherlands, where the government sectors did not grow substantially. Most elsewhere they grew between 1 and 3 percent, with the most startling increase in Austria (about a third), due perhaps to large numbers of undocumented workers. The nations with the largest shadow economies in 1998 were Greece (29 percent of GDP), Italy (27.8 percent), and Spain (23.4 percent), followed by the Belgians and Scandinavians (22 and 18 percent, respectively). At the bottom were Switzerland, the still generally aboveboard Austrians, the United States, and the United Kingdom – the latter with 13 percent. The report concludes that, with the exception of Spain, "the countries that had the largest shadow economy also had the highest tax and social security burden"; the converse, except in Austria, was also true.[127] It seems indisputable that off-the-books operations thrive in state-dominated economies and that the Commission is ill equipped to enforce prudential expenditure standards and practices, especially along the Mediterranean littoral. The Scandinavian example further suggests that higher taxes seem likely to aggravate the problem.

One would have thought that, for a Commission intent upon qualifying itself to serve as a future executive in a European federal government, the first priority would be to put its own house in order. However, Prodi's priority was to guard turf. He thus sought to parry threats to the Commission with a bold, two-pronged Delorean thrust and developed one scheme for burrowing bureaucratically outward from inside, another for arcing ideologically inward from outside. The former was, as noted earlier, the proposal for the European constitutional convention; the latter, the 26 July 2001 White Paper on Governance. Its specific purpose was to help overcome the Union's "democratic deficit" by "creating a sense of civil society" and "generating a sense of belonging to Europe." As Prodi put the matter, the White Paper responded to the need to "forge unity at the grass-roots level" and "promote a sense of shared interests, values and aspirations among citizens through activities in their home town, region or country" by means of "administrative coordination." The White Paper thus presents a program for creating the missing European *demos* by "organizing civil society," setting up new Europe-wide bureaucratic networks, making regulation more effective, and using foreign policy to strengthen the European sense of identity. This White Paper, a pathetic yet scary document, not only brooks a degree of interventionism and control unacceptable in contemporary Europe but is also completely unrealistic.

A response to the Nice debacle, the new program offered a way to build Europe by circumventing the member-states. It involved reviving long-held plans. The Parliament would be the big winner, as the first policy priority was to overcome the "democratic deficit" by assigning it powers now assigned to the Council of Ministers. But the Commission would also come out on top thanks to the adoption of "new methods of delegation to institutions and decentralization." These were spelled out in Prodi's White Paper.[128] The third priority would be a new "social and economic action program" conceived along Delorean lines. It would involve (among other things) a call for a new European tax and the special Commission appointment of a "Mr. or Ms. Euro" to supply political guidance to, and act as spokesperson for, the European Central Bank.[129] The final and most general aim was to "improve the lives of Europe's citizens."[130] In February 2002, Prodi set 2004 as the terminal date for the compilation of a new organizational framework (*Kompetenzkatalog*) for the Commission, the completion of the implementing legislation for the rights charter, a codification and simplification of EU legal texts, and a delineation of the rights and privileges of the European Parliament. The work was to support the capstone of the effort, a Euro-constitution.[131] On 26 April 2002, Prodi told a Bavarian audience that the time had come to break with a policy of small steps and "face the ultimate question of what the Union is aiming for."[132] He was ready to move.

The White Paper on Governance advances schemes for the administrative "coordination" of society to the centralizing power, as well as for creating influential new Euro-lobbies and leveraging Brussels' power at the national level. The German term *Gleichschaltung* comes closer to what the paper envisages than any English word. Jacques Delors introduced the (then still partly virginal) Community to the concept of "organized civil society." Conceived as all-embracing, it includes trade unions and employer associations (the "social partners"), trade associations, professional associations, and nongovernmental organizations that bring people together in a common cause. To these, Prodi's White Paper adds "community-based organizations" at the grass roots that pursue "member-oriented objectives – youth groups, family associations, and all others through which citizens participate in local and community life."[133] All of them should be encouraged to acquire a "European dimension," according to the White Paper. "From chess competitions between European towns, to mothers' unions knitting circles in village halls, everything," according to one critic, "is to be enlisted in the greater cause of European integration."[134]

Network governance is also touted as a method to "widen the unitary political space" and thus organize the European civil society. The approach requires training various Euro-elites, human "force multipliers" in the management of European integration, by offering courses to national civil servants in the EU's own European Institute of Public Management in Maastricht, in the proposed European Police College, at the European University Institute, and in more than 300 other educational and cultural institutions.[135] To this list must be added the loyalty-building effects of the Framework Programs for research and development as well as the extensive funding of academic projects, especially those concerned with the European Union itself. The Commission paper also places a new emphasis on the co-optation of nongovernmental organizations into network structures, especially those concerned with ecology. By seeding such groups – and at the same time insisting upon, and helping develop, cross-border partnerships – the EU can introduce a European dimension to "feel good" projects that enjoy general public support.[136]

On regulatory issues, the governance document makes several important recommendations. One is a new use of the so-called Framework Directive. In the manner of an enabling act, it broadens the authority of the EU to issue regulations that take effect automatically and that previously had been limited to "implementation." Such framework directives are meant to replace mere "directives," which require the adoption of secondary national legislation and which previously had been required for issues of policy. The new approach would permit Brussels to increase both the ability to impose new law and its identification with it. The White Paper also recommends creating new regulatory agencies that either implement particular Commission programs or enforce particular aspects of law; it also counsels the "devolution" of responsibility for enforcement to national agencies in fields like veterinary medicine. "Devolution" in the twisted Euro-meaning does not involve a transfer of authority or the grant of autonomy. The guidelines would continue to come from the Commission; the national organizations merely implement Brussels' policy. The final section of the White Paper advocates manipulative use of foreign policy in order to increase a sense of belonging to an imperiled political unit.[137] This is a variation on an old theme, one well played by Otto von Bismarck as a method of forging collective solidarity. The Iron Chancellor spawned many latter-day disciples: Need anything further be said about the dangers of invoking an external threat in order to inspire a feeling of membership in a political community – to create a *demos*? To paraphrase Marx, anti-Americanism is the Europeanism of fools.

The attempt to instill a sense of Euro-nationhood has caused much silliness. Delors, who regarded the patriotism-building effort as a species of industrial policy, referred to it as "culture management." In his maiden address to the European Parliament in 1985, the new Commission president pronounced that "the culture industry will tomorrow be one of the biggest industries, a creator of wealth and jobs."[138] Regretting that "under the terms of the treaty we do not have the resources to implement a cultural policy," he promised "to tackle the issue along economic lines." Committees of bureaucrats and marketing professionals soon met to discover how to "inject" unity into the masses, manufacture history as a "genealogy of progress" from Plato to NATO, and devise appropriately attractive symbols and rituals. The effort presupposed an essentialist concept of culture as a bounded, pure, and unproblematic entity. Also involved in this effort to create an imagined community was, in the words of Susan Sontag, "the Europeanization not of the world but of Europe itself."[139]

Nothing was to be spared in this high-philistine endeavor. "Mother Europe," as put in the big Commission-sponsored De Clercq report of 1993, "must protect her children." To "engrain Europe" in "peoples' minds," it stressed, "newscasters and reporters must *themselves* be targeted" to become agents of influence.[140] The same committee also recommended organizing a centralized Office of Communications ("so the Community speaks with a single voice"), founding a European Library and Museum, instituting a European Order of Merit, and issuing birth certificates granting "European citizenship." The De Clercq report followed on the heels of the previous Adonnino committee, whose recommendations included creating a Europe-wide "audio-visual area," organizing a European Academy of Science ("to highlight the achievements of European science in all its wealth and diversity"), forming European sports teams, setting up "voluntary work camps," introducing a stronger "European dimension" in education, and providing a Euro-lottery "with prize money awarded in ecus" in order to "make Europe come alive for Europeans."

The need to create a "People's Europe" elicited a host of additional suggestions: introducing European postage stamps with portraits of Monnet, Schuman, and other Founding Fathers; choosing an anthem ("Ode to Joy"); encouraging sporting competitions and teams; funding a youth orchestra; providing an EU "Woman of the Year" award; adopting a revolutionary new calendar with festive "European weeks," "European months of culture," and the designation of special, thematic "European years"; and creating new holidays to celebrate Jean Monnet's Birthday, the Schuman Plan Declaration, Walter Hallstein Day, and so on. Then, too, there was a need for new symbols like the flag with its deep blue field and famous twelve-star circle ("clock without hands"), which – as noted by consultant scholar-experts – had a mystical significance: "Twelve was a symbol of perfection and plenitude, associated equally with the apostles, the sons of Jacob, the tables of the Roman legislator, the labors of Hercules, the hours of the day, the months of the year, and the signs of the Zodiac."[141]

It was also necessary to broaden EU appeal at a more intellectual level. To create the proper frame of mind, gifted writers like Jean-Baptiste Duroselle (who authored *Europe: A History of its Peoples*) were commissioned to present Europe's story as a march of progress culminating in the benign leadership of the EU as guided by "founding fathers" and "visionary statesmen" like Monnet, Adenauer, De Gaspari, Spaak, and contemporaries cast in a similarly heroic mold. This potted history was but one episode in a much broader campaign to "Europeanize" education.

Finally, as if in self-fulfilling prophecy, Eurostat (the Commission's statistical office) fabricated a category of "European public opinion" in order to accustom the public to "thinking European."[142] The attempt to turn phantom into *demos* stood little chance, however. It had to compete with the internet and other new means of accessing information, sexual and gender liberation and empowerment, personal enfranchisement, increases in mobility and the ease of travel, the growth of leisure, added longevity and better health – to mention only a few of the trends abroad in the world that enhance human freedom, independence, opportunity, and variety; make contemporary life intricate, rich, and endlessly fascinating; and make a mockery of all attempts to shape the human personality by cookie-cutter methods.

The Convention on the Future of Europe, which opened on 28 February 2002, will probably turn out be just another talk shop. But that is no reason not to take it seriously. The convention represents, if nothing else, the most serious attempt currently under way to break through the present EU logjam. It can count on the good will of (and at least a measure of support from) integration well-wishers who recognize the seriousness of the breakdown of both functionalism and intergovernmentalism as well as the need to make Community institutions operational. For the first eight months of 2002, the convention operated in the dark. Not until 26 October – in the immediate aftermath of the 21 October Irish referendum and the critical Franco-German deal over Enlargement struck a few days later – did it reveal an outline of a future draft constitution. It was singularly the work of the chairman, Valéry Giscard d'Estaing, did not represent a consensus view even of the packed assembly, skirted most fundamental problems facing the Community, and proposed only a partial reform of its institutions.

A couple of cautionary points are still worth noting. The Commission has already been marginalized in the drafting process. The convention will conclude its work before Enlargement takes place and, if it amounts to anything, will present the eastern Europeans with still another *fait accompli*. Eventual ratification of any new constitution or framework document worthy of the name is less likely than a split-up of the Union as a result of heavy-handed attempts to impose it. However, the draft outline does contain two fruitful specific suggestions. The first is to replace the rotating presidency with an elected president as *primus inter pares* among the other Community heads of state and government convened as the European Council. The second is to create a "congress," conceived as a second house of the European Parliament and composed of delegates appointed by, and responsible to, national parliaments. Whether such potentially constructive reforms will be aired cannot be predicted. The usual rows broke out once the constitutional "skeleton" was revealed. Its reception does not augur well for the success of the convention.

The gathering brought together 105 delegates from 28 countries, the fifteen members and the thirteen aspirants. Only a handful of them were Euroskeptical. The 76-year-old Valéry Giscard d'Estaing – who last held high office in 1981, when he stepped down as prime minister of France – presided. Ridiculed by press and public as would-be "Grandfather of Europe," Giscard harbored well-prepared constitutional plans and was from the outset properly suspected of merely awaiting a propitious moment at which to spring them.[143]

Giscard's task as chairman was to produce a single coherent constitutional proposal that could be presented to the governments of Europe for ratification. Giscard's opening address made it clear that concern with public alienation prompted the convocation; that the choice delegates would be called upon to make would be between a United States of Europe (the German model) or a United Europe of States (the French); and that facing up to A****** presented "Europe" with its greatest challenge.[144]

The final text of "the organizational platform for the future," which is to be completed by mid-2003, will delimit the powers of the states and also redefine the powers of the European Council, the Commission, the European Parliament, and the European Court of Justice. The matter is supposed to be decided at an intergovernmental conference in 2004. The member-states will make the ultimate decision, but "they will not be able to brush aside as irrelevant the ideas of the various national parliaments, the Commission, and the European Parliament, as well as the delegates from the admission candidates that ... together make up the convention."[145] The way in which the ratification procedure will be bound into an *engrenage* package cannot be foreseen.

The convention finally gave President Prodi his day, a chance to pull out his six-shooter and blast away. Presenting his view to the European Parliament on 22 May, he challenged the EU governments to give successor Guardians sweeping powers over the Union's economic and foreign policy as part of a "grand political project that would lay the foundations of a supranational democracy." Prodi demanded new authority to issue "binding instructions to governments that deviate from the leading policy guidelines adopted by Euro-zone members" and to serve as sole representative of the monetary union at international meetings. He also called for the elimination of national vetoes on taxation (which, he maintained, must be coordinated in a single market) as well as an end to divided responsibility for foreign policy (which he wanted to vest solely with the Commission). Prodi further demanded elimination of the national veto and its replacement with qualified majority voting in a number of other issue areas, the bestowal on the Parliament "of the same powers as EU governments," and a "unity of views between Commission and Parliament."[146]

M. Giscard d'Estaing does not share Prodi's views. Understandably – in light of his close relationship with Helmut Schmidt – Giscard attributes the success of the first fifty years of European integration to Franco-German entente and blames the recent setbacks on "the failures of the Franco-German couple." To meet his overarching goal of making that "relationship cozy again" will be tantamount to qualifying as an Olympic gold-medalist in the upstream handpaddle event. Still, his first few strokes have not yet tired him out.

The first thing to note about the document presented by Giscard d'Estaing to the convention is that its official status remains unclear. It consists of a three-part outline of a preamble, ten headings, and 46 articles; though referred to as a "skeleton," it establishes basic "structures" that need only be "fleshed out." Although voting procedures have been kept secret, the draft is known to have won only "grudging support" rather than a ringing endorsement from the convention. The proposal of four possible names – European Union, European Community, United States of Europe, and United Europe – is symptomatic of underlying disagreement about ends and purposes, with Giscard himself having made known his preference for the last-mentioned choice.

By whatever name, the proposal calls – in the dry explanation of the EU press service – for a "Union of European states, retaining their national identity, closely coordinating their policies at the European level, and managing certain responsibilities along European lines .... Provided with a single legal personality, this entity would confer dual citizenship, European and national." Of critical importance, "the law upon which it is based would take precedence over national laws in the exercise of the various responsibilities allocated to it." In other words, European law would override national law in specific and enumerated areas when conflicting with "subsidiarity" – which, as Delors once cynically remarked, he would give anyone 1,000 euros to define.

The scope of European level jurisdiction was broad. Visa, asylum, and immigration policy would come under the "internal market." Commercial policy, common security and foreign policy, and the conclusion of all international agreements would fall under the rubric of "external action." All member-states were to be enjoined to "loyal cooperation" with Brussels in the spirit of "European loyalty."[147] The Charter of Fundamental Rights was to be packaged with the treaty, though whether as preamble or appendix was unclear. Also of critical importance, the text of the draft outline calls for financing entirely by "own resources" rather than state contributions – thus vesting the hypothetical future "Europe" with the power to tax.

The institutional configuration implied by the document is by no means straightforward or resolved, but it does include provisions for a president to replace the rotating presidency and for a congress – consisting of delegates appointed by national parliaments – to act as second house in a bicameral legislature. The Commission is apparently to lose both the power to initiate legislation and its special role as guardian and vanguard of the integration process.[148] The final section, perhaps the most significant in the treaty skeleton, stipulates takeover of the *acquis communautaire* and all previous treaties and enactments unless otherwise modified – but says nothing about reform of CAP, regional funds, industrial and R&D policy, or any of the other fundamental structural problems plaguing the EU.[149]

Giscard's constitutional sketch met with immediate angry protest from the British, with the proposed renaming of the EC/EU as "The United States of Europe" or "United Europe" touching a particularly sensitive nerve. The *Times* was unsparing in its criticism:

> When the notion of a constitutional convention for the European Union was first vented two years ago, Tony Blair assured British voters that there was nothing to worry about. There was something to be said ... for spring-cleaning the EU's overstuffed filing cabinet, and the happy result would be that many decisions that should never have been assumed by Brussels would be returned to national control. The convention [was supposed] to have no constitutional consequences for Britain or for the EU ... [but] the federalist intent is clear from the very first "article" ... the cardinal principle [of subsidiarity] that nothing should be decided centrally, is being stood upon its head.[150]

Yet some room for cooperation remained, according to Simon Jenkins:

> Common sense must agree with the recent call of [Foreign Secretary] Jack Straw, for a more stable framework in which to regulate European commerce. Even the skeptic cannot sidestep the challenge of the Giscard convention. The lurches toward "ever closer union" can only be stopped by treaty .... Those seeking a Europe of sovereign states surely have interest in discussing it.[151]

Prime Minister Tony Blair was, for the moment, not one of them. After an angry Blair denounced the Franco-German deal done behind his back over Enlargement – whose wrong-minded main purpose was to maintain CAP fully intact – Chirac revoked the prime minister's invitation to the traditional year-end Anglo-French summit. Relations between the two favorite enemies went into the deep freeze.[152] A seriously embarrassed Blair had to face up to the fact that – with the smirking Franco-German couple in front of him and an angry British public at his back – it would be necessary to scramble frantically, at least for a while, in order to maintain his favored EU posture of one foot in and one foot out.

The German government appears to be well disposed toward the Giscard draft and has even dispatched foreign minister Joschka Fischer to cheerlead at the convention. As a result of Schröder's squeak-through re-election in September and subsequent plunging popularity, he is ill positioned to take the initiative. The French have rather conspicuously remained silent on the draft of their former president, though Chirac (himself at most Euro-neutral) has at least not registered any objections to it. Much more important for the French at the moment was the need to protect the CAP–Enlargement coup and turn the momentary reconciliation with the Germans into something more enduring than a kiss on the run. The governments of both Italy and Spain, neither of them pro-federalist, have withheld comment on the constitutional text.

As the year 2003 opened, prospects for the convention seemed somewhat brighter. The days of scoffing are over, according to George Parker of the *Financial Times*: the imperious Giscard d'Estaing has "good reason to believe" that the substance of his draft (due to be produced by 2003) will "resemble the treaty [eventually] agreed upon by European leaders."[153] The judgment is overly optimistic. Although the "ardent federalist" Jean-Luc Dehaene (the Belgian author of an important committee report) has proposed creating a "Euro-Pentagon" and a single diplomatic service, and though Prodi has sponsored a draft constitution (code-named Operation Penelope) that would confront member-states with a take-it-or-leave-it ultimatum, consensus seems to have been approached on only a single point: the need for a president, elected by the member-states, to preside at the European Council.[154] Both Chancellor Schröder and Prime Minister Chirac incline to this British initiative. Such agreement may presage a shift in venue for institutional reform from the present special convention to the European Council. This turn of events would increase the likelihood that, as advocated by British Foreign Secretary Jack Straw, a new constitution would

start out with just a few lines, setting out what the EU is – a union of sovereign states [that] have decided to pool some of their sovereignty, better to secure peace and prosperity in Europe and the wider world [and] confirm that the Union exercises only those powers which are explicitly ... conferred on it by the member-states, ... the EU's primary source of democratic legitimacy.[155]

It could, with luck, provide the fresh start that the EU needs. The Convention on the Future of Europe has not provided it.

Nor has the attempt to salvage the special trans-Rhenanian relationship in the aftermath of the CAP deal over Enlargement. On 22 January 2003, the 603 delegates to the *Bundestag* met with their 577 French counterparts in a grandiose reaffirmation of friendship – staged at the palace of Versailles – to commemorate a treaty that, in fact, their predecessors had thirty years earlier all but repudiated as inconsistent with Germany's obligation to it allies: the notorious Elysée Treaty concluded by Adenauer and de Gaulle after the general's memorable veto of Britain's application for membership in the EC. On 23 January, the reciprocating French deputies joined their colleagues at a love-fest in the refurbished *Reichstag*. A couple of new bilateral arrangements for policy coordination accompanied the symbolic events, but they were inconsequential for the constitution-drafting exercise. The single initiative to result from it, a joint proposal for a "two-tower" structure featuring a reinforced Commission and a strengthened Council executive, was widely ridiculed as a calculated attempt to aggravate disagreement between the two bodies, met with vehement disapproval from all of the small member-states, and pleased only the British, who were happy to see German plans for a single strong federal authority sidetracked.[156]

There is little reason to conclude that support for Giscard's outline is any-thing other than thin. The galaxy of distinguished names assembled to take part in the constitution-drafting exercise has, in fact, set out on the wrong mission. What David Howell calls the "thread of democracy" – which should run from the individual citizen through elected national legislatures and then on up to European institutions – has either been broken or never even existed. The an-swer is not to strengthen the European Parliament, which suffers from the same chronic disease as the other European bodies that it seeks to monitor and is part of the same remote and unaccountable apparatus that has alienated the public; to do so would increase centralization, not control from the grass roots. If the Euro-delegates seriously intended to restore or create the Union's democratic links, Howell argues, they would be visiting national parliaments – rather than summoning delegates to their convocation – and trying to make the Union work by applying the subsidiarity principle as it was intended to operate, by devolving decision-making responsibility. The convention has actually got it backwards, has forgotten its source of its legitimacy "and where the Union's institutions stand in the hierarchy of governance."[157] They are "subordinate, not superior, the servants not the masters of the nation-states," deriving their authority "from the parliaments that brought them into being" and not, as stipulated at the Laeken summit (which authorized the convention), from "the democratic values it projects."[158]

The European conclave represents the most recent, and boldest, of successive attempts to stave off the consequences of policy-making failure by raising the ante. The results may be fewer and fewer, but the game gets bigger and bigger. The Convention on the Future of Europe has a misleading air of finality about it. Its sequel is less likely to be a new constitution than a Convention on the Fu-ture of Europe (II) or Convention on the Future of Europe Lite, except in the unlikely event that it generates enough rancor to split up the Union. In any case, its failure will not mark the end of attempts to build Europe by grand gesture.

The success of a constitutional project will also have to contend with the grow-ing public impression that the experiment in Euro-state building has been falter-ing badly. Monetary union has been a disappointment. The euro-enthusiasm engendered by the painless adoption of a new currency (and with the ease of making calculations in it) soon gave way throughout much of Europe to a wave of resentment at retail price-gouging, which – if Eurostat is to be believed – was largely imagined and far from inflationary. Willem Duisenberg, the Dutch pres-ident of the European Central Bank, has also been broadly criticized, perhaps unfairly, for maintaining excessive interest rates. Duisenberg could hardly be blamed that his mandate was asymmetrical: it required protecting the currency's integrity but was silent about promoting growth. The problems of the ECB were enormous and structural. None other than Romano Prodi – who, as Italian prime minister, could rightly lay claim to shoehorning his fiscally incontinent nation into the convergence criteria – admitted as much. In a press conference impropriety he blurted out the unpleasant truth that the EMU, "like all rules that are rigid," was "stupid." "He was right, obviously," the *Economist* editorial-ized, "hence the rending of garments in Europe's capitals .... What word better describes a regime that tells economies in recession to raise taxes and cut spending?" After less than a year of operation, it had become painfully evident that "the pact should be re-designed or else ignored." In January 2003 the Commission admonished the French (who merely shrugged off such criticism) and the Germans (who promised compliance) for exceeding allowable budget deficits. Barring far-reaching supply-side reform, deflation would slow economic growth in Germany to 0.2 from 0.5 percent.

In early October 2002 the EU finance ministers abandoned the goal of balancing their budgets by 2004, but more than a course correction will be required.[159] Reconfiguration will require a new treaty, something impossible before 2005, and until then "lurch and muddle" will have to continue and "Europe will rub along with the pact and semi-comply, destroying many jobs," albeit fewer than by strict obedience to the unrealistic conditions dictated by the stability and growth pact.[160] Under the circumstances, Europe will be lucky to grow at much more than a single percent in 2002.[161]

The governance problems of 1990s began with the failure to find a substitute for the Delorean agenda. In the post-Maastricht period, Council and Commission both turned away from the economic challenges of the day in favor of a "pillar erection" policy undertaken in pursuit of the chimera of building a European nation around a framework of centralized administrative institutions responsible only to themselves. The unwise and futile policy of "vertical" Europe building and the malfunctioning European Monetary Union have exacted a heavy price, politically and economically. The decision to pursue the institution-building agenda discredited and destroyed the effectiveness of the Commission over the 1990s. It is now toast.

Delors bequeathed his successors a badly running administrative machine. A few of its parts were good enough to be used elsewhere, but many others needed fixing. Oil leaked badly. Santer's effort to provide sealant failed. Prodi's attempt to "gun" the motor may only have caused it to break down faster. The unpopular president nevertheless did what he could to keep the Commission functioning: grabbed competences opportunistically, tried to pump up the Parliament, and launched a barrage of new initiatives. But without the compliance of the member-states – and, in particular, absent the cooperation of a wealthy Germany with a guilt complex – he could do little. The constitutional convention has not yet given Prodi many chances to develop his flair for dramatic gesture on the main stage. He still has little to show for the misguided attempt to overcome the "democratic deficit" by reviving Delors's programmatic "organization" of European society. As the new millennium opened, the Commission was obviously fast becoming expendable; the big member-states were ready to do away with it or at least reduce it to subservience. Regardless of the convention's outcome, the future European Commission will function more like an appendix than a brain.

Intergovernmentalism also broke down in the 1990s. It could lay at least some claim to being a victim of circumstance. The scandal that led to the downfall of the Santer Commission came at a time when, with considerable skill and luck, the member-states might have dealt with Enlargement and reform as part of a single package entailing the reorganization of Community institutions. As it was, the failure to re-nationalize CAP and redefine regional aid would eventually poison the Enlargement process. The Lisbon dot.com summit came too late to step up the pace of liberalization or to set the EU off in a new direction. That was partly a matter of bad luck but due also to such bad judgments as the choice of the "safe" Santer over the "dynamic" Brittan or Sutherland for Commission president and the decision to beat up on Austria.

Intergovernmentalism also was victim to German reunification. The staggering costs of "institution transfer" deprived the Federal Republic of both the willingness and wherewithal to serve as European paymaster. Chancellor Kohl was prepared to fork out whatever was needed to alleviate the fear and mistrust that merger with the former German Democratic Republic was expected to engender. Chancellor Schröder, lacking the means to do so, chose instead to "take the high road." The result was a succession of German proposals for a democratic federal government of Europe. Well-meaning, equitable, and perhaps – in the distant future – even feasible, they met with a frigid reception. The other member-states preferred the "fudge and drudge" of intergovernmentalism and Commission functionalism to government, even good government, by Berlin. The merest prospect of a democratic federalism – which Germany would dominate by force of numbers, national power, and geographic position – triggered a retreat to the arms of the nation-state.

The Franco-German couple's relationship did not survive the strain of reunification, though both parties tried to pretend otherwise. The linchpin of intergovernmentalism has been pulled. It will be hard to reinsert it into the trans-Rhenanian machinery – though there promises to be no lack of such attempts. An opportunity now exists for the member-states to restructure relationships between one another, to coalesce in a variety of ways around different projects and for new purposes. Over the near term, such a trend would almost certainly be directed toward practical, focused regulatory economic cooperation and could dovetail the EU into the developing international regulatory network. It will not, however, advance the vaulting ambition of organizing a federal democracy for Europe more than one step at a time.

The needed *demos* is missing. Attempts during the 1990s to impose a sense of European nationhood – from the top down using monnetist methods, extending it laterally across society by "coordinating" in the manner of Jacques Delors, and stimulating Euro-patriotism by fanning latent anti-Americanism – have led almost nowhere. The future impetus to integration will have to originate within national polities, through the market, or from the accession of new members. Developments in all three spheres are sources for future hope as well as present despair.

13

No Open-and-Shut Cases: Member-States and the European Community in the 1990s

THE CHAMPAGNE did not go flat everywhere in Europe during the 1990s. In Finland it bubbled over for ten years once the cork was pulled. In Britain it also kept sparkling into the new millennium. In Italy, the *prosecco* tasted great when first poured, though a little light, but had to be quaffed while cool and before losing its delicacy. It was in the great trans-Rhenanian areas of sparkling wine production, of *champagne* and *Sekt,* that the stuff lost the power to tickle the palate, enchant the spirit, and enliven the company. In France and Germany few folks really understood how the magic had been lost or what had gone wrong with the formula – why no one seemed effervescent and everyone morose – but *morosité* was indeed the word of the day. Perhaps the irrepressible Dutch had the answer. At least they had not forgotten how to laugh.

The party began as the new world economy opened. Why did some Europeans enjoy it and others remain glum? This is not a question for Trivial Pursuit but a pastime of another kind: the asymmetrical three-level interdependence game taking place internationally, regionally, and nationally and from which, in complicated and unpredictable ways, integration advances. The impasse at the EU signified neither its end nor its need – merely that the impetus to change would have to come from outside of official Brussels. Where the arrows of the future point is not always evident. One should never try to make an open-and-shut case. Let's open a few cases anyway. Listen for the pop, catch the flow, and raise the glass. The heart will be merry and the soul at peace.

Why smile as the European Union heads for disaster and the world economy weakens? Well, why not? The downturn is temporary, long-term trends are encouraging, and the EU has been resilient in the past. The EU of tomorrow will not be built by the Franco-German couple whose leadership was previously so important, by weak and discredited Eurocrats, nor by the delegates to the Convention on the Future of Europe – who, like the Projectors[1] Gulliver met in Lagoda (Balnibarbi), let their country lapse into rack and ruin while spinning out plans for perfect human institutions. Rather, its architect will be the work of those member-states that had adapted successfully to the international challenges of the 1990s by reforming both their public and private spheres. They were the nations with open economies that encouraged entrepreneurship, lowered taxes, placed curbs on union power, curtailed restrictive labor practices, provided strong work incentives, lightened the load of paperwork, enforced the rule of law, exposed governmental operations to public scrutiny, held their elected officials accountable, and encouraged frank and open discussion. Rewards went to the virtuous – or at least they should have and sometimes even did. Vice, at any rate, seldom went unpunished.

In the same years that M. Delors mounted his offensive for a European super-state, the coalesced nations of Europe engaged, across a long front, in strategic withdrawals from the mixed-economy welfare state. In most theatres of opera-tion and in most sectors of combat, the market onslaught made the inefficient provider of services simply too costly to maintain. Specific national strategies varied, but regrouping and consolidation were common to most of them. This kind of withdrawal was occasionally successful. The welfare state could be re-formed by adopting sound policies under the right conditions and by introducing the competition principle in sturdy democracies that enjoyed public support and were rich enough to pay for expensive public goods as defined and determined by electoral choice. Denmark and the Netherlands would seem to meet such cri-teria; others might be able to do so under somewhat different conditions. Still others had not a prayer. Outcomes would depend heavily upon specific national traditions. In France and Italy, as in Sweden and Spain, the overbearing power of the state – although exercised differently in each case – posed the central prob-lem and hindered the proper operation of democratic institutions. Reform of the economy was inextricably bound with reform of the state. Change in such places was possible but difficult.

Not all points along the line were weak. In some sectors of the front, de-fenses in depth were well prepared and an apparent calm prevailed. Such was the case with Germany, which remained unreformed even after reunification brought in new reserves. However, the market was not allowed to work and the improperly mobilized new manpower still had to be fed. Greater numbers did not strengthen but weakened. Here was a situation that, if left uncorrected, in-vited disaster. Germany was the greatest power among the coalesced nations. Finally, a couple of countries in dire straits crossed the line and, shifting to the other side, joined forces with the smiling lady, the indomitable Mrs. Thatcher, and her impish successor, the mercurial Blair. New Zealand – hardly a Euro-pean nation, but in important respects resembling one of them – went over early. So, too, did Finland. Such conversions could be consequential and even alter national identities. The repaired and revived nations would have reason to cele-brate, at least for a time.

But why should successfully reformed nations that thrive economically want to build the EU when they do well outside of it? In fact, each member-state, in-cluding the less successful, has a substantial (though quite different) stake in the Community's survival. Such stakes are at once economic, geopolitical, and psy-chological and at the same time rest on distinct national traditions. The future of the EU hinges, in part, upon understanding the nature of such varied interests and how to protect and increase them by the successful pursuit of common policies. Examination of Europe's diverse political cultures can shed at least some light onto what EU membership means to individual member-states – as well as on what can be done to build genuine loyalties to a European union. A few vignettes follow. Each will emphasize the distinctiveness of national politics in Europe.

A FINNISH FESTIVAL

Finland is an unlikely but fascinating place to begin the festivities. If any country should celebrate the 1990s it is that northern outpost of Finno-Ugric-Altaic language. When the decade opened, the Finns found themselves in the throes of the most severe depression to afflict any European nation outside of the former Soviet bloc since World War II, with three years of 20-percent unemployment and negative economic growth. Yet by the end of the decade the remote, traditionally insular, geopolitically exposed, and culturally dominated "big little" country was at the top of the GNP league tables and at the forefront of modern technology and social modernization.[2] The Finland of the year 2000 had become a model for both Europe and its Nordic and Baltic neighbors as well as a new influence in the world at large. The previously often overlooked nation simply forgot that it had ever suffered historically from a cultural inferiority complex. The extraordinary Finnish success story has many parts. It involves a historical egalitarianism, a strong sense of community, an innate practicality, the intelligent application of brains and brawn, farsighted leadership, and – for once in the nation's history – plenty of good luck.

The Finnish depression had causes similar to the catastrophe that hit Sweden at the same time.[3] It featured a bank lending binge, which led to excessive consumer indebtedness, a boom in home prices, a bursting credit bubble, and a collapse of the financial structure that was at least partly traceable to a loss in export competitiveness caused by wage rigidity, high labor costs, and productivity declines. The force of the downturn was horrific. By 1993, official unemployment was (under)estimated at 18 percent and output had declined 11 percent in two years. The depression was a wake-up call. The security of the welfare state had proved to be illusory, and all the main political parties recognized this fact.[4] But what was to be done? The Soviet collapse was a huge blessing. The loss of Finland's largest export market added fuel to the economic firestorm but at the same time created a new sense of possibility. The foreign threat had lifted. Finland could unwind for the first time since the war. The long-pursued "Paasikivi–Kekkonen Line" had bound the Finns to a pro-Soviet neutrality, forced them to remain at arm's length from the EU and NATO, encouraged a mood of national introspection, and restricted independence.[5] But the Line now belonged to the past. A young generation of leaders moved rapidly to the fore at the beginning of the 1990s and, in a quiet revolution, reoriented Finnish political life in a way that built on national strengths. No single individual can take credit for the accomplishments of these years; they were bipartisan and arose from within a country in which "solidarity" was not a byword for the politics of class but a mechanism of national survival.

On 17 March 1991, Esko Aho – then 36 years old and (within the then somewhat grayish context of Finnish politics) a dashing figure – was named prime
minister to head the first nonsocialist government in two decades, a four-party
cabinet dominated by his Center Party.[6] Aho set Finland on a course followed
after 1995 by Paavo Lipponen, a social democrat, who remains in office today. In
early 1992 Aho declared Finland's intention to seek EU membership. His motives
were primarily geopolitical rather than economic.[7] The Center Party represented
mainly the rural regions of the north, whose heavily subsidized farmers feared
competition from warmer climes and were thus set against the EU.[8] Aho would
later oppose Finnish participation in EMU on the grounds that the nation's special situation called for monetary flexibility, and he also objected strongly to the
Commission's bullying of Austria. Within the ardently pro-EU Finnish political
establishment, Aho was distinctly cool toward Brussels.

Cutting both taxes and the budget sharply, the young prime minister led the
suffering country out of the depression by following a course of deregulation,
privatization, and a general liberalization aimed at attracting foreign capital
and improving the country's export performance. A classic gale of creative destruction swept through the land. Aho broke with centralized wage bargaining
and the unions. His refusal to pad payrolls in order to sop up unemployment
encouraged labor mobility. He also lifted restrictions on foreign ownership of
stock, reduced levels of corporate taxation to the lowest in Europe, and provided
income-tax breaks for foreign managers. Privatization, a key policy, was a component of the broader plan for economic reorganization. Reform would become
a bipartisan issue.[9]

The state sector developed in Finland not for ideological reasons but for a
practical one: capital shortages. The same deficiency launched privatization.
The years 1988 and 1989 marked a "historical turning point" in the economy.
The prime minister of the day, Harri Holkeri, began expanding the ownership
base of public companies in order to increase their access to capital.[10] Aho then
introduced a policy of assessing their management performances with a view to
improving them by privatization when necessary. His successor continued the
policy. Two important rules were followed: the new companies had to be adequately capitalized; and income from the sale of shares had to promote industrial
competitiveness and strengthen public finance. These considerations alone determined the scale and timing of the program.[11]

It was hugely successful. The capital strength of the privatized companies increased, and profitability improved. Assets became marketable and the monetary
value of remaining state shareholdings increased. The Helsinki stock exchange
deepened and widened, while the number and diversity of Finnish investors increased. Foreign share ownership grew from virtually nothing to 20 percent
of overall capitalization value. The owners from abroad also brought valuable
management skills to Finland. Finally, the inflowing revenue both strengthened
the industrial base and shored up state finances.[12] The money was particularly

welcome in light of the huge costs of the government-led bank reorganization, which in 1993 consumed a full quarter of the budget.[13]

By the beginning of 1994, a corner had been turned. Exports – now competitively priced thanks (in part) to a 50-percent devaluation of the markka against the DM – enjoyed record increases; payments turned favorable; the budget was in surplus; unemployment, though still in double digits, was at least moving in the right direction; the national debt, though still excessive, was at least coming down; and private savings were up. The stock market advanced no less than 91 percent in 1993, the first in a streak of many bullish years to come. Within the economy, there was a notable shift from the public to the private, from primary production like wood and wood-pulp products to new high-tech fields, and from markets in the former Soviet Union to those in Europe and the West. A new era in Finnish history was at hand.

In a national referendum of October 1994, Finland opted for the EU. Aho directed the campaign, even though the majority of Centrists opposed entry. His electoral base weakened and – still not forgiven for "having taken the country by the scruff of the neck in 1991" – the man often misleadingly called "Finland's Kennedy" was voted out of office on March 1995, just as the party would really begin. Finland, a former backwater, would set the pace of change in Europe.[14]

Paavo Lipponen would be in office for the next eight years.[15] He received most of the credit for Finnish success and deserved much of it. Lipponen had declared back in 1970 that "socialism had lost out to the market" and can also take credit for insisting since the 1980s that "there is no Nordic alternative to the EU."[16] His consistent position has been that Finland cannot risk allowing Moscow and Brussels to determine the nation's fate. Although economic considerations were of secondary importance in the decision to join the EU, membership has benefited Finland materially because it coincided with the shift from a mixed economy (functioning on the basis of regulation) to an expectations-oriented market system.

National-patriotic considerations also contributed to the reform process. Finnish ethnic politics are among the least uncivilized of any in Europe. The Finns and the Swedes have never fought each other except on the ice. Yet until 1995 the Finns had not even once defeated their neighbor in the World Hockey Championships, which were always played in Stockholm. The losses were an unpleasant reminder to Finnish nationalists that the Swedes (after seven centuries of rule) had simply handed the country over to Imperial Russia in 1809 for another century of foreign domination and that the 6-percent Swedish minority still occupied the commanding heights of the economy and set the tone for high society. Frustrated by repeated defeats on the rink, the Finns swallowed hard and finally hired a Swedish coach, Curt Lindstrom. Thanks to his use of shrewd psychology instead of the iron discipline of the past, a confident and crafty team of uppity Finns upset the cool and confident Swedes, finally clinching their first title. It no longer seemed so important in Helsinki to turn tables on the "snobs" but instead to be reminded that one could still learn something from them.[17]

Take banking, for example. In Finland, the story involved a race to the bottom rather than one to the top. Yet the result was an even finish. Two banks dominated the economy: one Finnish, Kansillas-Osake-Pankki (KOP); the other ethnic Swedish, Union Bank of Finland (UBF). Both were badly run and in dire need of a government bailout after 1992. KOP was essentially a retail bank, and UBF was an investment bank with close ties to the Finnish National Bank. Bank employees and customers alike were vehemently opposed to any merger between the two. Overriding all parties, the government stripped the Swedish business community of privileged "relationship banking" and forced hardheaded super-patriotic Finns to deposit their money in the coffers of former "exploiters."[18] The new amalgamated Merita Bank was a giant in the Finnish economy, with half of all retail deposits and the bulk of the corporate banking business. It held shares in every sector of Finnish industry. After shedding a third of its work force, the combined bank managed to turn a profit by 1995. Change did not end there, however. In late 1997, Merita formed a joint holding company with Nordbanken, the third largest in Sweden, to become the biggest bank in Scandinavia. Danish and Norwegian partners were being actively courted as service providers "to the steadily internationalizing Nordic banking community." The politics of ethnicity may not have been completely transcended in Finnish banking, but its importance had diminished remarkably fast.[19]

The governments of Aho and Lipponen were not doctrinaire in their approach to industrial reorganization. Merita was poured into the mold of the German universal bank. The new Sampo-Leonia company, a near-rival in size, resulted from fusion between an insurer and the old postal savings bank and was more typical of a newer kind of financial services company. Fast-developing capital and credit markets competed with both. Privatization was both cause and effect of the growing importance of disintermediated finance. Large formerly public companies that were reorganized and brought to market included a single firm for the chemical industry; a merger between the national petroleum and electrical power companies; a new national telephone company, Sonera (which later fused with Telia, its Swedish counterpart); and Sponda, a real-estate holding company.[20] In the late 1990s the Helsinki exchange became among the most modern in Europe. It traded derivatives as well as stocks and bonds in a centralized and fully automated order-driven system linked with EUREX (for derivatives) as well as the Deutsche Börse. Membership in the EMU encouraged Finns to hope that, as the only Nordic country in the currency union, they could become "a sort of service bureau" for financial products in the northern region.[21]

The institutional changes that came over the Finnish economy provide a necessary though hardly sufficient condition for the amazing rise of Nokia. The private company, the largest in Finland, was a 135-year-old diversified manufacturer of rubber boots, diapers, and assorted consumer electronics when – after the suicide of its president in 1992 – Jorma Ollila took over the firm and turned it to the production of cellular telephones.[22] By 2000 Nokia had the highest capitalized value of any publicly quoted European company and accounted for about 10 percent of Finland's GDP, more than half the value of its stock exchange, and a fifth of its exports. Nokia holds over 20 percent of the world handset market and has steadily taken share from originally larger market incumbents like Motorola and Ericsson. About half of the company's employees are foreign, as are its owners. Only about 5 percent of its product is sold in Finland.[23]

Explanations of Nokia's extraordinary success usually emphasize the early lead of the northern-tier countries in setting up the first cellular network, the Nordic Mobile Telephone Group; the great executive gifts of Ollila; the egalitarian corporate culture of Finland; the technical skills of employees; and its heavy investment in research and development. Taken together they have produced a succession of more marketable – though not necessarily cheaper or technically better – products than the competition. As of 2000, Nokia had led *Industry Week*'s survey of the world's thousand best companies for five years in a row. It is an exemplar of best practices, provides powerful evidence that Europe can compete in the high-tech sector, and has served as spearhead of the new Finnish economy. Although Nokia has withstood the economic blizzard of the past two years and, like any other company, could be blown away tomorrow, it has already changed Finland fundamentally and irreversibly.[24]

The Finns have become a nation of "technoholics" who half-believe themselves possessed of a special e-chromosome.[25] "You only have to step off the airplane," enthused the *Economist*'s Adrian Wooldridge,

to realize that the Finns have a particular affinity with mobile phones. The air is a-twitter with personalized ringing tones. Telephone boxes stand empty, reduced to mere street decorations. On the average [evening], Helsinki's city center is the scene of a dozen drunken stag nights. The bridegrooms dress in peculiar buttock-exposing costumes and clatter from bar to bar on skis. Even so they manage to keep their mobile phones stuck to their ears.[26]

Not every Finn elects to participate in such chummy rituals, but at a penetration rate of 63 percent, the country does have the world's highest density of cell-phone ownership: 92 percent of all households have at least one device. Children normally receive their first cell phone at age 7, and "mobile parenting" has become commonplace. A recent newspaper cartoon depicted a baby calling his parents for a diaper change.[27] Forty-four percent of Finns are internet users. Two thirds of Finnish managers use e-mail for in-house messages and nearly half use it for external communication. Over 1,700 electronics and electrical firms have developed to supply Nokia – some of them Silicon Valley–type start-ups, still others the more traditional kind of specialized electronics and electrical equipment manufacturers. A supply trail leads to neighboring Estonia. Finland is the only European country with a substantial positive trade balance in the IT (information technology) field.[28]

The techno-bug has also infected traditional economic sectors. Though still state-owned, the old national telephone company Sonera "acts very much like a venture capital–funded outfit in Silicon Valley"; 65 percent of its revenue comes from mobile, new media, and other specialized telecom services. Sonera was also the first operator in the world to launch into wireless application protocols (WAP) phones, a billion-dollar venture whose wisdom, however, still remains to be demonstrated.[29] In banking as well, the MeritaNordbanken Group became among the most progressive and profitable in the world, with 710,000 customers. Half the bank's active clients in Finland pay bills, trade shares, purchase financial services, take out e-loans, and transfer funds over its on-line service. By comparison, only 2 percent of Citigroup's retail business is conducted over the net-bank.

In 2001, Finland ranked second only to the United States on the list – published by the Swiss-based Institute for Management Development – of the world's most competitive countries.[30] Thanks to its spurt in the late 1990s, it also won the race to be the fastest-growing economy in Europe during the twentieth century.[31] Finland is the rare example of a nation able to spawn a successful, entirely indigenous, multi–billion-dollar high-tech industry. How did change come so thoroughly and so quickly? One Finnish commentator, emphasizing the importance of distinctive national tradition, points to the impact of the most widely read Finnish novel since World War II, Vdinv Linna's *Unknown Soldier*. Linna, notes the commentator, reminds his readers that "the most prominent features of Finnish ... military organization were organic forms, improvisation, individual reliability and responsibility and fast reaction ... many of [them] still visible [in] high-tech firms" and, further, that Finns have "an ever-present understanding of a shared fate."[32] The culture thus "cherishes the consensus that helped the country through so many hardships," the most recent example of which was the severe depression of the early 1990s. The readiness for collective sacrifice, courageous and wise political leadership, and a deeply embedded need to prove oneself were instrumental in the dramatic Finnish turnabout.

Education policy was also important. Finland spends more per pupil than any European country at the primary and secondary level. Some 60 percent of the overall population is expected to complete tertiary education. Finnish universities are oriented to technical fields, especially to IT, and higher education is following a planned program of expansion. Information technology courses are taught in fifteen universities that graduate 600 students at the master's level annually, as well as in an extensive network of polytechnics that produce over 2,000 degrees in computing and engineering. There are exceptionally close ties between the academic and corporate worlds.[33]

A fundamental shift in educational philosophy underlies much of the raw data. As a result of the depression of the early 1990s – as well as the failure of the existing system to produce promised results – Finland shifted from a centralized, standardized state-run school system (operated to provide identical opportunities and to encourage equal outcomes) to one that, although still public, promoted "diversity," favored "giftedness," and "opened pathways for those with special [aptitudes] and inclinations." The old Nordic social-democratic educational ideology gave way, in brief, to a gospel of competition, accountability, and efficiency. School choice has been introduced. Outside funding is now possible. National self-evaluation procedures and school rankings have been launched. Competition is encouraged. Centralized educational bureaucracies have been dismantled. Finland has moved, according to Risto Rinne, toward an Anglo-Saxon model appropriate to a "networking society" and "connected with the great questions of world politics."[34] Whether the shift amounts to an unnecessary and undesirable abandonment of the Nordic model or rather an "organic," flexible, fast-moving, responsible, and characteristically Finnish adaptation to a world in motion cannot be determined on the spot.

Finnish membership in the European Union has been mutually beneficial. Taking the road to Brussels instead of that leading to Moscow helped the Finns break out of a provincialism born of fear that had stultified growth not only of the economy but of the national personality. Once open to the world, they astonished even themselves by the speed and extent of their participation – making a contribution to and helping to determine what went on in Europe and the world. "Technoholism" is not a vice requiring a twelve-step recovery program but rather a healthy and pleasantly quirky expression of national pride and identity that is welcome in a people historically subject to foreign domination. Membership in the EU increased the size of the Finnish market by a factor of 40; it has strengthened Nordic regionalism and, in anticipation of Enlargement, Baltic regionalism as well. Finland stands to benefit in the future as gateway to the East, and EU membership has undeniably broadened horizons. Yet the Finnish process of economic change began at home, did not require much foreign encouragement, and would most likely have continued even without membership in the EU. Finland moved early and fast to create the conditions under which entrepreneurialism could flourish. In one secondary but still important respect, EU membership did make a difference. The heavy subsidization of arctic and near-arctic agriculture was to be phased down to EU levels, reducing the size of the farm population two thirds by 2005 but at the same time lowering food prices and reducing inflation – a development paralleled in other lines of consumer products. Still highly competitive in key fields, Finland has not yet experienced the downside of EMS/EMU membership and – depending upon the fates of the other, still national Nordic currencies – may become a regional financial safe haven. The Finnish will not be unhappy to prove to their neighbors that it pays to be the "model European."

Exposed geographically and heavily dependent on the welfare of the high-tech industry, the "one size fits all" policy of the EMU may yet prove costly to Finland in a larger than purely economic sense. The Finns did not (and do not) need the external constraints of the convergence criteria, which their nation cleared with ease. In the 1990s Finland managed better than either its Nordic neighbor or other European welfare states – though still at the cost of high unemployment – to overcome Eurosclerosis by opening its economy to the animal spirits of competition. The achievement may not be easy to duplicate elsewhere. Thanks to it, however, Finland has migrated from the northeastern flank to the very center of European concerns and preoccupations. In so doing, it had broadened the definition of the word "European."

Finland's honeymoon with the EU may now be over, according to a recent survey of the Center for Finnish Business and Policy Studies. This survey detected a large gap between elite and public opinion, a rise in skepticism, and a growing disinterest in the Union. Finns want the EU to take a more active role in controlling crime, be more open and democratic, give greater consideration to the interests of small countries, encourage national cultures, and protect the welfare state. They are not enthusiastic about Enlargement, the project for an EU defense organization, the implementation of economic and monetary union, the adoption of a single currency, or the creation of a European federation. An alarming rise in voter apathy and a mood of political discouragement accompanied the lack of Euro-enthusiasm, an indication that perhaps even in Finland the party may be drawing to a close.[35]

THE FAILING ITALIAN MIRACLE

It started out well enough in Italy (save for the arrest of a celebrant or two for stealing the silverware) as the distinguished guests were ushered in; a pleasant, decent lot, though more accustomed to work than play. Yet nothing seemed to click. Light pleasantry gave way to false bonhomie and warm eyes to forced smiles. The atmosphere went dead before much *prosecco* could be downed. The real action seemed to be elsewhere. Everyone regretted that, for whatever reason, the party had become a drag. A new guest then arrived – a rich, flashy one with plenty of sparkling wine for all. No one knew quite what the stuff was or where it had come from, but they kept drinking anyway. It was, as things turned out, the only party in town.

In no other country has the relationship between the EU and national development been so close or consequential as in Italy of the 1990s. The implosion and collapse of the *partitocrazia* during the months between the fall of the Berlin Wall and the downfall and disappearance of the USSR created a political vacuum in Italy that a technocratic project would soon fill, or at least try to fill. The project antedates the events themselves and grew from the hopes of those with a hand in it *and* those against whom it was aimed: the politicians. Nearly all Italians recognized the need for reform, even though most of them were by dint of circumstance beneficiaries as well as victims of the system's myriad injustices, inefficiencies, corruptions, and petty iniquities: things could simply not be allowed to get worse. The wide north–south divide had to be closed and the mafia brought under control. The costs of corruption had to be reduced nationwide in order to protect the competitiveness of industry and create essential conditions for economic growth.

Brussels, the Great White Hope, was expected to clean up the mess the Italians had made of their system. As the veteran political commentator Indro Montanelli archly stated the matter: "Ours is a servile race, incapable of self-government, which is looking to Europe for salvation."[36] The budget cesspool was the source of the stench, but it pervaded much of Italian public life. In order to banish it, vast areas of the administration and the organized economic sphere also had to be aired out. Italian membership in the EMU was to have provided the incentive needed to bring public finances under control. Yet trust in the EU extended even beyond this single scheme. Italians looked to competition policy to end favoritism and clientage within the economy, raise levels of efficiency, and accelerate modernization in those many spheres where industry and finance lagged behind. They also looked favorably upon corporatist social partnerships, northern European schemes to reform the welfare state, and the "Dutch miracle" as possible development models for their own ramshackle system. The reformers counted on best practices to produce good government and dreamt of a second, reformed Italian Republic that would be as clean, responsive, and democratic as those in other member-states.[37] The technocratic project was noble, not shabby or self-serving. And it expressed the hopes of a nation.

They have not yet been fulfilled. Italy now suffers from a "democratic deficit" of its own, which is to be found on the political left. On the right Silvio Berlusconi has forged a national party–like movement (which developed early), has survived being in opposition, has a stable constituency, and today enjoys the largest parliamentary majority of any government in postwar Italian history. The Berlusconi phenomenon is one of a kind. How many men or women have enough money to buy not politicians – that's easy – but whole governments of one of the five or so richest nations of the world? How many heads of state can be likened to a sultan, a medieval despot, an emperor bokassa, a world-historical corrupter, an Italianate Potemkin, a glitterato without glitters, a star in his own B-grade movie, a waiter with attitude, and a buffoon – without seeming to mind? And who is the man's tailor, anyway? And what's his address? It is too early to predict whether his *Forza Italia* movement will head toward "Margaret or Musso" – or go no place at all. It is evident nevertheless that Berlusconi opposes the unstable political bargain upon which the technocratic project rests and will repudiate it if possible.[38] Big changes may then result.

The bargain in question is between the left-center expert administrators, who have headed all non-Berlusconi governments in the 1990s, and the Italian labor unions in their role as party surrogates. The technocrats are chiefs without Indians and will lack them until the squabbling tribes, the factional remnants of earlier leftist parties, can smoke the peace pipe, form a real electoral federation, and generate loyalties at the grass roots.[39] Their failure in this respect has enabled an economically weakening labor movement – one losing both members and wage-bargaining power – to survive politically by representing de facto the interests of the stranded left-voting electorate. The unions' side of the bargain calls upon them not to interfere with the technocratic project, indeed to enforce it.[40]

The deal is difficult for both parties to uphold. The technocratic project requires stripping organized labor of market influence, enforcing budgetary austerity, and imposing a policy that reduces economic growth in the interests of the
long-term objective of good government. Union cooperation must rest on trust
that the objective can be met and also needs guarantees that the labor movement will in some measure benefit once this happens. Otherwise, the power of
the unions will disappear. The disinflation dividend was to have provided the
incentive to cooperation. The reduction in the fourth of the budget required in
the 1980s to service the immense deficits, and which had turned whole swaths
of the middle class into rentiers, would serve labor's constituent interests: fund
pensions, provide work, and support financial transfers to the south.[41]

The aftermath of Liberation provides a precedent for cooperation between a
reformist government unsupported by a strong party and organized labor, but
there are significant differences as well. One is that the bargain is temporal –
and, with Italy's qualification for monetary union, in effect over. Another is the
intrinsic conflict between union monopoly on the one hand and the market, economic growth, and democratic government on the other. The final difference
is the present prime minister. Berlusconi was not privy to the previous governments' deal with the unions. To strengthen *Forza Italia* he must break out of its
constraints, repudiate the pact with labor, and regain the monetary and fiscal
authority needed to step up growth and prevent a repetition of the economically
"lost decade" of the 1990s.[42] If he succeeds, Italy may no longer be dependent
upon Brussels and may thus become less Europhilic.

Italy of the year 2002 remains only partly reformed. The Second Republic that
was happily announced in the early 1990s still remains in abeyance, the attempt
to write a new constitution long since abandoned. The old system continues to
operate, though with significant differences. Thanks to the replacement of pro-
portional representation with a Westminster-like first-past-the-post voting rule,
the earlier party-dominated system has given way to one featuring a strong executive, be it president or prime minister. The hard-fought battle to qualify for
monetary union has brought down inflation dramatically, lowered the budget
deficit, and resulted in substantial though partial labor market and pension reforms. The reduction in short-term note circulation has re-directed savings into
equity investment, strengthened and modernized financial markets, and given
rise to the possibility that some form of modern shareholder capitalism would
replace the existing dense networks of state- and family-dominated corporatism.
Privatization encouraged such hopes.[43] In this respect as well, reform has slowed
down since EMU qualification. So too has the campaign against corruption associated with the term *tangentopolis*. With the support of a new law limiting
the independence of prosecuting attorneys, Berlusconi has directed that no new
cases be opened. The power of the mafia remains uncurbed.[44]

Since 1992, presidentially appointed technocratic cabinets of the left-center
have alternated in power with the two popularly elected governments of Berlusconi: the short-lived 1994 alliance with the Lombard League and neofascists; and

the present, more durable one dating from April 2001. The Maastricht timetables provided the reference points for the budgetary targets of successive "presidential democracies": Giuliano Amato, who had been minister of the treasury; Carlo Azeglio Ciampi, a former Governor of the Bank of Italy; Lamberto Dini, a former director general of the Bank of Italy; Romano Prodi (whose administration, formed in 1996, included both Dini as foreign minister and Ciampi as minister of both budget and treasury); and, finally, Massimo D'Alema. The determination of these governments is hard to exaggerate. At great political risk, Prodi even slapped on a 9-percent Euro-surcharge to the income tax in order to qualify for the EMU.

Thanks to such exertions, the public deficit decreased from 10.2 percent of GDP in 1991 to 2.5 percent in 1998, low enough to qualify for the EMU. By 1998 inflation had been brought down to 1.5 percent, but so too had economic expansion, which in the aftermath of the 1992 devaluation had been at the highest rate in Europe. By 1996 it had been reduced to 0.7 percent and in 1997 improved to only 1.5 percent. For the decade as a whole, Italian economic growth was anemic, the second lowest among major European countries. Unemployment, averaging 10.5 percent, was second only to Spain in the final years of the decade and particularly severe in the south, where it ran at over 20 percent. The official Italian employment rate was actually the lowest in Europe, with only about one person in two between the ages of 15 and 64 pulling in a paycheck. The high number of noncontributors placed an enormous strain on the pension system. Almost no new jobs were created over the decade, at least in the legal economy. The income gap between north and south grew in the 1990s, the distinction between the protected "ins" and the overlooked "outs" faded only slightly, and the size of the black-market economy continued to be estimated at between 25 and 30 percent of GDP.[45]

The Maastricht constraints provided the technocratic cabinets with the political cover needed to start the reform process in two general areas: pensions and labor markets on the one hand; and privatization, deregulation, and restructuring on the other. The social reforms were tripartite in inspiration and featured negotiations between government and "social partners" that were anchored in union acceptance of "serial equity." For labor, "serial equity" meant "no gain without pain." Amato raised the retirement age for both men and women, lengthened the span of employment needed to qualify for a pension, stretched out the number of years worked that were used as a baseline for benefits determination (thereby reducing them), and cut "seniority premiums." Dini secured passage of a new contributions-based pension scheme – which, however, would only be phased in beginning 2013. In 1997 Prodi ran into heavy resistance from his Refounded Communist allies and could make little further headway. The reforms of the three governments nevertheless reduced the share of pensions in the budget from nearly a quarter to 16 percent, a huge savings. Labor market reform was also significant and included the elimination of wage indexing as well as the Treu Law of 1997; it thus broke the monopoly of the federal employment offices on job placement, portal to the lifetime job. No further reform of either pensions or labor markets has been possible since Italy qualified for monetary union.[46]

Financial reform was long overdue in Italy of the 1990s. A strong merchant banking sector was crucial for the strength of export-oriented family firms. Venture capital was needed for high-tech growth. Good governance was a must for stock market equity financing. Italy's banking system was one of the most disorganized and inefficient in the developed world. Most of the country's 1,000-plus banks were owned either by governmental agency or charitable foundation. Traditions of clientage and relationship banking made Italian financing among the most expensive in Europe. Overstaffing and high prevailing wage rates lowered profitability and reduced capitalization. Average return on equity averaged 4.13 percent at Italian banks, as opposed to 21.1 percent at their British counterparts. No Italian bank was among even the top sixty in Europe.[47] International financials like JP Morgan, Salomon Bros., and Morgan, Stanley dominated Italian investment banking – "bagged" three quarters of the merger and acquisition deals, 60 percent of stock underwriting, and over a third of leveraged buyouts.

The most important Italian bank, Mediabanca, owed its powerful role to connections rather than size, although also by means of cross-holdings it owned shares in many key financials and industrials.[48] What looks like a pyramid from one standpoint, however, resembles a cascade from another. Without the personal prestige of Enrico Cuccia, Mediabanca would have been merely one financial house among many. Until his death in 2000 at age 93, Cuccio served as a human flywheel in the family-dominated world of Italian paleocapitalism. He was the man who smoothed out the power surges, shifts in tempo, and temporary imbalances that might otherwise have broken it up. Although often described as a king-maker, Cuccio was actually more like a Holy Roman Emperor – essentially weak but recognized as the first among sovereigns. It was to his *salotto buono* or salon that the great territorial lords would come for mediation and approval and to pay court.

Pressure for bank reform came from the EU, Confindustria (the Italian employers' federation), and, most directly, from the Bank of Italy, which directed that the charitable foundations sell out within five years. The Bank also vetted mergers.[49] The introduction of cost control was a first step in financial reform and included not only early retirements but the introduction of performance-related pay. Bank dependence on lending also had to be reduced and sources of fee-based revenue tapped – such as insurance, credit cards, custody services, and payments systems. The back office had to be turned into a profit center. Furthermore, asset management had to replace deposit banking as a profit-center – hardly a revolutionary step, except in Italy. Above all, the banking industry had to be consolidated.

Developments in related fields paralleled those in banking. The decline in the inflation rate, dedication to debt reduction, and commitment to increasing investor value provided, according to one glowing account, "the cornerstone of a new era," which thanks to privatization and pension reform promised to get still better.[50] Capitalization on the Milan exchange doubled in the first six years of the 1990s and trading volume tripled. In October 1997 the Treasury transferred ownership of the exchange to private financial intermediaries such as banks, broker–dealers, and private investors. Driven by the fall in interest rates, success in meeting the Maastricht criteria, and a newfound confidence in equity markets, the stock indices hit ten-year highs in July 1997.[51] The beginning of securitization was another indication that Italian finance was modernizing. So, too, was the increasing prominence of American financial service companies in Milan and Rome.[52] However, Italy was not about to develop the modern, rule-based, transparent, and sophisticated "Anglo-Saxon" capital markets needed for economic modernization. Nor would the problem of corporate governance be solved overnight.[53] As in the realm of politics, restoration would only gradually displace reform.

Take privatization. The government's need for money dictated the timetable. There appears to have been no attempt either to create "shareholder democracy" along British lines or to re-constitute elites along French lines. Neither the EU nor the Italian state had the power to enforce its competition directives.[54] The tradition of clubbiness proved too deeply ingrained to dislodge. Instead of the arrival of new entrants, a reshuffling of Italian interests took place in industry and finance. The utilities provide instructive examples. By 2000, all of them had been re-constituted as quasi-monopolies. In the case of ENEL, the electricity monopoly, "instead of creating a competitive market, Italy has landed itself with a powerful, partly private monopolist that charges its customers far above the European average."[55] In the case of gas, the Italian government ended ENI's total domination of distribution but allowed it to keep most of its assets and contracts. ENI's share in shipments would decline only to 70 from 85 percent. Nor was ENI required to sell Snam, its distribution subsidiary. The shift of electrical power plants to combined-cycle gas turbine technology in any case guarantees ENI access to a growing market.[56] The privatization of Telecom Italia yielded the Italian state even more revenue than either the German or British government received from the sale of their national telephone networks. In "the biggest straight fight in European corporate history," Telecom Italia nonetheless fell to a predator a mere fifth of its size, the Olivetti office machine company,[57] which had been saved from bankruptcy only a few years earlier. Olivetti recently lost control to a consortium led by Pirelli, the tire manufacturer, and Benetton, the fashion house famous for trying to make AIDS chic. Because the utilities are privately owned at least in part, the Italian competition "watchdog" can only bark, not bite. He has stated publicly that, in the absence of a consumer outcry over pricing, he will remain toothless. The privatization of banking was also botched. The sales of Credito Italiano, Banca Commerciale Italiana, and Istituto Mobiliare Italiano in 1993 and 1994 did not create new banks with broad shareholder bases. Instead, the sales were "ensnared in complex webs of cross-shareholdings" and the boards of the new banks were dominated by outside private interests.[58]

Consolidation and re-grouping occurred in the private as well as the privatized sector. Mediabanca has been prominent in the reshuffling of corporate interests but is no longer dominant since the death of Cuccia. International banks have lined up behind Italian financials but seldom bid against them. The characteristically labyrinthine deals are often at least partly defensive and meant to acquire minority holdings of a company's own stock in order to foreclose possible hostile takeovers.[59] In the course of the 1990s, the mighty Agnelli family discreetly managed to shift the bulk of its assets out of the loss-making automobile industry (the source of its political power) and into diverse, preponderantly financial investments. Most recently, the family patriarch arranged the takeover of Montedison, a major electrical utility.[60] In banking and finance, Assicurazioni Generali acquired Istituto Nazionale della Assicurazioni, partly for defensive reasons. In the process, the already dominant firm became an even larger presence on Italian insurance markets.[61] Three banking groups are forming to rival the "universal banks" of Germany and France: Milan's Unicredito, Turin's San Paolo, and Intesa (also of Milan).[62] According to Luigi Spaventa – head of Consob, the Italian securities and exchange commission – the eclipse of Mediabanca has not resulted in openness but in widespread conflicts of interest and price manipulation throughout the country's financial system. Attacking the dominant role of the banks, Spaventa claimed that two thirds of Italy's publicly traded companies had failed to adopt rules designed to increase transparency and improve corporate governance, and he further accused consumer banks of pushing clients into buying "sophisticated products such as covered warrants and reverse convertibles whose prices [they] regularly manipulated to their own advantage."[63]

The presidential democracy of the 1990s nevertheless brought the budget under control. Inflation ended, and with it a corrupting and demoralizing political dynamic of give-and-take that favored the well-placed, the unscrupulous, and the violent at the expense of the good citizen. The new fiscal discipline enabled Italy to enter the European Monetary Union, a huge boost for confidence and an achievement upon which later governments could build.[64] The technocrat-dominated governments also launched overdue reforms of pensions and labor markets. The attempt to modernize the economy, the state, society, and politics still fell far short of the mark.[65] Taxes, labor costs, and labor market regulations became even more burdensome and restrictive over the 1990s.[66] Halfhearted liberalization left markets in the grip of monopolies.

There was also little sign of an emerging "new economy." The tradition of Italian entrepreneurship did not spill over into the high-tech field. Because Italian university education remained archaic and resistant to change, technical transfer to the private sphere was minimal. For their part, Italian specialty manufacturers faced intensified competition from East Asia but had trouble adapting to it. The lack of adequate legal and financial infrastructures limited access to capital and hindered corporate growth. Italy attracted the least per-capita foreign investment in Europe. Unemployment remained in double digits while the economy all but stood still. Serious effort to reform ended in 1998 once Italy was admitted to the EMU. After years of deferred promises, unrest within organized labor festered. Prodi's 1998 acquiescence in the demand for a 35-hour week indicates that the "social partnership" was beginning to fall apart.[67] The technocratic left-center had in the meantime failed completely to rally its voters to a platform that might have created a solid reform constituency. There remained only one organized electoral movement or party that could command citizen loyalty, *Forza Italia*.

Berlusconi would not have an easy time after taking office on 13 May 2001, if only because economic growth over the following twelve months ground to a halt. The media magnate came to power promising to turn the country's sluggish, underperforming economy around by slashing taxes, investing in infrastructure, privatizing state assets, and "reinventing Italy" in a "Copernican turn."[68] Once in the saddle, he relented. In October, the new prime minister put privatization and liberalization completely on ice, which led to a bitter protest from a disenchanted employers' association.[69] Unveiled in June, the tycoon's program seemed to point not to the future but to a return of the old Italy that technocrats had failed to force onto a more constructive course of development. As the *Times* put it, "for all the talk of restructuring, deregulation, transparency and competitiveness ... by the government of ... Berlusconi, Italy has never ceased to be what it was at the time of the Medicis: a cozy, intimate network of family dynasties who between them control the country's financial and economic life and even politics."[70]

Berlusconi proposed tax breaks for firms reinvesting profits, amnesty for tax evaders repatriating funds from abroad, and abolition of the inheritance tax. He thereby extended a warm clasp of friendship to the traditional middle-class voters of the old DC, who had elected him to office. It was a reassuring gesture to a public fed up with sleaze prosecutions, happy to relegate *tangentopolis* to history, ready to treat Euro-virtue as passé, and comfortable with a restoration of customary ways of doing business.[71] In such an atmosphere, even the mafia could return to semi-respectability.[72] Berlusconi won at least a measure of confidence from this Italy of tradition. The tax forgiveness repatriated some 50 billion euros, an estimated tenth of the amount squirreled away in foreign banks.[73] There was also plenty of the stuff left behind for future bargaining.

The introduction of fixed-term labor contacts was the second important point in Berlusconi's platform. The technical-sounding change implied the reversal of an existing labor market culture under which "everything is forbidden unless it is expressly allowed."[74] The measure was supposed to encourage employers to hire new employees by assuring the former of the right to dismiss the latter. In other words, it eliminated union-guaranteed job protection. The proposal was clearly intended to be the opening move in a long campaign to reduce union power. The brutal murder of Professor Mario Biaggi, the architect of the reform, was bloody prelude to a strike that had already become inevitable. A purported spokesman for the Red Brigade, now apparently revived after lying dormant for over a decade, claimed credit for the foul deed. Umberto Bossi nevertheless publicly pointed the finger at CGIL – the big, formerly communist union. Summarily sacked from the cabinet by Berlusconi, the impetuous leader of the *Lega* had given the union chief, Sergio Cofferati, the excuse needed to call a general strike for 16 April. It would be the biggest demonstration in twenty years.[75]

The strike failed to have the desired effect. The government compromised: the right to fire was to be limited to expanding firms that employed fewer than fifteen and was only to remain in effect provisionally, for three years. Berlusconi was hardly the Thatcherite he claimed to be. The flamboyant media magnate could nonetheless look forward to several more years in power. There would have to be plenty of bread and circuses before the half-step reverse march through the institutions could show results and the entrenched power of labor gradually crumble away. The tide had been reversed, if ever so slightly. The two smaller labor unions accepted Berlusconi's offer. Cofferati resigned, pledging a general strike in the fall.[76]

Time worked against the labor boss. The promise of "serial equity" had institutionalized the political power of the unions without benefiting the membership or halting the movement's erosion. Berlusconi did not need support from labor and would not unless he lost that of his natural constituency of former DC voters, which (except during the interlude of the 1990s) had maintained their grip on power for over half a century. The political left had failed in a Gramscian bid to capture institutions from within. A resort to armed struggle like that of the 1970s was no longer an option. The only one available was to create a real, single party of the left. To do so, its leaders would have to recognize that the audacious bid of the technocrats to solve the problems of Rome via Brussels had failed and then devise a broad strategy of democratic renewal as an alternative to it. Otherwise the patriotic Berlusconi could claim credit for their chief accomplishment. The governments of "presidential democracy" had ended Italy's servile dependence on "Europe" by demonstrating a public willingness to accept the hard choice of economic austerity if necessary to set their house in order. Too bad that the method adopted for the purpose was ill conceived and basically unworkable. If for some reason the austerity policy had succeeded then it would also have weakened the EU. For why would a people that had learned to govern itself properly from Rome still prefer to be ruled from Brussels? The only chance for a divided Italian left is a failure of the right that would demonstrate the inability of the country to stand on its own two feet and thrust it back into the arms of the Eurocrats.

A DIFFERENT DUTCHMAN?

No one can quite remember when the celebrating began in the Netherlands, because it never really stopped. The party was pretty good, though small, and – except for a brief period during the 1970s – nearly everyone behaved decently. The guests were long acquainted, or at least they knew each other well. Then someone unexpected, odd, and troubling showed up. A terrible thing happened.

The party broke up, at least for a while. It would take more than champagne to get it rolling. For once, Dutch courage would not do.

In no other country has the relationship between the EU and national development been so close and *in*consequential as in the Netherlands. Until quite recently it has seemed painless and unthreatening. The meteoric rise of the right-wing antiestablishmentarian Pim Fortuyn – and his senseless murder on the eve of the May 2002 election – has produced a political earthquake, which may in time be discovered to have occurred along a deeper and more extensive European fault line. The Netherlands has often been a bellwether of change. The Fortuyn phenomenon exposed an unsuspected degree of public disaffection deriving from the immobility, impersonality, unaccountability, remoteness, and unresponsiveness of government in The Hague – and with its apparent master in Brussels. The public, or at least a portion of it, felt disenfranchised, powerless, and at the mercy of events. The "unassimilable immigrant" was the symbol of the citizen's phobic fear of being overrun, having his rights trampled upon and his privacy violated. The surprising and unpleasant rise of Dutch nativism and the murder of Fortuyn took place in what is odds-on the most stable and contented country on the continent. The unfortunate upstart was actually the first victim of political assassination in the Netherlands since the seventeenth century.[77]

The Dutch have been not only good Europeans but the best Europeans. The largest of the small nations, located in the middle – geographically and culturally – of the triangular force field of Berlin–Paris–London, and democratically confident as well as politically intelligent, the Netherlands has served both as pivot of the EU and as lead indicator of contemporary European social and institutional development. The Dutch have always been at the vanguard of the group of small nations that favor strengthening the Commission, yet they have often mediated effectively between Germany, France, and Britain in the interests of intergovernmentalism. The two most recent EU treaties were negotiated in Maastricht and Amsterdam. The Netherlands has obviously been more important to the success of the EU than mere size would indicate.

Membership in the EU has not required much of the Dutch. Unlike the case of Italy or even France, adaptation to the customs union, the monetary union, and (in general) to the growing regulatory power of the Brussels institutions has presented few difficulties and caused little pain. The economy of the Netherlands, trade-based and maritime in orientation, has traditionally been open. Even before the Treaty of Rome and, in fact, prior to the Marshall Plan, the Dutch government recognized and fully accepted the implications of their economic dependence upon Germany. A national consensus developed early that the chief comparative advantage of the Netherlands vis-à-vis its big neighbor to the east was low labor costs and that the gulden should shadow – in effect, be pegged to – the Deutsche mark. This has been the case since 1958. Most of the time the Dutch currency has been undervalued in relation to the strong currency next door, giving the Netherlands a long-term trade advantage.[78] It has also been easy for the nation to adapt to "social Europe." Although its mechanisms are in many respects unique, the Dutch welfare state provides comparable benefits to its compeers in northern Europe.

A deeply inculcated, even hallowed political tradition of national tolerance is the mainspring of Dutch national strength. This apparent virtue represents an intelligent accommodation to a strong native streak of independent-mindedness and congenial stubbornness. The existence of this tradition has, over time, enabled disparate confessional and regional interests to arrive constructively at consensus on issues large and small without sacrificing their distinct identities. This "pillarization" has created a society in which it may take six months and complicated trade-offs between three to five coalition parties in order to form a new cabinet, yet it has also produced one that seems able to function smoothly even in the absence of a government. Once in place and able to act, Dutch government does so authoritatively. Sound practice has helped create a nation in which fundamentalist Calvinists coexist with potheads, as well as a society in which civil liberties are not merely paid lip service but ingrained in conscience and routine.[79]

Trust in the fundamentals of the system runs almost shamefully deep. Although few Dutch citizens can imagine living under a different political dispensation, many of them seem almost obliged to disparage their system in the presence of outsiders, as if embarrassed by pride but also to protect what they have. Satisfaction at living within a ramshackle system that works well as a consequence of a unique history is a special Dutch national conceit. "Consensus and accommodation," according to one expert,

are key words in any characterization of ... Dutch society ... the Dutch love to have meetings about everything and nothing. Sitting around the table seems [to be] a collective social habit and a quintessential feature of the consensus society .... Everyone can participate, have their day, and feel part of the decision-making process. But a decision once made is indeed accepted, even when it involves *gedogen,* a well-nigh untranslatable term that means looking the other way when you must .... Often carried over into English as "tolerance," [it] could also come close to meaning something like sogginess, fudge or even hypocrisy.[80]

The events of the recent past suggest that the limits of *gedogen* may have been reached.

Many foreigners have admired and sought to copy the Dutch model of good government, self-government, and civic activism, and some of the greatest minds of Netherlands political science have spent long years agonizing over the lessons that might be learned from it. Adriaan Lipjhart eventually arrived at seven, since famous, basic rules of Dutch politics: be practical; agree to disagree; solve crises at the top; include all parties in the settlement; turn ideological issues into technical ones; use secrecy to reach difficult compromises; and recognize the right of the government to govern.[81] The Wassenaar Agreement of 1982 embodied such approaches. It created that rare social partnership that actually produced sound results, indeed turned the "Dutch disease" into the "Dutch miracle," even gave rise to a so-called Polder Model that conjoined economic growth and the welfare state in a democratic politics of consensus. Wim Kok, head of the Labor Party, led the negotiations. He would become the dominant figure in Dutch politics for the next twenty years. The Wassenaar Agreement succeeded where other similar-sounding arrangements have failed, according to M. Peter van der Hoek, because it "has more to do with sociology than economics ... and especially with the key word national consensus," something "so rare that [it] cannot be replicated .... It is not a formula that can be copied elsewhere."[82]

The Dutch affliction of the 1970s was aberrant. It occurred under exceptional conditions, when the discovery of North Sea natural gas made it seem, for a time, as if natural and historical constraints had fortuitously been lifted. The scourge spread after the government of Joop den Uyl, the most left-leaning in the history of the Netherlands, gave the economy a strong fiscal goosing, dumped money massively into welfare schemes, jacked up the minimum wage, kite-tailed wages in the unproductive public sector to high flyers in the competitive private sector, and overgenerously indexed social security benefits. With the gulden already geared permanently to the sturdy DM, much of the export industry quickly became uncompetitive, bankruptcies rose perilously, unemployment soon soared to 800,000, and growth came to a juddering standstill. The unions soon lost 17 percent of their membership, and the public deficit rose to 6.5 percent of GDP.[83] The huge one-time yield from the sale of gas kept the orgy in full swing. The flows might as well have been flamed off for all the good they did.

By the 1990s, however, the only disease discursively connected with the Netherlands was the Dutch elm blight; talk of a "Dutch miracle" had by then become the rage. The Netherlands has, in fact, managed for nearly two decades to maintain a high level of noninflationary growth and a low budget deficit – while suffering little unemployment. The Wassenaar Agreement of 1982, the keystone of this success, put Dutch economic policy back on the traditional track.[84] Resting on a joint union–management promise to enforce wage restraint, it brought centralized bargaining to an end and opened the way for a release of market forces. The deal cut the Netherlands adrift from the turbo-Keynesian welfarism of the den Uyl years, let the economy float toward the open market, and was also part of a more general parting with the traditional semi-corporatist welfare state. The power of the social partners to manage the benefits system ended. Taxes came down, the provision of social benefits was decoupled from wage increases, collective bargaining was decentralized, medical benefits were reduced, and health insurance was privatized. The pact did not, as often misrepresented, vindicate the "Rhenish model" but was, instead, a decisive step away from it.[85] The share of public expenditure dropped from 66 percent of GDP in 1985 to 43 percent in 2000, wage costs fell relative to those in neighboring countries, the number of jobs increased at four times the European rate and on a par with the American, unemployment held steady at 4 percent (less than half the EU average), and annual growth increased at a rate 0.8 percent higher than the northwest European average.[86]

A couple of splotches mar the pretty picture. The new jobs were nearly all part-time, temporary, and held by women – the same group whose greater participation in the American labor force accounted for its overall increase in employment.[87] The really disfiguring splotch is disability leave. It can be taken at full salary for a year and, after a single day's work, is renewable for another year, and so on indefinitely. If one includes the disproportionate number of Dutch goldbrickers as unemployed, then the job-creation part of the miracle looks more like a magician's sleight of hand. Even though the Netherlands is at the very top of longevity charts, estimates of persons on disability run from 8 to 13 percent of the workforce – between two and three times the EU average.[88] They raise the true rate of Dutch unemployment into double digits.

Attempts to curtail abuses have been futile. An effort in the aftermath of the Wassenaar Agreement to pass a new law cutting sickness and disability benefits triggered the largest union protests of the postwar period. A subsequent administrative ruling to curtail abuses of "lower back pain" gave rise to an epidemic of "work stress" and did nothing to diminish the number of "disabled." No one seemed to object too strongly. Was it not better to be ill, or at least feel ill, than to suffer the shame of not holding a job?[89] Was not *gedogen* a humane interim solution to the unemployment problem? There was, of course, no lack of work – only of a willingness to do unpleasant jobs. New immigrants, many Muslim and illegal, made up for shortages in labor supply.

A 1997 study by the McKinsey consulting firm argued that further liberalization will probably be needed in the Netherlands for long-run growth.[90] Competition remains lax. Limits on hiring and firing, together with stringent collective bargaining agreements, conspire to keep the Dutch below even Denmark on OECD tables ranking labor flexibility. It is also difficult to set up new companies, social security benefits are still overgenerous, and the "disabled" must be put back to work in order to make the economy grow. The study concludes that the Dutch could raise output by 15 percent and create a million new jobs by lowering such barriers. The ground lost in the years of the "Dutch disease" could then be regained. In 1973, GDP per capita in the Netherlands was at the top of the eleven northwest European countries; by 1987, it was at the bottom. By 1997 the Dutch had climbed their way back to seventh on the list. According to one recent economic study, "the ... growth performance of the Netherlands has primarily been the result of a correction of the below-average performance during the 1970s ... brought about by significant wage moderation."[91] A slight rise in inflation and a fall in labor productivity together suggest, according to the OECD, that the wave may have crested by mid-2001. A slowdown should be expected.

The Dutch apparently were not worried that the tulip might have begun to wilt.[92] By 2002 the Netherlands had outperformed nearly every country in Europe for almost ten years, had a generous welfare state as well as a constructive commitment to European integration, and seemed to be developing into a successful multiracial society at peace with itself. If many Dutch chose not to work, so much the better: it meant that they had learned to value leisure more highly. The people of the polder, it seemed, had learned to live sensibly and had generated innovative ways of dealing with the collective stress, anger, and hostility that accompanies modern change. The Netherlands was a happy society, content with itself.

According to the journalist Roel Janssen, the Dutch were in fact entering a new Golden Age.[93] A budget surplus in 2001, the first in thirty years, facilitated the largest single tax cut since the war. The shift of wealth from the public to the private sector stimulated a boom in property values, making many feel rich. Other stuff also made life pleasant. Recreational drugs were legal and easily accessible. The same was true of abortion. Prostitutes were allowed to unionize.[94] Handicapped Dutch men, and women as well, were entitled to weekly servicing by unionized "sex workers," courtesy of the national medical service. Euthanasia was encouraged. Bill Clinton singled out the Netherlands as ideal exemplar of the Third Way.[95] The Pope made no comment.

Official politics were clubby and pleasant. According to the *Economist*:

The general election ... on 6 May 1998 ... promises to be the most mild-mannered – don't call it dull – parliamentary contest in Europe this decade. The two main opponents, the oh-so-responsibly left of center Labor Party, led by the prime minister Wim Kok, and the gently free-market Liberals, led by the (in Dutch terms) fearfully adversarial Frits Bolkestein have actually been getting along embarrassingly well as a ruling "purple" partnership for the past four years. To make matters even friendlier, most of Mr. Bolkestein's party supporters would apparently prefer Mr. Kok to go on running the show.

The Christian Democratic Appeal, the centrist Catholic party that ran the government from 1917 to 1994, did not even bother to challenge the "purple" coalition of Labor and Liberals because, according to the writer, "it is hard to find a burning issue for the Dutch to get angry about ... in Dutch politics ideology seems to be nearly dead."[96]

Foreign Minister Hans van Mierlo, not the "flying" but the "sighing" Dutchman, conveyed a similar impression. According to the *Economist*, Mierlo "keeps a close watch on the EU and the future of humanity, ... seems to care little about the possible loss of Dutch identity," and professed not to be in the least concerned that the country's traditions were disappearing under a European shroud. "What the hell are we losing?" he asked rhetorically. "The concept of the state, which isn't that old – 200 years or so – is being eroded," and the Netherlands, he added, had already been reduced from a state to a region.[97] Characteristic Dutch cautionary disparagement? Too secure to worry? Complacency? All the above, according to a part-time futurologist.

"Visions of the Twenty-first Century Dutch" presents journalist Roel Janssen's lighthearted glimpse into the future of the polder people. He imagines that a hundred years hence the Kingdom of the Netherlands will have disappeared as an independent nation and become a region in an expanded European Federation.

No one would really suffer as a result. The exiled House of Orange would rusticate comfortably on the Argentine pampas, while cows would graze in most parts of the Netherlands outside the conurbation known as the Randstad – the area roughly defined by the present-day cities of Amsterdam, Rotterdam, The Hague, and Utrecht. Three transportation corridors would pass through the bucolic scene, connecting the Randstad to the states of the former Germany and to Flanders as well as Wallonia and the other French-speaking regions to the south. Dutch would be spoken only by old folks.

The people of the former Netherlands would get an early lead into the large and growing market for leisure drugs in the early twenty-first century, Janssen predicts, but over time would lose out to French food conglomerates and German chemical giants – both financed by The City of London and able to provide cheap, reliable, upscale synthetic forms of consciousness-raising pharmaceuticals to the expanding population of pleasure-seeking senior citizens. Thanks to an abundance of capital and a strong position in the traditional field of electronics, what was left of Dutch industry will thrive producing software in "Polder Valley." The absence of manufacturing and an ecological ban on overcultivating farmland will reduce late twentieth-century pollution and restore the wonderful blue skies of seventeenth-century landscape painting. Early experience as a leisure society would put the Dutch at the cutting edge in the active and fruitful pursuit of pleasure, life's true purpose. At the end of the twenty-first century, the Dutch Reformed Church will be established as the official state religion and put under the administration of the cultural heritage commission. The Roman Catholic Church would disband itself in the former Netherlands. Islam would become the largest single faith.[98]

Janssen was hardly the first commentator not to predict the coming of Pim Fortuyn, but, in retrospect, someone should have done so. Haider, Kjaregaard in Denmark, Berlusconi, the rising power of Le Pen, the rightward drift in Germany, and the recent formation of conservative governments in Portugal and Norway all point in the same direction. Even in the prosperous and complacent Netherlands, political problems were mounting at the beginning of the twenty-first century, and neither resort to sex and drugs nor reference to clear skies, eco-agriculture, and the pleasure principle addressed them. The astonishing rise of Pim Fortuyn provides striking evidence of a public sense of disenfranchisement, helplessness, vulnerability, and powerlessness. A crisis of democracy seemed to be brewing in the very place the system was supposed to work best.

Pim Fortuyn may have provided a timely wake-up call to the Dutch, or perhaps something more in the nature of a warning shot. The populist right is hardly the place one might expect a character like him to crop up. Fortuyn bore scant resemblance to either the quiet, brown-suited (and recently "outed" gay) mayor of Berlin or any of the numerous officially repentant homosexual respectables of Westminster. He was an uncloseted, overt, completely unashamed flamer – who knew what he was and who he was, made no apologies, and reveled in his own theatricality – a striking man with shaved head, a pampered pooch on a string, an ostentatious monogram on his Bentley, a sashay, a professed desire to wield one of Mrs. Thatcher's handbags, and a snappy answer to any question. But he spoke in the name of traditional Dutch rights and privileges and in a straightforward manner wholly consistent with customary liberties – to do one's own thing, control one's own government, protect one's own community, and make one's own opinion heard.

Fortuyn was in certain respects a threatening figure. He had a dangerous penchant for the simplistic and an unhealthy taste for rabble-rousing as well as for young Arab men. Yet he argued in defense of openness and individualism, accountability, plain speaking, and a national political tradition that the establishment politicians either seemed to have forgotten or no longer took seriously. Immigrants – those who came mainly to do the dirty work for which the natives were too proud – were unfortunately his target, at least those of them whose values seemed by Dutch standards to be narrow and intolerant. But who, and precisely which groups they comprised, was never made clear. They were not targeted for individual scapegoating, harassment, or violence. Assimilation – not lack of it – was Fortuyn's goal. Racism as such was absent. The second-in-charge of Pim Fortuyn's List was a black businessman originally from the Cape Verde Islands. The problem with the immigrants, from the Dutch standpoint, was one of sheer numbers; Fortuyn's policy was to prevent any more from coming. The foreign born comprised some 40 percent of the population of Rotterdam – in a small, densely populated country like the Netherlands, a presence that was impossible to overlook and that made one feel a stranger in one's own community. The anti-immigrant appeal was a cheap way to get votes. It also warned politicians, both in The Hague and in Brussels, to forget for a moment their seemingly all-important plans, projections, and constructions and listen for once to the voices of their constituents: the failure to do so was demonstrably undermining the national tradition of self-determination by consensus and turning the Dutch, for the first time, into Euroskeptics.[99]

Pim Fortuyn's assassination on the eve of the Dutch election, according to John O'Sullivan, was "like the shaking of a kaleidoscope" that will produce "dramatically different new patterns of politics."[100] It is impossible to know what such configurations might have looked like if Pim Fortuyn were alive. Fortuyn was a political unknown prior to March 2002, when – campaigning under the slogan of "Liveable Rotterdam" – he took first place in city council elections. He then formed the List named after him in order to contest the May elections. In a television debate the day before his murder (by an extremist vegan protesting his refusal to support a ban on mink farming), Fortuyn seriously outpointed the other candidates: 40 percent of the viewers reckoned that he had "won," and another 26 percent were impressed by the candidate of the Greens. Ad Melkert, head of the Labor Party (the dominant force in the government coalition), impressed only 8 percent of the audience sample. In the last poll before he was killed as well as in the actual returns, Pim Fortuyn's List came in second only to the centrist Christian Democrats, who had been out of power for the previous eight years. Unlike Labor, the Catholics neither snubbed Fortuyn nor repudiated his stand on immigration.[101] Holding 26 seats, his List was included in the new coalition. The Dutch electoral results underscored that the mainstream parties overlooked voter alienation at their own peril. They did not point to the permanence of a right-wing insurgency. Fortuyn's followers proved, even by their own admission, unfit to govern and have left the cabinet in disgrace. The List vanished in the elections of 22 January 2003, but Pim's influence did not. "Out went political correctness," the *Economist* reported, "and into all three main parties' view of migration, openly, came much of what [Fortuyn's] voters had said." The politicians had apparently been forced to listen.[102]

CHIRAC TO CHIRAC: FRANCE ON HOLD

In France, too, a party was going on, but it was not open to the public. It took place in a back room, and only the politically connected could join in. There was plenty of champagne, the finest vintages, and more of it on the way. Everyone seemed eager to contribute in order to get on board. The guests all drank greedily, but even the finest varieties tasted stale. The problem was not old wine but old palates. It is depressing to think that the twelve-year period beginning in 1995 started out with one presidency of Jacques Chirac and will end with another. Chirac is

a consummate election winner who has not known what to do with victory.... He has advocated everything from Thatcherite-Reaganite economics to French laborism,... faced both ways on Europe, and he picks up and discards ideas like lint .... Surrounded by a wave of scandal allegations, Chirac is not exactly the man one would choose to lead a national revival around the core republican values of freedom, equality, and fraternity.[103]

Chirac's face has been before the French public since 1975, when he first became prime minister. His initial presidential term was wholly undistinguished, scandal-plagued, blundering, unimaginative, disingenuous, and occasionally demagogic. While it is hard to point to a single impressive positive achievement in the France of these years (unless entrance into the EMU be mistakenly claimed), it is easy to locate the most serious and persistent unsolved problem: unemployment, especially of young people. The phenomenon gave rise to much tut-tutting about "social exclusion," but nothing really consequential was done to end it. Far from being either necessary or inevitable, the wretched problem resulted from two reversible decisions: to defend the overvalued franc and to protect labor markets. Not globalization but rigid protectionist policy making is what gave rise to *les exclus*. No French leader could be found with the courage and foresight to do anything about it, at least openly.

The French preferred Chirac in 2002 as the lesser evil. He was probably the right choice. One alternative candidate was the aging know-nothing, quasi-racist populist from the National Front, Jean-Marie Le Pen. Le Pen was already a force to be reckoned with in 1995. He represented a stable constituency of the chronically disgruntled, many of them stranded former communists. Le Pen actually increased his vote in the preliminary ballot from 15 to 16 percent in the two elections of 1995 and 2002. It was enough to get him in the runoff. The Socialists, a voting bloc put together almost single-handedly by François Mitterrand, also put up a candidate. Virtually installed as "co-habiting" prime minister by President Chirac in 1997, Lionel Jospin's showing in the 2002 election was so dismal that, even though able to ride a miniwave of prosperity, he failed to qualify for the second round. He stood, it was complained, for nothing. The diagnosis was correct. Because official socialist economic policy did not work, unacknowledged "capitalist" expedients had to be found that did. Word and deed did not go hand in hand in policy making. The candidate thus swaddled himself in shades of gray. The future of French socialism now looks bleak, as does that of the present system. A few pundits have even detected the outlines of a Sixth Republic on the horizon.[104]

The chimera of grandeur is the source of France's current malaise. The quest for this elusive prize has trapped France in the coils of commitments it cannot meet and ends it cannot reach, raised expectations it has no chance of fulfilling, and deferred frank confrontation with the important challenges it faces. A pervasive *morosité* is the result. The Maastricht plan for French co-leadership of Europe never got off the ground. The effort to qualify for EMU weakened the economy, increased public insecurity and frustration, and gave rise to pusillanimity, panic, and hysteria. It is evident in both an excessive and sometimes ludicrous anti-Americanism and an introspective and sickly *souverainisme*.[105]

Shorn of intellectual adornment, *souverainisme* means merely favoring national interests. It excludes not only leadership of but also participation in any form of European federal government worthy of the name. It does not, however, foreclose two possible dangers: the creation of a new Europe-wide police authority and the waging of a prestige-based security policy. Both of them remain official French aims. What the country stands to gain from this pursuit, apart from "prestige" and psychic affirmation, is by no means obvious. In this respect the policy is a fit complement to that of the EMU, which in some unspecified way France expects to "capture" and operate to advantage. Yet any serious French attempt to impose a level of political control over the governing central bank directorate – in order, say, to introduce the easy money policies that France needs – would almost surely cause the Germans to bolt, and co-bolting with them would be the Low Countries, the eastern Europeans of the former Deutsche-mark belt, the Spanish, and so forth. The EMU would disappear. Only tinkering at the margins is possible unless the single currency bloc is re-configured as a monetary regime with competing national currencies floating against a "parallel" European one. Enlargement, which France would prevent altogether if possible, will dilute French influence in the future Union and presumably also its interest in federalizing Europe.

An eventual French realization that the huge, long-term investment in European leadership has been money squandered is not a pleasant matter to contemplate. The governing elite has typically presented the European Union to the public as a French accomplishment, but if in some respects it resembles the

État writ large, in other more important ones it does not. Brussels has been an even more powerful agent of liberalization. The EU is bound to disappoint the growing numbers of French voters who have apparently been persuaded by their politicians to view "Europe" as a barrier to globalization. France's obsession with national power has interfered with (but not seriously imperiled) France's ability to respond to world economic challenges. The nation has, of course, profited from the virtual elimination of trade barriers as well as many other agreements of the Uruguay Round. In spite of chronic French foot-dragging, Brussels has managed to force many domestic markets at least partly open and can take credit for having directly or indirectly promoted the creation of business-friendly institutions.[106] Entrepreneurship indeed survives within the French economy, in spite of official discouragement, but also in the face of a Gallic *gedogen* – the practice of looking the other way, or at least of obscuring economic realities from the electorate.[107] The old *Patronat* has re-constituted itself as the more modern and market-oriented MEDEF (*Mouvement des Enterprises Françaises*).[108] Significant economic and structural change is under way. The task facing France is to cope with such change politically. Adaptation will require shifting power from the state to the private sector; opening the dominant elites to fresh personalities, views, and interests; replacing the rigid intellectual mindset that aggravates problems it purports to solve; learning less doctrinaire approaches; eliminating the privileges enjoyed by insiders that exclude outsiders; opening markets to more competition; and restoring self-government to the people. Little development along these lines took place during the Chirac presidency.

He faced a standing dilemma: either to sacrifice the *franc fort* that had made France economically respectable or to trim back the welfare state – a choice between policies that would promote economic growth and strengthen the state on the one hand and those that would win elections on the other. There was no easy escape. France was "fragile" and feared for its national identity. The state itself had been "colonized" by militant public employee unions which, though relatively few, could be confident of support from public-sector stakeholders – the huge number of beneficiaries from transfer payments. Wary of confrontation, Chirac might earlier have heeded the words of the British Labour politician Dennis Healey: "If you can't ride two horses at once, don't join the circus." In the first five months of office, May to October 1995, Chirac (and his spear-carrying prime minister, Alain Juppé) promised to create 3 million jobs. Abruptly and without explanation, he then declared for austerity. With taxes already stratospheric and unemployment at 12 percent and rising, Chirac soon faced a serious threat to public order, possibly even along the lines of a 1968 upheaval. Although the massive 21 December 1995 strike of public employees was not supported by either the private sector or the two smaller unions, it dropped the Chirac–Juppé government to its knees in the first round. Juppé abandoned plans for pension reform, railroad privatization, and deregulation and then agreed to an "employment summit." Two days later, he abandoned what remained of the austerity package. Juppé never recovered.[109]

In April 1997, facing the need to freeze the budget in order to hew to the convergence criteria, President Chirac – to almost universal astonishment – called for a legislative election a year earlier than necessary, even though his government controlled an overwhelming 80-percent legislative majority. His motives remain puzzling. If one assumes that Chirac thought even this commanding margin insufficient to prevent a recurrence of the December 1995 disorders, his purpose might then have been either to turn an overwhelming into a crushing majority or to force the socialist "party of work" to share responsibility for pursuing an inflationary and economically ruinous policy that would discredit France in Europe. Chirac would win either way. The Socialists swept the boards. Five years of unpleasant, devious, and in some ways unpredictable cohabitation began. *Business Week* feared for the worst:

When Lionel Jospin's Socialist Party swept to victory in the recent election, business leaders were steeled for what they fear will be a dangerous step backward for the French economy. If the Socialists carry out their agenda, they will increase government intervention … stall privatizations, bolster a costly welfare state, and tighten labor market rules that are already too rigid.[110]

These were reasonable surmises on the basis of Jospin's promises. Two days before the election Jospin even joined forces with the German SPD's Marxist-fundamentalist party chairman, Oskar Lafontaine, to call for a continent-wide job-creation pact.[111] Workers in 23 European countries held rallies to shout the message that unemployment, not budget restraint, should be their governments' principal concern.[112]

But a funny thing happened on the way to the class confrontation. Jospin became a crypto-capitalist. The 35-hour week – the *réduction du terme de travail* (RTT) and centerpiece of Jospin's 1997 campaign – became the cause not of France's economic downfall (as almost universally predicted) but of its recovery at the end of the decade.[113] The surprises began with the implementation of the RTT. According to Christopher Caldwell, MEDEF (the revitalized employers' association) succeeded in

shaping … the 35-hour work week in ways [that] those who drafted the law would never have envisioned. As it stands, RTT actually increases the number of authorized overtime hours and decreases the overtime premium. What's more, companies have "annualized" the arrangement, so that those who need forty hours' work from their employees can get it – by giving back the five weekly hours as vacation time. Many mid-level employees … have discovered to their surprise … that they [are] entitled to five weeks of paid vacation.[114]

Employers also somehow managed, presumably with labor authorities turning a blind eye, "to re-negotiate, from the ground up, employment arrangements that were decades old" and to cut salaries, eliminate privileges, and win constraints on long-term bargaining agreements. As a result, unemployment fell from 13 to 9 percent in three years.[115] "The thirty-five hour week created jobs," according to best-selling author Alain Minc, but "for reasons other than the ones the government is citing. It created jobs because it held down wages" and has even introduced a measure of Dutch-style labor flexibility.[116]

"Stealth capitalism," as Minc calls the Jospin policy, was no oversight but resulted from a perceived political necessity. "We have labor savings," Minc snickers, "but you have to [make them] without claiming credit ... we have a kind of double language."[117] The 35-hour week was anything but an isolated example. Learning a lesson from Juppé's ill-fated effort to launch private plans, the government also introduced pension reform by stealth – in the form of "a voluntary long-term savings scheme ... whereby workers get tax-breaks and their contributions are deducted from wages, which are then topped up by employers." In the words of a Paris bank official, it amounted to "a pension fund in disguise, but the government avoided using that ideology-charged term."[118]

Jospin's clandestine relationship with the market mechanism was more than a succession of one-night stands. It was a lasting affair. Under three different finance ministers, Jospin totally or partially privatized more companies than his four predecessors combined, $40 billion worth.[119] In the end, the thing was too big to keep under the covers. In 2000 the third of his finance ministers, Laurent Fabius (who had "turned the wheel" for Mitterrand back in the early 1980s) presented his countrymen with "the largest change in tax structure in half a century." Made possible by the windfall sale of mobile telephone licenses, it took a whack of $5.5 billion out of the value-added tax, income tax, and local taxes. It was the Socialists' pre-election gift to the French people.[120]

The *fin de siècle* pro-market policies were a remarkable success. Economic growth averaged over 3.3 percent for the four years beginning in 1997, far outpacing Germany. More new jobs were created in France than in either Germany or Great Britain, some 450,000 in 1999 alone. The rate of unemployment came down to single digits. The *Bourse* jumped 50 percent in 1999, and the *Nouveau Marché* leapt an astonishing 135 percent. Had the good times continued to roll, Jospin might have able to been put a ring on his sweetheart and make his new relationship with the market "legit," but the world economic downturn that swept through France in mid-2001 ended any such reveries.[121] For the French left, capitalism remained an illicit pleasure.

There was a leaven to the *morosité* of Jacques Chirac's first presidential term, and he helped provide it. The leaven was scandal, with plenty to go around. In 1996 Jean-Claude Méry, a wealthy property developer and a senior official in M. Chirac's Gaullist RPR party, decided to make a video "as a form of protection" and "in case anything should happen to me." In September 1999, a year after Méry died of cancer, someone slipped a copy of the tape to *Le Monde*, which reported its contents beginning in October and continuing until the eve of the Nice summit in December. On the video, Méry claimed to have run a kickback scheme – 1.5 percent on all public contracts – that over a seven-year period provided in excess of $35 million of illicit funding to the RPR in the 1980s and 1990s (when Chirac was mayor of Paris), paying out 80 percent and keeping the rest for himself. Méry specifically recounts one instance when he forked over $600,000 to an aide in the presence of Chirac, at the time both mayor and prime minister. The president predictably denounced the charges on television as "abracadabra," but his deputy as mayor, the aide presumably in question, was placed under investigation and soon jailed for refusing to talk.[122]

Prime Minister Jospin played the injured party to the hilt, denouncing President Chirac as "the number-one opponent of the French government." Therewith ended any pretense of cooperation between the two gents. The campaign for the presidency began. The debacle at Nice provided a welcome diversion from mounting evidence of bursting RPR coffers. The press darling Dominique Strauss-Kahn, who earlier had been forced to step down as Jospin's finance minister for a relatively minor indulgence in corrupt practice, then came unwittingly to Chirac's rescue. Unable to deny leaked information that he had been given a copy of the Méry tape, Strauss-Kahn's improbable declaration that he had never actually seen the thing aroused ample suspicion that, for the Socialists, the scandal was only part of the game known as "politics as usual."[123] The matter reached stalemate. The crisis passed.

On an early February morning in the Philippines, a 74-year-old Frenchman facing police detention opened the back of his cellular telephone and calmly ate its memory chip. His name was Alfred Sirven. He had formerly been executive vice-president and bribemaster of the state-owned petroleum company ELF, was a fugitive from justice, and boasted that he had collected enough dirt to "topple the republic twenty times over."[124] The ELF scandal had a slow-drip quality to it – the investigation had been going on for nearly seven years – but had already brought down no less a figure than the "famously cunning lawyer and ladies' man" Roland Dumas, who had been foreign minister under Mitterrand as well as a close friend and confidante. At the time the investigation began, Dumas served as chief justice of the French equivalent to the U.S. Supreme Court.[125]

Even more entertaining than the spectacle of the defiant, uncooperative, and completely unrepentant ex-justice was his co-defendant, a woman who referred to herself as "The Whore of the Republic," his ex-mistress Christine Deviers-Joncours. She was a still sultry fifty-something "with the body of a goddess, a generous mouth, and big green eyes that are never lowered," whose pimping husband had put her up to the job of keeping Dumas well and properly seduced in order to help make something out of her otherwise pointless existence.[126] ELF paid Deviers-Joncours a modest salary for a position with no apparent purpose other than to keep a shit-eating grin pasted across Dumas's face, to which end she could bring to bear not only her evident physical attributes but also her access to an open expense account. From it she drew about $45,000 every four weeks. The two high-flying sybarites actually spent $42,000 in a single month at a posh Paris restaurant. Although Devier-Joncours's habit of flicking cigarette ashes on the Oriental carpets while draping her long legs over the arms of gilded chairs angered many mid-level company bureaucrats at the office, she was apparently worth the money and the extra efforts of the cleaning crew.

Dumas helped ELF bag several big contracts. For his part, Sirven pocketed many millions of dollars. Company president M. Loik Le Floch-Prigent, who was already in jail on related charges and legally in very deep water, claimed that Mitterrand warned him never to tamper with a system put in place during de Gaulle's era in order to win friends in high places. Le Floch-Prigent provided a long list of well-known French political names – including current cabinet ministers – who had been on the receiving end of the company's generosity. Sirven remained incarcerated and kept his mouth shut, with little apparent attempt being made by anyone to open it up. The defendants – the former chief justice, his self-proclaimed Whore, and the ex-CEO of ELF – received prison sentences.

The scandals amused as well as disgusted, produced *Schadenfreude* rather than anger, did not have *tangentopolis* and *mani pulite* as sequels, and in the end merely confirmed widespread and well-founded public suspicions that the system was incapable of reforming itself. Chirac's involvement in funding shenanigans would have come as a surprise to no one except perhaps his mother. More damaging than the president's being implicated in the sleaze – he, after all, enjoyed immunity from prosecution – was the spreading involvement of intelligent and comparatively youthful leaders like Dominique Strauss-Kahn who might otherwise have "made a difference." Here was a gifted man, a pragmatic realist with a popular touch, who understood the ins and outs of both economics and politics and was committed to modernization. Yet the vast hopes vested in him as savior of the Socialist Party came a cropper no less than three times by dint of association with corrupt practices.[127] A tragic scandal involving the careless use of AIDS-infected blood, which caused the death of more than 500 hemophiliacs, similarly tainted the career of Laurent Fabius – a technocrat's technocrat – for many years.[128] Even the name of Alain Madelin, the one genuine French cabinet-level economic liberal of the past two decades, was dragged into the ELF affair.[129]

The repatriation in February 2002 from another tropical country (the Dominican Republic) of still another fugitive well-placed former RPR bagman, Didier Schuller – who could confirm Méry's story of payoffs in Paris and testify that he had witnessed M. Chirac personally accept money from the (since deceased) land developer – had no discernible outcome on the election.[130] Nor, by the same token, did public knowledge of a potentially far more damaging (financially, and perhaps politically) scandal: the $30 billion public bailout of Crédit Lyonnaise. This bank was a *grand projet* of the late Mitterrand years. With unrestricted taxpayer funding and top-level enarch leadership (administered by the technocratic *Wunderkind* Jacques-Yves Haberer), it was supposed to have developed into the French answer to the Deutsche Bank. Haberer put the bank on an acquisition binge, which led to extraordinary misjudgments and asset fire sales of historic proportions, reeked of fraud as well as top-level stupidity, and took place behind a screen of total public unaccountability. A mysterious yet timely fire destroyed bank records in 1996, delaying prosecution for years. Indictments finally came in July 2002. Among those delivered writs was Jean-Claude Trichet, the designated successor to Willem Duisenberg as president of the European Central Bank. Trichet was finance minister in the early 1990s and thus responsible for the oversight of Crédit Lyonnaise.[131]

The April 2002 elections were a triumph for no one. Jacques Chirac was the first choice of less than 20 percent of a thinned-out electorate. Many of those who voted for him in the runoff went to the polls with clothespins on their noses. Chirac's first term provided France with seven hollow years during which he failed even to address the main problems facing the country. Not only were most of the old players still on hand in 2002, the election itself was a rerun of unresolved issues from 1995. Neither Chirac nor Jospin, elderly tin-eared men out of touch with the voters, came to grips with the tough issues: France's place in the world, its fear of globalization, the rigid bureaucracy, pensions, unemployment, or even – the hobbyhorses of M. Le Pen – crime and immigration. The failure to confront the geriatric ruffian on the latter issue, coupled with growing public resentment of the EU, probably provided the thin margin that brought him into the runoff and resulted in the resignation of Jospin as head of the Socialist Party. The defection of perhaps 10 to 15 percent of the normally left-wing vote into splinter parties provides the most persuasive evidence of Socialist debilitation. In this race of the decrepit, the party of Mitterrand kept only steps ahead of that of the winning bloc. The parties of the right, with the exception of Le Pen, were almost equally weak and disoriented. The turnout was the lowest on record. Voter apathy is the real story of the 2002 election.[132]

The brilliant critic and commentator Jean d'Ormesson thinks that "Europe" – the great cause of the past fifty years – might have changed the political mood, but he bemoans the fact that the "grand adventure" has turned into a mere "accounting exercise" without the life of legend and the power of myth, lacking an incarnation or any human representation at all. The introduction of the euro, the epiphany of the fifty-year adventure, occurred *sans* trumpets or fanfare; it just, as he puts it, slipped passionlessly into pockets. Ormesson's hope for a revived Euro-idealism is sadly misplaced. *Cris de coeur* meant to remind the French of the grand vision of Europe will fall on deaf ears.[133] Why should one expect the citizens of a nation that has nearly given up hope of governing itself to try to govern a continent?

The dirtiest little secret at the heart of Europe is that the people of France have not ever demonstrated any particular desire to play such a role. From the first, integration has been an elite project and has never subsequently developed into anything else. To set up the coal–steel community, Monnet had to circumvent the legislative process and hot-wire past the French bureaucracy. The French had to be dragged kicking and screaming into the European Economic Community. General de Gaulle made a singularly significant, and by no means unpopular, contribution to blocking its development. Mitterrand turned to Europe only after having nearly ruined the French economy and desperate for a political escape. The Maastricht treaty culminated an intense seven-year campaign of Jacques Delors to "build Europe," but it missed being rejected in France by only a hair's breadth – even after ferocious browbeating and media bombardment of the electorate, two thirds of which did not vote. The political consequences of the economic pain inflicted by EMU qualification made Chirac cower, as did each of the well-meant but threatening German initiatives for a federal Europe. All French political personalities and factions not associated with the Euro-establishment consistently and decisively rejected such proposals.

Whether featuring a "two-speed Europe," a "pioneer group," a "hardcore leadership" or some other clever variation on a tired old theme, French federal plans all boil down to proposals for irresponsible bureaucracies – backstopped by nuclear weaponry – designed to be run by Gallic techno-elites in order to leverage France's national power.

That the dogged commitment to pursuing such lopsided schemes exacts a high price in member-state resentment is an uncomfortable but unmistakable reality that must be reckoned with. Apart from France's Belgian clients, only the pre-Schröder Germans had any real taste for such plans. The spring 2002 elections suggest that, domestically, the chickens have finally come home to roost. French voters are unwilling to contemplate further futile sacrifice in the name of Europe. Any effort to instill a revived sense of special mission into them will either come up short or become counterproductive; it could only turn the nation further inward, slowly sealing it off from healthy interaction with the rest of the world, solidifying existing social divisions, and marginalizing the French within Europe. France surely has an important role to play in the enlarged future EU, but not as one of two dominant powers (or of even three, four, or five) but perhaps of six or seven medium-sized nations and blocs of small nations.[134] This reality will put to a severe test the conviction of Stanley Hoffman, the dean of American political science scholarship on France, that the French nation is making a gracious adjustment to the long-term shift from the powers and perks of great-power status to the more modest role of one among several still powerful midsized nations that can no longer lead.[135]

A turnabout will be required to arrest the decline in relative French power. It may also provide a formula to cure the sullenness, resentment, and resignation that afflicts the country. The state must get out of the economy and let the economy run itself to the greatest extent feasible. In a comparison between French and Italian per-capita growth over the past fifty years, Oxford economist Andrea Boltho recently demonstrated that Italy, starting with two thirds the GDP of France in 1950, has now closed the gap. Latecomer advantage provides part of the explanation, according to Boltho, who adds that the chaotic methods of Italian economic nonmanagement have proven to be more effective than the ordered hexagonal tradition of *dirigisme*.[136] The heaviest price that the French have paid in order to maintain the great-power illusion is in wasted brainpower. An opening of markets will unleash an immense capital of untapped talent, intellectual energy, and creativity, especially the dormant energies represented by the 20 percent of the currently unemployed (and still greater number of underemployed) young adults, who – along with the much-abused immigrants and rest of *les exclus* – have for over two decades borne the brunt of sacrifice exacted by weak and misguided political leaders from both sides of the aisle.[137]

UNITED GERMANY: WELL-MEANING BUT UNWISE

Unlike the exclusive private party organized by the French, the Germans prepared for a huge public celebration, the most spectacular such affair in Europe since World War II. They did everything possible. Location, budget, timetable, favors for the guests – the Germans worked out the arrangements in meticulous detail. Everyone was to be equally happy. Yet no one smiled. A large, elegantly attired party crowded in one corner. It provided the champagne. A smaller, less well-groomed bunch huddled in another. Bottles of the bubbly were regularly dispatched to it across the room by pulley. There was barely enough of the stuff to go around, a little more, to be sure, for those on the sending side, too little for anyone to get very tipsy. The opposing groups mumbled to themselves, occasionally nodding to but mostly just staring past the others. No one felt like staying. Few left happy.

The party of the 1990s went bad for three reasons. The West German economy had begun to get sclerotic at least ten years earlier, the Maastricht convergence criteria placed an additional burden upon it, and the "institution transfer" model that shaped reunification policy inflicted huge costs in a misguided attempt to equalize conditions in the two parts of the country. It overstretched the West economically and in the East produced a heavily subsidized, culturally colonized, resentful and stagnant society. Although feared as potential hegemon, the ability to lead slipped away from the united Germany, a victim of the very European stability policies it had championed. Not just a shortage of money but a lack of high spirits helped kill the fun. It was a special pity for Gerhard Schröder, chancellor since 1998. A genuine bon vivant and always out for a good time, he did his best to animate the festivities. But the party had been organized by his predecessor (Helmut Kohl), the event turned out to be badly planned, and there was little that Schröder could do about it.

The basic reasons for the weakness of the German economy in the 1990s are familiar: excessive taxation and other strong disincentives to work; overregulation, especially of labor markets; a lack of innovation; and institutional rigidity. A model that worked so well for so long should not be readily dismissed, however. In a 1995 Discussion Paper ("German Capitalism: Does It Exist? Can It Survive?"), Wolfgang Streeck provides a lucid cultural and economic analysis of why a system so brilliantly suited to the circumstances of the twentieth century's third quarter has had so much trouble adapting to those of the fourth. German markets are, Streeck emphasizes, "politically instituted and socially regulated, and regarded as creations of public policy deployed to serve public purposes."[138] Wolfgang Münchau of the *Financial Times* puts the matter somewhat less abstractly, noting that the term *Soziale Marktwirtschaft* as currently used "does not simply denote a market economy flanked by a social system, but a social system which penetrates every aspect of the economy itself."[139] German firms, Streeck adds, are "social institutions, not just networks of private contracts or the property of their shareholders. Their internal order is a matter of public interest and ... subject to extensive social regulation by law and industrial agreement."[140] Such practices, Münchau elaborates, "run deep in the veins of Germany's political and economic establishment."[141] The state itself, Streeck proceeds, "is neither *laissez faire* nor *étatiste*, but best thought of an *enabling state*, whose power to intervene is constitutionally hedged in by the powers of semi-public authorities."[142]

Policy responsibility is thus depoliticized and, in the important instance of wage bargaining and regulating work conditions, is shared by organized employer and employee associations, which for their part are obliged to respect both the competition and welfare principles. "Associative regulation," as Streeck calls the tradition, had maintained the "postwar settlement" longer in Germany than elsewhere, as indicated by low wage dispersion. It is profoundly conservative, he adds. Past social and economic success make it psychologically difficult to part with the system, even though its shortcomings have become increasingly evident.[143]

Adaptation is essential because the conditions Streeck cites as required for success of the German economic model are no longer present. Worldwide product markets for quality-competitive goods are not large enough to sustain full employment in an economy that has barred itself from serving price-competitive markets. Product innovation, furthermore, no longer proceeds fast enough to provide a sustained edge in quality-competitive markets. The labor supply, treated by Streek as if fixed, does not fit the volume and character of demand in such markets and specifically is overskilled relative to need. Because goods of equal quality can be produced outside of Germany, insufficient innovation and a surplus of high-skilled workers trained in the wrong fields lead to loss of market share, lack of new market entry, and unemployment. The only open choices are to let the market re-allocate, which takes courage, or to orchestrate some sort of a transition to *sauve qui peut*; the latter involves the convoy principle and is hard to organize, slow-moving, and subject to frequent breakdown.[144]

Bad policy has compounded the problem. Although the secular exhaustion of the German model might have brought on the crisis of the 1990s, the conduct of unification policy greatly added to its severity. No one has ever put the matter more succinctly than Streeck:

The West German response to unification was above all designed to protect the West German social order from being modified by the event. Unification was conceived and executed as a giant exercise in *Institutionentransfer,* a wholesale transplantation of the entire array of West German institutions to the former East Germany.[145]

Business, labor, and the government (as well as the opposition) supported the policy, which included the entire apparatus of associative regulation. The government, employers, and unions committed themselves almost immediately to phasing in wage equality, even though the certain outcome of it would be to make the industry of the new region – variously estimated as being from one half to one quarter as productive as that of the West – hopelessly uncompetitive as well as to create massive unemployment and thus require many years of subsidization. The transfer of West German institutions also resulted in the transfer of West Germans to run them – virtually everyone of any importance.

Living standards in the East improved dramatically from the wretched levels of the previous regime, with income up at least 50 percent, but the mood soured. Initial euphoria gave way in *die neue Bundesländer* to a sense of psychic exploitation or cultural capture from within.[146] Those who had gone East to find equal-status employment when jobs were tough to get in the advanced West resented lazy, cosseted Eastern "ingrates," spoiled by communism into un-Germanness. The economic system worked so poorly and property rights were so confused that carpetbagging was mercifully minimal in the territory of the former German Democratic Republic. So, too, was any spirit of idealism on the part of the *Wessis*, any joy at the exercise of newfound freedom on the part of the *Ossis*, or any real pride on the part of either in the immense achievement of peaceful reunification.[147] If there was a national communion it was, in the manner of early Christian celebrants in ancient Rome, kept secret.

Industrial output in the East fell 65 percent during 1990–1991, industrial employment by two thirds, and agricultural employment by three quarters. The birthrate dropped 60 percent and the marriage rate by 65 percent during the three years after the Wall came down – evidence of trauma.[148] Estimates of net national wealth also followed a sharply southern trajectory. Hans Modrow, the last "leader-of-the-people under real-existing socialism," guesstimated net national wealth at about DM 1.5 trillion. His Christian Democratic successor, Lothar de Mazière, halved the figure to DM 800 billion. The initial chief of the *Treuhand*, the agency set up to privatize the "People's Own Factories" (*Volkseigenebetriebsgenossenschaften*), figured that the assets on his books were worth about DM 600 billion. His successor, after having sold off the lot, came away with a minimum net loss of DM 300 billion.[149]

Chancellor Kohl had assured the public that reunification would be free of charge. Knees began to wobble when, even though serious discussion of the subject was discouraged, the costs gradually became known. Now approaching a trillion euros, they have averaged 4.5 percent of GDP and still run at the rate of 4 percent. An initial growth spurt – stimulated by the construction of transport and telecommunications infrastructures, the renovation of dilapidated cities and towns, and the refurbishment of half the seriously clapped-out housing stock – raised growth rates impressively for three years but then stopped. With labor productivity at no more than 75 percent of West German levels and wages supported at about 90 percent of them, unemployment in the East remains stuck at nearly 17 percent, over twice that in the West, even though meanwhile a million *Ossis* have left the region.[150] Industrial investment in "the new federal lands" is still agonizingly slow as well as heavily subsidized, and it has created little new wealth in the form of secondary industry. No company from the East is listed on the German stock exchange index.[151] The old factories are in ruins and few new ones have been built. Yet the rehabilitated cities are lovely and the views outside their walls pleasantly pastoral. And why not? "Labor Solidarity" has had the impact of a Morgenthau Plan on *Ostdeutschland*.

Gerhard Schröder became chancellor in February 1999. An outgoing crowd-pleaser with a distinctly contemporary lifestyle, he arrived as a welcome contrast to the *bürgerliche* backroom baron Helmut Kohl, who – notwithstanding his protean accomplishments – had been at the apex of European power for too long even for his own good. Although it is still too early to judge Helmut Kohl's legacy, the perspicacious political scientist and Adenauer biographer Hans-Peter Schwarz recognized as early as 1994 that Kohl had locked Germany into policy commitments that overstretched national power. The huge transfers to the *neue Bundesländer* (150 billion DM of a total budget of about 500 billion DM) assured public resistance to any new EU financial commitment, not least of all because social policy consumed another 125 billion DM. Heavy German borrowing in capital markets also put upward pressure on interest rates. Inescapably, Schwarz concluded,

Germany will find itself compelled ... to make its ... European policy more self-centered, more tightly budgeted, and less flexible than it has been, all in the service of ... rather narrowly defined national interests .... A political establishment that prided itself on its international outlook and "post-national and European" ideology is now coming to the painful realization that both at home and abroad such attitudes will no longer work.[152]

Schröder would find it increasingly hard to meet Kohl's commitments. Annual economic growth for the decade averaged only 1.5 percent, at the bottom of the European league and far below the American rate of 3.5 percent. Unemployment hovered around 10 percent, at the 4-million mark. The size of the labor force diminished slightly because of increased retirements on the one hand and falling birthrates on the other. The costs of unification kept the budget under current stress and doubled the national debt. The EMS and later the EMU kept the Deutsche mark (and later the euro) in the vise grip of overvaluation. However, this did not show up in the overall balance of payments – they remained positive because of continued strength in traditional export industries. Yet high taxes and social charges, along with supply-side disincentives, attenuated domestic demand. When the U.S. economy stopped growing in 2000, the German economy shrank as well. The Federal Republic's EMU commitments remained fixed because (1) it was bound to them by treaty and (2) the Bundesbank insisted upon the restrictive monetary and fiscal rules and cannot break them without wreaking havoc. The country was in a box. The external value of the currency could not fall as the economy idled. The convergence criteria, which Germany found increasingly difficult to meet, placed strict limits on the extent to which taxes could be reduced in order to return purchasing power to consumers. During the downturn of 2001–2002, it even appeared that the country was headed into a deflationary trap. Overdue structural reform is the only escape from Germany's plight.[153]

Chancellor Schröder's hands were seriously tied. No one doubted that labor was overpaid, underworked, and overprivileged – in fact, the most expensive in the world. Excessive regulation was a heavy cross for firms to bear. The injunction against dismissing employees created an unwillingness to hire and so increased unemployment. In product line after product line, excessively generous wage and benefits packages priced German goods out of the market. Without reform of the labor market, the economy would wither. Even though union membership had declined by a third since 1990, Schröder could not challenge the authority of the labor movement – still his largest single constituency. Moreover, the tradition of centralized wage bargaining had worked to the past mutual satisfaction of the bargaining partners and kept governments "above the fray," sparing them from intervening in the kind of interest conflict that could detract from authority, prestige, and popularity. In April 2000 the unions accepted moderate wage increases of 2.5 percent, in line with productivity growth, that established a two-year *Burgfrieden* or "peace in the castle." Labor peace ended with the expiration of the deal.[154] Striking then resumed.

Before Schröder could introduce serious economic reform he had to get rid of the incorrigible Oskar Lafontaine, standard-bearer for the hard left. Lafontaine had opposed unification on the grounds that the Federal Republic needed to be taught a lesson in socialist economics by its German "partner-state." He was belatedly forced out the door in March 1999 while still riding the hobbyhorse of European tax equalization.[155] Schröder could now press for the biggest tax reform in fifty years, which passed in December 1999. The omnibus bill included cuts – effective January 2002 – in the top income bracket from 51 to 42 percent and slashes in taxes on corporate earnings from 40 to 25 percent. Even more far-reaching was a provision ending the 50-percent tax on capital gains that had prevented banks, insurance companies, and other financials from selling their cross-holdings.[156]

The banks themselves had lobbied hard for the measure in order to unlock some $225 billion in dormant assets, the capital needed to make over traditional *Hausbanken* into state-of-the-art financial services companies. The new law held potentially revolutionary implications for German business.[157] The Deutsche Bank's sprawling portfolio included a 12.1 percent stake in Daimler-Chrysler, 7.8 percent of the tire manufacturer Continental, and 10 percent of Linde, an industrial gas producer. The rival Dresdner Bank held 30 percent of Linde, 21 percent of Heidelberger Zement, and 5 percent of BMW. The portfolios of big insurers like Allianz were even fatter.[158] Many of the industrial shares, it was hoped, would be snapped up by foreign firms, thus doubling their stake in the German economy to the 36-percent level prevailing in France and the Netherlands and providing a welcome capital infusion.[159] The end of passive *Hausbank* control was intended to force inefficient firms to respond to shareholder concerns and to either become competitive or face market disapproval. Schröder's tax reform was to be a winch for winding down Rhenish capitalism and turning German finance and industry into something resembling its freewheeling American and British counterparts.[160]

The path to the new capitalism was not unobstructed. Progress was slow. Backlash came from within a "traditionalist" segment of industry, spoiled by protection. The CDU aided and abetted this faction and nearly blocked the SPD reform bill. The states, whose interests were largely overlooked in the package, demanded the right to tax dividends. Facing pressure from unions and semipublic companies like Volkswagen, German delegates in the European

Parliament opposed an EU directive to harmonize and facilitate foreign take-over bids.[161] Berlin introduced legislation to strengthen company defenses. The unions pressured the government to toughen co-determination legislation in order to scare off foreign interests.

Schröder continued in the same antimarket vein.[162] He opposed efforts (of EU Competition Commissioner Mario Monti) to break up the manufacturer-supported dealer cartels and special licensing requirements that still fragment the European automobile market and elevate profit margins artificially. He objected to the creation of a price supervision authority for European energy markets. He tried to protect Deutsche Telekom's lucrative monopoly on local telephone hookups. He intervened to block the takeover of the failing and now bankrupt Kirch media network by "foreign interests" (in this case, Rupert Murdoch) and made a serious though eventually doomed attempt to rescue the huge Holzmann construction company. "Facing more than four million unemployed," according to press commentator Josef Joffe, the Schröder government "concluded that it can make electoral hay by keeping change and competition at bay. The chancellor may also calculate that telling Brussels where to get off will garner him votes [at the election] in September [2002]."[163] With the economy sagging to nearly zero growth after mid-2001 and with the commitment to eliminating the budget deficit by 2004 looming closer, a second tax cut – which was sought by many economists, businesses, and consumers – had to be ruled out. In the September 2002 election the theme of stakeholder protection, especially in the employment field, ran through the campaign rhetoric of both Schröder and the CDU chancellor candidate, Edmund Stoiber. Restrictive immigration policy featured prominently in both their electoral packages.[164]

Schröder owed his narrow victory at the polls chiefly to winning the swing vote in *Ossiland* and even more specifically to the flash flooding of the Elbe that began in late summer. A providential event, the flood provided plenty of headlines and photo-ops – a one-time public relations opportunity for Schröder to "take charge," "demonstrate compassion," and exploit on television his easygoing good looks as well as a certain down-to-earth charm with which Herr Stoiber was distinctly not blessed. Stoiber nonetheless managed to maintain a slight plurality in the West, and both candidates held on to traditional constituencies – the most important of which for the winner was, as predicted, organized labor.

The voters' message, as Schröder heard it, was that the German people preferred security to risk, even with stagnation and high unemployment and at the expense of economic growth. In his first post-electoral speech at the *Reichstag,* the chancellor thus stated that "the German people ... don't want the social welfare state to be abolished, benefits to be reduced or job protection to be cut back." Schröder vowed to heed their wishes "in spite of the weak economy."[165] Germany, he thought, needed "less bureaucracy and less reverence for the powers that be – but not less state."[166] At the same time, he stressed that "he had not been elected to serve Germany's business lobby." The Federation of German Industry, the Federation of Employers, the Chambers of Commerce, and the Central

Association of Skilled Workers replied to this declaration of war in kind – by releasing an unprecedented joint letter of protest.[167] "Rarely," reported the *Financial Times,* "have Germany's bosses been so angry." The chairman of Commerzbank complained of the government's "lack of civil courage," a member of the Allianz board predicted the ruin of Germany's reputation as a location for business, and the chief of a leading engineering group warned "that if the economy continues to be throttled,... Germany will turn from a restructuring case to a bankruptcy candidate."[168] Particularly irksome was the proposed new tax bill, which – in the name of "closing down loopholes" – raised corporate tax rates substantially in order to meet the EMU convergence criteria. With economic growth running at only 0.5 percent annually and no relief in sight, gloomsters and doomsters in the press asked increasingly, and with unmistakable *Schadenfreude*: "Is Germany Looking Like Japan?"[169]

The obstacles to German economic growth were by no means all political. Lack of innovation within Germany industry and finance had also been important. A 1996 study (by the McKinsey consultancy firm) of the electronics industry, a traditional pacesetter for the economy, pointed to alarming conclusions. The industry, it predicted, would lose three quarters of its 200,000 jobs by the year 2000 and without innovation (defined as the development of new processes or products) would virtually disappear. The innovation cycle was shortening dramatically: the typewriter lasted well over fifty years and the electric typewriter little more than ten; PC word-processing software is upgraded every six months. McKinsey's worldwide survey of 102 electronics companies indicated that German firms had to move rapidly to improve performance. Not only was the overall productivity of many producers only half that of the successful ones, the "innovation gap" was even wider. German firms generated only $1.3 million in average sales – as opposed to the $3 million of non-German industry leaders – because of lower revenues per product due to a lack of world market "hits." Process innovation, the source of two thirds of manufacturing cost savings, was even slower; and with competitors increasing innovation productivity by 7 to 10 percent annually, drastic measures were called for. Several poor practices had to be changed: firms would have to set higher sales targets, enter faster-growing markets, amalgamate in order to reach critical mass, improve access to sources of outside information, introduce flexible management practices, increase spending on R&D, and tighten their focus. Lacking were a unifying vision, open communications, a readiness to experiment, the use of innovative marketing techniques, and the promotion of entrepreneurship. McKinsey would presumably be happy (for a fee) to demonstrate how such virtues could be put into practice.[170]

Revisiting the scene four years later, the management gurus were encouraged. Although Germany had generated only a single high-tech company – the software powerhouse SAP – the Neuer Markt (a German version of the NASDAQ) had been launched by the Frankfurt stock exchange in 1997, and sufficient venture capital was available for the first time. Germans were finally learning to appreciate the importance of entrepreneurship. The first private business school in the country's history opened in 1998. Yet the young "start-up culture" needed nurturing, especially by large, established companies. BASF, Daimler-Chrysler, Deutsche Telekom, SAP, and Siemens pointed the way, according to the McKinsey experts, but still had far to go in order to catch up with competitors from the United States, where a quarter of new venture capital comes from established firms.[171]

Perhaps the McKinsey bromides lacked enough time to bring world management standards to Germany. The evidence suggests that the magic elixir of the new economy was more apt to cause upset stomachs than to bring relief. Most of the main German forays into the brave new world of global capitalism of the late 1990s have disappointed or gone belly up.[172] Germany has only three truly healthy world-class companies operating internationally as market leaders: Allianz Versicherung, SAP, and BMW. The less said about the remainder, the better. The Deutsche Bank – although still the sector trendsetter – is rudderless, has failed in successive attempts to merge itself into cutting-edge fields, and is in danger of falling out of the first tier of international financials. The DaimlerChrysler merger finally began to turn a profit in the second quarter of 2002 but still looks shaky and may yet become merely the latest in a series of failed Daimler acquisitions, the culmination of which may be to destroy the reputation of Mercedes, the most valuable brand of its era. The Deutsche Telekom story conjures up too many painful memories – especially for the 2 million Germans introduced to shareholder culture by purchasing it – to relate at this point; doing so would leave tearstains on the page. A single world-class German company, Allianz, has successfully "gone global" through international mergers and acquisitions, though by mid-2002 it was suffering severe indigestion problems from having swallowed the Dresdner Bank whole. The vast bulk of merger activity has involved national consolidation rather than multinational marriage.

Yet there is no alternative "best practice." The Rhenish model is not an export product. German organized capitalism, as Streeck trenchantly observes, developed in a specific national context of interwoven public and private institutions that cannot be replicated elsewhere, least of all at the European level. He adds that non-German trade unions and management both object to adopting German governance models for an EU company statute. Streeck also correctly points out that attempts to introduce the state-directed economic model invariably fail at the EU. He concludes that public power can be only be mobilized for market-modifying and market-correcting political intervention at a level where the state is strong – that of the nation. "Globalization ... favors national systems like the United States and Britain that have historically relied less on public-political and more on private-contractual economic governance, making them more structurally compatible with the emerging global system."[173] For Germany, a hard learning process lies ahead.

The decision to shut down the Neuer Markt in 2003 ended Germany's short-lived adventure in the new economy. Between 1996 and 1991, the number of German investors exploded from 9 percent of the German population to over 21 percent. Nearly all of them were badly burned when the market plunged

96 percent from its March 2000 peak amidst a series of scandals involving allegations of insider trading and accounting manipulation. The effort to build a German equity culture has been seriously discredited. The ambitions of the Deutsche Börse to merge with London in order to form a stock exchange on the scale of the NYSE seem far-fetched today.[174] The collapse of the Neuer Markt, conclude Bertrand Benoit and Alex Skorecki of the *Financial Times,* "deepens the uncertainty about the pace of corporate reform ... and raises questions about whether the emerging equity culture will ever take root."[175]

Contributing to Germany's weak economic performance have been the convergence and stability criteria, the high costs of reunification, and the large size (about 0.5 percent of GDP) of its net payment to the European Union. The Federal Republic now covers less than a quarter of the EU budget, in contrast to the one third supplied during the Kohl years. The CDU and SPD are both committed to reducing this contribution (in relative terms) still further after 2006. The paymaster era is drawing to an end. The failure of the Maastricht design to develop substantively, combined with the nearly universal mounting public opposition to the "European construction, " deprives Germany of important policy leverage. Schröder cannot speak in the name of Europe as Kohl once did. Nor is the idea of a single "European vision" credible, as it was in the days of close alignment of the Federal Republic with both France and the Commission. This will only change once the peoples of Europe agree to create a democratic federation, which Germany (by force of numbers and location) would dominate.

The 25 October 2002 Schröder–Chirac Enlargement–CAP deal was a fitting corollary to a new German bipartisanship based on protecting stakeholders and preserving the status quo generally. The deal involved backtracking on earlier commitments of Agenda 2000 and on the constructive though partial reforms initiated by Agricultural Commissioner Franz Fischler, deferred reform of CAP at least until 2007 (and probably until 2013), and sealed the decision to deprive accession countries of an equal share of farm subsidies and otherwise discriminate against them. Negotiated privately between the French president and the German chancellor on the eve of the official opening of the summit in Brussels, the *fait accompli* restored French leadership of the trans-Rhenanian duo – at least temporarily – and eliminated any chance that Germany, not to mention the candidate nations, would benefit from Enlargement. The Federal Republic would instead stave off competition, reform, and adaptation to a changing economic environment. Although the durability of revived Franco-German copartnership has yet to be demonstrated, Chirac-to-Chirac found its equivalent in Schröder-to-Schröder. Political stagnation lies ahead. The only antidote may be the remarkable plunge in Schröder's popularity – which by December 2002 had led to rumors that his own party was trying to force him out.[176]

BRITAIN: NO BEEF HERE

No one could quite recall when the booze began to flow in London. The lady believed to have organized the "do" was under a doctor's order to speak no longer about the matter. The man now in charge talks plenty, but his meaning is often hard to figure out. Not by chance does he resemble a Joker, the extra card in a deck. The giveaway is not the little wand he waves but the glint in his cagey blue eyes. Because he forever darts from place to place and says different things to different people, no one can really tell what he's got up his sleeve or at the back of his mind – or how the party might someday end. Every guest has strong views on the subject, however, and with champagne still pouring in from somewhere, they all clamor for attention. Shouting, jeering, mocking, raucous laughing – the din is almost unbearable. One can hardly think. Eyes have gone bleary and smiles tiddly, gestures loosen and grow expansive, legs get more rubbery, but the celebrating still goes on. Bu-urp, r-r-rumble r-r-rumble. Pf-schitt! (went the lady). Rrrrr-ip! (went the gent). There were oh so many bubbles, and ever so much gas. No one wanted the party to end because everyone feared that a hang-over would follow.

The economy kept the champagne flowing. "What Have Two Decades of British Economic Reform Delivered?" presents the best brief analysis of the subject to date. The authors of this recent National Bureau of Economic Research paper, David Card and Richard Freeman, conclude unequivocally that "during the 1980s and 1990s the United Kingdom arrested the relative decline in [both] GDP per-capita and labor productivity ... characteristic of earlier decades and partially closed the gap in income with France and Germany through relative gains in employment and hours." The United Kingdom further "combined high employment-population rates with rising real wages for workers: an achievement [that eluded] the U.S. ... until the 1990s."[177] The authors demonstrate that 1979 was the watershed date. Output growth per working-age adult had previously been slower in the United Kingdom than in either France or Germany but there-after became more rapid. Unlike Germany and France, employment in Britain continued to increase after 1979. The differential in average GDP growth rates between the United Kingdom and the other two shifted from −0.63 to +0.84 in the two decades on either side of the divide. Card and Freeman attribute the productivity changes to the decline in unionization (4.3 percent), a rise in priva-tization (1.1 percent), incentives to profit making and ownership (2 percent), and changes in self-employment (−0.4 percent); in sum, about 7 percent or 0.35 per-cent per year for 1979–1999) – a quarter of a point higher than in the previous twenty years.[178] The authors further suggest that reduced unemployment bene-fits provided an additional work incentive.

Although Prime Minister Blair signed the EU social charter and attempted to introduce a minimum wage, the Labourites held the line on the Thatcher reforms.[179] The only other important potential exception is the commitment of Blair and Chancellor of the Exchequer Gordon Brown to raise the standards of the National Health Service to the EU average of about 8.5 percent of na-tional income by scheduling increases of 6.4 percent annually between 1999 and 2004.[180] The two men, fierce long-time rivals, are known to disagree on the sub-jects of how best to deliver medical services and how much should be budgeted to pay for them. Closely linked to this problem is another one: the economics of British membership in the European Monetary Union, which Gordon Brown steadfastly opposes. The high costs of Brown's medical reforms could prevent Britain from meeting the convergence criteria for membership in the EMU – whether by accident or design is something known only to the Joker, whose master manipulations obscure intent.[181]

Tony Blair was the least overshadowed head of state during the 1990s, a remarkable accomplishment considering that the woman whose office he assumed was the commanding figure in Europe of the 1980s. During the five-year interregnum between their two governments, Blair transformed the Labour Party: he scrapped the governance rules rigged for trade-union domination; broke with the commitment to socialism, state ownership, and state-promoted social equality; and also made a firm commitment to "Europe." His motivation has often been called into question. Blair's forebears include a prominent actor and actress. At Oxford he is still remembered as the lead singer in an undistinguished rock band called The Ugly Rumours. The near collapse of the Labour Party under the ineffectual leadership of Michael Foot, as well as the inspiration of the otherworldly Anthony Benn, accelerated his rise in politics. Peter Mendelson has been the most formative influence on Blair's career. Spin-master supreme, the scandal-tainted Mendelson is a serious student of politics as marketing and also the father of *glitznost*. To his harshest critics – left and right – Blair, and the New Labour he represents, is sheer opportunism.[182]

Swept into power with a huge majority in 1997 – and retained with the loss of only a few seats four years later – the Labour prime minister stayed the economic course set by Mrs. Thatcher. Privatization and deregulation proceeded, as did the marketization of public services. The Bank of England was set free from Treasury control. The government created new tax incentives for employee share ownership programs and reduced disincentives to jobholding. Taxes remained relatively low compared to the rest of Europe. Blair did nothing to stanch the membership drainage from the unions. Britain would remain Europe's champion of flexible labor markets. In 2000, the Economist Intelligence Unit ranked Britain the second-best place in the world to do business. The OECD, in its first review of the United Kingdom in two years, called the Blair economic record "enviable."[183] Tony Blair did introduce two major institutional reforms with potentially important implications for Britain's relationship to Europe: abolition of the hereditary privilege of sitting in the House of Lords, and devolution of government to Scotland and Wales. Whether the purpose behind the latter was to prepare Britain for a federal Europe (or was in fact even related to it) is unknown and a source of confusion in policy discussion.[184] The outcome of the issue will depend partly upon developments in Europe.

Contrary to the fears and suspicions of the Euro-pessimists who dominated the opposition party, Britain under Blair would not be marginalized permanently into a state of impotent opposition to an inexorable rise of federalism. Consider the circumstances working against centralization: the Commission was feeble and discredited, intergovernmentalism was breaking down, the Franco-German marriage was unraveling, Germany was laboring under the huge costs of unification, France was disenchanted and demoralized, and throughout Europe there was mounting public opposition to remote, impersonal, and unaccountable government at both the national and transnational levels. Moreover, power had shifted (and would continue to shift) from center to periphery as new member-states joined the Union. Foreign Secretary Robin Cook "said it all" shortly after coming to office: "the high tide of integration [has] passed in Europe."[185]

There is still more to Blair's case. British growth far exceeds the EMU average. Inflation and unemployment are low. The head of the Confederation of British Industry, Digby Jones, characterizes the government's macroeconomic record as "superb" and better than that of any government, of whatever color, since World War II.[186] The United Kingdom is the only country to have passed through the regime change process. The open-market policies it favors are more easily transferable than those of France, Germany, or any other major member-state. The successful among the EU nations are those who, as neoliberals, have adapted "Thatcherism" to their special national traditions. Such nations will not thereby become less diverse, more tractable, or easily governable from the center unless their individual political cultures blend into a European *demos*. Until such a distant era, empiricism will trump rationalism. The only feasible growth models are those akin to the British – follow the scenario of evolutionary institutionalism as described by Andrew Shonfield or eventually even the liberal federalism of Ralf Dahrendorf's Third Europe.

Prime Minister Blair's European diplomacy presents a tactical alternative to the present EU – a structure built not on long-term alliances but resting on issue-based coalitions of convenience in which Britain plays a vital role for which no other nation can be substituted. The policy is officially called "the new bilateralism," and by means of it Blair has managed to exploit the special situation of Britain to execute a successful policy of constructive nonbinding commitment. Ideologically, he has bound himself to Schröder and the doctrine of the *neue Mitte* or (middle) Third Way.[187] Exemplary in its vagueness – the American humorist P. J. O'Rourke called it "a clarion call to do *whatever*" – the dispensation required a ritualistic nod toward socialism on the left followed by a knowing wink on the right to competitive markets. The former crypto-Trotskyite prime minister Jospin could not bend his knee for capitalism in public. He would, at least on this question, become an *exclu* from the Third Way duo.

Geopolitically, the British prime minister linked himself to France and made friendly noises (especially at the St. Mâlo bilateral talks) about the Paris-inspired European Defense Initiative. The sign that hung over this happy Anglo-French condominium harked back to the 1948 Treaty of Brussels; it read "Germans Need Not Apply." Yet by supporting U.S. security policy foursquare and participating in such flashy televised American military romps as the overthrow of the atavistic Taliban government in Afghanistan, Blair indicated by deed rather than mere word that France's long-term dual aim – keeping the Germans under control and replacing NATO by creating an independent Euro-army – could not be taken seriously except, perhaps, as a way to prevent post–Cold War staff planners from suffering early brain death due to boredom.[188] By 1 February 2003, Blair's unstinting support for the American policy of overthrowing the Iraqi dictator, Saddam Hussein, by military force (if necessary) had undermined EU efforts to form a solid independent front in the impending confrontation and had raised the personal status of the British prime minister to that of "the second most powerful man in the world" after the U.S. president.

With the inimitable *Signor* Berlusconi, whose ability to govern may well depend in the long run on reducing the unions, Blair staged a celebration of flexible labor markets that would have been politically suicidal for either the French or the Germans.[189] The Brit also stood by the Italian in opposing the creation of both a Euro-police force and Euro-restrictions on bank secrecy laws. Blair struck up a close relationship with the continent's warmest open admirer of Mrs. Thatcher, Prime Minister Jose-Maria Aznar of Spain.[190] Like his predecessors, the present prime minister has unstintingly supported Enlargement – a commitment that sharply distinguishes Britain from Germany, France, Italy, and Spain – which places him in good stead with the accession countries. The need to speed up the process was the main theme of his October 2000 Warsaw speech, the British reply to the earlier ones of Josef Fischer and Jacques Chirac.[191] To Prodi's mounting fury, Blair has simply bypassed the Commission.[192]

Within the European Union, the British prime minister has been as determined an economic liberalizer as his predecessor.[193] His policy can accurately be described as Thatcherism without the handbag. From the continental (as opposed to the British) viewpoint, the differences between the two prime ministers are largely ones of style. Such perceived similarities are common to the EU policies of every other member state: they are all essentially bipartisan, distinctly national, more similar to one another than to those of foreign ideological allies, and reflect deeply inculcated distinctive habits, values, mentalities, and loyalties. Prime Minister Blair's heterogeneous approach has served a traditional British aim: to prevent the formation of any union of continental powers that could threaten the isles' freedom and independence.

On monetary union, Blair wants to hold out until the drive toward federalism runs out of steam. He committed himself early in his first term to holding an EMU referendum by June 2003 if five economic criteria can be met by then. Blair knows full well that at least 60 percent of the British electorate firmly opposes joining the currency union.[194] He cannot be ignorant of the persuasiveness of the economic and political case against adoption of the euro. And, as attested by his running dispute with Gordon Brown, he is surely aware that the EMU membership issue is the most obvious wedge that could split Labour apart. Yet if Blair ceased professing personal support for British membership, he would no longer be an EU player. He would then – as John Major discovered when his Maastricht stalk-out enabled the others to adopt the Social Charter – have difficulty limiting interventionism. Blair could also lose leverage in Washington if Britain disavowed the monetary union. His best choice is to maintain fictive EMU enthusiasm until the project loses momentum and pressure for membership abates.[195]

Blair's actions point even more strongly than his official rhetoric to strong, bipartisan continuity in British integration policy. Like Mrs. Thatcher, he too favors a large, loose, purpose-based, informal, and sensible European confederation that can be constructed and deconstructed as needed.

Margaret Thatcher delineated the main lines of the approach in "Britain and Europe," a speech delivered in Bruges, Belgium, on 20 September 1988.[196] It raised discussion of the subject from the level of cost–benefit analysis to the plane of moral responsibility. Far from rejecting British membership in the Community, which for historical reasons would be futile and destructive, Mrs. Thatcher pleaded for a relationship that would enable Britain more effectively to discharge its traditional responsibilities as guardian of political freedom on the continent and outlet to the world. In the Bruges speech she expressed in unforgettable language the seldom heard (and then barely respectable) viewpoint that the attempt to "build" Europe ran the risk of destroying what is distinctive and of value about its civilization – national tradition, democracy, and enterprise. In a few choice words and phrases, Mrs. Thatcher dethroned the complacent belief that policy made in the name of Europe is ipso facto sound, just, and progressive; exposed it to principled criticism; and, though short on relevant specifics, offered an alternative to the reigning orthodoxy. Instead of the abstract model that M. Delors and his Brussels mandarins tried to superimpose upon Europe's peoples, she presented a positive, cosmopolitan vision of a wider, more democratic, generous, humane, enjoyable, comfortable, and practical Europe. Her vision was fully consistent with European tradition and the intent of the Treaty of Rome, not to mention the lessons of current history. The ebbing of Euro-federalism, Blair's diplomacy, the long-term trend toward globalization, and the spread of liberalization have brought Thatcher's goal within reach.

Europe is great, Mrs. Thatcher insisted, precisely because "it has France as France, Spain as Spain, Britain as Britain, each with its own customs, traditions and identity." It would, she added, "be folly to fit them into some kind of identi-kit European personality."[197] Thus "active cooperation between independent sovereign states is the best way to build a successful European Community. To ... suppress nationhood and concentrate power at the center of a European conglomerate would be highly damaging and jeopardize the objectives we seek to achieve."[198] The Community was but a single manifestation of European identity and, as she reminded the audience, did not yet include Warsaw, Prague, and Budapest, which were then still behind the Iron Curtain. Nor, she warned, should the Eurocracy try to stand in the way of close relationships between the individual nations of Europe and other parts of the world like the United States.

The Community existed to promote the welfare of its member-states and at their sufferance; it was not

an end in itself, or ... an institutional device to be constantly modified according to the dictates of some abstract intellectual concept ... but [provided] the practical means by which Europe can ensure the future prosperity and security of its people in a world in which there are many other powerful nations and groups of nations [and in] ... a world in which success goes to the countries which encourage individual initiative and enterprise, rather than those that attempt to diminish them.[199]

"We have not," she thundered, "rolled back the frontiers of the state in Britain only to see them reimposed at a European level, with a European superstate, exercising a new dominance from Brussels."[200] Intended as a charter of liberty, the Treaty of Rome had been misapplied, she argued. Central planning and detailed control could nevertheless be banished if the single market program could be encouraged by free enterprise within a framework of law and in the absence of central regulation from Brussels.[201]

The Bruges speech gave rise to what has become known as Euroskepticism but which might more accurately be called Euro-criticism or Euro-dissent. It cannot be equated with rejection of the EU (although Lady Thatcher herself has subsequently come close to such a position) but instead refers to an attitude that distinguishes the process of integration from a specific set of institutions, rejects the notion of transcendent purpose, and insists upon using traditional standards of democratic governance to evaluate it. Mrs. Thatcher invited the electorate to assert control over an institution that had been treated as personal property by Eurocrats and irresponsible governments.

The first principled Euroskeptic, Mrs. Thatcher lost both her job and the leadership of her party because of her outspoken views. Yet after Maastricht her successor John Major also grew increasingly Euroskeptical, as did his party. Since 1994 Euroskeptics have held the upper hand over the minoritarian and now profoundly disaffected Europhiles.[202] Tony Blair managed to keep the European issue out of the campaigns of 1997 and 2001, fully appreciating that it could split Labour just as surely as it had the Tories.[203] Today a clear electoral majority in Britain is Euroskeptical, which is not to say that a Europhile government could not someday be formed. It will nonetheless be difficult to maneuver Britain into the EMU. At the same time, a slight majority of the public remains opposed to withdrawal from the EU itself but also deeply dissatisfied with the way it operates.

Although the British pride themselves on their ignorance of the EU, and though foreigners (with the help of rigged Commission polling) generally take them at their word, nowhere has the issue of "Europe" been discussed at such length as in the United Kingdom.[204] A highly Euroskeptical press has subjected the Brussels institutions to an unremitting drumfire of withering criticism, exposed immense fraud, uncovered countless administrative absurdities, and revealed endless instances of intrusiveness, overregulation, bureaucratic empire building, official misrepresentation, obfuscation, stonewalling, and petty tyranny.[205] The journalists have also driven home to the readers of both tabloid and broadsheet the unsettling truth that the lofty, sometimes inscrutable pronouncements from Brussels are not mere "froth and bilge." Translated into directives and regulations, such edicts impose costs, change the rules of the marketplace, affect livelihoods, alter status, redistribute income, and modify the law of the land.[206] The basic message of this reporting is that Euro-government is undercutting the supremacy of the British Parliament by stealth and destroying traditional liberties and freedoms. The journalist skeptics have also raised a disturbing question. Where has the power stripped from British institutions been lodged? Has it been seized by anonymous bureaucrats? Is it embedded in the operating programs of soulless machines? Or has it simply been made subject to a system gone haywire?[207]

In *Statecraft: Strategies for a Changing World* (published in 2002), Lady Thatcher presents her plan for dispelling such fear, doubt, and confusion.[208] It is forthright and even foresighted, but it is also politically unrealistic and could be counterproductive. *Statecraft* is an alarming book, but not because of its strident tone; her critique is fair. She condemns the EU as a source of bad policy and for "existing for its own sake," hypocritically revering the idea of Europe while wallowing in "materialistic chicanery and corruption." She further notes that the "European social model" undermines the economy, the pensions crisis continues to mount inexorably with nothing done to address it, and the CAP remains unreformed. Lady Thatcher is contemptuous of the common defense and security policy as an expensive, demagogic, and irresponsible distraction from serious efforts to solve the world's problems. Her book cites instance after instance in which the Brussels institutions (and national governments) have defied democracies and states outright – noting that, like the EMU, many have been expressly designed for such a purpose.

Yet in *Statecraft* Mrs. Thatcher repudiates her greatest European accomplishment, the Single European Act. She maintains that the European Commission has wrecked the SEA by subverting the principle of subsidiarity embedded in the Maastricht treaty.[209] Although holding "that nothing should be decided by an upper tier of authority that can adequately be decided by a lower one, subsidiarity ... has not," she insists, "led to Europe relinquishing one single power to national governments. Nor will it."[210] Instead, Commission, Parliament, and Court have similarly and jointly exploited and widened "every loophole through which could be pushed upon Britain, through the back door, a host of undesirable corporatist and collectivist provisions."[211] Thus Mrs. Thatcher concludes that the United Kindgom cannot remain a member of the European Union as presently constituted and should walk out if it cannot be thoroughly reformed.

Mrs. Thatcher need not despair. Although there is much truth in her charges, the grasp of the Brussels institutions has always exceeded their reach. Jacques Delors did not invent the pretensions of the Commission: he inherited them from Walter Hallstein, who applied the Monnet method of "making Europe through the back door." Above all, the SEA has set in motion an inexorable liberalization process that Brussels can delay or divert but not stop. The EU's *Flucht nach Vorne,* the bid to reassert economic and political control through the instrument of a federal constitution, can produce only cloud castles. The member-states remain deeply divided. The Leviathan is still not in view. A British withdrawal from Europe could provide more than a fillip to federalism and even revive an effort to restore the "Europe" of Commission functionalism and Franco-German duopolist intergovernmentalism.

Aware of such dangers, Mrs. Thatcher favors a policy of semi-detachment. She wants to change Britain's relationship with the EU by means of negotiation or otherwise by withdrawal. Mrs. Thatcher would not only keep the pound and opt out of EMU, a sound idea, but refuse to enter any restrictive arrangements in the future. No problem here, either. As a first step toward a new policy, the British Parliament should pass an act reasserting its supremacy. Right again. Henceforth her scenario becomes somewhat questionable. Mrs. Thatcher insists that Britain play "hardball" with the EU, demand far-reaching concessions, threaten to walk out, and leave if necessary. At the same time, she wants Britain to adopt unilateral free trade and (as a second best) join NAFTA, which would be renamed the North *Atlantic* Free Trade Agreement and serve as an economic counterpart to NATO.[212] Because NAFTA is a free-trade arrangement, Britain could still join (or remain in) other trade organizations. Mrs. Thatcher maintains that, with a foot in the American as well as the European camp, Britain should be able to repeal objectionable EU features like CAP and CFP (Common Fisheries Policy) as well as eventually turn the organization back into what (she thinks) it was meant to be in the first place: an authority for implementing and maintaining a single market – a European free-trade area – albeit with a common external tariff.

The weakness of the scheme is obviously that the United States cannot be counted upon to support it. The American commitment to Euro-federalism, though varying in intensity from administration to administration, has remained unbroken since the days of the Schuman Plan. The situation is no different today. No opposition to the EU worth mentioning exists in official Washington; it remains the warp to the woof of NATO in American foreign and security policy toward Europe. Nor could any EU member-state be expected to support the design laid out in *Statecraft*. Would Spain sacrifice the right to deploy its huge fishing fleet in British waters or give up regional aid? Would France stop building up institutional ramparts to defend its national identity from Anglo-Saxon onslaught? Would Germany, surely from the American standpoint still the preeminent European power, relinquish the federalist option? Or would Italy – or for that matter the Netherlands, Belgium, Austria, Denmark, or Sweden – be prepared to loosen relations with their biggest trading partner, Germany? And would Britain ever really want to risk destroying an organization that, in spite of its many past shortcomings and potential future threats, has steered Europe ideologically away from nationalism and toward political and (sometimes in spite of itself) economic cooperation?

But why worry? The EU has already become the once-hoped-for combination of sixes and sevens that Britain championed in its free-trade area proposal of the mid-1950s. Chances are that it will eventually loosen further as new members enter after Enlargement. In the meantime, Blair is generally winning Britain's battle, albeit with methods less straightforward than those of the frank Lady

Thatcher. Disingenuousness does exact a price, and the current prime minister may have to pay it. Done behind his back, the one-sided and regressive Chirac–Schröder Enlargement–CAP deal of 24 October 2002 set negotiating parameters for the final phase of accession. Chirac's coup was a sharp rebuke to British policy as well as impressive evidence that when the trans-Rhenanian couple wants "to boogie" it can be unstoppable. The would-be reformers – the Swedes, Danes, Dutch, and even Brits – thus fell quietly into line at the summit opening the next day, and on the following Monday the accession candidates grudgingly accepted the *fait accompli*. Blair tried to finesse the debacle during the parliamentary question period but uncharacteristically ended up with egg on his face.[213] The issues arising from Enlargement remain far from being settled, however, if only because second-class citizenship will never be acceptable to the new member-states.

Blair seems increasingly likely to do better on EMU. Contrary to expectations, British tourists returned from continental vacations in 2002 unimpressed with the new currency, perhaps because of retail price increases but more likely because of the widening divergence between U.K. and Euroland economic performance.[214] By fall it had become painfully apparent that "Europe's grand experiment in a monetary union [was indeed] fraying badly – the victim of its own rigidity, an unforgiving global downturn, and national politicians who still put the interests of their own countries before those of a united Europe."[215] Commissioner Prodi's *Stupido!* ejaculation had the effect, according to Mark Landler of the *New York Times,* "of a hand grenade, igniting a debate that has been smoldering in corporate boardrooms and finance ministries across Europe."[216]

With the future of the monetary union in doubt by fall 2002, British polls indicated that two thirds of the public, though still resigned to eventual EMU membership, objected to it. A panel of forty economists estimated the chances of Britain adopting the euro by the end of 2004 at 5 percent, by the end of 2005 at 20 percent, and by the end of the following year at 35 percent.[217] Bob Worcester, chairman of Mori International (Britain's leading pollster) added his authoritative voice to the doubters by stating unequivocally in late October that "I no longer believe that in the life of this parliament Tony Blair will call a referendum on the euro, no matter the outcome of [Chancellor of the Exchequer] Gordon Brown's economic tests."[218]

As for the potentially even more important long-range issue facing Blair – the constitutional one – the Convention on the Future of Europe has not made enough progress to determine if anything will result from it. Giscard's "skeleton" has by no means received universal approbation, may not provide a template for future negotiation, and only skirts most critical issues. The big question is the hoary one still best posed in German: *Bundesstaat oder Staatenbund?* The lack of a consensus surrounding the matter frustrates sound assessment of the proposed institutional changes, the most important of which are an upper house ("congress") elected by national parliaments and a permanent council presidency. Regarding the presidency, the Giscard document makes no mention of terms, let alone powers. The constitutional role of the president will hinge partly upon the settlement of another outstanding issue, the relationship between existing and future Community institutions.

British spokespersons have already protested the proposed names for the future union as well as the lack of specificity in provisions concerning the proposed congress. So far, the envisaged permanent presidency has not been challenged, which only fuels long-standing suspicions that Blair covets the job. Does he? Except perhaps for Cherie, only the Joker knows for sure. Should he hold such a hypothetical office, the purposes to which he might put it cannot be foretold. However, if the past is any guide to the future then Blair will have time on his side. "The Euroskeptics have got it wrong," according to Norman Lamont, former chancellor of the exchequer. "It isn't superstate that's the problem; it's the entire dysfunctional nature of the European Union."[219]

Twenty years intervened between the founders' era and the "re-founding" of the mid-1980s. It may take another twenty to digest the gains of the re-founding and before re-re-founding becomes politically possible. Until then, Britain would be well advised to stay "in" and do the job it has always done best: protect the independence of the continental states, encourage cooperation in mutual problem solving, and keep open an avenue to the world. It is well positioned for such tasks. Mrs. Thatcher's reforms provided the model that the successful European states have since followed. Enlargement will eventually require decentralization and practical cooperation. Globalization, though hardly replacing the nation-state, continues to give rise to new forms of international cooperation. Evolutionary institutionalism could eventually become liberal federalism. In any case, Britain's European responsibilities will remain no less important in the near future than they have been in the recent past.

14

Shrinking Enlargement:
Betrayal of Pledge or Opportunity in Disguise?

IN THE same months that Great Europeans pondered at the Convention on the Future of Europe in Brussels, lower-level talks continued in nearby offices. Unless present trends should suddenly reverse, the upshot of these discussions will traduce the ideals upon which the European Community is based, make it even less viable as an institution, and create a host of new problems in eastern Europe. The talks in question concern the accession treaties defining EU entry for ten nations that either belonged to the former Soviet bloc or were carved out of the carcass of the USSR (plus Malta and Cyprus). Successive Community leaders and spokesmen have promised the nations once trapped behind the Iron Curtain that Enlargement will seal the transition from Soviet domination to national independence and re-entry into Europe. These hopeful peoples will not like being cheated.

The accession talks should have culminated a difficult but successful decade-long transformation process. The former captive nations have indeed reorganized, reshaped, and redrawn their economies, governments, public administrations, legal systems, and standards for public health, the environment, the workplace, and manufacturing as well as product norms, in accordance with what has been called the Washington Consensus (WC) and in a manner consistent with Brussels' guidelines for entrance into the European Union. The WC flushed away central planning and replaced it with functioning markets for goods and factors of production together with the legal and administrative frameworks required for their proper operation.[1] Ownership in eastern Europe shifted from the state to private hands, and recovery followed. The candidate states have by now also incorporated (or will soon) the entire and continuously evolving *acquis communautaire* – the EU's regulatory machinery – into their national institutions. The machinery of democratic governance is up and running. The victims of communism are ready to rejoin "Europe." But "Europe" has betrayed them.

Until recently, every democratically elected government in post-communist eastern Europe – left, right, and center – had committed itself unswervingly and unstintingly to the accession process, usually with strong public backing. The long-oppressed peoples of the East hardly doubted after the Iron Curtain came down that the path to the EU would lead to economic and political democracy. With little hesitation they seized the chance to re-enter a civilization that had often treated them as stepchildren and had all but forgotten them over the forty-plus wretched years of Soviet domination. Inclusion in the European community of nations was supposed to heal the wound from which Europe had bled, cause the Cold War to fade into memory, revive oppressed and dispirited peoples, and rejuvenate a weary civilization.

No one seriously doubted that the new members would be treated like the old ones – the rule had been followed in the past, and the possibility of breaking with it had never even been raised – or that the West would make a fair settlement with the East and, if necessary, reform the EU to do so. Anything less than a common European home, with one front door and no servants' entrance, seemed unthinkable. The EU Enlargement Commissioner Guenter Verheugen routinely described it as "a historical opportunity and an obligation for the European Union ... one of its highest priorities." Verheugen promised to find the right balance between "speed and quality" and committed himself to "joint work" in the common East–West cause.[2] "Wideners" and liberalizers within the EU welcomed Enlargement not only in order to rectify a historic injustice but as an opportunity to introduce long-overdue reform.[3]

Events cascading since fall 2001 made sadly apparent by mid-2002 that an immobilized and gridlocked EU would be incapable of accommodating the candidate nations on an equitable basis. Far from assuring fair treatment for the newcomers, the accession terms will actually cost them money and violate rights guaranteed by the Treaty of Rome. Those states that elect to join will become second-class citizens subject to administrative *apartheid*. The marriage between West and East will not take place. The former Soviet satellites will instead be condemned to live in concubinage. This status should not be confused with the idea of a two- or multi-speed Europe or a Europe *à la carte* in which individual nations can move ahead at the pace that best suits them or in the manner most appropriate for their interests: no, the candidate nations have received a simple *Diktat*. The fifteen established members do not necessarily desire the outcome but cannot prevent it. The problems are structural in nature.[4] According to Victoria Curzon Price, "because of the many and complex distributive aspects of the EU ... an Enlargement ... based on existing ... rules would bust the budget and be unacceptable from the standpoint of the main contributor, Germany."[5] Institutional gridlock prevents changing unpopular rules that benefit only a privileged few and harm the rest. The budgetary problem results from faulty institutional design, lack of leadership, and public pusillanimity.

For some eastern European countries, the wiser choice would probably be to stay out until the EU reforms itself and offers better terms. The *acquis,* it should be noted, generates additional expenses that must figure in the decision to join. The accession nations should, according to Curzon Price, "look carefully at the hidden costs of adopting the *acquis communautaire*."[6] For those peoples who have struggled their way out of the ruins of the communist system, a dream may well come to an end. The hopes aroused by it will not have been entirely misplaced, however, if through their own efforts the nations of eastern Europe can build on the achievements made since the breakup of the bloc. As emphasized by Laszlo Csaba,

much of the macroeconomic and regulatory benefits for acceding countries [was] realized during their preparation for full EU membership. Disinflation, consolidation of public finances, reduction of interest rates, the introduction of the rule of law ... the enforcement of auditing and disclosure requirements and environmental protection are all policies with virtues of their own.[7]

The course now set will be difficult to change. Each of the net EU contributors – Germany, Britain, Sweden, and the Netherlands – opposes raising the community levy above the total targeted maximum of 1.27 percent of GDP for the years 2000–2006. Higher levies would arouse the ire of the public. France – followed by the other net CAP beneficiaries – has consistently refused to consider reducing farm subsidies, which still consume nearly half the budget. There is no painless solution. EU price supports provide 40 percent of farm income Europe-wide, and without their benefit a country like Portugal would lose 80 percent of its farms.[8] The July 2002 proposals made by Agricultural Commissioner Franz Fischler – to phase out commodity price support in favor of income mainte-nance – would neither have reduced overall transfers to the West nor done the farmers of the East much immediate good. The easterners would initially still have received only a quarter of the support paid the West and nothing whatsoever for maintenance, leaving them at a huge competitive disadvantage. Nonetheless, the Fischler scheme would at least have moved CAP reform off dead center.[9] The Chirac–Schröder deal of late October eliminated even this possibility.

Regional fund allocation, about 30 percent of the community budget, will similarly be skewed because of a new rule that limits total EU payments to no more than 4 percent of a recipient nation's GDP. The per-capita income of the aspirants, at only 27 percent of the Community average, places them at an over-whelming disadvantage in the competition for such monies.[10] The Club Med nations, whose income levels are rapidly converging with the EU mean, will con-tinue to receive existing levels of support – even for "cohesion payments" made specifically to ease transition to the monetary union, which the recipients have since entered. It is politically unrealistic to expect Prime Minister Aznar of Spain, to mention only the largest beneficiary of such funds, to relinquish the bounty.

When outbound transfers are set against the meager inbound ones, the new entrants will (as things now stand) receive a paltry net gain of 0.05 percent of total Community GDP – not nearly enough to offset the direct and indirect costs of membership associated with incorporating the *acquis* and accepting increased economic regulation. The Chirac–Schröder deal sealed both the terms of the ac-cession arrangement and, for now, the fate of the accession countries. They will have to buy a full-price ticket in order to see only half the show. There is no eco-nomic justification for such stinginess. The argument that the aspirant nations cannot absorb inflows exceeding 4 percent of GDP is pure bunk: all the first-tier candidates receive several times as much foreign capital.[11]

The case against giving the eastern Europeans a meal ticket is a different one. More equitable treatment of the prospective entrants would strain the Community budget, require a painful un-entrenching of entrenched interests, and reduce resources that could be channeled to still poorer future entrants like Turkey. There is no reason to suppose that the first tier of candidates, now ten in number, would be more generous to newcomers than the Club Med has been to them. The evil of cross-payments feeds upon itself. Subsidies should be abolished altogether.

Consider the downside of equitable transfers. In a country like Poland – where more than a quarter of the population supports itself on small, under-capitalized, unproductive farms – the infusion of full price-support payments into agriculture would be highly disruptive: trigger a flight to the countryside, result in grotesque misallocations, and produce seas of milk where lakes once were and Alpine landscapes of butter instead of mere rolling hills. Nor is there any guarantee that EU subsidies, even if redirected from price supports, would be wealth-producing. In fact, the Greek case (not to mention that of the former German Democratic Republic) provides strong evidence to the contrary. The creation of new EU-standard economic and financial institutions that reduce risk outweighs the potential benefit of monetary transfers to the accession countries. Political stability is the asset of real value but at the same time the forfeit of the niggardly.

Stability may indeed be the chief casualty of Enlargement. The discriminatory accession terms are certain to nurture a sense of grievance. Restrictions on labor mobility – a right guaranteed by the Rome treaty – will be a volcanic source of anger and resentment, especially during recession, not least of all because Germany (the great official champion of *Osterweiterung*) is the real force behind the unjust labor restrictions.[12] At Chancellor Schröder's insistence, albeit with the willing (though often silent) acquiescence of most of the remaining fourteen, labor migration from the new member-states will be curtailed for a period of five to seven years. Easterners in search of a better life will have to seek it at home. Domestic opportunity may be limited by additional EU constraints. Not only do the high fixed costs imposed by the *acquis communautaire* strip low-wage countries of comparative advantage, the EMU convergence criteria also will inhibit growth because, following the Samuelson–Balassa axiom, in catch-up countries rapid development requires tolerating high inflation for the medium term. Thus, EU membership may retard the convergence process it is intended to promote.[13]

EU ENLARGEMENT POLICY

The political economy of EU Enlargement, in the words of Laszlo Csaba, is double-talk.[14] He is much too polite. The final declaration of the June 2001 Gothenburg Council would finally seem to have put the long-sought goal within easy reach. Confirming the decision reached at Nice, it set 2004 as the admission date for the first tranche of candidate nations, supposedly enabling them to participate in elections to the European Parliament to be held that year. Still to be worked out were the modalities of precisely when, how many, and which countries would be allowed to come on board, and under what conditions. The admission decision had little to do with the qualifications of candidates. Several of them (Hungary, Estonia, Slovenia, the Czech Republic, and Poland) were at the time already within hailing distance of the difficult and arcane requirements and had fulfilled nearly all of the 31 "chapters" and most of the 899 directives and regulations of the *acquis communautaire*. They also clearly met the three Copenhagen Criteria of basic rights and principles.

EU policy, the source of the Enlargement problem, has been one of big words and small deeds. The process has moved forward along two meandering tracks: one of paltry results ("backscratch track" or BAT), the other of lofty rhetoric ("bullshit track" or BUT).[15] The problem stems from M. Delors's obsession with Russian Dolls and "deepening" the Community, from which Enlargement represented an unwelcome diversion. Delors's viewpoint would survive his departure from the Commission. The Community first became involved in Enlargement thanks to the initiative of U.S. President George Bush, Sr. At the July 1989 G-7 summit, he proposed that the EC coordinate aid distribution from the wealthy so-called G-24.[16] Delors accepted the responsibility but did little to put the Community's relationship with the eastern European nations on a long-term footing. Credit for doing so belongs to Hans van den Broeck and Sir Leon Brittan – both "wideners" and liberalizers – who became the Community's two external relations commissioners in 1993.

A forceful advocate of the needs and claims of the eastern European countries, Brittan was also the chief designer of the accession strategy.[17] Club Med and French support for Enlargement hinged upon a general understanding that the EU would generate a new "Mediterranean program." With both the Germans and the British behind the program, it went ahead without much worry about cost or potential conflicts of interest between the old members and the new candidates, between the member-states themselves, or between them and the Commission. These issues would crop up later and with a vengeance. In the meantime, the EU kept its head in the sand, apparently untroubled that cost estimates of the Enlargement process varied from 27 billion to 63.5 billion ecus and from 15 to 25 percent of the total EU budget – eventually to 74 percent of it.[18] The additional expense entailed by the future Mediterranean program also went unmentioned because "the Commission [was] keen to keep the figures approximate, fearing that the more precise numbers would make the negotiations more difficult and antagonize member-states [unnecessarily]."[19]

Things started out well enough. Shortly after the fall of the Berlin Wall in 1989, the European Community established diplomatic relations with the new democracies of central Europe, removed quotas, extended the Generalized System of Preferences, and concluded a number of agreements for trade and cooperation. To support their efforts to reform and rebuild the economies of the former Soviet bloc nations, the Community next provided PHARE, a vast program of technical assistance and financial support. A number of bilateral "Europe Agreements" ensued over the next several years. Asymmetrical in design, these trade arrangements prevented EU imports from swamping eastern European markets and adversely affecting payments. The Community soon became the main source of east European trade and investment, each slightly less than half of the regional total. The Europe Agreements also aligned the east European partner nations with EU rules regarding capital movement, competition, intellectual and industrial property rights, and public procurement.[20] The Copenhagen Council of 1993 set the basic criteria for entrance into the Union.[21] Required were: political stability (defined as democracy, the rule of law, and respect for human rights, including those of minorities); the existence of a functioning market economy as well as an ability to compete within the Community; and a willingness to assume the obligations of membership, including "adherence to the aims of political, economic, and monetary union." In less than a decade, several accession countries easily met the Copenhagen Criteria.

Problems began with the accession process. The Commission set its parameters in Agenda 2000, the EU finance plan for the years 2000–2006. Long in preparation, the document came up for discussion before the Berlin summit in March 1999 but was not signed owing to the simultaneous disgrace and dismissal of the Santer Commission. Agenda 2000 linked Enlargement to reform of the EU and was thus fatally flawed, yet it provided reasonable cost estimates and located the necessary sources of funding. The Commission recognized the futility of trying to raise the "own funds ceiling" (1.27 percent of GDP) that constituted the upper limit of EU expenditure; they set enlargement costs at 80 billion euros for the six accession countries and factored in a reasonable rate of growth. By saving 7 billion euros from structural programs, enough money could be raised to meet applicant country needs without lifting the program ceiling of 46 percent. Less evident was the source of the additional 16 billion euros in savings supposed to be generated by shifting from price support to income maintenance in the CAP.[22] At no subsequent summit or IGC was any progress made toward meeting this goal. Except for having introduced a nit-picking "screening" program in order to bog down the accession process until the EU could get its act together, the Commission's subsequent influence on the course of events was zilch. Commission Enlargement policy would become, in fact, a one-man show run by Guenter Verheugen – a proxy for Chancellor Schröder – and thus largely a German affair.

In the meantime, the rounds of intergovernmental diplomacy kept wandering around the problem, as heads of state got snarled up with other issues and as worry and fear mounted about further alienating electorates. The negotiations for Enlargement ran afoul of the breakdown in governance. As a result of French pressure, the December 1999 Helsinki summit more than doubled the number of eligible candidate nations to twelve without providing additional funding.[23] This truly alarming development did not lead to any action. The main accomplishment at the following year's Nice brouhaha was to wave the yellow flag at the last minute. Enlargement could proceed – but under caution. "The compromises of Nice," according to the astute Csaba,

reflect the ongoing preoccupation with the domestic sellability of the deals, not with the improved workability of common organs .... When supranationalist institutions lack the public trust and respect ..., national legitimacy and the processes required of it (i.e. convincing the public and reflecting national constituency views) inevitably superimpose their logic over the concerns of integrational efficiency or functional rationality. This is truly bad news for the candidates.[24]

The Swedish presidency of early 2001 brought representatives of member-states and accession countries around a single table for the first time. Babble and incomprehension resulted.[25] The Stockholm summit's liberalization agenda also flagged badly.[26]

It might have been the weather, or perhaps the World Cup, or still more likely the forthcoming September elections in Germany, but the Madrid summit of 21–22 June 2002 was "the sleepiest in history," according to the *Economist*: "the grandees cleared their throats about illegal immigration, naval-gazed about how to run more effective summits in the future, got nowhere on plans for an EU rapid reaction force," and did nothing at all about what Guenter Verheugen described as "a historical opportunity and an obligation for the European Union and therefore one of its highest priorities."[27] Diplomacy now skipped back from the BUT to the BAT, according to Thomas Fuller of the *International Herald Tribune*:

More than a decade after the fall of the Berlin Wall, negotiations over the enlargement of the European Union have come to this: Brussels bureaucrats argue with their eastern counterparts over the legal definition of a dentist ... food experts debate the way Poles pickle their cucumbers ... [and] EU governments haggle among themselves over the future of farm subsidies while candidate countries watch from the sidelines.[28]

Berthold Kohler of the *Frankfurter Allgemeine Zeitung* commented with unusual directness:

The closer Europe moves toward removing the final frontiers, the less those in the borderless and highly prosperous western regions of the continent are willing to sacrifice for the ... ideal of a united Europe .... The growing reluctance to share affluence ... in the name of European solidarity is adding to the pressure of national governments to insist that all new member states have EU compatible economies and social standards prior to their admission.[29]

A poll conducted by Deutsche Bank Research confirmed this impression: German support for Enlargement dropped between 1999 and 2000 from 38 to 34 percent; support among the more upbeat British dropped from 44 to 40 percent. French support (at 26 percent) was at the bottom of the scale, a "sad commentary on a country which viewed itself as sentimentally attached to Poland (Napoleon and Maria Walewska, Chopin and George Sand, Pierre and Marie Curie)."[30]

To defuse the "sharing anxiety" of the rich, the Commission sponsored a study, later frequently cited in official pronouncements, entitled "The Impact of Eastern Enlargement on Employment and Wages in the EU Member States." No problem, it concluded (contrary to the human evidence obvious on any street corner to every big-city pedestrian in Europe): there was no great foreign interest in making easy money in the West. Only 335,000 immigrants would enter the EU once the barriers were lifted, and most of them would penetrate no farther than the border regions – presumably to facilitate going home for weekends with the family. Restriction of mobility? No way, according to Anna Diamantopoulos, head of the DG for employment: free movement "is one of the four basic freedoms of the EU treaty which the Commission upholds and supports." Asked for possible derogations, she waffled pitifully: "there have been [previous] temporary arrangements to ensure a smooth process of integration and it will be for the negotiations to look at this on the basis of evidence about the whole situation across the EU and in individual member states and regions."[31] The real number of those desiring work in the West was at least 6 million. Public opposition to allowing them freedom of mobility was, within Germany and most other rich countries, nearly total.[32]

Three things could to be done to stave off dealing with the "migration problem." One was to bash the applicants in order to delay their admission. Thus, on 26 July 2000, Commissioner Verheugen announced to an audience of Brussels office-grandees that "in all applicant countries of central and eastern Europe there are damaging links between the old political structures – the *nomenklatura* – and the new economic structures .... This is not very transparent, and I am not sure which controls which, but it is a real danger to foreign direct investment."[33] He must have felt like General Perón upon discovering that his beloved betrothed, Eva, was no longer a virgin. Another approach was to "tighten up" on the applicant countries. Thus, in 1998–2000 the Commission adopted "delaying tactics by unexpectedly introducing the phase of *acquis* screening, turning the entry bargain into a kind of comprehensive examination of applicants."[34] The harassment only spurred them to make a greater effort.

Finally, a taboo could be placed on political discussion concerning labor movement from the East. Powerful incentives existed in Germany for keeping things quiet.[35] The historical ones require no elaboration. The economic ones were equally powerful. Since *Mitteleuropa* made good sense, all organized economic interests in the *Bundesrepublik,* including farmers, initially supported prompt inclusion of the aspirants. With a declining population, Germany furthermore needed 300,000 new immigrants annually to promote economic growth and help cover gaping future deficits in the paygo pension system.[36] Geopolitically, the last thing the country needed was trouble on its borders. Of all European countries, the Federal Republic stood to gain – or lose – the most through *Osterweiterung*.[37] On the Enlargement question, the German chancellor indeed had no choice but to look like a good guy before God, the world, and Europe. But could he do so and still be re-elected by an anti-immigrant public?

Commissioner Verheugen forced the issue. In a newspaper interview of 2 September 2000, he regretted

that there was little chance of a referendum on Enlargement in ... Germany, and by urging the EU members not to leave to the Commission what he called the "dirty work" of selling the Enlargement idea to public, he managed to belittle his job, upset his Commission colleagues, irritate the German government, annoy almost every other EU government, and dismay all the thirteen countries queuing up to join the club.[38]

This was not the mother of all gaffes that it first appeared to be. Rather, it was a calculated attempt to force hidebound political elites to explain the historical opportunity of Enlargement to increasingly skeptical electorates – instead of (as customary and most recently demonstrated in the case of the EMU) simply presenting them with *faits accomplis*. Verheugen might have thought that without such an effort Enlargement could fail. Perhaps his purpose was to spread responsibility for the adoption of nativist approaches throughout the Community, recognizing that opposition in Germany to "immigration" had grown too strong to keep out of the political arena much longer. "When it comes to Enlargement," he told an interviewer, "we must not make decision[s] above the heads of people again."[39]

His trial balloon burst almost at once. Although foreign minister Josef Fischer disowned Verheugen on the spot, the "coalition of silence" once broken could not be restored. Spokespersons from both parties soon found themselves rushing pell-mell to become champions of the hard line on "immigration," which became a central issue in the September 2002 election campaign. The farmers' association predicted disastrous overproduction and financial ruin if the accession lands were granted full access to CAP subsidies. The president of the Bundesbank called for tougher stability and convergence criteria for EMU applicants from the East.[40] Although honeyed words continued to flow from the mouths of Schröder, Fischer, Verheugen, Prodi, and other official spokespersons, the seriousness of the situation was hard to conceal.[41] Writing months after Verheugen's famous "gaffe," the Hungarian economist Laszlo Csabo pointedly warned that "the split between the pro-European and pro-Enlargement elites and business circles and an electorate orientated mainly by tabloids and infotainment fearing basically crime and major costs, has reached the point where it may become prohibitive."[42] Neither East nor West wanted to admit that the situation had spun out of control because each had too much to lose. Thus the critical decisions concerning Enlargement – on CAP, structural funds, and free movement of labor – would be postponed until the last possible moment, the Danish presidency that began in July 2002. The whole issue would have to be settled under the gun.

The situation deteriorated badly over the first six months of 2002, a period that coincided with Spain holding the rotating EU presidency. In February the Commission presented its first detailed plans for accommodating the new members.[43] It was now revealed that CAP subsidies would be limited to a quarter of those paid in the West, that income supports would not be provided, and also that structural payments would hew to the "4 percent of GDP" rule. In the new scheme of things, payments would total 40.1 billion euros (for ten rather than six entrants) and structural payments would be limited to 114 euros per capita (as opposed to 231 per capita in the Club Med countries). The total package would equal an estimated net 0.05 percent of the European Union's GDP annually, or 3 billion euros of the 6-trillion EU economy.[44] Per-capita Marshall Plan aid was fifteen times as great in real terms, and the U.S. assistance was of course sent abroad rather than allocated within the same political unit.[45] An analysis of the Commission package by staff members of the Hamburg Institute for World Trade concluded that " the proposal ... can be seen as trying to achieve the impossible."[46] Inequitable and inadequate in making provision to meet requirements for incorporation of the *acquis,* it did manage to keep the costs below budget. It was, *auf gut Deutsch,* stingy.

The French and Dutch elections would provide persuasive evidence of the rise of a new provincialism. Policy already reflected the new attitude. The French refused to commit to an accession date, wanted CAP to be treated as sacrosanct, feared future German domination, and hinted unsubtly that the indefinite postponement of Enlargement would not make them unhappy. In an EU of 25 members, according to political scientist Daniel Gros, "France is an also-ran."[47] For his part, Delors griped that "expansion was crowding out other projects." *Le Monde* "fretted that an enlarged union would become simply a free-trade area on lines that would represent a 'British victory over the previous Franco-German vision.' "[48]

The German campaign for the 22 September election evinced a similarly unwelcome trend. It was evident that *Ossiland* would determine the outcome, because voter loyalty there was weak.[49] The three previous general elections had witnessed wild swings in sentiment. The economy was thought to be the critical issue in September 2002. The East had grown at only half the national rate since 1997 and in early 2002 was actually in negative territory. Unemployment was stuck at an appalling 18 percent, with per-capita income at only three quarters of the West's level. Voter resistance to wage competition from "immigrants" was strong. Schröder and Stoiber ("Schroiber") both tried to capture the anti-immigrant vote by outdoing each other in lambasting obfuscating Eurocrats, refusing ostentatiously to pay more into the EU, and promising to restrict the free movement of labor "for the time being."[50]

In the attempt to burnish his European credentials, each also aggravated existing problems. The SPD man tried to kick German concerns upstairs to the EU; he advocated "renationalizing" it yet also asserted that the "antidote" to renationalization was a simultaneous widening and deepening into federal union – the "stuff of Euroskeptic nightmares," sniffed the *Guardian*'s correspondent.[51] For his part, Stoiber did a spectacular flip-flop. In an 8 June speech he demanded thoroughgoing reform of both EU regional and farm policy and railed against the exclusion of the aspirant nations from the CAP. "Repatriation" – or restoring responsibility for farm subsidies to the member-states – was, he insisted, the solution to the farm problem.[52] Five weeks later, on 28 July, he unexpectedly appointed as shadow minister for agriculture an unabashed champion of the unreformed CAP, publicly committing himself to maintaining existing support levels.[53] A CDU/CSU victory would have ended any chance of the candidate nations for a better deal.

The last remaining shot for the easterners to avert second-class EU citizenship was, it seemed, an SPD triumph convincing enough to leave in office the Green agriculture minister, Dr. Renate Künast. Künast had masterfully manipulated the quasi-hysteria created by the outbreak of "mad cow disease" – which in medieval fashion spread throughout much of northern Europe during 2000 and 2001 – into a generalized campaign against the wicked force supposedly behind the scourge, "commercial agriculture." The astonishing instant prominence of a media-savvy French boho-peasant with a boutique farming operation named José Bove – who in 2000 had, for the benefit of a national television audience, publicly bulldozed a franchised McDonald's restaurant – attests to the powerful appeal of the eco-shibboleth. By exploiting it, Künast provided a much-needed pop-ideological justification for reforming the CAP. In the name of safe food, a clean environment, and the European Way of Life, the handouts from Brussels could be detached from crop and animal production and put to better alternative uses: either beautification of the countryside to please the public and the politicians (for, like structural or cohesion funds, it provided an open invitation to boondoggling) or income maintenance, which was less costly than the continuous subsidizing of overproduction.[54]

On 10 July 2002 the EU agriculture commissioner, Franz Fischler, presented his income maintenance program. Although withholding little from present beneficiaries, it reflected the new anxiety of the food-consuming public and also partly opened the door to long-run change.[55] The Fischler plan guaranteed farm incomes but allowed the market to determine what to grow, bringing costs down. The stipends were not to have been portable and thus would eventually be phased out. Payment was to be contingent upon (1) fulfilling environmental obligations, which may have been intended as a tricky way of re-diverting public money back to public purposes; and (2) co-financing by national governments. Although capped as a sop to progressives, the income-maintenance rights were to appertain to owners rather than lessees working the land. Fischler's program can be regarded as a middle-class entitlement. Mediterranean products like oil and wine were exempt from the scheme for political reasons. The farm-reform proposal offered nothing to the accession countries other than the prospect of fairer treatment in the future.[56] Although a Stoiber electoral victory would have killed the Fischler program immediately, Schröder's squeak-through win enabled it to survive for another month.

THE ACCESSION COUNTRIES: THE FRONT-RUNNERS

Each of the five front-running accession nations of eastern and central Europe can claim to have made extraordinary progress over the past decade. All of them have replaced their former monopolies with private market traders. By 1996, imports and exports with the former USSR had declined from over 30 percent to just 12 percent of the total. The Czech Republic and Estonia have more liberal trade regimes than the EU, and those of Poland, Hungary, and Slovenia were on a par with it.[57] Moreover, the 899 specific targets of the 80,000-page *acquis* have, at enormous cost, largely been digested. The economics and politics of the accession countries have varied enormously, but they share the miserable legacy of communist misrule: an absence of democratic tradition, paleolithic economies, endemic corruption, and fear. The progress that has been (and can be) made in overcoming them varies substantially from country to county, but in none of them should stability and trouble-free development be taken for granted. Nearly all of the accession countries are still fragile and will be for a long time to come. To get a handle on the challenges and perils of Enlargement, it is necessary to get down to cases.

Slovenia is the closest exception to the general hardship rule and is almost too easy to discuss. It is a nation pre-cast by history for the role of good European. Slovenia lacks any prior history of independence, a unique case, but has strong traditions of local self-government. The Slovenes are socially and economically egalitarian and are ethnically as well as religiously homogenous (Catholic). They are also well-educated and highly industrious. For most of its history Slovenia has maintained cultural independence within some form of broader union dominated by foreigners; it is protected by secure borders and has had little conflict with its neighbors (except perhaps with Italy over Trieste). The Slovenes maintain close commercial and institutional ties with adjacent countries, have no minority problem, possess a modern (though small) industrial sector, benefit from a generally efficient and modern class of smallholders, and are (including the large gray–black economy) about as wealthy per capita as the bottom group of EU states. Slovenia should be a shoo-in for membership, but it is not. In a recent interview, Prime Minister Janez Drnovsek regretted that "the European Union is not an ideal any more .... It certainly represents a lot of advantages, but also some problems."[58] Drnovsek's voters particularly resented "double standards in Brussels."[59] Why, they wondered, should Greece be flush with EU handouts while Slovenia went empty-handed? The nation had little hope of becoming a net recipient and worried that its Alpine farms would fall victim to CAP-subsidized western producers.

The *Czech Republic* is too problematic to deal with in a few lines. The remarkable and complicated personalities who have placed their special imprints on events there require detailed discussion. Special historic grievances against Austrians and Germans have figured prominently in Czech diplomacy; they, too, require extensive description, as does the "velvet divorce" from the Slovaks – to date the only peaceful secession in post-communist eastern Europe. A majority of Czechs opposes EU accession.[60]

Estonia cannot escape historical scrutiny in these pages as easily as the former two aspirants. One of the three eastern Baltic nations to regain national independence from the Soviet empire, it is the pacesetter for the region. Not officially

independent until the breakup of the USSR in August 1991, the small nation of
1.5 million speakers of a Finno-Ugric tongue soon became another New Zealand, a laboratory of successful free-market reform. For Estonia, the adoption
of the *acquis* and the acceptance of other EU constraints has been costly and
may even require taking a step backwards. It might be best for it to stay out.

Hungary's transformation has been no less successful than that of the little
Baltic state. Second only to Slovenia among the accession front-runners, this
highly urbanized nation of 10.5 million is now strong enough to take or leave
the EU. The bipartisan consensus supporting membership has eroded. Politics
rather than economics may in the end be decisive in settling the issue of whether
or not to join. The recent revival of irredentism is coupled to mounting hostility
toward Brussels and could be destabilizing.

Poland may not have the luxury to pick and choose. A nation of 39 million
and hence large enough for the status of France, Britain, Italy, or Spain, it faces
huge problems. Poland is poor and deeply divided between economic winners
and losers, weighted down with Europe's largest and least productive sector of
peasant agriculture, has insecure borders and an unresolved history of ethnic
and national conflict with its neighbors, struggles with low (though improving)
living standards, and remains vulnerable to political breakdown. The large number of unknowns rules out speculation about outcomes. If the EU's Enlargement
policy boils down to "Germany and the others," its concern can be reduced to
"Poland and the others." A Polish problem will be a problem for Europe.

ESTONIA: NEW ZEALAND OF THE BALTIC

The first great Estonian act of state after the official break with the Russian federation in August 1991 was to restore the kroon as the national coin and set up
a currency board to enforce a peg to the DM, making the new money immediately convertible and (according to the governor of the national bank) "good for
anything from the latest model of a western car to a call girl."[61] The decision to
adopt such a board, which required hard-currency backing for the national circulating medium, held immense implications for the small nation. It virtually
committed Estonia to the classical liberal agenda: open borders, balanced budget, the competition principle, privatization and deregulation, low taxes, and a
minimal state. According to Johns Hopkins professor Steve Hanke, economic
adviser to Estonia at the time, purely patriotic motives prompted the adoption
of the currency board. Indeed, the young nation virtually lacked trained economists. The government may have proceeded blindly, but its economic program
has worked so well that Estonia's decision to seek EU membership, one made for
overriding political reasons, requires substantial economic sacrifice.

The introduction of the new national circulating medium in place of the de-
tested Soviet ruble became the occasion for a national holiday and set the stage
for a wave of reform. The government abolished tariffs, freed prices (including
those in agriculture), adopted a balanced budget requirement, compressed the

tax schedule (which included a flat income and corporation tax) to eighty pages, and established the law of property and contract. It further privatized industry and sold it off to foreigners and did likewise with the banks, virtually all of which passed into the hands of Swedes and Finns. Estonian capital inflows would soon become the highest per capita in post-Soviet eastern Europe. The combination of a currency board (which eliminates monetary policy), an open economy, and simple but rigid tax laws means that labor has borne the burden of adaptation to economic change.[62] Unions have been weak and wages relatively low.

Estonia was the first patient cured by economic "shock therapy." The economy took a tumble after the collapse of the USSR, but it rebounded sturdily in 1993 and has continued to grow at the highest rate in Europe ever since; even during the recession of 2001–2002, it expanded at rates of 4 and 5 percent annually. The meltdown of the Russian economy in 1998 caused barely a ripple, and its revival in 2002 has begun to benefit the whole Baltic region. Estonian unemployment has been brought down to 6 percent. Inflation remains high but is lower than in other transition economies.

Thanks in considerable measure to the proximity of Finland, structural change has been dramatic. Estonians use more computers and cell phones per capita than the French. Central Tallinn has been restored and is prosperous, but conditions deteriorate as one moves away from it.[63] The suburbs are studded with ramshackle Soviet-era apartments, and much of the countryside is a shambles. A 30-percent Russian minority remains monoglottic and is ghettoized. Wages (about $300 per month) are low but higher than those prevailing elsewhere in the Baltic. The influx of foreign capital owes more to cheap labor than to high productivity. With the help of the EU, the governments in office since 1996 have given highest priority to upgrading the bench and reforming the civil service, but corruption (of the Soviet-era type) remains rife. The previous decade is nevertheless the proudest in Estonian history.[64]

During this decade Estonia re-aligned itself with the West: with NATO, which it is now joining; but above all with the EU, which (according to Mart Laar, prime minister during 1992–1996 and 1999–2001) "is not only an economic union but has a cultural and historical identity."[65] Laar thinks "Europe should concern itself deeply with what it is about, so that for the [Estonian] people the European Union does not merely stand for a Euro-currency. It must also be an idea, a dream." For him, as a Christian, it must also rest on the foundations of religion. Laar hopes the EU will respect the fact that "nowhere else on earth do so many cultures live together on such a small territory."[66] Estonia claimed to qualify for – and sought to gain admission into – the Union as early as 2000.

Laar and the rest of the political establishment faced a problem: freedom, prosperity, and national independence were associated with policies that would have to change if the country were to join the EU. The kroon would disappear (an issue more emotional than economic), the public sector would have to expand substantially, the simple tax code would have to be scrapped, corporatist labor relations machinery would have to be cranked up, and a measure of subsidization and tariff setting would be introduced. Those practices that had lent distinctiveness to Estonia and made it prosperous would inevitably be superceded by directives from Brussels.[67] Already, according to Razeen Sally, "regulation is increasing in quantity and complexity, presaging ... a departure from the simpler, more straightforward classical liberalism of the 1990s in the direction of something closer to the EU mainstream. The most visible sign of this trend is the end of free trade."[68]

It is difficult to fathom Estonian public opinion on EU membership.[69] A poll published on 20 February 2002 found that only a third of the electorate would have voted to join the EU if a referendum had been held in December 2001.[70] The government's office responsible for negotiating with the EU, which had commissioned the poll, said that the result amounted to a rise since the previous June, when only 27 percent said they would vote "yes."[71] A March 2002 poll found that only 33 percent of the public supported EU membership and that Estonia, "like the other Baltic republics, feared being governed centrally from Brussels as earlier from Moscow."[72] Much of the opposition seems to have come from neglected rural areas, where unemployment remains high. The main business journal, *Aripaev,* also complained frequently of interference from Brussels. Those supporting EU entry were resigned rather than enthusiastic.[73] Estonians often regretted that their country was too poor to be a Norway, which rejected EU membership; Estonia's one natural resource of note (apart from forestry) is sub–commercial grade shale oil – hardly a match for the bulging seams under the North Sea.[74]

The conservative government of Siim Kallas, which took office in February 2002, appears to be shifting gradually from Euro-enthusiasm to Euro-wariness. In March the Commission ordered Kallas to change the fiscal code and in particular "the popular policy of not taxing reinvested corporate profits," even though direct taxation does not fall within the realm of the accession negotiations.[75] The question kept "cropping up" owing to pressure from France, Italy, and Spain. Kallas, like most Estonians, resented being bullied by Brussels. The head of the international affairs department at the Ministry of Finance, pointedly noting that the IMF had approved the tax policy as well as attested to its effectiveness, argued that "[it] is a symbol of the country ... and should not be changed." *Aripaev* editorialized on 11 March that Estonia should pull out of the negotiations if the EU did not give in, since "Estonia ... is not requesting special treatment, [but] ... merely removing obstacles that were restricting faster growth."[76] In subsequent remarks, Prime Minister Kallas warned that EU entry was "not an end in itself, but a way of improving living standards and that protection of the national culture and economy would remain the first priorities of Estonian policy."[77] Feeling vulnerable, the strongly pro-European opposition (the Moderate Party) proposed de-linking the planned 2003 referendum on EU membership from the national elections. A veteran EU-watcher reported that "Estonia was deliberately slowing down the [accession] process, an impression reinforced by the larger number of transition periods ... and exceptions ... requested ....

Further doubts were raised by the sudden resignation in January ... of Mart Laar, who had pioneered the Estonia application."[78] A July 2002 poll indicates that, while fewer Estonians were "neutral" about EU membership, the shift was decisively into the camp of opposition.[79] Estonia could easily turn out to be another Denmark or Ireland. There could well be a surprise "no" on the accession referendum.

Estonia may have been the first of the front-runners to recognize that EU membership has a downside, but it was not alone. By April 2000 it had become evident to Brian Caplan, reporting in the British financial weekly *Euromoney,* that

senior officials from governments in Poland, Hungary, the Czech Republic, Estonia and Slovenia ... are starting to ... fear that the EU's heavy-handed bureaucracy and its onerous regulations could stifle the entrepreneurial spirit that has been unleashed in their countries since the fall of communism. Imposing first-world environmental standards in what still are emerging markets could lose them their competitive edge, complain officials.

International investors were said to share similar concerns, and "the prospect of east European tigers growing up fat and listless on a diet of EU subsidy is not one that enthralls [them]."[80]

Adaptation costs were indeed an issue. To meet EU standards on water purity would theoretically cost Poland $40 billion, a staggering sum equal to about 40 percent of the country's GDP. And water was only one of the areas covered by the 2,000 or so EU environmental directives and regulations, which also concern air purity, pesticide residues, waste management, chemical hazards, and biotechnology. The requirement for full adoption of the *acquis* also neglects one fundamental point, according to Victoria Curzon Price:

high standards of safety, like high wages and shorter working hours are "presents" [consumption goods] that rich countries give themselves, not handicaps which stupidly reduce incomes and maim "competitiveness." They *reflect* real high incomes [and] ... are the *result* of productivity ... [and] *ways of consuming that reflect the results of high productivity.*[81]

For the weaker and poorer nations, by comparison, these ways of consuming are a curse.

Resentment was also growing as a result of struggles with incorporating 80,000 pages of rules and regulations into national legislation, an entry requirement not faced by the nations of the southern enlargement. Administrative reform was nevertheless necessary throughout post-communist eastern Europe, and the infusion of EU pre-accession subsidies like PHARE (equal in value to 2–3 percent of GDP) was irresistible: "No government anywhere in the world ... could possibly turn down that kind of largesse and the short-term economic boost it would provide, even if administrators believed in the long term some of the economic effects could be negative."[82] Yet in the rush for the money the candidate nations risked being deprived of flexibility and forced into "a straitjacket that constrains policy choices." The adoption of EU labor standards, according to the Commission's own economists, will force many small businesses out of operation, and strict environmental standards will destroy the steel and chemicals industries. Without the lure of the EU fund transfers, membership begins to look like an economically bad proposition. Arguments for "getting out while the getting is good" are becoming ever more tempting. By early 2002, according to *Euromoney,* "bankers [had] started to think aloud about the future of the central and eastern European countries if they do not win membership in the club. Their tentative conclusion is that the prospects for a clutch of states on the outside could be surprisingly rosy."[83] Countries that have restructured their economies will do well regardless of whether they join, according to a leading Deutsche Bank economist, and can outperform the rigid EU if they remain independent.[84]

The refusal of the EU for several years to provide definitive completion dates increased the chances of Estonia's staying out. The decision (made as a result of French pressure) to expand the candidate list to ten – including Roumania and Bulgaria, which are obviously unsuited for membership according to the Copenhagen Criteria – had the same effect. The move has prompted at least one reporter to question French motives since "no country has less to gain than farmer-dominated France from an eastwards shift in the center of gravity within the EU by taking in poor agricultural states. Hence some suspect [France] of a ploy to hobble Enlargement by showing just how idiosyncratic the Brussels' selection of fast-track countries has been."[85] By doubling the number of claimants to the accession funds without augmenting them, the French threw a monkey wrench into the works.

According to an EU poll released in March 2002, only in four accession countries – Hungary, Poland, Slovakia, and Cyprus – do a majority of people view the Union as a "good thing"; the rest are either undecided or feel it is bad. Politicians generally prefer to avoid entering into debate on the subject.[86] The continuing economic downturn – coupled with persistent EU high-handedness, ineptitude, and gridlock – invites the populist right to play the Euroskeptic card. Brussels-bashing could be a springboard to power. A negative Estonian vote in an EU referendum would do little damage to the Community and perhaps benefit a nation that has done well by becoming a New Zealand of the eastern Baltic. Estonia also has influential supporters in Finland as well as in the "Nordic Five" (into which it has sidestepped) and the "Baltic Eight," which also includes Latvia, Lithuania, and Poland. At least for the moment, relations are amicable with Russia. Prospective Estonian membership in NATO should provide an additional measure of security. Estonia might then even become a Hong Kong of the Baltic. Yet this scenario is unlikely. Security considerations are, according to Sally, overriding: "The EU is seen as the strongest anchor for Estonia's return to the West .... Even Estonian economic liberals argue that the EU's protective cloak is worth the sacrifice of full-blooded liberal economic policies, if that indeed is what EU membership requires."[87]

HUNGARY: RIGHT WAY OR RIGHTIST WAY?

A Hungarian refusal to enter the Union would also have few direct economic consequences either for it or Europe. However, a decision to stay out would represent a triumph for the restive and increasingly militant Hungarian right wing – which, after its recent electoral defeat, is currently being reorganized as Forward Hungary! by Viktor Orban along lines at least superficially similar to the Berlusconi movement in Italy. In view is apparently the revival of claims for a greater Magyar state.

Hungary was the first Soviet-bloc country to reform its economy and, to date, has been among the most successful. Yet the transition from one to the other has not been trouble-free. First introduced in 1968, "goulash communism" was a consumption-oriented variation of the command economy, an improved version of the production-oriented Leninist model. The self-serving character and unimpressive operation of the Hungarian system nonetheless require a public choice explanation, according to János Kornai. In Hungary, the slow-moving governmental machinery generated what he terms a "premature welfare state" characterized by quasi-independent economic bureaucracies subject only to "soft constraints" and by inadequate rates of savings and investment. Gradualism was its keynote. The economy stagnated through the 1980s and, though not subject to the quasi-collapse that occurred elsewhere, wallowed through the early 1990s as well. Decisive change did not occur immediately following the overthrow of communism but only five years later, once the failures of the complacent system long in place had become too glaring to overlook.[88]

A spate of measures introduced by the Socialist Party government of Gyula Horn (1984–1988) achieved the critical breakthrough. The Horn government represented the interests of the old but partly "goulashed" *nomenklatura* along with the ideas of a small and economically liberal Alliance of Free Democrats, formerly a persecuted opposition group. Together they had the two-thirds majority needed to push the stabilization legislation through the parliament. Horn adopted the neoliberal agenda: devalued the forint by 9 percent and fitted it into a "pre-announced crawling peg" based on DM parity; cut back the budget sharply; and reduced public-sector wages. He further restricted consumption in order to encourage investment, and he revoked paternalist welfare transfers and entitlements.

Such measures resulted in a punishing austerity and howls of pain but little public protest. Yet in the first year they yielded the kinds of results that economists respect. The monthly budget deficit fell, inflation slowed down after an initial spurt of price increases, and the gap on current account shrank substantially. The policy also had positive long-term consequences. One was a thorough overhaul of the welfare state, another the reform of public finances (adopting French accountability standards), a third the setup of a partly privatized three-tier pension system. Consolidated government spending declined from 62 percent of

GDP in 1990–1994 to 45 percent by 1998. Domestic public debt peaked at
83.6 percent of GDP in 1993 and had diminished to 65 percent by 1998. Privatization, which followed the British auction model, stuck. Utilities, telecoms,
and the big banks all went under the hammer. The unions, post-communist
survivors, were too weak to influence labor markets, which remained flexible.
Thanks to the Europe Agreements of 1992, Hungary's acceptance of GATT deliberations and agreements, and accession to the OECD, liberalization has proceeded along several fronts. International banking standards have been adopted
and enforced, and risk has been reduced to levels prevailing in western Europe.[89]

A huge influx of foreign direct investment (FDI) followed the reform, something of extraordinary importance to Hungary's modernization. Hungary was
the uncontested FDI leader in central and eastern Europe over the ten-year period 1989–1999, garnered twice as much per capita as the Czech Republic, and
over the same years enjoyed a sixfold increase in annual inflows. This investment
is keyed into the operation of multinationals. Some 70 percent of Hungarian exports, as well as a high percentage of imports, are intrafirm. The composition of
this trade includes a high and increasing degree of value-added labor. According
to Bartlomiej Kaminski, Hungary benefits from a

> virtuous circle ... [that] represents a very advanced process of economic restructuring ...
> [and] has moved beyond the stage of marginal supplier of manufactures ... into the field
> of technology and human capital-intensive products, with their aggregate share rising
> from 32 percent in 1989 to 39 percent in 1992, and 66 percent in 1997.[90]

The Hungarian transition is now over. Redistribution by the state, though
high, is lower than in Denmark, Sweden, or France. The Hungarian capital
market is "gradually evolving into a solid and defining institution of the [com-
petitive] order," is intertwined with both London and New York, and is more
prominent in shaping allocation decisions and in corporate financing than its
counterparts in Austria, Italy, or even Germany. Financing costs are low. The
main economic indices are healthy. Unemployment is consistently below double digits, and "thanks to the weakness of the social partners," at Polder levels.
Inflation is comparatively modest, hovering around 10 percent. At about 4 to
5 percent over the past five years, growth has been both impressive and steady.
Hungarian workforce productivity is 80 to 100 percent that of German, depending on the sector. The output of university-trained graduates has doubled since
1995 and, as the chief of the national trade and development office can properly
boast, "we've now reached the stage where investors come here for the productivity benefits, not cheap labor." Hungary is indeed so well hooked into the
economy of western Europe that "actual EU membership will not bring substantial changes."[91] The story of the late 1990s is not merely one of high economic
performance but of institution building and structural reform, development of
efficient forms of corporate governance, privatization of monopoly rents, and
adoption of high standards of fiscal accountability and bookkeeping.[92]

The political situation provides fewer grounds for optimism. The Socialist government of Peter Medgyessy – in office since April 2002 as the result of a narrow victory – is staunchly pro-EU but already weakened by revelations of the prime minister's *gestapiste*-type past.[93] No post-communist government of Hungary has ever been voted back into power, including the Fidesz predecessor of the present one. This right-wing crew held what was thought to be a decisive edge: it had been generous with handouts and giveaways; was headed by a young and nearly charismatic leader, Viktor Orban; and benefited from a booming economy. The rule in Hungary nevertheless has been: alternation of the Socialists and Fidesz; cabinets of the left and cabinets of the right; Budapest one time, the countryside the next; and leadership of progressive intellectuals and professionals today, guidance by nostalgic national-patriots and traditionalists tomorrow. As long as Hungary stood to benefit economically from the large annual transfer payments, Orban and his party, Fidesz, operated under constraint and could not oppose entrance into the EU – though negotiations were often difficult and relations with Brussels sometimes poor.[94] The disappearance of those payments and also its newfound economic strength enable Hungary to accept or reject EU membership with a degree of equanimity. The path may open for a new departure in foreign policy.

Orban is no friend of the open society. He objects to further privatization as a sellout to foreigners, supports bans on land ownership by non-Hungarians, denounces foreign bankers and international capital, and supports "social partnership." When Orban replaced the ex-communist Socialists in 1998, shares dropped 17 percent on the Budapest exchange. When they in turn replaced him in 2002, shares jumped 7 percent to the high of the year.[95] Orban shrewdly did not challenge the policies established by the Horn government until early 2002 when, in order to provide goodies for the electorate, he cranked up spending. In the first four months of the year he handed out enough to raise the cumulative monthly deficit to four fifths the amount targeted for the whole twelve-month period. A corporatist–populist of a traditional stripe, Orban is now busily upgrading into something more formidable and troubling.

When Victor Orban speaks of Hungary, it is often about the "cultural and spiritual renewal of a nation of fifteen million," 5 million of whom, in approximately equal numbers, are Magyarophone citizens of neighboring Slovakia and Roumania. He enjoys referring to Transylvania as "Hungary's living space in the Carpathian Basin."[96] As a step toward reuniting the foreign population to the mother country, the Fidesz government enacted a so-called status law – which opposition Socialists felt obliged to support – entitling fellow Magyars in the two neighboring nations to partake of Hungarian social benefits. Orban generally disarms the criticism that the bestowal of such privileges is a step toward granting citizenship rights with the throwaway line that the issue is moot because, once Hungary is within the EU, the importance of national borders will disappear anyway. To underscore what he really means, on 3 April 2002 Orban paid a visit to Komarom/Komarno (Slovak), a traditionally Magyar area of settlement divided by the Danube, announcing there that the EU would bring a

big change in resident's lives .... We will re-unite the town of Komarom .... We want to join the EU so that at long last the state borders which separate Hungarians from Hungarians lose their significance, and with this act of joining we will turn from a 10-million medium-sized European country into a 15-million-strong nation.[97]

Such talk rattled cages in Brussels. So, too, did the ostentatious hand of friendship that Orban extended to Jörg Haider during the "Austrian crisis" – as well as his refusal to disavow the possibility of forming an electoral coalition with the anti-Semitic Justice and Life Party of Istvan Csurka. "Danny the Red" Cohn-Bendit, presently incarnated as a Green member of the European Parliament representing France, denounced Orban as a Jew-baiter.[98] The Commission would be well advised to pay attention to the budding friendship between Mr. Orban and Mr. Berlusconi. The latter came to power in part because of public opposition to the austerity policy adopted by the Italian technocratic left in order to qualify Italy for the European Monetary Union. Berlusconi's policy is to assert Italian power within the EU and at the same time weaken it. Orban threatens to do likewise, if not leave it altogether.

There is another reason for examining the Italo-Hungarian connection. Denouncing his April electoral defeat as due to fraud, Orban has – though continuing to respect democratic proprieties – begun to turn Fidesz into a mass political movement. *Hijra Magyarorsag!* or Forward Hungary! was obviously inspired by *Forza Italia!* but rests organizationally on new "civic circles." Resembling communist cells, they have apparently been set up to enable his supporters to mobilize on a moment's notice. For what purpose is not clear.[99] Orban stated in a 22 July interview that

the value of this movement is that it is above parties. Although mostly right-wing or center-right people are in it, left-wing people can also find their place in it .... By standing separately from, and above, the world of parties, we offer opportunities to all people with so-to-speak national feelings. There must be something that holds us, the 15 million Hungarians, together.

He elaborated, somewhat ominously, that

the civic circles are not just about the question of who is in government [because] ... we would like to re-build Hungary's social fabric ... re-knit and reinforce this fabric so that Hungary becomes a strong country, a strong national community, regardless of government. The civic circles' aim is not [only] to gain power ... its real meaning goes beyond this.[100]

Anti-EU appeals will figure strongly in Forward Hungary! propaganda. In fact, relations between Budapest and Brussels nearly broke down in February 2002 after the Commission presented plans that would cut the eastern European aspirants out of most farm aid and regional assistance. On 22 March a Hungarian government official suggested deferring accession until 2007, when the new EU budgetary cycle was scheduled to begin. On the eve of the April election, Hungarian radio reported that "the stance of the European Union and Hungary regarding the joint budget issues are miles apart," and the Hungarian delegate rejected membership outright if Hungary became a net contributor from the outset.[101]

As leader of Forward Hungary! Orban has said little about the dollars and cents of the accession arrangement but has delivered dire warnings that the EU will wipe out the Hungarian cultivator. Yet only 3 percent of Hungary's working population actually supports itself exclusively by agriculture, though another 5 percent supplement income by part-time work in the sector. Economic stakes in the farm issue are not particularly large. The emotional ones are. "Yesterday," said Orban in a 22 July 2002 interview, "I met farmers. I can tell you that they are embittered .... It is not worth hiding the truth .... [I]f the current government does not return to the agricultural policy supporting family farms and private farms, tens of thousands of Hungarian farmers and families will go bankrupt after EU entry .... This must be prevented."[102]

The present socialist government stands between Hungary and a course of development that could set it apart from the EU and let loose old-style prewar politics and regressive economics. If Orban comes to power, the "thundering herd" of world capital markets may be the chief remaining obstacle to such a disastrous turn of events. As prime minister, Orban had the good sense not to challenge the sound economic policies of the previous administration by actively pursuing corporatism or pushing irredentism much beyond the rhetorical. A threat to prosperity could well provide a one-way ticket out of the prime minister's office. The rotten deal that the EU is offering the accession countries threatens the welfare of the present somewhat compromised but well-disposed government in Hungary – which, if faithful to the Horn legacy, will act not only in the nation's best interest but in those of Europe as well.

THE POLISH QUESTION: AS ALWAYS, UNANSWERED

For Poland, and Europe, the harsh EU accession terms could be devastating. The socialist government now in power is weak and has neither strong party backing nor public support. After years of expansion, the country has slipped into a serious recession whose end is not in sight and which could be disastrous for a country as poor as Poland. Support for EU entry is lukewarm and waning, and a powerful antidemocratic movement is being organized to oppose it. Neither this group nor any other organized political faction, however, is yet strong enough to take over the reins of power from the unpopular incumbent. The prime minister, Leszek Miller, has promised to resign if the EU referendum fails. Unless a satisfactory replacement for the present government can be assembled and bolted together, turmoil may ensue. If the referendum on the EU passes,

Polish membership could also become highly problematic for both Poland and Europe. If it does not psss, matters could become still worse.

The problems of post-communist Poland began with Solidarity itself. It freed Europe from communism but could not liberate Poland from its history of internal weakness.[103] Now in disarray, Solidarity was a heterogeneous grass-roots movement, at once democratic-socialist and Christian-conservative, bound together by idealism but without the experience and know-how required either to reform the economy or govern a modern nation. Universally admired by the conservative and liberal/libertarian right in the West, Solidarity – once installed in office after heroic and painful compromises with the martial-law communist dictatorship of General Jaruzelski during the 1980s – followed a socioeconomic agenda as radical as any on the post–World War II western European left.

Less important than whether it be described as socialist or corporatist in inspiration is the fact that Solidarity's policy rested on worker control of the productive process – on an across-the-board application of the co-determination principle (*Mitbestimmung*).[104] The European left largely overlooked the importance of this experiment, which was conducted in the name of the Christian ideals and anticommunism that progressive-minded Westerners held in contempt; among the politically correct, especially in West Germany, the Polish peoples' movement met with less friendly support than worried disapproval. At the same time, the political right overlooked the economic side of Solidarity in favor of the greater stake in play: the collapse of the Soviet empire. Almost unnoticed, the Solidarity experiment – the effort to reform and govern a modern nation by applying interwar European economic ideology – failed thoroughly.[105]

No one could fill the vacuum. Solidarity was a mass movement, supported at first overwhelmingly by nearly all classes and regions. Yet Poland lacked strong quasi-communist managerial cadres, like those in Hungary, into whose hands economic authority might gradually be placed. The country was also too large (39 million), too diverse (the amalgamation of regions and provinces from the three central European empires of the nineteenth century), and too poor (lowest per-capita income within east central Europe, $3,500/year in 1996) to be easily administered from a single center of power.[106] The nation also lacked a legitimate political opposition with moral authority.[107] Like the new economic and political governance machinery, it would have to be invented.

Poland gave birth to "shock therapy" – the prescription for state economic controls to be lifted at once and across the board, enabling prices to find their own level, sending the signals needed to make markets self-generating, and channeling investment into meeting demand. The structural changes needed to consolidate and extend the gains of the market economy could then be designed and put into place: law based upon the principles of property and contract; financial institutions providing access to capital; rules that increased predictability and reduced transactions costs; fiscal systems that were fair and transparent; efficient administration; and sturdy democratic political institutions for public control of government. The list of reform items was long and some have yet to be checked off – perhaps because only a single pencil has been used and only one man has been able to use it.[108]

Leszek Balcerowicz can claim credit, or take the blame, for having been the director of Poland's economic transformation.[109] Regardless of the specific offices he has held over the past ten years, this brilliant and forceful man has defined and implemented the economic policy of every government in power up to the present. He has not followed a grand design but proceeded opportunistically, as allowed by political constraints and according to tacit (though sometimes contested) agreements that governments in power have made in recognition of the "special situation facing Poland." Balcerowicz's extraordinary role, which lacks any parallel in post-communist eastern Europe, has something to do with the tough nature of the job.[110]

Shock therapy requires inducing a Schumpeterian wave of destruction that must destroy before it can create. In poor and structurally weak Poland, such a policy inevitably causes great human suffering, produces more short-run losers than winners, embitters the public, and shortens the lives of elected governments. The shock therapist's job is a thankless one best conducted by a nonelected authority "above politics" and shielded from voter control – ideally, a central banker able to operate autonomously and without either the overt approval or sanction of the government in power. Lacking any real economic policy of their own, successive Polish governments have until quite recently accepted an arrangement by which, whatever the rhetoric of public policy, Balcerowicz has made the tough economic decisions for them. It is the biggest open secret in Warsaw.

As in Hungary and much of the rest of post-communist eastern Europe, Polish traditionalists and modernizers have alternated in office: Solidarity and its remnants on the one hand; overhauled communists parading as social democrats on the other. At this point the similarity ends. Instead of Hungarian gradualism, a state of cold (and sometimes hot) war existed during the ten years of struggle between the beneficiaries of the communist system and those who had suffered from the misrule of the stupid and privileged *nomenklatura*. The Polish high command ran the country for several years under martial law. The inept and discredited communist party had to be given early retirement.

The simple and relatively clear divisions in Hungary between city and countryside that had created strong, reliable constituencies for single large parties of the left and right are not to be found in Poland. Vast differences exist between class and region that are hard to bridge, resulting in party fragmentation, frequent shifts in voting behavior, and large variations in outlook and interest. Government has alternated between left and right coalitions – formed along the communist–anticommunist divide by ill-disciplined parties and their shifting allies – and remains subject to the demands of confrontation-minded interest groups such as farmers, unions, public-sector employees, and regional advocates.

Post-communists replaced Solidarity from 1993 to 1997. A neo-Solidarity government remained in power until October 1999, when it gave way to the cabinet formed by Leszek Miller and consisting of Socialists and their partners from the Peasants' Party, the successor to a communist-era client of the same name. Twenty pounds lighter, fitted out in an Italian suit, and retooled as a socialist, the former communist Aleksander Kwasniewski began his five-year presidential term in 2000. Like the other *ancien régime* powers, Solidarity and the Communist Party, the Catholic church is undergoing an identity crisis and also losing its political authority. A situation of underlying political instability is present.

After ten years of impressive growth at just under 7 percent, the Polish economy stalled in 2002. The new prosperity left many behind but made Poland the envy of its neighbors and became a source of national pride and hope. The current recession was mainly caused by the world downturn of 2001–2002 but was aggravated by policy mistakes; it is the exception in eastern Europe, where strong growth still prevails. Polish unemployment is approaching 20 percent. New money and modern lifestyles in the city stand in jarring contrast to the poverty and insecurity prevailing in much of the countryside. "Disco Poland" – the nonideological folk who demand little more than a decent opportunity to get by and enjoy themselves – still holds the upper hand politically. Yet the growing misery has rekindled deep-seated historical resentments that have begun to take bizarre and threatening political form – to wit, the meteoric rise of the populistic peasant demagogue, Andrzej Lepper. The European Union is the favorite object of his strident complaint. Until a few months ago his emotional appeal had no basis in the dollars and cents of accession. The EU's avarice has nevertheless validated Lepper's screeds and simplified the task of arousing the angry, confused, and profoundly conservative public. The peasant rabble-rouser has now rallied about 20 percent of the electorate to his strange standard, and support for him is growing. The almost leaderless left is having trouble defending both itself and the pro-EU policy. The small but influential pro-enterprise right is also becoming increasingly disenchanted with its "European commitment." Though wary and disaffected, it has not yet tried to link up with the angry small farmers, unemployed workers, "informal economy" street vendors, and idle youth who have flocked to the Lepper movement.

The Polish transition has passed through three phases, each with a different impact. The first was the famous phase of pure shock therapy. Advised by Jeffrey Sachs of Harvard and often opposed by powerful forces within Solidarity, Balcerowicz – then acting as minister of finance – took advantage of the current confusion, the naïveté of the movement's political leadership, and voters' readiness for sacrifice and rammed twenty major laws and constitutional amendments through the Sjem, or parliament, in the last three months of 1991. He used this "window of opportunity" to free prices, slash government spending, privatize shops and services, liberalize foreign trade, and let the zloty float.

As in the occupied former German *Reich* of 1948, kiosks sprouted up everywhere, queues vanished, and consumer goods came out of the woodwork. The protected, jury-rigged, nonmarket official economy imploded. Prices began to rise at once. Real wages declined 20 percent in two years as unemployment climbed into double digits. Factories closed. Those unable to find work returned to the country to subsist on miniplots. A quarter of the working population drew some form of pension, devouring 15 percent of GDP. By mid-1992, 6,000 strikes had taken place.[111] This, then, was the phase of necessary destruction.

Following it came a phase of creativity, of self-generating market growth and institutional consolidation. It did not so much replace the poor "Poland B" with a more affluent and progressive "Poland A" as rejuvenate and strengthen the latter. This creative phase coincides, politically, with the first post-communist Socialist government (1995–1997) and the first post-Solidarity government (1997–1999). Winning the election thanks to self-destruction by the right, the Socialists garnered a two-thirds parliamentary mandate with only 36 percent of the vote of the 42 percent of the electorate that actually went to the polls. Utterly devoid of ideas, the reconstructed communists – previously members of the ridiculed "stonehead" (*beton*) faction – shrewdly let the Balcerowicz reforms stand. Acting contrary to official rhetoric, their finance minister (Grzegorz W. Kolodko) cut pensions, halved the budget deficit, hacked back taxes enough to reduce black-market activity substantially, reduced subsidies to public corporations, continued to encourage foreign direct investment, and did not interfere with the expanding private sector of entrepreneurs, small firms, and new "greenfields" operations of all sizes that were the real motor of the Polish economy. By 1997, some 1.8 million private firms employed 30 percent of the workforce and produced nearly half the national output.[112]

A fall in the Socialist vote and the near collapse of the Peasants' Party brought a post-Solidarity government to power in September 1997 under the colorless Jerzy Buzek. Elected as a candidate of a new, pro-European liberal party called the Freedom Union (FU), Leszek Balcerowicz was nonetheless again the real power behind the government. As deputy prime minister and finance minister, Balcerowicz had a largely free hand. The combination of FU secular liberals and what remained of the conservative Catholics and labor activists was an odd one – but no stranger than the other alternative, the amalgamation of free marketeers and ex-communists. Spoils rather than ideology divided the two factions.[113]

A new middle-class sensibility made its presence felt in Poland of the late 1990s. Even with living standards at a third of western European levels, no less than half the Polish people proudly considered themselves as "belonging to the middle class." In the 1995 presidential election, the tricked-out ex-communist Kwasniewski whipped the international hero and icon Lech Walesa in humiliating fashion. The Primate of the Polish Church, Cardinal Glemp, soon did a turnabout and no longer denounced the "godlessness" of the EU.[114] Disco Poland seemed attuned to the prospects of the future, not legacies from the past.

Meanwhile, back in Poland B, things had not been going so well. Solidarity opposition to the dismantling of worker self-management resulted in a wave of strikes in 1992 and "impeded the development of effective privatization strategies." Some 560 companies were simply allowed to go bankrupt. Most big firms remained in the public sector and under at least partial control of worker councils. They, too, have run up against hardened constraints, been forced to shed labor, and have acquiesced in a gradual shift of control to management while turning to the government for subsidies. According to the former director of privatization, "the strength of Solidarity created a special pressure for insider-oriented ownership transformation, with the participation of employees and managers."[115] The situation remains murky.

Poland had inherited, in the words of Carolyn Campbell, "an industrial structure characterized by excessive development and geographical concentration of heavy industries, underdevelopment of high technology, service and consumer industries, and extreme horizontal and vertical integration." The "implementation of radical economic reforms did not," she deadpans, "result in the adjustment of this structure."[116] Much of this Stalinist industry was indeed fit only for the scrap pile. Although the prevailing wisdom in Poland held that the best industrial policy is no industrial policy, there were practical limits beyond which it could not be pushed. The industries of petroleum refining, steel, pharmaceuticals, fertilizer, banking, and insurance all lobbied the government for some form of protection and were at least partially successful.[117] The "kleptoklatura" was also alive and well. The tattered public sector of the economy remained rife with patronage.

The steel industry was a disaster area. This supposed showpiece of communist economics was overbuilt, obsolete, and employed 123,000 – 2.3 percent of the entire labor force. The Association Agreement with the EU called for the total elimination of tariffs by 2000, but the point was moot because the more efficiently produced western European steel easily surmounted existing barriers and flooded the Polish market in the mid-1990s. The EU refused the Poles restructuring assistance like that paid in the West under the Davignon Plan on the grounds that only firms able to make a profit should benefit from it. The Polish government then developed its own "rationalization" plan, the most important features of which included a reduction of raw steel capacity by a third (to 11.7 million annual tons), the introduction of continuous casting (which was nearly universal outside of the ex-bloc), the closure of all open-hearth furnaces (an obsolete technology), the privatization of profitable firms, and the dismissal of 80,000 workers. The social costs of the plan were too high for its completion. The EU nevertheless continued to exert pressure. Thanks perhaps to this "shield" from political responsibility, the rationalization program could be revised and extended to 2006. It shut down nearly all the open-hearth furnaces and seven electric furnaces, some 8.3 annual tons of capacity. The dilapidated and subsidized processing industry remains intact, however, and still limps idly along. Its capital goods inventory is forty years old on average.[118]

Textiles were another large and hopelessly uncompetitive sector of industry, employing 7.3 percent of the industrial labor force – less, to be sure, than in Portugal at 33 percent. Concentrated in Lodz, the Polish industry was only 42 percent as productive as the EU average and unable to compete even at the pitifully low prevailing wage levels. After the EU refused to give Poland a special break (dérogation) like the earlier one granted the Portuguese, the government "privatized" 96 percent of the sector by letting it, in effect, die off.[119]

After many delays, the Poles adopted a rigorous restructuring plan for the key and once strategically vital coal sector in 1998. It called for eliminating 118,000 of Poland's 237,000 mine jobs and the shutting down 24 of its 65 mines. The $4.4 billion of incurred costs roughly equal the total prospective subsidy that would have had to be paid to operate the mines until 2002. Drafted by Balcerowicz as finance minister and vice–prime minister in the post-Solidarity government, the plan represented a crushing defeat for the labor-union wing of the unstable movement, in which the miners had been a powerful element.[120]

The problems facing agriculture were more serious yet. Poland is home to 2 million individual plots, which employ 27 percent of the working population (as opposed to a 6.2-percent EU average). There are more farmers in Poland than in Germany, France, Italy, and the United Kingdom combined and over twice as many as in the other accession countries. Like his predecessors of fifty years ago, the average Polish farmer owns only two or three cows and is for the most part unacquainted with modern methods of breeding, sanitation, or using herbicides and pesticides. Most producers are at the quasi-subsistence level and market only locally.

The smallholdings are particularly numerous in regions of the former Russian and Austro-Hungarian empires, where large landowners were expropriated after the war. Squatters then occupied and subdivided the estates. Rather than collectivize and risk Church-led resistance, the government left them alone. Under the ancient Marxist regime, they were represented by the predecessor of the Peasants' Party (PSL) now in coalition with the Miller government. The social and economic situation in agriculture differs significantly in formerly West Prussian areas, where medium-sized farms were the rule prior to polonization. Agriculture is most advanced in the Wielkopolska region, where western European–type methods are standard. The overpopulation characteristic of the eastern and southern regions of Poland is absent. In the thinly populated estate country of East Prussia taken over by Poland, Soviet-type *kolkhoz* and *sovkhoz* are worked by state employees who are largely secular in outlook and support the Socialists. These big operations cover a fifth of total farm acreage.[121]

EU policy has been completely unmindful of the problems of rural Poland.[122] The Europe Agreements opened the country to a flood of subsidized farm products, worth about $500 million per year. EU surpluses were also dumped in Russia, depriving Polish agriculture of its most important foreign market. The Polish Peasants' Party estimated that only 600,000 of the country's 2 million farms would survive accession. Smallholders of the south and east are expected to comprise the bulk of those forced off the land; they will likely face a slow death. EU grain, meat, and milk exports wrought disproportionate havoc on midsized modernizers of the former West Prussia, forcing them to operate at huge losses.[123] According to the owner of one model farm, an 87-hectare spread 150 miles south of Warsaw with 450 pigs and an additional 100 hectares of wheat grown on leased land, "if they'd given me the subsidies the EU farm gets, I'd survive. But I won't survive another three years of the current economic situation."[124] It has deteriorated steadily since then. In 1980, farm incomes equaled 80 percent of urban ones; by 2002, the figure had declined to 40 percent. At about 1.4 million persons, 42 percent of Poland's joblessness was rural. The situation would be still worse without the 23 percent of farm household income that derives from social insurance and welfare benefits.

The EU farm-product export offensive has rekindled old fears of a forced sell-out. The harsh accession terms are fanning them into flames. Polish land prices are a tenth of Germany's. Much desirable acreage is located in ethnically and nationally contested regions. Herr Stoiber pointedly insisted during the 2002 electoral campaign on a restoration of the rights of recovery for former German owners.[125] To Polish patriots, "land is not [only] a good, but a heritage never to be betrayed. For many of them, Slimak is a role model. A dim-witted peasant in a nineteenth-century novel, "Slimak is slow, incoherent, and useless, but he knows one thing: not to sell his tiny plot to the Germans."[126] All Polish governments have attempted to incorporate a ban on foreign farm ownership into the accession treaty. In late 2001, Miller gained EU assent to a twelve-year delay.

Unemployment (including underemployment) is the most severe medium-term problem faced by the government of Poland. New jobs will have to be found for about 350,000 workers made redundant in traditional industry and 400,000 in light industry. Another 2.8 million farm workers are underemployed and will gradually be displaced.[127] The baby boom of the early 1980s will, moreover, create a bulge of youthful job-seekers in the early 2000s. By one estimate, "young Poles will soon make up about 40 percent of all people looking for employment in both central and western Europe."[128] Some 700,000 Poles work abroad, only 200,000 of them legally. Surveys indicate that as many as 40 percent of working-age Poles would like to emigrate.[129] The magnitude of this figure, as opposed to derisory official EU estimates, helps explain the determination of German government resistance to the free movement of labor. It underscores even more forcefully the strong pressure that will be felt within Poland once the safety valve of emigration is capped.

Appointed in October 2001, Prime Minister Leszek Miller won the election by default. Only 46 percent of the electorate went to the polls. Buzek's outgoing neo-Solidarity government captured a mere 6 percent of the vote, spelling an end to the anticommunist front that had stirred hearts and minds for eleven years. The Lepper party, Self-Defense (Samoobrona), captured a substantial portion of the Peasants' Party electorate, with each of them receiving about 10 percent of the total vote. Balcerowicz's Freedom Union, which previously had captured an 11 percent share, lost all its seats.[130]

Leszek Miller is a canny survivor from the communist past, the only European head of government who was once a member of a politburo and an enthusiastic apparatchik.[131] An unrepentant supporter of General Jaruzelski, Miller publicly stated as late as March 1990, even after the Communist Party had been defeated in national elections, that "the withdrawal of Soviet troops from Poland would do no one any good."[132] Miller spent his 1991 summer holidays in the Crimea at the same hotel with Boris Pugo and Gennady Yanayev, both leaders of the anti-Gorbachev putsch. Had it succeeded, Anne Applebaum bitterly remarks, "Miller might well have become prime minister of Poland a good deal earlier."[133] For over two years, he was under investigation for having received over a million dollars from the Kremlin in order to tailor the Communist Party to fit the new specifications of social democracy. Whenever he spoke in parliament, the opposition understandably walked out in protest.[134] The case was dropped after the reborn Communist Party came to power. As minister of interior in the first socialist government, the "sly and slippery" Pole was suspected of keeping an open line to the Kremlin. The foreign minister in the present government, Tadeusz Iwinski, was a prominent Communist Party ideologist in his previous incarnation and is openly anti-Semitic. A chapter in one of his books is entitled "The Zionist Version of Bourgeois Expansionism."

The cagey Polish prime minister may not be quite the "dancing monkey auditioning for a part" that – as the socialist head of a democratic government seeking entry into the EU – he appears to many to be. His mantra has been: "Let the economy grow faster. Taxes on business must be cut. It should be easier to hire and fire. Joining the EU will be Poland's third greatest moment in history since its conversion to Christianity a millennium ago." Miller kept Balcerowicz in harness, this time as president of the central bank. His administration also appointed a hard-line socialist as minister of treasury, who restocked the boards of public companies with party loyalists; consolidated government holding companies in steel, coal, arms, and other industries; and declared an end to privatization, most notably that of banks.[135] The design behind the policy seems to be that of state capitalism rather than the free market.

Both as democrat and economic liberal, Miller's credentials are suspect to the public. His pro-Europeanism is popularly ascribed to his training as a Soviet stooge. After taking orders from Moscow, how hard could it be for him to take orders from Brussels? Even if Miller manages to dispose of his heavy ideological baggage as easily as his colleague Kwasniewski shed excess pounds while running for office, his unsavory past undercuts his credibility and could fatally undermine it as hardships mount. His vulnerability jeopardizes the EU accession campaign. Adam Michnik, editor of *Gazeta Wyborcza* and former dissident, delayed for several months (until late December 2002) his newspaper's reporting on a $17.5-million bribe offered to Miller – on the grounds that public exposure of such corrupt practices would jeopardize EU accession.[136]

When Miller entered office, the economy was projected to grow at a rate of 5 percent. Over the following eight months it would slow to a crawl. In July 2002, unemployment moved past the 17-percent mark and was expected to reach 20 percent by the end of the year.[137] Growth sputtered forward at just 1.5 percent (when 5 percent would be needed for full employment). By June 2002, Miller's approval rating had dropped to 14 percent, almost two thirds less than the remarkable 40 percent of the sample who thought the old Communist Party had done a good job.[138]

The EU did not give an inch to the accession countries in 2002. Official Polish policy alternated between placatory suggestions to the public that things would improve after the German elections in September and warnings to the EU that, if they did not, then Poland would stay out of the union.[139] The official Polish negotiator, Jan Truszcynski, stated unequivocally: "It is clear that without direct payments we won't go in and there will be no Enlargement."[140] Even if Poland entered with a slight positive balance, it would be far exceeded by the costs of membership. Fading hope for change combined with rising unemployment and material hardship to strengthen Polish opposition to the EU, which until 2000 did not even officially exist. None other than Andrzej Lepper himself had long claimed to be for accession, so long as the Polish peasant received a fair shake. The best crude estimates agree that sentiment is too close to call on the accession issue. Support is nonetheless "shallow" and dwindling.[141]

"With his quiff, puckered scowl and solarium tan, Mr. Lepper ... used to be likened to Elvis Presley," but the similarity stops there. He is a professed admirer of the iron-headed Belarus strongman Alexander Lukashenka. Lepper's foulmouthed outbursts cost him his position as deputy speaker in the Sjem. He has accused members of the Polish government of conniving with the Taliban to smuggle anthrax into the United States. (Whether Mr. Lepper plays the guitar is unknown at this time.)[142] His political style is straightforward: He shows up wherever there is strife – at a Szczecin shipyard, at a Lublin car factory – journalists in tow. Where there is no strife, he is ready to stir it up – ransack offices, dump grain in the street, set up blockades, beard ministers on the run, and so on.[143] According to a careful observer, Lepper is "an amazingly good communicator [who] perseveres with a few simple slogans .... He has cunningly targeted small street traders, low-skill working class and the unemployed as his prime [market] .... [Lepper] has dared to speak what others are thinking."[144]

The program of the pompadoured peasant boils down to a few crude slogans: Balcerowicz must go; Poland has been looted by its political leaders; there must be a middle way between capitalism and communism. Lepper is vague about where such a passage might be found. Cynically convinced that the EU, like other powerful foreign influences in the nation's past, will never give Poland a fair deal, he has not needed to come out unconditionally against entry. Lepper's appeal, in any case, has little to do with a specific policy: it is that of the angry outsider bent upon rocking the boat of the cozy, mistrusted, corrupt political elite. So unpopular is the government that even 60 percent of the "modern" farmers support the Self-Defense Party. The movement is believed to have the support of about 20 percent of the Polish public.[145]

The spread of "Lepprosy" is not necessarily bad news for the Polish political establishment – if only because it siphons off pressure from the frustrated Polish working class, whose unions have largely collapsed. These losers of the 1990s now want "to establish a communist-like economy." Led by figures historically linked to Solidarity like Marek Jurczyk and Andrzej Gwizda, they have tried to revive the National Protest Committee at the troubled Szczecin shipyards.

Their appeal is nationalist-nativist and collectivist-socialistic.[146] The movement is united only by "nostalgia for communism, ... intense dislike for Leszek Balcerowicz, ... a lack of ideas for the future of business, [a belief that] Poland is governed by alien elements, and that the most precious [national treasures] are sold for nothing by the political elite to foreign moguls."[147] The revived movement has virtually nothing in common with the only other surviving Euroskeptical element in the country, called Civic Platform, the successor free-market party to Balcerowicz's Freedom Union (FU).[148] The repackaging was probably a mistake. In the present foul mood of the country, any organized group that could refer to itself as the F*** **u party would probably improve its chances.

Political fragmentation might be reduced in the run-up to the referendum. On 9 May 2002, the government launched its official pro-accession campaign. A day earlier, the 31-year-old Roman Giertych – leader of the small, right-wing League of Polish Families – had preemptively countered by forming a movement to oppose it. A serious student of western Euroskepticism, Giertych is intent upon taking Poland down the road of hard-line nationalism. Economic issues will have high billing in his campaign.[149] "At the beginning," according to the political commentator Tomasz Zukowski, "the Europhiles generally talked about money and the opponents about ideas. Now proponents talk about European civilization and united experience, and their opponents talk about money."[150] As put succinctly by Giertych: "We believe that in the current economic situation Poland's entering the EU simply does not pay off."[151] Mention must finally be made of the Law & Justice Party, headed by the identical twins Jaroslaw and Lech Kaczynski. Affectionately remembered as child television actors, the "Kacz Twins" are rising fast to the top. Recently elected mayor of Warsaw, Lech may well run to succeed Kwasniewski as president. Lech and Jaroslaw (the latter the less public of the two) are deeply suspicious of Brussels and are politically positioned between the "leppers" and the free-market liberals.[152]

As things now stand, Poland makes no net gain from EU membership. Poles will not (except in Britain, Sweden, the Netherlands, and Greece) be able to work abroad or remit money back home. Poland will face unfair competition from the EU on foodstuffs, where the nation's low land prices and cheap labor would normally provide comparative advantage. The country also faces huge conversion costs in industry as well as heavy charges associated with the *acquis*. They are anything but nontrivial. Danuta Hubner, the Polish official responsible for accession, estimates that the social chapter will consume 2–3 percent of GDP per year and environmental cleanup another 2 percent for at least a decade. To them must be added the heavy costs of the single currency standard, should Poland enter the EMU.

The question facing Poland is not whether the country stands to gain more by staying out than by going in, but whether it stands to lose more. Polish protectionism raises one set of dangers; EU retaliation poses still another threat. Overhanging these issues is another: given instability at the top, could any democratic Polish government survive popular rejection of the EU? It seemed evident to Mrs. Hubner back in 1997 that "we have to negotiate membership ... not just with Brussels but with the Poles."[153] The process that should have been, as promised the public, a matter of give-and-take has instead been dictated. West European morosity and nativism and EU inflexibility have deprived their Polish interlocutors of legitimacy.

In June 2002, the Miller government changed course. The shutdown of the famous Szczecin shipyards, the anchor of the regional economy, apparently provided the necessary trigger.[154] The government broke with the program "Work – Development – Entrepreneurship," which in theory had guided policy up to then. Associated with Marek Belka, the minister of finance and deputy prime minister, the sound policy linked spending increases to rises in GDP, froze public-sector wages, began to roll back the Kafkaesque tax bureaucracy, and cut red tape. Future plans included policies to facilitate the hiring of part-time labor and accelerate capital depreciation.[155]

Neither the electorate nor the government was in the mood to wait for the long-term benefits yielded by the classical remedies of economic liberalism. The pro-accession Balcerowitz, who had not cut rates fast enough to please an angry public, had to be sacrificed.[156] In June the government thus proposed a bill to pack the monetary council overseeing central-bank operations. In early July, it replaced Belka with the more compliant former treasury minister, Grzegorz Kolodko, whose lax fiscal policies bankers blamed for rekindling inflation earlier. The top priority of his "anti-crisis action plan" is to create employment by means of tax incentives, debt forgiveness, and injection of liquidity into the banking system. Almost surely it will involve throwing good money after bad – particularly into state-sector operations run on a patronage basis – and be inflationary.[157] The zloty immediately lost a percentage point against both dollar and euro. On 1 August 2002, Standard & Poor's downgraded the rating on the two largest issues of Polish bonds.[158]

Although the inflationary bias of the Kolodko policy could complicate Poland's accession to the EU, the shift in course may also have an overriding benefit. As pointed out by the political commentator Piotr Zarembka, "All new regimes since 1989 have left the bulk of public opinion convinced that little is really changing – that however they vote, out of the ballot box pops Balcerowicz and monetaristic fiscal conservatism. Here, finally, we have the opportunity to test out [an] alternative theory."[159] Poles will at long last be getting the kinds of economic policies for which they had voted. If opening monetary and fiscal floodgates does not produce economic chaos, the democratic process may well be strengthened, increasing political stability over the long run. However, EU policy stacks the odds against any such positive outcome.

The Chirac–Schröder deal of 24 October 2002, the stringer for *Agence France Presse* blithely reported, "removed the last major obstacle to expansion expected to be approved in December with a funding [arrangement] thrashed out at a two-day summit following a last-minute compromise on the crucial issue of farm subsidies."[160] Other observers took a distinctly less sanguine view of what had transpired. Simon Jenkins of the *Times* called the understanding "perfidious and ... a conspiracy against the Third World and eastern Europe" in which "a bad-tempered French president browbeat a weak German chancellor into reneging on commitments to farm reform, reached with Britain in the lead, last year." Jenkins found it hard to imagine "a more tawdry plot, even in recent European diplomacy."[161] By holding the eastern Europeans up for ransom, the French – with the acquiescence and compliance of the other westerners – have won the Enlargement endgame. The 12–13 December Copenhagen summit would be handed a *fait accompli*. Enlargement can proceed as scheduled and on French terms. The accession countries will have a high price to pay. So will Europe.

The deal is a standstill agreement that eliminates any opportunity for reform. Nothing will be done prior to 2007 to reduce the 50 percent of the Community budget that CAP consumes. The five-year guarantee to western European farmers will leave little for the accession countries and give unfair competitive advantage to the rich farmers of the West over the poor ones of the East. The deal also leaves in place a gradual phase-in of the support payments, with increases from 25 percent in 2004 in 5-percent increments until reaching 40 percent by 2006–2007. Thereafter CAP can rise by only a single percent annually (for inflation) until 2013, by which time the rates paid the new members will have been brought to parity with the level of the original fifteen. Even then, the accession states will be able to claim only a tiny fraction of the largesse. By 2006 some 2.5 billion euros in "market spending and direct aids" would accrue to the accession countries as opposed to about 43 billion euros to the farmers of the Fifteen. By 2013, the ten new members' share can grow to 5 billion euros – which does not, however, "mean a reduction in subsidies for the present members." According to EU experts, the growth of funds for new members can be provided "through indexing the global sum with inflation."[162] Not included in the farm package is a big unknown, rural development funding. Even under the most optimistic assumptions, however, the agriculture of eastern Europe – the main sector of production in which the accession nations should enjoy a competitive advantage – will face serious economic discrimination.[163]

The overall settlement, as presented at Copenhagen, contains no offsetting compensation to the prospective new members. The new kids on the block received mere verbal assurance that "they will not be worse off as ... members than as candidates."[164] Indirect, opportunity, and administrative costs are nowhere taken into account. Structural and cohesion funds, supposed to provide an offset, were actually cut (upon German insistence) from the Commission-proposed 25.6 billion euros, to be paid over 2003–2006, to 23 billion euros.[165] Worst of all from the eastern European standpoint, the previously West-dictated restrictions placed upon labor mobility still stand. Nothing has been conceded to the accession nations.

The 24 October deal is, in fact, the greatest coup in the history of European integration. Without providing a quid pro quo of any kind and in the teeth of overwhelming public opposition, Chirac single-handedly brought a shuddering halt to a decade of effort to reform the CAP. On the losing side were the WTO, the European Commission, the British-led net contributors, and the would-be "wideners" and liberalizers of the Community. The sole beneficiaries of the deal are the cosseted, disproportionately French farmers of western Europe. Schröder's real reasons for yielding to Chirac remain obscure. The British interpretation – that he was "stitched and outfoxed," tricked by a smarter and tougher negotiator – is not completely convincing. Schröder had already gone quite soft on CAP reform during the election campaign. That the British-led faction immediately acquiesced in the Franco-German deal is only slightly less surprising.

The eastern Europeans tried to put the best face on the setback. Initial reaction was one of relief that accession had not been derailed or hopelessly delayed. The have-not governments of the former Soviet bloc could not, of course, repudiate their own work without risk of being thrown out. They could merely try to contain the certain backlash. On 28 October 2002, negotiators for the ten accession candidates met in Copenhagen for collective tongue-clucking.[166] "Only when we are an EU member and the new budget exists," admitted the chairman of the Sjem European Committee, Jozef Oleksy, "will it be possible to talk about the further fate of direct subsidies." He sheepishly hoped that "the reform of the Common Agricultural Policy will be launched in the meantime."[167] On 30 October, thousands of Czech farmers marched on Prague with a petition signed by 100,000 protesting the ruination of the nation's farming in the face of unfair EU competition.[168] It surely will not be the last such event of its type.

The Chirac-engineered deal is utterly indefensible.[169] Apart from the harm done in eastern Europe, it perpetuates trade discrimination against Third World producers, stimulates ecologically damaging overproduction, adds 1,000 pounds per year to food costs for a family of four, has eliminated at a stroke any hope that Enlargement will result in Community reform, makes a mockery of both EU procedures and the exercise in constitution drafting currently under way, and has also divided the Community even more seriously than before. The prospect is dim that a reconciled Franco-German couple will manage, as in the 1980s, to give the EU direction and purpose in the future. The Chirac–Schröder deal was anything but a fresh initiative; it only preserved the status quo. Present public petty-mindedness stands in the way of anything more ambitious. There are other Franco-German problems as well. The "lordly President Jacques Chirac and the informal, almost laddish" Chancellor Gerhard Schröder despise each other, according to EU-watcher Ambrose Evans-Pritchard, "and disagree on almost every policy ... [because] Paris, like London, wants to ensure that national capitals gain the whip hand over Brussels [whereas] Germany is pushing for a 'federalist' model at the ... Convention on the Future of Europe."[170]

Prime Minister Blair's straddling, tightrope walking, dancing, and dodging proved to be less than nimble-footed at the recent summit: he took a severe beating. Before stalking out in fury, however, he administered a memorable tongue-lashing to the imperious French president. Professing "never having been spoken to like this before," Chirac thereupon dis-invited the prime minister to the annual pre-Christmas "Anglo-French summit" in Le Tourquet.[171] At present the outside man at the EU, Blair looks in desperation to the Doha WTO round to liberalize international trade in agricultural commodities and restart the CAP reform process.[172] For now, his policy is in ruins. The hopes of "wideners" and liberalizers that Enlargement would bring reform have gone up in smoke. The accession nations have been badly burned. Blair has failed not only their deeply compromised governments but also their understandably disgruntled electorates.

Those who have been cheated will not make life within the Community pleasant. If left outside it, however, they could be destabilizing and disruptive. Ten years of hard work, sacrifice, and idealism in the East have met with callousness, petty-mindedness, and duplicity on the part of the West. The nations abandoned at Yalta must soon face a harsh truth: they have fallen victim to yet another historic betrayal. It drags the name of Europe into the mud.

15

The New Market Economy
and Europe's Future

THE European Union may be seriously dysfunctional, but it is surely real. One might legitimately wonder about the "new market economy" after the stock market implosions of 2000 and 2001 and over two years of slow-motion or no-motion growth whose end is not in sight. Does it even exist, or was it a delusion? The collapse in asset values that followed the bursting of the NASDAQ bubble in April 2000 has infected markets worldwide. The Silicon Valley start-ups were the first casualties. Emulators and offshoots in Europe got hit next, and soon thereafter high-tech giants on both sides of the water like Intel and Nokia. They remain subject to market pummeling but will surely survive. Many others may not be so lucky. A distressing number of high-flying market leaders cooked their books and now have reason to regret it. Other tottering giants, like the debt-laden European telecoms, got drawn into making made bad business decisions and have gone nearly or altogether bankrupt.

The Masters of Destiny who ran such once-proud firms have had to learn the hard way that this new market economy is still subject to the old rules of supply and demand. Few indeed were the "players" impervious to the lures of the boomer *Zeitgeist,* even though time and again irrational exuberance has been the precursor of bust. An economic era has come to a predictably inglorious end and with it the hope that a new and better age was near at hand. It is in fact, but only the dawn has yet broken. It may take many years to reach high noon. The day is long.

The 1990s was an impressive decade of enduring accomplishments, some of which spilled over into low-growth Europe. The development of powerful new technologies gave rise to a broad array of advances in product and process that spread through much of industry. The world of finance, though not revolutionized, was substantially reformed. Fresh business models modernized patterns of work and social behavior. Structural change increased the size and importance of the amorphous entity known as the service sector, where hierarchy gradually gave way to initiative and obedience to job performance. Risk taking, innovation, and entrepreneurship were rewarded, and punished, as never before – at least in the twentieth century. Intellectual capital increased. Structural change raised the potential for long-term growth.[1]

And in the background was China, since the reforms of the late 1980s growing at an unprecedented rate even for a developing country: upwards of 12 percent annually for over a decade and still above 8 percent. Unlike the Russians, who failed in an attempt to introduce capitalism from the center, the Chinese have moved from the outside in – starting from the village on the one hand and the coastal enterprise zone on the other – spreading deregulation and the impact of market change by the oil-slick principle. The process is still only starting: some 70 percent of the industrial economy remains within the state sector, but as it erodes, the purely capitalist revolution taking place within this civilization of 1.3 billion people will place unrelenting pressure on the sluggish economies of the West.[2]

Why, then, has the economy of the West been stuck in a "slo-gro, no-gro" rut for the past two years? What went wrong? Overheating and inflation followed by rate increases, rising unemployment, falling productivity and investment – the usual scenario – did not play out. Instead, an investment-led boom resulted not in higher interest rates but in steady reductions even below expected yield, which fueled a surge in credit, equity, prices, and investment. The value of investment doubled as a share of American GDP from 1997 to 2000, causing the return on capital to decline. The fall in real rates of profit (partly masked by not treating options as a cost) after 1998 should have influenced investing but did not. Instead, investment rates continued to increase, creating excess capacities and setting the stage for a painful shakeout process. A monetary explanation would point the accusing finger at the Fed for not raising rates early and fast enough to discourage overinvestment. An Austrian explanation, such as Hayek elaborated shortly before the onset of the Great Depression, would argue that the downturn was the predictable result of the business cycle – something governed by the partial liquidity of capital investment, which impedes and delays reaction to market signals and produces the uneven patterns associated with boom and bust. The question of which theory better fits the circumstances of the current downturn cannot be settled tomorrow. The same holds with regard to the next question: What, if anything, can be done to reverse the trend?[3]

Europe must provide some of its own answers, especially in the matter of the structural problems responsible for low rates of long-term growth. A powerful engine of liberalization, sometimes even in spite of itself, the European Union requires far-reaching reform lest in the future it impede economic growth, breed social unrest, and aggravate existing political problems. The overhaul may take many years, especially if the EU also insists upon pursuing counterproductive policies. The EU should cease to pretend that the creation of a federal government for Europe is realistic politically, drop the attempt to engender Euro-patriotism (especially when it requires the invention of a foreign threat), stop promoting ideas for the purpose of building bureaucracies, terminate the practice of governing by stealth and manipulation, eliminate inequitable and harmful income transfer programs like CAP and most of the regional policies, and return to first principles. In order to thrive, the EU must be depoliticized and allowed to develop only when serving a demonstrably useful function; must eliminate market-hostile policies across the board; and, above all, must concentrate on building the institutions designed to maintain economic competitiveness.

In April 2001, in the immediate aftermath of the optimistic Lisbon summit, the *Financial Times* produced "Europe Reinvented," an insightful four-part survey of the economic opportunities being opened up by the EU as it entered the new millennium. Observing that the summit committed the EU to an ambitious agenda of social and economic reform, the survey's general editor (Lionel Barber) noted that not politics but rather the private sector had been the real agent of change since the Single European Act, a reflection of international developments. Privatization and the launch of the euro had accelerated the trend, but driving it was an "explosion of information technology and telecommunications."[4] Shaping change were the giant American investment banks, plus one or two European imitators, which "put together multi–billion-dollar cross-border deals [that] are changing Europe's corporate landscape beyond recognition." The four-part series dealt subsequently with the development of a new equity culture, the modernization of stock markets, the standardization of accounting and other regulatory practices, the creation of a single financial market, and the growth of the old as well as the new economy; it also investigated specific examples of change at the national level.

The various articles in the series, each a model of journalistic precision, pointed to a somewhat more guarded conclusion than intimated by the overall theme. These contributions suggested that, far from being settled, the competition – between politics and economics, institutions and market, old ways and new, and member-state and Brussels – had become increasingly entangled, making the prediction of any outcome problematic. The articles nevertheless corroborated the three fundamental contentions of the series. Liberalization had driven progress in Europe; economic growth had been spearheaded by innovation in the fields of telecommunications and finance; and such changes had left a permanent legacy.[5]

The Lisbon summit turned out to be a false start for the EU. A year after the Community's leaders set out to create "the most competitive and dynamic knowledge-based economy on the planet within ten years," a progress report was to be delivered during the Swedish presidency. The results were disappointing, as was the Stockholm summit itself. In truth, Community economic reform needed resuscitation. As noted by *Die Welt*'s Nicholas Blome, the summit was to have been "an ordinary economic [one] of the old-fashioned variety, but from the first moment gave the impression of being an unhealthy combination of politics and economics. Schröder, Blair, Chirac, and the others danced at Stockholm as if at many different weddings."[6] "We cannot," he added editorially, "continue to go on like this much longer."[7] Blome's concerns for the Community were warranted.

The Stockholm summit should be remembered for what it failed to do rather than its several cosmetic "accomplishments" – or even the single solid one, the opening of postal services to competition. The summit did not manage to deregulate gas and electrical markets because of French objections; *Electricité de France* thus continued to benefit from a protected domestic market, the profitability of which generated much of the wherewithal to buy up foreign suppliers on the other European national markets that had been previously opened up. Nor could the member-states agree to set up a single air-traffic control system, because the United Kingdom and Spain differed about airspace jurisdiction over Gibraltar. They also deferred a decision to build a multi–billion-dollar satellite network (Galileo) because private funding was insufficient, and they postponed action on a long-awaited common patent law because the Iberians felt slighted. Even amidst the "mad cow" panic, they could not decide whether to establish a European food safety agency.[8]

The Stockholm summit may have overlooked the cyber-issues arising from Lisbon because of the cloud overhanging them after the tech-stock collapse of the previous twelve months.[9] The same excuse cannot be made for disregarding other points on the liberalization agenda. Much backsliding had taken place since Lisbon. First, a major report drafted after a year of investigation by the Lamfalussy committee for reform of the European financial system met with too many national objections to be given serious consideration and hence was tabled. Second, at German insistence, the Commission's attempt to forbid the issuance of "golden shares" (which enable favored interests to retain corporate control and so frustrate cross-border takeovers) was relegated to the back burner. The special effort of innovation commissioner Erkki Liikanen to win endorsement of his efforts to "unbundle the local loop," thus opening local telephony and internet access, also made no headway. Surveying the meager conference results, the Swedish host, Prime Minster Goran Persson, commented limply: "This is how life is. You don't get everything at once."[10]

Others were less charitable. Noting that the EU leaders had failed to back any of the forty free-market initiatives put forth to meet the Lisbon agenda, the gruff and outspoken single market commissioner, Frits Bolkestein, complained that "we're seeing too much poetry and not enough motion. It will not do to issue these elevated statements [and] then not ... act upon them."[11] In the final minutes of the conference, which nearly broke up over French refusal to open energy markets, Bolkestein publicly reprimanded both President Chirac and Prime Minister Jospin; and in a later press interview he asked angrily: "Why does the French government have this fear of modernity? Why are they so slow in reforming the public sector?" He opined that "They [needed] to get over this mental block."[12]

Able and determined like Brittan and Sutherland, Bolkestein was finding himself increasingly isolated in the Commission – as was the other leading liberalizer, Mario Monti, the head of the competition directorate. To protect his turf, the deeply committed free-marketeer and former economics professor was even occasionally forced to don an anti-American mask. The *Economist* ruefully had to recognize that, since Lisbon, "social Europe" has been making progress in ways that make European labor markets more, not less rigid. New and tougher labor regulations are looming that will make it harder and harder for employers to fire – and therefore make them more reluctant to hire .... In coming months the liberalizers may find that their biggest battles involve not so much making progress as holding the line against rolling back measures already agreed [upon] .... Opposing bailouts would use up a lot of the Commission's political capital and may make it harder to persuade public opinion of the virtues of further liberalization.[13]

In fact, economic opening continued largely without benefit of a push from Brussels. The legacy of the Single European Act is complicated and difficult to disentangle. The SEA has, on the one hand, provided an excuse for nit-picking and costly re-regulation that has made a travesty of the notion of subsidiarity and has often resulted in both higher cost and the reduction of competition. Yet it has also reduced traditional national restraints on trade, prevented their reimposition, and encouraged tariff reduction. The usual theoretical explanations do not account for these results. The high unemployment of the 1990s should have produced a resurgent protectionism unless: international competition had eroded uncompetitive sectors; or dependence on international trade had shifted the sectoral balance to firms dependent on the global as opposed to the domestic market; or, more broadly, the increase in international trade flows was great enough to have generated a suprasectoral constituency of sufficient size and strength to override sectoral protectionist opposition – something that would require powerful ideological underpinnings.

None of these conditions obtained, according to Brian T. Hanson.[14] The SEA did not necessarily enshrine free trade. It had the more limited initial purpose of creating a single European market for European producers in the face of global competition. What both the European Roundtable and the French have fought for, Hanson underscores, more closely resembled Fortress Europe than anything that has subsequently developed. He might have mentioned that Mrs. Thatcher's winning bet on the market was right. Liberalization indeed took hold.

In the 1990s, the EU would enter 26 bilateral free-trade treaties, among them the Europe Agreements with the eastern European accession states. Domestically, restrictive arrangements like those in the highly vulnerable and protectionist automobile industry gradually loosened. The counterintuitive rise of international trade and even greater increase in capital mobility in the face of high unemployment was, as Hanson might further have noted, also a phenomenon of the late 1970s and early 1980s and thus antedated the SEA. He nevertheless correctly concludes that SEA cast the EU into an essential new role. Brussels gained the authority to override the reimposition of national protectionism, and the requirement for a weighted Council majority to oppose the advance of liberalization made reversal of the process almost politically impossible.[15] The process of economic change could not be easily suppressed or re-directed and had to be left to work itself out. Under present circumstances, EU gridlock is more a precondition than an obstacle to liberalization. As long as the Union cannot impose policies destructive of the market, the competition-induced, self-generating process of change will continue.

THE NEW AND THE OLD IN THE EUROPEAN ECONOMY

The economic growth of the 1990s should indeed be associated with the rise of the high-tech sector, according to a recent National Bureau of Economic Research (NBER) working paper. In it, Martin Baily and Robert Lawrence argue that structural productivity increased at about 1.6 percent above trend, of which 0.6 percent resulted from capital deepening within the high-tech sector (including software and communications), another 0.2 percent from the computer manufacturing industry, and 1.0 percent from industries other than information technology (IT). The large residual may be due to innovations facilitated by IT. Much of the acceleration in labor productivity stemmed from the service sector, they find, in particular retail trade and finance and business services. Service-sector branches that invested heavily in IT enjoyed a 50-percent faster rate of productivity growth than those that did not. The authors conclude that "the economy has changed [structurally] in the [1995–2000] expansion and a new technology has played a substantial role in [the] transformation."[16] Other indicators support the thesis. Even at the depressed levels of early 2001, stock valuations reflected the increased value of intangible capital. They coincided with a wave of innovation that ran parallel to increased expenditure for research and development and a rise in the number of registered patents. Another indicator of the importance of innovativeness to growth is the mounting number of scientific researchers employed at companies with fewer than 500 employees: 23 percent of the total, as opposed to 16 percent in 1993.[17]

Several conditions have been propitious to growth. Noting that nearly 70 percent of all IT products are purchased by wholesale and retail trade, finance, and communications, the authors argue counterfactually that competitiveness – especially in the big global service industries (e.g. banking) – is an important driver of innovation in the high-tech field: if IT sales were entirely the result of a random surge in the flow of innovation, then all countries would be expected to have shared in it proportionally. This is not the case. The availability of venture capital and the development of supply-chain management, along with fiscal discipline and low interest rates, have produced the right policy environment for growth and innovation, they suggest. The authors close with a reminder that productivity gains occurred before either the explosive growth of the internet or the NASDAQ crash. This wave of innovation, they conclude, substantially improved economic performance in both old and new firms in ways that otherwise cannot be explained, and for this reason it is appropriate to speak of a new "e-economy."[18]

Nor did the new economy disappear after the mid-2000 downswing. From 1999 to the end of 2001, employment in the top-100 boom companies climbed 26 percent, by 177,000 jobs; as of July 2002, only eight of these companies had failed, only three had experienced falling revenues, and the remainder had enjoyed an increase in combined sales of $99 billion in the past three years. Robust productivity increases – the closest that economic statistics comes to measuring the wealth of a nation – have rolled in from 1999 to the present.[19] Third-quarter 2002 American nonfarm productivity rose an impressive 4 percent, a remarkable result especially in a "growth" recession.[20] For the year 2002, U.S. GDP actually rose 2.8 percent.

What are the implications of the new economy for Europe? According to David B. Audretsch and A. Roy Thurik, the idea that job growth leads to low wages – a truism of the European left – has no basis in fact. "If higher wages can only be gained at the cost of fewer jobs, [then] how," they ask, "could the average income in Silicon Valley be 50 percent greater than the rest of the country and at the same time have created 15 percent more jobs between 1992 and 1996?"[21] The answer is that no such trade-off between wages and jobs is necessary under the emerging economic system. The old managed economy is outmoded, they argue, because routinized tasks can no longer be performed competitively in high-cost locations. Globalization has shifted the comparative advantage of high-cost locations to knowledge-based labor – that is, to the new entrepreneurial economy in which failure is an externality of the learning process. In this emerging system, the positive virtues of long-term relationships, stability, and continuity give way to flexibility, change, and turbulence. A liability in one becomes a virtue in another.[22]

The shift from "managed" to "entrepreneurial" economy, according to Audretsch and Thurik, implies a different rather than a lesser role for government policy: they must target inputs in order to create and commercialize knowledge rather than outputs, such as particular firms. Largely concerned with the issue of control, policy making in the *managed* economy aimed at determining what to produce, how to produce, and who would produce in order to constrain the power of big corporations, which – though needed to capture scale economies – threatened democracy. The methods applied were antitrust policy and public ownership.

By comparison, in the *entrepreneurial* economy the task facing the government, according to Audretsch and Thurik, is enabling in character: to foster the production and commercialization of knowledge, encourage labor mobility, and facilitate firm start-ups. The 1988 Cecchini Report measured the gains of the single market in terms of cost reductions through mergers, consolidations, and rationalization, whereas the real gains that Audretsch and Thurik argue for derive from the economics of diversity. A shift away from mega-corporations to smaller, more dynamic company operations occurred from the mid-1970s to the early 1990s, they observe, in all the OECD countries. The quick little guys are more competitive and promote higher economic growth than the slow big ones; success, in short, will continue to reward "those countries which have introduced a greater element of entrepreneurship."[23] The message of these two authors was familiar but still hard for the EU to heed.

"Old industry" is often disparaged, and incremental improvements in product or reduction of manufacturing costs often go unrecognized. Yet in their various forms and guises, the metal benders remained the major EU employer outside the service sector. That much said, developments during the 1990s in the traditional sectors of European industry are of only secondary interest. Europe lost its historical lead in chemicals and pharmaceuticals but kept up with the emerging American mega-firms, thanks largely to merger. The most successful of them, GlaxoSmithKline, imitated American models. In the related and budding new field of bio-tech, Europe barely got its toes in the water. Ideological opposition from the ecology movement contributed substantially to the dismal outcome. To mention only the largest branch of manufacturing, automobiles was a stagnant or declining field except for German builders of luxury-class vehicles, who exported heavily to the United States. European producers on the whole held on to traditional slow-growth manufacturing markets, as they also did in the expanding ones for luxury goods.[24] The beginnings of Silicon Valleys could be detected in various places – in Sweden and Finland, around Cambridge, and in Paris and Munich – but their economic role was slight except along the European periphery.[25] The declining industries of coal, steel, shipbuilding, and textiles continued their predictable decline.

The real action in Europe was in deregulated government monopolies (postal service, airlines, and railroads) or other once highly protected fields like road haulage – and especially in the privatized or partially privatized network industries of gas, electrical power, and telecommunications. In such fields, change of ownership and control produced huge economies, opened passages to product development, led to the reconfiguration of markets and firms, and – perhaps of still greater importance – spawned new relationships between the public and private spheres. In the network industries, control of infrastructure determined market access or lack of it. Such fields were traditionally considered to be natural monopolies. To make them competitive required active public policy intervention, a new kind of re-regulation. The Brussels authorities would play a large, though by no means completely successful, role in the process.[26]

There was also plenty of action in the financial field. The impetus was provided largely by the Wall Street mega-firms operating in The City.[27] The extraordinary power of such financials derived from their high-paid expertise and easy access to huge pools of dollars. The source of the liquidity was something still missing in Europe: a shareholder culture. Institutions – pension and mutual funds, in which the majority of Americans participated – provided this vast amount of readily mobilized wealth.[28] To approximate anything like a European equivalent would require converting the state-controlled or regulated paygo pension programs of the continent into funded, privately owned systems like those of the United States and Great Britain.[29]

The U.S. financial presence was big in Europe during the 1990s. The legions of young, short-haired, dark-suited, London-dwelling janissaries of economic change – most of whom were not, in fact, American citizens – sent shock waves reverberating throughout the European financial system. Their hard-driving determination to turn a buck caused markets to replace institutions and brought about the development of mysterious new financial products for lending, leasing, hedging, and stripping. Traditional lines between banking and other fields would also disappear in a race for new customers and capital, national champions would fuse in order to remain competitive, and rationalization would take place at every level of operation in attempts to reduce costs and increase speed of operation. Cyber-banking raised a host of new issues ranging from customer access to the definition of money itself. Many European banks broke from the German model and – instead of trying to serve as industrial directorates – adapted themselves to meeting client demand. Earnings at the bottom line largely displaced the exercise of control as the overriding strategic objective.

The American banks posed a challenge not only to other financial institutions but to the EU itself. The rise of the so-called Euro-dollar market in the 1960s is what first sparked discussion of monetary union. A desire to regain control over national levers of monetary policy and to reduce dependence upon an unstable dollar-based world economy gave rise to this discourse. The turbulence settled down in the 1990s. Thereafter, the perceived needs to discipline national governments and promote Euro-patriotism partly displaced the creation of a European capital market as motivations for monetary union. A common currency is only the first step toward a single financial market; regulatory machinery must also be put in place. Progress to date is not encouraging. Success may eventually offset the disadvantages of euro adoption. Failure will surely aggravate them.

THE 3G TELECOM DEBACLE

If there were no Silicon Valley in Europe, then one would have to be invented to enable the ancient civilization to stand up to the U.S. upstart. That is the rationale behind the policies that ultimately led the telecommunications industry, the leading growth sector of the European economy, to make an all-or-nothing commitment to a technology that will eventually bankrupt most firms in the field. The industry provides a case study that might have been invented by Audretsch and Thurik to demonstrate what can happen when the challenge of the entrepreneurial economy is met with the methods of the managed economy. It also proves that the EU has difficulty with trial-and-error learning.

The technology in question is 3G, shorthand for third-generation wireless transmission (cellular telephones employ 2G technology). Europe, and more specifically Nokia, is the world's largest manufacturer of the handheld devices. The Finnish phone maker dominates the European market, where penetration (about 70 percent) is half again as dense as in the United States. The Nordic giant is also taking a leading role in the development of 3G, the technology developed in order to market a computer the size of a telephone, a pocket-sized mobile minilaptop that can be held and operated on the run. The demand for 3G handsets was believed to be huge. If Europe could mobilize its strengths and dominate it, perhaps even Microsoft (which was converging on 3G from the software angle) could be nudged aside and technological victory be claimed for the old-world champion.[30] Or such was the hope of the Commission.

Problems with the concept have mounted. An early version of the mobile, handheld computer – WAP (wireless application protocol) – flopped. The devices have not yet become marketable, are too costly and heavy, and consume too much power; moreover, adequate software for them does not exist in the standard UMTS (Universal Mobile Telecommunications System) operating system. Microsoft, which has access to UMTS, is backing a different horse. The market for the 3G product has not even been adequately tested or established, but initial evidence indicates that it is much smaller than predicted. The costs of building infrastructure, on the other hand, are far higher than anticipated. Astonishingly, neither network nor manufacturing companies apparently thought it necessary to develop business models.[31] No one either within or outside of the industry seriously challenged the presuppositions upon which the 3G program was based – a fatal error.[32]

Chief among them was that Europe could adopt a single standard as it had done earlier with the GSM (Groupe Spécial Mobile, or global standard for mobile) system for the cellular telephone, which enabled "roaming" from one country to another. The single product market brought Nokia and Ericsson into international prominence, and the European standard became the world's. The first problem with the single standard adopted for 3G (W-CDMA) is that it does not yet work properly and will not until 2004 at the earliest. It is also too heavy, too slow, and requires too many battery changes. Another problem is that a second system – developed by Qualcomm, an American company – actually does work and is compatible with different vendors' equipment. The Qualcomm system can, moreover, operate on 2G as well as 3G bandwidth and does not necessarily require expensive new infrastructure. Although experts disagree on whether the U.S. system (CDMA2000-1X) can properly be labeled as 3G, the question is moot from the consumer standpoint: it operates equally well on either. In the tech-crazy pioneering Japanese market, the operator using the European system has – even with the encouragement of the pro-European U.S. State Department – signed up only about 135,000 subscribers; its competitor, using the American system, has 2.3 million. The Japanese (and Koreans) thus ironically demonstrated the superiority of the U.S. standard.[33]

The European adoption of the W-CDMA standard has had still another dire consequence: it created an artificial shortage of broadband and set off a bidding war. Broadband is the radio spectrum needed to handle the huge flow of digital information that mobile 3G would have to generate in order to become profitable using W-CDMA. To make matters still worse, increases in speed and operational efficiency reduce broadband requirements, depleting the value of the asset. This fact, together with the ability of the U.S. system to operate at either 2G or 3G, opens up for the latter the possibility of shifting to flat-rate pricing – the critical step toward the mass adoption of wireless internet access – and a move that would also favor content providers like Microsoft over equipment manufacturers like Nokia and Ericsson.[34]

The most pressing problem facing the European industry is financial. Under the terms of their licenses, operators must provide services by particular deadlines. However, owing to the excessive prices (over $100 billion) paid for licenses at government-held auctions, the big network companies are either strapped for cash or on the verge of bankruptcy. Most of the survivors will have to be subsidized or require debt forgiveness and in either case will lack the capital strength to build the necessary infrastructure – even in the (unlikely) event that 3G becomes commercially feasible on a large scale.

Broadband, moreover, lacks any other comparable large-scale application that cannot be replicated by wireline. The industrialized world now suffers from immense overcapacities in fiber-optic cable, the main data carrier. Absent a craze for the 3G W-CDMA handset like earlier ones for the hula-hoop or pet rock, the big telecommunications companies will have purchased a will-o'-the-wisp of no economic value. The size of the numbers is daunting – at latest reckoning, $115 billion purchased at government auction and payable by the network companies in cash (rather than inflated stock capitalization) over a period of twenty years. If acquisitions and infrastructures are added, total cost comes to $500 billion.[35] To recoup this staggering investment, the operators will need to reap the equivalent of thousands of dollars from every man jack in Europe.

The enormity of the situation is only now becoming evident to the public. Early manifestations of the cascading problem include the sacking of the celebrity chiefs of Deutsche Telecom (DT) and Vivendi (the former Lyonnaise des Eaux) – with many other shaky thrones now ready to topple – as well as the decision by Sonera (the Finnish telecom and 3G pioneer) to postpone entry into the first big market, Germany. Other operators have "mothballed" their networks and one, Norway's Mobile, has simply handed its license back to the government. The Commission has authorized providers to share networks, a clearly anticompetitive practice, in order to stave off disaster.[36] 3G will not be launched in Europe until 2005 and perhaps never. Network equipment providers like Ericsson face catastrophe, and the makers of handsets may also be looking at lean times.[37]

The humbling of these giants involves far more than purely monetary losses. Telecom stocks were purveyed to the masses. In Germany, for instance, the Deutsche Telecom privatization increased size of the stockholding public by 50 percent. Now trading at a mere tenth of its issue price, it has discredited shareholder and, more broadly, equity culture: where innovation is needed, risk aversion has been strengthened. Hence, the telecom collapse has discredited pension reform also. Similar stories could be told elsewhere. A once brilliantly orchestrated EU policy has become FUBAR.

The Union played a leading role in telecommunications policy during the 1990s. According to Russell Carlsberg, "Europe's 3G policy is part of a larger focus on the technological sector as a solution to Europe's economic problems … as the [EU] believes that there will be a convergence of various strands of electronic commerce and [intends] to move itself into a more competitive position with the United States."[38] Initially, the Commission had little luck. Government postal services (PTTs) virtually monopolized European telecommunications until the 1980s, when the big users of long distance – the international banks and multinational corporations who generated about half the transmissions – began to recognize the huge savings that could be made through digitalization. For the big banks, savings could amount to 5–10 percent of turnover. Impressed by the breakup of Ma Bell, the financials lobbied hard both nationally and in Brussels to separate telephones from the PTTs.[39] The campaign came as a godsend to a Commission unable to make any headway in the communications field, because overcharging by the bloated PTTs enabled them to provide kickbacks to governments.

A 1979 report drafted at the behest of the commissioner for industrial policy, Viscount Étienne ("Steve") Davignon – who was aided and abetted by the European Roundtable – first pointed to the competitive disadvantages caused by the telephone monopolies and described "telematics" as "strategically important."[40] A second report made the case for building a harmonized, Europe-wide network. A Commission directive of 1983 provided the breakthrough. The directive set up a committee of representatives from member-state ministries of economics and finance to establish a program to develop the new technologies. This group supplied the material for the 1984 Bangemann Report, "Europe and the Global Information Society," which emphasized the need for deregulation in order to draw private investment into the construction of integrated broadband information highways. The following year witnessed the launching of the RACE component of the Framework Program for the research and development of broadband.

The EU policy was carefully crafted. It created a powerful new competence for the Commission, required no public funding, and opened a huge new field of responsibility for competition policy, which now extended beyond the enforcement of rules to include the building of new institutions.[41] Telecommunications became a model "European" policy, one designed and guided from Brussels with a view to building up an economic growth sector – an industrial policy on a grander scale than anything previously conceived.[42] Two key measures, one for telecom services and the other called the Open Network Provision, date from 1990. As implemented along the way by successive papers, directives, and regulations, they set a timetable calling for fully competitive telephone markets (both fixed and mobile), as well as for network supply, by 1 January 1998. This "phase-in" approach allowed incumbent monopolies time to adjust their market positions. While the European Commission laid down overall policy guidelines, national governments would determine the conditions of competition in each country and either set the actual prices or establish a process for setting them.[43] In practice, liberalization involved a constant tug-of-war, with a groaning Commission – at the head of its team – pulling hard on one end of the rope and the sweating French (and national monopolists) yanking just as vigorously on the other.[44]

The move toward privatization and liberalization triggered a boom in both telecommunications services, which grew at the rate of 6 percent annually to

$169 billion and were expected to reach $223 billion by 2000, and infrastructure equipment, which was expected to grow to $28 billion by 2000. A wave of
mergers and corporate alliances swept through Europe, the pace forced by the
entrance of American giants like WorldCom, which was "frantically constructing fiber-optic rings ... in Europe's cities." Indeed, "every market segment of
the [PTTs] ... [found itself] savagely under attack."[45]

From an early date the Commission vigorously promoted wireless telephony,
a technologically promising field that provided the tonic of competition for the
telephone monopolies and opened an opportunity to promote transnational networks. A 1997 Green Paper enthused that "mobility is at the very heart of ...
the Union for the free movement of goods, people, services, and capital .... The
prospect of Europe-wide advanced mobile communications services will support ... success ... in the mass market."[46] The Commission lobbied hard for the
adoption of the digital GSM standard in 1992, which simplified and reduced the
cost of international phone calls.

GSM gave the Europeans – and especially the Nordics, who were admitted in
1995 – a commanding lead in the field. The Swedes had set up the first contemporary cellular system in the early 1980s. By the late 1990s, digital was taking
over from the earlier analog system at a rapid rate, and GSM penetration was
increasing worldwide and in eastern Europe. With about 40 percent of global
market share, it was well on the way to becoming the global standard by 2000.
By 2002, that share figure would reach 65 percent.[47]

The boom in mobile phones produced the greatest business success story of
the 1990s, Nokia, which controlled nearly a third of the cellular market worldwide. Nokia's product was neither markedly better nor cheaper than that of
the competition, but the firm "outperformed rivals in getting product to market
quickly and efficiently [because] ... it has understood customers better, designing fashionable phones that people want to use, and creating different phones
for different customer groups."[48] Taking advantage of scale economies, the sophisticated product was highly profitable. Even after the downturn of mid-2000
Nokia continued to generate earnings, though not often hitting targets. Worth
about $500 million in 1991, the company had a capitalization of about $200 billion by 2000.

But as European markets approached saturation, it became increasingly difficult to sell additional cell phones. Needing a new product, Nokia thus invested
heavily in the new UMTS system designed for 3G and created its own operating
system for it.[49] The technology would have many bugs. Although the success of
Nokia inspired and enriched Finland – and built European self-confidence – the
Finnish giant was, at the end of the day, still only a highly successful manufacturing company with a single world-class product. It was not a process innovator
whose spillovers could stimulate the rise of a new sector of industry, and it would
never become an engine of growth like Intel or a service spawner like Microsoft.
The welfare of the company is bound part and parcel to the development of the
3G network, whose failure may leave it dead in the water.

In pursuit of the Lisbon-set goal of "becoming the most competitive and dynamic knowledge-based economy in the world," the EU adopted "eEurope action plan 2002."[50] It was something more than a cutesy-pie face-lift on the hagridden visage of R&D Framework Policy. A new package for telecoms, then growing at a rate of 12 percent, was at the heart of the Lisbon agenda.[51] The plan called for the industry to enter the second phase of the wireless revolution by 2002, thereby providing "a plethora of new data-centric services that would have us permanently connected to just about anything imaginable."[52] In spite of the best efforts of the innovation commissioner, Erkki Liikanen, the EU vision of cyber-Europe would not materialize.

Yet by early 2000, nearly everyone had caught the e-bug.[53] The rapid spread of the disease had something to do with the economics of the industry: huge sunk capital costs, low operating expenses – and from there, endless streams of gravy on the upside. Scale of operations is what really counted in both wireless and wireline networks. Huge overcapacities were created as a result. Europe's backbone upstarts "collectively built 100 times more capacity than the market could absorb."[54] Only 10 percent of the fiber-optic cable laid in Europe has ever been activated.

The new version of the flu that the telecoms caught actually originated, like an earlier epidemic, in Hong Kong. After a whirlwind of deal making, the old Chinese trading house of Hutchison, Whampoa sold its European wireless phone business, Orange, to Mannesmann (a veteran German steel-pipe producer) for the seemingly outrageous price of $30 billion. Swallowing a $30 billion poison pill, Vodaphone, the mighty young British upstart, then bought Orange from Mannesmann and – together with the French Vivendi – formed a company to create a single portal to serve the entire digital world – television, music, e-commerce, and cell phones. Zippo-flasho: the wireless phone big boys were prepared to face off with the e-giant Microsoft in his own lair.[55]

Even as the dot-com bubble popped and the tech market caved in, the broadband auction process turned into a juggernaut. Advised by an economist from the London School of Economics about how best to sell radio spectrum, the British government raised $33 billion in April before the last hammer drop.[56] In August, Germany raised another $45 billion, and by the end of the year the telecom industry would throw over $100 billion into 3G licenses. "It was," thought the chief of the communications giant KPN, formerly part of the Dutch post office, "the last chance to step into a new world .... We had to be a global player."[57] "If we had dropped out," explained an executive from Spain's Telefonica, "our market cap would have fallen by more than the price of the license."[58]

Alarmed at the vast sums being spent, a Nokia executive "went to Chris Gent [CEO of Vodaphone and the heaviest plunger of the lot] and told him it was madness .... [Gent] shrugged his shoulders and said 'What can you do?'"[59] When Mr. Fok (managing director of Hutchison, Whampoa) unexpectedly broke with his partners and conspicuously exited amidst a late round of the German auction, just after the $45-billion figure had been reached, the bottom dropped out of the market. Telecom stocks plunged throughout Europe; the rating agencies quickly downgraded the ballooning debt of Deutsche Telekom, France Télécom, and KPN; and the entire industry slammed the brakes on spending.[60]

An article in the Winter 2002 issue of the *McKinsey Quarterly* predicted that, over the next five years, a huge consolidation will have to take place.[61] Because the UMTS system failed to take off, the authors argued, there was no chance that a sharp revenue increase could offset the high interest charges. The five large integrated incumbents (built on old PTT platforms) and ten smaller integrated companies would soon be reduced to "two or three large integrated ... companies holding majority stakes in data, wireless and wireline services." It would be hard to determine which of them would survive, because it would cost tens of billions of dollars to purchase even a 5-percent share of the mobile telephone market. Scale economies dictated that two or three large integrated operators would eventually dominate the wireless field. The integrated producers best able to generate revenues were the former PTT incumbents who, in spite of privatization, still controlled the profitable link to the individual consumer. Since all of the ex-PTTs remained at least partly owned by the governments, they were also well-positioned to solicit bailouts.

If the incumbents put the challengers to rout, then integrated telephone networks will remain only partially competitive and rates will stay high. The outcome will not resemble anything in Silicon Valley. Unhappy about the situation, the Commission continues to campaign vigorously, but to little effect, in an effort to "unbundle the loop" – open existing phone lines to competing service providers. In another blow to eEurope, DSL service capable of providing high-speed access to the internet is expected to remain unnecessarily expensive for the next several years.

By mid-1992, the grim McKinsey scenario was playing itself out. As *Business Week* reported:

> The bulk of telecom service is back in the hands of the former state monopolies, which are staggering under their own debt loads. Worst of all, the rush to build long-haul highways was not matched with equal investment in local and regional infrastructure, leaving Europe's network rife with bottlenecks. It's as if the Continent were crisscrossed with vast autobahns, but the on- and off-ramps remained rutted dirt paths. Prices for local connections remain high, while only 7 percent of homes across Europe have zippy broadband connections – half the rate in the U.S.[62]

Things were hardly better for the equipment producers: by July 2002, the market capitalization of Ericsson had dropped 95 percent in little over two years. Surveys indicated that fewer than half of the cell-phone owners surveyed in late spring expressed any interest in upgrading to 3G, which (even without the financial problems facing the industry) would have delayed large-scale product rollout until 2005. The supreme irony is that the eventual success of broadband may depend upon Microsoft, which has developed its own operating system and is having it built into low-priced 3G sets manufactured in Asia. The history of the

PC may then repeat itself: standardization will knock down profit margins, software leadership replace that of hardware, and eEurope rest on American product innovation.[63]

Could anything be done to save the situation? The *Financial Times*'s expert, Peter Martin, thought not. "It is time," he wrote in a 30 July 2002 editorial, "for the European telecommunications industry to think the unthinkable and abandon 3G .... But pulling back from a clearly hopeless investment ... is not enough for the industry."[64] Most wireless operators are still pressing ahead with 3G plans, he proceeded, hoping that a burst of handset sales and service revenues will reverse the industry's fortunes. The decision represents "a complete misreading of the future .... Networks should abandon the dream that handsets will become mobile media terminals with lucrative content and e-commerce revenues .... The wireless business will be what it has always been: communication between individual customers."[65] European bureaucrats, Martin concluded, would have to give up hopes of a one-shot leap into technological leadership, companies like Ericsson and Nokia must recognize that revenue streams will not be forthcoming from base station and product rollouts, and content providers can forget about future windfalls. "Think the unthinkable," Martin concludes, "Turn off 3G!"[66]

The 3G story resembles a rerun of HDTV in important respects. Once again the Commission sought to pick a winner in order to displace the United States from high-tech leadership. In play again was not only a product but a network meant to set the standard for Europe and the world. As previously, failure required immense write-offs. Success once again will reward risk taking, flexibility, and backup strength rather than forceful executive leadership and "vision." The two cases were not, however, identical. The stakes in 3G were larger, the relationships with and among producers less cozy, and concern with social welfare much more substantial. Indeed, the thorough rewiring of society proposed in the Lisbon agenda was part of a larger concern with improving educational standards and equipping the public with the skills needed for the future. The 3G debacle also had a different cause. If technical obsolescence doomed HDTV, irrational exuberance will prove fatal to the mobile handset. The EU-led campaign to adopt a single operating system limited to 3G broadband may have created a situation of artificial scarcity, but without a pell-mell rush into the market the intangible product could never have been sold. Excessive demand as well as artificially constrained supply sealed the fate of 3G. The precise reasons for the market failure are still obscure, but the disaster can serve as a jarring reminder of the pressing need for better institutional design.

NOT YET A SINGLE FINANCIAL MARKET

The same thing is true in the field of finance. The creation of the European Monetary Union did not, and for many years may not, have as a sequel a single financial market (SFM) for Europe. So far one exists only for bonds. The matter is important chiefly because the lack of a single market for equities costs Europe an estimated 1-percent growth annually.[67] It is thus an essential prerequisite of a strong, competitive European economy. The incompleteness of the Euro-financial market has little strategic significance, however. Contrary to French misconceptions, a *Finanzmacht Europa* actually complements rather than threatens the dollar. Competition between greenback and euro would promote stability, reduce borrowing costs, and expand liquidity. The nationality of money furthermore has little to do with financial power in an open economy. Patriotic loyalty to a particular currency is a matter of sovereign indifference to borrowers and lenders; their only concern is cost or benefit on the one hand and risk on the other. The determinants of these on the supply side are capital and credit availability as well as banking expertise. Although the truism applies at every level of finance, it is now of particular importance at the top.

A single financial market should reduce borrowing costs by stimulating competition, promoting convergence, and encouraging transparent, Europe-wide pricing. The creation of a SFM requires eliminating sheltered markets, driving inefficient lenders out of business, and expanding the operational scope of those left standing. What happens at the top guides the process. Here the big money is made.[68] At such stratospheres, use of the word "bank" can lead to confusion. The ownership share of U.S. banks in capital assets is much smaller than in Europe, and a larger portion is controlled by nonbanks and thence "disintermediated" or provided across markets. Companies holding the high ground of finance control this wealth by means of market wizardry and the ability to leverage their vast assets into structured "deals" (mergers and acquisitions, underwriting, initial public offerings, etc.) that are profitable both to others (because well priced) and to themselves. The handful of big financials that dominates the field normally distributes two thirds of annual gross profit in this highly lucrative business to senior and middle management in the form of year-end bonuses.

The firms in question are what used to be called the "bulge bracket banks": Goldman Sachs; Merrill Lynch; Morgan, Stanley; Citicorp; Morgan Chase; Lehman Brothers; Deutsche Bank; and Credit Suisse–First Boston. Six of them are American; the other two became players by acquiring American investment banks through mergers. Staffed multinationally, each operates in essentially similar fashion.[69] Since contemporary investment banking is utterly dominated by Wall Street and The City, the creation of a SFM can only increase the power of the mega-firms. For the "Anglo-Saxons," a single financial market presents a win–win situation. It will increase liquidity and European self-esteem on the one hand and, barring some catastrophic event, line their already deep pockets on the other. The SFM would be Wall Street's sandbox. That is why the big U.S. banks are its greatest enthusiasts.

Only the market-based reform of European society challenges the dominance of the giant New York–London financials. Access to the vast pension and mutual fund assets tapped by Wall Street and The City is, in theory, unrestricted.[70] The advantage of U.S. (vs. non-U.S.) money-center borrowers derives from proximity, knowledge, "track record," and capital strength. European-based borrowers would enjoy like advantages over time if such vast amounts of liquidity could be mobilized locally. The development of a shareholder culture would bring them closer to the goal. Movement in the right direction was under way when the stock market collapse began in mid-2000. Many years will have to pass until the burnt fingers of small investors heal, memory of pain fades, and the damage can be undone.

Long-run European financial competitiveness will require the privatization of pensions – a regulatory task of immense difficulty even in a single nation, *a fortiori* in a union of fifteen or twenty-seven. And this task pales by comparison to the painful political decision that must be made prior to it: to break with the welfare state. The single financial market confronts the peoples of Europe with a choice between three alternatives, ranked from most to least desirable:

1. accept an American-dominated SFM market in order to generate the growth needed to support the welfare state; or
2. part with the welfare state in a bid to regain financial sovereignty; or
3. pitch the SFM altogether and accept a status quo in which mergers have reduced the number of potential banks to two or three per country, an outcome that would resemble the telecom scenario.

Financial reform began in the 1980s with the restoration of capital mobility, the various "big and little" bangs on equity markets, and the first wave of (often government-sponsored or -encouraged) bank mergers.[71] The single market for banking began to develop in early 1993 as a consequence of the "1992" SEA program, when the Second Banking Coordination Directive took effect. It enabled any Community bank to set up operations in another member-nation if able to meet the standards prevailing in its own national market. This "single passport" opened the portal to cross-border mergers and the establishment of foreign operations, thus setting in motion a second great wave of consolidation and reorganization. At the same time, a "home country" loophole in the directive enabled the host nation to impose higher prevailing standards under certain, loosely specified conditions. The decree allowed ample wiggle-room to enable incumbents to settle with insurgents.

Two types of national situations arose, according to the analyst of the *Banker*:

those in which capital is provided in most, if not all, sectors, of the economy by private investors, with the consequence that capital markets are strong and legal and accounting systems have been developed with the requirements for the creation of tradable securities and liquid markets in mind, and those in which the provision has been dominated by state funding.[72]

The former were capitalized by various species of hybrid assets such as subordinated debt and preference shares, which lowered costs, reduced risk, and stabilized returns. Disclosure rules were generally good in such cases, according to the expert. In the latter case – in which banks and industrials have been relieved of any need to entice outside investors – the legal, accounting, and fiscal systems were less suited to liquid capital markets and disclosure rules less stringent. Banks in such places (Italy, Iberia, and France) would require propping up by the government in the near term.

The European banking industry was deeply troubled in the early 1990s.[73] The situation was worst in the Nordic countries, which were struggling with the crises that broke with the bursting of the real-estate bubble. Elsewhere the removal of restraints on markets formerly regulated by cartels, fixed-interest pass-throughs, and other distortions created an epidemic of rate cutting under severe price competition. At the same time, foreign banks made deep inroads into formerly sheltered markets, and the sectoral boundaries between various kinds of banking institutions eroded. In the 1980s European banks had failed, it seemed, to keep up with their increasingly international corporate customers, who turned elsewhere and became less dependent on intermediated bank finance. Disintermediation continued and savers began to discover equity alternatives to traditional bank accounts.[74] Although a couple of big banks (Deutsche Bank and Crédit Lyonnaise) moved quickly into cross-border retailing, for most credit institutions sheer necessity dictated a "much greater number of defensive mergers and acquisitions ... within the same country. At one end of the scale ... are a series of mergers in Italy, Spain, Austria, and among the German *Landesbanken* and savings banks ... [and] at the other end [are] the 'mega-mergers' transforming Europe's smaller markets." They included the formation of ABN-AMRO in the Netherlands, the consolidation of six Danish banks into Den Danske Bank and Unidanmark, and the marriage of Banco Bilbao and Banca Viscaya in Spain.[75]

The news was little better for Europe's investment banks, according to an exhaustive McKinsey report.[76] They specialized in underwriting securities, trading, and advising (especially on mergers and acquisitions) but suffered from undistinguished product, high costs, and lack of adequate distribution resulting from their failure to keep abreast of capital globalization, growing issuer and investor sophistication, and the mounting tide of dollar flows. They had also wrongly tried to remain one-stop lenders while "failing to recognize that the skills involved in ... structuring, pricing, and researching equities have little in common with those needed for success in commercial banking products such as syndicated lending."[77] By comparison, U.S. banks had "unbundled" services and concentrated on developing product expertise. The McKinsey experts concluded that the main beneficiaries have been the "bulge bracket firms," which successfully transferred competencies developed in the tough U.S. market – in advisory services, securities and distribution, and currency and interest-rate management – to Europe. "Together with their worldwide placing capability, their long-standing relationship with investors in the United States, and the breadth of their product range," the report added, "they [can] offer broad-based solutions rather than simple products."[78]

In addition to being spread too thin and suffering from a legacy of national champions and overcapacity, European investment banks faced a problem common to the industry as a whole. As they commanded an increasing share of institutionally managed money (pensions and funds), top-tier investors were demanding "even tighter margins" and in many cases bypassing intermediaries altogether. As spreads continued to shrink, volumes counted for more, because "presence in multiple financial markets entails cost structures – particularly in information technology and operations – that can be prohibitively high." The inescapable McKinsey logic indicated that "there is room for only a few global, broad-based players."[79] Routine-bound European investment banks, incapable of nimble adaptation to the fast-moving situation, would soon have to disappear.

With or without the adoption of a single currency in 1999, "Europe's capital market and big banks," according to the Dresdner's chief economist, Dr. Klaus Friedrich, "are going to experience greater change than at any time in the past 200 years."[80] Friedrich expected a reduction in the number of banks by a quarter, a doubling in the size of the continental stock exchanges, the emergence of an American-style corporate bond market, and a head-on battle between London, Paris, and Frankfurt to become the trading center of the new Europe. Dr. Friedrich overshot the mark, but not badly. Stock exchange volume would grow by about 50 percent but level out in late 2000. The corporate bond market has just begun to take hold. The battle still rages among the exchanges over who should be Number One, but the only successful merger to date – EURONEXT, between the Paris, Brussels, and Amsterdam exchanges – is better thought of as an alliance than a fusion.[81] Even so, 1997 did witness the greatest number of bank mergers ever. Some of them featured combination with insurers, but nearly all of them were (as previously) intranational: in Germany, France, Austria, Belgium, Switzerland, and Italy. The amalgamation of the Finnish Merita Bank and the Swedish Nordbanken was the only important exception.[82]

The prospect of a single currency was a huge threat to the position of European finance. As crudely stated by one American financier, "European monetary union has opened a killing ground for large U.S. banks ... the only institutions that [had] put pan-European banking systems into place over the previous decade."[83] The Europeans faced a bundle of additional problems relating to the EMU. The single currency would wipe out whole chunks of traditional wholesale businesses of foreign exchange, corporate banking, and government bond trading – which had accounted for about 40 percent of bank revenues – and so reduce profits further. In 1997, the volume of such activity totaled $100 billion. As for specific fields, the $800-billion foreign exchange–conversion business normally yielded earnings of from $6 billion to $8 billion annually, the lion's share of it by commercial banks. Foreign exchange *trading,* the source of $3 billion of these earnings, would disappear altogether. Another third in revenue losses will occur because loss of scale advantages adds to transaction cost.

Corporate lending presented a different problem. Increasing borrower resort to the bond market and persistent overcapacity had cut margins to the point at which banks were pulling out and buying back their own shares in order to raise the value of the new "currency," market capitalization. The $21-billion (annually) deposit and money market business – in which banks hold foreign currency deposit accounts for each currency used by corporate customers – would also fall as customers settled in euros. Correspondent banking, worth $14 billion annually, would also shrink when banks need not hold accounts with other banks simply in order to make and receive payment in foreign currencies. Trading in government bonds on behalf of customers, a source of 2–3 billion dollars in annual revenue, would also decline, as would own-account trading. The fall in interest rates, the "convergence play" in the EMU run-up, had made this activity a major profit center – an easy, one-time opportunity to offset losses in other fields. Above all, banks would lose the expertise gained through familiarity with local market conditions.

New market opportunities, according to the McKinsey report, would open only to the "vibrant few,... a handful of banks."[84] Wholesale revenue growth would be concentrated in investment banking: equities, bonds, and mergers and acquisitions, "areas in which most local banks would be hard pressed to match the skills and global reach of U.S. banks already operating in Europe."[85] The prognosis turned out to be sound. Although 1999 brought a record number of mergers in the banking field (440, worth 200 million euros), very few of them were transnational and increasing numbers of them were with non-EU partners. The number and prominence of failed merger attempts mounted. While the integration of wholesale banking and money markets had increased, noted one analyst, "a strong segmentation of national retail banking markets ... [remained because of] linguistic and cultural barriers as well as politically induced market access barriers, such as differences in consumer protection regulations and taxation."[86] The sudden rise in the popularity of credit (as opposed to charge or debit) cards in spring of 2002 was the main integrator of European markets at the retail level.[87]

The recession that had set in by 2001 was a disaster for investment banking, halving earnings from the European merger and acquisition business. The year 2002 was given up as a lost cause by July. Bonuses for the big "rainmakers" were off by 70 percent. The sevenfold increase in deal making since 1993 was now a thing of the past.[88] Europe had become "a growth market in hibernation."[89] Smallish players looking vulnerable are ABN-Amro and Commerzbank;[90] their days are numbered. "Big boys" like Goldman can be expected to shed pricey labor – it nearly doubled staff in The City to 4,500 between November 1999 and November 2000. (Look for a real-estate bust in central London!) The lull does not fundamentally change the European banking picture. Retail remains sick, overpopulated, highly regulated, and partly protected – as well as besieged by new competition from e-banks, equity investment, and credit cards.

According to a recent study by a New York firm of banking consultants, a few behemoths like Citigroup will dominate the field.[91] Some large investment banks can use their balance sheets to sell credit products, like MorganChase and Barclays. Others – like Goldman, Merrill, and Morgan, Stanley – can still thrive as specialists in equity and advisory work. The midsized European challengers can nonetheless be expected to disappear over the next ten years. Given the situation on the demand side, the bounty will continue to flow upward. As put by a senior Goldman partner,

the biggest institutions in fund management ... spend $1 billion every year on Wall Street and in The City. Most of them are consolidating the number of brokerage firms that they do business with. Some are saying "We will pay $1 billion to our suppliers." So the top five get $100 million each, and the others get the rest. We can't afford not to be in the $100 million club.[92]

Rule making for a governance framework in the sprawling, heterogeneous, and diverse financial sector is at the epicenter of the single market project. "The modernization of the European economy must ... begin," according to Christa Randzio-Plath, economist and chair of the European Parliament's finance committee, in the "financial services markets, [by] reducing the cost of capital, [facilitating] cross-border financing ... and offering better return on investment to institutional and private investors."[93] Institutional design, or the setup of regulatory machinery, is an incredibly boring subject if considered in isolation – abstract, legalistic, and at times overly technical. The subject is also often difficult to follow because the universe in which it exists is detached from reality and can, at best, make only an imperfect accommodation to it. Rules do count, however: they are independent variables that, if respected and observed, become ingrained and institutionalized as patterns of behavior and thus part of a self-regulating mechanism. The mechanism itself may work well and advance progress but also can impede it, be neutral, re-direct the path of change, or modify contexts in unexpected ways. The consequences are difficult to anticipate for the very reason that such institutions are built to deal with contingencies that may or may not arise. How could the "irrational exuberance" be predicted that led to the financial ruination of the 3G project? Which policy consultants argued during the negotiating process that a future monetary union – far from freeing Europe from "dollar tyranny" – would actually increase the power of the American financial community within it?

Such surprising outcomes suggest a need to examine the workings of the single market project in detail. The U.K. Economic and Social Research Council undertook one such effort in the 1990s. Ambitious though far from comprehensive, the survey underscored the point that the single market has by no means always developed as intended. Apart from the fact that the gradual shift to qualified majority voting has changed the rules in effect at the program's inception, the regulatory measures adopted have often taken on a life of their own. The European playing field, though "more level" than previously, is consequently neither quite flat nor entirely smooth across the surface. The only kind of rules that work, the Council concluded, are the "shalt-nots" of "negative integration"; prescriptive measures are essentially unenforceable.

The regulatory system of the EU is distinctive. The compromises needed in order to make enactments binding often do not result in rules that reflect the wishes of the sponsoring member-states. Mutual recognition of standards, the operational method preferred in Community rule making, can be achieved from a variety of distinct approaches – through effective bargaining outcomes between different parties, from within a consensus-anchored epistemic or interest-based community, or by means of an imposed standard – as well as at any of the three tiers in play: national, Euro-regional, and international. Indirect rule is another important characteristic of EU governance. The EU makes a regulation and then requires each member-state to transpose it into national law and enforce compliance. If this avoids the problem of "one size fits all," it also risks producing quite different outcomes because enforcement is one step removed and thus involves agency problems. The U.K. survey further emphasized that – because the reporting requirement of directives shifted power from the local to the national level – enforceability varies substantially from country to country.[94] The survey nonetheless found that, "where the community measures are concerned with trade liberalization and emphasize decentralization and self-regulation," implementation presented few difficulties.[95]

Outside the area of trade liberalization, according to the survey, the EU occupies "contested space" and has little real authority over such diverse matters as population movement, television without frontiers, or the setting of common standards for pornography or privacy. This non–trade liberalization universe features "considerable institutional resistance to implementation, even though formally the Community does have the power to regulate."[96] The resistance remains largely unacknowledged because high legal costs, the risk of losing, and the time needed to secure relief limit cases "to questions of importance to an enforcement agency, a wealthy pressure group, or business."[97] Litigation gives rise to the enunciation of principles but operates only at the margin of Community regulation. The EU is thus really consequential in only one main respect: imposing a trade regime on a "negative" basis.

Along with many other important responsibilities, the Single Financial Market belongs to the portfolio of Frits Bolkestein, commissioner for the internal market and taxation since September 1999. Bolkestein is an unusual figure. The oldest commissioner presently serving, he has two careers behind him: as managing director at Shell; and, after retirement, in the hurly-burly of Dutch politics, an arena he entered because he was fed up with civic disorder and collectivism. The closest thing in official Brussels to a classical liberal, Bolkestein is famous for being outspoken, especially as regards the "federalist vision." He warned that German plans involve "a good chance of failure, and Europe might then end up on the road to disintegration as a kind of reaction."[98] To him, Enlargement amounts to "the greatest supply-side exercise ever in world economics, [one] that will stimulate production, increase competition, reduce prices, and increase demand within the European Union" if common rules, including with regard to labor, are adopted Community-wide. Bolkestein has pressed hard for a common corporation tax in order to improve "transparency," thereby demonstrating a need for tax reduction, and he has taken a particular interest in designing a European pension plan both to relieve the fiscal burden on member-states and to provide necessary liquidity for the single financial market.[99] A forceful liberalizer and "widener," Bolkestein is also deregulator- and re-regulator-in-chief for the network industries of gas, electricity, and postal services (whose lack of recent progress has been disheartening) as well as communications and finance.[100]

The influence of the dogged Dutchman may have peaked at the Lisbon summit of April 2000, at which the member-states adopted the Financial Services Action Plan (FSAP) as a central "pillar" of the economic modernization agenda, chose 2003 as the completion date for an overall reform program, and targeted 2005 as the date for full implementation of the reform. The same month, the market collapse inexorably started tearing down the budding confidence of the new European investor. If anything can be salvaged from the debris, it is Bolkestein's proposal for an institutional European pension fund, which could improve though not fundamentally change the structure of financial markets. In such a case, demographic reality would have to drive institutional reform.[101]

The Lisbon targets for financial reform will not be met. Progress in the field, slow though not altogether discouraging, owes something to the distinctive arm's-length approach that the Commission has generally followed in dealing with the banking sector: "Rather than establishing uniform regulation and supervision for a single financial market, the principles of home country control, harmonization of essential principles, and mutual recognition were applied, assuming that mutual recognition and market forces would interact to yield convergence in the regulatory environment."[102] Such an approach has also implied incremental change resulting from compromises between aggressive insurgents and protected incumbents and slow progress toward the SFM.

A euro market in government bonds developed with the simple reissuance in 1999 of outstanding notes in the new currency. The new market for corporates had emerged by the beginning of 2002, a distinctly promising trend, though their value had risen only to 11 percent of GDP (as opposed to 27 percent in the United States). Stock market capitalization had also increased to about 80 percent of GDP in the Euro-zone, compared to 135 percent in the United States. Most corporate borrowers still continued to rely on domestic capital markets because of company law considerations and the lack of common disclosure standards. The infrastructure for settling payments for securities transfer remained fragmented and inefficient. Their costs were eight times as high as in the United States, and domestic settlements were four times as expensive. The lack of a multilateral payments system and the heavy expenses of existing manual operations constricted market development and caused delays in the introduction of processing machinery.[103]

Trends at the retail level leave an impression of lethargy, impaction, and gradual slippage for banks operating in domestic markets. The merger pattern remained national – banking–banking followed by banking–financial services – rather than cross-border, because the risk-adjusted returns on in-country mergers continued to exceed those from cross-border fusions. Although disintermediation continued to erode the traditional banking business, neither its number of branches nor overall employment declined. European banks continued to hold a far higher share of total financial assets (49 percent vs. only 18 percent) than their U.S. counterparts, a good index of the "competitiveness gap."

According to a recent OECD study, lack of harmonized consumer protection rules and "the related issue of [poor] transparency of retail banking" are the main hurdles for cross-border activities of retail banks, which "do not reach out for cross-border prospective customers, nor do customers shop around for credit."[104] The same held for the corporate sector. In 2001, the Commission initiated anti-cartel proceedings against 120 banks in each of the member-states for conspiring to maintain high cross-border transfer and conversion fees, but the matter remains under discussion. At the same time, the wider use of benchmark, euro-denominated products at the wholesale level strengthened both "commodification" and the handful of big money-center banks while weakening former lenders of national currencies.[105]

Protecting the non–money-center banks was a

mosaic of European regulatory structures, over forty of them, with different powers and competencies. The ... system is ... too slow, too rigid, and ill-adapted to the needs of modern financial markets. Even when it does work, which is rare, it often produces texts of legendary ambiguity – along with little or no effort to transpose the agreed texts consistently – nor enforce their proper application.

This harsh verdict stems from the committee of "Wise Men" headed by the distinguished Belgian economist and central banker, Baron Alexandre Lamfalussy. The board was set up in June 2000 to launch a sweeping review of the effort to create a single market in financial services and, more specifically, to implement the Financial Services Action Plan after many fruitless months of committee work – directed by the Commission and with the extensive participation of the financial community.[106] Responsible for the impasse were "protectionism, a fear that once the floodgates are opened the Anglo-Saxons will dominate financial services, turf wars within the ... Commission, and turf wars between the fifteen member-states."[107]

The FSAP identified forty problem areas, the most important of which were different governance structures, the lack of a single prospectus (presenting basic financial information) for securities issuance, the absence of standards for defining abuses like insider trading, and high costs of cross-border payments.[108] Submitting its report in February 2001, the Lamfalussy committee proposed setting up a two-tiered committee structure outside the Commission: one dealing with principles and responsible for supervision, the other with the details of implementing regulations and legislation.[109] The recent collapse (due to German opposition) of a thirteen-year effort to pass a takeover directive through the Parliament provided a timely reminder of the need to distinguish matters of principle from administrative detail. The huge setback stemmed from a refusal to countenance the idea that shareholders should have the final word on takeovers – an issue that should have been tackled up front instead of being left dangling until the end.

The prospectus directive was another fiasco.[110] It had the simple and unchallengeable purpose of providing a standard format ("a single passport") to facilitate raising capital Europe-wide. The detailed provisions of the bill, which was compiled without adequate consultation, aroused the ire of much of the financial industry. The European Shadow Financial Committee, which represented the money-center banks, rejected the draft as burdensome and for increasing the costs of raising capital. The committee had other complaints as well. It preferred a one-tier structure, sought a greater role for the Commission and the European Parliament, and advocated moving to the next stage of planning – beyond the question of "how" to speed up legal reform to "what" needs to be reformed.[111] The big bankers concluded that the Lamfalussy report would delay the single financial market until past 2004 and called upon the European Parliament to block it.[112] The Parliament did so. The Commission still has plenty of draft proposals in the pipeline, each of them with a distant due date.[113] Pension reform was the most important among them.

Pension reform was, of course, primarily a member-state matter.[114] Although national systems varied enormously, one in four employees in EU nations benefited in part from a private plan. There was a compelling reason for raising discussion of the demographic time bomb to the EU level: no member-state could defuse it. By 2040, the ratio of workers to pensioners would decline to one in two from one in four. Unfunded pension liabilities, if budgeted, totaled twice the sum of Community GDP. Even with recent reforms, spending for public pensions will increase between 3 and 5 percent annually. Raising eligibility thresholds in order to increase the available supply of labor will ameliorate the situation, but privatization will be required over the long run – optimally at the European level – in order to spread risk and reduce administrative expenses. Bolkestein strongly advocated pooling contributions into a prudential fund framework to promote affordability. Long-term stock investment in such a fund, with actuarially ascertainable withdrawals, would support an adequate schedule of pension payout at the rate of 3 percent of salary. To produce the same yield from government bonds, the cost would rise to 15 percent.[115] The harsh demographic realities presented at least some grounds to hope, even against the discouraging backdrop of plunging markets, for the injection of new capital into European financial markets.

"If God," screeched an angry *Euromoney* journalist,

Niccolo Machiavelli, or Isambard Kingdom Brunel had designed the single European market, they would now be standing in the corner with a dunce's cap on. It is as if the launch of the single market in 1992 and the introduction of a pan-European currency have added nothing to the quality of services that retail [banking] consumers or even the average company can enjoy.[116]

The lack of forward momentum in financial reform is striking when compared to the 1980s. Progress then occurred at more than one level. The threatened Mexican default of 1982 precipitated the organization of the Basle Committee of the Group of Ten, which worked out an improved standard for capital reserve requirements. The European Community incorporated it into the Second Banking Directive, an example of the process that economist George Pagoulatos called "leapfrogging," whereby a crisis generates an organized effort to anticipate future problems.[117] The big national reforms of the 1980s – the restoration of capital mobility and the opening of stock markets – were organized quickly and brought about results in short order.

The regulatory reforms needed to create the SFM should not be any more difficult to introduce. They are legal in character, do not involve the immediate creation of new institutions, and neither incur great political risk (by requiring large-scale layoffs) nor cause other immediate dislocations. Every word in the text of every draft regulation can, however, impinge on particular interests and redistribute earning power. Unless present trends are reversed, losers will continue to outnumber winners. Someone's ox must be gored. Yet the regulatory challenge facing this sector is somewhat less daunting than that facing many others if only because – unlike, for instance, the network industries – only a single economic community is involved. Agreement does not have to be negotiated between providers and consumers or with competing outside interests.[118]

However, policy-making machinery has broken down at several levels: within the financial community itself, within the Commission, between it and the member-states, and between the member-states themselves.[119] Although the conflicts have become almost impossible to unravel, a few basic cleavages are present. The big money-center banks envisage a European Securities and Exchange Commission operating "transparently" with a single set of rules. Smaller national banking corporations – savings and loans as well as state, regional, communal, and "nonprofit" banks – seek protection through national regulation.[120] Having created a new Financial Services Authority and loath to relinquish City power, the British oppose centralization in the name of federation and mutual recognition of standards. Behind this move, according to the *Economist,* "is a bargaining game between the European financial centers – London, Frankfurt, and Paris. Champions of a pan-European capital market, especially the big banks based in London are afraid ... that the French [may] steal the prize."[121] France's "hidden agenda?" queries the commentator: "a pan-European regulator based in Paris."[122]

The interests of Commission and Parliament align, ironically, with those of the money-center banks; the states, predictably, align with the Council. The European Parliament disowned the Commission's creation, the Lamfalussy committee; the British still struggle to reach some sort of agreement with the "losers" opposed to the rise of The City in their campaign to resist centralization; and, in the absence of action, the "losers" continue to lose. It all makes very little sense. Europe's banks continue to operate on their home ground and at a competitive disadvantage to powerful American interests. They will continue to do so until EU capital markets of equivalent strength to those in the United States develop through the spread of shareholder culture and the privatization and "Europeanization" of pensions. This will not happen until the "wideners" and liberalizers displace the "deepeners" and institution builders – who, however, remain outspoken advocates of the Single Financial Market as a European necessity, a way to face up to American power, and a step toward political federation.

THE EUROPEAN UNION: AN INTERNATIONAL MARKET-CONFORMING REGULATORY AGENCY?

Go figure. In a 1999 paper written for the NBER, Alberto Alesina and Romain Wacziarg ask: "Is Europe Going Too Far?" Recognizing that the Community has claimed "attributions which, in the rest of the world, are in the domain of national governments," they argue, as does this book, that EU-specific institutions are complex, clumsy, and need reform.[123] The authors add that such institutions have developed suboptimally – lacking a coherent blueprint and adequate policy coordination – as a result of power grabbing by the Commission and the often unstable compromises of European Councils. Alesina and Wacziarg conclude that today such institution building is producing unintended and nonbenign consequences. They also underscore the point made by Martin Feldstein and others that conflict avoidance within the monetary union requires political resolution by means of a European-level bargaining process because of inadequate compensatory interregional transfers.[124]

The two economists attribute the shortcomings of the EMU, which are characteristic of EU-specific institutions, to the intellectual fallacy that the Community must deepen in order to widen. Under conditions of free trade, the contrary is the case. Even a small nation can have a large market: the world. The connection between market dimensions and political borders disappears, as Hayek argued on the eve of the Second World War, under the economic conditions of interstate federalism. The optimal size of a country declines as economic integration advances. Political agglomeration is not required to create large markets. Countries and political unions can be small and still prosper.[125]

Over the past fifty years, according to the co-authors, economic integration and political separation have developed hand in hand. The relative importance of the international market has, as Gottfried Haberler first predicted, continued to rise. As put by Alesina and Wacziarg, "the volume of trade, as measured by the ratio of imports plus exports to GDP averaged over a sample of sixty-one countries, has increased from 43.2 percent in 1950 to 60.6 percent in 1992."[126] Financial markets have also expanded rapidly, and the mobility of capital has accelerated even faster. At the same time, the authors add, the number of countries has risen from 74 in 1946 to 192 in 1995, more than half of which are smaller than Massachusetts.

The central problem of the EU, according to Alesina and Wacziarg, is twofold: "Europe is going too far on many issues that would be better dealt with in a decentralized fashion, while it is not going far enough on policies that guarantee the free operation of markets both across and within the countries of the Union."[127]

If, on the one hand, the result is due to the misapplication of the subsidiarity principle, on the other it can also be attributed to a failure to provide "international public goods." Such goods can be infrastructural (physical in character) but also intellectual – the laws, rules, standards, regulations, and conventions without which transactions in international markets cannot be conducted properly.[128] Appropriate institutional design is needed. Can the EU develop into a market-conforming regulatory agency for both Europe and the world?

Not everything in the 1990s was all that bad at the EU. The competition directorate was a bright spot. Competition Commissioner Mario Monti can be criticized for not cracking down hard enough on state aid – only 10 percent of public contracting within the EU is open to competitive bidding – but he has, in fact, been the most active "cartel cop" yet to walk the beat. In 1999 he took action against restrictive agreements in the industries of shipping, steel pipe, cement, and beer. He also broke up the WorldCom–Sprint merger, scotched another one between the Swedish truck builders Volvo and Scania, and caused a deal to collapse between two aluminum companies, Alcan and Pechiney. Monti has attacked the wireless operators for excessive roaming fees, broken up a completed merger between two French electrical companies, and gone vigorously after the big telecoms for refusing to "unbundle the loop." His tireless campaign to end the practice of dealership tie-ins within the automobile industry was finally crowned with success in August 2002.[129]

The active Italian's most spectacular, highly criticized, and courageous initiative has been, according to the *Spectator,* to "break up the corporate copulation of the two U.S. giants," General Electric and Honeywell. By blocking the deal, " 'Super Mario' twisted the tail of the legendary tycoon Jack Welch [CEO of GE],... alpha male of the macho school of American management and living god."[130] Fair enough: Welch's deal would have joined Honeywell's avionics to GE's aero-engine business, enabling him to put together a package that could drive the conglomerate's only other two serious international competitors – Pratt Whitney and Rolls Royce – out of business. That, indeed, was the purpose of the deal! Monti has also kept a constant low-flame fire burning under the feet of Bill Gates – uncomfortable for Bill but healthy for the market and, given the current American administration's decision to downgrade antitrust enforcement, good for the United States as well. Monti has recently faced some tough sledding. In June 2002 the ECJ reversed breakup orders in the cases of Air Taurus–First Choice, Schneider–Legrand, and Laval–Sidel. To rise to the high standards of the court, the competition commission proposed introducing a new internal procedure and the creation of a new position for a chief economist. That office remains no less pro-active than prior to the setbacks.[131]

The Single European Market (SEM) remains far from complete. A recent survey conducted by the Confederation of British Industry and the British Chamber of Commerce found that most barriers to trade remain in place. An Institute of Directors study indicated that SEM has increased costs. These results were not exceptional. Only 12 percent of Portuguese firms, 17 percent of Dutch, and

20 percent of French firms agreed that the single market had worked for them. The community average was only a third. Problems arise from cheating (non-enforcement) and from nonimplementation due to disagreements about standards. State aid (producer subsidies), public procurement, and technical standards – which for the most part remain national concerns – continue to cause major headaches. Compliance costs have been prohibitive for small businesses. Labor mobility, still limited by language barriers and the nonportability of benefits, has actually declined since the 1970s. Finally, there is the red-tape factor. "Often," sighs one commentator, "the process of achieving a satisfactory result can take years .... It took two [years] for Spanish authorities to drop new restrictions on bottle sizes that would have forced a U.K. soft drinks producer to completely change his production lines."[132]

Yet some progress *has* been made toward the Single European Market. Victoria Curzon Price helpfully reminds the pessimist that "whole swaths of industry completely impervious to market forces in energy, transport, water supplies, and communications have been or are still being opened to competition through trade and investment."[133] Cozy railway and energy monopolies continue to come under attack, as do air transport duopolies and road transport cartels. The exposure of protected sectors and monopolies to market forces has revealed high levels of state-funded debt and vast featherbedding. Where large-scale striking has impeded reform – in France, Italy, and Spain – the public has now at least been exposed to the problem. If pressure for the elimination of abusive practices does not relent and political breezes someday shift, decartelization, deregulation, and privatization may have better luck in the future.

Market-induced change has also continued within the broadened context created by the Single European Act. Between 1997 and 1998, the value of intra-European foreign investments doubled. Cross-border investments also hit a new high. Retail price convergence increased, although at a slower pace than in the early 1990s; price dispersion for private consumption in the fifteen EU nations fell from 22.3 percent in 1990 to 14.7 percent in 1998, though not always to lower price levels. Gas, electrical, and telecommunications prices declined sharply in anticipation of deregulation, but they still remained high by international standards. The number of air carriers grew from 132 in 1993 to 164 in 1998 while the market share of incumbent national carriers shrank. The continuation of such long-term incremental change indicates that the EU is still far from being a spent force in the field of liberalization.[134]

Hope also remained alive that the EU could still play a constructive role in world economic governance. Brussels initially opposed the opening of the Uruguay Round, but it took the initiative in pressing for the Millennium Round that opened in Seattle. If anything, the EU finds itself in the tariff-reduction driver's seat more often than the United States, where trade policy is more politicized and Congress presents the executive with a hurdle not faced by the trade commissioner. The balance between the two powerful negotiating parties fulfills the aims of wartime American free-traders as well as the goals of the Marshall Plan.

A Trans-Atlantic Business Dialogue now complements, extends, and even competes with the WTO. A November 1994 speech by the American commerce secretary, the late Ron Brown, catalyzed the new body into existence. Composed of businessmen and supported by both the United States and the European Union, it has several main tasks: adopting and enforcing a common competition policy, cooperating on setting of standards on the basis of mutual recognition, promoting (with the WTO) liberalization by the removal of nontariff barriers, and developing common regulatory systems. The organization made steady progress at several top-level meetings in the late 1990s. Its proudest achievement, which falls under the mutual recognition rubric, is saving $1.37 billion by reducing approval times for certifying the electromagnetic compatibility of telecommunications equipment and by streamlining inspections in the process of making pharmaceuticals.[135]

In March 1998, EU Trade Minister Sir Leon Brittan proposed expanding the new transoceanic business relationship into a New Transatlantic Marketplace Agreement (NTMA) aimed at reducing all industrial tariffs on a most-favored-nation basis, negotiating a free-trade area in services, extending WTO liberalization rules to the field of public procurement, and removing technical barriers to trade.[136] The proposal is still pending. Although such arrangements can be criticized on the grounds of discriminating against nonmembers and (in the American case) of excluding the larger Asian trade partner – as well as for incompatibility with standing international regulatory agencies like the WTO – developments have not proceeded to the point that any such issues have arisen. The new mood of caution prompted by Seattle has temporarily stalled the NTMA. Lionel Barber's judgment is still sadly premature that "Americans and Europeans are witnesses to the creation of a new, post–Cold War order ... embracing new concepts such as economic security and competitiveness [in which] business-to-business contacts ... count as much as traditional diplomacy in managing the relationship."[137] The need for progress toward voluntary global self-regulation remains pressing. The inability of the EU to make headway through the regulatory morass may dictate resort to the NTMA in the future. How, and whether, a new U.S.–EU partnership would move the latter in the direction desired by Mrs. Thatcher also remains to be seen. The emergence of China as a world trading power will provide a goad to it.

Giandomenico Majone thinks that the EU can meet the challenge of globalization. In "The Credibility Crisis of Community Regulation," he argues that it should become a competitive regulatory regime. Regulation is, he reminds readers, the central policy mechanism – be it legal or administrative – of the Community. Its tiny budget eliminates any other real means for the exercise of authority. The Single European Act's delegation of powers has increased rather than diminished the authority of the Commission, Majone argues. It created an enforcement lever, enabled the Euro-executive to draw on otherwise unavailable expertise, and allowed the transfer of compliance responsibilities to national bodies.

The system has now surpassed the limits of effective operation, he adds. The Commission has too many tasks to handle with the administrative instruments at hand and must contend with an "increased level of politicization and parliamentarization." It has also inadvertently complicated the policy-making process by bringing in self-regulating standard-setting bodies and producer associations, which were designed for the purpose of setting up their own rules rather than making accommodations to external norms or views. The regulatory capacity of the various member-states furthermore varies substantially. The enforcement problem, according to Majone, has become severe. To solve it, regulation must be divorced from politics, and equal measures of power and responsibility must be built into policy making.[138] This calls, he thinks, for new institutions.

Majone's solution is to delegate authority to independent European agencies embedded in transnational networks of national regulators and international organizations, which then compete in rule setting. The approach is consistent with Anne-Marie Slaughter's transgovernmentalism; can take heart from the progress of the Uruguay Round, which for the first time harmonized "national rules and policies [into] ... GATT agreements as a norm of international relations"; and fits in with the evolutionary institutionalism scenario laid out by Andrew Shonfield for the future development of the European Community. Majone also cautions that "the fragmentary character and diverse nature of the EU's external competencies represent a serious threat to the credibility of [its outside] commitments" and emphasizes its failure to keep pace with an evolving and improving international regulatory system.[139] In other words, what the EU does not do for itself, others may well do for it. The exercise of regional power will then pass up to the international level.

Majone doubts that the American model – centralized federal agencies operating independently of state regulatory authority – can be transposed to Europe; instead, he advocates the decentralized rule making and enforcement needed to assure that consensus and compliance go hand in hand. Three conditions must be satisfied: mutual trust, a high level of professionalization, and a common regulatory philosophy. The creation of such networked, self-regulating bodies is the essential prerequisite to EU credibility. Majone concludes that to survive the EU must become the hub of such a rule-making system.[140]

Can such a system escape regulatory capture? The recent past is no guide to the future. Regulatory design has traditionally been a reply to the notion of market failure caused by monopoly power, negative externalities, incomplete information, and insufficient provision of public goods. Its purpose was to offset one or more of the conditions needed to arrive at a Pareto-optimal allocation of resources.[141] The priorities of macromanagement and redistribution that prevailed after World War II turned "market failure" into an excuse for intrusive state interventionism such as centralized capital allocation and nationalization of industry. However, the Keynesian and social democratic consensus about the beneficence of the positive state and the wisdom of technocratic government came apart in the 1970s as a result of stagflation and unemployment.

The regime change that followed shifted the main approach taken toward regulatory problems. The purpose remains fundamentally the same – to make capitalism work – but it now centers on *institutional* failure. At its core is the notion of *lex mercatoria,* the law of the marketplace developed within the medieval trading community, where contractors first recognized that honesty rather than cheating best served their self-interest because – as a result of repeat dealing – a good reputation reduced transaction costs. Interaction then generated spontaneously into convention and was later codified into a framework of law. Based on property and contract, *lex mercatoria* originated in trial-and-error learning. Self-regulation on this voluntary basis worked better and more cost-effectively than could any ant army of external enforcers. The new institutional economics studies the evolution of such "internal institutions."[142] The apportioning of responsibilities between them and the external government enforcement mechanisms is of immense current interest, but it is difficult to determine in specific instances and also controversial. A new paradigm has not yet replaced the earlier one.

Still, historical institutionalists like Paul Pierson have recently analyzed the slow-moving nature of bureaucratic change and pointed out the importance of unintended outcomes. Public choice theory has created a new awareness of the inevitably self-interested bias of bureaucratic action as well as the importance of rent seeking by interest groups that benefit by spreading costs through a diffuse public and over generations. The key mechanism at work here is "information asymmetry," a situation that favors insiders and leads to regulatory capture; these tendencies contribute, in the view of John Blundell and Colin Robinson, to a "momentum [that] has little to do with considerations of public interest" but instead shifts high and "nontransparent" regulatory costs to others.[143]

Such costs can be monumental, if the fragmentary evidence available is any indication. A report by the Center for the Study of American Business estimated that in 1995 "compliance" cost the U.S. economy $15 billion, or 9 percent of GDP, which took $7,000 from the budget of a typical American family and of which the government itself covered only 2 percent. A 1998 McKinsey study claimed that, in Britain, "regulations imposed to achieve socially desirable outcomes [also] had the unintended impact of damaging employment and growth." The problem of overregulation is not going away. EU legal acts in force rose from 1,947 in 1973 to 14,729 in 1990 and 23,027 in 1996. The number of pages produced by the EU Publication Office more than doubled between 1989 and 1996: from 886,996 to 1,916,000.[144]

Blundell and Robinson make a couple of helpful suggestions for improving the situation. "Voluntary self-regulation" is their keynote. One is to provide liberalization incentives to regulators to encourage them to meet competition policy standards, an approach that has proved useful in British utility regulation. Another is to empower insurers with accreditation authority, which has proved effective, for instance, in British bridge building. A third suggestion comes from New Zealand, where the government entrusted road haulers with assuring safety compliance and limited its own role to supervision. Each example of voluntary self-regulation presumes that repeat dealing rewards good behavior at the bottom line. The theory is adaptable as well as inexpensive, and it avoids cost shifting as well as bureaucratic empire building.[145] As an approach to restoring the EU's regulatory credibility, it is worth taking seriously.

The survival of the EU may require such legitimization. The small budget, according to Majone, rules out the alternative – welfare state building, redistributionist social policy, and macroeconomic stabilization.[146] Neither the SEA nor the Maastricht and Amsterdam treaties have, moreover, "provided true legislative competencies in the social field." Instead, European voters "support far-reaching economic integration but continue to see in the nation-state the principle focus of their loyalty and the real arena of democratic politics."[147] To establish the EU's legitimacy as a competitive regulatory regime, he continues, the organization should follow the "Next Steps" policy laid out for Mrs. Thatcher, which is based upon four principles: decentralization and regionalization, the breakdown of monoliths to single-purpose entities, the delegation of governmental service delivery to private entities, and competitive tendering.[148] The technical-sounding but powerful suggestions of all who argue for the EU as market-conforming international regulator set out a future agenda that is consistent with past practice and present world trends as well as the interests of member-states, their citizens, and the needs of Europe itself.

Conclusion to Part IV

Needed: A New European Union?

THE HISTORY of European integration in the 1990s might lead one to such a conclusion. The process was not a driver of change but a drag on it, causing Europe to miss some of the opportunities of the decade and stifling many others. The source of the problem was not passivity or inactivity but rather a misplaced policy of "deepening," "positive integration," and institution building. The European Union deferred overdue reform and created bigger problems than any it might have solved. The botching of Enlargement is the worst mistake in the history of integration; it has discredited European idealism and will yield a harvest of future problems. The way out of the EU's difficulties is not to scrap it – or even for any single nation to walk out – but to learn from the mistakes of the 1990s.

Innovation was the decade's great story, and Silicon Valley was its symbol. Digital technology was a liberating force of such strength that one must reach back centuries to find apt comparison. It moved the spirit as well as the economy, rehabilitated the word "progress," and created a common denominator of human interest, value, and achievement. The high-tech revolution threatened the status quo everywhere yet improved the odds that change would be peaceful and constructive. The decade provided ample evidence of progress. China and India began to make their weight felt in the world. The American economy boomed, as did industry and agriculture almost everywhere outside of sub-Saharan Africa and (until the end of the decade) the Russian "near abroad." Contrary to fears and expectations, the collapse of the Soviet Union did not sweep in revolution, civil war, or chaos; bloodshed was, with certain painful exceptions like Chechnya, sporadic rather than endemic. Successor states emerged in eastern Europe, politically fragile perhaps, but committed to peace and democracy. Even Russia eventually stabilized. Though still very much alive, European nationalism did not cause war and upheaval except in the Balkans. A new global order – of unprecedented prosperity and protracted peace, of self-generated and self-sustaining order and governance, and of heretofore unimagined richness of cultural and intellectual interchange – had become possible.

Yet Europe came up short in the 1990s because of mistakes made at Maastricht. They can be blamed chiefly on the Delorean agenda, the attempt to "deepen" the Community. The deflationary economic policies adopted to qualify member-states for monetary union were an important part of the background. They lowered growth, impeded structural change, hardened social divisions, soured the political atmosphere, and produced festering public resentment. The effort to build a "social Europe" was a costly waste of time. If ever successfully launched, such a program would reproduce on a continental scale the constipated labor–management systems that had caused high unemployment, low industrial investment, and lack of innovation at the national level. "Social Europe" would, in addition, strip the less wealthy member-states of their main comparative advantage. A Euro-corporatism would also strangle in red tape. A "European social and economic space" à la Jacques Delors was chimerical, grounded in approaches that were already failing nationally, and without any real support except from within the Commission and the beggar-thy-neighbor French and Belgians. Never more than a serious annoyance, the corporatist building programs of Delors and others helped widen the gap between European and American economic performance. By the start of the new millennium, the spread had become larger than at any time since the early 1960s.

The bid to organize an embryonic federal Europe around a domestic and foreign security policy ("pillars two and three") made only limited progress. To be sure, 2003 would witness the EU's first-ever military operation (in Macedonia), the takeover of peacekeeping from NATO; the EU prepared to take over "fully flagged" responsibilities in Bosnia as well.[1] This welcome and cooperative engagement should not be confused with the development of an autonomous strike force – independent of NATO command, communications, and logistics – put to the service of "projecting European" world power. Such dangerous plans have precedents in the earlier European Defense Community and the Multilateral Force ("Euro-navy") and would repeat the mistake made at the inception of the integration process, when the Coal and Steel Community was founded: create a remote techno-bureaucratic authority unaccountable to the public.

The post-Maastricht effort to "deepen" was also seriously diversionary. It distracted the EU from its mounting internal problems, and it encouraged missteps and claims to the exercise of powers and responsibilities it could not meet. The EU became intrusive while remaining weak; in the process of making policy, it often looked both threatening and ridiculous. Small wonder it lacked credibility. The EU's shortcomings included bureaucratic bloat and lethargy; Byzantine, opaque, and dishonest methods of operation; dependency upon (and often subservience to) powerful interest groups; and sleaze that oozed from the hub, along the spokes, to the periphery and back. The Community did not reform inequitable and wasteful policies like CAP, corrupting ones like regional policy, or ineffective, extravagant, and misguided ones like the Framework Programs for research and development. Brussels remained complacent, self-serving, and ill equipped to tackle the problems of the day. Its policy failures, except in the Balkans, were those of omission rather than commission. Muddle and drudge was the norm for an institution that worshiped the god of technocracy.

Inactivity and weak performance become alarming only when coupled to conceit and overweening ambition. They, too, put in appearances. The Austria-bashing episode, the persecution of van Buitenen, and the 2001 White Paper on Governance are warning signs. One should be reminded in light of the EU's recent record of incompetence and underhanded politics that "These people demand the right to govern us!" The purpose behind the constitutional exercise now under way in Brussels is neither to clean the slate nor simplify governance but rather to produce a framework of federal institutions that would turn national democracies into regions and subregions of a powerful centralized state for which no *demos* exists and of which no electorate (save possibly in Germany, Belgium, and Luxembourg) would possibly endorse if given a bona fide opportunity to do so.

The problems of the EU in the 1990s were not necessarily those of its leaders. Romano Prodi has had a knack for making himself look bad, and he failed to inspire or set his personal stamp on the Commission. In assessing his presidency, however, one must not overlook his brilliant track record, determination, and integrity. Yet Prodi failed to reform the Commission and at best waged only a holding action. Although individual commissioners, operating autonomously, have remained major players, the Commission itself has been reduced to a *quantité negligible*. When Prodi talks, almost no one listens. The same thing happens when he shouts.

Nor were the heads of state a notably evil or weak lot. A weighted average aggregate measurement would probably tell us that they were neither much better nor worse than their predecessors. Yet in the 1990s the machinery of intergovernmentalism broke down; the most serious casualty was the European Council, by whose means M. Giscard d'Estaing and Herr Schmidt had revived the Community a decade earlier. Intergovernmentalist institutions did not work for two reasons. One was the failure of the Franco-German marriage, which resulted from the weakening of the German economy, the stubbornness of France, the fundamental difference between the French and German visions of the future Europe, and the expansion of the Community. These differences will not be easily bridged in the future, institution-drafting exercises not withstanding.

Intergovernmentalist institutions broke down also because they were poorly equipped to withstand the stresses and strains of the burdens placed upon them. The reform of EU governance would remain a zero-sum game if individual players could not discover new advantages of cooperation. The Delorean institution-building agenda failed to provide such incentives. The member-states eventually became unable to agree on anything other than – in the case of the monetary union – buck-passing. National conflicts mounted over the decade and cooperation markedly decreased. Promising beginnings (e.g., on Enlargement) failed to develop. Problem solving was deferred, deal making became progressively more difficult, deceitfulness increased, and policy making parted company from reality. As the machinery of integration broke down, ambitions escalated to the point that a damage-control operation like the Convention on the Future of Europe parades as a constitutional convention. A mere stopgap, it cannot overcome Community immobilism.

Underlying the problems of the 1990s was the pursuit of a long-outdated idea. Although no feasible alternative existed after World War II to the construction of Europe from the top down, the need for it has long since passed. A new generation is in power for which the events of 1939–1945 are history rather than a personal experience. Memories of the Cold War are also fading fast. Western Europe has for over a generation been stable, peaceful, and prosperous. The publics of Europe can be trusted to decide what is in their own best interest and should be given a chance to make this determination. They do not need self-serving Eurocrats to tell them what to do. The nations and peoples of Europe are no longer at each other's throats; they just need to get along a bit better. The EU of the 1990s contributed little to increasing mutual understanding and respect. A *demos* thus did not develop and, unless Enlargement is renegotiated, has little chance of doing so soon.

The shortcomings of the EU during the 1990s could readily be forgiven if, in the end, it delivers as promised to the people of eastern Europe and makes an honest effort to mend the historic division of the continent into a rich and elegant West and a poor and shabby East. As things now stand, a happy ending is only for fairy tales. More than heroic statesmanship will be required for an Enlargement turnabout. The EU would have to reform itself, beginning with CAP. Powerful interest groups and sullen publics will resist such a deal. The French now lead the charge for the EU status quo, and – as earlier in the "empty chairs" crisis – the other member-states follow quietly behind.

Western Europe's Enlargement derelictions will inflict a high price. For nearly a decade the candidate nations have made single-minded efforts, at substantial cost, to qualify for accession. For the citizenry of the former Soviet bloc, the prospect of a return to the civilization from which they were cut off for a generation outweighs the importance of even the material gains initially promised them. It is now evident not only that the manna will not descend from upon high but that the easterners will be only junior members of the European partnership. Once the former victims of communist misrule realize that they have been led down a garden path, there will be hell to pay. Their political establishments – fragile constructions for the most part though everywhere busily burrowing into state and economy – will feel the first force of the wave, but it will carry much more before it. One fact is painfully evident. The EU has undone what should have been its greatest accomplishment of the 1990s – the democratization of the satellites and captive European nations of the former Soviet Union – and has instead destabilized the region. The first real Euro-foray into a common defense and security policy is heading toward disaster.

How can Brussels be reformed? Cross the fingers and proceed cautiously; the fog is heavy. Only outlines are visible. The impetus to change may come from something farther away (e.g., changes in the international economy) or something too hard to see, such as a bottom-up market process at work within individual nation-states. Nonetheless, six surmises concerning the Community itself come to mind.

1. Unless Enlargement stops altogether, the EU will become more differentiated.
2. No big country except Germany wants federalism.
3. Common defense and security policy will go nowhere until European taxpayers are willing to foot the bill for it; it lies in the distant future.
4. Little progress has been made in institutionalizing central police powers in such presently "hot-button" areas as control of narcotics trafficking, white slavery, and terrorism, but this field remains fertile ground for bureaucratic growth.
5. A wider membership will not speed up decision making – a larger union will more permanently immobilize an already temporarily immobilized smaller one.
6. As the decision-making process slows down, the *acquis communautaire* will cease to grow.

Change is nonetheless possible. Member-states that want to go beyond what already exists can do so by means of special treaties between them, whether bi-, tri-, or multilateral. The resulting Community will more closely resemble the "multi-speed Europe" that Mr. Blair has in mind than the formally structured (though verbally meaningless) arrangement referred to as the "Europe of variable geometry." Although it will be difficult to find an appropriate image to describe such a Community (for none exists), one can conjure up memories of the "sticky marbles" that Lord Shonfield imagined more than 25 years ago. The most prominent features of the future organization will (as foreseen by Giandomenico Majone) be voluntary competitive regulatory agencies created to do Europe's – and part of the world's – necessary work, agencies that will (as Anne-Marie Slaughter anticipates) be bound by common principle and national law, will (as Sir Leon Brittan advocates) be managed by concerned stakeholders, and will (as many economists have suggested) develop as market-conforming international institutions in a manner consistent with the long-term secular trend toward liberalization. Under such conditions and then *perhaps* over decades such functional arrangements, if made subject and properly answerable to national parliaments, can develop along institutional evolutionary lines into organs of representative federal government as projected nearly three decades ago by Lord Dahrendorf. Globalization points toward such a line of development.

The creation of regulatory entities outside the existing EU institutional framework is neither new nor unusual, but customary. The CAP was recognized and accepted as being a necessary political side deal that was inconsistent with the Treaty of Rome. Giscard and Schmidt created the European Council as an extra-treaty organization in order to circumvent the Brussels machinery. The European Central Bank was designed to be removed from the supervision and direction of both Brussels and the states. New regulatory authorities should be judged by three standards: intent, operation, and impact. If they are properly designed to make markets work, "Europe" may someday develop from what it is today – a liberal framework agreement, a common customs area, and a single market governed by the competition principle – into a confederation of convenience, good sense, and common spirit embedded in a world market order resting on legal principle, guided by competition, and bettered by the invisible hand. Only the member-states can advance integration in such a direction. The future of integration rests upon the views and decisions of the European peoples.

Envoi

ENVOI is a pretty word that comes from medieval French. It describes a post-script attached as the final stanza of a ballad and includes both a dedication and a commendation. This envoi is dedicated to those who have built Europe. It also commends them in the sense of *thanking*. A commendation must also *recommend*. To participants in the historical drama it recommends that they view their own work in light of the grand project to which they and their successors have contributed or will contribute. This envoi also recommends their work as a subject to those whom it commends to undertake the pleasant task of writing the future history of European integration. This is the first book to deal with the matter comprehensively and over its entire fifty-year history. The author hopes to encourage others to write better accounts in the future by challenging those written in the past and presenting a new version of the story.

The process of European integration is a suitable subject for the social scientist but really belongs to the historian. Although a force shaping the world of today, it has become part of the past – has been woven into the fabric of civilization, and rewoven it as well. European integration is an epiphenomenon of broad and lasting change and thus cannot be understood in isolation. The nature of its impact also varies from time to time and place to place and can be either good or bad depending upon circumstance. The European integration process has evolved over the past half-century, is not static, will change in the future, cannot be treated as a constant, and should no longer be discussed in the language of the 1950s. Finding the appropriate idiom in which to describe the subject is not easy. The search for it involves more than simply reducing characterizations of the Founding Fathers to human proportions and requires something in addition to intellectual liberation from mythology, theology, a contrived official vocabulary, and political jargon. To discover the real meaning of past events, it is necessary to break with accepted theory, devise a new one, and even – because the subject extends beyond the present – occasionally place bets on the future. Integration must be discovered for what it is rather than what it purports to be in order to ascertain what it can become. This book is no more than a low rung on a continuous ladder leading into the future.

Political science theory claims to explain the alpha and omega of European integration, the essentials of its origins, course, and destination. Although the analytical force of its logic has advanced understanding of the subject to its current state, partial explanations are still the best it can offer. The weightiest of political science theories – liberal intergovernmentalism – drives Andrew Moravcsik's brilliant and relentless *The Choice for Europe*, the most important single book in the broad field of integration studies. Moravcsik has gone deep into the historical record in order to explain how European heads of state reached the Big Bargains that produced institutions like CAP, SEA, and EMU. In doing so he has demonstrated that national decision makers, the heads of government, collectively advanced the integration process. The impetus to change derived, in other words, from outside the institutional framework of Brussels.

Intergovernmentalist theory nevertheless leaves much unsaid. It neither explains why the negotiators arrived at particular types of grand bargains, nor compares the bargains in question to possible alternatives, nor indicates why certain of them could be struck at one time and not another, nor reveals why those Big Bargains arrived at have had different consequences from those intended, nor sheds light on why they can result in the relinquishment rather than the transference of power. Nor does liberal intergovernmentalism analyze integration developments taking place outside the institutional and economic context of Big Bargains or investigate change occurring in the temporal intervals between them. Nor does the approach examine the structure of standing bodies and institutions or explain their influence on the integration process.

No other political science theory does these things either. The functionalism of the 1950s rested on a provocative and fruitful hypothesis – the spillover dynamic – that stimulated research for thirty years. As a predictive scientific theory, however, it has demonstrably no value and has never recovered from the twenty-year hiatus that set in after the empty chairs crisis of 1965. It cannot be too strongly emphasized that the empirical work of political science – cited profusely (though still inadequately) in these pages – is of immense value to the future historian, who will find vast numbers of stimulating, intellectually rigorous, eminently useful, and often invaluable studies on nearly every aspect of the organized life of the Community. Political scientists have grappled long and hard with monetary, fiscal, commercial, technological, and legal subjects buried deep in the recesses of political economy. Most historians recoil in horror from such painstaking investigation. Although leaving many big questions unanswered, the Battle of the Paradigms within political science and international relations has propagated a healthy dialectic: functionalism begat liberal intergovernmentalism, which in turn begat the historical institutionalism that is moving political scientific theory closer to both history and economics.

Economics also lacks a general theory to explain the European integration process. It is often stated as truism that the subject is "economic" because its benefits are economic in character. The proposition may be sound, but neoclassical economics cannot demonstrate it convincingly – has never isolated an integration variable or generated a theory of endogenous economic integration development. Two basic explanations account for the situation. Neoclassical economics or *microeconomics* is, first of all, static and factors out those variables that cause temporal change. The second point concerns the nature of the context-shifting Big Bargains. Though often dealing with economic issues, they are fundamentally political in character. The coal–steel pool's rationale of efficiency, progress, and growth provided a convenient fiction for an essentially diplomatic arrangement struck to convince hostile publics in France and Germany that the enmity between them was not inevitable and could be overcome through cooperation. The Treaty of Rome's rationale was not, according to Jacques Pelkmans, grounded in the economics of free trade – a subject not even discussed at relevant negotiations – but grew out of the simple conviction that modern industrial development required markets as large as those of the United States. The preeminently "economic" Single European Act derived only partly from pressures felt by the international marketplace. The SEA was due also to Mrs. Thatcher's initiative and to trend-spotting heads of government who were troubled by policy failure and intent upon reform. The relevance of neoclassical economics to the project at hand is nevertheless great. The discipline provides an intellectual framework without which discussion becomes anecdotal, supplies an indispensable analytical and statistical methodology for all social science, and creates the aggregates needed for historical analysis. It is, however, of limited value in explaining how history shifted from "a" to "b" and even less so regarding how it might have moved from "a" to "j," "v" to "x," or especially "x" to "v."

For guidance as to how markets drive progress over time one must turn to the *classical liberal economic* school associated with Hayek and kindred approaches. Although it also lacks a general theory, the logic of spontaneous order creates, moves, shapes, shifts, alters, and eliminates markets in the real world with which historians must deal. Classical liberalism also, in various ways, joins economics with politics, diplomacy, and law, and in doing so it becomes partly prescriptive as well – provides insights not only into what has happened but also into what can and should happen. The conditions under which the process of change occurs have been the special concern of classical liberal offshoots like ORDO, public choice theory, the new institutional economics, and the young political science–based historical institutionalism. Such approaches have also influenced the thinking of social scientists specializing in the integration field who are not normally associated with (or do not associate themselves with) classical liberalism.

Relationships between seminal integration theorists and classical liberalism vary. Hayek, of course, developed the basic logic of market and institutional interaction in "The Economic Conditions of Federalism." Wilhelm Röpke devised the classical liberal solution to the German Problem, but he is associated most closely with ORDO-liberalism. Although the economic historian Gottfried Haberler – who first appreciated the thematic importance of liberalization for the present era – was originally an "Austrian" economist by nationality as well as training, Jacques Pelkmans – the political economist who applied the logic of integration to the real-world situation of contemporary Europe – was neither. Pelkmans, however, drew heavily from public choice theory. The same could be said of Jan Tumlir's demonstrations of the interdependence of representative government and open markets, although this argument also rested on classical liberal theories of constitutional order. The relationship of other major figures cited in this book to the classical liberal tradition can be less direct, as in the case of Dahrendorf; largely implicit, as for Pierson (except as regards the influence of Douglass North); or partial and even unrecognized, as in the case of Shonfield. Connections are also evident in the work of other important thinkers cited in the book but too numerous to name. The relevance of the classical liberal tradition of economics to this study has barely been touched upon in these pages. The author can no more than hint at its broader applicability given the constraints of the present volume.

Yet one cannot demonstrate the workings of change in the integration process without moving beyond the limited universes of purely social scientific inquiry. The most important event in its history – the regime change that began in the 1970s – was in fact exogenous, not endogenous, and resulted from both the breakdown of the international embedded liberal regime organized at Bretton Woods and its replacement with a new one resting on flexible exchange rates. This switch-over had implications that reached far beyond the realm of monetary economics. It decoupled nation-states from an international order built for the primary purpose of guaranteeing full employment, which both rested on and buttressed the controlled and regulated mixed economy of the welfare state. Within states, regime change irreversibly weakened the all-important link between governmental bureaucracy and the economy.

In the transformation that followed, economic stability replaced full employment as the overriding objective of policy. In addition, decision-making authority within states shifted from labor and the public sector to central economic and financial institutions, markets opened, and the competition principle began to work on a scale that had been impossible earlier. Controls broke down (or were abandoned) on the movement of capital, investment, and labor; in lieu of them, a network of market-enhancing (*Marktkonform*) regulatory institutions began to develop. Quasi-, pseudo-, "organized," and otherwise skewed capitalist economies retreated as properly functioning exchange mechanisms overpowered and broke through restraints and controls built to immobilize them. The competition principle would become the governing authority of the new market-guided era. The regime change – which was also part and parcel of a still broader trend, globalization – created the context of the present era in the West.

Regime change gave the European Community not only a new lease on life but a real life. What for twenty years had been chiefly a paper project would henceforth have an immediate and dynamic impact on the existence of individual Europeans. New rules adopted both in Brussels and nationally unleashed the force of competition, whose power could be resisted but not overcome. Opponents of the new liberal order have since found themselves waging a rear-guard action. With socialism discredited internationally (except in North Korea), they are no longer armed with ideas. Their only defense is self-interest.

The organization of this book reflects the greater importance of the recent history of integration. This back-loaded approach raises an immediate question. Might integration have moved faster or better? The answer is, "Yes and no." The deconstruction of the postwar embedded liberal system, itself the stepchild of early twentieth-century war economies, was a long-term process. As constraints have been lifted and opportunity has increased, the scope for making policy choices has broadened. However, the right ones have not always been made, and many wrong ones continue to be made. The gap between the potential and the actual has spread, as progress has become relatively slower and as the costs – of missed opportunities, accumulated resource misallocation, and misdirected decision making – increase. The historical record is unambiguous: only "negative" market-based integration policy works in the absence of a *demos*. The "positive," institution-centered alternative – based upon the fallacy that economic widening and political deepening go hand in hand – merely complicates and delays the integration process. The EU's breakdown in the 1990s has driven this point home.

There is much to lose should the integration process be reversed or undone. One might apply a kind of step theory to the fifty-year history of this temporal movement toward European cooperation. No stage in its complicated and unpredictable development has yet been regressive; each has eventually built on the prior one. Progress has occurred, in a successful sequence of challenge and response, as a result of a learning process – a gradual winnowing out of bad ideas by means of accumulated knowledge. The worst such ideas appear in the early history of integration. By comparison to some of the wild and irresponsible proposals then in circulation, the threats of the early 2000s are modest. They stem not from radical efforts to accelerate the process of change but from the mundane one of bringing it to a dead stop. That the locus of such efforts is the traditional political left may cause surprise but is nonetheless true. The effort to protect the status quo centers in groups – entrenched in the system of embedded liberalism created after World War II – that now face the threat of the global marketplace. This clinging to power is, however, producing collateral damage that discredits the European Union and creates future problems for Europe.

How might the process of European integration have been better or faster? At the first stage of integration, only one option was open. Europe needed ten years to recuperate from the war and adapt to the new conditions of the postwar world. Although the framework for the present liberal world system dates from World War II, it could only begin operation later. Lack of currency convertibility, the chief bottleneck, left the Bretton Woods institutions a hollow shell until 1958, when the cross-border circulation of national moneys (at least on a limited basis) became possible. The early history of integration involves both the deconstruction of the statism bequeathed by the era of the World Wars and the gradual substitution of a better alternative for it. Shock therapy could not have shortcut the process because the scary but necessary wave of creative destruction it entailed would have hit the societies of postwar Europe with gale force and left only ruins in its wake. With the Soviets at the gate, the risks of shock therapy far outweighed possible benefits.

The Schuman Plan of 1950, the diplomatic breakthrough that made integration into a European tradition, climaxed the drama of postwar reconstruction and marked the onset of a new era. Monnet was the indispensable man. Only he had the vision and the backing to make the diplomatic breakthrough needed for Franco-German reconciliation. Yet the founding of the coal–steel pool was a one-time event and far less important over the long run than the liberalization trend set in motion by German recovery. Over time, the West German boom activated other European economies as well as the institutions set up to regulate the international trading system, and thus it led the way to the future.

The next stage of integration, marked by the Treaty of Rome and the European Economic Community, took a turn in the right direction but also led to many detours that in vexing ways delayed the integration process, whose pace would now be set at two steps forward, one step back. The Treaty of Rome, a "liberal framework document" (in the words of Andrew Moravcsik), outlined basic procedures for creating a customs union and established the competition principle as an enforcement mechanism to regulate its operation. Economic integration proceeded with surprising ease. The common external tariff came down earlier than planned. The Community itself was soon flanked by extending ramparts of association agreements allowing the reciprocal duty-free entry of goods from surrounding nations outside the EEC. By the 1980s, the EEC (in its later incarnations as EC and EU) eventually had become stronger and more steadfast than its American partners in maintaining and developing the world trading system. Such an outcome had been sought by American postwar planners and was the goal of the Marshall Plan, reflecting the survival of a lingering nineteenth-century southern Democratic Party free-trade tradition. It also pointed to the future – the Single European Act and, less immediately, the emerging liberalized global order.

The Treaty of Rome unfortunately also included the Common Agricultural Policy, the core Brussels institution, which has warped the subsequent political and economic development of the Community. It has become a Frankenstein monster. The Community managed to assert control over the CAP only once, in 1988, by reducing its share in the budget from three quarters to a half – but to make that cut politically acceptable it had to create a new layer of income transference, regional policy. CAP impedes reform, perpetuates injustice, saps the moral and political strength of the Community, and today threatens to turn Enlargement from a triumph of hope and ambition into a defeat of betrayal and despair. Reform of the EU must aim above all at repatriating the farm price-support system. The end of the keystone revenue reallocation scheme should eventually bring down the others.

A policy choice, as opposed to a theoretical alternative, existed at the initialing and ratification of the Rome treaty, something that was not true at the founding of the coal–steel pool. The nineteen states of the OEEC, the Marshall Plan organization created to develop trade rules, might well have formed a free-trade area in the late 1950s. The proposal was widely supported by producers and economists because it was limited in aim and easy to set up. The subsequent history of EEC/EU expansion indicates that it was not economically "too big" and would probably have also produced quick and large one-time gains by opening closed markets. Trade theory supports such a view. Above all, it would have prevented the development of CAP.

The farm sector was wisely excluded from negotiations for a free-trade area as well as from the eventual European Free Trade Area (EFTA). The individual member-states could set their own standards for price support and protection, which did not involve transfer payments. Such payments produced the traditions of horse-trading and *engrenage* that introduced bad government into the Brussels institutions. Although the subsidization of farm products was in fact higher in the Nordic countries than in the EEC/EC, EFTA did not ratchet up overall food price levels. Nor did any price support scheme influence EFTA's institutional development.

The free-trade alternative failed for lack of political leadership: from a United States committed, for purported security reasons, to the eventual federation of Europe; from Great Britain, the ostensible but demoralized official leader of the cause; and from a Federal Republic whose chancellor (Adenauer) attached more importance to the newfound intimacy with France than to any economic arrangement whatsoever. The modest, even obscure EFTA nevertheless shadows the EU long after the former's eclipse. As a large free-trade association whose political development is limited to making markets work, it provides a model framework for an expanded EU. The EFTA experience demonstrates that a common market does not necessarily need more than minimal institutions; by the same token, it provides scant guidance on how future market-conforming institutions can be created that will improve the exchange process.

The integration process had "hit the wall" prior to regime change and could advance no further because, as first noted by the great Swedish social scientist Gunnar Myrdal, national bureaucrats in the welfare state – as well as the citizens they served – faced overpowering disincentives to the transference of policy-making authority to a centralized external institution; if and when this happened, it could only be on their own terms. Cooperation was not necessarily ruled out – but integration was. Nothing could therefore come of the many successive efforts of the 1960s and 1970s to build Europe either by planning or by its somewhat less robust stepchild "economic coordination." Such efforts resulted only in new public discourse, Swiftian Projection, and Euro-pessimism.

The adoption of the Single European Act (1986), the third great stage in the integration process and the second of a predominantly economic character, is arguably also the most important one. The worldwide regime change, the national adoption of Thatcherite and neoliberal policies, and the EC's promulgation and implementation of the program to eliminate nontariff barriers set in motion the wave of change that – thanks also to increasing pressure from the world marketplace – subsequently (albeit slowly and unevenly) set Europe on a course of liberalization. This outcome was only partly intended. Jacques Delors sponsored the Single European Act for two reasons, one of them close at hand: the internal market provisions supply the strongest centralization leverage in the Rome Treaty. He needed to take advantage of them in order to bolster Commission power. The longer-range consideration involved a wager: that he could direct the development of a new European economy from Brussels. Like his sponsor, French President Mitterrand, Delors aimed to win the battle in Europe that appeared to have been lost in France. He wanted to create a corporatist–socialist system to protect "a distinctive European way of life" and strong enough to stand up to the United States.

Margaret Thatcher (the true "mother" of the SEA) bet, for her part, that markets once unleashed would produce a cascade of self-generating change, which though unpredictable in pace and amplitude could not be turned back and would thus open the way to progress. M. Delors had indeed struck a Faustian bargain, a pact with the devil that he could not win. Even so, neither he nor those who still share his views – the technocracy, entrenched incumbents in circles of management (as represented at the European Roundtable), and the organized labor union movement throughout much of Europe and its client political parties – have ever managed to concede defeat. They have instead fought back hard nationally, at the level of Europe, and (whenever possible) internationally. The conflict between the proponents of markets and institutions has resulted neither in standoff nor compromise but in continuous struggle, sometimes "hot" and sometimes "cold," waged across many fronts.

The resistance of the traditional left – since the "regime change" a defender of the eroding corporatist–socialist status quo – has not been healthy. The ambitious attempt of Jacques Delors to create a federal-bureaucratic Europe by "deepening" failed miserably, thwarted Community development in the 1990s, and created serious future institutional problems like the European Central Bank and political problems as in the case of Enlargement. The bank could book one important achievement: its convergence criteria wrung inflation out of the European economy. That being accomplished, the ECB has no further value. The restrictive criteria by which it must operate retard growth. Furthermore, the bank's monopoly on European monetary and fiscal policy guts national self-government, democracy, and legislative tradition – facts evident in the present political demoralization of much of Europe.

Enlargement should have been the EU's great glory but has become a monumental disgrace. Instead of being welcomed into the Community and treated as equals, the eastern Europeans are being put on the second track in a two-track Europe. The wealthy West will remain wealthy because, in part, it can beggar the poor East. This unintended outcome – dictated by the shamefaced member-states – can be traced directly to the power of vested interests within the Community: the farmers, France, and all other recipients of transfer payments. The EU must reform its fundamental operating mechanisms and structures, as earlier promised the candidate nations, or risk being morally discredited.

Euro-idealism today sells at a huge discount in spite of the Community's ideological price-maintenance policy. More immediately, the "shafting" administered the East will be repaid – if not in kind (for the accession candidates are too weak to attempt such a thing) then by the instability resulting from adoption of a policy ruinous to the credibility of eastern European governments, nearly all of which "committed to Europe" and now must face angry backlash from cheated electorates. The EU is at this point no longer solving European problems but creating them. The compromise struck to soften the blow dealt the eastern Europeans – the unilateral opening of national job markets by Britain, Sweden, the Netherlands, Ireland, and Greece – is a practical (though still partial) solution that, however, sets the discredited EU in bold relief.

The technocratic bid to "organize" Europe around a bureaucratic nucleus has run its course. The great centralizing campaigns – at the ECSC, under Hallstein, and during the Delors presidency – have all failed, and countless lesser ones have never gotten off the ground. Each of the big pushes has, moreover, generated counterpressures that have produced unintended consequences. The Coal and Steel Community did not "functionally" generate the European Defense Community but rather the European Economic Community, a "liberal framework organization" based upon a different principle of organization. Hallstein's agitated attempts to inseminate the Commission somehow instead pollinated the member states. The European Council and "liberal governmentalism" resulted in the creation of the European Monetary Union – an unprecedented abdication of national political power.

Deloreanism has also been self-defeating. M. Delors's attempt to stand up to the Big Guy, A******, has only increased Europe's dependence upon the United States. "Policy networking" and high-tech corporatism transformed big-business lobbying from a Washington vice into a Brussels growth industry. A combination of Eurocratic overregulation and the deflationary euro bogged down the European economy, making recovery and expansion dependent upon transoceanic trends and events. The eventual creation of a single European financial market will, as uncharitably put by a senior Wall Street bulge-bracket banker, turn the European "social and economic space" into "a killing ground for us." The inability of the Commission to draw the appropriate lessons from the unbroken and calamitous failures of its industrial *cum* R&D policy continues to impair European innovation and competitiveness, skews incentive structures, and promotes bad science. The same holds for a slew of additional wrong-minded initiatives: subsidizing the entrepreneurship of small and medium-sized businesses, promoting "active labor market policy," discouraging biotech research, and so on. Commission industrial policy has delayed necessary adaptation, and the efforts to pick winning technological *grands projects* have produced heavy losers. Nearly all such policies have weakened rather than strengthened Europe. The EU's attempts to "play" in the high-stakes games of international security – in order to stimulate a feeling of Euro-nationhood – merely makes the Community look foolish.

Such failures may be troubling but are not life-threatening because they are corrected in part by the (to be sure, imperfect) workings of an economic, political, and intellectual competition process now under way in a liberalizing Europe. The gravest threats to Europe's future antedate regime change and belong to the era in which American hegemony was unbroken in the West, the Cold War was accepted as permanent, and the U.S. government supported a trans-Atlantic, monnetist coalition of institution builders for whom the future of "Europe" was too critical a matter to subject to democratic decision making. Their policies were truly frightening. The European Defense Community would have generated a military–industrial complex at the core of the European economy and polity. By comparison to this irresponsible idea, CAP seems a minor inconvenience. Kennedy's Grand Design, developed by Monnet's epigones, was even worse than EDC. The multilateral pseudo-nuclear navy anchoring the proposal would have locked Europe into dependence upon a semipermanent transatlantic atomic strategy controlled from Washington, stripped the ancient civilization of the ability to develop independently, and turned it into a permanent captive of American policy. The collapse of the Bretton Woods system and the end of dollar hegemony was the equivalent of a real "declaration of independence" for Europe – not the Declaration of *Inter*dependence patronizingly called for by President Kennedy in Constitution Hall on 4 July 1962. Greasy hamburgers and bad Hollywood blockbusters are a small price to pay for Europe's new freedom. Sustaining it, worldwide, are networks of institutions conceived and operating with a view to cooperative power sharing. Europe's authority has increased in (and by means of) them, especially at GATT/WTO, and can continue to do so by becoming an international market-conforming regulatory authority unless its own self-defeating policies stand in the way of such a development. It can also provide a link to the emergent third force of non-Western capitalism.

A federal Europe can be created democratically, functionally, and through the market – or not at all. Only with genuine public assent built upon constructive, market-induced change can "positive integration" eventually create a political Europe. Hayek described long ago how the process works. It matters little whether it begins in politics or economics; the two constructively interact, feed upon each other, and produce beneficial outcomes. European integration – in its economic phases the product of a three-level game – has indeed been a mutable process. The first great part in its history was political, the reconciliation of France and Germany by way of the Schuman Plan. The second, the adoption of the Treaty of Rome and its provisions for a common customs area, was economic. Once the Community was up and running and with a single external tariff in place, regime change set the stage for the third part: the spread of neo-liberalism, Thatcherism, and globalization. The Single European Act, the most important single development in the history of European integration, unleashed the market process across the Community. How the competition principle – once allowed to work – has moved Europe toward a closer union is a special concern of this book.

The mechanism of this agency is not easy to describe except in general terms. Change is not transmitted through "the" market but through myriad constantly shifting markets. The precise way they operate can only be subjectively understood by participants in transactions. The relationship between market-induced and market-conforming institution-induced change is an issue of profound theoretical debate and cannot be resolved in these pages. However, in the absence of a *demos,* European integration can only take place (as demonstrated logically and empirically) by means of "negative integration" – in other words, by "shalt not" rules designed to prevent market interference, in some cases reinforced by laws and institutions tailored to their proper operation.

Future integration progress, which would involve creation of a feeling of European nationhood, can only occur by means of empirical, commonsense, need-dictated development of the EU into an institution that improves the operation not only of the market mechanism (and hence of the economy) but also of the society and polity. Powerful trends work in such a direction: the revolution in technology and in business philosophy, the long-term secular increase of world trade, continued liberalization, the new appreciation for the market and market-supporting institutions, and the ever-increasing consumer demand for a better world. Such influences might, in the medium term, cause the Community to evolve institutionally into an EFTA-like mechanism with new regulatory powers. The EU would not thereafter be a "a mere trade area" but an engine of self-sustaining growth that would erode pointless hierarchies, encourage the emergence of an enterprise society, create opportunities only dreamt of today, and even give rise via Shonfield's institutional evolutionism or Dahrendorf's liberal federalism to some form of future European union. Far from resembling the "identikit Europe" built around the "European social model" of M. Delors, the future would be richer and more culturally diverse than anything either preceding it or readily imaginable by the mostly pessimistic present-day Europeans. The Europe of tomorrow is less likely to be the monotonous planed and leveled human landscape conceived and governed by technocrats in Brussels than a less tame, more variegated, dynamic terrain shaped by the exercise of human freedom – the indispensable companion of, and necessary prerequisite for, free markets. It then might also become a genuine community.

The future of Europe, and European integration, is today in jeopardy. The EU has accomplished little or nothing in the past ten years, the public is alienated from it, and policy makers have shown themselves unable to head off disaster over Enlargement. Privatization and marketization have come close to a standstill. The regulatory authority of the EU, indeed its very legitimacy, is contested. Renewed impetus to integration could come either from changes in the international sphere or from advances or breakthroughs in technology, but recovery from the present growth recession seems likely to be protracted. Change could also come, as with Erhard's Germany and Thatcher's Great Britain, like a bolt out of the blue. Yet it is hard to be optimistic on this score. The traditional left can neither provide economic solutions of its own nor abandon the political shibboleths of the past. Neoliberalism is a dull weapon. The term must be at least implicitly quoted because it implies the adoption of pro-market policies without openly admitting the fact – except tactically, as dictated by European necessity. Liberal parties, even in Britain where the pro-market Mr. Blair has taken over Labour from within, remain insubstantial. There is no serious, organized, political constituency for classical liberalism anywhere in Europe today, even on the conservative political right.

There is, in fact, an ideological vacuum. With the lingering death of socialism and the collapse of the left in several countries, influence on that portion of the spectrum has by default shifted to the union movement, which – although shrinking and less representative of blue-collar interests – is growing more powerful by serving two new constituencies: in a narrow sense, public employees (a growing percentage of unionized workers almost everywhere); in a broader sense, recipients of government transfer payments, whose interests the demoralized parties of the left can no longer represent adequately. As the former strikes, the latter acquiesces, half-smiling. The trend is not healthy. Issues are decided in the streets by threats of violence and disruption rather than by the thrust and parry of legislative debate, and in bodies that are neither representative of nor accountable to those in whose interests (blue-collar workers) they purportedly act. Time and again, attempts of wary governments to introduce long-overdue welfare-state reform have been turned back by mass union-led protest. The classic example is the single Dutch attempt to curtail abusive violations of the notoriously lax sick-leave policy. It triggered the biggest demonstration in the history of the politically advanced Netherlands.

Nor can much be expected from the political right. It is presently either in disarray (United Kingdom), out of power (Germany), answerable to a sullen public (France), immobile (Italy), or slowly turning away from the market in attempts to shore up defenses. The conservatives are no more likely than the left to provide the leadership needed to break through present gridlock. It may be foolish to conjecture, but a shock of some kind – like the 1979 Winter of Discontent – may be needed to trigger serious political change at the domestic level in present-day Europe. But who would hope for such a thing?

It should be obvious that any historian who ventures to speculate about the future soon finds himself on thin ice. The past is the playground where a person so trained is familiar and most comfortable. The historian re-creates memories of events imaginatively and intellectually by means of extensive documentation and a prior knowledge of outcomes. In the absence of such knowledge, a member of the guild must apply different methods. The early chapters of the book rest largely on the use of customary ones; the other chapters cannot. Bridgeworks of political and economic theory provide the structure spanning the book's middle sections. The final ones, which deal with the 1990s, rely upon information in the public domain and require not only the application of theory to analysis of events but also an aptitude for reading tea leaves or for catching straws blowing in the wind. The historian is thus able to speak with greater confidence about the past than the present – and to discuss hard theory more comfortably than disputable circumstance. The language of the book, which runs the gamut from stringently abstract to merely whimsical, reflects these intellectual strengths and weaknesses.

It is important – particularly in light of Europe's present problems – to try to maintain a sense of proportion with respect to the subject at hand. What has integration really accomplished over the past fifty years? First of all, the EU has not itself produced viable democracies in the less-privileged states of Europe: credit for that honor belongs primarily to the citizens of such countries. But unless Community prestige becomes utterly discredited, no alternative political system (representing values contrary to what it has stood for) can replace parliamentary government. As things now stand, the route to dictatorship has been foreclosed. The Enlargement debacle could, however, reopen it.

Nor has the EU prevented the outbreak of war in Europe. The right to such a claim belongs to NATO, which has obviated the need of its members to guard their borders and shifted the burden of defending Europe to the United States. NATO is the guarantor of the conditions that make integration possible and should not be taken lightly or otherwise trifled with. The European Union deserves credit, nonetheless, for transforming a situation of nonwar into one of enduring peace. The EU has shifted the focus of diplomacy from wary defensiveness and emergency troubleshooting to a search for common ground and constructive solutions to mutual problems – and has found plenty of them. Historic enmities have been marginalized, the foreign policies of member-states Europeanized, and conflict resolution institutionalized. Traditional flash points have flickered out. War between European states has become almost unthinkable. Still, dilettantish tampering with the well-functioning security machinery could eventually lead to future intra- and extra-European difficulties.

The EU and its predecessors have not always been a force for economic progress, but on balance the record is good. The customs area is deeply engrained in history, NTBs continue to come down, and competition policy remains vitally in force. If history continues as before, present trends toward "neo-neoprotectionism" will succumb to market pressure over time. The run-up to the European Monetary Union has indeed helped governments bring down deficits and get inflation under control. That, however, is a matter of history. The EMU will have to be gradually modified, loosened, or replaced by an EMS-like monetary regime once its ill effects are better understood publicly. The EMU can be downsized and reduced – more easily than is generally supposed and far more rapidly than it was built.

This book would not be worth its salt if its author shied away from attempting to draw up an integration balance sheet, nation by nation. The EU, far from being a federation or even a confederation, is today still an arrangement of convenience held together by its aggregate components: sticky marbles. Why do they adhere? There is no single answer because each national case is a thing unto itself: stakes vary, as do the positives and negatives in each of them. For practical reasons, only crude comparison is possible here. It is worth noting how different "Europe" looks from different national vantage points. Every member-state benefits in some manner, though to different degrees.

Those at the top of the list are nations that have profited both economically, through liberalization and subsidization, and politically, by being drawn out of provincialism or authoritarianism and into the dynamic democratic mainstream. Such nations have experienced not only quantitative but qualitative improvements in their ways of life. The big gainers are Finland, Greece, Spain, Portugal, Ireland, and Italy. For the Mediterranean nations, the EU has also provided a much-needed fiscal and monetary whip hand. Next in line come a couple of special big gainers that have not changed qualitatively. Belgium has been a large net beneficiary if only because it hosts "Europe's capital city." Super-rich Luxembourg, the biggest per-capita recipient of Community funds, has in addition – through EU membership – gained a voice in European affairs that is altogether disproportionate to its tiny size.

A Euro-neutral group comprises a third category. It consists of small, wealthy nations that are closely aligned with Germany and for whom adjustment to the Community has not required much material or political sacrifice or change in domestic institutions – but for whom the economic benefits of membership have also been slight and could have been attained bi- or multilaterally. Membership for this group – the Netherlands, Denmark, and Austria – is on balance beneficial because, as evident in borrowing rates, predictability and stability reduce transaction costs. Furthermore, membership – in this case, an ability to act in the name of Europe – can provide welcome political camouflage for an uncomfortable economic dependence upon a powerful neighbor. However, the EU stake of this group is not large and could disappear (to be replaced bilaterally) if the EU becomes burdensome.

A case apart, France has over the years been a substantial net beneficiary of Community transfer payments thanks chiefly to the CAP, but other membership rewards have been less tangible. "Europe" has also served France as a convenient fiction. The most important French decision of the post-de Gaulle era has been to align with the DM and German fiscal practice. The oversized role played by French governing elites in the life of the Community has yielded few tangible public rewards; if anything, it has strengthened the authority of an already overpowerful ruling caste. The decades-long attempt to saddle the rest of Europe with France's high benefit levels (in order to protect French jobs) has had little impact. Without the CAP, French membership would cease to be either economically or politically advantageous. The public will have to be convinced that *grandeur* is worth the price.

The membership reward of the Federal Republic, by far the largest net Community contributor, has been overwhelmingly political in character. Though not yet trusted enough to be considered for Community leadership – which should normally accrue to it by virtue of size, population, power, achievement, and good behavior – Germany has become a respected member of Europe. In the future, citizens need atone only in private. Hitler, the war, and the Holocaust are no longer relevant public policy matters. If only for enabling the ex-Reich to overcome the legacy of the past, membership in the Community has been worthwhile. Whether it will remain so, now that respectability has been regained, remains an open question.

Neither Sweden nor Britain – both net payers within the Community that opted out of the monetary union – can claim to have gained much from accession. For Sweden, adjustment to "social Europe" has been unproblematic. Indeed, the nation entered the EU largely to weaken the grip of the welfare state. Community membership has not, however, smoothed out economic reform or adaptation to the post–welfare-state environment. Even though it continues to fall in the OECD league tables, Sweden remains a net contributor and has, in truth, gained little from membership. The faster rate of growth the country enjoys relative to the Community today derives from the decision *not* to enter the monetary union. National control of monetary policy remains an important economic lever.

The United Kingdom has gained the least from membership in the EU club. The cost of adjusting to Europe has involved real sacrifice of both parliamentary tradition and economic interest. Britain has always been a net contributor, even with the embarrassing rebate. The United Kingdom has also been a reform pacesetter that does not need Brussels' help but still must accept and pay for it. The economic case for British membership is probably the weakest of any member-state. However, the security rationale is strong. Britain's withdrawal from the EU could open the door to single-power domination of the continent. For this reason alone, the prudent decision would be to influence events from within the organization. Geographical expansion and the healthy solvent of the market should enable the future Community to evolve along lines more consistent with British views than in the recent past.

Binding together the EU as a whole is not only the self-interest of its national components but also the reality that no feasible alternative exists in the absence of a willingness to relinquish Europe's identity as a distinct civilization. Not even the farsighted Mrs. Thatcher has come up with a suitable alternative plan – and she would also be among the first to reject colonization by a former colony, a threat that exists even with the best of intentions on all sides.

The United States is not, like Britain or France, a centralized state where rules (transmitted into laws and institutions) guide national development. Instead it is an emergent young civilization that, though committed to underlying principle, generates new rules along the way and then tries to adapt them to rapidly changing circumstance. President Reagan did not invent supply-side economics – whose very existence is still disputed by experts – nor could he have predicted its outcome: a new market-based economic era. Nor can his successors direct the course of the American future, except loosely. If (on the one hand) the way is open to dynamic change, then it is also (on the other) open to large-scale disaster.

Some form of a "political Europe" is needed if only as a hedge against such a contingency. The organization of Asia along the lines of competitive capitalism presents Europe with a second compelling challenge, as well as a further argument for the TINA ("there is no alternative") doctrine – at least in a restrictive sense. To defend the values of Europe as a civilization, the EU has no choice but to adopt the economics and politics of classical liberalism; otherwise, it faces political strife and economic decline.

Over the past fifty years, Europe has used the integration process to meet and surmount a succession of historical challenges. They are, by this time, familiar. The coal–steel pool reconciled the French and the Germans. The EEC institutionalized the course of liberalization upon which Europe had been moving since the war. The Single European Act adapted the economy to a global age of high technology and open markets. The reconciliation of Europe's peoples and the existence of an expanding single European market are established facts, historical outcomes, and the givens of tomorrow's history. Although its path has been littered with the detritus of misconceived policy, integration is a long-haul process.

Past progress has nevertheless alternated with long periods of inactivity and failure. Five years elapsed between the conclusion of the Schuman Plan and the Messina negotiations that led to the EEC, another twenty between the empty chairs crisis and the conclusion of the Single European Act, and another fifteen between its adoption and the present. The current world economic downswing – the consequence of a cyclical crisis – has darkened but cannot move the horizon. When the sun eventually rises, it will expose a new human landscape featuring an innovative and increasingly productive economy driven by technological change and competition, an emerging international structure of regulations to reduce transaction costs, and an impressive body of international law. Like the historians who write about such subjects, the men and women who have devoted their lives and careers to building Europe have also had only partial and imperfect knowledge. They have nevertheless managed to create something that is solid, greater than the sum of its known parts, and of enduring value. It is to such earnest workers that this envoi, this happy little ending, is appropriately dedicated.

Notes

PREFACE

1. David Calleo, *Rethinking Europe's Future* (Princeton, 2001); Desmond Dinan, *Ever Closer Union* (Boulder, 1999); Keith Middlemas, *Orchestrating Europe* (London, 1995); Alan Milward, *The European Rescue of the Nation-State* (London, 1993); Andrew Moravcsik, *The Choice for Europe* (Ithaca, 1998); Neill Nugent, *The Government and Politics of the European Union* (London 1999); John Pinder, *The Building of the European Union* (Oxford, 1998); Peter Stirk, *A History of European Integration Since 1914* (London, 1996); Loukas Tsoukalis, *The New European Economy Revisited* (Oxford, 1997).
2. Daniel Yergin and Joseph Stanislaw, *The Commanding Heights: The Battle between Government and the Marketplace That Is Remaking the Modern World* (New York, 1998).

INTRODUCTION TO PART I

1. Robert Skidelsky, *John Maynard Keynes: Fighting for Britain, 1937–1946* (London, 2000).
2. John Gerard Ruggie, "International Regimes, Transactions, and Change: Embedded Liberalism in the Postwar Economic Order," *International Organization* 36/2 (1982), 379–415.
3. Alan S. Milward, *The European Rescue of the Nation-State* (London, 1993).

CHAPTER 1

1. See Alan Ebenstein, *Friedrich A. Hayek: A Biography* (New York, 2001).
2. See Ronald M. Hartwell, *A History of the Mont Pèlerin Society* (Indianapolis, 1995).
3. Ebenstein, *Hayek*.
4. Friedrich A. Hayek, *The Road to Serfdom* (London, 1944).
5. Ebenstein, *Hayek*.
6. See Israel M. Kirzner, "How Markets Work: Disequilibrium, Entrepreneurship and Discovery" (unpublished manuscript, 2000); see also Israel M. Kirzner, *The Driving Force of the Market* (New York, 2000).
7. Ludwig von Mises, *Human Action* (New Haven, 1949).
8. Friedrich A. Hayek, "The Economic Conditions of Interstate Federalism," reprinted in F. A. Hayek, *Individualism and Economic Order* (Chicago, 1948), 255–72.
9. Friedrich Meinicke, *Die deutsche Katastrophe* (Wiesbaden, 1949).
10. Ibid.
11. Friedrich A. Hayek, "Historians and the Future of Europe," (28 February 1944), R. M. Hartwell Papers, 4/0, Hoover Institution Archives.
12. Ibid.
13. Ronald M. Hartwell, "The Re-emergence of Liberalism? The Role of the Mont Pèlerin Society," R. M. Hartwell Papers, 4/0, 6–7, Hoover Institution Archives.
14. Friedrich A. Hayek, "The Problem of Germany" (1945), Friedrich A. Hayek Papers 107/2, Hoover Institution Archives; see also Friedrich A. Hayek, "Opening Address to the Mont Pèlerin Society" (1 April 1947), Friedrich A. Hayek Papers, 84/10, Hoover Institution Archives.

15. Patrick M. Boarman, "Wilhelm Röpke: Apostle of a Humane Economy," *Society* 37/6 (September 2000), 57–73. See also in *ORDO* 50 (1999): Hans-Günter Krüsselberg, "Wilhelm Röpkes Lehre von der Politischen Ökonomie," 3–19; Hans-Peter Schwarz, "Wilhelm Röpkes Neuordnungsideen von Deutschland, 1942–1948," 37–46; Razeen Sally, "Wilhelm Röpke and International Economic Order," 47–59.
16. Wilhelm Röpke, *The Solution of the German Problem* (New York, 1946).
17. Ibid., 259–61.
18. Sally, "Wilhelm Röpke," 49.
19. Victor Gollancz, *In Darkest Germany* (Chicago, 1947).
20. See Anthony J. Nicholls, *Freedom with Responsibility: The Social Market Economy in Germany, 1918–1963* (Oxford, 1994).
21. Ibid., 150–8.
22. Nicholls, *Freedom with Responsibility*, 178–223.
23. Gottfried Haberler, "Economic Aspects of a European Customs Union," *World Politics* 11/4 (July 1949), 431–41.
24. Gunnar Myrdal, *An International Economy* (New York, 1954).
25. Haberler, "Economic Aspects," 436.

CHAPTER 2

1. See Jean Monnet, *Mémoires* (Paris, 1976); François Duchêne, *Jean Monnet: First Statesman of Interdependence* (London, 1994); Eric Roussel, *Jean Monnet* (Paris, 1995).
2. See John Gillingham, "Jean Monnet and the New Europe," in Stephen A. Schuker (Ed.), *Deutschland und Frankreich. Vom Konflikt zur Aussöhnung* (Munich, 2000), 197–209.
3. Roussel, *Jean Monnet*, 880–903.
4. Harry Bayard Price, *The Marshall Plan and Its Meaning* (Ithaca, 1955).
5. Henry Hazlitt, *Will Dollars Save the World?* (New York, 1947).
6. John Ikenberry, "A World Economy Restored: Expert Consensus and the Anglo-American Postwar Settlement," *International Organization* 46/1 (Winter 1992), 289–321.
7. Robert Skidelsky, "Keynes's New Order," in Skidelsky, *Keynes* (see intro. I, n. 1), 179–232.
8. See Harold James, "The IMF and the Creation of the Bretton Woods System, 1944–1958," in Barry Eichengreen (Ed.), *Europe's Postwar Recovery* (Cambridge, U.K., 1995).
9. Douglas A. Irwin, "The GATT's Contribution to Economic Recovery in Postwar Western Europe," in Eichengreen, *Europe's Postwar Recovery*, 127–51.
10. John Gillingham, "Jean Monnet et le 'Victory Program' americain," in Gérard Boussuat and Dominique Wilkens (Eds.), *Jean Monnet et les Chemins de la Paix* (Paris, 1998), 97–109.
11. John Gillingham, "'Wollt Ihr den totalen Krieg?' Reflections on Joseph Goebbels' Propaganda Triumph in Light of the Thing Itself," forthcoming in Roger Chickering et al. (Eds.), *A World at Total War: Global Conflict and the Politics of Destruction, 1937–1945*.
12. "Robert R. Nathan, 92, Dies; Set Factory Goals in World War II," *New York Times*, 10 September 2001; Robert R. Nathan, "An Unsung Hero of World War II," in Douglas Brinkley (Ed.), *Jean Monnet: The Path to European Unity* (New York, 1991), 67–85.
13. Mark Skousen, *The Making of Modern Economics* (Armonk, NY, 2001), 371.
14. Wassily Leontief, "The Structure of the United States Economy," *Scientific American* 212/4 (April 1965), 11–12.
15. Gillingham, "Jean Monnet and the New Europe."
16. See Chiarella Esposito, *America's Feeble Weapon: Funding the Marshall Plan in France and Italy, 1948–1950* (Westport, CT, 1994).
17. John Gillingham, "The Marshall Plan and the Origins of Neo-Liberal Europe," in Hans Labohm (Ed.), *The Marshall Plan Fifty Year Later: Problems and Perspectives* (The Hague, 1999), 11–14; Harry Bayard Price, *The Marshall Plan and Its Meaning* (Ithaca, 1955).
18. John Gillingham, *Coal, Steel and the Rebirth of Europe, 1945–1955: The Germans and French from Ruhr Conflict to Economic Community* (Cambridge, U.K., 1991), 228–99.
19. Ibid., 299–348.
20. Ibid.

21. John Gillingham, "Coal and Steel Diplomacy in Interwar Europe," in Clemens A. Wurm (Ed.), *Internationale Kartelle und Aussenpolitik* (Stuttgart, 1989), 83–101.

22. John Gillingham, "De la coopération a l'integration: la Ruhr et l'industrie lourde francaise pendant la guerre," *Histoire, économie, société* 11/3 (1992), 369–97.

23. Gillingham, *Coal, Steel,* 359.

24. Ibid., 205–17.

25. Hans-Peter Schwarz, *Konrad Adenauer: A German Politician and Statesman in a Period of War, Revolution and Reconstruction,* vol. 1, *From the German Empire to the Federal Republic, 1876–1952* (Providence, 1995), 435–88.

26. Schwarz, "Wilhelm Röpke," 37.

27. Gillingham, *Coal, Steel,* 228–98.

28. Ibid.

29. Ibid., 313–19.

30. Ernst B. Haas, *The Uniting of Europe: Political, Social, and Economic Forces, 1950–1957* (Stanford, 1958).

31. John Gillingham "American Monnetism and the European Coal and Steel Community in the 1950s," *Journal of European Integration History* 1 (1995), 21–36; see also Theodore Achilles, "How Little Wisdom: Memoirs of an Irresponsible Memory" (unpublished manuscript, 1974).

32. Marc Trachtenberg, "The Nuclearization of NATO and U.S.–European Relations," in Francis H. Heller and John Gillingham (Eds.), *NATO: The Founding of the Atlantic Alliance and the Integration of Europe* (New York, 1992), 413–31.

33. Wilhelm Maier-Dornberg, "Die Planung des Verteidigungsbeitrages der Bundesrepublik Deutschland im Rahmen der EVG," in Militärgeschichtliches Forschungsamt (Ed.), *Anfänge westdeutscher Sicherheitspolitik 1945–1955,* Bd. 2 (Munich, 1990), 717.

34. U.S. National Archives, RG 469/15, "Aid to EDC, Draft Statement for Mr. Wood, 5 February 1952."

35. John Gillingham, "David K. E. Bruce and the European Defense Community Debacle" (unpublished manuscript), 33–6; U.S. National Archives, RG 84/9, "EDC and Related Organizations, 1951–1966."

36. Michael M. Harrison, *The Reluctant Ally: France and the Atlantic Alliance* (Baltimore, 1981), 33.

37. *Foreign Relations of the United States, 1952–1954/VI:* "The Director of the Office of Regional Affairs (Moore) to the Deputy United States Representative to the European Coal and Steel Community (Tomlinson)," 13 January 1953; Sherrill Brown Wells, "Unofficial Partners: The Cooperation of Treasury's William Tomlinson and Jean Monnet on Advancing European Integration, 1947–1954" (unpublished manuscript), 17.

38. Townsend Hoopes, *The Devil and John Foster Dulles* (Boston, 1973), 164.

39. Gillingham, "David K. E. Bruce," 37–52.

40. Diaries of David K. E. Bruce, Virginia Historical Society, Entry 27 August 1954.

41. Hoopes, *Devil and Dulles,* 246.

42. Bruce Diaries, Entry 26 September 1954.

43. Werner Abelshauser, "Rüstung. Wirtschaft, Rüstungswirtschaft: Wirtschaftliche Aspekte des kalten Krieges in den fünfziger Jahren," in Klaus A. Maier et al. (Eds.), *Das Nordatlantische Bündnis 1949–1956* (Munich, 1993), 90–1.

44. Gillingham, "David K. E. Bruce," 48–9.

CHAPTER 3

1. Victoria Curzon, *The Essentials of Economic Integration: Lessons of EFTA Experience* (London, 1974), 33.

2. See Christian Deubner, *Die Atompolitik der westdeutschen Industrie und die Gruendung von Euratom* (Frankfurt, 1977); see also Peter Weilemann, *Die Anfänge der Europäischen Atomgemeinschaft: Zur Gruendungsgeschichte von Euratom 1955–1957* (Baden-Baden, 1982).

3. U.S. National Archives, U.S. Department of State (840.00/10-2656), "Paris to Sec. State," 26 October 1956.

4. Jean Delmas, "Naissance et développement d'une politique nucleare militaire en France (1945–1956)," in Maier, *Nordatlantische Bundnis* (see chap. 2, n. 43), 263–72.
5. Curzon, *Economic Integration*, 28–39.
6. Alan Kramer, *The West German Economy* (New York, 1990), 181–3.
7. Irwin, "GATT's Contribution," 143.
8. Ibid., 134–40, 143–9.
9. Herman van der Wee, *Prosperity and Upheaval: The World Economy, 1945–1980* (Berkeley, 1987), 354.
10. Ibid., 140–1.
11. Milton Friedman, "The Case for Flexible Exchange Rates," in Milton Friedman, *Essays in Positive Economics* (Chicago, 1953), 157.
12. Barry Eichengreen, "The European Payments Union," in Eichengreen, *Europe's Postwar Recovery*, 171–82.
13. Ibid., 187–91.
14. Ibid., 173–9.
15. Ibid., 190–1.
16. Gottfried Haberler, "Integration and Growth of the World Economy in Historical Perspective," *American Economic Review* 54/2, part 1 (March 1964), 1–22.
17. Kramer, *West German Economy*, 181, 183, 189.
18. Ibid.; see also Holger C. Wolf, "Post-war Germany in the European Context," in Eichengreen, *Europe's Postwar Recovery*, 323–52.
19. Milward, *European Rescue*, 134–73.
20. Herbert Giersch, Karl-Heinz Pacque, and Holger Schmieding, *The Fading Miracle: Four Decades of Market Economy in Germany* (Cambridge, U.K., 1992), 88.
21. Kramer, *West German Economy*, 195–213; see also Richard Overy, "The Economy of the Federal Republic Since 1949," in Klaus Larres and Panikos Panayi (Eds.), *The Federal Republic of Germany: Politics, Society and Economy before and after Unification* (London, 1996), 26–7.
22. Giersch et al., *Fading Miracle*, 109.
23. Ibid.; see also Henry C. Wallich, *Mainsprings of the German Revival* (New Haven, 1953), 113–41.
24. Giersch et al., *Fading Miracle*, 114.
25. Stuart Holland, *The Uncommon Market* (London, 1980), 12.
26. Andrew Moravcsik, *The Choice for Europe: Social Purpose and State Power from Messina to Maastricht* (Ithaca, 1998), 139.
27. Ibid.
28. See Hanns-Jürgen Küsters, *Die Gründung der europäischen Wirtschaftsgemeinschaft* (Baden-Baden, 1982); see also Andrew Moravcsik, "Finding the Thread: The Treaties of Rome, 1955–1958," in Moravcsik, *Choice for Europe*, 86–158.
29. Ibid., 139.
30. Ibid.
31. Robert Marjolin, *Architect of European Unity: Memoirs, 1911–1986* (London, 1989), 276.
32. Morvacsik, "Finding the Thread," 140.
33. Marjolin, *Architect*.
34. Ibid., 285–6.
35. Moravcsik, "Finding the Thread," 90–9; van der Wee, *Prosperity and Upheaval*, 358–9.
36. See Federico Romero "Migration as an Issue in European Interdependence and Integration: The Case of Italy," in Alan S. Milward et al., *The Frontier of National Sovereignty: History and Theory, 1995–1992* (London, 1993), 32–58.
37. Marjolin, *Architect*, 281.
38. Ibid.
39. Ibid., 297–307.
40. Frances Lynch, "Restoring France: The Road to Integration," in Milward et al., *Frontier*, 72–7.
41. See Gilbert Noel, "Les Groupes de Pression agricoles Française et le Projet d'Organisation et de l'Europe agricole entre 1950 et 1954," EUI Colloquium Papers, DOC. IUE 315/90 (Col 49), 1–44.
42. Marjolin, *Architect*, 301–2.
43. Ibid., 302.

44. U.S. National Archives, U.S. Department of State (840.00/6–565), "The French Patronat and the Re-launching of Europe," 5 July 1956.
45. Ibid.
46. Ibid.
47. U.S. National Archives, U.S. Department of State (840.00/6–156), "France, the Common Market, and the Franc Area," 1 June 1956.
48. Schwarz, *Konrad Adenauer,* vol. 2, *The Statesman, 1952–1957* (Providence, 1997), 242.
49. Moravcsik, "Finding the Thread," 144.
50. Marjolin, *Architect,* 301.
51. Ibid., 300.
52. Ibid., 318.
53. See Reginald Maudling, *Memoirs* (London, 1978), 79–80, 111–12.
54. See Harry Johnson, "Introduction," in Victoria Curzon, *Economic Integration,* 1–13.
55. Moravcsik, "Finding the Thread," 130.
56. Maudling, *Memoirs,* 72–3.
57. Ibid., 69–71.
58. Giersch et al., *Fading Miracle,* 121, 122.
59. Curzon, *Economic Integration,* 32.
60. Ibid.
61. See articles by Stanley Hoffman, John T. S. Keeler, Alan S. Milward, John Gillingham, Jeffrey Vanke, and Marc Trachtenberg re/ Andrew Moravcsik, "De Gaulle between Grain and Grandeur: The Political Economy of French EC Policy, 1958–1970," parts 1 and 2, *Journal of Cold War Studies* 2/2 and 2/3 (Spring and Fall 2000).
62. Jacques Rueff, "Die französische Wirtschaftsreform. Rückblick und Ausblick," *ORDO* 12/1660 (1961), 111–26; "Zur Wirtschaftsreform in Frankreich: Bericht zur Finanzlage ... 30. September 1958," *ORDO* 11 (1959), 3–67.

CHAPTER 4

1. Dennis Swann, *The Economics of the Common Market,* 6th ed. (London, 1990), 11–13, 87–94.
2. Curzon, *Economic Integration,* 66–7.
3. Miriam Camps, *What Kind of Europe?: The Community since de Gaulle's Veto* (London, 1965), 77–8, 82–3.
4. John Gillingham, "Jean Monnet and the Origins of European Monetary Union," in Dean J. Kotlowski (Ed.), *The European Union from Jean Monnet to the Euro* (Athens, OH, 2000), 79–86.
5. Camps, *What Kind of Europe?,* 40.
6. Swann, *Economics,* 176.
7. Marjolin, *Architect,* 314.
8. Maudling, *Memoirs,* 72.
9. Walter Hallstein, *Europe in the Making* (London, 1972), 24–5, 37–8.
10. Ibid., 34.
11. Ibid., 37.
12. Ibid., 46.
13. Ibid., 42.
14. Walter Hallstein, *United Europe: Challenge and Opportunity* (Cambridge, MA, 1962), 46.
15. Plato, "Guardians and Auxiliaries," in *The Republic* (trans. Desmond Lee; London, 1987 reprint), 177–224.
16. Hallstein, *Europe in the Making,* 58.
17. Ibid., 59.
18. Jean-Jacques Servan-Schreiber, *The American Challenge* (New York, 1967).
19. *Foreign Relations of the United States, 1958–1960/IV,* "Memorandum of Conversation with President Eisenhower," 30 November 1960.
20. Johnny Laursen, "Growing Together? The Internationalization of the West European Economy, 1950–1971" in Richard T. Griffiths and Toshiaki Tachibaniki (Eds.), *From Austerity to Affluence: The Transformation of the Socio-Economic Structure of Western Europe and Japan* (London, 2000), 32.

21. Servan-Schreiber, *American Challenge*.
22. Lawrence G. Franko, *The European Multinationals: A Renewed Challenge to American and British Big Business* (Stamford, CT, 1976), 157–8.
23. Morris Mendelson, "The Eurobond and Capital Market Integration," *Journal of Finance* 27/1 (March 1972), 110–26; Oscar L. Altman, "The Integration of European Capital Markets, *Journal of Finance* 20/2 (May 1965), 209–21.
24. Altman, "Integration," 209–12; Mendelson, "Eurobond," 125–6.
25. Brian Tew, *The Evolution of the International Monetary System, 1945–1988* (London, 1988), 138–47.
26. Hallstein, *Europe in the Making*, 150–6.
27. Robert Triffin, *Gold and the Dollar Crisis: Yesterday and Tomorrow*, Essays in International Finance, vol. 132 (Princeton, 1978); Robert Triffin, *Gold and the Dollar Crisis: The Future of Convertibility* (New Haven, 1961), 131–45.
28. Robert Mundell, "Capital Mobility and Stabilization Policy under Fixed and Flexible Exchange Rates," *Canadian Journal of Economics* 29 (November 1963), 475–85.
29. Holland, *Uncommon Market*, 33–8.
30. Malcolm C. MacLennon, "The Common Market and French Planning," *Journal of Common Market Studies* 3/1 (1965), 23–46.
31. Ibid., 40–1.
32. Jean Monnet, "A Ferment of Change," *Journal of Common Market Studies* 1/3 (1962), 205.
33. Étienne Hirsch, "French Planning and Its European Application," *Journal of Common Market Studies* 1/2 (1962), 125.
34. Andrew Shonfield, "Stabilization Policies in the West: From Demand to Supply Management," *Journal of Political Economy* 75/4-2 (August 1967), 440–2.
35. Ibid.
36. Holland, *Uncommon Market*, 37.
37. Moravcsik, *Choice for Europe*, 156, 157, 236–7.
38. W. R. Lewis, *Rome or Brussels? An Economist's Comparative Analysis of the Development of the European Community and the Aims of the Treaty of Rome* (London, 1971), 8.
39. Ibid., 5.
40. Hallstein, *Europe in the Making*, 226.
41. Paul Pierson, "Increasing Returns, Path Dependence and the Study of Politics," *American Political Science Review* 94/2 (June 2000), 251–80; Paul Pierson, "Big, Slow-Moving, and Invisible: Macro-Social Processes in the Study of Comparative Politics" (Speech, Harvard University Center for European Studies, November 2000).
42. Hallstein, *Europe in the Making*, 224.
43. Ibid., 226.
44. Ibid., 193.
45. Ibid., 206.
46. Ibid., 213.
47. Ibid., 169.
48. Ibid., 171.
49. Ibid., 169–77.
50. Ibid., 239.
51. Ibid., 241.
52. Ibid., 304.
53. Ibid., 245.
54. Ibid.
55. George Ball, *The Past Has Another Pattern: Memoirs* (New York, 1982), 208f.
56. Ibid., 197–8.
57. John Gillingham, "Foreign Policy as Theology: The Failure of Kennedy's Grand Design" (unpublished manuscript, October 1994); Ball, *Another Pattern*, 262–3.
58. Bruce Diary, Entry 5 February 1963, Virginia Historical Society.
59. Bruce Diary, "Preliminary Report on European Policy," 11 February 1963, Virginia Historical Society; Lawrence Kaplan, "The MLF Debate," in D. Brinkley (Ed.), *John F. Kennedy and Europe* (Baton Rouge, LA, 1999), 51–66.

60. Bruce Diary, "William R. Tyler to David Bruce," 19 September 1964, Virginia Historical Society.
61. Bruce Diary, Entries 6 December 1964 and 12 January 1965, Virginia Historical Sociey.
62. Miriam Camps, *European Unification in the Sixties: From the Veto to the Crisis* (New York, 1966), 29–80.
63. Ibid., 60; Moravcsik, *Choice for Europe*, 193–4.
64. Ibid., 197.
65. Camps, *Unification*, 81.
66. Ibid., 84.
67. Ibid., 88.
68. Ibid., 105.
69. Ibid., 105–6.
70. Ibid., 8–124.
71. Ibid., 112.

INTRODUCTION TO PART II

1. The European Economic Community (EEC) became the European Community (EC) in July 1967.
2. Desmond Dinan, *Ever Closer Union*, 2nd ed. (Boulder, 1999), 59–64.

CHAPTER 5

1. Donald J. Puchala, "Europeans and Europeanism in 1970," *International Organization* 27/3 (Summer 1973), 387–92.
2. Ibid., 390.
3. Ibid., 391.
4. Henry R. Nau, "From Integration to Interdependence: Gains, Losses, and Continuing Gaps," *International Organization* 33/1 (Winter 1979), 119–47.
5. Stuart A. Scheingold, "Domestic and International Consequences of Regional Integration," *International Organization* 24/4 (Autumn 1970), 978–1002.
6. Ibid., 981.
7. "The Administrative Implications of Economic and Monetary Union within the European Community. Report of a Federal Trust/UACES Study Group," *Journal of Common Market Studies* 12/4 (1973/4), 414–20.
8. Ibid., 421–2.
9. Ibid., 423.
10. Ibid.
11. Ibid., 438.
12. Alec Cairncross et al., *Economic Policy for the European Community: The Way Forward* (New York, 1975).
13. Ibid., xv.
14. Ibid., 50.
15. Ibid., 60.
16. Ibid., 58–63.
17. Ibid., 233–9.
18. Ulrich Everling, "Possibilities and Limits of European Integration," *Journal of Common Market Studies* 18/3 (March 1980), 217–28.
19. Andrew Shonfield, *Europe: Journey to an Unknown Destination* (London, 1973); Ralf Dahrendorf, *Plädoyer für die europäische Union* (Munich, 1973).
20. Shonfield, *Journey*, 80–1, 88–9.
21. Ibid., 17.
22. Ibid.
23. See Anne-Marie Burley and Walter Mattli, "Europe Before the Court," *International Organization* 47/1 (Winter 1993), 432–76.
24. Ibid., 67–82.

25. Dahrendorf, *Plädoyer,* 76–85.
26. Ibid., 83.
27. Ibid., 195–6, 209–10, 222–3.
28. Jacques Pelkmans, "Economic Theories of Integration Revisited," *Journal of Common Market Studies* 18/4 (June 1980), 333–54.
29. Ibid.
30. Ibid., 336 (emphasis in original).
31. Melvyn B. Krauss, "Recent Developments in Customs Union Theory: An Interpretive Survey," *Journal of Economic Literature* 10/2 (June 1972), 413–36.
32. Pelkmans, "Economic Theories," 337–41.
33. Ibid., 341.
34. Jacques Pelkmans, "The Assignment of Public Functions in Economic Integration," *Journal of Common Market Studies* 21/1 and 2 (September and December 1982), 98–125.
35. Ibid., 100.
36. Ibid., 100–1.
37. Ibid., 98–9.
38. Ibid., 100.
39. Ibid., 104–8.
40. Ibid., 108–9.
41. Ibid., 113–14.
42. Ibid., 115.
43. Ibid.
44. Ibid., 119.
45. Douglas J. Forsyth and Ton Notermans (Eds.), *Regime Changes: Macroeconomic Policy and Financial Regulation in Europe from the 1930s to the 1990s* (Providence, 1997).
46. Douglas J. Forsyth and Ton Notermans, "Macroeconomic Policy Regimes and Financial Regulation," in Forsyth and Notermans, *Regime Changes,* 18–65.
47. Ibid., 39.
48. Ibid., 33.
49. Ibid., 35–6.
50. David Henderson, *The Changing Fortunes of Economic Liberalism: Yesterday, Today and Tomorrow,* IEA Occasional Paper 105 (London, 1998).
51. "Coming Home to Roost" (Special Report: Privatization in Europe), *Economist,* 29 June 2002.
52. Ibid., 18–26.
53. Gottfried Haberler, *International Trade and Economic Development* (San Francisco: International Center for Economic Growth, 1988).
54. Daniel Yergin and Joseph Stanislaw, *The Commanding Heights: The Battle between Government and the Marketplace That Is Remaking the Modern World* (New York, 1998).
55. Dany Rodrik, *Has Globalization Gone Too Far?* (Washington, DC, 1997).
56. Henderson, *Changing Fortunes,* 42–53, 65–6.
57. "Is Margaret Thatcher Winning in Europe?," *Economist,* 1 June 2002.
58. David Calleo, *The Imperious Economy* (Cambridge, U.K., 1982), 7–79.
59. Ibid., 44–58.
60. Ibid.
61. Ibid., 58.
62. Ibid., 29–37, 58–61, 62–78, 78–102, 118–38.

CHAPTER 6

1. Carole Webb, "Variations on a Theoretical Theme," in Helen Wallace et al., *Policy Making in the European Communities* (London, 1977), 25.
2. See Joshua Muravchik, *Heaven on Earth: The Rise and Fall of Socialism* (San Francisco, 2002).
3. Razeen Sally, *Classical Liberalism and the International Economic Order: Studies in Theory and Intellectual History* (London, 1998), 156.
4. Jan Tumlir, *Protectionism: Trade Policy in Democratic Societies* (Washington, DC, 1985), 11.
5. Ibid., 3–10.

6. Jan Tumlir, "International Economic Order – Can the Trend Be Reversed?," *World Economy* 5/1 (March 1982), 29–42.

7. Ibid.

8. Ibid., 31.

9. Tumlir, *Protectionism*, 38–9.

10. Ibid., 39–44.

11. Jan Tumlir, "Who Benefits from Discrimination?," *Schweizerische Zeitschrift für Volkswirtschaft und Statistik* 121 (1985), 249–58.

12. Ibid.

13. Ibid., 331.

14. Lisbet Hooghe and Gary Marks, "The Making of a Polity: The Struggle over European Integration," Robert Schuman Center, 97/31 (June 1997), European University Institute, Florence.

15. Henrik and Michele Schmiegelow, "The New Mercantilism in International Relations: The Case of France's External Monetary Policy," *International Organization 29/2*, 367–91.

16. Christain Sautter, "France," in Andrea Boltho (Ed.), *The European Economy: Growth and Crisis* (Oxford, 1982), 451–71.

17. Ibid., 467–8.

18. Giersch et al., *Fading Miracle*, 213.

19. Ibid., 342–3.

20. Ibid., 226–7, 234–5.

21. Ibid., 213–14.

22. Paul Ginsborg, *A History of Contemporary Italy: Society and Politics, 1943–1988* (London, 1990), 285–6.

23. Ibid., 356.

24. Ibid., 359–60, 379–80; Guido M. Rey, "Italy," in Boltho, *Growth and Crisis*, 503–27.

25. John Haycroft, *Italian Labyrinth: An Authentic and Revealing Portrait of Italy in the 1980s* (London, 1985), 105; Rey, "Italy," 518.

26. Rey, "Italy," 522.

27. Ginsborg, *History of Italy*, 389.

28. Ibid.

29. Ibid., 401–2; Rey, "Italy," 525.

30. Rey, "Italy," 523–4; Ruggero Ranieri, "After the Rewards of Growth, the Penalty of Debt," in Bernard J. Foley (Ed.), *European Economies Since the Second World War* (London, 1998), 75–101.

31. Michael Surrey "United Kingdom," in Boltho, *Growth and Crisis*, 528–53.

32. Andrew Gamble, *The Free Economy and the Strong State: The Politics of Thatcherism*, 2nd ed. (London, 1994), 75–6.

33. See Alec Cairncross, *The British Economy Since 1945*, 2nd ed. (Oxford, 1995), 182–225.

34. Surrey, "United Kingdom," 539–40.

35. Cairncross et al., *Economic Policy*, 141–2; Gamble, *Politics of Thatcherism*, 83.

36. Surrey, "United Kingdom," 550.

37. Tumlir, *Protectionism*, 39–44.

38. See Andrew Gamble, *Britain in Decline* (Boston, 1981).

39. Surrey, "United Kingdom," 543–4.

40. Gamble, *Politics of Thatcherism*, 85.

41. Ibid., 88–9.

42. Surrey, "United Kingdom," 550–1.

43. Ibid.; Cairncross et al., *Economic Policy*, 211.

44. Richard Cockett, *Thinking the Unthinkable: Think-tanks and the Economic Counter-revolution, 1931–1983* (London, 1995), 187.

45. Michael Davenport, "The Economic Impact of the EEC," in Boltho, *Growth and Crisis*, 234–58; Richard Howarth, "The Common Agricultural Policy," in Patrick Minford (Ed.), *The Cost of Europe* (Manchester, 1992), 51–83; Tim Josling, "Agricultural Policy," in Peter Coffey (Ed.), *Economic Policies of the Common Market* (London, 1979), 1–21.

46. Howarth, "Common Agricultural Policy," 52.

47. Davenport, "Economic Impact," 235.

48. Howarth, "Common Agricultural Policy," 54.
49. Davenport, "Economic Impact," 235–7; Howarth, "Common Agricultural Policy," 57–62.
50. Howarth, "Common Agricultural Policy," 57.
51. Josling, "Agricultural Policy," 20.
52. Elmar Rieger "The Common Agricultural Policy," in Helen Wallace and William Wallace (Eds.), *Policy-Making in the European Union,* 4th ed. (Oxford, 2000), 179–210.
53. Neill Nugent, *The Government and Politics of the European Community,* 2nd ed. (Durham, NC, 1991), 321.
54. Ibid., 315.
55. Brigid Laffan and Michael Shackleton, "The Budget," in Wallace and Wallace, *Policy-Making,* 210–41.
56. Michael Shackleton, *Financing the European Community* (New York, 1990), 65–6.
57. Nugent, *Government and Politics,* 314–15; Schackleton, *Financing,* 1–2.
58. Nugent, *Government and Politics,* 325–6.
59. Dieter Biehl, "A Federalist Budgetary Policy Strategy for the European Union," *Policy Studies* (October 1985), 66–76.
60. Ibid., 68–9.
61. Nugent, *Government and Politics,* 333.
62. Ibid., 323–34.
63. Ibid., 327.
64. Shackleton, *Financing,* 38.
65. Ibid., 40.
66. Commission of the European Communities, "Report of the Study Group on the Role of Public Finance in European Integration" (MacDougall Report) (Brussels, April 1977).
67. Steven J. Warnecke, *The European Community in the 1970s* (New York, 1972).
68. Ibid.
69. Dahrendorf, *Plädoyer,* 90–1.
70. Ibid., 151–2.
71. See Hussain Kassimand Anand Menon, *The European Union and National Industrial Policy* (London, 1996); see also David B. Audretsch, *The Market and the State: Government Policy Towards Business in Europe, Japan and the United States* (New York, 1989).
72. See Michael Hodges, "Industrial Policy: A Directorate General in Search of a Role," in Wallace and Wallace, *Policy-Making,* 113–35.
73. Loukas Tsoukalis and Antonio da Silva Ferreira, "Management of Industrial Surplus Capacity in the European Community," *International Organization* 34/3 (Summer 1980), 355–76.
74. Ibid., 361.
75. Victoria Curzon Price, *Industrial Policies in the European Community* (London, 1981), 90.
76. Tsoukalis and da Silva Ferreira, "Industrial Surplus Capacity," 363.
77. John Gillingham, "The American Minimill: Challenge to European Steel in Light of the Present World Financial Crisis" (unpublished manuscript, September 1998); Julian Szekely and Gerardo Trapaga, "Zukünftsperspektiven für neue Technologien in der Stahlindustrie," *Stahl und Eisen* 114 (1994), 43–4.
78. Curzon Price, *Industrial Policies,* 105–15.
79. Tsoukalis and da Silva Ferrara, "Industrial Surplus Capacity," 367.
80. Ibid., 369.
81. Ibid., 369–70; Curzon Price, *Industrial Policies,* 98–100.
82. Alan Riley, "The ECJ: A Court with a Mission?," *European Policy Analyst* 4 (1996), 69–76.
83. Donna Starr-Deelen and Bert Deelen, "The European Court of Justice as a Federator," *Publius* (Fall 1986), 81–97.
84. Ibid.
85. Burley and Mattli, "Europe Before the Court."
86. Starr-Deelen and Deelen, "European Court of Justice," 90–3.
87. Hjalte Rasmussen, "Between Self-restraint and Activism," *European Law Review* (1988), 128–38.
88. Karen Alter, "The European Union's Legal System and Domestic Policy: Spillover or Backlash?," *International Organization* 53/3 (Summer 2000), 489–518.

89. Kris Pollet, "EU Lawmaking: Less, Better and Simpler," *European Policy Analyst* 2 (1997), 63–77.
90. Fritz W. Scharpf, *Governing in Europe: Effective and Democratic?* (Oxford, 1999), 2.
91. Keith Middlemass, *Orchestrating Europe: The Informal Politics of the European Union, 1973–1995* (London, 1995), 285–8.
92. Moravcsik, *Choice for Europe*, 310.
93. Robert W. Russell, "Snakes and Sheiks: Managing Europe's Money," in Helen Wallace and Alisdair Young, *Participation and Policy-Making in the European Union* (Oxford, 1997), 69–90; Moravcsik, *Choice for Europe*, 291–5.
94. John B. Goodman, *The Politics of Central Banking in Western Europe* (Ithaca, 1992), 118–26.
95. Moravcsik, *Choice for Europe*, 295–302.
96. Ibid., 287.
97. Helen Milner, "Resisting the Protectionist Temptation: Industry and the Making of Trade Policy in France and the United States During the 1970s," *International Organization* 41/4 (1988), 639–65.
98. Ibid., 641, 642, 643.
99. Ibid., 662.
100. Ibid.
101. Werner Feld, "Political Aspects of Transnational Business Collaboration in the Common Market," *International Organization* 24/2 (Spring 1970), 209–38.
102. See Peter Robson and Ian Wooton, "The Transnational Enterprise and Regional Economic Integration," *Journal of Common Market Studies* 31/1 (March 1993), 71–90.
103. Ibid., 63.
104. Ibid., 64.
105. See Cockett, *Thinking the Unthinkable*.
106. Gamble, *Politics of Thatcherism*, 107–20.
107. Margaret Thatcher, *The Downing Street Years* (London, 1993), 173–235.
108. Gamble, *Politics of Thatcherism*, 120–1.
109. Ronald Tiersky, *François Mitterrand: The Last French President* (New York, 2000), 130–41; Jonah Levy, *Tocqueville's Revenge: State, Society and Economy in Contemporary France* (Cambridge, MA, 1999), 43–1. See also George Ross, Stanley Hoffman, and Sylvia Malzacher (Eds.), *The Mitterrand Experiment: Continuity and Change in Modern France* (Oxford, 1987).
110. Koichi Nakano, "The Role of Ideology and Elite Networks in the Decentralisation Reforms in 1980s France," *West European Politics* 23/13 (July 2000), 97–110; Bob Jessop, "Twenty Years of the (Parisian) Regulation Approach: The Paradox of Success and Failure at Home and Abroad," *New Political Economy* 2/3 (November 1997), 503–26.
111. Cockett, *Thinking the Unthinkable*, 131.
112. Ibid., 139.
113. Ibid., 150.
114. Ibid., 155.
115. Ibid., 283.
116. Ibid.
117. Ibid., 237–8.
118. Ibid., 278.
119. Ibid., 245–6, 274–5.
120. Gamble, *Politics of Thatcherism*, 108.
121. Ibid., 110, 112.
122. Ibid., 114.
123. Thatcher, *Downing Street Years*, 108–14.
124. Ibid., 143–7, 389–96; Gamble, *Politics of Thatcherism*, 116–17.
125. Frederic London, "The Logic and Limits of *Désinflation competitive*: French Economic Policy from 1983," *Oxford Review of Economic Policy* 14/1 (Spring 1998), 96–114.
126. Levy, *Tocqueville's Revenge*, 47.
127. London, "Logic and Limits," 99.
128. Ibid.
129. Ibid., 111.

130. Ibid., 112.
131. Ibid., 114.
132. Ibid., 101.

CHAPTER 7

1. Wolfgang Streeck, "The Internationalization of Industrial Relations in Europe: Problems and Prospects," *Politics and Society* 26/4 (December 1998), 429–64.
2. Jeffry A. Frieden, "Invested Interests: The Politics of National Economic Policies in a World of Global Finance," *International Organization* 45/4 (Autumn 1991), 425–51.
3. Robert F. Bartley, *The Seven Fat Years* (New York, 1992).
4. Ibid.
5. See Roy C. Smith, *Comeback: The Restoration of American Banking Power in the New World Economy* (Cambridge, MA, 1993).
6. Paul and Volcker and Toyoo Gyohten, *Changing Fortunes: The World's Money and the Threat to American Leadership* (New York, 1992), 166–7.
7. Ibid., 248–9; Adam Clymer, "Rethinking Reagan: Was He a Man of Ideas After All? A Gathering of Scholars Looks at His Place in History," *New York Times*, 6 April 2002; Martin Feldstein, "Supply Side Economics: Old Truths and New Claims," *American Economic Review* 76/2 (May 1986), 26–30.
8. Feldstein, "Supply Side Economics," 27.
9. See also Brink Lindsey, *Against the Dead Hand: The Uncertain Struggle for Global Capitalism* (New York, 2002).
10. See Charles Grant, *Delors: Inside the House that Jacques Built* (London, 1990); George Ross, *Jacques Delors and European Integration* (New York, 1995).
11. Roland Vaubel, "The Political Economy of Centralization in the European Community," *Journal des Économistes et des Études Humaines* 3/1 (March 1991), 21.
12. Philip Revzin, "World Business (A Special Report): United We Stand .... Europe Moves toward Unity in 2002. The Brussels Bureaucrat in the Driver's Seat," *Wall Street Journal*, 22 September 1989.
13. Vaubel, "Political Economy of Centralization," 29.
14. Ross, *Jacques Delors*, 157–65.
15. Ibid., 163–4.
16. Sir John Hoskins, "1992 and the Brussels Machine," in Sir Ralf Dahrendorf et al. (Eds.), *Whose Europe? Competing Visions for 1992* (London, 1992), 11–14.
17. Grant, *Derlors*, 153–4.
18. Ralf Dahrendorf, "A Little Silver Lining on a Dark Horizon," in Ralf Dahrendorf (Ed.), *Europe's Economy in Crisis* (London, 1981).
19. Ross, *Delors*, 4.
20. Kenneth Dyson and Kevin Featherstone, *The Road to Maastricht: Negotiating Economic and Monetary Union* (Oxford, 1999), 88–90.
21. Grant, *Delors*, 12–13.
22. Michel Albert, *Capitalism vs. Capitalism: How America's Obsession with Individual Achievement and Short-term Profit Has Led It to the Brink of Collapse* (New York, 1993).
23. Dyson and Featherstone, *Road to Maastricht*, 701.
24. Streeck, *Internationalization*, 432.

CHAPTER 8

1. Victoria Curzon Price, "1992: Europe's Last Chance? From Common Market to Single Market" (19th Wincott Memorial Lecture, London, 1988), 41.
2. Ibid., 12–24.
3. Ibid., 23.
4. See Hugo Young, *This Blessed Plot* (New York, 1999).
5. Thatcher, *Downing Street Years*, 536–59, 727–67.

6. Nigel Lawson, *The View from No. 11: Britain's Longest-Serving Cabinet Minister Recalls the Triumphs and Disappointments of the Thatcher Era* (New York, 1993), 960–5.

7. Ibid., 322–3; Thatcher, *Downing Street Years*, 557–8.

8. Thatcher, *Downing Street Years*, 344–78.

9. John Pencavel, "The Surprising Retreat of Union Britain" (unpublished manuscript, Department of Economics, Stanford University, November 2000), 2.

10. Gamble, *Politics of Thatcherism*, 209.

11. Ibid., 225.

12. See Eamonn Butler et al. (Eds.), *The Omega File* (Adam Smith Institute, 1982); Cockett, *Thinking the Unthinkable*, 305.

13. Gamble, *Politics of Thatcherism*, 247.

14. Virginia Byfield, "Privatization Politics," *Alberta Report/Newsmagazine* 21/34 (8 August 1994): review of Madsen Pirie, *Blueprint for a Revolution* (London, 1994).

15. Pencavel, "Suprising Retreat," 19.

16. Ibid., Thatcher, *Downing Street Years*, 272–6; Gamble, *Politics of Thatcherism*, 233.

17. Thatcher, *Downing Street Years*, 559–605; Lawson, *View from No. 11*, 566–7.

18. Thatcher, *Downing Street Years*, 278–9, 570–1, 591–2; Lawson, *View from No. 11*, 599–610.

19. Thatcher, *Downing Street Years*, 598–9.

20. Richard Disney, Carl Emmerson, and Sarah Smith, "Pension Reform and Economic Performance in Britain in the 1980s and 1990s," EEP/IFS/NBER Conference, "Seeking a Premier League Economy" (8–9 December 2000); Lawson, *View from No. 11*, 612–19.

21. Ibid., 367–71.

22. Ibid., 676–87.

23. Cited in ibid., 199.

24. Ibid., 197–211.

25. Thatcher, *Downing Street Years*, 114–21.

26. Lawson, *View from No. 11*, 211–12, 216–20.

27. Ibid., 226–8.

28. Ibid., 224.

29. Ibid., 222–4.

30. Ibid., 213–16.

31. Ibid., 230–4.

32. Ibid., 236–40; Richard Green and Jonathan Haskel, "The Role of Privization," CEP/IFS/NBER Conference, "Seeking a Premier League Economy" (7–8 December 2000), 17.

33. Green and Haskel, "Role of Privatization," 23.

34. Ibid., 24–7; Geoffrey Howe, *Conflict of Loyalty* (New York, 1994), 237–40.

35. Green and Haskel, "Role of Privatization," 18.

36. Ibid., 23.

37. Ibid., 23–7, 29–32.

38. Lawson, *View from No. 11*, 41.

39. Ibid., 627–8.

40. Smith, *Comeback*, 168–9, 198–201.

41. Ibid., 201.

CHAPTER 9

1. Herman Schwartz, "Small States in Big Trouble: State Reorganization in Australia, Denmark, New Zealand, and Sweden in the 1980s," *World Politics* 46/4 (July 1994), 527.

2. Ibid.

3. Ibid., 528.

4. Ibid., 532.

5. Lewis Evans, Arthur Grimes, Bryce Wilkinson, and David Teece, "Economic Reform in New Zealand 1984–95: The Pursuit of Efficiency," *Journal of Economic Literature* 34 (December 1996), 1856.

6. Ibid., 1857–60.

7. Schwartz, "Big Trouble," 540–1.

8. See Hannes Suppanz, "New Zealand: Reform of the Public Sector," *OECD Observer* 200 (June/July 1996), 40–2; Adrian Orr, "New Zealand: The Results of Openness," *OECD Observer* 192 (February/March 1995), 51–4.

9. Ibid., 51.

10. Evans et al., "Reform in New Zealand," 1870–2.

11. Ibid., 1893–5.

12. Torben Iversen and Anne Wren, "Equality, Employment, and Budgetary Restraint. The Trilemma of the Service Economy," *World Politics* 50 (July 1988), 507–46.

13. Torben Iversen, "The Choice for Scandinavian Social Democracy in Comparative Perspective," *Oxford Review of Economic Policy* 14/1 (Spring 1998), 60.

14. Ibid., 59–76.

15. Ibid., 69.

16. See Sven Jochem, "Nordic Labour Market Policies in Transition," *West European Politics* 23/13 (July 2000), 115–23.

17. Iversen, "Choice," 67.

18. Ibid.

19. Jochem, "Nordic Transition," 119.

20. Richard H. Cox, "The Consequence of Welfare Retrenchment in Denmark," *Politics and Society* 25/3 (September 1997), 303–27.

21. Ibid., 313.

22. Ibid., 314–15.

23. Ibid., 318–19.

24. Ibid., 319.

25. Ibid., 17, 19.

26. Assar Lindbeck, "The Swedish Experiment," *Journal of Economic Literature* 35/3 (September 1997), 1273–1319.

27. Ibid., 1275–6.

28. Ibid., 1297–8.

29. See Bertram Silverman, "The Rise and Fall of the Swedish Model: Interview with Rudolf Meidner," *Challenge* (January/February 1998), 69–90.

30. Lindbeck, "Swedish Experiment," 1276, 1291–2.

31. Ibid., 1292.

32. Ibid., 1294.

33. Ibid., 1297.

34. Ibid., 1308.

35. Sherwin Rosen, "Public Employment and the Welfare State in Sweden," *Journal of Economic Literature* 34/2 (June 1996), 729–37.

36. Eric Lundberg "The Rise and Fall of the Swedish Model," in Dahrendorf, *Europe in Crisis* (see chap. 7, n. 18), 200.

37. Gregg M. Olsen, "Re-modeling Sweden: The Rise and Demise of the Compromise in the Global Economy," *Social Problems* 43/1 (Febrary 1996), 8.

38. Ibid., 5–6; Mark Blaisse, "Sweden: Remaking the Model," *European Affairs* (November/December 1991), 56–61; "Mensheviksson," *Economist,* 1 April 1989, 42–3.

39. Lindbeck, "Swedish Experiment," 1285, 1291.

40. Ibid., 1297–8.

41. Ibid., 1308.

42. Ramana Ramaswamy, "The Structural Crisis in the Swedish Economy," *International Monetary Fund Staff Papers* 41/2 (June 1994), 367–80.

43. Ibid., 368.

44. Mike Marshall, "The Changing Face of Swedish Corporatism: The Disintegration of Consensus," *Journal of Economic Issues* 30/3 (September 1996), 843–57.

45. Olsen, "Re-modeling Sweden," 33–4.

46. "Sweden: The Economic Watchwords Are Fiscal Restraint and Austerity until the Wheels of Industry Begin to Pick Up Speed Again," *Business America,* 27 July 1992, 22–6.

47. "Mensheviksson" (see n. 38).

48. Ibid.

49. Charles Silva, "Europe or Bust? European Integration in Recent Swedish Historiography," *Scandinavian Studies* 69/3 (Summer 1997), 367–81.
50. Blaisse, "Sweden."
51. John Madeley, "The Return of Swedish Social Democracy: Phoenix or Ostrich? *West European Politics* 12/2 (April 1995), 422–3.
52. Lindbeck, "Swedish Experiment," 1303, 1313–14.
53. Jonas Agell, Peter Englund, and Jan Sodersten, "Tax Reform of the Century – The Swedish Experiment," *National Tax Journal* 49/4 (December 1996), 643–64.
54. Assar Lindbeck, Per Molander, Torsten Persson, Olof Petersson, Agnar Sandmo, Birgitta Swedenborg, and Niels Thygesen, *Turning Sweden Around* (Cambridge, MA, 1994).
55. Levy, *Tocqueville's Revenge*, 48–9; Vivien A. Schmidt, *From State to Market: The Transformation of French Business and Government* (Cambridge, U.K., 1996), 139–46.
56. Levy, *Tocqueville's Revenge*, 58–69.
57. Schmidt, *From State to Market*, 271–6.
58. Ibid., 348–9.
59. Levy, *Tocqueville's Revenge*, 69–70.
60. Schmidt, *From State to Market*, 348–9.
61. Suzanne Berger, "French Business from Transition to Transition," in Ross et al., *Mitterrand Experiment* (see chap. 6, n. 109), 191.
62. Berger, "French Business," 193.
63. Ibid., 193–7.
64. Schmidt, *From State to Market*, 112–14.
65. Ibid., 141–7.
66. Ibid., 147–64.
67. Levy, *Tocqueville's Revenge*, 66.
68. Ibid., 67.
69. Schmidt, *From State to Market*, 157–8.
70. Ibid., 155.
71. Ibid., 262–76.
72. Ibid., 275.
73. Ibid., 437–47.
74. Levy, *Tocqueville's Revenge*, 69–86.
75. Ibid., 71–2.
76. Ibid., 71.
77. Ibid., 82.
78. Giersch et al., *Fading Miracle*, 194–5.
79. Ibid., 202–5.
80. Ibid., 202.
81. Ibid., 206.
82. "Introduction," in Mario Baldassari (Ed.), *The Italian Economy: Heaven or Hell?* (London, 1994), 7–18.
83. Dyson and Featherstone, *Road to Maastricht*, 464–5.
84. Patrick McCarthy, *The Crisis of the Italian State: From the Origins of the Cold War to the Fall of Berlusconi* (New York, 1995), 2–4, 61–80, 82, 91–2, 94, 103, 174–5.
85. See Fiorella P. S. Kostiris, *Italy: The Sheltered Economy: Structural Problems in the Italian Economy* (Oxford, 1993), 17–33, 75–6, 91–2, 115–16.
86. Bernard Connolly, *The Rotten Heart of Europe* (London, 1955), 258–61.
87. Dyson and Featherstone, *Road to Maastricht*, 466–80.
88. Connolly, *Rotten Heart*, 259.
89. Ibid.
90. Dyson and Featherstone, *Road to Maastricht*, 499–500.
91. McCarthy, *Crisis of the Italian State*, 81–101.
92. Cited in ibid., 93.
93. Stefano Misossi and Pier Carlo Padoan, "Italy in the EMS. After Crisis, Salvation?," in Mario Baldassari and Franco Modigliani (Eds.), *The Italian Economy: What Next?* (New York, 1995), 131–8.

94. Ibid., 144–8.
95. Ibid., 148–51.
96. Kostiris, *The Sheltered Economy*, 4.
97. Ibid., 4–5.
98. Ibid., 5.
99. Ibid., 8.
100. Ibid., 6.
101. Ibid., 6–7.
102. Kostiris, *The Sheltered Economy*.
103. Ibid., 9–13.
104. Mario Baldassarri, "Italy's Perverse Enveloping Growth Model between Economic Reform and Political Consensus: The 1992 Crisis and the Opportunity of 1993," in Baldassari and Modigliani, *What Next?*, 85.
105. Ibid., 86.
106. Ibid.
107. McCarthy, *Crisis of the Italian State*, 123–38.
108. Ibid., 128.
109. Ibid., 134–5.
110. Ibid., 130–4.
111. Victor Pérez-Diaz, *Spain at the Crossroads: Civil Society, Politics, and the Rule of Law* (Cambridge, MA, 1999), 44.
112. Ibid., 24.
113. "Thank You and Goodbye: A Strong Democracy, Spain Now Needs a Reformed Economy," *Economist*, 24 February 1996, 17.
114. Ibid., 8–9.
115. See Pérez-Diaz, *Spain at the Crossroads*.
116. Ibid., 20.
117. Thatcher, *Downing Street Years*, 546.
118. See Albert Recio and Jordi Roca, "The Spanish Socialists in Power: Thirteen Years of Economic Policy," *Oxford Review of Economic Policy* 14/1 (Spring 1998), 139–59.
119. Miguel Martinez Lucio and Paul Blyton, "Constructing the Post-Fordist State? The Politics of Labour Market Flexibility in Spain," *West European Politics* 18/2 (April 1995), 340–61.
120. "The Socialist of the Year 2000," *Economist*, 30 January 1988, 32.
121. Paul Heywood, "Power Diffusion or Concentration? In Search of the Spanish Policy Process," *West European Politics* 21/4 (1998), 103–28.
122. Omar Encarnation, "Social Concertation in Democratic and Market Transitions: Comparative Lessons from Spain," *Comparative Political Studies* 30/4 (August 1997), 387–420.
123. Ibid., 9.
124. Ibid., 8.
125. Ibid., 5–10.
126. Ibid., 17.
127. Pérez-Diaz, *Spain at the Crossroads*, 110–11.
128. Recio and Roca, *Spanish Socialists*, 8.
129. Mary Farrell, *Spain in the EU: The Road to Economic Convergence* (London, 2001), 178.
130. Pérez-Diaz, *Spain at the Crossroads*, 40–1; Heywood, "Diffusion or Concentration," 110–11; Recio and Roca, *Spanish Socialists*, 140–1.
131. See Bob Anderton, "Spain: Evaluating the Effects of Macropolicy using an Econometric Model," *National Institute of Economic Research* 146 (November 1993), 76–90; Jordi Catalan, "Spain, 1939–96," in Max-Stephan Schulze, *Western Europe: Economic and Social Change Since 1945* (London, 1999), 365–7.
132. Heywood, "Diffusion or Concentration," 106.
133. Ibid., 107.
134. Ibid., 111–13; "Social Concertation," 5–7.
135. See Sofia A. Pérez, "From Labor to Finance: Understanding the Failure of Socialist Economic Policies in Spain," *Comparative Political Studies* 32/6 (September 1999), 659–89.
136. Farrell, *Spain in the EU*, 25.

137. Mary Beth Double, "Privatization Changes Spain's Business Environment, and Creates Opportunities for U.S. Business," *Business America* 114/4 (22 February 1997), 8–11.
138. Ibid.
139. Sofia A. Pérez, *Banking on Privilege: The Politics of Spanish Financial Reform* (Ithaca, 1997).
140. Ibid., 131, 136, 137.
141. Ibid., 158.
142. Ibid., 165.
143. Ibid., 152.
144. Ibid., 152–8.
145. Ibid., 155.
146. Ibid., 159–66.
147. Farrell, *Spain in the EU*, 22–5.
148. Ibid., 26.
149. Ibid., 29.
150. Ibid., 30, 32.
151. Ibid., 35, 39.
152. Ibid., 40.
153. Pérez-Diaz, *Spain at the Crossroads*, 28.
154. Ibid., 4.
155. Ibid., 41, 78.
156. Paul Heywood, "Sleaze in Spain," *Parliamentary Affairs* 48/4 (1995), 726–38.
157. Pérez-Diaz, *Spain at the Crossroads*, 85–7.
158. Ibid., 85–6.
159. Heywood, "Sleaze," 731.
160. Ibid., 727.
161. Ibid., 728; Pérez-Diaz, *Spain at the Crossroads*, 45.
162. Francisco Torres, "Lessons from Portugal's Long Transition to Economic and Monetary Union," in Francisco Seixas da Costa et al., *Portugal: A European Story* (Cascais, 2000), 99–130.
163. Luis de Sousa "Political Parties and Corruption in Portugal," *West European Politics* 24/1 (January 2001), 157–80.

CHAPTER 10

1. Alfred Tovias, "A Survey of the Theory of Economic Integration," in Hans J. Michaelmann and Panayotis Soldartis (Eds.), *European Integration: Theories and Approaches* (Lanham, MD, 1994), 58–75; Richard E. Baldwin and Elena Seghezza, "Growth and European Integration: Towards and Empirical Assessment," Center for Economic Policy Research, 1393 (May 1996); Luis A. Rivera-Batiz and Paul M. Romer, "Economic Integration and Endogenous Growth," *Quarterly Journal of Economics* 106/2 (May 1991), 531–55.
2. Paul Pierson, "The Path to European Integration: A Historical Institutionalist Analysis," *Comparative Political Studies* 29/2 (April 1996), 123–63.
3. Paul Pierson: "Increasing Returns, Path Dependence and the Study of Politics," *American Political Science Review* 94/2 (June 2000), 251–80; "When Effect Becomes Cause: Policy Feedback and Political Change," *World Politics* 45/4 (July 1993), 595–628; "Big, Slow-moving, and Invisible: Macro-Social Processes in the Study of Comparative Politics" (Speech, Harvard University Center for European Studies, 10 November 2000). See also Simon Bulmer, "New Institutionalism, the Single Market and EU Governance," ARENA Working Paper no. 97/25 (1997).
4. Stephen Liebfried and Paul Pierson, "Social Policy," in Wallace and Wallace, *Policy-Making* (see chap. 6, n. 52), 267–92.
5. Manfred E. Streit and Werner Mussler, "The Economic Constitution of the European Community: From 'Rome' to 'Maastricht'," *European Law Journal* 1/1 (March 1995), 5–30.
6. Herbert Giersch, "EC 1992: Competition Is the Clue," *European Affairs* 3 (1989).
7. Margaret Thatcher, *Statecraft: Strategies for a Changing World* (London, 2002), 360–411; Suzannah Herberts, "Delors Ready to Disown EU over Euro," *Daily Telegraph*, 21 March 1997.

8. Hoskins, "1992"; Laffan and Shackleton, "The Budget," 215.

9. Moravcsik, *Choice for Europe,* 325; Thatcher, *Statecraft,* 373–6.

10. Garry Blanchard, "The Single Market Revisited," Economist Intelligence Unit, 95/3 (1995).

11. Single European Act (OJ L 169, 29.6.1987). (Text of the Treaty.)

12. Moravcsik, *Choice for Europe,* 358–9.

13. Ibid., 357.

14. Interview, Lord Cockfield, 11 February 1993; Arthur Cockfield, "Beyond 1992 – The Single European Economy," *European Affairs* 4 (1988), 66–74.

15. Malcolm Salter, "Europe's New Industrial Revolution," *European Affairs* 3 (1988), 98–113.

16. Thatcher, *Statecraft,* 372–3.

17. Thatcher, *Downing Street Years,* 547.

18. Howe, *Conflict of Loyalty,* 409.

19. Ibid., 408–9.

20. Thatcher, *Downing Street Years,* 548–54.

21. Peter Brimelow, "Counterrevolution," *Forbes,* 3 November 1998, 114–20.

22. See George Ross, "French Social Democracy and the EMU," ARENA Working Paper no. 98/19 (1998).

23. Dyson and Featherstone, *Road to Maastricht,* 274–305.

24. Tommaso Padoa-Schioppa, *The Road to Monetary Union in Europe: The Emperors, the Kings and the Genies* (Oxford, 1995), 170–81.

25. Adam S. Posen, "Why the EMU Is Irrelevant for the German Economy," Institute for International Economics, Working Paper no. 99-5 (April 1995), 7.

26. Dyson and Featherstone, *Road to Maastricht,* 165–6, 184, 225, 234, 417, 480, 614.

27. Thatcher, *Downing Street Years,* 609–705, 709–18; Lawson, *View from No. 11,* 483–508.

28. Maria Green Cowles, "Organizing Industrial Coalitions: A Challenge for the Future?," in Wallace and Young, *Participation and Policy-Making* (see ch. 6, n. 93), 121.

29. Wayne Sandholtz and John Zysman, "1992: Recasting the European Bargain," *World Politics* 42/1 (October 1989), 95–128.

30. Cowles, "Organizing Industrial Coalitions," 117–20.

31. Wisse Dekker, "Keeping Up Europe's Guard," *European Affairs* (November/December 1991).

32. Interview, Lord Cockfield, 11 February 1993.

33. Moravcsik, *Choice for Europe,* 355–6.

34. Jacques Delors, "The Single Act and Europe: A Moment of Truth," (EUI, Florence, Italy, 21 November 1986).

35. Gilberto Sarfati, "European Industrial Policy as a Non-tariff Barrier," *European Integration Online Papers* 2/2 (13 May 1988), 1–11.

36. Ibid.

37. Les Metcalfe, "The European Commission as a Network Organization," *Publius* 26/4 (Fall 1996), 43–62.

38. "Maintaining Vigilance over Quality of EU Research," *Lancet* (3 April 1999), 1111.

39. Keith Pavitt, "Technology, International Competition, and Economic Growth: Some Lessons and Perspectives," *World Politics* 25/2 (January 1973), 183–205; Margaret Sharp and Keith Pavitt, "Technology Policy in the 1990s: Old Trends and New Realities," *Journal of Common Market Studies* 31/2 (June 1993), 129–51.

40. Stephen Woolcock, "Information Technology: The Challenge for Europe," *Journal of Common Market Studies* 22/4 (June 1984), 315–31.

41. Ibid., 324–7.

42. John Peterson, "Technology Policy in Europe: Explaining the Framework Program and Eureka in Theory and Practice," *Journal of Common Market Studies* 19/3 (March 1991), 519–39.

43. Antonio Ruberti and Michel Andre, "The European Model of Research Cooperation," *Issues in Science and Technology* 11/3 (Spring 1995), 17–20.

44. C. G. Kurland, "Beating Scientists into Plowshares," *Science* (2 May 1997), 761–2.

45. Ibid.

46. Deborah Mackenzie, "Framework Becomes a Pawn in Europe's Politics," *New Scientist* (23 March 1991), 14.

47. Judy Redfearn, "Report Card on European Science," *Science* (23 May 1997), 1186.

48. Nigel Williams and Alexander Hellemans. "Cracks in Europe's Framework?," *Science* (11 April 1997), 188.
49. Nigel Williams, "Framework: 'Unfocused, Underachieving'," *Science* (7 March 1997), 1.
50. Redfearn, "Report Card."
51. "A Mixed Report Card for Critical Technology Projects," *Science* (18 June 1993), 1736–9; Joseph C. Rolla, "The European Community's Technological Dilemma: Is a Regional Solution Possible in a Global Economy?," *National Forum: Phi Beta Kappa Journal* 72/2 (Spring 1992), 34–6; David P. Hanson, Conway Lackman, and Christine Grande, "EU Politics in High Technology: Promotion, Trade, or Protection?," *Review of Business* 16/1 (Summer/Fall 1994), 3–7.
52. "Europe's Technology Policy: How Not to Catch Up," *Economist,* 9 January 1993.
53. Colleen Shannon, "Industry Looks for a New Direction," *Chemistry and Industry* 128 (17 February 1992), 128.
54. Ingo Beyer von Morgenstern et al., "Europe's Structural Weakness," *McKinsey Quarterly* 1 (1994), 33–4, 37.
55. Deborah MacKenzie, "Delors to Push Science Funds into Arms of Commerce," *New Scientist* (8 February 1992), 16.
56. Grant, *Delors,* 156.
57. "A Europe Divided," *New Scientist* (2 January 1993), 3; Deborah MacKenzie, "Europe under New Management," *New Scientist* (2 January 1993), 12–14.
58. Luc Van Dyk, "Research in the EU: Better Times to Come?," *Lancet* (12 May 2001), 1465.
59. "Directives of the Future: Television Without Frontiers," *European Trends* (1978), 13–17.
60. Xiudian Dai, Alan Cawson, and Peter Holmes, "The Rise and Fall of High Definition Television: The Impact of European Technology Policy," *Journal of Common Market Studies* 34/2 (1996), 149–66.
61. See Xiudian Dai, *Corporate Strategy, Public Policy and New Technologies: Philips and the European Consumer Electronics Industry* (Oxford, 1996), 191–259.
62. Dai et al., "Rise and Fall," 154–6.
63. Peter Curwen, "High Definition Television: A Case Study of Industrial Policy versus the Market," *European Business Review* 94/1 (1994), 17–23.
64. Dai et al., "Rise and Fall," 220–8.
65. Ibid., 235.
66. Ibid., 236.
67. Mat Toor, "BskyB Lashes EC's Push for D2 Mac," *Marketing,* 28 May 1992, 10.
68. Ibid.
69. Ibid.
70. Leon Brittan, *A Diet of Brussels: The Changing Face of Europe* (London, 2000), 14.
71. Ebenstein, *Hayek,* 23–7.
72. David J. Gerber, *Law and Competition in the Twentieth Century: Protecting Prometheus* (New York, 1988).
73. Frances MacGowan, "Unmasking a Federal Agency: The European Commission's Control of Competition Policy," *European Business Review* 96/5 (1997), 13–26.
74. Ricardo Petrella, "The Limits of European Union Competition Policy," *New Political Economy* 3/2 (July 1998), 292–5.
75. MacGowan, "Unmasking."
76. Ibid., 333–5; Mark R. A. Palm, "The Worldwide Growth of Competition Law: An Empirical Analysis," *Antitrust Bulletin* 43/1 (Spring 1998), 105–45.
77. Hans-Werner Sinn, "The Competition between Competition Rules," National Bureau of Economic Research, Working Paper no. 7273 (July 1999).
78. Grant, *Delors,* 160.
79. Brittan, *Diet of Brussels,* 195.
80. Ibid., 161
81. Ibid., 161–2.
82. Leon Brittan, *Globalization versus Sovereignty? The European Response – The 1997 Rede Lecture and Related Speeches* (Cambridge, U.K., 1998), 2.
83. Ibid., 150–80; Leon Brittan, *The Europe We Need* (London, 1994), 19.
84. Brittan, *Globalization.*

85. Ibid., 29.
86. Brittan, *The Europe We Need*.
87. Ibid., 17.
88. Brittan, *Diet of Brussels*, 48, 54–84.
89. See Peter A. Hall and Robert J. Franzese, "Mixed Signals: Central Bank Independence, Coordinated Wage Bargainng, and European Monetary Union," *International Organization* 52/3 (Summer 1998), 505–35; Adam S. Posen, "Why EMU Is Irrelevant for the German Economy," Institute for International Economics, Working Paper no. 99/5 (April 1995).
90. Thatcher, *Statecraft*.
91. Grant, *Delors*, 154.
92. Ibid.
93. Ibid., 155.
94. Ibid.
95. Brittan, *Diet of Brussels*, 93–9; Alexis Jacquemin, "The International Dimension of European Competition Policy," *Journal of Common Market Studies* 21/1 (March 1993), 91–101.
96. Brittan, *The Europe We Need*, 82.
97. Peter Holmes, "Towards a Common Industrial Policy in the EC?," *European Business Journal* 5/4 (1993), 25–40.
98. Brittan, *Diet of Brussels*, 101–2.
99. Ibid., 98.
100. See Jan Host Schmidt et al., "Part A: Liberalization of Network Industries: Economic Implications and Main Policy Issues" (European Commission, n.d.), 1–149; Chris Doyle, "Liberalizing Europe's Network Industries: Ten Conflicting Priorities, Part I," *Business Strategy Review* 7/4 (Autumn 1998), 55–67.
101. Brittan, *Diet of Brussels*, 104.
102. Ibid., 103–96.
103. Ibid., 106–7.
104. Ibid., 107–10.
105. Loukis Tsoukalis, *The New European Economy Revisited* (Oxford, 1997), 92–102.
106. Harry Flam, "Product Markets and 1992: Full Integration, Large Gains?," *Journal of Economic Perspectives* 6/4 (Autumn 1992), 7–30.
107. Ibid., 27.
108. "Thatcherites in Brussels," *Economist*, 15 March 1997.
109. Alexis Jacquemin and Andre Sapir, "Europe Post-1992: Internal and External Liberalization," *American Economic Review* 81/2 (May 1991), 166–70.
110. Alexis Jacquemin and David Wright, "Corporate Strategies and European Challenges Post-1992," *Journal of Common Market Studies* 31/4 (December 1993), 525–37.
111. "Thatcherites in Brussels."
112. Jacques Pelkmans, "A Grand Design by the Piece: An Appraisal of the Internal Market Strategy," in Roland Bieber et al. (Eds.), *1992: One European Market? A Critical Analysis of the Commission's International Market Strategy* (Baden-Baden, 1988), 359–83.

CHAPTER 11

1. Ross, *Delors*, 39–50.
2. Ibid., 40.
3. Ibid., 41.
4. David Allan, "Cohesion and the Structural Funds," in Wallace and Wallace, *Policy-Making* (see chap. 6, n. 52), 244–65.
5. Ross, *Delors*, 216.
6. Alvero de Vasconcelos, "Portugal the European Way," in Alvero de Vasconcelos and Maria Joao Seabra (Eds.), *Portugal: A European Story* (Lisbon, 2000), 12.
7. Ross, *Delors*, 43.
8. Pierson, "Path to European Integration," 148.
9. Ross, *Delors*, 44–5.

10. "Lobbying for the EU: The Search for Ground Rules" (Economist Intelligence Unit), *European Trends* 3 (1994), 74; Sonia Mazey and Jeremy Richardson, "Effective Business Lobbying in Brussels," *European Business Journal* 5/4 (1993), 14–27.

11. David Coen, "The Impact of U.S. Lobbying Practice on the European Business–Government Relationship," *California Management Review* 41/4 (Summer 1999), 27–44.

12. Shirley Williams, "Sovereignty and Accountability in the EC," in Robert Keohane and Stanley Hoffmann (Eds.), *The New European Community: Decision-making and Institutional Change* (Boulder, 1991), 155–75.

13. Ibid., 28.

14. Ibid.

15. Ibid., 30–3.

16. Mazey and Richardson, "Business Lobbying," 16.

17. Ibid., 28.

18. Metcalfe, "Commission as Network"; Middlemass, *Orchestrating Europe,* 435–612.

19. Ronald Facchinetti, "Global Lobbying in the New Europe," *Corporate Board* 16/90 (January/February 1995), 19–25.

20. Cowles, "Organizing Industrial Coalitions," 124–34.

21. Coen, "Lobbying Practice," 134.

22. Marieke de Koning, "Taking Care of Business," *European Affairs* (August 1991), 29–31.

23. Ibid., 29, 30, 31.

24. Ibid., 31.

25. Coen, "Lobbying Practice," 33.

26. Ibid., 34.

27. Ibid., 41.

28. Barry Eichengreen, "European Monetary Unification," *Journal of Economic Literature* 31/3 (September 1993), 1321–57.

29. See Robert A. Mundell, "A Theory of Optimum Currency Areas," *American Economic Review* 51/4 (September 1961), 657–65; Barry Eichengreen, "European Monetary Unification: A Tour d'Horizon," *Oxford Review of Economic Policy* 14/3 (Autumn 1998), 24–51; Rudi Dornbusch, "Euro Fantasies," *Foreign Affairs* 75/5 (September/October 1996), 110–25; Martin Feldstein, "The Political Economy of the European Economic and Monetary Union," *Journal of Economic Perspectives* 11/4 (Fall 1997), 23–42.

30. Dornbusch, "Euro Fantasies," 22.

31. Michael Camdessus, "Europe's Coming of Age," *Banker* (May 1997), 12–14.

32. Tommaso Padoa-Schioppa, "The Genesis of EMU: A Retrospective View" (Speech, European University Institute, Florence, 29 June 1995).

33. See Roland Vaubel, "Currency Competition and European Monetary Integration, *Economic Journal* (September 2000), 936–46.

34. Padoa-Schioppa, *Road to Monetary Union,* 69–77.

35. Ibid., 50–2.

36. Dyson and Featherstone, *Road to Maastricht,* 784–6.

37. Ibid., 34, 677–8; Eichengreen, "European Monetary Unification," 1324; Padoa-Schioppa, *Road to Monetary Union,* 159–60.

38. Eichengreen, "European Monetary Unification," 1322.

39. Padoa-Schippa, "Genesis of EMU," 2.

40. Ibid.

41. Padoa-Schioppa, *Road to Monetary Union,* 188–9.

42. Richard N. Cooper, "Will an EC Currency Harm Outsiders?," *Orbis* 80 (Fall 1992), 517–29.

43. Eichengreen, "European Monetary Unification," 1343.

44. Dyson and Featherstone, *Road to Maastricht.*

45. "A Survey of EMU: Maastricht Follies," *Economist,* 11 April 1998.

46. Ibid.

47. Padoa-Schioppa, *Road to Monetary Union,* 8.

48. Eric Helleiner, "One Nation, One Money: Territorial Currencies and the Nation-State," ARENA Working Paper no. 97/17 (1997).

49. Padoa-Schioppa, *Road to Monetary Union,* 8.

50. Ibid.
51. Ibid., 7.
52. Ibid.
53. Martin Feldstein: "EMU and International Conflict," *Foreign Affairs* 76/6 (November/December 1997), 60–73; "Europe's Monetary Union: The Case Against EMU," *Economist*, 13 June 1992; "The Political Economy of the European Economic and Monetary Union: Political Sources of an Economic Liability," *Journal of Economic Perspectives* 11/4 (Fall 1997), 23–41.
54. Feldstein, "EMU and International Conflict."
55. Ibid., 64.
56. Ibid., 68.
57. Ibid., 69.
58. Ibid., 72.
59. Ibid., 73.
60. Ian Begg, "Wrong Questions, Wrong Answers: The EU Economic Policy Debate Since 'Maastricht'," *European Business Journal* 8/4 (1966), 37–44.
61. Ross, *Delors,* 232.
62. Charles Jenkins, "The Maastricht Treaty" (Economist Intelligence Unit) (March 1992), 1–35.
63. Dornbusch, "Euro Fantasies," 117.
64. Grant, *Delors,* 181; Ross, *Delors,* 237–47.
65. Grant, *Delors,* 188.
66. Ibid., 189.
67. Ibid., 194.
68. Zbigniew Brzezinski et al., "Living with a Big Europe," *National Interest* 60 (Summer 2000), 17–32; "Robertson: NATO Allies Can't Replicate U.S. Capabilities Soon," *Defense Daily* (23 June 2000), 1–2; Martin Walker, "Europe: Superstate or Superpower?," *World Policy Journal* 17/4 (Winter 2000) 1–10; "The European Rapid Reaction Force," *Guardian,* 11 April 2001; "Europe's Rogue State," *Daily Telegraph,* 29 May 2001.
69. Grant, *Delors,* 185.
70. Ibid.
71. Ibid., 191.
72. Ibid., 192.
73. Ibid.
74. Ibid., 197.
75. Ross, *Delors,* 188–95.
76. "Constitutional Reform after Maastricht" (Economist Intelligence Unit), *European Trends* 1 (1994), 59–69.
77. Ross, *Delors,* 190.
78. Ibid.
79. Ibid., 191.
80. Ibid.
81. Ibid.
82. Jack Straw, "A Constitution for Europe," *Economist,* 12 October 2002.
83. Ross, *Delors,* 198.
84. Ibid.
85. Ibid., 199; Stephen Smith, "Financing the European Community: A Review of Options for the Future," *Fiscal Studies* 13/4 (November 1992), 98–121.
86. Ross, *Delors,* 203.
87. Grant, *Delors,* 214.
88. Ibid., 205–8.
89. Ibid., 216.
90. Ross, *Delors,* 207.
91. Grant, *Delors.*
92. Ross, *Delors,* 209.
93. Grant, *Delors,* 221–5.
94. Connolly, *Rotten Heart.*
95. Ibid.

96. Thatcher, *Downing Street Years*, 705, 713–15.
97. Lawson, *View from No. 11*, 1208–10.
98. Young, *This Blessed Plot*, 439.
99. Ibid., 412–71.
100. Posen, "EMU Is Irrelevant"; Amity Schlaes, "Germany's Chained Economy," *Foreign Affairs* 73/5 (September/October 1994), 109–18.
101. Barry Eichengreen, "Who Mislaid the *Wirtschaftswunder?*" (Speech, AIGCS, November 1999).
102. Grant, *Delors*, 228–9; Ross, *Delors*, 211–17.
103. Peter Ludlow, "Delors II: Continuity or Discontinuity," *European Affairs* 2 (1989), 36–9.
104. Grant, *Delors*, 241.
105. Connolly, *Rotten Heart*.
106. "White Paper on Growth, Competitiveness and Unemployment: A Fervent Appeal for European Cohesion," *International Labour Review* 133/1 (1994), 1–7; Ross, *Delors*, 221–6.
107. "White Paper on Growth."
108. Ross, *Delors*, 224.

CONCLUSION TO PART III

1. "A Fortress Against Change," *Economist*, 23 November 1996.

INTRODUCTION TO PART IV

1. William R. Buck, "Historic Trade Pact Is Signed, Laying New Foundations for World Trade," *Business America* 115/12 (December 1994), 30–1.
2. Francis Fukuyama, *The End of History and the Last Man* (New York, 1992).
3. Daniel Gros, "Europe's Problem Is Not the Stability Pact," *Financial Times*, 24 October 2002.
4. Razeen Sally, "Developing Country Policy Reform and the WTO," *Cato Journal* 19/3 (Winter 2000), 403–23.
5. Chris Shore, "European Union and the Politics of Culture," Bruges Group Occasional Paper no. 43 (London, 2001), 4.
6. Timothy Garton Ash, "Europe's Endangered Liberal Order," *Foreign Affairs* 77/2 (March/April 1998), 51–66.
7. C. Fred Bergsten, "Fifty Years of the GATT/WTO: Lessons from the Past for Strategies for the Future," Institute for International Economics, Working Paper no. 98/3 (1998), 1–8.
8. Ibid., 2.
9. Ibid.
10. Ibid., 4.
11. Bergsten, "Fifty Years."
12. Ibid., 6.
13. Leon Brittan, *Diet of Brussels*, 117–49.
14. Ibid., 133; Bergsten, "Fifty Years," 2.
15. John McLaughlin, "Bush Regains Power to Fast-Track Bilateral Trade Deals," *Lloyd's List*, 7 August 2002.
16. Anne-Marie Slaughter, "The Real New Order," *Foreign Affairs* 76/5 (September/October 1997), 183–98.
17. Ibid., 185.
18. Ibid., 186–8.
19. Ibid., 89–98.
20. Brian T. Hanson, "What Happened to Fortress Europe? External Trade Policy Liberalization in the European Union," *International Organization* 52/1 (Winter 1998), 55–86.
21. Ibid., 69.
22. Ibid., 70.
23. Ibid., 59.
24. Hanson, "What Happened."
25. Razeen Sally, "Hayek and the International Economic Order," *ORDO* 51 (2000), 98–118.

26. Wolf Sauter, "The Economic Constitution of the European Union," *Columbia Journal of European Law* 4/27 (Winter/Spring 1998), 1–42; Manfred E. Streit and Werner Mussler, "The Economic Constitution of the European Community," *European Law Journal* 1/1 (1995), 5–30.
27. Jeffrey Sachs, "Consolidating Capitalism," *Foreign Policy* 98 (Spring 1995), 50–9.
28. Ibid., 58.

CHAPTER 12

1. Hooghe and Marks, "Making of a Polity" (see chap. 6, n. 14).
2. William Wallace, "Collective Governance," in Wallace and Wallace, *Policy-Making* (see chap. 6, n. 52), 523–42.
3. Middlemass, *Orchestrating Europe*.
4. Jeremy S. Bradshaw, "Constitutional Reform after Maastricht" (Economist Intelligence Unit), *European Trends* 1 (1994), 59–69.
5. Charles Jenkins, "Unfinished Business" (Economist Intelligence Unit), *European Policy Analyst* 3 (1997), 7–9; "Cheer Up, Europe!," *Economist*, 21 June 1997.
6. Andreas Middel, "Ein neuer Anlauf für die Reform: Gipfel von Amsterdam scheiterte an nationalen Eitelkeiten und Rivalitäten," *Die Welt*, 11 November 1999.
7. Elizabeth de Bony, "Agenda 2000: A Blueprint for Enlargement" (Economist Intelligence Unit), *European Policy Analyst* 2 (1997), 65–73.
8. Christian Wernicke, "Solo für Schröder. Beim Berliner EU-Gipfel sur Agenda 2000 steht der Bundedkanzler allein da – ohne Rückentdeckung der Kommission," *Die Zeit*, December 1999.
9. John Vinocur, "New Chance for Schröder: German Presidency of EU Offers Opportunity for a Success That Has Been Elusive at Home," *International Herald Tribune*, 14 December 1998.
10. Barry James, "Crisis Helps Bonn's EU Presidency," *International Herald Tribune*, 22 April 1999.
11. "Crisis in Brussels, Goodbye to Berlin," *Economist*, 20 March 1999.
12. "Edith Cresson, Europe's Controversial Commissioner," *Economist*, 6 March 1999.
13. Suzanne Lowry, "Blunder Woman: The Fighter They Love to Hate," *Daily Telegraph*, 3 April 1992.
14. Julian Corman, "EC Clears Whistleblower Who Exposed Brussels Fraud," *Daily Telegraph*, 12 September 1999.
15. Christian Wernicke, "Gewissen der Eurokrtie. Der kleine Buchalter Paul van Buitenen wurde zum Kronzeuge der Brüsseler Misswirtschaft," *Die Zeit*, March 1999.
16. "EU-Kommission suspendiert Autor eines Betrugsberichts," *Die Welt*, 5 January 1999.
17. Ibid.
18. Ibid.
19. Cited in Shore, "Politics of Culture," 21.
20. Ibid.
21. Ibid.
22. Toby Helm, "Cresson Savaged by Wise Men," *Daily Telegraph*, 16 March 1999.
23. Shore, "Politics of Culture," 22.
24. Helm, "Cresson Savaged."
25. Andreas Middel, "EU-Kommission und Parlament kommen nicht zur Ruhe. Viele Abgeordnete zornig über Abstimmungsausgang – New Vorwürfe gegen einen Kommissar," *Die Welt*, 16 January 1999.
26. Barry James, "EU Commission's Future at Stake in Fraud Inquiry," *International Herald Tribune*, 15 March 1999.
27. Toby Helm, "EU Crisis as Santer's Team Quits in Disgrace," *Daily Telegraph*, 16 March 1999; Andreas Middel, "Weisen-Bericht könnte Schicksal der EU-Kommission besiegeln," *Die Welt*, 16 March 1999.
28. "Overview: Supplement: The Guide to Portuguese EU Presidency," *Euromoney* (July 2000), 2–4; Stephan-Götz Richter, "Eyes Wide Shut in Lisbon," *Globalist*, June 2000; Peter Hort, "Think Twice before Surrender," *Frankfurter Allgemeine*, 20 June 2000.
29. Vito J. Racanelli, "European Trader, EU Could Tread Uncharted Ground in Fight with Austria," *Barron's*, 7 February 2000; "The Perils of Austracism," *Economist*, 17 June 2000.

30. "The Union Expects Europe's Voters to Fit Its Political Space," *Economist*, 11 March 2000.
31. "Louis Michel, Belgium's Moralistic Diplomat," *Economist*, 26 February 2000.
32. Barry James, "Proliferation of Government Jobs Becomes Bad Joke in Belgium," *International Herald Tribune*, 19 July 1999.
33. Ibid.
34. Dick Leonard, "Belgians Face Confidence Crisis," *Europe* 363 (February 1997), 16–18; Jay Branegan, "The Nightmare Goes On," *Time*, 2 December 1996; Daniel Dombey, "The High Price of Waiting for Justice in Belgium," *Financial Times*, 20 March 2002.
35. Olenka Frienkel, "Belgium's Silent Heart of Darkness," *Guardian*, 5 May 2002; "Something Rotten," *Economist*, 14 September 1996; Ambrose Evans-Pritchard, "Child Murders Could Provoke New Revolution," *Daily Telegraph*, 23 January 2002; Harry McGee, "Dutroux Trial Is Over Six Years in the Making," *Sunday Tribune*, 2 June 2002.
36. Frienkel, "Heart of Darkness."
37. Leonard, "Confidence Crisis."
38. Ibid.
39. Stephen Castle, "Belgian Royal Family Dismisses Paedophile Claims over King," *Independent*, 18 September 2001.
40. Dombey, "High Price."
41. "Louis Michel,…".
42. Andreas Middel, "Prodi will Österreich nicht diskriminiert sehen. Bilaterale Isolierung ja, Schikanen nein. EU-Kommssionschef empfängt Bundespräsident Kleistl," *Die Welt*, 9 March 2000.
43. "Overview" (see n. 28).
44. "Overview"; "Europe in Cyberspace," *Economist*, 1 April 2000.
45. "The Row over the EU's Market Isn't Over," *Economist*, 31 March 2001. "From Lisbon to Stockholm," *Economist*, 31 March 2001; Erkki Liikanen, "Europe's Strategy for Catching Up with New Economy Rivals," *International Herald Tribune*, 19 June 2000; Frits Bolkestein, "The Follow-up to Lisbon – Building a Knowledge Economy" (Speech, Brussels, 18 September 2000).
46. Peter Hort, "Think Twice before Surrender," *Die Welt*, 20 June 2000.
47. Nikolaus Blome and Andreas Middel, "Wo bitte ist der Chef? Unter den EU-Kommissaren wächst der Unmut über Romano Prodi," *Die Welt*, 28 February 2000.
48. Mike Bracken, "Who is Romano Prodi?," *Guardian*, 24 March 1999; "Prodi – A Respected Academic," *Eurotimes* (Ireland), 11 October 2000.
49. Romano Prodi, "The European Union: A Hard but Successful Venture" (Speech, Florence, 20 June 1996).
50. "Speech by Professor Romano Prodi: Schumpeter Award of 1999" (Vienna, 10 May 1999).
51. Romano Prodi, "European Industry and Finance in International Competition" (Speech, Florence, 20 March 1998).
52. Romano Prodi, "The Age of the Euro" (Speech, Bologna, 22 February 1999).
53. "The Challenge Awaiting Romano Prodi," *Economist*, 3 April 1999.
54. "Bruxelles veut une reforme institutionnelle rapide et vaste," *Le Tribune*, 19 October 1999.
55. "Romano Prodi: Europe's First Prime Minister?," *Business Week*, 11 October 1999; "Prodi, un Patron sous tutelle," *Nouvel Observateur* 1800 (n.d.).
56. Christian Wernecke, "Prodis Sternenkrieger," *Die Zeit* 29/1999 (n.d.).
57. "New Broom Sweeps Half-Clean," *Economist*, 10 July 1999; "Prodi Imperator," *Economist*, 18 September 1999.
58. "Der einsamste Mann in Bruessel," *Der Spiegel*, 3 April 2000.
59. Barry James, "Prodi and Revamped European Commission Struggle to Take Reins," *International Herald Tribune*, 19 April 2000.
60. Nikolaus Blome, "Prodi lebt," *Die Welt*, 4 May 2000; James, "Prodi."
61. Lionel Barber, "Romano's Reformation," *Europe* 394 (March 2000), 8–9.
62. Nikolaus Blome, "Brüssel 'verkauft' sich schlecht," *Die Welt*, 23 February 2000.
63. "L'Europe: Cinq annees de banalites?," *Le Tribune*, 11 February 2000; Franklin Dehousse, "Sur le bilan livre venredi par la Commission Prodi …," *Le Soir*, 29 July 2000.
64. Roman Prodi, "Shaping the New Europe" (Speech, Strasbourg, 15 February 2000).
65. Ibid.

66. Ibid.
67. Ibid.
68. Ibid.
69. Andreas Middel, "Die neue EU-Kommission gleicht einer Baustelle. Kaum Wandel ein Jahr nach Prodis Amtsantritt," *Die Welt*, 20 September 2000; "Schlechtes Zeugnis für die EU Kommissionschef Prodi," *Vorarlberg-Online*, 10 July 2000; "Jahreserzeugnisse für die EU-Kommissare," *Die Welt*, 24 July 2000; Peter Hort, "Prodi's Second Chance," *Frankfurter Allgemeine Zeitung*, 6 August 2000; Andreas Oldag, "Prodi geht die Puste aus," *Süddeutsche Zeitung*, 16 September 2000; Nikolaus Blome, "Ein Jahr Prodi," *Die Welt*, 20 September 2000.
70. "La Commission livre le bilan de sa premier année de fonctionemment: Tout va très bien chante Romano Prodi," *Le Soir*, 16 September 2000.
71. Hort, "Prodi's Second Chance."
72. Hajo Friedrich, "Brussels Seen as Toothless Tiger," *Frankfurter Allgemeine Zeitung*, 17 September 2000.
73. "Anniversary of the Prodi Commission's Arrival in Office," *Die Welt*, 15 September 2000.
74. Romano Prodi (Speech, Plenary Session of the European Parliament, 3 October 2000).
75. Ibid.
76. Nikolaus Blome, "Schröder will die EU-Kommission schwächen," *Die Welt*, 12 October 2000; Julian Coman, "Prodi Snub for Britain over EU Blueprint," *Daily Telegraph*, 17 October 2002.
77. Peter Hort, "Prodi Lashes Out at EU Governments," *Frankfurter Allgemeine Zeitung*, 3 October 2000; "Prodi veut devenir le patron économique de la zone euro," *La Tribune*, 4 October 2000; Andreas Middel and Nikolaus Blome, "Prodi Schlägt zurück," *Die Welt*, 4 October 2000.
78. Peter Hort, "Schröder and Prodi on Cool, Yet Collected Terms," *Frankfurter Allgemeine Zeitung*, 21 November 2000.
79. Ambrose Evans-Pritchard, "Prodi Warns of EU Deadlock," *Daily Telegraph*, 1 December 2000.
80. Christian Wernicke, "Klempnern für Europa," *Die Zeit* 44/2000 (n.d.).
81. "A Treat from Nice," *Economist*, 14 December 2000; Michaela Wiegel, "The Chirac Show in Nice Has Europe Bemused," *Frankfurter Allgemeine Zeitung*, 11 December 2000.
82. Joe Murphy and Julian Coman, "Blair Isolated as Nice Turns Nasty," *Daily Telegraph*, 10 December 2000.
83. Guenther Nonnenmacher, "Mission Impossible," *Frankfurter Allgemeine Zeitung*, 19 January 2001; Eric Dupin, "Chacun pour soi dans la grande Europe," *La Libération*, 13 December 2000; Ambrose Evans-Pritchard, "Blair Pledges to Maintain Britain's Veto," *Daily Telegraph*, 13 December 2000; Michaela Wiegel, "Chirac Is No Mitterrand," *Frankfurter Allgemeine Zeitung*, 6 December 2000.
84. Ambrose Evans-Pritchard, "EU Leaders Scramble to Fix a Deal," *Daily Telegraph*, 11 December 2000.
85. Ambrose Evans-Pritchard, "Blair Pledges."
86. John Vinocur, "Europe without Direction," *International Herald Tribune*, 12 December 2000.
87. "La Chronique de Jacques Juilliard: Europe: le modèle Thatcher," *Nouvel Observateur* 1888 (n.d.).
88. Joachim Fritz Vannahme, "Ein Ganzer Europäer: Belgiens Premier Guy Verhofstadt," *Die Zeit*, 2000 (n.d.).
89. Klaudia Prevezanos, "The EU Conference in Nice: More Than a Minimum Consensus for Europe and Germany," American Institute for Contemporary German Studies, 4 January 2001.
90. Ibid.
91. "Prodi: 'Nous avons perdu le fil," *Le Soir*, 15 February 2001.
92. "Divorce After All These Years? Not Quite, but …," *Economist*, 25 January 2001; Peter Hort, "How More Than a Poisoned Chalice Soured Franco-German Relations at Nice," *Frankfurter Allgemeine Zeitung*, 13 December 2000..
93. "Lob für Schröder," *manager-magazin*, 12 December 2000.
94. Patrick Bishop, "French EU Presidency 'A Failure'," *Daily Telegraph*, 28 December 2000.
95. Ibid.
96. Michaela Wiegel, "Chirac Calls for European Constitution in Ringing Speech to Bundestag," *Frankfurter Allgemeine Zeitung*, 27 June 2000; Helmut Bünder, "France Must Steer EU through

Tough Agenda," *Frankfurter Allgemeine Zeitung*, 2 July 2000; "European Union: Chirac Outlines French Program," *European Report*, 5 July 2000.

97. Michaela Wiegel, "French Unveil Blueprint for European Constitution," *Frankfurter Allgemeine Zeitung*, 16 June 2000.

98. Ibid.

99. "Ein Trauriges Bild der Uneinigkeit: Die Zeitungskommentatoren bewerten das Gipfeltreffen von Nizza überwiegend negative," *manager-magazin*, 12 December 2000.

100. Ibid.

101. "Big Issue: Ireland Votes 'Yes'," *Independent*, 26 October 2002.

102. Dietrich Alexander, "Ein Debakel als Geburtsstunde eines europäischen Wertekataloges. Mach dem Korruptionsskenal der EU-Kommission um Jacques Santer beschlossen die Mitgliedstaaten, eine EU-weit gültige Grundrechte-Charta zu erstellen," *Die Welt*, 14 September 2000.

103. "Draft Charter of Fundamental Rights of the European Union," *Daily Telegraph*, 21 September 2000.

104. "The Founding Fathers Maybe: The EU's Constitutional Convention," *Economist*, 23 February 2002.

105. Ambrose Evans-Pritchard, "EU Must Be Federal State with Elected President," *Daily Telegraph*, 15 June 2000.

106. Michael Barnier, "Europa muss wieder auf Touren kommen," *Die Welt*, 26 February 2001.

107. Peter D. Sutherland, "The European Union – More Than a Market," *European Journal* 9/3 (Autumn 1997), 29–30.

108. Nikolaus Blome, "Prodis Verfassung," *Die Welt*, 11 November 1999.

109. "Vom Staatenbund zur Föderation – Gedanken über die Finalitaet der europäischen Integration. Rede von Bundesaussenminister Joschka Fischer am 12. Mai 2000 in der Humboldt-Universität Berlin," *Die Zeit*, 12 May 2000.

110. John Vinocur, "Fischer Tries to Give Depressed EU a Lift: Vision of a Federalized State Leaves Smaller Nations Skeptical," *International Herald Tribune*, 18 May 2000; "Nein zum Bundesstaat. Der französische Aussenminister Hubert Védrine über die Zukunft Europas, die Erneuerung der Union und seine Sympathie für den deutschen Kollegen Joschka Fischer" (Interview), *Der Spiegel*, 5 June 2000.

111. Tony Peterson, "Anger over German Plan to Unite Europe," *Daily Telegraph*, 28 May 2000.

112. Toby Helm and Patrick Bishop, "French Face German Federalist Ultimatum," *Daily Telegraph*, 24 January 2001.

113. "L'Europe de Gerhard Schröder," *Le Monde*, 7 May 2001; "Rèpondre a Schröder," *Le Monde*, 7 May 2001; "M. Hollande Critique le Projet européen de M. Schröder," *Le Monde*, 8 May 2001; "Schröder Plan for EU Central Govt. Set for Test at European Socialist Congress," *Financial Times*, 6 May 2001; Tony Paterson, "Cook's EU Post Pleases Germans," *Daily Telegraph*, 6 May 2001; Toby Helm and George Jones, "EU Socialists Move to Tip Balance of Power," *Daily Telegraph*, 8 May 2001.

114. Edmund L. Andrews, "Germany's Ruling Party Backs Single Federal System for EU," *New York Times*, 30 April 2001; John Hooper and Kate Connolly, "Germany Wants EC to Be a Government," *Guardian*, 1 May 2001; "European Superstate," *Guardian*, 30 April 2001; "It's Revolutionary but Britons Will Rush to Build Their Air-raid Shelters," *Guardian*, 1 May 2001.

115. "Europe by Stealth," *Daily Telegraph*, 8 March 2001.

116. "Euro Government Gets Cool Reception" (BBC News, 29 April 2001); "Alarm over Call for EU Government," *Times*, 30 April 2002; Imre Karacs, "Germany Isolated on EU Government," (Independent.co.uk).

117. John Schmid, "Paris Shuns Schröder's EU Reform Proposals," *International Herald Tribune*, 3 May 2001.

118. Ibid.; "Jospin lehnt Schröders Vision ab," *Spiegel.on line*, 28 May 01.

119. "A Eurovision Song Contest," *Economist*, 2 May 2001.

120. "Belgium's Verhofstadt Says Agrees with Schröder on EU Reform, Bar Farming," *Financial Times*, 2 May 2001.

121. Andreas Oldag, "Zu Normal für Brüssel. Der Freundliche Kommissionspräsident wird von den Staats- und Regierungschefs mehr belächelt als beachtet und droht, zum Statisten zu verkommen," *Süddeutsche Zeitung*, 22 March 2001.

122. Julian Coman, "Mismanagement and Fraud Cost EU Taxpayers 4 Billion Pounds," *Daily Telegraph,* 19 November 2000.
123. Ibid.
124. "Budget: Sharp Increase in Fraud and Irregularities in 2000," *European Report,* 16 May 2001.
125. Ibid.
126. Ibid.
127. Friedrich Schneider, "Dimensions of the Shadow Economy," *Independent Review* 5/1 (Summer 2000), 81–2.
128. Nigel Farage, "Democracy in Crisis: The White Paper on Governance," Bruges Group Occasional Paper no. 44 (London, 2001).
129. Roland Watson and Charles Bremner, "Cook Dismisses Prodi Call for European Tax," *Times,* 30 May 2001; Ambrose Evans-Pritchard, "Prodi Urges Brussels to Tighten Grip on the Euro," *Daily Telegraph,* 30 May 2001.
130. "Romano Prodi préconise une nouvelle gouvernance européene," *La Tribune,* 10 February 2000.
131. Andreas Middel, "Romano Prodi plant bereits die Reform nach der Reform," *Die Welt,* 14 February 2001.
132. "Prodi Urges Debate on EU's Ultimate Goal" (Reuters, 26 April 2001).
133. Farage, "White Paper," 5.
134. Ibid., 6.
135. Martin Ball et al., "Federalist Thought Control: The Brussels Propaganda Machine," Bruges Group Occasional Paper no. 45 (London, 2001), 28–37.
136. Farage, "White Paper," 6–8.
137. Ibid., 8–11.
138. Shore, "Politics of Culture," 9.
139. Ibid., 14.
140. Ibid., 10–11.
141. Ibid., 8.
142. Ibid., 12.
143. Michael Stabenow, "How an Aging Architect of Europe Came Back into the Limelight," *Frankfurter Allgemeine Zeitung,* 16 December 2001.
144. "Re-launching Europe," *Economist,* 1 March 2002; Ambrose Evans-Pritchard, "Superpower Europe Goes on the Agenda," *Daily Telegraph,* 1 March 2002.
145. Klaus-Dieter Frankenberger, "A Unique Chance for the EU," *Frankfurter Allgemeine Zeitung,* 27 February 2002.
146. Rory Watson, "Prodi Tells EU to Give His Successor Sweeping Powers," *Times,* 23 May 2002.
147. "Sitzung des Reformkonvents in Brüssel," *Süddeutsche Zeitung,* 29 October 2002.
148. Daniel Dombey, "Giscard Warned on EU States," *Financial Times,* 30 October 2002.
149. "European Convention: Mixed Reception for Draft Constitution" (European Information Service), *European Report,* 30 October 2002; "Les Grandes lignes de la première partie de l'esquisse constitutionelle," *Le Monde,* 30 October 2002.
150. "Europe's Future," *Times,* 29 October 2002.
151. Simon Jenkins, "Blair Finally Comes Up Against the Old Enemy," *Times,* 30 October 2002.
152. Ibid.
153. George Parker, "Comment and Analysis," *Financial Times,* 31 December 2002.
154. "The Perils of Penelope," *Economist,* 14 December 2002; Ambrose Evans-Pritchard, "EU Convention Goes off the Rails," *Daily Telegraph,* 28 December 2002.
155. Straw, "Constitution for Europe."
156. "Franco-German Relations: Spectacle or Substance," *Economist,* 25 January 2003.
157. David Howell, "Yawning Democratic Deficit between Grass Roots and Nations," *Daily Telegraph,* 4 February 2002.
158. Ibid.
159. "Growing and Slowing," *Economist.com/Global Agenda,* 9 October 2002.
160. "Restoring Europe's Smile," *Economist,* 24 October 2002.
161. "Germany Drags Europe Down," *Financial Times,* 27 September 2002.

CHAPTER 13

1. Jonathan Swift, *Gulliver's Travels* (part III: "A Voyage to Laputa ...") [reprint of original edition] (London, 1906).
2. Leo V. Ryan, "Finland Aspires to European Union Small Country Leadership," *European Business Journal* 9/1 (1997), 43–50.
3. Jack W. Osman, "The Finnish Economic Depression of the 1990s: Causes, Consequences and Cure," *Scandinavian Review* 86/1 (Spring 1998), 17–22; Frances Cairncross, "In Sweden's Wake," *Economist*, 5 November 1994.
4. "Nordic Countries: Farewell," *Economist*, 23 October 1993.
5. Jason Lavery, "Finland at Eighty: A More Confident and Open Nation," *Scandinavian Review* 85/2 (Autumn 1996), 13–18.
6. Matti Huuhtanen, "Thirty-six-year-old Premier Named to Non-Socialist Finnish Government" (Associated Press, 4 April 1991); Robert J. Gutman, "Finland's Prime Minister: Esko Aho," *Europe* 319 (September 1992) 28–31; Robert Koch, "Esko Aho, Finland's Conservative 'Kennedy of Kannos' " (*Agence France Presse*, 6 February 2000); "Europe Aho: Finland," *Economist*, 14 September 1991.
7. Charles Goldsmith, "Aho Takes a Cautious View as Finnish Vote on EU Nears," *Wall Street Journal Europe*, 28 September 1994.
8. "Very First Lady: A Feisty Finnish President," *Economist*, 12 February 2000.
9. "The Finnish Economy," *Kansallis-Osake-Pankki Economic Review* 1/16 (1994), 16–25; John Roberts, "Finland in Search of a Cure," *Euroweek* (June 1993), 17–23.
10. Erkki Viirtanen, "Privatization Has Achieved Its Goals," *Unitas* 71/1 (1999), 4–7.
11. Matti Vuoria, "Seeking Efficiency by Privatization," *Unitas* 68/2 (1996), 4–9.
12. Philip Eade, "How Long Can Helsinki Keep on Climbing?," *Euromoney* 299 (March 1994), 182–7.
13. Osman, "Finnish Economic Depression"; "The Finnish Economy" (see n. 9).
14. David Arter, "The March 1995 Finnish Election: The Social Democrats Storm Back," *West European Politics* 18/4 (October 1995), 194–205.
15. Thomas Romanschuk, "Finland: Lipponen Implements Tough Policies," *Europe* 376 (February 1998), 16–20; Robert J. Guttman, "Prime Minister of Finland, Paavo Lipponen" (Interview), *Europe* 361 (November 1996), 8–11.
16. Ryan, "Finland Aspires," 45.
17. Risto E. J. Penttila, "Finland's Quiet Revolution, 1989–1999," *Scandinavian Review* 87/3 (Winter 2000), 10–17.
18. Steven Irvine, "Don't Mention the War," *Euromoney* 314 (June 1995), 144–50.
19. "Finland: Restructuring the Banking Sector," *Institutional Investor* 6/28 (June 1994), 20–3.
20. Tarja Wist and Nina Rosenlew, "Finland: Capital Markets," *International Financial Law Review* (July 1999), 10–13; Ian Scales, "Why Sonera/Telia Could Be an Anomaly," *America's Network* 106/8 (15 May 2002), 23–5.
21. Roman Romantschuk, "The Helsinki Stock Exchange," *Europe* 388 (July/August 1999), 13–16.
22. Joanne Mason, "The Labors of Ollila," *International Management* 47/7 (July/August 1992), 52–5; Richard C. Morais, "Smoked Reindeer and WAP Phones," *Forbes*, 27 December 1999.
23. Justin Fox, "Nokia's Secret Code," *Fortune* 191/9 (May 2000), 160–74.
24. Janet Guyon, "Nokia Rocks Its Rivals," *Fortune* 145/5 (4 March 2002), 115–18; John S. McClenahen, "Leading the Field in Financials," *Industry Week* 249/13 (21 August 2000).
25. Marcus Gibson, "Wired Up: The Growth of Finland's High-Tech Sector," *Scandinavian Review* 85/2 (Autumn 1997), 21–7.
26. Adrian Wooldridge, "Telecommunications: To the Finland Station," *Economist*, 9 October 1999.
27. Sarah Lyall, "Jacks? Dolls? Yo-Yos? No, They Want Cellphones," *New York Times*, 24 October 2002.
28. John Warner, "Lessons from the European Tigers," *Business Week*, 6 July 1998.
29. Dan Sabbagh, "WAP Is Kwap, But Keep Hoping," *Spectator*, 30 September 2000.
30. "Finland Takes Second Place in Competitive Economies Study," Nordic Business Report, 30 April 2002.

31. Riitta Hjerppe, "Finnish Growth Was Europe's Fastest in the Twentieth Century," _Unitas_ 72/2 (2000), 19–23.
32. Kalle Lyytinen, "Finland: The Unknown Soldier on the IT Front," _Association for Computing Machinery. Communications of the ACM_ 42/4 (March 1999), 15.
33. Risto Rinne, "The Globalization of Education: Finnish Education on the Doorstep of the New EU Millennium," _Educational Review_ 52/2 (June 2000), 131–41; Kathryn Tully, "On Top of the World," _Corporate Location_ (January/February 1999), 74–7.
34. Rinne, "Globalization of Education," 140.
35. Paal Aarsaether, "Finnish Political Parties Struggle to Overcome Voter Apathy" (_Agence France Presse_, 7 June 2002).
36. Cited in John Hooper, "A New Italian Renaissance," _Wilson Quarterly_ 22/2 (Spring 1998), 75.
37. See Martin Bull and Martin Rhodes, "Between Crisis and Transition: Italian Politics in the 1990s," _West European Politics_ 20/1 (January 1997), 1–14.
38. Mark Donovan, "Election Report: A New Republic in Italy? The May 2001 Election," _West European Politics_ 24/4 (October 2001), 193–206; "Can Berlusconi Renew the Nation?," _Business Week_, 28 May 2001; Martin Woollacott, "The Berlusconi Disease Can Spread throughout Europe: Italy Has Been Mired in Chauvinism and Buffoonery," _Guardian_, 19 April 2002; Joe Klein, "The Prince: Is Silvio Berlusconi a Medieval Throwback ...?," _Guardian_, 6 June 2002; Nicholas Farrell, "Maggie Not Musso," _Spectator_, 20 April 2002; "Berlusconi's Dolce Vita," _Investors Daily_, 16 May 2001.
39. Donovan, "Election Report," 194.
40. Maurizio Ferrera and Elisabeta Gualmini, "Reforms Guided by Consensus: The Welfare State in the Italian Transition," _West European Politics_ 23/2 (April 2000), 187–210; "Berlusconi's Battle," _Financial Times_, 16 April 2002.
41. Luigi Federico Signorini, "Italy's Economy: An Introduction," _Daedalus_ 130/2 (1998), 67–77.
42. "Berlusconi's Battle" (see n. 40).
43. Vincent Della Sala, "Hollowing Out and Hardening the Italian State," _West European Politics_ 20/1 (January 1997), 14–33; "Better Future after Prodi's Job," _Euromoney_ 374 (June 2000), 176–8.
44. John Dickie, "Is the Italian Mafia about to Surrender?," _The Business_, 1 June 2002.
45. Signorini, "Italy's Economy."
46. Ferrara and Gualmini, "Reforms."
47. Stephen Jewkes, "Italy's Merchant Banks Take Stock," _Europe_ 368 (July/August 1997), 20–1; Philip Moore, "The Quest for a Risorgimento," _Euromoney_ 329 (September 1996), 356–60.
48. "Italian Banking, the Final Curtain," _Economist_, 22 April 2000; "Mediobanca on the Back Foot: Investment Banking in Italy," _Economist_, 23 June 2001; "No Renaissance: Italian Banking," _Economist_, 15 July 1995.
49. "Italian Banking: Spaghetti Junction," _Economist_, 27 March 1999.
50. Banca Akros, "A New Era for the Italian Stock Market," _Euromoney_ 342 (October 1997), 26.
51. Ibid.
52. Christopher O'Leary, "Finalmente! Italian Structured Finance Has Arrived at Last," _Investment Dealers' Digest_, 13 March 2000, 5–6.
53. Andrea Goldstein and Giuseppe Nocoletti, "Italy: Corporate Governance," _OECD Observer_ 192 (February/March 1995), 4–7; Fred Kapner, "Italian Banks' Role under Fire," _Financial Times_, 6 April 2001; "Flattering to Deceive: Italian Capitalism," _Economist_, 4 August 2001.
54. "Italy's Unfinished Business," _Economist_, 14 October 2000.
55. Ibid.
56. Patrick Crow, "Italian Gas Decontrol," _Oil and Gas Journal_ (21 February 2000).
57. "Europe's Wave of Offers," _Privatisation International_ (1 November 1997); Marcus Walker, "The Sack of Italia Telecom," _Euromoney_ 363 (July 1999), 30–46.
58. "No Renaissance" (see n. 48).
59. "The Final Curtain" (see n. 48).
60. "A Hostile Bid That's Dandy for Italy," _Business Week_, 16 July 2001.
61. John Roussant, "Twilight of the Gods," _Business Week_, 19 August 1996.
62. "The Final Curtain."

63. "Italian Banks' Role under Fire" (see n. 53).
64. "Summer Respite: Italy," *Economist*, 26 July 1997.
65. See H. M. Scobie, S. Mortali, S. Persaud, and P. Docile (Eds.), *The Italian Economy in the 1990s* (London, 1996); Signorini, "Italy's Economy"; "Better Future" (see n. 43); "Many Mountains Still to Climb," *Economist*, 8 November 1997.
66. "Can Berlusconi Renew the Nation?" (see n. 38).
67. "Now for a Party?," *Economist*, 4 April 1998.
68. "Broken Promises of Economic Revival," *Guardian*, 21 June 2002.
69. "So Much for 'Reinventing' Italy," *Business Week*, 19 November 2001; James Blitz, "Employers Seek Reform in Italy," *Financial Times*, 26 September 2001.
70. "Dynasties Run Italy from Politics to Finance," *Times*, 4 August 2001.
71. "Is There Less Than Before? Italy and Corruption," *Economist*, 16 February 2002.
72. Dickie, "Mafia to Surrender?"
73. "Italian Tax Amnesty Success," *Retail Banker International*, 28 May 2002.
74. James Blitz, "Berlusconi in Bid to 'Stir Up' Italy's Economy," *Financial Times*, 29 June 2001.
75. James Blitz, "Berlusconi's Battle," *Financial Times*, 16 April 2002.
76. "Berlusconi Two, Cofferati One," *Economist*, 29 June 2002.
77. "The Legacy of Pim Fortuyn," *Economist*, 11 May 2002; "A Wind of Change in the Netherlands," *Economist*, 18 May 2002; "Do the Right Thing," *Time International*, 27 May 2002; John O'Sullivan, "The Death of an 'Extremist': The Assassination of Pim Fortuyn Should Make Us Think Hard," *National Review*, 3 June 2002.
78. Peter van der Hoek, "Does the Dutch Model Really Exist?," *International Advances in Economic Research* 6/3 (2000), 397.
79. J. C. H. Blom, "Pillarisation in Perspective," *West European Politics* 23/3 (July 2000), 153–63.
80. Van der Hoek, "Dutch Model," 388.
81. Blom, "Pillarisation."
82. Van der Hoek, "Dutch Model," 395.
83. Anton Hemerijk and Jelle Visser, "Change and Immobility: Three Decades of Policy Adjustment in the Netherlands and Belgium," *West European Politics* 23/2 (April 2000), 234–5; Van der Hoek, "Dutch Model," 391.
84. Ibid.
85. "The High Road That Leads out of the Low Countries," *Economist*, 22 May 1999.
86. Bart van Ark and Jakob de Hahn, "The Delta Model Revisited: Recent Trends in the Structural Performance of the Dutch Economy," *International Review of Applied Economics* 14/3 (July 2000), 312.
87. Robert C. Kloostermann, "Three Worlds of Welfare Capitalism? The Welfare State and the Post-industrial Trajectory in the Netherlands after 1980," *West European Politics* 17/4 (October 1994), 172.
88. "Economic Illusions," *Economist*, 4 May 2002.
89. Fraser Bailey, "Dutch Treat," *Spectator*, 24 November 2001, 22–4.
90. Hans van Alebeek, Alexander P. W. van Wassenaer, and William W. Lewis, "Boosting Dutch Economic Performance," *McKinsey Quarterly* 4 (1997).
91. Van Ark and de Haan, "Delta Model," 312.
92. Barbara Smit and Julian Coman, "The Tulip Economy Starts to Wilt," *European*, 18 September 1997, 14–15.
93. Roel Janssen, "A New Golden Age," *Europe* (February 2001), 6.
94. "Red Light Revolt," *Maclean's*, 15 October 2001, 15.
95. "The High Road That Leads out of the Low Countries" (see n. 85).
96. "And the Winner Is … Cozy Consensus: The Dutch Election Is Issue Free …," *Economist*, 2 May 1998.
97. "Hans van Mierlo, Sighing Dutchman," *Economist*, 2 May 1998.
98. Roel Janssen, "Visions of the Twenty-first Century Dutch," *Europe* (December 1999), 35–6.
99. "The Political Legacy of Pim Fortuyn" (see n. 77).
100. O'Sullivan, "Death of an 'Extremist'."
101. "A Wind of Change in the Netherlands" (see n. 77).

102. "Dutch Set to Return to Polls on January 22," *Het Fiancielle Dagblad*, 11 October 2002; Andrew Osborn, "Party is Over as Fortuyn's Heirs Feud," *Guardian*, 20 October 2002; "Sighs of Relief," *Economist*, 25 January 2003.

103. Jonathan Fenby, "The Longest Journey: Chirac Will Face a Tough Time – and Task – If He Is to Repair French Politics," *Time International*, 13 May 2002.

104. David Lawday, "France, Lies, and Videotape," *New Statesman*, 9 October 2000.

105. See Sophie Meunier, "The French Exception," *Foreign Affairs* 79/4 (July/August 2000), 104–16.

106. "The French Connected," *Time International*, 12 June 2000, 40; "Single Market: Sweden Best at Implementing EU Law, France Worst," *European Report*, 18 May 2002, 488.

107. "Analysis: French Economy Better Than Most" (United Press International, 20 November 2001).

108. "France's Not So Social Partners," *Economist*, 22 January 2002.

109. "A Historic Defeat," *Wall Street Journal Europe*, 19 December 1995.

110. Bill Javetski and Gail Edmondson, "Long Live the Welfare State," *Business Week*, 16 June 1997.

111. Bill Javetski and Joan Warner, "A New Maginot Line," *Business Week*, 9 June 1997.

112. Ibid.

113. "Something Odd in France," *Economist*, 1 April 2000.

114. Christopher Caldwell, "Europe's 'Social Market'," *Policy Review* (October/November 2001), 29–37.

115. Ibid.

116. Ibid., 34.

117. Ibid.

118. "Still a Dirty Word: Private Pension Funds in France," *Economist*, 8 June 2002.

119. Ibid.; "French Economy Better Than Most" (see n. 107).

120. Lionel Barber, "France and Germany Take Different Approaches," *Europe* 396 (May 2000); Barry James, "France Joining EU Trend of Tax Cuts, Fan Growth," *International Herald Tribune*, 31 August 2000.

121. Barber, "France and Germany."

122. Patrick Bishop, "Mery Affair Seen as One Exposure Too Many," *Daily Telegraph*, 27 September 2000; Julian Coman, "The Scandal Surrounding Chirac Is Dismissed with a Gallic Shrug," *Sunday Telegraph*, 2 October 2000; "Tax, Lies and Videotape," *Time International*, 9 October 2000; Jon Henley, "Flames of Scandal Close in on Silent Chirac," *Guardian*, 5 December 2000.

123. "Tax, Lies, and Videotape."

124. "The Key to a Scandal," *Economist*, 10 February 2001.

125. Ibid.; John Roussant, "A 'Clean Hands' Campaign for France?," *Business Week*, 19 February 2001; "Affaire Elf," *Le Figaro*, 5 February 2001; "Les nombreuses pistes des affaires Elf convergent vers Alfred Sirven," *Le Monde*, 7 February 2001; "L'ancien patron Elf s'explique sur les emplois fictifs, les commissions occultes et le role des politiques aupres de la compagnie petroliere," *Le Figaro*, 18 May 2002.

126. Susannah Herbert, "A True Courtesan: The Whore of the Republic," *Economist*, 7 November 1998; "Naughty Business: Whore of the Republic Shakes the French Establishment," *Maclean's*, 2 April 2001.

127. "Encore, Encore! Former French Economy and Finance Minister Dominique Strauss-Kahn Returns to National Politics," *Time International*, 16 April 2001.

128. Deepak Gopinath, "Absolutely Fabius," *Institutional Investor* 34/9 (September 2000), 126–36.

129. "Alain Madelin, Failing for France," *Economist*, 2 February 2002.

130. "Official Quizzed over Chirac Sleaze Confirms Allegation" (*Agence France Presse*, 9 March 2002); "Exiled Fugitive Threatens to Tell All in Chirac Case," *International Herald Tribune*, 5 February 2002.

131. Jane Sasseen, "French Go for Broke in Europe (Credit Lyonnais' International Ambitions)," *International Management* 47/9 (October 1992); "Banking's Biggest Disaster," *Economist*, 5 July 1997; David McClintock, "The Bank Scandal That Keeps on Growing," *Fortune*, 7 July 1997; "The Scandal Continues," *Economist*, 17 May 2001.

132. "Chirac's Last Chance," *Economist.com/Global Agenda*, 3 May 2002; "Goodbye Reform?," *Business Week*, 6 May 2002.

133. Jean d'Ormesson, "L'ecrivain acheve son analyse de la derniere anne du XXe siecle," *Le Figaro*, 1 January 2001.

134. "A Big Country Directoire for Europe?," *Economist,* 23 March 2002.

135. Stanley Hoffmann, "Shorn of Its Grandeur, France Is Succeeding as a Modern, Middle-size Power," *Time International,* 12 June 2000.

136. Andrea Boltho, "Economic Policy in France and Italy since the War: Different Stances, Different Outcomes?," *Journal of Economic Issues* 35/3 (September 2001), 713–39.

137. "France: Who Speaks for Youth?," *Business Week,* 22 April 2000, 48.

138. Wolfgang Streeck, "German Capitalism: Does It Exist? Can It Survive?," MPIFG Discussion Paper 95/5 (November 1995), 9.

139. Wolfgang Münchau, "Germany Falling," *Spectator,* 20 October 2001.

140. Streeck, "German Capitalism."

141. Münchau, "Germany Falling."

142. Streeck, "German Capitalism," 10.

143. Ibid., 11.

144. Ibid., 15.

145. Ibid., 20.

146. Ibid., 21–2.

147. Barbara Kienbaum and Manfred Grote, "German Unification as a Cultural Dilemma: A Retrospective," *East European Quarterly* 31/2 (June 1997), 223–31; "A Berlin Wall of the Mind," *Time International,* 160–1; "Germany's Mezzogiorno," *Economist,* 21 May 1994.

148. David Shirreff, "The Achilles Heel of Europe," *Euromoney* 324 (April 1996), 50–9.

149. Eric von der Heyden, "Privatization in East Germany: The Delivery of an Economy," *Columbia Journal of World Business* 30/3 (Fall 1995), 42–55.

150. "More Cash Please," *Economist,* 12 May 2001.

151. "Das Land War tot" (Interview with Klaus von Dohnanyi), *manager-magazin* (n.d.).

152. Hans-Peter Schwarz, "Germany's National and European Interests," *Daedalus* 123/2 (Spring 1994), 81–106.

153. Tom Buerkle, "The German Dilemma," *Institutional Investor* 36/1 (January 2002), 47–53; David Marsh, "Behind a Healthy Facade Germany Is Crumbling," *Sunday Times,* 27 April 2002; "The Economics of the Madhouse," *The Business,* 17 February 2002; Alicia Wyllie, "Germany's Economic Miracle Turns to Dust," *The Business,* 20 January 2002; "Wanted: A Turnaround Artist for Germany," *Business Week,* 28 June 1999.

154. "Metall Buckles," *Economist,* 1 April 2000; "Metalworkers' Union Set for 100,000 Strike," *Frankfurter Allgemeine Zeitung,* 7 April 2002.

155. "Das Land War tot" (see n. 151).

156. "Architect of Reform: Hans Eichel's Success in Rewriting the Tax Code Will Have Far-reaching Impact on German Economy," *Time International,* 28 August 2000.

157. Bruce Barnard, "Germany's Tax Reform," *Europe* 410 (1 October 2001), 22–3.

158. Jo Wrighton, "The Global Ambitions of Allianz," *Institutional Investor* 34/6 (June 2000), 102–10; David Fairlamb, "The Player," *Business Week,* 24 January 2000.

159. Trevor Thomas, "Tax Law Could Spur German Acquisitions," *National Underwriter Property and Casualty – Risk & Benefits Management* 104/34 (21 August 2000), 9.

160. Stephan-Götz Richter, "Globalization Hits Corporate Germany," *Globalist* (2001), 1–32.

161. Ambrose Evans-Pritchard, "Germans in Move to Block Hostile Company Takeovers," *Daily Telegraph,* 13 December 2000.

162. Andrew Gimson, "Lady Thatcher's Views May Be Unmentionable – But She Has Plenty of Help from Gerhard Schröder," *Spectator,* 23 March 2002.

163. Josef Joffe, "Schröder's New Europe," *Time International,* 25 February 2002.

164. Toby Helm, "Immigration to Be Key Election Issue," *Daily Telegraph,* 25 March 2002.

165. "Schröder Vows No Radical Reform of the Welfare State" (*Deutsche Presse-Agentur,* 29 October 2002).

166. Ibid.

167. "Business Boos, Unions Cheer Schröder Policy Speech" (*Deutsche Presse-Agentur,* 29 October 2002).

168. Daniel Bogler, "German Business Sees Red: The Newly Elected Coalition's Tax and Spending Measures Have Upset Nearly Everyone," *Financial Times,* 25 October 2002.

169. Mark Landler, "Is Germany Looking Like Japan?," *New York Times,* 31 October 2002.

170. Jürgen Kluge, Rupert Deger, and Juergen Wunram, "Can Germany Still Innovate?," *McKinsey Quarterly* 3 (1996), 142–53.

171. Jürgen Kluge, Jürgen Meffe, and Lother Stein, "The German Road to Innovation," *McKinsey Quarterly* 2 (2000).

172. Brian Bloch and Klaus J. Groth, "German Managerial Failure: The Other Side of the Globalization Dilemma," *European Business Review* 98/6 (1998), 311–21.

173. Streeck, "German Capitalism," 27.

174. Richard Tromans, "Neuer Markt Set to Close in 2003," *Legal Week*, 3 October 2002; John Schmid, "Germans Give Up on Neuer Tech Exchange," *International Herald Tribune*, 27 September 2002; Heather Stewart and Charlotte Denny, "How Germany Paid for the Boom," *Guardian*, 11 October 2002.

175. Bertrand Benoit and Alex Skorecki, "Since April 2000 Germany's Neuer Markt Had Shrunk by EUROs 211 bn," *Financial Times*, 27 April 2002.

176. Mark Landler, "Schröder Says He Won't Quit Despite Strife in His Party," *New York Times*, 12 December 2002.

177. David Card and Richard B. Freeman, "What Have Two Decades of British Economic Reform Delivered?," National Bureau of Economic Research, Working Paper no. 8801 (February 2002), 2, 167.

178. Ibid., 18, 19, 20.

179. Ibid., 3.

180. "Continental Drift," *Economist*, 20 April 2002; "Gordon's Gamble," *Economist*, 20 April 2002.

181. Larry Elliott, "Brown's 'Hands Off' Warning to Brussels," *Guardian*, 7 May 2001; Larry Elliott, "Brown Slaps Down EC," *Guardian*, 8 May 2001. See also "A Dangerous Game," *Economist*, 7 December 2002; "Tonier Than Thou," *Economist*, 12 October 2002.

182. Muravchik, *Heaven on Earth*, 301–9.

183. "New Labour's Report Card," *Economist*, 10 June 2000.

184. Neil Berry, "Anxious Anatomists of Blair's Britain," *Contemporary Review* (March 2001), 135–43; Peter David, "Britain Is Different," *Economist*, 6 November 1999.

185. "Britain, Out of Harmony Again," *Economist*, 28 November 1998.

186. "Whine, Gripe, Bluster: Business and Government," *Economist*, 23 November 2002.

187. Reginald Dale, "What the 'Third Way' Is Really About," *International Herald Tribune*, 4 April 2000.

188. George Jones and Ambrose Evans-Pritchard, "Chirac Angers Blair by Backing EU Army," *Electronic Telegraph*, 8 December 2000.

189. "Berlusconi, Blair and the Italian Connection," *Daily Telegraph*, 16 February 2002.

190. "Spanish Daily Sees Revival of Spanish–UK Alliance" (BBC Monitoring, 4 January 2002), *La Vanguardia*, 2 January 2002; "Aznar's Ascent: The Spanish Prime Minister Tells Leslie Crawford, Lionel Barber, and Tom Burns of His Twin Goals: A Seat for His Country at Europe's Top Table and a Balanced Budget at Home," *Financial Times*, 18 July 2000.

191. "Analysis: Britain's Blair and Europe" (United Press International, 26 September 2000); "Blair's Vision," *Economist*, 30 September 2000.

192. "The Spleen of Europe: Why Brussels Is Angry with Blair," *Economist*, 24 March 2001.

193. Brian Groom and Ed Crooks, "Gordon Brown's Global Vision for the EU," *Financial Times*, 18 January; Ellen Kelleher and Ruth Sullivan, "Gordon Brown," *Financial Times*, 15 February 2001.

194. "The Debate That Will Not Die," *Economist*, 17 June 2000; "The Euro Could Cost Tony Blair Dearly," *Business Week*, 3 July 2000.

195. "Britain, A Power in the World," *Economist*, 6 November 1999. See also "Blair Denied Backing in Euro Campaign," *Times*, 4 June 2001; "Blair Sacks Pro-Euro Cook," *Daily Telegraph*, 9 June 2001.

196. "Britain and Europe" (20 September 1988), in Martin Holmes (Ed.), *Bruges Revisited* (London, n.d.), ⟨http://eurocritic.demon.co.uk/bruges.htm⟩.

197. Ibid., 5.

198. Ibid., 4.

199. Ibid., 4.

200. Ibid., 5.

201. Ibid., 6.
202. "Standing Firm on Europe," *Economist,* 19 April 1997; "The Flight of the Tory Pro-Europeans," *Economist,* 1 June 1996.
203. Patrick Wintour, "Blair Asks French to Be Quiet on EU," *Guardian,* 23 May 2001.
204. Ian Black, "Britain's Are Dunces on Europe," *Guardian,* 30 April 2001.
205. Ambrose Evans-Pritchard, "It's Now Blasphemy to Mock Europe," *Spectator,* 18 November 2000; Anthony Jay, "All Bureaucracies Are Bad, but the EC Is a Federalizing Behemoth," (www.euro-sceptic.org).
206. George Jones, "The 34 Areas Where Power Was Given Up," *Daily Telegraph,* 13 December 2000.
207. Christopher Booker, "Europe and Regulation: The New Totalitarianism," in Martin Holmes (Ed.), *The Euroskeptical Reader* (London, 1996), 186–204.
208. Thatcher, *Statecraft.*
209. Ibid., 372–6.
210. Ibid., 380.
211. Ibid., 375.
212. Ibid., 403–8.
213. "A Hard Bargain," *Times,* 26 October 2002; "Gerhard Fumbles, Tony Fumes, Jacques Wins, We Lose," *The Business,* 27 October 2002; "Blair, Chirac Clash over Agriculture" (Associated Press, 28 October 2002).
214. "Poll Suggests Public Hostility Likely to Push Back Euro Entry," *Evening News* (Edinburgh), 18 October 2002.
215. Mark Landler, "Europe Strains to Put Laggards Back in Line," *New York Times,* 27 October 2002.
216. Ibid.
217. "Poll Suggests Public Hostility" (see n. 214).
218. Bob Worcester, "Reluctant Europeans: Forget Tony Blair's Election Promises – There Will Be no EURO Referendum This Parliament," *Guardian,* 21 October 2002.
219. Norman Lamont, "Why Europe Can't Be a Democracy," *Spectator,* 20 October 2001.

CHAPTER 14

1. Michael Ellman, "The Political Economy of Transformation," *Oxford Review of Economic Policy* 13/2 (Summer 1997), 33–43.
2. European Commission, "European Union Enlargement: A Historic Opportunity" (1999).
3. Ulrich Sedelmaier and Helen Wallace, "Eastern Enlargement," in Wallace and Wallace, *Policy-Making* (see chap. 6, n. 52); Victoria Curzon Price, Alice Landau, and Richard G. Whitman, *The Enlargement of the European Union: Issues and Strategies* (London, 1999); Leszek Balcerowicz, "Europe Growing Together," in Curzon Price et al., *Enlargement.*
4. Curzon Price, "Reintegrating Europe Economic Aspects," in Curzon Price et al., *Enlargement,* 45–6.
5. Ibid., 50.
6. Ibid., 35.
7. Laszlo Csaba, "Double Talk – The Political Economy of Eastward Enlargement of the EU," *Intereconomics* 36/5 (September/October 2001), 235–43.
8. "Portugal's Farms Will Not Survive without EU Aid," *Diario de Noticias,* 24 July 2002.
9. "Farmer Franz Fischler," *Economist,* 6 July 2002.
10. "To Get Them In, Cut the Costs: Enlarging the European Union," *Economist,* 2 February 2002.
11. Rosemary Righter, "EU Entry Will Cost Big Bang Ten Too Much," *Times,* 25 June 2002.
12. Andreas Middel, "Neue Runde Im Beitrittspoker," *Die Welt,* 26 May 2000.
13. Leszek Balcerowicz, "Why Wait for the Euro?," *Financial Times Information,* 30 May 2002.
14. Ibid., 235–43.
15. Harry Epp, "Myth and Reality: EU Enlargement Policy (unpublished manuscript, July 2002); see also Sedelmaier and Wallace, "Eastern Enlargement," 431–3.
16. Sedelmaier and Wallace, "Eastern Enlargement," 433.

17. Ibid., 440; "Hans van den Broek, Europe's Expander," *Economist*, 6 June 1998.
18. Curzon Price, *Enlargement*, 15.
19. Ibid.
20. European Commission, "Historic Opportunity."
21. Sedelmaier and Wallace, "Eastern Enlargement," 440–1.
22. European Commission, "Agenda 2000: Strengthening the Union and Preparing for Enlargement" (n.d.); "Just Small Change: The EU Budget," *Economist*, 18 October 2000.
23. "Fahrplan der EU," *Die Welt*, 5 September 2000.
24. Csaba, "Double Talk," 238.
25. Stephen Castle, "Expansionist Dream Turns into Nightmare for Europe's Leaders," *Independent*, 7 May 2001.
26. "Stockholm Syndrome," *Times*, 27 March 2001; "Europe: Liberalize? Regulate? Both," *Economist*, 10 March 2001.
27. "Europe: Snore, Snore: After the EU Summit," *Economist*, 29 June 2002.
28. Thomas Fuller, "At What Price a Bigger EU?," *International Herald Tribune*, 14 June 2002.
29. Bernard Kohler, "No Criticism without Praise," *Frankfurter Allgemeine* (Archive), 9 November 2000.
30. Roger Boyes, "German Enthusiasm for Bigger EU Shrinks in the Wash," *Times*, 14 March 2001.
31. "EU Enlargement Study Quells Worst Migration Fears," Europe Information Service – Euro East, 27 June 2000.
32. "Deutschland muss mit Zuwanderungswelle rechnen," *Handelsblatt.com*, 22 April 01.
33. "EU Enlargement: Verheugen Warns on Political Intrusion into EU Economics," *European Report*, 26 July 2000.
34. Csaba, "Double Talk," 240.
35. "EU-Osterweiterung: Die Koalition des Schweigens bricht," *Die Welt*, 5 September 2000; "Verheugens Rabubruch," *Die Welt*, 5 September 2000; "Merkel: Regierung versagt in Europa-Politik," *Die Welt*, 7 September 2000.
36. European Commission, "The Free Movement of Workers in the Context of Enlargement" (6 March 2001), 10.
37. "Growing Pains: The European Union Must Solve Many Internal Problems Before It Can Begin to Admit New Members from the East," *Time International*, 22 March 1999; "Die Jahrhundert Chance … In Wahrheit profitiert kaum ein Land so start wie Deutschlend," *manager-magazin*, December 2000.
38. "Europe: A Row about a Bigger EU," *Economist*, 9 September 2000; Nikolaus Blome, "Kämpfen für die EU: Verheugen had nicht in aller Ruhe bis zu Ende gedacht," *Die Welt*, 5 September 2000.
39. "Germany Rejects Referendum on EU's Eastward Enlargement," *Frankfurter Allgemeine* (Archive), 3 September 2000.
40. "Bundesbank-Chef Welteke warnt vor Gefahren durch EU-Osterweiterung," *Die Welt*, 4 December 2000; "EU-Osterweiterung kommt nicht vom Fleck," *Die Welt*, 10 March 2001.
41. "Verheugen Gives Poles Hope for EU Aspirations," *Frankfurter Allgemeine* (Archive), 30 October 2000.
42. Csaba, "Double Talk," 236.
43. "To Get Them In" (see n. 10).
44. Ambrose Evans-Pritchard, "New EU Countries Facing 'Second Division' Status," *Daily Telegraph*, 15 June 2002.
45. Thomas Fuller, "At What Price."
46. Klaus Frohberg and Monika Hartmann, "Financing Enlargement: The Case of Agriculture and Rural Development," *Intereconomics* (March/April 2002), 75.
47. Cited in Fuller, "At What Price."
48. Giles Merritt, "It's Time Now to Find Out What Europeans Want," *International Herald Tribune*, 6 February 2001.
49. "In the Dumps Again: Eastern Germany's Economy and Voters," *Economist*, 16 March 2002.
50. "The Schroiber Conundrum," *Financial Times*, 3 June 2002.
51. Edward Pilkington and John Hoper, "Schröder Puts New Berlin Center-stage," *Guardian*, 11 May 2002.

52. "Konferenz zur Osterweiterung. Stoiber fordert radikale Reform der EU," *Süddeutsche Zeitung,* 8 June 2002.
53. Martin Walker, "Europe's Farming Follies" (United Press International, 28 July 2002).
54. Claire Wilkenson, "Sowing Dissension," *Barron's,* 22 July 2002; Michael Mann and Lionel Barber, "An Appetite for Change," *Financial Times,* 9 April 2001.
55. "To Get Them In."
56. "Farmer Franz Fischler" (see n. 9).
57. Curzon Price, *Enlargement,* 27.
58. Cited in Fuller, "At What Price."
59. "Ready to Join but not Keen," *Economist,* 14 December 2002.
60. Cited in Fuller, "At What Price."
61. Andrew Stuttaford, "Back to Normal: Estonia's Effort to Overcome Fifty Years of Soviet Control," *National Review,* 1 November 1993, 22–5.
62. "In the Fast Lane: Seven Years after Regaining Independence, Estonia Is Well on the Way to Joining the EU," *Baltic Review,* 10 December 1998.
63. "Estonia: A Shining Example of Economic Transformation," *Business America* 118/8 (August 1997); John Hoag and Mark Kasoff, "Estonia in Transition," *Journal of Economic Issues* 44/4 (December 1999), 919–20; International Monetary Fund, "Estonia: Second Review under the Standby Arrangement – Staff Report," *Country Report* 1/14 (January 2001).
64. "Estonia's Latest Challenge," *Economist,* 13 March 1999.
65. "Mart Laar: Estonia's Punchy Prime Minister," *Economist,* 24 February 2001.
66. Ibid.
67. "In the Fast Lane" (see n. 62).
68. Razeen Sally, "Estonian Trade Policy, 1991–2000," *World Economy* 25/1 (January 2002), 79–106.
69. "Estonians Divided over EU Accession," *Financial Times,* 7 November 2001.
70. "Enlargement: Polls Say Estonians Are Euroskeptic. Other Candidates Pessimistic," *European Report,* 2 March 2002.
71. Ibid.
72. Ibid.; "Estonian Press Article Tells Businessmen EU No Different from USSR" (BBC Monitoring, 30 May 2002).
73. "Newspaper Urges Estonia to Consider Staying Out of EU" (BBC Monitoring, 10 May 2002).
74. Ibid.
75. "EU Calls for Tax Policy Changes: Talinn Seethes," *Baltic Times,* 14 March 2002.
76. Ibid.
77. "Estonian Prime Minister Calls on Government and Parliament to Intensify Efforts for Entry into EU" (Interfax, 11 April 2002).
78. "Estonia Lags Behind in EU Negotiations," *Europe,* May 2002, 3.
79. "Percentage of Euroskeptics increases in Estonia" (Baltic News Service, 27 July 2002).
80. Brian Caplan, "Out of the Frying Pan into the Fire," *Euromoney* (April 2002), 76.
81. Curzon Price, *Enlargement,* 51 (emphasis in original).
82. Caplan, "Into the Fire," 54.
83. Ibid.
84. Ibid.
85. Jonathan Fenby, "Germany, France Have Second Thoughts on European Union Enlargement," *Knight-Ridder Business News,* 10 February 2002.
86. Fuller, "At What Price."
87. Sally, "Estonian Trade Policy," 99.
88. János Kornai: "The Postsocialist Transition and the State: Reflections in the Light of Hungarian Fiscal Problems," *American Economic Review* 82/2 (Papers and Proceedings of the 104th Annual Meeting of the American Economic Association, 4 May 1992), 1–21; "Paying the Bill for Goulash Communism: Hungarian Development and Macro-stabilization in a Political-economic Perspective," *Social Research* 63/4 (Winter 1996), 943–1004.
89. Laszlo Csaba, "A Decade of Transformation in Hungarian Economic Policy: Dynamics, Constraints and Prospects," *Europe-Asia Studies* 50/8 (December 1998), 1381–91.
90. Bartlomeij Kaminski, "Industrial Restructuring as Revealed in Hungary's Pattern of Integration into European Union Markets," *Europe-Asia Studies* 52/3 (2000), 465.

91. Ernest S. McCrary, "Hungary Headed for the EU," *Global Finance* 16/3 (March 2002), 57.
92. Csaba, "Decade of Transformation."
93. "He Admits He Spied But It Was Long Ago: Hungary's Embattled Prime Minister," *Economist*, 22 June 2002.
94. "Central Europe/Baltic Media Roundup on EU-related Issues," 21–27 March 2002 (BBC Worldwide Monitoring).
95. "Is Central Europe, along with Hungary, Turning Right?," *Economist*, 30 May 1998.
96. "Viktor Orban, an Assertive Hungarian," *Economist*, 2 March 2002.
97. "Central Europe/Baltic Media Roundup on EU-related Issues," 4–10 April 2002 (BBC Worldwide Monitoring).
98. "Viktor Orban."
99. "Beaten but Not Abashed; Hungary's New Right," *Economist*, 15 June 2002.
100. "Hungarian Ex-premier Says No to Privatization," 22 July 2002 (BBC Worldwide Monitoring).
101. "Central Europe/Baltic Media Roundup on EU-related Issues," 27 March and 11 April 2002 (BBC Worldwide Monitoring).
102. "Hungarian Ex-premier."
103. Neal Ascherson, "The Ghosts of Past Invasions That Still Haunt Poland," *Guardian*, 21 February 1999; Tomasz Zarycki, "Politics in the Periphery: Political Cleavages in Poland Interpreted in their Historical and International Context," *Europe-Asia Studies* 52/5 (July 2000), 581–910.
104. Janusz Lewandowski, "Privatizing the Communist State," *Quadrant* 43/4 (April, 1999), 23–30; Eric Hanley, "Cadre Capitalism in Hungary and Poland: Property Accumulation among Post-Communist Elites," *East European Politics and Society* 14/1 (Winter 2000), 150–1.
105. Elizabeth Pond, "Miracle on the Vistula," *Washington Quarterly* 21/3 (Summer 1998), 210.
106. See George Blazyca, "Polish Socioeconomic Development in the 1990s and the Scenarios for EU Accession," *Europe-Asia Studies* 51/5 (July 1999), 799–825.
107. Ibid., 805–6.
108. Vladimir Popov, "Shock Therapy versus Gradualism," *Comparative Economic Studies* 41/1 (Spring 2000), 1–45.
109. Balcerowicz, "Europe Growing Together"; Leszek Balcerowicz, "Poland's Transformation," *Finance and Development* 37/3 (September 2000), 14–20.
110. Pond, "Miracle," 310–11; Balcerowicz, "Poland's Transformation"; Balcerowicz, "Europe Growing Together," 3–9.
111. Pond, "Miracle," 213–14; Blazyca, "Socioeconomic Development," 805–6.
112. Pond, "Miracle."
113. Ibid., 216.
114. Ibid., 217.
115. Lewandowski, "Privatizing"; Mark J. Bonamo, "Poland's Privatization Process: A View from the Inside," *Journal of International Affairs* 50/2 (Winter 1997), 573–80.
116. Carolyn Campbell, "The Impact of EU Association on Industrial Policy Making," *East European Quarterly* 35/4 (Winter 2001), 502.
117. Ibid., 504.
118. Ibid., 506–7.
119. Blzyca, "Socioeconomic Development," 801; Campbell, "Impact of EU Association," 509.
120. "Solidarity versus Solidarity," *Economist*, 25 April 1998.
121. Zarycki, "Political Cleavages," 866.
122. Tony Paterson, "Polish Farmers Declare War over EU Membership," *Guardian*, 18 April 2000; David Walker, "Ploughshares," *Guardian*, 20 April 2000.
123. "Poland's Angry Second Nation," *Economist*, 1 October 2000.
124. Andrew Nagorski, "A Bumper Crop of Despair: Warsaw Wants to Join the Club by 2003. The EU's Policies Will Crush Many Polish Farmers before Then," *Newsweek International*, 29 November 1999.
125. Toby Helm, "Let Germans Return to Poland, Says Stoiber," *Daily Telegraph*, 25 June 2002.
126. "A Most Emotional Issue: Polish Land," *Economist*, 23 March 2002.
127. Janusz Mucha and Marek S. Szczepanski, "Polish Society in the Perspective of its Integration with the European Union," *East European Quarterly* 35/4 (Winter 2001), 485.

128. Blazyca, "Socioeconomic Development," 803.
129. Mucha and Szczepanski, "Polish Society," 486.
130. "The Left is Back – In the Center: Poland's Election," *Economist,* 29 September 2001.
131. "Leszek Miller: Poland's Wily Man of the Future," *Economist,* 21 April 2001.
132. Anne Applebaum, "Slippery Pole," *Spectator,* 31 August 2002.
133. Ibid.
134. Wojciech Kosc, "Poland: Government vs. Balcerowicz" (PAP News Wire, 1 July 2002).
135. John Reed, "Poland's Plum Jobs Go to Ministers' Allies," *Financial Times,* 19 February 2002; John Reed, "Probe Launched into 14 Polish State Concerns," *Financial Times,* 9 May 2002.
136. "Polish Tale of Bribery," *New York Times,* 12 February 2003.
137. "Nice Holiday, Pity about the Job: Poland's Economy," *Economist,* 27 July 2002.
138. "Poles Prefer Old Communists to Ex-communists: Poll" (*Agence France Presse,* 31 July 2002).
139. "Miller: Cabinet Reshuffle Poses No Threat to EU Negotiations" (PAP News Wire, 11 July 2002); "Miller on Stoiber's Demand" (PAP News Wire, 25 June 2002).
140. "Poland Talks Tough on Farm Subsidies" (*Deutsche Presse-Agentur,* 17 June 2002); Elzbieta Kawecka-Wyrzykowska, "Merits and Shortcomings of the Commission's Financial Framework for Eastward Enlargement," *Intereconomics* 37/2 (March/April 2002).
141. "Over Half of Poles Support Integration with EU" (PAP News Wire, 13 March 2002).
142. "Poland's Populist: Andrzej Lepper," *Economist,* 29 June 2002.
143. Maja Czarnecka, "Polish Opposition Calls on Government to Abandon EU or Resign" (*Agence France Presse,* 25 June 2002); Roger Boyes, "Polish Farm Hands Show Solidarity against EU," *Times,* 26 June 2002; "Maverick Polish Populist Spills German Grain in Protest against Imports" (*Deutsche Presse-Agentur,* 6 June 2002).
144. Chris Mularczyk, "The Rise of Andrzej Lepper" (*Warsaw Business Journal* Global News Wire, 27 May 2002).
145. Charles Clover, "Pig Farmer Blocks EU Stampede," *Daily Telegraph,* 6 July 2002.
146. "The End of Work and a New Beginning for Polish Trade Unions," *Gazeta Wyborcza,* 7 April 2002.
147. Ibid.
148. Anna Kocinska, "Anti-EU Voices Talking Louder but Not Agreeing" (*Warsaw Business Journal* Global News Wire, 20 May 2002).
149. "Giertych Set to Ride Euroskeptic Boiling Point to Rightwing Leadership" (Polish News Bulletin, 2 May 2002); Andrew Nagorski, "Backlash in the East: Polish Right Wing," *Newsweek International,* 13 May 2002; "Right-wing Sympathizers Stage Anti-EU Demo" (BBC Monitoring).
150. Tomasz Zukowski, *Spektakl na zamkniecie sezonu. Wybory w teatrze polityki* (Wiez, 1996), 104.
151. "Giertych Set to Ride."
152. "On the Rise: Poland's Right-wingers," *Economist,* 14 December 2002.
153. "Unfinished Business: Poland Prepares for Europe," *Economist,* 20 September 1997.
154. Ian Fischer, "As Poland Endures Hard Times, Capitalism Comes under Attack," *New York Times,* 12 June 2002.
155. John Reed, "Race Is on to Reform Finances … Speed and Recovery Is Crucial to EU Membership," *Financial Times,* 17 June 2002.
156. Balcerowicz, "Why Wait."
157. John Reed, "Wobbles in Warsaw: The Appointment of Grzegorz Kolodko … Has Unsettled Investors," *Financial Times,* 9 July 2002; Piotr Zarembka, "The Unpleasant Arrogance of Grzegorz Kolodko," *Rzeczpospolita,* 9 July 2002; "Finance Minister Proposes Measures to Stimulate Economy (BBC Monitoring Europe, 16 July 2002).
158. "Finance Chief Puts on Brave Face as Poland Is Downgraded," *Financial Times,* 1 August 2002.
159. Zarembka, "Grzegorz Kolodko."
160. James Hossack, "EU Starts Countdown to Enlargement after Crucial Deal on Funding" (*Agence France Presse,* 26 October 2002).
161. Jenkins, "Blair against the Old Enemy."
162. "EU Accession Breakthrough?," *Financial Times,* 3 November 2002.
163. "European Council: Brussels Cuts a Curious Deal to Open Doors to Enlargement" (European Information Service, 30 October 2002); Axel Mönch, "Dämpfer für Agrarreform vor 2007.

Obligatorische Modulation dürfte nach Brüsseler EU-Gipfelspäter kommen," *Deutscher Fachverlag GmbH. Agrarzeitung Ernährungsdienst,* 22 October 2002.

164. "Brussels Cuts a Curious Deal."
165. Ibid.
166. "Poland Suggests Summit with All EU Candidates," *Financial Times,* 29 October 2002.
167. "EU Accession Breakthrough?"
168. "Czech Farmers March on Prague, Threaten to Vote down EU" (*Deutsche Presse-Agentur,* 30 October 2002).
169. Robert Graham, "Cock of Europe's Roost," *Financial Times,* 2 November 2002.
170. Ambrose Evans-Pritchard, "Farm Deal Keeps EU Enlargement Plans on Track," *Daily Telegraph,* 26 October 2002.
171. Jenkins, "Blair against the Old Enemy."
172. David Charter and Rory Watson, "Britain Attacks France over EU Subsidies," *Times,* 26 October.

CHAPTER 15

1. Michael Lewis, "In Defense of the Boom," *New York Times Magazine,* 27 October 2002, 44–5.
2. George Gilder, "The Coming Capitalist Reversal," *American Spectator* (online), November/December 2002.
3. "The Unfinished Recession: A Survey of the World Economy," *Economist,* 28 September 2002, 3–28.
4. Lionel Barber, "Europe Seeks a Third Way to Prosperity," in *Europe Reinvented* (Part I: The New European Political Order), *Financial Times* (March 2001). See also "Part II: The New Rules of the Game"; "Part III: The Challenge of Globalisation"; "Part IV: Europe's New Capitalism."
5. Ibid.
6. Nikolaus Blome, "Der erschöpfte Gipfel," *Die Welt,* 24 March 2001.
7. Ibid.
8. Barry James, "Agreeing on Little, EU Leaders Muddle Ahead," *International Herald Tribune,* 26 March 2001.
9. "So Much for Dynamic: European Liberalisation," *Economist,* 3 November 2001.
10. James, "Agreeing on Little."
11. Ambrose Evans-Pritchard, "Blair Faces Free Market Struggle at EU Summit," *Electronic Telegraph,* 22 March 2001.
12. Julian Coman, "France Sabotages Summit over Free Market Reforms," *Electronic Telegraph,* 25 March 2001.
13. "So Much for Dynamic" (see n. 9).
14. Hanson, "What Happened."
15. Ibid.
16. Martin Neil Baily and Robert Z. Lawrence, "Do We Have a New E-conomy?," National Bureau of Economic Research, Working Paper no. 8243 (April 2001).
17. Ibid.
18. Ibid.
19. Lewis, "In Defense of the Boom."
20. Daniel Altman, "Productivity Is Up Sharply, in Good Sign for Long Term," *New York Times,* 8 November 2002.
21. David B. Audretsch and A. Roy Thurik, "Sources of Growth: The Entrepreneurial Economy versus the Managed Economy," Centre for Economic Policy Research, Discussion Paper Series, no. 1710 (October, 1997), 1–73.
22. Ibid., 2.
23. Ibid., 3, 4.
24. Peter Marsh, "The Old Economy Strikes Back," in *Europe Reinvented* (Part IV) (see n. 4); Tim Burt, "The End of the Road," ibid.; David Pilling, "U.S. Dominance Creates an Irresistible Attraction," ibid.
25. "Finance and Economics: Swedes Chopped: Europe's High-tech Economies," *Economist,* 8 September 2001.

26. Doyle, "Liberalizing Networking Industries; Michael L. Katz and Carl Shapiro, "Systems Competition and Network Effects," *Journal of Economic Perspectives* 8/2 (Spring 1994), 93–115.
27. Charles Pretzlik, "U.S. Banks Take Europe by Storm" in *Europe Reinvented* (Part IV) (see n. 4).

28. Frits Bolkestein, "Defusing Europe's Pensions Timebomb" (Speech, Brussels, 6 February 2001).
29. Frits Bolkestein, "Integration of Financial Markets in Europe" (Speech, Prague, 23 September 2000).
30. Russell Carlberg, "The Persistence of the *Dirigiste* Model: Wireless Spectrum Allocation *a la francaise*," *Federal Telecommunications Journal* 54/1 (December 2001), 129–30.
31. "The Faulty Connection: Wireless: Why Europe's Telcoms Stumbled and Fell in the Race to Build Third Generation Services," *Newsweek,* 17 September 2001.
32. Graham Lynch and Tony Chan, "3G's Financial and Technical Booby Traps," *America's Network,* 1 June 2000; Stephen McClelland, "Europe's Wireless Futures," *Microwave Journal* 42/19 (September 2000), 78–9; "The Tortoise and the Hare," *Economist,* 16 March 2002; Stephen Baker et al., "Telcom Tremors: Will 3G Flop or Fly?" *Business Week,* 16 October 2000.
33. Gilder, "Capitalist Reversal."
34. Brian Carney, "Europe: The Great Unwired," *American Spectator,* May/June 2002; "Time for Plan B: Mobile Telecoms," *Economist,* 28 September 2002; "Let Europe's Operators Free: 3G Telecoms," *Economist,* 28 September 2002.
35. "Tale of a Bubble: How the 3G Fiasco Came Close to Wrecking Europe," *Business Week,* 3 June 2002.
36. Julian Bright, "Playing for Time," *Communications International* (September 2002), 42–4; Emma McClune, "Mothball Mania," *Communications International* (September 2002) 35–6; "3G on Hold," *Business Europe,* 18 September 2002.
37. Ibid.; "Broadband Bust: Vast Overcapacity Has Europe's Upstart Providers Going Under," *Business Week,* 17 June 2002; Peter Martin, "Lazy, Hazy, Crazy Thoughts: Old Models of Corporate Growth Are Dying," *Financial Times,* 30 July 2002.
38. Carlberg, "Persistence of *Dirigiste*," 135.
39. See Peter F. Cowhey, "The International Telecommunications Regime: The Political Roots of Regimes for High Technologies," *Industrial Organization* 44/2 (Spring 1990), 169–99; see also Wayne Sandholtz, "Institutions and Collective Action: The New Telecommunications in Western Europe," *World Politics* 45/2 (January 1993), 242–70.
40. Josef Esser and Ronald Noppe, "Private Muddling Through as a Political Program? The Role of the European Commission in the Telecommunications Sector in the 1980s," *West European Politics* 19/3 (1996), 547–8.
41. Ibid., 552.
42. Paul Gannon, "Europe: Regulating Across Borders," *Telecommunications* 31/10 (October 1997), 29–30.
43. Leonard Waverman and Esen Sirel, "European Telecommunications Markets on the Verge of Liberalization," *Journal of Economic Perspectives* 11/4 (Fall 1997), 113–36.
44. Jonathan Solomon and Dawson Walker, "The Transformation of the Telecommunications Industry in Europe," *European Business Journal* 8/2 (1996), 22–7.
45. Myles Denny-Brown, "Privatization and Liberalization in the European Union," *Business America* 118/7 (July 1997), 19–20.
46. Bhawani Shankar, "Boundless Europe: The Wireless Revolution," *Telecommunications* 31/11 (November 1997), 60.
47. Ibid., 59–64.
48. Christopher Brown-Humes, "Nokia Sets the Standard," in *Europe Reinvented* (Part III) (see n. 4).
49. Ibid.
50. Erkki Liikanen, "eEurope – An Information Society for All" (Speech, Dublin, 23 April 2001).
51. "European Commission Unveils new eEurope Plan," *Europemedia,* 30 May 2002; Bruce Barnard, "e-Europe," *Europe* (May 2002).
52. Ibid.
53. Malcolm Penn, "A Fiasco in the Making?," *Electronic Engineering Times,* 13 May 2002, 32–3.
54. "Broadband Bust" (see n. 37).

55. "Tale of a Bubble" (see n. 35).
56. "Faulty Connection" (see n. 31).
57. Ibid.
58. Ibid.
59. Ibid.
60. "Tale of a Bubble."
61. Josep Isern and Maria Isabel Rios, "Facing Disconnection: Hard Choices for Europe's Telcos," *McKinsey Quarterly* (Winter 2002), 92–3.
62. "Broadband Bust."
63. "Tortoise and the Hare" (see n. 32); Christopher Brown-Humes, "A Meeting of the Minds as Microsoft Sets Up a Challenge," *Financial Times,* 17 July 2002; Mark Halper, "Steve and Jorma Make the Hard Call," *Fortune,* 29 April 2002.
64. Martin, "Lazy, Hazy."
65. Ibid.
66. Ibid.
67. See Geert Bekaert, Campbell R. Harvey, and Christian Lundblad, "Does Financial Liberalization Spur Growth?," National Bureau of Economic Research, Working Paper no. 8245 (April 2001).
68. Pretzlik, "Banks Take Europe by Storm."
69. Ibid.
70. Bozidar Djelic, Andrew Doman, and John R. Woerner, "Investing in Europe," *McKinsey Quarterly* (Winter 2000), 14.
71. Chris Davison, "Euro Awaits Single Financial Market," *Euromoney* 392 (December 2001), 76–82.
72. Sarah Smith, "Europe's Bumpy Fields," *Banker* 143/814 (1992), 34; see also Anthony D. Loehnis, "EC on Its Way to Integrating Markets," *American Banker* 156/240 (December 1991), 1–3.
73. "Banking's Chequered Future," *International Management* 47/9 (October 1992), 64.
74. Ibid.
75. Ibid., 65.
76. David Hunt, "What Future for Europe's Investment Banks?," *McKinsey Quarterly* (Winter 1995), 104–5.
77. Ibid.
78. Ibid.
79. Ibid.
80. Adrian Hamilton, "Euromarkets Face Big Bang," *European,* 26 June 1997.
81. David Rothnie, "Growing Up in Public: The Vision for EURENEXT Was Unfurled during March 2000 in the Teeth of the Technology Slump," *European Venture Capital Journal* (1 May 2002), 42–3.
82. "Penetrating Europe's Retail Banking Market," *European Banker,* 22 May 2002.
83. James R. Kraus, "Big Banks Are Expected to Make a Killing on the Euro," *American Banker* 163/29 (12 February 1998), 20.
84. Jonathan A. Davidson, Alison R. Ledger, and Giovanni Vanni, "Wholesale Banking: The Ugly Implications of EMU," *McKinsey Quarterly* (Winter 1998), 66–82.
85. Ibid.; see also, Hamilton, "Euromarkets Face Big Bang."
86. Ibid.
87. "Suddenly, All Europe Is Saying, 'Charge It!'," *Business Week,* 8 April 2002.
88. "The Big Chill in Europe," *Business Week,* 25 March 2002.
89. "Europe Is a Growth Market in Hibernation," *Business Week,* 25 March 2002.
90. "Big Chill in Europe."
91. "Finance and Economics: Big, Bigger, Biggest: Strategies for Corporate and Institutional Banking," *Economist,* 6 April 2002.
92. "Growth Market in Hibernation."
93. Christa Randzio-Plath, "Challenges and Perspectives for a Single Market for Financial Services in Europe," *Intereconomics* (July/August 2000), 192.
94. Iain Begg and Imelda Maher, "The Inconsistent Single Market," *European Business Journal* 10/2 (Summer 1998), 47–56.
95. Ibid.

96. Ibid.
97. Ibid.
98. "Frits Bolkestein, An Almost Skeptical EU-Commissioner," *Economist,* 3 May 2001.
99. Bolkestein, "Defusing" (see n. 28).
100. "Face Value: The Bruiser from Brussels," *Economist,* 22 April 2000.
101. Bolkestein, "Defusing."
102. OECD, "Economic Surveys. Euro Area" (Geneva, July 2002), 57.
103. Ibid., 64–71.
104. Ibid., 70.
105. Ibid., 66.
106. Ibid., 58–9.
107. David Shirreff, "Disgrace at the Heart of Europe," *Euromoney* (October 1999), 75.
108. Ibid., 11–12; "The Regulation of the European Securities Markets: The Lamfalussy Report," *Journal of International Banking Regulation* 3/1 (October 2001).
109. OECD, "Economic Surveys" (see n. 102).
110. Chris Davison, "Euro Awaits Single Financial Market," *Euromoney* 392 (December 2001).
111. Ibid.
112. Emma Daly, "EU Plan Called Overambitious," *International Herald Tribune,* 27 March 2001.
113. Frits Bolkestein, "The Financial Services Action Plan" (Speech, Brussels, 3 June 2002).
114. Bolkestein, "Defusing."
115. Ibid.
116. Shirreff, "Disgrace."
117. George Pagoulatos, "European Banking: Five Modes of Governance," *West European Politics* 22/1 (January 1999), 68–88.
118. Sveinbjorn Blondal and Dirk Pilat, "The Economic Benefits of Regulatory Reform," *OECD Economic Studies* 28 (Spring 1997), 2–47.
119. "Don't Bank on Brusssels: Botching Bank Regulation," *Economist,* 21 April 2001.
120. "What Single Market?," *Banker* 148/872 (October 1998), 7.
121. "Finance and Economics: Scrapping over the Pieces: European Financial Services," *Economist,* 9 March 2002.
122. Ibid.
123. Alberto Alesina and Romain Warcziarg, "Is Europe Going Too Far?," National Bureau of Economic Research, Working Paper no. 6883 (January 1989), 1–45.
124. Ibid., 1, 3, 12.
125. Ibid., 13.
126. Ibid.
127. Ibid., 3.
128. Ibid., 14.
129. William Echickson, "The Equalizer," *Business Week,* 9 October 2000; "Spaghetti Monti," *Economist,* 81; Janet Guyon, "Why Europe Makes Microsoft Nervous," *Business Week,* 12 November 2001; "Invasion of the Cartel Cops," *Business Week,* 8 May 2000; "When Monti Spoke, Everyone Listened," *Business Week,* 25 March 2002; Mario Monti, "Local Loop Unbundling"(Speech, 8 July 2002); "Monti Braves the Catcalls," *Economist,* 15 December 2001.
130. Ivo Dalway, "How Monti Riled the Yanks," *Spectator,* 7 July 2001, 16.
131. Mario Monti, "By Invitation," *Economist,* 9 November 2002.
132. David Smith, "How Single the Single Market?," *Management Today* (January 1990), 54–8.
133. Victoria Curzon Price, "Britain's Future in Europe: A Personal View," *Journal of the Institute of Economic Affairs* 17/1 (March 1997), 16–22.
134. "Economic Reform: European Commission's Second Annual Report (Highlights)," *European Business Journal* 12/2 (2000), 63–6; Doyle, "Liberalizing Network Industries."
135. Paula Stern, "New Paradigm for Trade Expansion and Regulatory Harmonization: The Trans-Atlantic Business Dialog," *European Business Journal* 9/3 (Autumn 1997), 35–47.
136. Brittan, *Diet of Brussels,* 161–71.
137. Lionel Barber, "The New Transatlantic Dialog," *Europe* 369 (September 1997), 6–9.
138. Giandomenico Majone, "The Credibility Crisis of Community Regulation," *Journal of Common Market Studies* 38/2 (June 2000), 273–302.

139. Ibid., 278.
140. Ibid., 290–1.
141. Giandomenico Majone, "From the Positive to the Regulatory State: Causes and Consequences of Changes in the Model of Governance," Estudio Working Paper no. 1957/53 (June 1997).
142. Martin Ricketts, cited in John Blundell and Colin P. Robinson, "Regulation without the State," Institute for Economic Affairs (London, May 1999).
143. Ibid., 7.
144. Ibid., 3, 4, 5.
145. Ibid., 10–18.
146. Giandomenico Majone, "The Regulatory State and its Legitimacy Problems," IHS Wien, Political Science Series no. 56 (July 1988).
147. Ibid., 21.
148. Giandomenico Majone, "From the Positive to the Regulatory State," 10.

CONCLUSION TO PART IV

1. "And for My Next Task: The European Union's Institutional Dynamism Is Marred by Its Economic Sloth," *Economist,* 4 January 2003.

Bibliography

Abelshauser, W., "Rüstung, Wirtschaft, Ruesstungswirtschaft: Wirtschaftliche Aspekte des kalten Krieges in den fünfziger Jahren," in K. A. Maier et al. (Eds.), *Das Nordatlantische Buendnis 1949–1956* (Munich, 1993).

Akros, B., "A New Era for the Italian Stock Market," *Euromoney* 342 (October 1997).

Albert, M., *Capitalism vs. Capitalism: How America's Obsession with Individual Achievement and Short-term Profit Has Led It to the Brink of Collapse* (New York, 1993).

Alesina, A., and Wacziarg, R., "Is Europe Going Too Far?," National Bureau of Economic Research, Working Paper no. 6883 (January 1999).

Alter, K., "The European Union's Legal System and Domestic Policy: Spillover or Backlash?," *International Organization* 53/3 (Summer 2000).

Altman, O. L., "The Integration of European Capital Markets," *Journal of Finance* 20/2 (May 1965).

Ambler, J. S. (Ed.), *The French Welfare State: Surviving Social and Ideological Change* (New York, 1991).

Anderson, C., "When in Doubt, Use Proxies: Attitudes toward Domestic Politics and Support for European Integration," *Comparative Political Studies* (October 1998).

Anderton, B., "Spain: Evaluating the Effects of Macropolicy Using an Econometric Model," National Institute of Economic Research, 146 (November 1993).

Arter, David, "The March 1995 Finnish Election: The Social Democrats Storm Back," *West European Politics* 18/4 (October 1995).

Artis, M., Buti, M., Fanco, D., and Ongena, H., "Fiscal Discipline and Flexibility in EMU: The Implementation of the Stability and Growth Pact," *Oxford Review of Economic Policy* 14 (Autumn 1998).

Audretsch, D., *The Market and the State: Government Policy towards Business in Europe, Japan and the United States* (New York, 1989).

Baily, M., and Lawrence, R., "Do We Have a New Economy?," National Board of Economic Research, Working Paper no. 8243 (April 2001).

Balassa, B., Kreinin, M., Resnick, S., Thorbecke, E., and Truman, E. (Eds.), *European Economic Integration* (Amsterdam, 1975).

Balassa, B., *The Theory of Economic Integration* (Homewood, IL, 1961).

Balcerowicz, L., "Poland's Transformation," *Finance and Development* 37/3 (September 2000).

Baldassari, M. (Ed.), *The Italian Economy: Heaven or Hell?* (London 1994).

Baldwin, R., and Seghezza, E., "Growth and European Integration: Towards an Empirical Assessment," Center for Economic Policy Research, 1393 (May 1996).

Ball, G., *The Discipline of Power: Essentials of a Modern World Structure* (Boston, 1968).

Ball, G., *The Past Has Another Pattern: Memoirs* (New York, 1982).

Barber, L., "Romano's Reformation," *Europe* (March 2000).

Barber, L., "France and Germany Take Different Approaches," *Europe* (May 2000).

Barnard, B., "e-Europe," *Europe* (May 2002).

Barnes, I., and Barnes, P., *The Enlarged European Union* (London, 1995).

Bartley, R., *The Seven Fat Years* (New York, 1992).

Baun, M. J., *An Imperfect Union: The Maastricht Treaty and the New Politics of European Integration* (Oxford, 1996).

Begg, I., "Wrong Questions, Wrong Answers: The EU Economic Policy Debate since 'Maastricht'," *European Business Journal* 8/4 (1966).

Bekaert, G., Harvey, C., and Lundblad, C., "Does Financial Liberalization Spur Growth?," National Bureau of Economic Research, Working Paper no. 8245 (April 2001).

Berger, S., "French Business from Transition to Transition," in G. Ross, S. Hoffmann, and S. Malzacher (Eds.), *The Mitterrand Experiment: Continuity and Change in Modern France* (New York, 1987).

Bergsten, F., "Fifty Years of the GATT/WTO: Lessons from the Past for Strategies for the Future," Institute for International Economics, Working Paper no. 98/3 (1998).

Berry, N., "Anxious Anatomists of Blair's Britain," *Contemporary Review* 278/1622 (March 2001).

Biehl, D., "A Federalist Budgetary Policy Strategy for the European Union," *Policy Studies* (October 1985).

Blanchard, G., "The Single Market Revisited," Economist Intelligence Unit, 95/3, 1995.

Blazyca, G., "Polish Socioeconomic Development in the 1990s and the Scenarios for EU Accession," *Europe-Asia Studies* 51/5 (July 1999).

Bloch B., and Groth, K., "German Managerial Failure: The Other Side of the Globalization Dilemma," *European Business Review* 98/6 (1998).

Blom, J., "Pillarisation in Perspective," *West European Politics* 23/3 (July 2000).

Boarman, P. M., "Wilhelm Röpke: Apostle of a Humane Economy," *Society* 37/6 (September 2000).

Boltho, A. (Ed.), *The European Economy: Growth and Crisis* (Oxford 1982).

Boltho, A., "Economic Policy in France and Italy since the War: Different Stances, Different Outcomes?," *Journal of Economic Issues* 35/3 (September 2001).

Bonamo, M., "Poland's Privatization Process: A View from the Inside," *Journal of International Affairs* 50/2 (Winter 1997).

Booker, C., "Europe and Regulation: The New Totalitarianism," in M. Holmes (Ed.), *The Euroskeptical Reader* (London, 1996).

Bordo, M., and Lars, J., *Lessons for EMU from the History of Monetary Unions* (London, 2000).

Boussuat, G., and Vaicbourdt, N. (Eds.), *The United States, Europe and The European Union: Uneasy Partnership (1945–1999)* (Brussels, 2001).

Boussuat, G., and Wilkens, D. (Eds.), *Jean Monnet et les Chemins de la Paix* (Paris, 1998).

Bradshaw, J., "Constitutional Reform After Maastricht" (Economist Intelligence Unit), *European Trends* 1 (1994).

Brennan, G., and Buchanan, J. M., *The Reason of Rules: Constitutional Political Economy* (Cambridge, U.K., 1985).

Brigues, P., Jacquemin, A., and Sapir, A., *European Policies on Competition, Trade and Industry: Conflict and Complementarities* (Aldershot, 1995).

Brittan, L., *A Diet of Brussels: The Changing Face of Europe* (London, 2000).

Brown, M., "Privatization and Liberalization in the European Union," *Business America* 118/7 (July 1997).

Brzezinski, Z., et al., "Living with a Big Europe," *The National Interest* 60 (Summer 2000).

Buchanan, J., *Liberty, Market and State: Political Economy in the 1980s* (Brighton, Sussex, 1986).

Buchanan, J. M., *The Economics and the Ethics of Constitutional Order* (Ann Arbor, 1994).

Buchanan, J., and Congleton, R., *Politics by Principle, Not Interest: Toward Nondiscriminatory Democracy* (Cambridge, U.K., 1998).

Buchanan, J., Poehl, K., Price, V., and Vibert, F., *Europe's Constitutional Future* (London, 1990).

Buchanan, J. M., and Tullock, G., *The Calculus of Consent: Logical Foundations of Constitutional Democracy* (Ann Arbor, 1965).

Buck, W., "Historic Trade Pact Is Signed, Laying New Foundations for World Trade," *Business America* 115/12 (December 1994).

Buerkle, T., "The German Dilemma," *Institutional Investor* 31/1 (January 2002).

Buigues, P., Jacquemin, A., and Marchipont, J. (Eds.), *Competitiveness and the Value of Intangible Assets* (Cheltenham, 2000).

Bull, M., and Rhodes, M., "Between Crisis and Transition: Italian Politics in the 1990s," *West European Politics* 20/1 (January 1997).

Bulmer, S., "New Institutionalism, the Single Market and EU Governance," ARENA Working Paper no. 97/25 (1997).

Bulmer, S., and Scott, A., *Economic and Political Integration in Europe: Internal Dynamics and Global Context* (Oxford, 1994).

Burley, A., and Mattli, W., "Europe Before the Court," *International Organization* 47/1 (Winter 1993).

Butler, E., et al. (Eds.), *The Omega File* (Adam Smith Institute, 1982).

Cairncross, A., *The British Economy Since 1945*, 2nd ed. (Oxford, 1995).

Cairncross, A., *Living with the Century* (Bath, 1998).

Cairncross, A., Giersch, H., Lamfalussy, A., Petrilli, G., and Uri, P., *Economic Policy for the European Community: The Way Forward* (New York, 1975).

Caldwell, C., "Europe's 'Social Market'," *Policy Review* (October/November 2001).

Calleo, D., *The Imperious Economy* (Cambridge, U.K., 1982).

Calleo, D. P., *The Bankrupting of America: How the Federal Budget Is Impoverishing the Nation* (New York, 1992).

Calleo, D., *Rethinking Europe's Future* (Princeton, 2001).

Camdessus, M., "Europe's Coming of Age," *The Banker* 147/855 (May 1997).

Campbell, C., "The Impact of EU Association on Industrial Policy Making," *East European Quarterly* 35/4 (Winter 2001).

Camps, M., *What Kind of Europe?: The Community Since de Gaulle's Veto* (London, 1965).

Camps, M., *European Unification in the Sixties: From the Veto to the Crisis* (New York, 1966).

Caplan, B., "Out of the Frying Pan into the Fire," *Euromoney* (April, 2002).

Card, D., and Freeman, R., "What Have Two Decades of British Economic Reform Delivered?," National Bureau of Economic Research, Working Paper no. 8801 (February 2002).

Carlberg, R., "The Persistence of the *Dirigiste* Model: Wireless Spectrum Allocation *a la francaise*," *Federal Telecommunications Journal* 54/1 (December 2001).

Caves, R., *Multinational Enterprise and Economic Analysis* (Cambridge, U.K., 1982).

Chakravarty, S., and Molyneux, P., "The Single European Market in Financial Services," *European Business Review* 96/5 (1996).

Cini, M., *The European Commission Leadership: Organization and Culture in the EU Administration* (Manchester, 1996).

Cipolla, C. (Ed.), *Contemporary Economies,* part I. Fontana Economic History of Europe, vol. 6 (Sussex, 1977).

Cockett, R., *Thinking the Unthinkable: Think-tanks and the Economic Counter-revolution, 1931–1983* (London, 1995).

Cockfield, A., "Beyond 1992 – The Single European Economy," *European Affairs* 4 (1988).

Coffey, P. (Ed.), *Economic Policies of the Common Market* (London, 1979).

Commission of the European Communities, "Report of the Study Group on the Role of Public Finance in European Integration" (MacDougall Report), Brussels (April 1977).

Cooper, R., "Macroeconomics in an Open Economy," American Association for the Advancement of Science, 1986.

Cooper, R., "Will an EC Currency Harm Outsiders?," *Orbis* 80 (Fall 1992).

Corbet, H., and Jackson, R. (Eds.), *In Search of a New World Economic Order* (London, 1974).

Cowles, M., "Organizing Industrial Coalitions: A Challenge for the Future?," in H. Wallace and A. Young (Eds.), *Participation and Policy-Making in the European Union* (Oxford, 1997).

Cowles, M., Caporaso, J., and Risse, T., *Transforming Europe: Europeanization and Domestic Change* (Ithaca, 2001).

Cowles, M., and Smith, M., *The State of the European Union,* vol. 5, *Risks, Reform, Resistance, and Revival* (Oxford, 2000).

Cox, R., "The Consequence of Welfare Retrenchment in Denmark," *Politics and Society* 25/3 (September 1997).

Csaba, L., "A Decade of Transformation in Hungarian Economic Policy: Dynamics, Constraints and Prospects," *Europe-Asia Studies* 50/8 (December 1998).

Csaba, L., "Double Talk – The Political Economy of Eastward Enlargement of the EU," *Intereconomics* 36/5 (September/October 2001).

Curzon, G., and Curzon, V. (Eds.), *The Multinational Enterprise in a Hostile World* (London, 1977).

Curzon, V., *The Essentials of Economic Integration: Lessons of EFTA Experience* (London, 1979).

Curzon Price, V., *Industrial Policies in the European Community* (London, 1981).

Curzon Price, V., *1992: Europe's Last Chance? From Common Market to Single Market* (London, 1988).

Curzon Price, V., Landau, A., and Whitman, R., *The Enlargement of the European Union: Issues and Strategies* (London, 1999).

Cuwen, P., "High Definition Television: A Case Study of Industrial Policy versus the Market," *European Business Review* 94/1 (1994).

Dahrendorf, R., *Die Chancen der Krise über die Zukunft des Liberalismus* (Stuttgart, 1983).

Dahrendorf, R., *Plädoyer für die Europäische Union* (Munich, 1973).

Dahrendorf, R., "A Little Silver Lining on a Dark Horizon," in R. Dahrendorf (Ed.), *Europe's Economy in Crisis* (London, 1981).

Dai, X., *Corporate Strategy, Public Policy and New Technologies: Philips and the European Consumer Electronic Industry* (Oxford, 1996).

Dai, X., Dawson, A., and Holmes, P., "The Rise and Fall of High Definition Television: The Impact of European Technology Policy," *Journal of Common Market Studies* 34/2 (1996).

Davenport, M., "The Economic Impact of the EEC," in A. Boltho (Ed.), *The European Economy: Growth and Crisis* (Oxford, 1982).

DeBony, E., "Agenda 2000: A Blueprint for Enlargement" (Economist Intelligence Unit), *European Policy Analyst* 2 (1997).

Dekker, W., "Keeping Up Europe's Guard," *European Affairs* (November/December 1991).

Della Sala, V., "Hollowing Out and Hardening the Italian State," *West European Politics* 20/1 (January 1997).

Delmas, J., "Naissance et développement d'une politique nucleare militaire en France (1945–1956)," in K. A. Maier et al. (Eds.), *Das Nordatlantische Buendnis 1949–1956* (Munich, 1993).

Deubner, C., *Die Atompolitik der westdeutschen Industrie und die Gründung von Euratom* (Frankfurt, 1977).

Dinan, D. (Ed.), *Encyclopedia of the European Union* (Boulder, 1998).

Dinan, D., *Ever Closer Union,* 2nd ed. (Boulder, 1999).

Disney, R., Emmerson, C., and Smith, S., "Pension Reform and Economic Performance in Britain in the 1980s and 1990s," EEP/IFS/NBER Conference: "Seeking a Premier League Economy," 7–9 December 2000.

Dixit, A., *The Making of Economic Policy: A Transaction-Cost Politics Perspective* (Cambridge, U.K., 1996).

Dolan, M., "European Restructuring and Import Policies for a Textile Industry in Crisis," *International Organization* 37/4 (Autumn 1983).

Double, M., "Privatization Changes Spain's Business Environment and Creates Opportunities for U.S. Business," *Business America* 14/4 (22 February 1997).

Doyle, C., "Liberalizing Europe's Networking Industries: Ten Conflicting Priorities, Part I," *Business Strategy Review* 7/4 (Autumn 1998).

Drobak, J., and Nye, J. (Eds.), *The Frontiers of the New Institutional Economics* (San Diego, 1997).

Duchene, F., *Jean Monnet: First Statesman of Interdependence* (London, 1994).

Dyson, K., and Featherstone, K., *The Road to Maastricht: Negotiating Economic and Monetary Union* (Oxford, 1999).

Eade, P., "How Long Can Helsinki Keep on Climbing?," *Euromoney* 299 (March 1994).

Ebenstein, A., *Friedrich A. Hayek: A Biography* (New York, 2001).

Eichengreen, B., "European Monetary Unification," *Journal of Economic Literature* 31/3 (September 1993).

Eichengreen, B. (Ed.), *Europe's Postwar Recovery* (Cambridge, U.K., 1995).

Eichengreen, B., "European Monetary Unification: A Tour d'Horizon," *Oxford Review of Economic Policy* 14/3 (Autumn 1998).

Eichengreen, B., "Who Mislaid the *Wirtschaftswunder?*" (Speech, AIGCS, November 1999).

El-Agraa, A. M., (Ed.), *The Economics of the European Community*, 2nd ed. (New York, 1985).

Ellman, M., "The Political Economy of Transformation," *Oxford Review of Economic Policy* 13/2 (Summer 1997).

Encarnation, O., "Social Concertation in Democratic and Market Transitions: Comparative Lessons from Spain," *Comparative Political Studies* 30/4 (August 1997).

Erhard, L., *Prosperity through Competition* (London, 1962).

Erhard, L., *The Economics of Success* (Princeton, 1963).

Esposito, C., *America's Feeble Weapon: Funding the Marshall Plan in France and Italy, 1948–1950* (Westport, CT, 1994).

Evans, L., Grimes, A., Wilkinson, B., and Teece, D., "Economic Reform in New Zealand 1984–95: The Pursuit of Efficiency," *Journal of Economic Literature* 34 (December 1996).

Everling, U., "Possibilities and Limits of European Integration," *Journal of Common Market Studies* 18/3 (March 1980).

Farage, N., "Democracy in Crisis: The White Paper on Governance," Bruges Group Occasional Paper no. 44 (London 2002).

Farrell, M., *Spain in the EU: The Road to Economic Convergence* (London, 2001).

Feld, W., "Political Aspects of Transnational Business Collaboration in the Common Market," *International Organization* 24/2 (Spring 1970).

Feldstein, M., "Europe's Monetary Union: The Case Against EMU," *The Economist,* 13 June 1992.

Feldstein, M., "The Political Economy of the European Economic and Monetary Union: Political Sources of an Economic Liability," *Journal of Economic Perspectives* 11/4 (Fall 1997).

Feldstein, M., "EMU and International Conflict," *Foreign Affairs* 76/6 (November/December 1997).

Ferrera, M., and Gualmini, E., "Reforms Guided by Consensus: The Welfare State in the Italian Transition," *West European Politics* 23/2 (April 2000).

Foley, B. (Ed.), *European Economies Since the Second World War* (New York, 1998).

Forsyth, D., "Restoring International Payments: Germany and France Confront Bretton Woods and The European Payments Union," Estudio Working Paper no. 1997/111 (December 1997).

Forsyth, D., and Notermans, T., *Regime Changes: Macroeconomic Policy and Financial Regulation in Europe from the 1930s to the 1990s* (Providence, 1997).

Franko, L., *The European Multinationals: A Renewed Challenge to American and British Big Business* (Stamford, CT, 1976).

Fransen, F., *The Supranational Politics of Jean Monnet* (Westport, CT, 2001).

Frieden, J., "Invested Interests: The Politics of National Economic Policies in a World of Global Finance," *International Organization* 45 (Autumn 1991).

Friedman, M., "The Case for Flexible Exchange Rates," in M. Friedman, *Essays in Positive Economics* (Chicago, 1953).

Friedrich, C. J., *Europe An Emergent Nation?* (New York, 1969).

Frohberg, K., and Hartmann, M., "Financing Enlargement: The Case of Agriculture and Rural Development," *Intereconomics* (March/April 2002).

Furubotn, E. G., and Richter, R., *Institutions and Economic Theory: The Contribution of the New Institutional Economics* (Ann Arbor, 1997).

Gamble, A., *Hayek: The Iron Cage of Liberty* (Boulder, 1966).

Gamble, A., *Britain in Decline* (Boston, 1981).

Gamble, A., *The Free Economy and the Strong State: The Politics of Thatcherism,* 2nd ed. (London, 1994).

Garton Ash, T., *History of the Present: Essays, Sketches, and Dispatches from Europe in the 1990s* (New York, 1999).

Garton Ash, T., "Europe's Endangered Liberal Order," *Foreign Affairs* 77/2 (March/April 1998).

Gerber, D., *Law and Competition in the Twentieth Century: Protecting Prometheus* (New York, 1988).

Gibson, M., "Wired Up: The Growth of Finland's High-Tech Sector," *Scandinavian Review* 85/2 (Autumn 1997).

Giersch, H., "Eurosclerosis – What Is the Cure?," *European Affairs* 4 (1987).

Giersch, H., "EC 1992: Competition is the Clue," *European Affairs* 3 (1989).

Giersch, H. (Ed.), *Fighting Europe's Unemployment in the 1990s* (Heidelberg, 1996).

Giersch, H., Pacque, K., and Schmieding, H., *The Fading Miracle: Four Decades of Market Economy in Germany* (Cambridge, U.K., 1992).

Gilder, G., *Wealth and Poverty* (New York, 1981).

Gillingham, J., "Coal and Steel Diplomacy in Interwar Europe," in C. A. Wurm (Ed.), *International Kartelle und Aussenpolitik* (Stuttgart, 1989).

Gillingham, J., *Coal, Steel and the Rebirth of Europe, 1945–1955: The Germans and French from Ruhr Conflict to Economic Community* (Cambridge, U.K., 1991).

Gillingham, J., "De la cooperation a l'integration: la Ruhr et l'industrie lourde francaise pendant la guerre," *Histoire, economie, societe* 11/3 (1992).

Gillingham, J., "American Monnetism and the European Coal and Steel Community in the 1950s," *Journal of Economic Integration History* 1 (1995).

Gillingham, J., "Jean Monnet et le 'Victory Program' americain," in G. Boussuat and D. Wilkens (Eds.), *Jean Monnet et les Chemnins de la Paix* (Paris, 1998).

Gillingham, J., "The Marshall Plan and the Origins of Neo-Liberal Europe," in H. Labohm (Ed.), *The Marshall Plan Fifty Years Later: Problems and Perspectives* (The Hague, 1999).

Ginsborg, P., *A History of Contemporary Italy: Society and Politics, 1943–1988* (London, 1990).

Goldstein, A., and Nocoletti, G., "Italy Corporate Governance," *OECD Observer* 192 (February/March 1995).

Goodman, J., *Monetary Sovereignty: The Politics of Central Banking in Western Europe* (Ithaca, 1992).

Gowan, P., and Anderson, P., *The Question of Europe* (London 1997).

Grant, C., *Delors: Inside the House That Jacque Built* (London, 1990).

Green, R., and Haskel, J., "The Role of Privization," CEP/IFS/NBER Conference: "Seeking a Premier League Economy," 7–9 December 2000.

Griffiths, R., and T. Tachibaniki (Eds.), *From Austerity to Affluence: The Transformation of the Socio-Economic Structure of Western Europe and Japan* (Hampshire, 2000).

Gros, D., and Thygesen, N., *European Monetary Integration* (London, 1992).

Haas, E. B., *The Uniting of Europe: Political, Social, and Economic Forces, 1950–1957* (Stanford, 1958).

Haberler, G., "Economic Aspects of a European Customs Union," *World Politics* 11/4 (July 1949).

Haberler, G., "Integration and Growth of the World Economy in Historical Perspective," *American Economic Review* 54 (March 1964).

Hall, P. (Ed.), *The Political Power of Economic Ideas: Keynesianism across Nations* (Princeton, 1989).

Hall, P., and Franzese, R., "Mixed Signals: Central Bank Independence, Coordinated Wage Bargaining, and European Monetary Union," *International Organization* 52/3 (Summer 1988).

Hallstein, W., *United Europe: Challenge and Opportunity* (Cambridge, MA, 1962).

Hallstein, W., *Europe in the Making* (London, 1972).

Hanley, E., "Cadre Capitalism in Hungary and Poland: Property Accumulation among Post-Communist Elites," *East European Politics and Society* 14/1 (Winter 2000).

Hanson, B., "What Happened to Fortress Europe? External Trade Policy Liberalization in the European Union," *International Organization* 52/1 (Winter 1998).

Harrison, M. M., *The Reluctant Ally: France and the Atlantic Alliance* (Baltimore, 1981).

Hatzichronoglou, T., "The Globalisation of Industry in the OECD Countries," *STI Working Papers* 2 (1999).

Haycroft, J., *Italian Labyrinth: An Authentic and Revealing Portrait of Italy in the 1980s* (London, 1985).

Hayek, F. A., "The Economic Conditions of Interstate Federalism," reprinted in F. A. Hayek, *Individualism and Economic Order* (Chicago, 1948).

Hayek, F. A., *The Constitution of Liberty* (Chicago, 1960).

Hayek, F. A., *Law, Legislation and Liberty: A New Statement of the Liberal Principles of Justice and Political Economy*, vol. 2, *The Mirage of Social Justice* (Chicago, 1976).

Heath, E., *Old World, New Horizons: Britain, Europe, and the Atlantic Alliance* (Cambridge, MA, 1970).

Helleiner, E., "One Nation, One Money: Territorial Currencies and the Nation-State," ARENA Working Paper no. 97/17 (1997).

Hemerijk, A., and Visser, J., "Change and Immobility: Three Decades of Policy Adjustment in the Netherlands and Belgium," *West European Politics* 23/2 (April 2000).

Henderson, D., *The Changing Fortunes of Economic Liberalism: Yesterday, Today and Tomorrow* (London, 1998).

Henderson, W., *The Genesis of the Common Market* (London, 1962).

Heywood, P., "Power Diffusion or Concentration? In Search of the Spanish Policy Process," *West European Politics* 21/4 (1998).

Heywood, P., "Sleaze in Spain," *Parliamentary Affairs* 48/4 (1995).

Hirsch, E., "French Planning and Its European Application," *Journal of Common Market Studies* 1/2 (1962).

Hjerppe, R., "Finnish Growth Was Europe's Fastest in the Twentieth Century," *Unitas* 72/2 (2000).

Hoag, J., and Kasoff, M., "Estonia in Transition," *Journal of Economic Issues* 44/4 (December 1999).

Hodges, M., and Wallace, W., *Economic Divergence in the European Community* (London, 1981).

Hodges, M., "Industrial Policy: A Directorate General in Search of a Role," H. Wallace and W. Wallace (Eds.), *Policy Making in the European Union*, 4th ed. (Oxford, 2000).

Holland, S., *The Uncommon Market* (London, 1980).

Holmes, M., *European Integration: Scope and Limits* (New York, 2001).

Hooghe, L., and Marks, G., "The Making of a Polity: The Struggle over European Integration," Robert Schuman Center, 97/31 (June 1997), European University Institute, Florence.

Hooper, J., "A New Italian Renaissance," *The Wilson Quarterly* 22/2 (Spring 1998).

Hoopes, T., *The Devil and John Foster Dulles* (Boston, 1973).

Hoskins, J., "1992 and the Brussels Machine," in R. Darhendorf (Ed.), *Whose Europe: Competing Visions for 1992* (London, 1989).

Howarth, R., "The Common Agricultural Policy," in P. Minford (Ed.), *The Cost of Europe* (Manchester, 1992).

Howe, G., *Conflict of Loyalty* (New York, 1994).

Huber, E., and Stephen, J., "Internationalization and the Social Democratic Model," *Comparative Political Studies* 31 (June 1998).

Hulsman, J., *The World Turned Rightside Up: A New Trading Agenda for the Age of Globalisation* (London, 2001).

Ikenberry, J. G., "A World Economy Restored: Expert Consensus and the Anglo-American Postwar Settlement," *International Organization* 46/1 (Winter 1992).

Ingersent, K., Rayner, A., and Hine, R., *The Reform of the Common Agricultural Policy* (Hampshire, 1998).

Isern, J., and Rios, M., "Facing Disconnection: Hard Choices for Europe's Telcos," *The McKinsey Quarterly* (Winter 2002).

Iversen, T., "The Choices for Scandinavian Social Democracy in Comparative Perspective," *Oxford Review of Economic Policy* 14/1 (Spring 1998).

Iversen, T., and Wren, A., "Equality, Employment, and Budgetary Restraint. The Trilemma of the Service Economy," *World Politics* 50 (July 1988).

Jacquemin, A., and Pench, L. (Eds.), *Europe Competing in the Global Economy: Reports of the Competitiveness Advisory Group* (Luxembourg, 1995).

Janssen, R., "A New Golden Age," *Europe* (February 2001).

Janssen, R., "Visions of the Twenty-first Century Dutch," *Europe* (December 1999).

Jenkins, C., "The Maastricht Treaty," Economist Intelligence Unit, March 1992.

Jenkins, C., "Unfinished Business," Economist Intelligence Unit, March 1997.

Jochem, Sven, "Nordic Labour Market Policies in Transition," *West European Politics* 23/13 (July 2000).

Jonas, A., Englund, P., and Sodersten, J., "Tax Reform of the Century – The Swedish Experiment," *National Tax Journal* 49/4 (December 1996).

Josling, T., "Agricultural Policy," in P. Coffey (Ed.), *Economic Policies of the Common Market* (London, 1979).

Kaminski, B., "Industrial Restructuring as Revealed in Hungary's Pattern of Integration into European Union Markets," *Intereconomics* 52/3 (2000).

Kassim, H., and Menon, A. (Eds.), *The European Union and National Industrial Policy* (London, 1996).

Kienbaum, B., and Grote, M., "German Unification as a Cultural Dilemma: A Retrospective," *East European Quarterly* 31/2 (June 1997).

Kirzner, I. M., *The Driving Force of the Market* (New York, 2000).

Klausen, J., *War and Welfare: Europe and the United States, 1945 to the Present* (New York, 1998).

Kloostermann, R., "Three Worlds of Welfare Capitalism? The Welfare State and the Post-industrial Trajectory in the Netherlands after 1980," *West European Politics* 17/4 (October 1994).

Kluge, J., Deger R., and Wunram, J., "Can Germany Still Innovate?," *The McKinsey Quarterly* 3 (1996).

Kluge, J., Meffe J., and Stein, L., "The German Road to Innovation," *The McKinsey Quarterly* 2 (2000).

Kornai, J., "The Postsocialist Transition and the State: Reflections in the Light of Hungarian Fiscal Problems," *American Economic Review* 82/2 (Papers and Proceedings of the 104th Annual Meeting of the American Economic Association, 4 May 1992).

Kostiris, F., *Italy: The Sheltered Economy: Structural Problems in the Italian Economy* (Oxford, 1993).

Kotlowski, D. (Ed.), *The European Union from Jean Monnet to the Euro* (Athens, 2000).

Kramer, A., *The West German Economy, 1945–1955* (New York, 1990).

Krauss, M. B., "Recent Developments in Customs Union Theory: An Interpretive Survey," *Journal of Economic Literature* 10/2 (June 1972).

Krugman, P., *Rethinking International Trade* (London, 1990).

Kuesters, H. J., *Die Gründung der europäischen Wirtschaftsgemeinschaft* (Baden-Baden, 1982).

Kurland, C., "Beating Scientists into Plowshares," *Science* 276/5513 (2 May 1997).

Kurzer, P., *Business and Banking: Political Change and Economic Integration in Western Europe* (Ithaca, 1993).

Kuznets, S., *Postwar Economic Growth: Four Lectures* (Cambridge, MA, 1964).

Laffan, B., and Shackleton, M., "The Budget," in H. Wallace and W. Wallace (Eds.), *Policy-Making in The European Union,* 4th ed. (Oxford, 2000).

Larsson, T., *The Race to the Top: The Real Story of Globalization* (Washington, DC, 2001).

Laurent, P., and Maresceau, M., *The State of the European Union*, vol. 4, *Deepening and Widening* (Boulder, 1998).

Lavdas, K., *The Europeanization of Greece: Interest Politics and the Crises of Integration* (London, 1997).

Lavery, J., "Finland at Eighty: A More Confident and Open Nation," *Scandinavian Review* 85/2 (Autumn 1996).

Lawson, N., *The View from No. 11: Britain's Longest Serving Cabinet Minister Recalls the Triumphs and Disappointments of the Thatcher Era* (New York, 1993).

Leaman, J., *The Political Economy of West Germany, 1945–1985: An Introduction* (New York, 1988).

Leonard, D., *The Economist Guide to the European Union*, 8th ed. (London, 2002).

Leontief, W., "The Structure of the United States Economy," *Scientific American* 212/4 (April 1965).

Levy, J., *Tocqueville's Revenge: State, Society and Economy in Contemporary France* (Cambridge, MA, 1999).

Lewandowski, J., "Privatizing the Communist State," *Quadrant* 43/4 (April 1999).

Lewis, W. R., *Rome or Brussels? An Economist's Comparative Analysis of the Development of the European Community and the Aims of the Treaty of Rome* (London, 1971).

Lindbeck, A., "The Swedish Experiment," *Journal of Economic Literature* 35/3 (September 1997).

Lindbeck, A., Molander, P., Petersson, T., Petersson, O., Sandmo, A., Swedenborg, B., and Thygesen, N., *Turning Sweden Around* (Cambridge, MA, 1994).

Lindsey, B., *Against the Dead Hand: The Uncertain Struggle for Global Capitalism* (New York, 2002).

Locke, R., *Remaking the Italian Economy* (Ithaca, 1995).

London, F., "The Logic and Limits of *Désinflation compétitive*: French Economic Policy from 1983," *Oxford Review of Economic Policy* 14/1 (Spring, 1998).

Loth W., Wallace, W., and Wessels, W. (Eds.), *Walter Hallstein: The Forgotten European?* (London, 1998).

Ludlow, P., "Delors II: Continuity or Discontinuity," *European Affairs* 2 (1989).

Lundestad, G., *Empire by Integration: The United States and European Integration, 1945–1997* (New York, 1998).

Lynch, F., "Restoring France: The Road to Integration," in A. Milward et al. (Eds.), *The Frontier of National Sovereignty: History and Theory* (London, 1993).

Lyytinen, K., "Finland: The Unknown Soldier on the IT Front," *Association for Computing Machinery. Communications of the ACM* 42/4 (March 1999).

Macharzina, K., and Staehle, W. H., *European Approaches to International Management* (Berlin, 1986).

Mackenzie, D., "Framework Becomes a Pawn in Europe's Politics," *New Scientist* 129/1761 (23 March 1991).

Mackenzie, D., "Delors to Push Science Funds into Arms of Commerce," *New Scientist* 133/1807 (February 1992).

Mackenzie, D., "Europe under New Management," *New Scientist* 137/1854 (2 January 1993).

MacLennon, M. C., "The Common Market and French Planning," *Journal of Common Market Studies* 3/1 (1965).

Maddison, A., *Phases of Capitalist Development* (Oxford, 1982).

Maier-Dornberg, W., "Die Planung des Verteidigungsbeitrages der Bundesrepublik Deutschland im Rahmen der EVG," in Militärgeschichtglishes Forschungsamt (Ed.), *Anfänge westdeutscher Sicherheitspolitik 1945–1955*, Bd. 2 (Munich, 1990).

Marjolin, R., *Architect of European Unity: Memoirs, 1911–1986* (London, 1989).

Marks, G., Hooghe, L., and Blank, K., "Integration Theory, Subsidiarity and the Internationalisation of Issues: The Implication for Legitimacy," EUI Working Paper, RSK no. 95/7 (1995).

Martin, C., *The Spanish Economy in the New Europe* (Hampshire, 2000).

Maudling, R., *Memoirs* (London, 1978).

McCarthy, P., *The Crisis of the Italian State: From the Origins of the Cold War to the Fall of Berlusconi* (New York, 1995).

McDougall, I., and Snape, R. (Eds.), *Studies in International Economics: Monash Conference Papers* (Amsterdam, 1970).

McNeill, W., *The Metamorphosis of Greece Since World War II* (Chicago, 1978).

Meade, J., *Problems of Economic Union* (Chicago, 1953).

Meinecke, F., *Die deutshe Katastrophe* (Wiesbaden, 1949).

Mendelson, M., "The Eurobond and Capital Market Integration," *Journal of Finance* 27/1 (March 1972).

Metcalfe, L., "The European Commission as a Network Organization," *Publius* 26/4 (Fall 1996).

Meunier, S., "The French Exception," *Foreign Affairs* 79/4 (July/August 2000).

Middlemas, K., *Orchestrating Europe* (London, 1995).

Milner, H., "Resisting the Protectionist Temptation: Industry and the Making of Trade Policy in France and the United States during the 1970s," *International Organization* 41/4 (1988).

Milward, A., *The European Rescue of the Nation-State* (London, 1993).

Milward, A., "From EC to EU: An Historical and Political Survey," *Journal of Common Market Studies* (June 1998).

Milward, A., Lynch, F., Ranieri, R., and Sorensen, V., *The Frontier of National Sovereignty: History and Theory 1945–1992* (London, 1993).

Minford, P. (Ed.), *The Cost of Europe* (Manchester, 1992).

Mishkin, F., "International Experiences with Different Monetary Policy Regimes," National Bureau of Economic Research, Working Paper no. 7044 (March 1999).

Misossi, S., and Padoan, P., "Italy in the EMS. After Crisis, Salvation?," in M. Baldassari and F. Modigliani (Eds.), *The Italian Economy: What Next?* (New York, 1995).

Monnet, J., "A Ferment of Change," *Journal of Common Market Studies* 1/3 (1962).

Monnet, J., *Memoires* (Paris, 1976).

Moravcsik, A., *The Choice for Europe: Social Purpose and State Power from Messina to Maastricht* (Ithaca, 1998).

Moravcsik, A. (Ed.), *Centralization or Fragmentation? Europe Facing the Challenges of Deepening, Diversity, and Democracy* (New York, 1999).

Mucha, J., and Szczepanski, M., "Polish Society in the Perspective of Its Integration with the European Union," *East European Quarterly* 35/4 (Winter 2001).

Mundell, R., "A Theory of Optimum Currency Areas," *American Economic Review* 51/4 (September 1961).

Muravchik, J., *Heaven on Earth: The Rise and Fall of Socialism* (San Francisco, 2002).

Myrdal, G., *An International Economy* (New York, 1954).

Nakano, K., "The Role of Ideology and Elite Networks in the Decentralisation Reforms in 1980s France," *West European Politics* 23/13 (July 2000).

Nathan, R. R., "An Unsung Hero of World War II," in D. Brinkley (Ed.), *Jean Monnet: The Path to European Unity* (New York, 1991).

Nau, H. R., "From Integration to Interdependence: Gains, Losses, and Continuing Gaps," *International Organization* 33/1 (Winter 1979).

Neal, L., and Barbezat, D., *The Economics of the European Union and the Economies of Europe* (Oxford, 1998).

Newhouse, J., *Europe Adrift* (New York, 1997).

Nicholls, A. J., *Freedom with Responsibility: The Social Market Economy in Germany, 1918–1963* (Oxford, 1994).

Noel, G., "Les Groupes de Pression agricoles Francaise et le Projet d'Organisation et de l'Europe agricole entre 1950 et 1954," EUI Colloquium Papers, DOC.IUE 315/90 (Col 49).

North, D., *Structure and Change in Economic History* (New York, 1981).

North, D. C., *Growth and Welfare in the American Past* (Englewood Cliffs, NJ, 1966).

Nugent, N., *The Government and Politics of the European Union* (Durham, 1999).

Olson, M., *The Rise and Decline of Nations: Economic Growth, Stagflation, and Social Rigidities* (New Haven, 1982).

Orr, A., "New Zealand: The Results of Openness," *OECD Observer* 192 (February/March 1995).

Osman, J., "The Finnish Economic Depression of the 1990s: Causes, Consequences and Cure," *Scandinavian Review* 86/1 (Spring 1998).

Overy, R., "The Economy of the Federal Republic Since 1949," in K. Larres and P. Panayi (Eds.), *The Federal Republic of Germany: Politics, Society and Economy before and after Unification* (London, 1996).

Padoa-Schioppa, T., *The Road to Monetary Union in Europe: The Emperor, the Kings, and the Genies* (Oxford, 1994).

Pavitt, K., "Technology, International Competition, and Economic Growth: Some Lessons and Perspectives," *World Politics* 25/2 (January 1973).

Peacock, A., and Willgerodt, H. (Eds.), *Germany's Social Market Economy: Origins and Evolution* (New York, 1989).

Pelkmans, J., "Economic Theories of Integration Revisited," *Journal of Common Market Studies* 28/4 (June 1980).

Pelkmans, J., "The Assignment of Public Functions in Economic Integration," *Journal of Common Market Studies* 21/1 and 2 (September and December 1982).

Pelkmans, J., *Market Integration in the European Community* (The Hague, 1984).

Pelkmans, J., *European Integration: Methods and Economic Analysis* (Essex, 1997).

Penttila, R., "Finland's Quiet Revolution, 1989–1999," *Scandinavian Review* 87/3 (Winter 2000).

Perez, S., *Banking on Privilege: The Politics of Spanish Financial Reform* (Ithaca, 1997).

Perez, S., "From Labor to Finance: Understanding the Failure of Socialist Economic Policies in Spain," *Comparative Political Studies* 32/6 (September 1999).

Pérez-Diaz, V., *Spain at the Crossroads: Civil Society, Politics, and the Rule of Law* (Cambridge, MA, 1999).

Peterson, J., "Technology Policy in Europe: Explaining the Framework Program and Eureka in Theory and Practice," *Journal of Common Market Studies* 19/3 (March 1991).

Pierson, P., "When Effect Becomes Cause: Policy Feedback and Political Change," *World Politics* 45/4 (July 1993).

Pierson, P., "The Path to European Integration: A Historical Institutionalist Analysis," *Comparative Political Studies* 29/2 (April 1996).

Pierson, P., "Increasing Returns, Path Dependence and the Study of Politics," *American Political Science Review* 94/2 (June 2000).

Pierson, P., "Big, Slow-moving and Invisible: Macro-Social Processes in the Study of Comparative Politics," (Speech, Harvard University Center for European Studies, 10 November 2000).

Pindar, J., *The Building of the European Union* (Oxford, 1998).

Pond, E., "Miracle on the Vistula," *Washington Quarterly* 21/3 (Summer 1998).

Pond, E., *The Rebirth of Europe* (Washington, DC, 1999).

Popov, V., "Shock Therapy versus Gradualism," *Comparative Economic Studies* 41/1 (Spring 2000).

Portillo, M., *Democratic Values and the Currency* (London, 1998).

Posen, A., "Why the EMU Is Irrelevant for the German Economy," Institute for International Economics, Working Paper no. 99/5 (April 1995).

Preeg, E., *Traders in a Brave New World: The Uruguay Round and the Future of the International Trading System* (London, 1995).

Prevezanos, K., "The EU Conference in Nice: More than a Minimum Consensus for Europe and Germany," American Institute for Contemporary German Studies, 4 January 2001.

Price, H. B., *The Marshall Plan and Its Meaning* (Ithaca, 1955).

Puchala, D. J., "Europeans and Europeanism in 1970," *International Organization* 27/3 (Summer 1973).

Ranieri, R., "After the Rewards of Growth, the Penalty of Debt," in B. Foley (Ed.), *European Economies Since the Second World War* (London, 1998).

Rasmussen, H., "Between Self-restraint and Activism," *European Law Review* (1998).

Recio, A., and Roca, J., "The Spanish Socialists in Power: Thirteen Years of Economic Policy," *Oxford Review of Economic Policy* 14/2 (April 1995).

Redfearn, J., "Report Card on European Science," *Science* 276/5316 (23 May 1997).

Rieger, E., "The Common Agricultural Policy," in H. Wallace and W. Wallace (Eds.), *Policy-Making in the European Union*, 4th ed. (Oxford, 2000).

Riley, A., "The ECJ: A Court with a Mission?," *European Policy Analyst* 4 (1996).

Rinne, R., "The Globalization of Education: Finnish Education on the Doorstep of the New EU Millennium," *Educational Review* 52/2 (June 2000).

Rivera-Batiz, L., and Romer, P., "Economic Integration and Endogenous Growth," *Quarterly Journal of Economics* 106/2 (May 1991).

Robertson, P. (Ed.), *Reshaping Europe in the Twenty-First Century* (New York, 1992).

Rolla, J., "The European Community's Technological Dilemma: Is a Regional Solution Possible in a Global Economy?," *National Forum: Phi Beta Kappa Journal* 72/2 (Spring 1992).

Romero, F., "Migration as an Issue in European Interdependence and Integration: The Case of Italy," in A. Milward et al., *The Frontier of National Sovereignty* (London, 1993).

Ross, G., Hoffmann, S., and Malzacher, S., *The Mitterrand Experiment: Continuity and Change in Modern France* (Oxford, 1987).

Ross, G., *Jacques Delors and European Integration* (New York, 1995).

Ross, G., "French Social Democracy and the EMU," ARENA Working Paper no. 98/19 (1998).

Roussel, E., *Jean Monnet* (Paris, 1995).

Ruberti, A., and Andre, M., "The European Model of Research Cooperation," *Issues in Science and Technology* 11/3 (Spring 1995).

Rueff, J., "Die französische Wirtschaftsreform. Rückblick und Ausblick," *ORDO* 12 (1960).

Rueff, J., "Zur Wirtschaftsreform in Frankreich: Bericht zur Finanzlage ... 30. September 1958," *ORDO* 11 (1959).

Ruggie, J., "International Regimes, Transactions, and Change: Embedded Liberalism in the Postwar Economic Order," *International Organization* 36/2 (1982).

Russell, R., "Snakes and Sheiks: Managing Europe's Money," in H. Wallace and A. Young (Eds.), *Participation and Policy-Making in the European Union* (Oxford, 1997).

Ryan, L., "Finland Aspires to European Union Small Country Leadership," *European Business Journal* 9/1 (1997).

Sachs, J., "Consolidating Capitalism," *Foreign Policy* 98 (Spring 1995).

Sala, V., "The Retreat of the State: The Diffusion of Power in the World Economy," *West European Politics* (July 1997).

Salter, M., "Europe's New Industrial Revolution," *Economic Affairs* 3 (1988).

Sandholtz, W., "Institutions and Collective Action: The New Telecommunications in Western Europe," *World Politics* 45/2 (January 1993).

Sandholtz, W., and Zysman, J., "1992: Recasting the European Bargain," *World Politics* 42/1 (October 1989).

Sapir, A., "Regional Integration in Europe," *The Economic Journal* 102/415 (November 1992).

Sarfati, G., "European Industrial Policy as a Non-tariff Barrier," European Integration Online Papers, 2/2 (13 May 1988).

Sasseen, J., "French Go for Broke in Europe: Credit Lyonnais' International Ambitions," *International Management* 47/9 (October 1992).

Sauter, W., "The Economic Constitution of the European Union," *Columbia Journal of European Law* 4/27 (Winter/Spring 1998).

Sautter, C., "France," in A. Boltho (Ed.), *The European Economy: Growth and Crisis* (Oxford, 1982).

Scharpf, F., *Governing in Europe: Effective and Democratic?* (Oxford, 1999).

Scheingold, S. A., "Domestic and International Consequences of Regional Integration," *International Organization* 24/4 (Fall 1970), 978–1002.

Schlaes, A., "Germany's Chained Economy," *Foreign Affairs* 73/5 (September/October 1994).

Schmidt, H., *Men and Power: A Political Retrospective* (New York, 1989).

Schmidt, V., *From State to Market: The Transformation of French Business and Government* (Cambridge, U.K., 1966).

Schuker, S. A. (Ed.), *Deutschland und Frankreich. Von Konflikt zur Aussöhnung* (Munich, 2000).

Schumpeter, J. A., *Essays* (Cambridge, MA, 1951).

Schwartz, H., "Small States in Big Trouble: State Reorganization in Australia, Denmark, New Zealand, and Sweden in the 1980s," *World Politics* 46/4 (July 1994).

Schwarz, H. P., "Germany's National and European Interests," *Daedalus* 123/2 (Spring 1994).

Schwarz, H. P., *Konrad Adenauer: German Politician and Statesman in a Period of War, Revolution and Reconstruction*, vol. 1, *From the German Empire to the Federal Republic, 1876–1952* (Stuttgart, 1989).

Schwarz, H. P., *Konrad Adenauer: German Politician and Statesman in a Period of War, Revolution and Reconstruction*, vol. 2, *The Statesman, 1952–1957* (Providence, 1997).

Scobie, H., Mortali, S., Persaud, S., and Docile, P., *The Italian Economy in the 1990s* (London, 1996).

Sedelmaier, U., and Wallace, H., "Eastern Enlargement," in H. Wallace and W. Wallace (Eds.), *Policy-Making in the European Union*, 4th ed. (Oxford, 2000).

Servan-Schreiber, J. J., *The American Challenge* (New York, 1967).

Shackleton, M., *Financing The European Community* (New York, 1990).

Shankar, B., "Boundless Europe: The Wireless Revolution," *Telecommunications* 31/11 (November 1997).

Sharp, M., and Pavitt, K., "Technology Policy in the 1990s: Old Trends and New Realities," *Journal of Common Market Studies* 31/2 (June 1993).

Shonfield, A., "Stabilization Policies in the West: From Demand to Supply Management," *Journal of Political Economy* 74/4-2 (August 1967).

Shonfield, A., *Europe: Journey to an Unknown Destination* (London, 1973).

Shonfield, A. (Ed.), *International Economic Relations of the Western World, 1959–1971* (Oxford, 1976).

Siebert, H., "Labor Market Rigidities: At the Root of Unemployment in Europe," *Journal of Economic Perspectives* 11/3 (Summer 1997).

Siebert, H., "European Entrepreneurial Capitalism: The Schumpeterian Secret to Higher Growth," *The International Economy* (Spring 2002).

Siedentop, L., *Democracy in Europe* (London, 2000).

Signorini, L., "Italy's Economy: An Introduction," *Daedalus* 130/2 (1998).

Silverman, B., "The Rise and Fall of the Swedish Model: Interview with Rudolf Meidner," *Challenge* (January/February 1998).

Skidelsky, R. (Ed.), *The End of the Keynesian Era: Essays on the Disintegration of the Keynesian Political Economy* (London, 1977).

Skidelsky, R., *John Maynard Keynes: Fighting for Britain, 1937–1946* (London, 2000).

Skousen, M., *The Making of Modern Economics* (Armonk, NY, 2001).

Slaughter, A., "The Real New Order," *Foreign Affairs* 76/5 (September/October 1997).

Smith, R., *Comeback: The Restoration of American Banking Power in the New World Economy* (Cambridge, MA, 1993).

Smith, S., "Financing the European Community: A Review of Options for the Future," *Fiscal Studies* 13/4 (November 1992).

Solomon, J., and Walker, D., "The Transformation of Telecommunications Industry in Europe," *European Business Journal* 8/2 (1996).

Solomon, R., *The International Monetary System, 1945–1976: An Insider's View* (New York, 1977).

Sousa, L., "Political Parties and Corruption in Portugal," *West European Politics* 24/1 (January 2001).

Spaak, P., *The Continuing Battle: Memoirs of a European, 1936–1966* (Boston, 1971).

Spinelli, A., *The Eurocrats: Conflict and Crisis in the European Community* (Baltimore, 1966).

Spinelli, A., *The European Adventure: Tasks for the Enlarged Community* (London, 1972).

Stanbrook, C., "The Maastricht Treaty: Maastricht's Double Jeopardy," *International Corporate Law* (May 1993).

Starr-Deelen, D., and Deelen, B., "The European Court of Justice as a Federator," *Publius* (Fall 1986).

Strange, S., "International Monetary Relations," vol. 2 in A. Shonfield (Ed.), *International Economic Relations of the Western World, 1959–1971* (London, 1976).

Strange, S., "The Management of Surplus Capacity: How Does Theory Stand Up to Protectionism 1970s Style?," *International Organization* 33/3 (Summer 1979).

Strange, S. (Ed.), *Paths to International Political Economy* (London, 1984).

Streeck, W., "German Capitalism: Does It Exist? Can It Survive?," MPIFG Discussion Paper no. 95/5 (November 1995).

Streeck, W., "The Internationalization of Industrial Relations in European: Prospects and Problems," *Politics & Society* 26 (December 1998).

Streeck, W., "Competitive Solidarity: Rethinking the 'European Social Model'," MPIFAG Working Paper no. 99/8 (September 1999).

Streit, M., and Mussler, W., "The Economic Constitution of the European Community: From 'Rome' to 'Maastricht'," *European Law Journal* 1/1 (March 1995).

Stuttaford, A., "Back to Normal: Estonia's Effort to Overcome Fifty Years of Soviet Control," *National Review,* 1 November 1993.

Sullivan, M., "Corporate Governance and Globalization," *Annals of the American Academy of Political and Social Science* (July 2000).

Suppanz, H., "New Zealand: Reform of the Public Sector," *OECD Observer* 200 (June/July 1996).

Swann, D., *The Economics of the Common Market* (London, 1990).

Tew, B., *The Evolution of the International Monetary System, 1945–88* (London, 1988).

Thatcher, M., *The Downing Street Years* (London, 1993).

Thatcher, M., *Statecraft: Strategies for a Changing World* (London, 2002).

Thomas, T., "Tax Law Could Spur German Acquisitions," *National Underwriter Property and Casualty – Risk & Benefits Management* 104/34 (21 August 2000).

Tiersky, R., *François Mitterrand: The Last French President* (New York, 2000).

Torres, F., "Lessons from Portugal's Long Transition to Economic and Monetary Union," in F. Sexas da Costa et al. (Eds.), *Portugal: A European Story* (Cascais, 2000).

Torstensson, R., "Growth, Knowledge Transfer and European Integration," *Applied Economics* 31 (January 1999).

Tovias, A., "A Survey of the Theory of Economic Integration," in H. Michaelmann and P. Soldartis (Eds.), *European Integration: Theories and Approaches* (Lanham, MD, 1994).

Trachtenberg, M., "The Nuclearization of NATO and U.S. European Relations" in F. H. Heller and J. Gillingham (Eds.), *NATO: The Founding of the Atlantic Alliance and the Integration of Europe* (New York, 1992).

Triffin, R., *Gold and the Dollar Crisis: Yesterday and Tomorrow,* Essays in International Finance, vol. 132 (Princeton, 1978).

Tsoukalis, L., *The New European Economy Revisited* (Oxford, 1997).

Tsoukalis, L., and Ferreira, A., "Management of Industrial Surplus Capacity in the European Community," *International Organization* 34/3 (Summer 1980), 355–76.

Tumlir, J., *Protectionism: Trade Policy in Democratic Societies* (Washington, DC, 1985).

Tumlir, J., "Who Benefits from Discrimination?," *Schweizerische Zeitschrift für Volkswirtschaft und Statistik* 121 (1985).

Urwin, D., *The Community of Europe: A History of European Integration Since 1945* (London, 1995).

Van Alebeek, H., van Wassenaer, A., and Lewis, W., "Boosting Dutch Economic Performance," *The McKinsey Quarterly* 4 (1997).

Van Ark, B., and de Hahn, J., "The Delta Model Revisited: Recent Trends in the Structural Performance of the Dutch Economy," *International Review of Applied Economics* 14/3 (July 2000).

Van der Hoek, P., "Does the Dutch Model Really Exist?," *International Advances in Economic Research* 6/3 (2000).

Van der Wee, H., *Prosperity and Upheaval: The World Economy, 1945–1980* (Berkeley, 1987).

Van Dyk, L., "Research in the EU: Better Times to Come?," *The Lancet* 357/9267 (12 May 2001).

Vaubel, R., "The Political Economy of Centralization in the European Community," *Journal des Économistes et des Études Humaines* 3/1 (March 1991).

Vaubel, R., *The Centralisation of Western Europe* (London, 1995).

Vaubel, R., "Currency, Competition and European Monetary Integration," *The Economic Journal* 100/402 (September 2000).

Verdier, D., and Breen, R., "Europeanization and Globalization: Politics against Markets in the European Union," *Comparative Political Studies* 34 (April 2001).

Vernon, R., *Sovereignty at Bay: The Multinational Spread of U.S. Enterprises* (London, 1971).

Volcker, P., and Gyohten, T., *Changing Fortunes: The World's Money and the Threat to American Leadership* (New York, 1992).

Von der Heyden, E., "Privatization in East Germany: The Delivery of an Economy," *Columbia Journal of World Business* 30/3 (Fall 1995).

Von Morgenstern, I., et al., "Europe's Structural Weakness," *The McKinsey Quarterly* 1 (1994).

Walker, M., "Europe: Superstate or Superpower?," *World Policy Journal* 17/4 (Winter 2000).

Wallace, H., and Wallace, W. (Eds.), *Policy-Making in the European Union*, 4th ed. (Oxford, 2000).

Wallace, H., Wallace, W., and Webb, C. (Eds.), *Policy Making in the European Communities* (London, 1977).

Wallace, H., and Young, A., *Participation and Policy-Making in the European Union* (Oxford, 1997).

Wallace, W., "Collective Governance," in H. Wallace and W. Wallace (Eds.), *Policy-Making in the European Union*, 4th ed. (Oxford, 2000).

Wallich, H. C., *Mainsprings of the German Revival* (New Haven, 1953).

Warnecke, S., *The European Community in the 1970s* (New York, 1972).

Waverman, L., and Sirel, E., "European Telecommunications Markets on the Verge of Liberalization," *Journal of Economic Perspectives* 11/4 (Fall 1997).

Webb, C., "Variations of a Theoretical Theme" in H. Wallace et al. (Eds.), *Policy Making in the European Communities* (London, 1977).

Weilemann, P., *Die Anfänge der Europäischen Atomgemeinschaft: Zur Gründungsgeschichte von Euratom 1955–1957* (Baden-Baden, 1982).

Williams, N., and Hellemans, A., "Cracks in Europe's Framework?," *Science* 276/5310 (11 April 1997).

Wist, T., and Rosenlew, N., "Finland: Capital Markets," *International Financial Law Review* (July 1999).

Woolcock, S., "Information Technology: The Challenge for Europe," *Journal of Common Market Studies* 22/4 (June 1984).

Yergin, D., and Stanislaw, J., *The Commanding Heights: The Battle between Government and the Marketplace That Is Remaking the Modern World* (New York, 1998).

Young, H., *This Blessed Plot* (New York, 1999).

Zarycki, T., "Politics in the Periphery: Political Cleavages in Poland Interpreted in Their Historical and International Context," *Europe-Asia Studies* 52/5 (July 2000).

Zeiler, T. W., *Free Trade, Free World: The Advent of GATT* (Chapel Hill, 1999).

Zysman, J., and Schwartz, A. (Eds.), *Enlarging Europe: The Industrial Foundations of a New Political Reality* (Berkeley, 1998).

Index